**Jon Latimer**

Jon Latimer served for many yea[...] [...]lished widely in military journals [...] *Compass 1940, Tobruk 1941, Decepti[...]* acclaimed *Alamein*. He lives in Wal[...]

08/05

C000226840

*Other books by the author*

Operation Compass 1940

Tobruk 1941

Deception in War

Alamein

# Burma

*The Forgotten War*

## JON LATIMER

JOHN MURRAY

© Jon Latimer 2004

First published in Great Britain in 2004 by John Murray (Publishers)
A division of Hodder Headline

Paperback edition 2005

A CIP catalogue record for this title is available from the British Library.

ISBN 0 7195 6576 6

Typeset in Monotype Bembo by Servis Filmsetting Ltd, Manchester

Printed and bound by
Clays Ltd, St Ives plc

Hodder Headline policy is to use papers that are natural, renewable and recyclable products and
made from wood grown in sustainable forests. The logging and manufacturing processes are
expected to conform to the environmental regulations of the country of origin.

John Murray (Publishers)
338 Euston Road
London NW1 3BH

To Tilly and Rob

# Contents

| | |
|---|---|
| *Illustrations* | ix |
| *Maps* | xi |
| *Acknowledgements* | xii |

| | |
|---|---|
| Introduction | 1 |

## Part I – Defeat

| | | |
|---|---|---|
| 1. | Burma and the British | 11 |
| 2. | Japan and China | 27 |
| 3. | Invasion | 42 |
| 4. | Disaster on the Sittang | 58 |
| 5. | Enter Slim | 72 |
| 6. | Struggle on the plains | 88 |
| 7. | Retreat | 105 |
| 8. | Plans | 121 |
| 9. | Donbaik | 137 |

## Part II – Stalemate

| | | |
|---|---|---|
| 10. | Wingate | 155 |
| 11. | Supremo | 170 |
| 12. | The march on Delhi | 186 |
| 13. | Stilwell in the north | 204 |
| 14. | The Admin Box | 221 |
| 15. | Thursday | 239 |
| 16. | Kohima: the siege | 256 |
| 17. | Imphal | 272 |
| 18. | Kohima: the battle | 290 |

## Part III – Victory

| | | |
|---|---|---|
| 19. | Monsoon | 309 |
| 20. | Myitkyina and Mogaung | 325 |

CONTENTS

21. Pursuit                         341
22. Arakan                          359
23. Across the Irrawaddy            374
24. Mandalay and Meiktila           391
25. Rangoon                         407
26. Return                          423

    Notes                           435
    Bibliography                    544
    Index                           589

# Illustrations

1. Japanese troops entering Rangoon railway station, 7 March 1942
2. Japanese troops fighting among the oil derricks of Yenangyaung
3. Men and mules of the RIASC follow a *chaung* in Arakan
4. Australian POWs carrying sleepers for the Burma–Thailand railway
5. Gurkha navigators building a road
6. The three-power conference in Cairo, November 1943
7. Air despatchers waiting to unload Christmas dinner
8. Men of the Rajput Regiment waiting to go on patrol
9. A wounded Gurkha being carried by his colleagues
10. Men of the Bombay Sappers and Miners carrying out road maintenance
11. Soldiers loading a horse onto an aircraft
12. Model 92 70mm battalion gun used by the Japanese
13. A ground crew re-arming a Hurribomber
14. A Lee tank of 3rd Carabiniers crossing a river at Imphal
15. The 2nd Division bath unit
16. The aftermath of battle as seen around the 'Scraggy' position
17. An RAF Beaufighter attacking a Japanese merchant vessel near Rangoon
18. Men of 2nd Durham Light Infantry meet the Sikh crew of a Stuart tank on the Kohima–Imphal road
19. A 75mm pack howitzer pounds the Myitkyina garrison
20. Jeeps modified for use by 36th Division in the 'Railway Corridor'
21. Air attack on a bridge
22. Slim being knighted by Wavell, Viceroy of India
23. An auxiliary group carrying goods by head in traditional African manner
24. Men relaxing by playing cricket
25. The bridge across the Chindwin at Kalewa
26. Landing craft with troops wading ashore to capture Akyab
27. MV *Ontario*

28. Young Burmese guerrilla armed with a Sten sub-machine-gun
29. A 5.5-inch gun of 134th Medium Regiment RA engages Fort Dufferin over open sights
30. A Stinson L-5 communications aircraft landing at an airstrip on the Arakan front
31. Dead Japanese soldier at the bottom of a pit
32. Japanese officers surrendering their swords

The author and publishers would like to thank the following for permission to reproduce illustrations: Plates 1 (HU 2773), 2 (HU 2778), 3 (IND 1885), 7 (CF 227), 8 (IND 2917), 9 (IB 283), 10 (IND 3612), 12 (STT 3562), 13 (CF 196), 15 (SE 2115), 16 (HU 88977), 18 (HU 88980), 20 (SE 2870), 22 (SE 2815), 23 (SE 2996), 24 (SE 1474), 25 (SE 2830), 27 (SE 3633), 28 (SE 3901), 29 (IND 4537) and 31 (IND 4740), Trustees of the Imperial War Museum, London; 4 (AWM P00406.026), 6 (AWM 128480), 11 (AWM P02491.115), 17 (AWM SUK12576), 21 (AWM SUK13875), 26 (AWM SUK13683) and 30 (AWM SEA0202), Australian War Memorial, Canberra; 5, 14 and 32, Gurkha Museum; 19, US Army.

# *Maps*

1. South-East Asia and ABDA Command, December
   1941–February 1942   36
2. The Japanese invasion of Burma, February–April 1942   44
3. The evacuation of Burma, May–October 1942   92
4. Northern Arakan Operations, November 1942–May 1943   138
5. The first Chindit expedition: Operation Longcloth,
   February–May 1942   160
6. Lines of communication, China–Burma–India, 1943–5   183
7. The March on Delhi, March 1944   192
8. The Admin Box, February–March 1944   227
9. Northern Burma, March–August 1944   244
10. The Kohima battlefield, April–June 1944   257
11. The Imphal battlefield, March–July 1944   274
12. Advance to the Chindwin, July–November 1944   345
13. Arakan operations, 1945   362
14. Extended Capital, December 1944–April 1945   376
15. The fall of Rangoon and breakout of 28th Army,
    May–August 1945   408

## KEY TO MAPS

**TROOP MOVEMENTS** (except as marked otherwise)

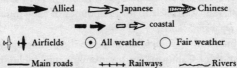

# Acknowledgements

When embarking on this project, the title was a natural one given the feelings of participants on both sides regarding their place in history. Yet if the Desert Campaign has been described as over-written, Burma is not so lacking in literature as one might expect. While I have found few general accounts or overall military histories apart from the official ones and the mammoth *Burma: The Longest War*, by Louis Allen – to whom I am deeply indebted for both this and his other work on the subject – over the last twenty years a great many individual memoirs have been published by former participants, and I have encountered many superb accounts of life in Burma that I have found of great value. Also invaluable have been those books by Major-General Sir Julian Thompson based on personal accounts held by the Imperial War Museum, and John Nunneley's *Tales from the Burma Campaign*. Indeed, I wish to thank all those participants who have taken the time to record their memories and deposit them at the IWM or with the Burma Campaign Memorial Library and other libraries around the world; this book would be nothing without them. I am also deeply indebted to Dr Tamayama Kazuo for the honour of allowing me to quote from *Tales by Japanese Soldiers*.

In tracing many of the books that make up the bibliography I must also thank Brad Smith of California for his monumuental bibliography, courtesy of his CBI Info website. And for helping me to locate these myriad titles, I wish to extend my warmest thanks to the staff of the library at the School of Oriental and African Studies in London, especially Lisa Cole, Yaye Tang, Lesley Price, Lance Martin and Rosemary Seton of the Special Collections reading room, who patiently recovered practically the entire Burma Campaign Memorial Library for my perusal. Once again my thanks to John Hall of University of Wales, Swansea, for his support, and to the library staff at UW Swansea, Swansea Central Library, the British Library, the National Army Museum reading room and all the staff at the Departments of Documents, Printed Books, Sound Recordings and the Photographic Archive of the Imperial War Museum; also the staff of the

Quaker International Centre and my old friends John McHugh, Angie Bennett and Graham Jenkins for accommodation in London, and Stan and Elaine Greaves, Alison Kahler, Lucy Jones and Laurie Hannigan for the same in Sydney and Canberra. Permission for quotations from Rudyard Kipling's *Mandalay* and *From Sea to Sea* by A.P. Watt Ltd on behalf of the National Trust for Places of Historic Interest or Natural Beauty.

Special thanks to Mrs Joyce Cruise, Collette Carroll, David Murray, Frank Maynard, Finny O'Sullivan, Kevin Enright, Brigadier John Randle and Tony McClenaghan of the Indian Military Historical Society and to Chris Peterson for his *Unparalleled Danger Unsurpassed Courage*; to Dr David Omissi of the University of Hull; to Ian Wilson of 9th Border Regiment Association, Captain Marcus Bennett RRW TD and Roger Evans; to Brigadier Nick Ridley for his grandfather Lieutenant-General Sir Philip Christison's memoir; to Sally and Lucy Jaffé for their history of the WAS(B); to Neville Hogan and Lesley Cartwright-Taylor of the Burma Forces Luncheon Club; to Gavin Edgeley-Harris of The Gurkha Museum; to Jacqui Minchinton, Paul Robinson and Sarah Orton at Northampton Borough Council and to Jon-Paul Carr of the Northamptonshire Regiment Association.

Also thanks to Lieutenant-Colonel Munish Nanda, the Garwhal Rifles Regimental Centre; Major Vivek Chaun of the Madras Regimental Centre; Colonel Narinder Pal Singh of 7th Light Cavalry; Mr Kaushik Roy; Chris Carson; Elizabeth Adey at Luton Museum Service; Martin Crowther at the Royal Museum and Art Gallery, Canterbury; Lorraine Chester and Simon Jones of the Museum of Liverpool Life; Karl Noble, Clifton Park Museum, Rotherham; David Hopkins, Curator of the Museum of The Manchester Regiment; Bill Norman of The Duke of Wellington's Regiment Museum; Martin Everard of the South Wales Borderers Museum; Dr S. Bull of Lancashire County Museum Service; Philip R. French, Newarke Houses Museum; Terry Mackenzie of The Cameronians Museum; Lieutenant-Colonel Anand Surma of the Jat Regimental Centre; Lieutenant-Colonel R. A. Leonard of The Keep Military Museum, Dorchester; Peter Crocker of The Royal Welch Fusiliers Museum; Major W. Shaw of The Royal Highland Fusiliers Museum; Lieutenant-Colonel W. D. Eliot, Light Infantry Office, Taunton; Pete Starling and the staff of the Army Medical Services Museum; Major C. M. J. Deedes, Light Infantry Office, Pontefract; George Streatfeild of the Soldiers of Gloucestershire Museum; Captain John Lee BEM at Headquarters The Royal Anglian Regiment (Lincolnshire); Lieutenant-Colonel Tony Scott and CSgt Willie Turner of The Staffordshire

Regiment Museum; Katherine Boyce of the Royal Air Force Museum; Matthew Buck and Chris Evans of Firepower, The Royal Artillery Museum; Major (Retd) J. O. M. Hackett and Major R. S. Prophet, The Worcestershire and Sherwood Foresters Museum; Lieutenant-Colonel Roger Binks, Major Jimmy Scott, Captain Jimmy Springthorpe and Peter Slater of The Royal Scots Dragoon Guards Museum; Ian Hook of the Essex Regiment Museum; Mr Harding, Queen's Royal Surrey Regiment Museum; Richard Callaghan of the Redoubt Fortress Museum, Eastbourne, and Bert Maile of 9th Royal Sussex Regiment; Taranjit Singh of the Sikh Cyber Museum; Major Sadanand Shelke of the Maratha Light Infantry Regimental Centre; David Murphy of The Royal Scots Museum; Captain J. O'Grady, The Lancashire Fusiliers Museum; George Fraser, Harry Moses of the Durham Light Infantry Museum and Steve Shannon, the curator, for his *Forgotten No More*; Major Roger Chapman of The Green Howards Museum; Lieutenant-Colonel T. C. E. Vines, Prince of Wales' Own Regiment of Yorkshire Museum; W. W. Smith of The Gordon Highlanders Museum; Colonel H. B. H. Waring of The Queen's Own Royal West Kent Regiment Museum, Maidstone; Tim Stankus at the Royal Signals Museum; Rod McKenzie of the Argyll and Sutherland Highlanders Museum; Lieutenant-Colonel Angus Fairrie of the Queen's Own Highlanders Museum; Dr Peter Liddle and Tracy Craggs of The Second World War Experience Centre in Leeds and once again to David Fletcher, Historian at the Tank Museum: with sincere apologies to anyone I may have overlooked.

Thanks also to Dai Power for website design, Grant McIntyre, Roland Philipps, Sam Evans, Helen Guthrie, Lucy Dixon, John Murray, Caroline Westmore, Jane Blackstock and Matthew Taylor at John Murray; to Martin Collins for drawing the maps and to Mike Levett for compiling the index; and as ever, to my agent Andrew Lownie, without whom this book would not have been possible.

*Ferryside, June 2004*

# Introduction

All honour to him, friend or foe,
Who fought and died for his country.
May the tragedy of his supreme
Sacrifice bring to us, the living,
Enlightenment and inspiration:
Fill with ever-mounting zeal
For the all-compelling quest for peace
World peace and universal brotherhood.

'Yesterday's Enemy is Today's Friend'
Recorded at Reizan Kannon Temple, Kyoto


'IN A LITTLE-KNOWN corner of Asia there was once a land as fair as any that a traveller could hope to discover', wrote Stephen Brookes of the land of his birth. 'It is still there, though you would have difficulty in relating what you see to the splendour of how things used to be before the armies of Japan, Britain and China fought over it for four years and left it broken and brutalised.'[1] This is the story of a war that was to have a profound, lasting and deleterious effect on its unwilling host. While what is presented here is fundamentally a military history, the war in Burma does not lend itself well to a single treatment. Nevertheless, a single theme runs through it: the struggle of the Burmese people for independence after sixty years of occupation.[2]

For the British it represented a colossal expenditure in treasure and blood (most of which, it must be said, was Indian) for a colony that within three years and largely as a result of the war gained independence. But it is wrong to belittle the efforts of the men that fought it, whose achievement nothing can diminish. Some time after the war a memorial was unveiled near Rangoon dedicated to the '27,000 men of the Commonwealth forces who died in Assam and Burma in the defence of freedom to whom the fortunes of war denied the ordinary rites accorded to their comrades in death'. Given the terrible regime in Burma for most the time since, one might question whether the war fought between 1941 and 1945 was for 'freedom'. Looking back now, sixty years since the war's end, its purpose seems more obscure than ever. For Tom Brooks of 215 Squadron RAF, the Burma Star means

> trying to find an airstrip on Akyab Island during the monsoon rains. It means flying over the Himalayas when the sun is setting. It means doing a radio let-down in Kunming in dense cloud, circling the airfield in a petrol-laden air-craft while other aircraft were in the vicinity. And, finally, it means having the responsibility of taking ten blokes across the Indian Ocean to the target and bringing them back safely, not once but many times.[3]

The war was a real and important part of the lives of hundreds of thou-sands of soldiers, and millions of ordinary people, whether engaged in it directly or not. Beautifully preserved though they are, the graves of British and Indian soldiers tell only part of that story.* Many more died who have no known grave: the ground where they fell consumed them. Indeed, Professor Raymond Callahan asks who, besides Field Marshal Viscount Slim, accomplished what they set out to do in Burma?

> No one. The British, from the Prime Minister [Winston Churchill] to [the Supreme Allied Commander, Vice-Admiral Lord Louis] Mountbatten, had never wanted to stage a campaign there. They were constrained to do so nevertheless, both by the inability to provide resources for the amphibious strategy they preferred, and American insistence upon re-opening the road to China ... Slim [with the Commander-in-chief, Field Marshal Sir Claude Auchinleck, and the Director of Infantry, Major-General Reginald Savory] forged an army that won a victory, immense and almost meaningless, except that it vindicated the Indian Army's honour and traditions before that army marched into the shadows.[4]

He goes on to say that victory did, at least, make Mountbatten's subse-quent task of winding up British rule in India easier, enabling the British, unlike the Dutch or French, to leave Asia with some dignity. Meanwhile the 'great China' of American sentiment turned out to be something quite different and convulsed American politics. Louis Allen calls these conclu-sions 'uncompromising and not easily acceptable', before concluding much the same thing. But in his preface he contemplates Japanese success: Britain forced to make a separate peace and a world in authoritarian militaristic darkness.[5] For the Japanese it was mainly a matter of wartime expediency,

---

* American dead were buried in temporary cemeteries and disinterred at war's end. Depending on next of kin, they were either returned to the USA for reburial or buried in the American Military Cemetery and Memorial in Manila.

undermined by more pressing demands. The Japanese government of the time was brutal and aggressive, dominated by the military.[6] Somebody had to defeat it, and not simply by naval blockade or atomic bomb. The Imperial Japanese Army had to be defeated to avoid a Germany post-First World War style claim of betrayal. The Japanese military regime in Burma threatening India and China was one such place, and Slim and Fourteenth Army achieved this, in the face of colossal difficulties – a truly great feat of arms.[7]

In 1941 Japan invaded Burma for two principal reasons: to secure all that she had already won in Malaya and Singapore, vulnerable along the Kra isthmus; and to cut the Burma Road from Rangoon to Lashio and over the border to Kunming, along which the Chinese received supplies. Like so many wars fought by the British, it began disastrously. 'Burma was lost before the first shot was fired', wrote Callahan. 'Neither trained troops nor the aircraft to hold it were available.'[8] The British Army's retreat across Burma – at some 900 miles the longest in its history – was utterly catastrophic, overshadowed though it was at the time by the loss of Singapore. Another American historian, Barbara Tuchman, noted that no nation other than the British 'has ever produced a military history of such verbal nobility ... win or lose, blunder or bravery, murderous folly or unyielding resolution, all emerge alike clothed in dignity and touched with glory'.[9] Hopefully the intervening years have revealed a little more of what created this disaster, but beneath the reasons remains a human story, of hundreds of thousands of participants and millions more swept up by events. And coming hard on the heels of defeat in Europe and the Mediterranean, with the fight against Nazism taking precedence over the Far East, it did little for British prestige in the USA. But fortunately defeat in Burma included the seeds of future success, as Slim held together the remnants of Burma Army from which was forged the winning formula.

The primary objective of the Prime Minister, Winston Churchill, was the recovery of Singapore, which would both be a genuine strategic victory and go some way to restoring British face throughout Asia. Always assuming sufficient shipping could be garnered, it also made Burma a strategic backwater. But while President Franklin D. Roosevelt, and America in general, may have been pro-British, they were not pro-British Empire. Roosevelt was as determined to see the end of empires as Churchill was to preserve the British one, so that strategic priorities diverged widely. In America the China lobby was strong: China remained a cornerstone of American policy, not only in terms of the defeat of Japan but also for the post-war stability she sought for the region. She would be one of four great powers Roosevelt hoped would preserve peace. However, 'myth and illusion were the dominant features of American perceptions of China.'[10] During the 1930s her 'self-appointed role as China's disinterested guardian had been the principal factor in the widening gap between the United States and Japan'.[11] Meanwhile the Chinese were engaged against both the Japanese and themselves. The Nationalists under Generalissimo Chiang Kai-shek were first of all concerned with survival, having had the worst of the war with Japan since the latter's invasion of Manchuria in 1931, and at greater intensity since Japan attacked China proper in 1937. But the Japanese were a temporary curse; Chiang's main objective was to destroy the Communists under Mao Tse-tung (Zedong), and armies lost in fighting the Japanese were lost to the battle against Mao. Chiang was prepared to await foreign help to defeat the Japanese, since the use of barbarians 'to defeat other barbarians was a traditional principle of Chinese statecraft'.[12]

When Mountbatten was appointed Supreme Allied Commander, South-East Asia Command, in 1943 he visited many of the troops. After the war one commanding officer reminded him of what he had said to them: 'I hear you call this the Forgotten Front, I hear you call yourselves the Forgotten Army. Well, let me tell you that this is not the Forgotten Front; you are not the Forgotten Army. In fact, nobody has even *heard* of you.'[13] The British were not alone in this feeling: Americans shared it at the time.[14] Indian soldiers after independence were forced to live in the shadow of members of the Japanese-sponsored Indian National Army against whom they fought, because the political situation deemed the latter to have fought for freedom and their own efforts to have been in the service of British imperialism. Yet the Forgotten War 'gathered to itself like a whirlpool, men from the ends of the earth'.[15] Some half of the 61,000 men forming the operational strength of the air force were American but, despite the illusion created by the American press and film industry since the war, with 12,000 troops by April 1945 they formed only 1.7 per cent of the total of 690,000 men involved on the ground, and considerably less than 1 per cent of combat strength as only a quarter of these were combat troops. The Chinese provided 72,000 and the Commonwealth 606,000.[16] The Anglo-Indian Fourteenth Army must have contained more diverse races than any other, perhaps in history. All the races of Burma were swept up by the war – Burmans, Chins, Kachins, Shans, Mons, Nagas and Karens – while men from every county in England, Scotland, Ireland and Wales fought alongside Australians, New Zealanders, Canadians, Newfoundlanders, South Africans and the peoples of west and east Africa: Hausas, Yorubas and Ibos from Nigeria; Kanjarga, Dagartis and Ashantis from

Ghana; Mandis and Timinis from Sierra Leone; Mandingos from Gambia; Nyasas and Yaos from Malawi; Manyamwezi and Manyema from Tanzania; Akamba, Nandi and Kavirondo from Kenya; Baganda and Achole from Uganda; Somalis from Somaliland; Awamb and Angoni from Zambia. But overwhelmingly, the majority of Fourteenth Army came from India; Rajputs, Dogras, Sikhs, Jats, Punjabis, Garwhalis, Biharis, Ahirs, Amirs, Chamars, Rawats, Minas, Mahars, Coorgs, Assamese, Adibasis, Kumaonis, Pathans, Brahuis, Mers, Tamils, Telegus, Paraiyahs, Brahmans, Hindustani Mussulmans, Punjabi Mussulmans, Madrassi Mussulmans and Gurkhas from Nepal, representing practically every race and caste on the subcontinent – all of whom volunteered to fight for the king–emperor.

The great pity is that most of these men were illiterate and have not left behind memoirs, as have so many British and American participants. The accounts we have of Indian soldiers are told via their officers, British and Indian. Therefore, and given the limits of space, the story here is fundamentally an Anglophone one, although as 2nd Lieutenant Charlton Ogburn Jr, an American participant, noted:

> In the similarity of their ordeal and the pitiful sense of duty or – equally pitiful – acceptance of the lack of an alternative that drove them on, there was little to distinguish among the nationalities assembled in that unlikely theatre, Japanese, Indians, Gurkhas, British, East and West Africans, Chinese and Americans.[17]

Equally in such a colossal maelstrom, it is impossible to provide details of every action, since far exceeding the 'big battles' were thousands of smaller fights involving isolated and independent patrols, companies, columns and the many guerrilla units sponsored by the Allies. Names appear throughout regimental histories of places where some grim fight took place: dozens of them, significant to the participants if to nobody else, and it is impossible to describe them all. It was ever thus.

Among British veterans feelings towards the former enemy remain mixed. John Winstanley 'had experienced fighting the Japs in the Arakan, [where they were] bayonetting the wounded and prisoners. So whereas we respected the Afrika Korps, not so the Japanese. They had renounced any right to be regarded as human, and we thought of them as vermin to be exterminated.'[18] William Pennington agreed: 'I would always hate the Japanese, even in my declining years. Ask any man who fought against the Japanese in that campaign: we all carry the same abiding hatred.'[19] But this is not so. John Hill, writing forty years later, wondered if those who fought still felt antagonism, animosity and hatred towards the Japanese.

The answer from me is 'No', but then I wasn't tortured as some were. I wasn't beaten or starved … I have great sympathy for those who were personally involved with the worst aspects of the Japanese behaviour in war. If they must continue to wage active or passive vendettas against the Japanese, their actions should be understood; for the rest of us, we should stand aside.[20]

Fifty years on, George MacDonald Fraser's feelings were somewhere in between. 'As to old grudges and hatreds … well one cannot help what one feels, and guilt and regret just don't come into it.' But seeing Japanese veterans interviewed on television, he felt 'a curious sort of recognition of the wrinkled old bastards'.[21]

The Japanese that died are even less well remembered than the Allied dead. David Wilson as Chairman of the Burma Star Association welcomed his former enemies to his home and to the 2nd Divisional Memorial at York, a replica of the Naga Stone at Kohima. He observes: 'It is hard to think of these men, impeccably dressed in smart suits, as the savage enemy they once were, and their emotion is quite genuine when they lay their wreaths of chrysanthemums on our memorial.' When he asked why they held a British memorial in such high esteem, he was told, 'because it is part of our history too now. We have nothing in Japan to remind us of our friends and comrades who lie with yours in Burma. It is our privilege to remember them here.'[22] John Nunneley expanded:

> My sympathy for the suffering endured by those many thousands of troops captured in the Far East and treated with ruthless brutality was undiminished and I remained profoundly grateful that I had not had to share their long ordeal. Would I have possessed the moral strength, the nobility of spirit, which distinguished those few former prisoners who brought themselves to forgive, I wondered? … In the Burma Campaign Fellowship Group I saw the spiritual rewards of reconciliation, and an opportunity to help rebuild a former relationship so that the two countries might go forward as friends and partners, each with a better understanding of the other's culture and way of life, and thinking.[23]

As a member of the post-war generation my own feelings are that we must move on. The only Japanese I have ever met were rugby fans, and I like rugby fans. Besides, the war was to have its most lasting effect on the peoples of Burma, and many of those who fought on the Allied side throughout, especially the Karens, Kachins and Chins in Burma, but also the Nagas and Assamese in India, have not known peace since.

Some former British soldiers have since returned to pay respects to those fallen, but travel restrictions make this difficult and most have not, while the plight of the former King's Burmese soldiers is often desperate.[24] In January 1945 Winifred Beaumont of 41st Indian General Hospital visited the Imphal cemetery and picked up a piece of tin with the words 'Lest We Forget' printed in holes with a nail and the heel of a boot.

> A great surge of emotion swept over me, making my hands tremble and I cried: 'Their courage must not be forgotten. This piece of tin should be placed in the House of Commons so that the nation can remember them!' The men laughed. 'A soldier is always forgotten until the next war.'

A friend said that they were the forgotten Fourteenth Army and it was up to them to remember. Even more reason, said Winifred: '"Then members can look at it and remember the cost in human life, and think again before embarking on another." They continued to laugh.'[25] Yet the words most often conjured up in relation to this war, from the Kohima Memorial, are still moving:

> When you go home,
> Tell them of us and say
> For their tomorrow,
> We gave our today ...[26]

## Note on pronunciation and spelling

In Romanized Burmese *au* is pronounced *ow*, *gy* is pronounced *j* and *ky* becomes *ch*. Thus Kyaukse is *Chowk-see*, Taukkyan is *Towkcharn* and Myitkyina is *Mit-cheena*; Ba Gyaw is *Ba jaw* and Maymyo is pronounced *Mymew*. The stress in Karen is on the second syllable. Chinese spelling in English used to be based on the Wade-Giles method, and has since been replaced in the west by the more accurate Pin-yin: thus the capital city of China used to be rendered Peking but is now Beijing. However, many names will be unfamiliar to readers when written in Pin-yin: for example, Chiang Kai-shek becomes Jiang Jieshi. I have therefore retained the Wade-Giles system except in cases where readers may already be familiar with Pin-yin. Similarly, distances are in the otherwise archaic imperial system rather than metric since almost all accounts – at least, Allied ones – use this.

# PART I
# DEFEAT

# I

## Burma and the British

I love the Burman with the blind favouritism of first impression.
When I die I will be a Burman, with twenty yards of real King's silk,
that has been made in Mandalay, about my body.

Rudyard Kipling

'**B**URMA IS DIFFERENT!' thought Lieutenant James Lunt. India, that land of colour, was drab in comparison. 'Rangoon's gardens bloomed with tropical profusion – bougainvillaea, poinsettias, laburnum and tall delphiniums of piercing blue. The Gold Mohur trees flamed like golden candles against the green foliage.' And not only Burma's botany caught the eye; 'above all the gaily dressed Burmese in their brightly-coloured *lungyis* (skirts) all combined to make Burma a moving pageant'.[1] The Shwe Dagon Pagoda's cupola 'gave radiance to the clear air and the blue sky; in the daylight it shone forth like a blaze of gold, burning and pure; in the evenings it tinkled its bells, and filled the heart with a gentle sadness which is not grief but a sweet perception of unearthly things'.[2]

Burma is a country of magnificent contrasts: high jungle, coastal mangrove swamps, alluvial deltas and a central dry triangular plain walled in by mountains to west, north and east. Larger than France, it is elongated and extends through Tenasserim as a finger along the Malay peninsula. Four main rivers running north–south dictate that communications run similarly: the Irrawaddy – a name derived from the Sanskrit, meaning 'river of refreshment' – is 1,300 miles long, up to 3 miles wide and navigable as far as Bhamo (800 miles). It was regularly served by large river boats of the Scottish-based Irrawaddy Flotilla Company, beyond which river boats could take the traveller as far as Myitkyina.[3] Its tributary the Chindwin is navigable by shallow-draught steamers. To the east the Sittang has a tidal bore that made crossing it difficult, although there was a railway bridge taking the line from Rangoon down to Tenasserim; and further east still the Salween, rising in China and longer than the Irrawaddy, follows the Thai border. Unnavigable, it was crossed only by ferry.

Roads were few and poor. The Arakan coastal strip – mostly swamp and bamboo forest – was more easily reached by boat from Chittagong or Calcutta than from the interior. Off the coast, Akyab island had an airstrip, a link on the Calcutta–Singapore route.[4] There was no complete road to Moulmein, although the railway went as far as Ye. Only tracks connected Thailand and India. However, one significant road did exist: the so-called Burma Road to China, 770 miles long from Kunming to Lashio, where it met the railway from Mandalay and Rangoon, taking supplies in a five-day journey.[5] Like all Burma's roads, it was in poor condition: liable to be impassable in the rainy season, when flooded *chaungs* (streams and rivers) might wash away a hillside, taking the 'road' with it.[6] The south-west monsoon blows from mid-May to mid-October, turning vast areas into swamp and dumping up to 200 inches of rainfall on parts of coastal Arakan. But from October to March the climate is pleasant, even in crowded towns. Not that many towns were significant, apart from Rangoon and Mandalay; most were little more than a few streets of wooden houses and shops with a pagoda.

In 1941 Burma teemed with wildlife, while its 17 million people included: 10 million Burmans,* whom the British regarded as pleasant and easygoing, but impulsive and excitable; some 4 million Karens, whose main home was the wild jungle-covered territory between the Sittang and Salween rivers, with sizeable communities in the Irrawaddy delta; and 1½ million Shans in the Shan states east of the central plains, where the very mixed population included Taungthus, Taungyos, Palaungs, Padaungs, Black Karens, Striped Karens, Lahus, Lisus, Ekaws, Inthas, Chinese Shans, Hküns and Miaos, and where perhaps half of Burma's 126 languages and dialects might be heard.[7] In the mountainous far north-east lived the Kachins, fond of opium and with a typical hillman's contempt for the people of the plains. Among the first tribes to enlist in British service, they maintained their loyalty the longest. West of the Chindwin lay the Chin Hills, a tangled mass of razor-backed ridges and bottomless forest-covered valleys 8,000 feet high, rain-drenched and feverish, beyond where, just inside India, lived the Nagas. From outside had come Indians – mostly Tamils from south India – to man the docks and carry out all manner of menial work Burmans deemed beneath them. But many were rich money-lenders, which fed a deep mutual antipathy with the Burmese.[8] There were also some 300,000 Chinese quietly making money and a small but signifi-

* The term 'Burman' is used to denote ethnic Burmese, as opposed to the myriad ethnic minorities that make up the population.

cant Japanese community, including many doctors and dentists. For the 20,000 Anglo-Burmans there was not the social stigma Anglo-Indians felt in India, and many held important positions in the administration.

The administration was a recent development. Friction between British India and Burma began after 1784, when a common frontier was established between Burma's newly acquired Arakan province and British-administered Chittagong. The First Burma War (1824–6) was a punitive response to raids from Assam and Arakan into territory controlled by the East India Company. The British seized Arakan and Tenasserim. Following more border incidents and mistreatment of traders, the Second Burma War (1852) saw them annexe the southern province of Pegu, including Rangoon. What remained was the kingdom of Ava under King Thibaw, a weak monarch dominated by his half-sister – one of four wives – Queen Supayalat ('Soup-plate' to British troops). The Third Burma War (1885–6) came after Thibaw raised fears among the British of French interference from their newly acquired territories in Indo-China.[9] In the war and subsequent pacification, lasting almost five years, one unit, 1st Royal Welch Fusiliers, lost only 4 men killed by enemy action, but 84 died of disease and another 350 had to be invalided out of the country.[10] Burma became a province of India promoting British and Indian economic interests, leading inevitably to Burmese social demoralization. The Burman sense of superiority to other races did not help to cement national feeling. Karen nationalism saw the establishment of the Karen National Association in 1881, strengthened by their receptivity to Christian missionaries, especially American Baptists.[11] When anti-British Burman dacoits (bandits) went on the rampage in 1886, the Karens resisted them. Distrust between Burmans and Karens never diminished, and the Karens would pay a heavy price for national aspirations come independence in 1948.[12]

In the years leading up to the First World War Burma underwent a transformation. Most significant was the vast increase in rice production as commercial methods replaced subsistence farming, and much land ended in the possession of *chattyars* (Indian moneylenders).[13] Not only did Indians work in agriculture, but the government-owned railway system was largely built by Indian funds. The other principal businesses were the teak forests of the north and the Burmah Oil Company, organized in 1886 and unique in making extensive use of Burmese labour. Between 1914 and 1942 British industrial investment in Burma tripled, with the addition of mining and rubber interests in the south-east setting the tone of European settlement.[14] Travelling to Rangoon in 1912, Maurice Collis noted of his mercantile companions that 'their lives were devoted ... to conducting to

London the streams of profits, on which the very existence of England depended.'[15]

Meanwhile, Burma suffered severe cultural and religious decline: apart from continued deference to *pongyis* (Buddhist monks), traditional society disintegrated and even the prestige associated with government service evaporated. Crime increased and social mobility for most Burmans tended to be downwards.[16] Although the First World War had little effect on the country, Burma followed in the wake of revolutionary upheaval centred on India, awakening political forces only dormant before. In 1920 the founding of the University of Rangoon was accompanied by a national school movement that marked the birth of revolutionary nationalism, culminating in racial violence during the Saya San rebellion of 1930–1.[17] Burman resentment of Indian coolie labour exploded and rioting was widespread in Lower Burma. Maurice Collis, now a judge in Rangoon, described their mood:

> The Burmese proletariat walked with a lighter step. They had shown the Indians their place. This was Burma, a land which had been independent for hundreds of years before it fell to the English. Too many Indians had crowded into it from their starving villages across the bay. They could ... undersell the Burmese, and there was a swarm of them too in the public services, particularly in the railways and the prison department. Well, they had been taught a lesson.[18]

Inevitably the British also ran foul of increasing nationalism and relations grew increasingly tense as the 1930s progressed. However, few had direct contact with Burmese people, so there was little personal animosity.[19]

Based on Rangoon University, the All Burma School Movement developed, though its importance was limited to the small middle class. It was closely associated with the Dobama Asionye ('We Burmese' Society), whose members referred to themselves as *thakin* (meaning 'lord' or 'master'), customarily used for addressing Britons in Upper Burma and now a symbol of youthful defiance. They also associated with the Communists, although theirs was essentially a nationalist rather than a Communist organization.[20] In 1936 there was another strike at the university, like many campuses a pleasant place to make friends of both sexes and work hard only around exam time. 'What splendour there was', noted student Mi Mi Khaing, 'in the richness of Burmese dress, food, companions, religious celebration, music, dancing and wit.'[21] Some of the more zealous male students, backed by *pongyis* in their 'saffron' robes – which in reality ranged from dusty yellow to deep orange – decried the 'degradation' of

14

Burma's young women resulting from the fashion for transparent muslin blouses. But few paid any attention until a lecturer was accused of 'immorality'. When Thakin Aung San was then disciplined for refusing to reveal the author of an inflammatory article in the journal of the Students' Union, strikers lay across the entrances of buildings where final examinations were due to be held. Since it is an unpardonable insult to tread on the body of a male Buddhist, no one dared cross the picket line. To Burman nationalists in particular the strike was of great importance, although Karens, Indians and Chinese regarded it as an abominable nuisance.[22]

Change was coming, however: there was a new constitution with an elected House of Representatives and a Senate, although the Governor reserved powers on foreign affairs and defence, and with the election of a nationalist coalition Cabinet under Dr Ba Maw in April 1937 Burma was separated from India. Ba Maw 'used quaint words, like an Englishman using Burmese and his well cultivated stutter and musical voice were effective'.[23] Colin McPhedran was an eleven-year-old Anglo-Burmese whose mother, Daw Ni,* was a Mon ('the educators of Burma') and a graduate of the University of Calcutta. She was also Ba Maw's cousin, and he recalled a visit to their house when a heated exchange arose over the future of the British, and his educated mother took sides with his Scottish father.

> I remember Uncle Ba Maw saying, 'One day we will have you British out of our country'. It hit a raw nerve with my father, and when Uncle Ba Maw followed it up with 'Archie, without Daw Ni you are nothing in this cultured country and the regard in which you are held is entirely due to the union with my cousin', my father almost exploded.[24]

In most Anglo-Burmese marriages the Burmese side normally came a poor second, and Daw Ni's background was unusual. Indeed, Eurasians were often condescended to as being 'café au lait', or 'two of coffee, one of milk', and often tried to compensate by being more pukka than genuine sahibs. George Robertson, son of a Scottish forester and a Shan woman, enlisted in the tiny Burma Royal Navy Volunteer Reserve. On his first day he went with an expatriate fellow officer in the latter's car, and 'I tried to strike up a conversation, but he would have none of it. He neither spoke nor took any notice of me ... even though we were so-called brother-officers.'[25] This was symptomatic of the pervasive European racial arrogance, which relegated all Asians to a lower tier.[26]

The political temperature throughout Asia rose rapidly during the late

---

* 'U' is the Burmese title of respect for an older or outstanding man; the corresponding title for a woman is 'Daw'.

1930s, and the anti-European aspects of the Kuomintang revolution in China contributed to Burmese nationalism. China had suffered revolution in 1911 with the overthrow of the last emperor. After 1923 the Kuomintang and Communists demanded unity and the overthrow of Western imperialism, the chief target of their animosity being Britain. In 1927 Chiang Kai-shek rose to prominence as leader of the ramshackle Kuomintang, and rupture with the Communists reduced opposition to foreign interference. Chiang was a devout, puritanical Methodist who did not smoke and rarely drank. He was also a neurotic, power-hungry despot whose treatment of those close to him was startlingly heartless. He abandoned his first wife, gave his second venereal disease on their wedding night and, despite her exemplary conduct, discarded her in favour of an advantageous match with Soong Mei-ling, the youngest of the fabulously wealthy Soong sisters.[27] When the Japanese expanded their war from Manchuria to mainland China in 1937, tension rose perceptibly, with Burmese opinion supporting the Chinese.[28] To most Asian intellectuals the war created the same passionate ideological rivalry between left and right as the Spanish Civil War produced for Europeans; while Japan repelled those of the left, it attracted those for whom ridding Asia of white imperialists was the more important goal. It was on this issue that Jawarlal Nehru broke with his rival to lead post-war India, Subhas Chandra Bose. Nehru backed China while Bose, an admirer of Mussolini, backed Japan.[29] Aware of Ba Maw's anti-British sentiments through his Japanese doctor, the Japanese consul in Rangoon approached him about stopping the flow of munitions to China along the Burma Road, now 'the most dangerous, most confused, and most important road in the world'.[30] But this was beyond Burmese jurisdiction; the Burmese were not yet ready for armed revolt against the British, and Ba Maw failed to get funding.[31]

In 1938 peasant demonstrations in Rangoon demanding agrarian reform were accompanied by serious anti-Indian rioting in the 'Revolution of 1300' (the date according to the Burmese calendar). At Mandalay seventeen people died under police fire, and Ba Maw's downfall in February 1939 only strengthened his Anglophobia. When H. G. Wells arrived on a lecture tour to convince people of the merits of a confederation of free people sustaining a world law, 'a free-thinking, free-speaking liberal world', he was disappointed with the answer he received.

> But our government won't let us. Our censorship won't let us. Our schools prevent us. The past stands in our way. Our boys learn more by striking, argument and reading forbidden literature, than by sitting in classrooms. They are learning to feel responsible for Burma.[32]

A new ministry was formed, headed by U Pu, but conflict in Europe had a sobering effect, with the general condemnation of fascism. It also saw the establishment of the 'Freedom Bloc', based on the Thakin Party, which subordinated ideology to nationalism and included Ba Maw and Aung San as general secretary. Then in September 1939 war came to Europe. The *Gazette of India* simply announced that 'I, Victor Alexander John, Marquess of Linlithgow, Governor-General of India ... do hereby proclaim that war has broken out between His Majesty and Germany.' 'One man,' wrote Nehru, 'and he a foreigner, plunged four hundred millions of human beings into war without the slightest reference to them.'[33] A similar declaration was made on behalf of the Burmese.

In May and June of 1940, with the German invasion of the West, the Freedom Bloc increased its overt anti-war propaganda, and also in May a Japanese agent arrived, disguised as a correspondent of the *Yomiuri* newspaper and general-secretary of the Japan–Burma Association. Colonel Suzuki Keiji of Imperial General Headquarters (IGHQ), using the pseudonym Minami Masuyo, had instructions to sound out Burmese political opinion with a view to cutting the Burma Road. He told Ba Maw that Chandra Bose had already requested 10 million rupees and 10,000 rifles. 'We want half that amount in Burma to begin with,' Ba Maw said, 'and we shall also want Japanese instructors.'[34] But agitation increased and more Thakin leaders were arrested. In a dramatic move, Ba Maw resigned from the House of Representatives and attacked U Pu's policy of supporting the war. His arrest on 6 August and subsequent one-year gaol sentence were a martyr-toned political sensation.[35] But by the end of September U Pu had been replaced by the more vigorous U Saw, who suppressed internal unrest with enthusiasm. Burma's third premier since separation was, according to Maurice Collis, a 'demagogue of mediocre education, ambitious for himself and without scruples'.[36]

In late 1940 Aung San departed for China in disguise aboard the Norwegian freighter *Hai Lee*, ostensibly to seek Chinese Communist support for Burmese independence. The Thakins were deeply split over collaboration with the Japanese; many implacably opposed it. But this madcap adventure saw Aung San arrested by the Japanese in Amoy, and he obtained his release only when the pro-Japanese Ba Sein made urgent representations to Japanese agents in Rangoon that Aung San was really seeking Japanese aid.[37] Suzuki now had evidence supporting active intervention in Burma to show IGHQ. He proposed to take thirty members of Aung San's party, arm them and infiltrate back into Burma through Thailand. The Minami Kikan (Minami Organization) was duly set up in February 1941.[38]

In a brief and furtive ten-day return to Burma, Aung San formed the pro-Japanese People's Revolutionary Party and the cadre trained at Hainan island before assembling at Bangkok. What Japan promised the 'Thirty Comrades' (or 'Thirty Heroes', as the Burmese press later styled them) remains unclear, but must have involved some form of independence for Burma.[39] The bond between Suzuki and his young charges was cemented with the *thwe thauk* (blood-drinking) ceremony, in which they cut their fingers and mixed their blood in a silver bowl with strong liquor, then drank, swearing 'to be indissolubly bound together by this blood when fighting the British enemy'.[40] They took fresh titles with the rank of *Bo* (colonel); Suzuki became *Bo Mogyo* (Colonel Thunderbolt), a name adapted from a Burmese saying concerning lightning striking the sphere of the palace, symbolic of the destruction of British rule.[41]

British defence policy in the Far East rested on the naval base at Singapore, but financial strictures meant Britain simply could not afford war with Japan, which left diplomacy as the main defence. When British requests for joint action against Japan were rejected by the USA in 1939, she was forced instead to improve relations while co-operating with the USA in assisting China via the Burma Road – 'to reconcile the manifestly irreconcilable'.[42] In 1940 the Chiefs of Staff believed it impossible to hold Singapore in isolation, but action was deemed necessary and Air Chief Marshal Sir Robert Brooke-Popham was appointed Commander-in-Chief Far East in April 1941.[43] His principal concerns remained Singapore and Malaya, and he pressed vainly for reinforcements, especially in the air, but Prime Minister Winston Churchill refused. Churchill regarded North Africa as the top priority for the defence of Great Britain, and 'as for an attack on Singapore, he did not believe anything of the sort was contemplated'.[44] Consequently, on 28 April 1941 he issued a directive – without referring it to the Chiefs of Staff – that there was 'no need at the present time to make any further dispositions for the defence of Malaya and Singapore beyond those modest arrangements which are in progress'.[45] Although the Singapore Defence Conference in October found serious deficiencies throughout the Far East, and recommended the deployment of 336 aircraft for Burma/Malaya, that figure was never approached.[46]

Meanwhile, the position of America remained obscure. Isolationism was strong and, while the British and Dutch were regarded as preferable to the Japanese, the anti-imperial sentiments bequeathed by the Founding Fathers and suspicion of Limey duplicity, combined with support for China and ignorance of the kind of war looming, hindered combined planning for it. Besides, America's principal concern was China. On 16

May 1941 President Franklin D. Roosevelt declared the defence of China vital to the USA, and the first military assistance by the USA soon followed in the form of an air mission at the request of Chiang, which was expanded to a full Military Mission in July.[47]

Since separation from India, Burma had been responsible for her own defence, financing whatever forces she kept and equipping them through the War Office in London. But preparations were wholly inadequate and a newly created defence department did not make for efficiency, with inevitable omissions.[48] The Governor was Vice-Admiral the Hon. Sir Archibald Cochrane, a descendant of the great naval hero Thomas Cochrane. The General Officer Commanding Burma was Major-General D. K. McLeod, whose main work was 'Burmanizing' the army – ensuring its independence from the Indian Army, although this had not progressed very far.[49] But Burma's administration remained complacent; an ex-governor reported that Burmese volunteering was good, that government ministers were co-operating and that the jungle frontiers of Thailand were formidable.[50] And Lieutenant I. C. G. Scott with the Burma Frontier Force (BFF) noted the colonel and his wife 'dressed for dinner every night, even when dining on their own'.[51]

Since she linked India and Malaya, Burma's security was vital to both. India was responsible for Burma's defence administration, yet it was operationally under Brooke-Popham's command at Singapore, and whether operations came under the Commander-in-Chief Far East or the Commander-in-Chief India became contentious when General Sir Archibald Wavell was appointed to the latter post in July 1941.[52] Wavell had been Commander-in-Chief Middle East until Churchill's impatience saw him swap places with General Sir Claude Auchinleck.[53] Although Wavell's strategic planning had been 'excellent' according to his opponent Generalleutnant Erwin Rommel, he had been unable to overcome the systemic failings of the British Army, and was now faced with an equally forlorn situation: shortages of everything and a confused chain of command.[54] On a visit to London in September 1941 Wavell tried to get Burma placed under his operational command, but the Chief of the Imperial General Staff, General Sir John Dill, told him 'the political set-up with regard to Chiang required that it should be part of the Command at Singapore'.[55] McLeod never took the threat from across the Thai border seriously, believing that only small forces could operate on the Raheng–Kawkareik–Moulmein axis.[56] When Wavell visited Rangoon in October, he met McLeod and the new Governor, the Rt. Hon. Sir Reginald Dorman-Smith, who heavily discounted the possibility of war: in any case, he said, if the Japanese invaded the Burmese would rise up against them, while under the new Defence of Burma Act prominent Freedom Bloc members were arrested.[57] Wavell found that the staff and intelligence organization was woefully poor, although this was not a situation peculiar to Burma. He signalled Dill that the defence of Burma was vital to the defence of India but not of Malaya, and he requested reinforcements and a revision of the command question, later noting in his despatch the continuation of this arrangement as 'the cardinal mistake'.[58]

Naval forces comprised five motor launches of the Burma Royal Naval Volunteer Reserve.[59] The air force was equally weak: when the Japanese invaded, the RAF had only 60 Squadron's Blenheim light bombers and 67 Squadron's antiquated Buffalo fighters to defend the precious airfields at Victoria Point, Moulmein, Tavoy and Mergui on the vital air reinforcement route to Malaya, although many people shared the contemptuous view of the Japanese expressed by Russell Spurr's father: 'Their eyesight is so bad they can't fly fighter planes. That's assuming the little bastards could even build them.'[60] For some reason 517 Air Ministry Experimental Station at Moulmein, the only radar unit in the Far East, was also in Burma rather than at Singapore. They sent regular reports to the Far East Intelligence Bureau at Singapore, all seemingly ignored.[61] And since Burma had never been deemed threatened by a major power, the army was pitifully weak: only two British battalions were maintained (1st Gloucestershire Regiment and 2nd King's Own Yorkshire Light Infantry – KOYLI), while it was considered imprudent to enlist Burmans in a force that might be used against their fellow countrymen. In 1939 the Burma Defence Force included only 372 Burmans but 3,197 Karens, Chins and Kachins.[62] They formed four battalions of Burma Rifles, formerly the junior regiment of the Indian Army, all stationed around Rangoon and Maymyo districts, with Indian artillery and engineers.[63] For internal security duties there were nine battalions of Burma Military Police, six of which converted to the BFF after separation remaining under civil control.[64] In 1941 the BFF formed columns numbered 1–8, mostly of two-company size, largely Indian* in composition, with Chins, Kachins and Karens. There was also the part-time volunteer Burma Auxiliary Force (BAF) of four battalions and a field artillery battery (with First World War vintage 18-pounders) drawn from the British, Indian,

---

* Including Punjabis and Sikhs but mainly Gurkhas, descendants of many who settled around Maymyo as market gardeners after discharge. 10th Gurkha Rifles was originally raised at Maymyo from Gurkhas living in Burma.

Anglo-Burmese and Anglo-Indian communities.[65] When war broke out in Europe, the BFF was made responsible for airfield security and the BAF was embodied. Expansion began, severely hampered by lack of resources and instructors.

Officers were mainly seconded from the regular British Army. The strict social hierarchy of the time meant a young man needed 'good' family and private means to serve in a fashionable regiment: Guards, Greenjackets (Rifles) or cavalry. Apart from the technical corps, most officer candidates had to find their way in the 'line' infantry regiments, where a private income was less important. But it remained extremely difficult for many to live on their pay, and one alternative was to go 'bushwhacking', as it was sometimes called: taking secondment to colonial forces such as the Royal West African Frontier Force, King's African Rifles, Sudan Defence Force, Trans-Jordan Frontier Force or Burma Rifles.[66] The Burma Rifles doubled in size as officers were recruited from the British civilian population. A Burma Corps of Sappers and Miners was raised, and a BAF heavy anti-aircraft regiment formed (despite the total absence of anti-aircraft guns in Burma). Demands for greater Burman recruitment led to companies being integrated into the newly raised battalions of Burma Rifles, but there was a desperate shortage of small arms of all kinds and practically no personal equipment, maps, mines, machine-guns, mortars, radios or field telephones, transport, grenades or ammunition.[67] The lack of practical experience that service on the North-West Frontier provided the Indian Army was widely noted. 'On parade they were extremely smart, but they had become too civilized. They had forgotten their jungle lore – had indeed been encouraged to put it behind them.'[68] Serving with 4th Burma Rifles in 1940, James Lunt noted that wartime expansion halved efficiency. He recalled:

> no tactical instruction of any kind … [On exercise w]e attacked in line up the gentle slopes, the commanding officer galloping to and fro as he adjured us to 'keep our dressing'. Afterwards, during the critique, he told us that British officers should always lead the line, waving their walking sticks. I wonder what the Japanese were being told around about the same time? Perhaps they did not carry walking sticks?[69]

Certainly the jungle was never mentioned in polite military circles: that was for snakes, elephants and timbermen. All talk was of how the war would be won in the deserts of North Africa and the North European plain.

The Singapore Defence Conference had recommended Burma be

reinforced by seven battalions with artillery and engineer support, but the Chiefs of Staff thought this an overestimate; 13th Indian Brigade arrived in Rangoon in March/April 1941 and moved to Mandalay. Over the summer 1st Burma Division was formed under Major-General J. Bruce Scott, comprising 1st and 2nd Burma Brigades and 13th Indian Brigade but with only 27th Mountain Artillery (a regimental headquarters sent to control four batteries already in country), which never operated as a regiment, 1st Burma Field Company and 56th Indian Field Company for engineers, and practically no signals, transport or provost staff. In August Brooke-Popham recommended to the War Office that another Indian brigade be sent, and Wavell agreed; 16th Indian Brigade was still arriving when the Japanese invaded.[70] Thus the two distinct bodies of soldiers in India, armies that once conquered Burma, were now charged with her defence.

In India the British Army provided forty-eight infantry battalions, four cavalry regiments and most of the artillery (control of which they had taken great care to retain since the Mutiny of 1857–8). But service overseas was not much fun. Two-thirds of a soldier's normal engagement was spent abroad; many did six years in India without a break. As one chronicler noted: 'Years without a hope of seeing home and family until the end.'[71] And during this time the government did nothing for them. For officers there were clubs, messes and a few women, but for the private soldier nought but a flyblown bar and grill on the outskirts of the bazaar – lousy food, adulterated booze and poxy women.[72] The Indian Army was about three times as large, with Indian soldiers (sepoys) and NCOs (lance-naiks and naiks equivalent to lance-corporals and corporals; havildars and havildar-majors equivalent to sergeants and sergeant-majors). An Indian battalion normally had about twelve British officers (King's Commissioned Officers, or KCOs); the rest were Indians (Viceroy's Commissioned Officers, VCOs), who had three ranks: jemadars (risaldars in the cavalry), who wore one star like a British 2nd lieutenant; subedars, who wore two like a lieutenant, and the subedar-major, who wore a crown like a British major. Platoons were commanded by VCOs and although the subedar-major commanded nothing he was omnipresent and omnipotent, effectively second-in-command of the battalion, with responsibility for all matters of morale and well-being. The whole taken together was the Army in India, with Commander-in-Chief provided alternately by British and Indian Armies. The military problems were roughly divided so that the British kept peace amid race riots and religious disorder, while Indian troops defended the frontiers. Both trained for war, although government parsimony meant this was seldom above brigade level, and always 'for War in Europe, with a wholly imaginary supply of modern weapons and equipment'.[73] In addition were the Indian State Forces. Before partition almost one quarter of the population lived not in 'British India' but in the princely states controlled by hereditary rulers with contract relations to the East India Company (and subsequently the Crown).* These maintained forces, some of which saw Imperial service, and in 1920 this arrangement was formalized when the Crown undertook to arm and equip a number of State Forces units as Field Service Units, which would then be available to the Crown on Indian Army establishments, with others available on lower states of readiness. In all, forty-nine states took part in the scheme, although this did not stop recruitment taking place within them for the Indian Army, which ultimately recruited some 350,000 men there against 50,000 for State Forces.[74]

The Indian Army had, like India herself, evolved. Originally, sepoys were mercenaries in the pay of the East India Company. However, 'John Company' was fatally undermined by the Mutiny, a brutal conflict with savagery from both sides, but one that haunted the remainder of British rule. Although some Indian historians regard the Mutiny as the first patriotic war, this is a serious oversimplification, and regiments from the Punjab recently added to the Raj during the Sikh Wars of the 1840s, together with Nepalese Gurkhas, were prominent in its suppression.[75] Afterwards the British government brought the Company's regiments under Crown control, sepoys swore allegiance to the Queen–Empress and her successors. And while the army represented many races, religions and languages, the British recruited largely from western and north–western areas which were believed to be 'martial': men of peasant stock and sound physique, simple and obedient (and loyal during the Mutiny).[76] The injustice and even impudence of this classification was proved in both World Wars, when men from all over India proved that, when well trained and led, they were a match for any soldiers in the world.[77] But in the meantime, Burma's conquest was largely carried out by this army, including units raised in the Punjab for the purpose.†

---

* India in fact comprised British India and 565 Indian states, large and small, ruled by maharajahs, rajahs and nawabs with on average 11 titles, 5.8 wives, 12.6 children, 9.2 elephants, 2.8 railway cars and 3.4 Rolls-Royces and who had killed on average 22.9 tigers (L. Collins and D. Lapierre, *Freedom at Midnight*, p. 136).

† The 89th, 90th, 91st and 92nd Punjabis and 93rd Burma Infantry were amalgamated in 1922 as 8th Punjab Regiment, which took for its cap badge the *chinthe*, the legendary beast that stood guard outside Burmese temples.

By 1939 regiments had been grouped into larger regiments, some based on a single class or race – Sikhs, Dogras, Garwhalis – while others were mixed. Regiments were 'family' affairs, with sons often following fathers into the ranks, and recruited by pensioners. John Shipster joined 7th/2nd Punjab Regiment, which like most Punjabi units was of mixed race: two companies of Punjabi Mussulmen ('Muslims who smoked, but abhorred pigs and did not drink alcohol'), one of Sikhs ('drank like fishes, but were forbidden to smoke'), and one of Dogras ('orthodox Hindus who worshipped the cow, but drank and smoked. It was all rather confusing').[78] The army's lingua franca was Urdu (meaning 'camp' or 'army'), a form of Hindustani incorporating many Persian and Arab words written in roman script for Morse code purposes, and now the official language of Pakistan. English was never used. In addition there were ten regiments of Gurkhas from Nepal. After the Anglo-Nepalese War in 1814–16 ended with a treaty of alliance and perpetual friendship, the Nepalese rulers agreed that their subjects could enlist as mercenary volunteers in the East India Company's service. During the Mutiny the dictatorial Nepalese prime minister, Jung Bahadur, threw his full weight behind the British and they became renowned for their courage and loyalty – to their friends, their regiments and their officers. Gurkhas are great mimics and enjoy a somewhat slapstick sense of humour, which seldom deserts them; they somehow always contrive to grin.[79]

The First World War underlined the Indian Army's ambiguous status, and indeed that of India herself. 'Neither was fully independent nor fully subordinate to London. India and the Army followed policies partly originating in India, partly in London, and with no clear responsibility or control of events.'[80] No attempt at modernization was made, partly owing to government frugality: Congress politicians grudged every anna spent on the army (16 annas made 1 rupee). Besides, internal security required lots of men with rifles, not tanks and technicians.[81] However, with the promise of eventual independence came 'Indianization'. By 1939 Indians were slowly gaining positions of authority within the Civil Service, although the army moved more slowly. Officers granted King's Indian Commissions (with British rank structure) began with an Indian intake to the Royal Military College, Sandhurst, in 1918. An Indian Military Academy was opened at Dehra Dun in 1932, and by 1939 a leavening of KICOs had been achieved.[82] Statistics vary, but one author reports that in October 1939 there were 3,031 British and 697 Indian officers serving, and by the war's end

18,752 British and 13,947 Indian officers (VCOs and KICOs), with another 14,000 officers on secondment from the British Army.[83]

From a pre-war strength of 194,373 the Indian Army would grow to 2,499,909 by its end (with 8 million people working on defence tasks and 6 million in war industries and the expanding railways). In addition, by 1945 Indian State Forces provided 41,463 men to serve the Indian Government from a strength of 99,367. Expansion in 1940 saw an armoured division raised from existing units (many still horsed), five new infantry divisions and a divisional headquarters. However, units were raised by 'milking' existing units for drafts, severely reducing their efficiency by replacing experienced men with raw recruits. In 1941 another five infantry divisions were raised and an armoured division, requiring 50 new battalions, and the steady drain of pre-war experienced men continued. In addition, new regiments such as the Assam and Mahar regiments were raised from classes not previously recruited, while severe shortages of equipment and technically qualified personnel hampered modernization.[84] Thus in 1941 the Indian Army was at its weakest in terms of cohesion. Many junior officers, still far from perfect in Urdu, had only just emerged from officer cadet training units. In many recently formed units, including Burmese ones, 85 per cent of soldiers were barely out of recruit training and few *jawans* (literally 'lads') had ever left their home villages before. It may seem odd that Indian and Nepalese soldiers should be willing to fight and die for a foreign cause, but their loyalty was less mysterious than might appear. The Army had evolved great internal strength, partly from the regimental system, the product of quality officers. Britain's best served in the Indian Army; in peacetime it was necessary to pass out in the top thirty at Sandhurst to get a vacancy. As a wartime officer noted: 'Courtesy and good manners between all officers, British and Indian, was at the heart of the happiness and security which was a normal part of their life.'[85] Training was generally of a high standard, at least at individual and unit level, and often tempered by active service on the Frontier. But perhaps most significant was the concept of personal honour: once a man had eaten 'the salt' he was bound by its code, which entailed never bringing shame on one's kin, village, comrades, regiment or class. Death was preferable.

For a great many it was not far away. On 12 May 1940 Harold Rattenbury, having wandered for 291 days through China and Burma, was flying between Rangoon and Akyab, looking down at the rivers and fields below. He noted several ladies and a child on the plane. One woman from Rangoon had been back to Britain to fetch her two sons, and he 'thought "What a mother won't do for love." That's what we all thought of Britain and Burma that day. How little could we foresee, Britain, scarred and bleeding, never knew invasion: Burma, lovely Burma, overflowed with blood and burned with fire.'[86]

# 2

# Japan and China

Summers and winters had gone – how many times?
And suddenly the Empire was wrecked.
The Imperial Army met the barbarian foe,
The dust of the battlefield darkened the sky and sea,
And the sun and moon were no longer bright,
While the wind of death shook the grass and trees
And the white bones were piled up in hills.
Ah, what had they done – the innocent people?

Li Po

UNTIL EMPEROR MEIJI overthrew the Tokugawa shogunate in 1868 Japan had been a closed society for 250 years. The new powers in the land realized Japan must modernize quickly, a process only possible with the aid and advice of the industrialized West, although the social values of the nation remained largely feudal, with strict adherence to rigid hierarchies and the demands of self-sacrifice and hard work.[1] For necessary raw materials Japan began to look abroad, especially at Korea, and this immediately brought her into potential conflict with China, which claimed suzerainty over Korea. When a Korean rebellion occurred in 1894 and China sent troops, Japan intervened, drove them from the country and seized the Liaotung peninsula in southern Manchuria, securing Korea's western flank. China sued for an armistice and accepted the independence of Korea (in reality, dominance by Japan), also ceding Formosa (Taiwan) and Liaotung. But within days of signing the treaty Russia, France and Germany insisted Japan give up Liaotung. Following the 'triple intervention' she viewed the European powers and especially Russia with deep suspicion; this was at once heightened when, in 1898, Russia leased the ports she had so recently forced Japan to abandon, and then moved troops through Manchuria into China during the Boxer rebellion of 1900.

In Europe the rise of the Triple Alliance between Germany, Austria–Hungary and Italy drew France and Russia closer together while Britain looked on with alarm. Britain's imperial power rested on her navy, and in 1902 she sought a naval alliance with Japan. Both sides gained but Japan gained more: not least, implicit acceptance at the top table of nations. The alliance also gave her the confidence to attack Russia in February 1904. With a crushing victory over the Russian fleet at Tsushima in 1905 she regained Liaotung and had her 'special interests' recognized. Significantly, America's gaze was also directed towards Asia with her newly acquired territories of the Philippines and Hawaii. In the same year President Theodore Roosevelt declared: 'Our future history will be more determined by our position on the Pacific facing China than by our position on the Atlantic facing Europe.'[2] When war erupted in Europe in 1914, Japan quickly came to Britain's aid, seizing the German Pacific possessions and her concessions in China, including the port of Tsingtao. Within months she issued the so-called 'Twenty-One Demands' to the Chinese government to give her access to the vast natural resources of the mainland, but in doing so she overplayed her hand. The strong pro-Chinese element in American society was offended and the US government began to look suspiciously at her, while British protests only reduced British popularity in Japan.

After the First World War Japan gained a League of Nations mandate over some former German possessions and wide influence from Manchuria almost to the equator. In 1922 the Washington Conference signalled the 'Four-Power Treaty', ending the Anglo-Japanese Treaty and fixing naval tonnage between Britain, France, Japan and the USA. Having been admitted to the club of world powers under British sponsorship, Japan now felt she was being elbowed out. As Admiral of the Fleet Lord Chatfield later commented: 'We had weakened most gravely our Imperial strategic position. We had turned a proved friend ... into a potential and powerful foe.'[3] Yet the elimination of British influence on Japan did nothing to strengthen the security of the United States; and it greatly weakened the strategic position of Australia and New Zealand, to say nothing of Hong Kong and other British possessions in the Far East. In 1927 a banking crisis saw the rise of a class of extremely chauvinistic officers in the Japanese Army, whose position was bolstered by the world economic crisis of 1929–30 and who fixed their eyes even more firmly on the rich natural resources of China, itself in deep turmoil.[4]

Then in September 1931 the Japanese Kwantung Army concocted the so-called 'Manchurian Incident' – the seizure of Mukden – and created the puppet state of 'Manchukuo', thereby replacing Britain as China's main enemy.[5] The League of Nations condemned the action, but in 1932 the

Japanese Navy attacked Shanghai, ostensibly to 'protect' Japanese traders there.[6] When a League of Nations investigation in Manchuria found Japan at fault, she peremptorily left the League. A year later she abrogated the disarmament treaties and in 1935 withdrew from the London Naval Conference.[7] She was now unfettered by international obligations.

The succession of Hirohito to the throne in 1926 intensified nationalism, and following a series of assassinations of senior officers and politicians in 1935–6 the Army became the dominant force in political life.[8] During the 1930s the Japanese Army was split into factions which were mostly dedicated to overthrowing parliamentary government but differed in the methods they were prepared to adopt. The 'Control Faction' comprised officers prepared to work with politicians and capitalists if the latter would do as they were told. The 'Imperial Way Faction', on the other hand, was more radical and prepared to resort to assassination to achieve its aims. A mutiny by officers from this faction in 1936 was quelled only by the direct intervention of the Emperor.[9] Hirohito's true position has since been debated, but he undoubtedly inspired fanatical loyalty, integrally linked to the state religion, Shintoism. By the time Japan renounced the Washington Treaty in 1936, she was completely under the control of the military, allied to big business, and she drew closer to Nazi Germany by signing the Anti-Comintern Pact, which she believed would protect her from attack by the USSR. According to the constitution, the ministers for the navy and army had to be serving officers and if they objected to other members of the government it could not be formed. This gave them enormous power and by 1937 half the national budget was allotted to defence.[10] After Japan had nibbled at China for four years the Marco Polo (or Lukouchiao) Bridge incident in July 1937 saw the beginning of full-scale war.

The Sino-Japanese War was 'the most inhuman, the most brutal, the most devastating war in Asia's History'.[11] For many Japanese these were matters of self-preservation. The issue of raw materials was paramount in a world carved up between European powers which resented Japan and would deny her access to them. 'Please kill Chinese people quickly, and then come home again', wrote the little son of one Japanese soldier as they seized Peking (Beijing), followed later that year by Shanghai.[12] The sinking of the USS *Panay* on the Yangtze river almost provoked war with the USA, and HMS *Ladybird* was also attacked; only a rapid apology and the offer of compensation from the Japanese government defused the situation, but American opinion was now firmly pro-Chinese. In 1938 the capital of the Chinese government of Chiang Kai-shek at Nanking (Nanjing) was captured. This tragic episode was marked by systematic atrocities of the most brutal and appalling kind, in sharp contrast to the universally admired Japanese behaviour during the Russo-Japanese War of 1904–5, but which were to become a feature of the Japanese Army's behaviour throughout its wars of conquest.[13] Yet neither side declared war: the Chinese knew that to do so would invoke the American Neutrality Act, which would hurt them far more than their enemy, while the Japanese wanted to maintain the pretence that they were not violating the Paris Pact outlawing war.[14]

In 1938 General Tojo Hideki became Vice-Minister of War, a position from which he exerted massive influence.[15] But as the Japanese continued to defeat Chinese field armies reaching Wuhan province, so Chinese guerrillas became more and more effective and the war dragged on. The foreign correspondent Nym Wales wrote:

> The Japanese army and its samurai officer caste has shown itself to be the vestigial remains of feudalism ... It is not a colonizing force, but a looting and raping expedition in the traditions of the Huns and the Spanish Conquistadores. Already it has demonstrated that it is trying to establish, not a true imperialist colony, but groups of feudal Shogunates, all quarrelling for power among themselves.[16]

Japan's immediate reaction to war in Europe in September 1939 was non-involvement; the German–Soviet Pact of August was a slap in the face and led to a brief *rapprochement* with Britain.[17] But following the fall of France in June 1940 renewed confrontation over the Burma Road highlighted Japanese ire over British support for China and the weakness of British regional defences. The Road had been the main route for supplying China since 1937, though little actually came from Britain.[18] With the Vichy French regime in Indo-China frightened into closing its rail link, Japan exerted pressure on Britain to close the Burma Road, which she agreed to do for three months in July 1940. Although the USA was sympathetic to Britain it was disappointed, while the Chinese were predictably bitter, but with the threat of invasion looming over Britain she could simply not afford to assume Japan was bluffing.[19]

The desire to keep the Chinese in the war was more Roosevelt's idea than Churchill's; the British considered the Chinese to be in a perpetual state of confusion and riddled with corruption and incompetence. The Americans, on the other hand, and Roosevelt in particular, believed they enjoyed a special relationship with Chiang and his American-educated wife. Brigadier-General Frank 'Pinky' Dorn, a Chinese-speaking US officer with long experience of China, thought the connection emotional, given that Roosevelt's grandfather made a fortune in China: 'Because of what was considered to be American self-interest – as well as because of sentimentality – the so-called government of China had to be kept in the war as an active ally. A political and economic mess ... China had to be perpetuated in the mistaken belief that it could and would help the United States defeat Japan.'[20] Chiang was a man of great intelligence and resourcefulness, but he was not as powerful or effective in controlling China's political forces as his detractors sometimes claimed. He outwardly exuded confidence, having trained at a Japanese military college in 1909 and served in the Japanese 13th Artillery Regiment. But despite this excellent preparation, his lack of experience at higher levels and his willingness to put political considerations above military ones reduced his effectiveness. Not that he had much option if he was to maintain control over his disparate forces: Lung Yun of Yunnan, for example, had made a fortune from opium, issued his own currency and kept his own army, and would wait until Madame Chiang arrived at his provincial capital as a hostage before he would go to meet Chiang himself.[21]

Japanese military strategists were divided into 'northerners' and 'southerners'. The former focused on the Soviet threat and on strengthening the position in China, while the latter advocated seizing the oilfields of the Dutch East Indies (Indonesia) and the rubber and minerals of British Malaya – part of a scheme for a Greater East Asia Co-Prosperity Sphere, with Japan as leader. Japan considered herself alone among Asian nations in having the industrial, political and military power to throw off the centuries-old yoke of Western dominance. A Co-Prosperity Sphere was therefore needed, operating under Japanese protection and direction. Component nations would be 'independent' only within the framework as designed by Imperial Japan; Japanese would become the lingua franca and the Japanese monetary system its economic basis; Japanese business and technology would develop the natural resources and underpin its trade.[22]

With the collapse of the Allies in the West the southerners' hand was greatly strengthened, although this also prompted the USA to begin a major rearmament programme and to impose a limited embargo on the export to Japan of certain strategic materials. In September 1940 Japan signed the Tripartite Axis Pact with Germany and Italy and invaded northern Indo-China. On 18 October, with the threat of invasion having receded, Britain reopened the Burma Road. On 2 November Hugh Woods of the China National Air Corporation, with the CNAC's operations manager, William L. Boyd, flew for the first time over 'the Hump', the China–Burma air route. Like the Burma Road, this traced its origin to the eighth-century Silk Road. Boyd proposed using it for supply operations, although he appreciated the hazards this entailed.[23] That month the German raider *Atlantis* boarded the Blue Funnel liner *Automedon* off the Nicobar Islands, and found a copy of a Top Secret paper in which the British Chiefs of Staff detailed their weakness in the Far East and their inability to remedy it in the foreseeable future. The Germans handed this to the Japanese and in meetings in March 1941 urged the Japanese to attack Singapore as soon as possible (but to avoid a conflict with the USA).[24]

In April 1941 Chiang had agreed to the formation of volunteer American air squadrons to serve in China, under Brigadier-General Claire L. Chennault. After finding fame in an aerobatic circus known as 'Three Men on a Flying Trapeze', by 1937 Chennault was living with his wife and eight children in frustrated retirement in Waterproof, Louisiana, having being invalided out of the Air Corps for partial deafness. He figured that, with the USA not at war, the next best thing was to fight for China, and a visit to Chiang and his wife convinced him.[25] He began scouring the services for volunteers and was overwhelmed. His men would receive $600 a month, and there would be a bonus of $500 for every Japanese plane confirmed destroyed. The American Volunteer Group (AVG) began assembling at a San Francisco hotel in June and by November three squadrons with P. 40 Tomahawk fighters had formed at Toungoo. Chiang allowed two squadrons to remain in Burma and assist in the air defence of Rangoon while the other went north to Kunming. The AVG was the one of the most colourful units of this or any other war. The Chinese referred to it as the 'Flying Tigers' from a proverb – 'Like tigers with wings, their strength is irresistible' – although the pilots themselves preferred simply 'American volunteers'.[26] They might have walked straight off a Hollywood film set, with zip-up leather jackets, Hawaiian shirts and brash manners. Yet however much they might convey an impression of playboys let loose, they were tough professional flyers. 'They were my angels,' said Madame Chiang, 'with or without wings.'[27] They painted the noses of their Tomahawks with red mouths and flashing teeth, and each squadron had an emblem: the 1st had 'Adam and Eve' locked in an embrace, the 2nd a predatory-looking Panda bear, and the 3rd a nude woman 'Hell's Angel'.[28] In the spring the US Congress had approved the first instalment of what would become $5 billion worth of lend-lease to China, and by the time journalist Leland Stowe arrived in Burma he had already heard disquieting rumours regarding its fate. What he saw on investigation shocked him: the greatest racket in the Far East. North of Lashio all rules ceased: trucks were driven to destruction without oil in the sumps or air in the tyres, then abandoned;

General Lung Yun was amassing a fortune taxing the traffic, and Stowe found much equipment had nothing to do with the war effort. The Chinese were getting the Americans to underwrite industrialization. Lend-lease was a huge capitalist bandwagon ridden by Chinese entrepreneurs, and black marketeers were thriving on stolen petrol, cigarettes and booze. Stowe filed a series of stories to the *Chicago Daily News* and fifty syndicated papers which caused an immediate furore, but it was eighteen months before he learned from an American liaison officer of their effect: 'Your stories were the one thing that got immediate action out of the Chinese. Do you know that more tonnage was transported over the [Burma] road in the next two months than at any time in its history?'[29]

Japanese policy makers were reluctant to make war on the USA if they could help it. Only when the Japanese move into southern Indo-China in July 1941 prompted the USA, followed by the British and Dutch, to impose full-scale economic sanctions against Japan was latent confrontation brought into the open.[30] The British ambassador to Tokyo, Sir Robert Craigie, believed the combination of America's determination to enforce a crippling blockade and Britain's weakness made war in South-East Asia inevitable.[31] But there was considerable disagreement within the Japanese government of Prince Konoye Fumimaro: Tojo, now War Minister, and new Foreign Minster Matsouka Yosuke were fully prepared for war with Britain and America, while the Navy's Admiral Yamamoto Isoruku warned on the signing of the Tripartite Pact that Japan should avoid war with the USA. Consequently mixed messages emerged from Tokyo during early 1941. In October 1941 the Army replaced Konoye with Tojo in a government plainly dedicated to complete military victory in China and against other enemies.[32] Then from late November events moved rapidly. Between 10 and 18 November the task force that was to attack Pearl Harbor left the Kurile Islands, and on 1 December Tojo declared that 'our Empire has no alternative but to begin war against the United States, Britain and the Netherlands', continuing that 'our Empire stands at the threshold of glory or oblivion'.[33]

Burma was of minor importance in Japan's early plans for a new order in East Asia; she wanted a settlement in China and access to Malayan tin and rubber and Indonesian oil. The Philippines and French Indo-China were of secondary strategic and economic importance, Thailand was not regarded as essential to Japan's ends and remote Burma distinctly less so. Japan's first concern in any imperialist adventure was the area bordering the South China Sea, and while this entailed war with Britain, it might not necessarily entail war with the USA. The Japanese Navy was wary of both British and American naval power, and Burma was considered an unnecessary risk. However, the total destruction of French and Dutch power and dangerous weakening of the British during the summer of 1940 made such an adventure plausible. In September, with German pressure on the new Vichy regime in France, Japan occupied Tonkin. Only the failure of Germany to invade Britain in 1940 persuaded the Japanese of the need to occupy Thailand as a prelude to any attack on Malaya, but this would require another eight months' preparation. The final decision to take over South-East Asia in July 1941 included arrangements for collaboration with Aung San and his youthful associates in the expulsion of the British from Burma. Before this, Tokyo displayed little interest in an invasion of Burma, although contingency plans were drawn up.[34]

Burmese nationalists were a tool for the destruction of British rule, and any concerns they might have over Burma's integrity could be ignored. Tokyo offered to 'restore' to Thailand Burma's eastern Shan States and parts of Cambodia, a bribe it honoured in due course. Only Malaya was to be ruled directly; the Japanese would rule other states through local agencies, including resident French and Dutch authorities, all depending on circumstances.[35] Japanese objectives in late 1941 were to ensure freedom of movement and access to the resources of South-East Asia but to avoid governmental problems, and to shift the allegiance of Chinese communities in these countries from Kuomintang to the puppet regime in Nanking. Nevertheless, the Japanese had been gathering intelligence regarding Burma since the mid-1930s. Following a visit to Tokyo in 1935 U Saw bought the *Sun* newspaper, probably with Japanese money, and it produced a stream of pro-Japanese propaganda, as did Thein Maung's *New Burma* following his visit in 1939. Until 1940 the Japanese believed Burma need be only neutralized, rather than occupied militarily, while German or Russian influence was expected to neutralize India. Certainly Japan did not have the forces necessary to overrun India if it was not to overstretch itself in the Pacific.[36] Ba Maw had already been sounded out through his dentist, another Suzuki, who put him in touch with various naval officers. One reserve naval officer whose wife practised dentistry in Rangoon, Kokubu Shozo, had published books on Burma and his knowledge of the country had genuine depth, unlike that of a secret agent. In company of a Japanese consulate official he was caught snooping around the sensitive Gokteik viaduct on the Burma Road to Yunnan. The consul apologized and the two were freed, and the consulate warned Ba Maw that Kokubu was unreliable. But Kokubu was also friendly with Thakin Ba Sein, who led a splinter group excluded from the Freedom Bloc, and he recommended Ba Sein to Tokyo, which told him to smuggle Ba Sein out of the country and make contact with the military attaché at Bangkok. Ba Sein was arrested at the border, but Aung San heard of this attempt and this turned his attention towards the Japanese.[37]

In Burma itself by October 1941 all hostile newspapers had been silenced by U Saw, who agreed to extend the Lashio branch of Burma Railways to the Chinese border. But his nationalism also saw him visit London in November to ask for a definite promise of post-war dominion status. Churchill was vague, however, and U Saw's claim to have left Britain without bitterness was belied by statements attributed to him in the USA. He spent several weeks there before being stopped at Hawaii by the outbreak of the Pacific war. Forced to reroute via Europe, he was detected communicating with the Japanese while at Lisbon, and after being arrested by British police in Egypt on 19 January 1942 spent the next four years as a prisoner in Uganda. The Anglophile Sir Paw Tun became premier and subsequently the ministry remained loyal to the governor.[38]

The Japanese were wary of becoming involved in hostilities with the Thais, through whose territory they would have to pass to attack Malaya and Burma. The Thais were proud of their independence, being the only country in the region to have maintained it, but knew they were in danger of being caught between the British and Japanese. But with the defeat of the Allies in the West and victory for the Axis seemingly imminent (together with bribes of territory promised by the Japanese), the Thai prime minister, Phibun Soggram, agreed verbally in October 1940 to support them in any invasion of Malaya and Burma. Until such time, however, the Thai government sat carefully on the fence and when the Japanese invasion fleet approached on 7 December, Phibun disappeared on a 'tour of inspection'.[39] In January 1942 Thailand declared war on the Allies, which the USA disregarded as unconstitutional and invalid, since the declaration was made under occupation. The British took it more seriously, which was a pity since within days of the Japanese arrival a pro-Allied Free Thai movement developed that in view of developments in western Thailand during 1942–3 could have been exploited.[40]

Now preparations for war finally began; 1st Glosters mobilized on 7 December, although it was painfully apparent that the men were not fully trained to use what little war equipment they had: 36 men of the battalion had been allowed to throw one grenade each in three years. They were 14 officers and 340 men understrength.[41] On 8 December 1941 Lance-Corporal Kawamata Koji was at Sukshien railway station in China

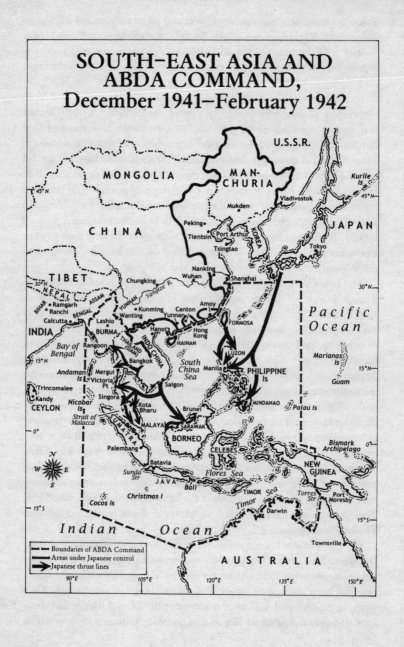

# SOUTH-EAST ASIA AND ABDA COMMAND,
## December 1941–February 1942

U.S.S.R.

MONGOLIA

MAN-
CHURIA

Kurile
Is

Mukden

Vladivostok

45° N

45° N

Peking

JAPAN

CHINA

Tientsin

Port Arthur

KOREA

Tsingtao

Tokyo

Nanking

TIBET

Chungking

Wuhan

Shanghai

30° N

Yangtze R.

NEPAL

BIHAR  Ramgarh

ASSAM

YUNNAN

Kunming

Canton

Amoy

30° N

Pacific
Ocean

Ranchi

Calcutta

BENGAL

Lashio

Wanting

Yunnan

Hong
Kong

FORMOSA

INDIA

BURMA

Hanoi

THAILAND

Rangoon

Bay of
Bengal

HAINAN

LUZON

Marianas
Is

15° N

Bangkok

Mergui

INDO-CHINA
(SIAM)

South
China
Sea

Manila

PHILIPPINE
Is

15° N

Andaman
Is

Victoria
Pt

Saigon

Guam

Trincomalee

Nicobar
Is

Singora

Kandy

CEYLON

Kota
Bharu

Brunei

MINDANAO

Palau Is

Strait of
Malacca

MALAYA

SARAWAK

Bismark
Archipelago

0°

Palembang

SUMATRA

BORNEO

CELEBES

0°

NEW
GUINEA

Batavia

Flores Sea

Sunda
Str

JAVA

Bali

Christmas I

TIMOR

Sea

Timor

Torres
Str

Port
Moresby

Cocos Is

15° S

Darwin

15° S

Indian — — Ocean

— — — Boundaries of ABDA Command
▬▬▬ Areas under Japanese control
▶▶▶ Japanese thrust lines

Townsville

AUSTRALIA

90° E

105° E

120° E

135° E

150° E

expecting to receive his discharge after three years in the army. He hoped
to get a job with the North China Railway Company.

> I explained this to a man at the station who stared at me in amazement and
> said to me, 'Your discharge is most unlikely. Look at this.' He handed me a
> newspaper with a headline saying that Japan had declared war against the
> USA and Britain. What a terrible situation! I ran back to my Company and
> I told my fellow soldiers 'Discharge is out of the question. It's war with the
> white people!'[42]

His comrades refused to believe him until he showed them the paper; all
they said was, 'Oh!' Malaya had been invaded, followed soon afterwards by
the attack on Pearl Harbor, concurrent with which Japanese forces attacked
Hong Kong, which fell only after two weeks' bitter fighting.[43] However,
Pearl Harbor filled the Chinese leadership with fresh enthusiasm: Chiang
ordered all his armies to attack systematically on a rotational basis to tie
down Japanese forces, and was able finally to declare war on Japan the following day.[44]

From Headquarters Southern Army in Saigon, commanded by General
Count Terauchi Hisaichi, the plan was for 25th Army under General
Yamashita Tomyuki to invade Malaya, while 15th Army, commanded by
Lieutenant-General Iida Shojiro, with 55th Division was to secure the right
flank of the forces invading Malaya and to capture the Tenasserim airfields
at Victoria Point, Tavoy and Mergui; 56th Division would be in reserve in
Japan until shipping was available.[45] After this Iida would be able to deal
with Moulmein, and at some point 33rd Division, then still engaged in
central China, would join 15th Army. If Malayan operations were successful, it would then seize crossings on the Salween and advance on Rangoon.
It was not planned at this stage to capture the whole of Burma.[46]

The Malayan campaign started badly for the British and got progressively
worse. The High Command was less than inspiring: Brooke-Popham had
been due to be replaced by Lieutenant-General Sir Henry Pownall, while
the army commander, Lieutenant-General A. E. Percival, proved deeply
unsatisfactory. On 10 December the battleship *Prince of Wales* and battle-
cruiser *Repulse*, sent by Churchill to impress the Japanese against the advice
of the Chief of the Naval Staff, Admiral Sir Dudley Pound, were sunk by
air attack. The carrier *Indomitable*, intended to accompany them, had run
aground off the West Indies. Air strength amounted to barely 141 aircraft,
many of them obsolescent, and Brooke-Popham was so worried by lack of
efficiency and morale that he issued a statement reminding personnel of service traditions.[47] It did nothing to help, and forward airfields (previously

sited without consulting the army, who were responsible for their defence) were abandoned with undue haste. Roosevelt and Churchill met in Washington on 22 December (the Arcadia Conference) and drafted a joint declaration on the 25th to fight the common enemy and not make separate peace. The declaration was made public on New Year's Day and endorsed by twenty-six countries, with the USA, UK, USSR and China listed first and the remaining twenty-two countries in alphabetical order, marking China as one of the four great powers.[48]

According to a Japanese Army pamphlet of 1934: 'War is the father of creation and the mother of culture. The testing of one's ability against hardship is the motive and stimulus for the development of life and the creation of culture, both in individuals and competing nations.'[49] By 1941 the Imperial Japanese Army was to outward appearances a technologically advanced, Westernized organization. It was, however, built on very different values from the individualistic and increasingly materialistic ones of the West. The Japanese soldier was drawn from a society that venerated group responsibility rather than individual freedom. Obligation to ancestors and superiors was the cherished principle on which the Japanese government added fresh burdens: the life of the Japanese soldier belonged to the Emperor, and his highest duty was to die an honourable death in that service. Field service regulations forbade soldiers to allow themselves to be taken prisoner alive; if captured wounded and unconscious, they were to commit suicide immediately consciousness was regained.[50] If a soldier 'consummated tragic death in battle', he was deemed to have joined the gods and his soul was enshrined in the Yasukuni Temple in Tokyo. For this reason the Japanese took great care to try and recover the bodies of those killed for cremation. But if this was not possible, a small portion of the body, even nail clippings, would suffice, so that ashes could be returned to the bereaved family at home. Twice a year during the war period an elaborate ceremony was held at Yasukuni when the names of the war dead were placed in an ark and carried in torch-lit procession to the altar where the names were deified. Thereafter the soldier reputedly continued to fight for Japan in the spirit world.[51]

Training for the conscript emphasized 'a fetish of self-discipline and the cultivation of will-power', and institutionalized the popular belief 'that sufficient will-power can overcome any obstacle'.[52] The result was a regime of brutal harshness not seen since the early days of the Prussian Army. A failure to learn a tactical lesson or reach an appropriate standard might see a recruit ordered to stand to attention all day. If he collapsed, he would be punished for disobeying orders, and officers and NCOs would regularly beat subordinates for the slightest infraction. Every gradation of rank was minutely observed and even private soldiers required to salute other privates of a higher grade. 'Kangaroo courts' were commonplace where junior ranks would try and punish recruits whose performance was deemed below standard, an unofficial system tacitly encouraged by the authorities. Such practices were most common in, but not exclusive to, recruit training establishments. Yet many recruits from peasant backgrounds found these impositions easier than the fields they left, and as late as 1935, although half the population lived in towns, 80 per cent of recruits came from the rural peasantry.[53] By 1941, with 1¼ million men in China and 1 million in Formosa, Korea and the home islands, Japan lacked large manpower reserves and to provide five armies (corps) to strike south meant scraping the sides of the barrel, with age limits widened in both directions and student deferments cancelled. Brutality in training became yet more harsh and standards of discipline diluted, resulting in an attitude that crime against superiors was far more serious than crimes against natives. Despite its modernity, much Japanese equipment compared unfavourably with Western models: they never had enough artillery, for example: an important reason for their defeat. But the funnelling of manpower into the infantry and their ability to live off the land meant the Japanese appeared far more numerous than Allied forces.[54] They also lacked effective medium tanks, and the Arisaka rifle was very long, designed to achieve high muzzle velocity and therefore accuracy. Ironically this probably went some way to explain the Japanese notorious reputation for bad shooting. It was almost as tall as many Japanese soldiers and, especially with the bayonet fixed, would be very difficult to aim properly. Plainly the Imperial Japanese Army was not on a par with that of 1905, or even 1937.[55]

Much has been made of the *samurai* origins of the Imperial Japanese Army and its associated code of *bushido*, 'the way of the warrior'. But beyond this were traits called *dukudan senko* and *gekokujo*. *Dukudan senko* implied the use of initiative and originality in emergencies, but did not condone unauthorized or unilateral action – a subtle distinction – while *gekokujo* signified the dominance of juniors by seniors, and is close to the meaning of insubordination in English. They had been prominent features of the behaviour of middle-ranking officers during the 1930s, especially in the Kwantung Army in Manchuria.[56] These traits gave officers in difficult situations in distant commands a justification for insubordinate behaviour that would have been intolerable in Western armies and, coupled with the Japanese belief that an individual acting with 'sincerity' of motive for (what

39

he believes) justifiable purposes could not be held culpable, was to provide a basis for much excessive behaviour in far-flung and remote commands, such as Burma. However, despite the technologically advanced nature of the Army, the harshness and frugality of the Japanese soldier's life set him apart from his Western counterpart: his rice-based diet was nothing compared to the protein-rich one customary in the West.

Contrary to the widely held belief, the Japanese had no previous experience or training in jungle warfare, although a team of staff officers had done all it could to learn about local conditions. To collate intelligence for fighting in the 'southern area' a small planning staff had assembled in Formosa at the end of 1940, with the task of finding out as much as possible about the countries of South-East Asia, and produced a pamphlet; but that was the sum total of specialist preparation.[57] However, the Japanese were well-trained, experienced fighters, unlike many of their opponents, especially the Indian Army units, who were poorly trained and all of whom were short of equipment. The Japanese made great use of bicycles to increase mobility and were not road-bound, as the British were.[58] The willingness of individual soldiers to endure great physical hardship was essential to the economies the High Command had to make, while their obedience underwrote tactics and their sense of invulnerability their offensive spirit.[59] Shortly before the final ignominious surrender of Singapore with some 130,000 Allied prisoners on 15 February 1942, Pownall reflected sadly that 'we were frankly out-generalled, outwitted and outfought. It is a great disaster for the British arms, one of the worst in history, and a great blow to the honour and prestige of the Army.'[60]

When Roosevelt and Churchill adopted the 'Europe First' policy for pursuing the war at the Arcadia conference in late 1941, they were afraid that in the meantime China might collapse, releasing the Japanese to overrun Australia, New Zealand and the rest of the Pacific. The American government therefore wanted to send a high-ranking general to China to assist militarily when on 31 December Roosevelt cabled Chiang to say that he had obtained agreement from Britain, Australia, New Zealand and the Netherlands for the formation of a China Theatre of War, with Chiang as Supreme Commander. Chiang needed a Chief of Staff for his new command, which included parts of Thailand and Indo-China, and cabled Roosevelt on 2 January 1942 asking him to nominate a trusted American general for the task. The Americans suggested the appointment should combine the functions of Chief of Staff China Theatre with Commander of China-Burma-India Theatre and supervisor of lend-lease material. Brigadier-General John Magruder of the American Military Mission to

China (Ammisca) was not senior enough and was already disillusioned with the Chinese. So when Lieutenant-General Hugh A. Drum turned down the post, believing its policy too passive, Chiang received Major-General Joseph W. Stilwell, who, while distinctly unenthusiastic, agreed to 'go where he was sent'.[61] However, his position was somewhat at odds with the wishes of Chiang, who instructed his personal representative and Madame Chiang's brother Soong Tze-vun (T. V. Soong) to clarify the power and status of his new Chief of Staff.[62] But Soong accepted American arrangements without question, which in due course would lead to serious misunderstanding and be the cause of subsequent disputes between Stilwell and Chiang.[63]

Stilwell was a 59-year-old West Point graduate who had served in China for several years – as language officer, with 15th Infantry Regiment, and as US military attaché. An eyewitness to the 1911 revolution, he spoke Chinese, although one Chinese critic noted that he 'lacked real knowledge of Chinese culture, politics, the aspirations of the Chinese and the ability to evaluate them'.[64] Significantly, his experiences gave him a low opinion of Chinese military and political leaders; he contemptuously called Chiang 'Peanut' (because of the shape of his skull, as revealed by his close haircut). His short temper and rudeness to superiors went some way to explaining why he had risen no higher than command of a division, but he was also regarded as a skilful trainer of troops and courageous. As an instructor at the infantry school, his caustic critiques of students led one to draw a caricature of him rising out of a vinegar bottle labelled with three Xs, and he was known forever after as 'Vinegar Joe'.[65] More importantly, he was a close friend of the Army Chief of Staff, General George C. Marshall, who viewed him as 'immensely capable and remarkably resourceful'.[66]

The position he now took was complicated, and an indication of his distaste for it – and of his ineptitude for its subtleties – was his failure for the first fifteen months to use the title Chief of Staff, which was so important to Chiang.[67] Stilwell's anti-diplomacy was astonishing, even extending to those Americans who showed signs of Allied co-operability.[68] He 'had developed hatred into a fine art, and seemed to dislike his own countrymen almost as much as the "Limeys"', noted Brigadier L. F. Field, who served in Peking as British liaison officer. Besides, Chiang 'wasn't really interested in fighting the Japanese, so long as they kept a respectful distance away from Chungking ... What he wanted was to build an army copiously stocked with modern weapons with which he could eventually fight the Communist Chinese.'[69] Stilwell faced an unenviable task.

# 3

## Invasion

Where was I when the war was on?
I can hear a faint voice murmur.
Where was I when the war was on?
In the safest place – in Burma.

Music-hall song of the 1920s

ON 8 DECEMBER 143rd Infantry Regiment of 55th Division (under command of 25th Army) landed on four beaches in southern Thailand. They were fiercely opposed by the Thais in the area, who, unaware at this stage of the agreement to allow the Japanese free passage, inflicted 79 dead. But they quickly reached the Kra river, which marked the Thai–Burma border, and occupied Victoria Point on the 14th.[1] Meanwhile the British implemented Operation Yacht, a plan to destroy two bridges linking Thailand with Malaya, to be carried out by the BFF's Field Force 2 (FF2) under Major S. W. A. Love – nicknamed 'Bwana' after many years' service with the King's African Rifles. Love divided his column – almost entirely Gurkha in composition with mule and pony transport – into three groups and set off through thick, rugged, jungle-covered country. However, one group ran into the Japanese while another searched in vain for a bridge that did not exist. The whole operation proved 'needless and blundering', and its end was tragic. On return to Burma, Love was ordered to clear the Japanese from the police station, during which he was killed; two days later a company of 2nd Burma Rifles easily took the post.[2] On 20 December two RAF Buffalo fighters attacked Victoria Point barracks, which the pilots described as 'full of Japanese troops', killing many.[3] Shortly afterwards 143rd Regiment, less a battalion at Victoria Point, moved to rejoin 55th Division at Bangkok.

On 12 December Churchill signalled Wavell, 'You must now look east. Burma is placed under your command', promising four fighter and six bomber squadrons and *matériel* reinforcement, together with 18th Division and the retention of 17th Indian Division, or what remained of it since two brigades had already been diverted to Singapore.[4] Churchill's vigorous but touchy exuberance was all too familiar to Wavell, who replied courteously but with a hint of reproach that he had pressed for this, and requested Bren light machine-guns and anti-aircraft guns, making a second detailed request ten days later. He also informed Dorman-Smith that he or his Chief of General Staff, Lieutenant-General Thomas Hutton, would visit shortly and that construction would begin of a road linking Assam with Burma via Imphal in Manipur State.[5] In addition he sent sixty-one technical staff officers to Army Headquarters Burma, including Major-General Eric Goddard to take charge of administration.[6] On 18 December Wavell received a telegram from Chiang sent via the Foreign Office, which had taken eight days to arrive. The Generalissimo offered to join any plan proposed by the Allies. Wavell reached Rangoon on 21 December, already aware that most of his promised reinforcements had been diverted to Malaya, although he still hoped for two East African brigades from Kenya and most of 17th Indian Division. When the American Lieutenant-General George H. Brett of the Air Corps arrived in Rangoon on the way to visit Chiang at Chungking, Wavell decided to go too, but not before telling Hutton to take over from McLeod after McLeod's proposed replacement was found to be sick.

Chiang, Wavell later wrote, 'was not a particularly impressive figure at first sight: he speaks no English but makes clucking noises like a friendly hen when greeting one. Madame, of course, speaks perfect English. We had long discussions until midnight.'[7] Chiang offered two Chinese armies (each equivalent to a weak British or Japanese division) to help defend Burma. However, at this point Wavell believed that Burma should be defended by Imperial troops if possible, and only accepted 93rd Division. He later explained that the Chinese were totally deficient in administrative services and could not arrive any sooner than they ultimately did, though this ignored the reality of Chinese methods and infuriated Chiang, who lost face.[8] Besides, from his own previous experience Wavell was surely over-optimistic in expecting all the reinforcements promised. While Chinese moves were slow, had they been accepted immediately they might have defended the Shan States, freeing 1st Burma Division for operations in Tenasserim, where reinforcements were badly needed.[9]

The return journey proved something of mystery tour when the American pilot got lost and eventually landed at Rangoon on Christmas Day in the middle of an air raid. Wavell shared a short trench with one of Brett's staff and two other Americans. 'I cannot say that I was enjoying it, but the abject terror of my companion had the effect of heartening me.

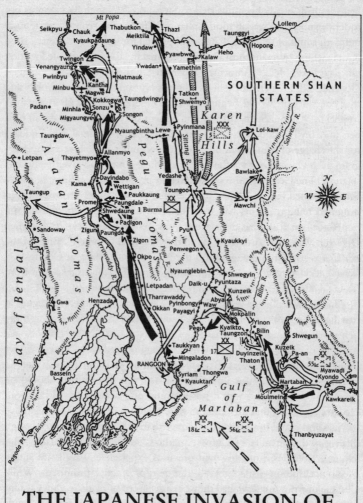

# THE JAPANESE INVASION OF
# BURMA,
### February–April 1942

When it was all over I counted seventeen bombs which had fallen within fifty yards of the trench, the nearest about a dozen yards away.'[10] This was the third Japanese air raid on Rangoon, the targets being Mingaladon airfield and the city itself. Leading Aircraftsman J. Helsdon Thomas of 67 Squadron had been quite sanguine at first. The sky

> appeared to be full of aircraft. I knew they were not ours, we didn't have that many. Clambering off the mainplane, I walked around the machine and picked up my respirator and tin hat. At that moment a short burst of machine-gun fire shattered the quiet morning. I looked up again and saw a large number of silver darts leaving the machines flying above me, 'Christ almighty,' I thought, 'they really mean business.' I turned away and ran.[11]

He was blown over by the bomb blast and, when he picked himself up, saw that the Buffalo he wanted oil for would no longer need it; nor would two others.

The effects of these raids were catastrophic: in the first, on 23 December, 1,250 people were killed and another 600 died of wounds (there was no civil defence organization or air raid precautions); during the third raid only 60 were killed and 40 wounded, much of the population having already fled.[12] Daw Sein was a midwife only vaguely aware of the war, so that she thought the first sound of bombs was an approaching storm. Her husband burst in, yelling, 'Out! Quick! We must get away!' She was in such haste to flee that she was half-way to the railway station before realizing she was half-naked. Her husband ripped his *longyi* in half and she clutched this to herself as they tumbled on to a packed train heading for Moulmein. After an hour the train stopped; children sobbed and women wailed, and an old man vomited on her. After some hours a man walked along the side of the train calling out, 'Moulmein has been destroyed! Bombs are falling everywhere! The train isn't going any further!' Rumours abounded that Rangoon had also been destroyed, and her husband suggested they make for India. But Daw Sein's children were with relatives in Arakan and, afraid she would never see them again, they instead made for Mandalay.[13]

Much of the Indian dock labour began the trek home via the Taungup track in Arakan, virtually paralysing the city. It was left to 1st Glosters to provide desperately needed labour as nominal rolls were scoured with particular attention to the 'trade prior to enlistment' column. Armed patrols roamed the streets ordered to shoot looters on sight.[14] But reinforcements were arriving, including 8th Heavy and 3rd Light Anti-Aircraft Batteries, Indian Artillery, and Air Vice-Marshal Donald Stevenson arrived on New Year's Day to become Air-Officer-Commanding in Burma.[15] Stevenson then received further reinforcements of 113 Squadron with Blenheim light bombers sent to Toungoo (later joined by 45 Squadron), and 30 elderly Hurricane I fighters in crates, followed shortly by 17 Squadron with Hurricane IIAs. These raided Japanese forward bases in Thailand and at Bangkok, although claims of destroying 58 aircraft on the ground proved optimistic.[16] Thereafter, the three Hurricane squadrons of 267 Group could barely maintain 10 machines in the air between them, plus a few Buffaloes and 10 AVG Tomahawks (later rising to 25, of which 18 were serviceable), and were constantly outnumbered by the Japanese. 'The whole of the RAF ground organization was a complete mess', recalled Squadron Leader Monty 'Bush' Cotton.[17]

Hutton assumed command of Burma Army on 28 December. A former gunner and a highly competent staff officer, he was conscientious and efficient, if perhaps lacking imaginative drive.[18] He was responsible for the great expansion of the Indian Army but had not commanded troops for twenty years and made little impression on James Lunt, to whom he seemed 'more like a head gardener'.[19] Meanwhile, at the Arcadia Conference Churchill and Roosevelt 'differed strongly' on China's war contribution.[20] Roosevelt firmly believed the days of empire were ending and wanted China to fill the vacuum that would be left by Japan; his views on the end of British rule in India were firmly rebuffed by Churchill, who had not taken office to preside over the liquidation of the British Empire and who reacted so strongly to this 'that he never raised it verbally again'.[21] But these differing aims necessarily impacted on strategy: American focus was on China, British on Singapore and India, with Burma caught in-between, and Churchill reluctantly agreed to the creation of ABDA Command (American-British-Dutch-Australian) under Wavell, encompassing South-East Asia in its entirety. Wavell assumed this new and massive responsibility on 30 December 1941 and signalled the new CIGS (Dill having been replaced by General Sir Alan Brooke only five days earlier) that he 'had been handed not just a baby but quadruplets', before setting off on another marathon journey to his new headquarters in Java.[22]

Burma was included in Wavell's vast operational responsibilities but for administrative purposes it remained under General Headquarters, India (GHQ(I)): 'the whole scheme wild and half-baked', according to Brooke.[23] Towards the end of January Stevenson was further reinforced by Hurricane IIAs of 135 Squadron and two army co-operation squadrons (28 RAF and 1 Indian Air Force), whose Lysanders were used as light bombers. This may have encouraged Hutton in his declaration of 28 January that Moulmein would be held; a prospect that far from pleased

2nd Burma Brigade, tasked with its defence.[24] Moulmein (*Maul-la-Myaing* to the Burmese) was a city of some 50,000, prosperous from rice and teak and fair with Portuguese influences on its architecture from pre-British days; surrounded by ridges and rivers with waterfalls and caves, its great pagoda was immortalized by Kipling.[25] Now Headquarters 2nd Burma Brigade was there, but its units were widely spread; 2nd Burma Rifles at Mergui and 6th Burma Rifles at Tavoy. To add to the confusion, it would soon lose these units from command, to be replaced by 7th and 8th Burma Rifles and two companies of 3rd Burma Rifles together with 4th Battalion, 12th Frontier Force Regiment, which had spent three weeks in Mandalay.[26] As 'Piffers' (Punjab Frontier Force), many a hard-pressed commander had previously been grateful for their presence. In the months to follow, 4th Sikhs as they referred to themselves (having been so called until 1903), under Lieutenant-Colonel W. D. 'Donny' Edward, would prove invaluable. Sikh soldiers were not always easy to command, but to their British officers they were less a regiment than a state of mind, and none would exchange them for another.[27] Meanwhile, jungle warfare training 'was carried out in a rather half-hearted manner owing to very little direction being given in the subject. We were to pay the cost of this later.'[28]

Also assembling at Moulmein was Headquarters 17th Indian Division under Major-General J. G. (Jackie) Smyth VC. James Lunt thought him 'tremendous', 'a bright, perky and friendly little man'. But he was not fully fit, having recently undergone surgery, and the strain would later reduce his efficiency.[29] However, 17th Indian Division was incomplete: originally comprising 44th, 45th and 46th Indian Infantry Brigades, only 46th under Brigadier Roger Ekin reached Burma; the others were diverted to Malaya. Smyth also received extra engineers in 24th and 60th Field Companies, but his only artillery was 5th and 12th Mountain Batteries and four Bofors from 3rd Indian Light Anti-Aircraft Battery. The excellent mule-borne 3.7-inch howitzer of the mountain batteries screwed together (hence the 'Screw Guns' of Kipling), and fired a 19½ pound shell 6,000 yards with great accuracy. On the command 'Action Front' the battery's eight mules and eight ammunition mules formed a circle facing outwards when, to the uninitiated observer, three minutes of total confusion suddenly resolved into a line of four guns.[30] However, Smyth realized Moulmein was virtually indefensible. 'From the start of the campaign', he later recalled, Wavell insisted 'my 17th Division should fight as far forward as possible and this objective was passed on literally to Hutton'.[31] Hutton was, in any case, under enormous pressure from Dorman-Smith, supported by Stevenson, to keep the

Japanese as far from Rangoon as possible and was prodded from London to keep supplies flowing to China.

'They say they are going to turn [Moulmein] into a second Tobruk', wrote James Lunt in his diary; 'they must be crazy!'[32] The Salween was not easily defendable; at Moulmein it would require a full division with complete artillery, which was simply not available. Fifty miles to the west was the formidable obstacle of the Sittang with its solitary railway bridge, and Smyth was convinced this offered the only realistic defence line; but he was overruled, he believed, because Dorman-Smith was afraid for Burmese morale.[33] Hutton was certainly strongly opposed to a premature withdrawal, and he believed Smyth wanted 'to scuttle back across the River Sittang as quickly as possible'.[34] Hutton had seemingly good reasons for the policy of forward defence strongly supported by Dorman-Smith and Wavell. But Wavell was 2,000 miles away in Java and both underrated the Japanese and overrated the defenders' ability and strength. He could hardly have been more out of touch in London and was in no position to impose himself on Hutton and Smyth, who were clearly not getting on.

Once at Moulmein, Smyth took under command 16th Indian Brigade and 2nd Burma Brigade. 'Will your Burma Rifles fight?' he asked Brigadier John Bourke of the latter. 'I'm not sure', was all Bourke could reply.[35] Apart from 8th Burma Rifles, which was mostly Indian, none of the other battalions could be relied on in combat, and Smyth recommended they only be used for reconnaissance. Furthermore, communications were woefully inadequate. Throughout the campaign it proved impossible to lay line, and wireless was subject to both large distances and the screening effects of jungle and plantation, as well as severe shortages of charged batteries. Distances everywhere were large, and while in 1940 the civil post and telegraph service had 8,400 miles of telegraph line, mostly along rail embankments, it was particularly vulnerable to bombing; worse, many infantry units jettisoned or lost bulky signals equipment, forcing reliance on despatch riders. Messages could take anything up to five days to get through so that, combined with a serious lack of information about the Japanese, command and control was dangerously weak. One signalman, Syed Ghonse, in order to save his despatches when faced with capture, ate them.[36]

Commanded by Lieutenant-General Takeuchi Yutaka, 55th Division assembled at Bangkok on 22 December. Takeuchi issued operation orders for crossing the border and capturing Moulmein and requested maps from 15th Army before moving to Pitsanuloke. But although he obtained quite accurate maps of Burma through members of Minami Kikan, he received only inadequate coverage of the Thai side. Fortunately the locals helped as guides and porters and in procuring the large numbers of horses and oxen needed to replace his mechanical transport along the rough tracks leading to the border. The routes west became increasingly difficult over two ranges of hills 2–3,000 feet high covered in dense tropical forest: 'We moved ahead in single file,' noted Captain Honjo Seikei in his diary, 'watching for tracks and tree roots; if you missed your footing, you'd be engulfed in the bottomless jungle floor. We climbed painfully, step by step, hauling ourselves up by holding on to creepers.' The days were intensely hot and nights bitterly cold, and inevitably the units became strung out. 'We only made about ten miles a day and finally reached Raheng on 17 January.'[37]

Meanwhile III Battalion, 112th Infantry Regiment, laboriously approached Tavoy, each man carrying seven days' rations. Several elephants had been provided by the Thai army, together with horses and oxen, but progress was extremely slow, sometimes just 2 miles per day. By the time they reached the crest of the jungle-covered Tenasserim range on 14 January there were practically no cattle left. Corporal Nakai Buhachiro of 55th Mountain Artillery Regiment recalled that the Thai ox was unlike that of Japan: 'Its meat was too tough and after two meals my gums were swollen and ached so I could take only beef soup. Then, as we could not carry the ammunition which had been carried on the ox, we left some shells to be picked up later.'[38] The following day they reached a grassy plain 34 miles from Tavoy, but with a motorable road. Tavoy, a town of some 30,000, was held by 6th and two companies of 3rd Burma Rifles, plus elements of the Kohine Battalion BFF. Action was joined on 16 January but by 1500 on the 18th the Japanese occupied the town, having lost 23 dead and 40 wounded. Although small, this action had serious consequences for the morale of the Burma Rifles, and the Japanese swiftly followed up towards Mergui, where 2nd Battalion was isolated. Army Headquarters (AHQ) in Rangoon saw no point in holding Mergui and ordered the non-Burmese to evacuate, which was accomplished by 22nd January. The power station and other installations were demolished and its stocks of rubber and tungsten removed by sea.[39]

Behind the Japanese came the Burmese nationalists: on 28 December the 'Thirty Comrades' and some 300 recruits lined up in front of Suzuki, who read an order announcing the disbandment of the Minami Kikan and the formation of the Burma Independence Army (BIA). They split into six columns to accompany the invasion forces, and by mid-January all were over the border in what most regarded as 'the fourth and final Anglo-Burmese War'.[40] On 17 January Takeuchi issued orders for the division to move on Kawkareik and attack Moulmein. On 20 January the divisional advance guard crossed the border heading for Moulmein. Kawkareik was defended by 16th Indian Brigade under Brigadier J. K. 'Jonah' Jones and widely dispersed, covering the tracks leading to the border 38 miles away. Two Indian battalions had no radios of their own and only a small section detached from Divisional Signals, but their sets worked only sporadically.[41]

The Japanese first encountered 1st/7th Gurkha Rifles near Myawadi. This unit had arrived in Rangoon the previous day and been quickly diverted.[42] The first brief encounter battle at Kawkareik was a foretaste of what was to follow; the Gurkhas were quickly outflanked and forced to withdraw. All troops took some time to learn how to handle night attacks by the Japanese in the forest; rumours abounded and there was much shooting at shadows. One commanding officer noted 'the effect of the jungle on these young soldiers was most marked as they, including British and Indian officers, actually showed me enemy moving in the jungle which was nothing more than the effect of light and shade on trees and under-growth. There was no enemy in the vicinity.'[43] Within forty-eight hours the rest of 16th Indian Brigade was forced to follow, during which time 1st/9th Jat Regiment fled from the ferry station at Kyondo after destroy-ing their transport and ammunition, taking much of Brigade Headquarters with them, although as their war diary acidly noted, 'no clear picture can be painted of this [occasion] as it was nothing short of a panic'.[44]

Wavell was disgusted and, visiting Hutton on 24/25 January, demanded vigorous offensive action. He thus continued to underestimate the Japanese and his own troops' desperately poor training. Hutton wanted to sack Jones but was persuaded not to by Smyth (Jones won a Distinguished Service Order (DSO) later in the campaign); the Commanding Officer of 1st/9th Jats was, however, replaced. Between 23 and 29 January the Japanese made a determined effort to establish air superiority and there was much fight-ing over Rangoon, during which 17 Japanese planes were shot down and 10 badly damaged for the loss of 2 AVG and 10 RAF machines, forcing the Japanese temporarily to concede.[45] Chennault was insisting on withdrawal from Rangoon by 25 January unless he received reassurances on replace-ment aircraft, which were eventually forthcoming.[46] British fighter strength was down to practically nil when three squadrons of Hurricanes flew in from Egypt (fitted with long-range tanks and having made nine three-hour hops from Iraq to Rangoon led by a Blenheim as navigator).[47] But the planes were obsolescent Mark Is, and spares shortages meant that never more than 30 were available, a number that steadily dwindled.

Hutton ordered Smyth to hold Moulmein at all costs despite the total lack of defence stores, including barbed wire and sandbags, although 2nd KOYLI were ordered south from the Shan States. European women and children were already being evacuated and the back-loading of stores began; rumour spread like wildfire and following air attacks Moulmein was quickly deserted by the remaining inhabitants. James Lunt noted:

> Japanese aircraft were overhead for most of the daylight hours ... At night howling packs of pi-dogs, roaming the streets in search of food, made the air hideous. The few people remaining flitted from place to place, arousing suspicion as fifth columnists, while out in the countryside villages burnt, mostly the work of dacoits or evidence of settling of grudges. Law and order had completely broken down.[48]

Soon after war's outbreak some officers were sent from Singapore to Rangoon to organize special operations in Burma, known as Oriental Mission. In the northern Shan States this task fell to a Burma Frontier Service officer, Noël Stevenson, who began training Kachin levies without waiting for government sanction. Dorman-Smith was sufficiently impressed by his efforts to commission him lieutenant-colonel and give him powers to organize a Burma-wide levy force, which Hutton accepted, although few senior staff officers showed any enthusiasm for the scheme. Some money and arms were, however, made available through Oriental Mission. The potential for a guerrilla group among the largely Karen population of the area prompted Stevenson to ask for the services of Major Hugh Seagrim of 1st Burma Rifles, who spoke the language fluently and was deeply attached to them. Seagrim enthusiastically agreed to stay behind and organize this, but unfortunately the British had retreated so fast he could not be supported.[49]

To the south and east of Moulmein 2nd Burma Brigade deployed 7th and 8th Burma Rifles, with 3rd in the north watching the crossings at the Ataran river, flowing into the Salween north-east of the town.[50] In reserve was 4th/12th Frontier Force Regiment, with 12th Mountain Battery, a troop of 3rd Indian Light Anti-Aircraft Battery and 60th Field Company in support. The Japanese attacked during the night of 30 January and 'managed to force a position on the left of the ridge', noted Lieutenant-Colonel I.A.J. Edwards-Stuart. 'We learned a valuable lesson on the challenging of sentries. At one place the Japs gave the correct password, entered the area and began firing in the direction of their own troops. Having thus reassured the garrison, they then turned on them and massacred all except one.'[51] Throughout the following day the Japanese increased the pressure on the perimeter, and by nightfall it was in danger of cracking. At Brigade

Headquarters the Brigade Major and his successor had collapsed and the Commander, Brigadier Ekin, who had been sent to replace Bourke, signalled Smyth that he doubted if the town could be held during daylight. Smyth gave permission to retire when he so chose and, with Brigade Headquarters under fire, a mad scramble was made for the ferries at the riverside jetties. James Lunt was busy destroying documents and

> found myself alone in the building, the house under heavy machine-gun fire, and the Japs yelling their heads off from the far side of the park about 800 yards away. My car had fortunately not been hit but the starter motor was inclined to be temperamental. We beat a hasty retreat down the drive, Rifleman Amrit Bahadur pushing like hell while I manipulated the choke. With luck we made it. Shortly after 0200 hours I located brigade headquarters in the old telephone exchange, surrounded by blazing buildings. All Moulmein seemed to be burning.[52]

Amazingly, the brigade got clean away with only one small ferry slightly damaged by a shell. The brigade lost 617 men (mostly missing): Major John Hume of 12th Mountain Battery managed to recover all four of his guns, but the anti-aircraft Bofors were overrun (2nd Lieutenant Mehar Dass managed to get one down to the jetty but it could not be loaded onto the ferry).[53] The most unfortunate outcome was the damaging effect on the already shaky morale of the Burma Rifles. Apart from the largely Indian 8th Battalion, most had not performed well thus far. Given their low standard of training and involvement in full-scale war with a foreign enemy while subject to the pressures of an anti-British priesthood, it is easy to see why many deserted. Yet many remained, and the Chins and Kachins did so throughout the campaign.[54]

Meanwhile Roosevelt suggested to a Cabinet meeting on 20 January that an air freight and alternative land route be considered to supply China and added to Stilwell's responsibilities. In March Ferrying Command was activated under Brigadier-General William D. Old USAAF as part of Tenth Air Force. The airfields, aircraft and personnel necessary would have to be put in place, although the difficulties entailed paled in comparison with those necessary for the 'back-country road' from India to China that would become inseparably connected with Stilwell and approved before he even arrived.[55]

On 31 January Wavell was appalled to learn of the ease with which the Japanese had driven 2nd Burma Brigade from Moulmein, although defending the far side of a wide river with few boats or ferries was never tactically sound, whatever the political considerations. Nor was he aware that Smyth was sick and only kept going by strychnine injections. Now both he and Hutton were injured; Hutton was flying to meet Chiang on 2 February when his Lysander crash-landed near Lashio. Although not seriously injured, the badly shocked Hutton was in a poor state to meet the Generalissimo and then received a signal saying Wavell expected to meet him in Rangoon on 4 February. He returned by rail. Wavell's turn came a week later when, returning from Singapore, he fell over a sea wall in the dark.[56] He insisted on returning to duty before he was really fit to do so, although at fifty-nine he was extremely robust and his mental capacity was not impaired; his attention was fixed on Singapore and the hopeless fight to save the Dutch East Indies.[57] But it was Smyth's health that most concerned 17th Indian Division. Hutton insisted on a visit by Major-General Treffry Thompson, Deputy Director Medical Services at Army Headquarters, who recommended a medical board. This was convened under Colonel Kenneth Mackenzie, senior medical officer of 17th Indian Division, who, doubtless under pressure from Smyth himself, found him fit to continue but also, crucially and in absurd fashion, requested that he also be given two months' sick leave at the first opportunity. Smyth wrote to Hutton on 8 February that there was 'nothing wrong with me that a few months' comparative rest wouldn't put right', although this was not an option. In the meantime 'I shall carry on here perfectly happily as long as you like. So sorry.'[58]

On 6 February Wavell visited 2nd Burma Brigade. 'Take back all you have lost!' he barked, continuing to believe the Japanese were overrated. He also decided *en route* from Pegu to the Sittang that armour could operate in the open country and to request an armoured brigade be sent to Burma.[59] The same day Japanese 33rd Division* under Lieutenant-General Sakurai Shozo (or Seizo) crossed the frontier some 20 miles north of Moulmein to cover the northern flank of 55th Division.[60] At the same time Iida moved 15th Army Headquarters forward to Moulmein to co-ordinate operations. Hutton insisted that on leaving Moulmein, Martaban on the west bank of the Salween must be held 'to the last round and last man'. Smyth put Ekin back in charge of 46th Indian Brigade and reinforced it with 2nd KOYLI, now arrived from the Shan States although little more than 250 strong, with no heavy weapons or transport except 7 lorries and 48 mules.[61]

---

* The 33rd Division were known as the 'White Tigers' after the seventeen-year-old sons of *samurai* forced to retire into the castle of Wakamatsu by Imperial soldiers in 1868, twenty of whom committed suicide when they believed the castle had fallen, and in time became national heroes. They called themselves *Byakka-tai* or 'White Tiger Band'.

Martaban was held by 3rd/7th Gurkhas with a Yorkshire company under command, while 7th/10th Baluch Regiment held the ferry crossing at Kuzeik–Pa'an. However, with 16 miles of bank to defend it was inevitable that the Japanese would infiltrate across the river, and on 7 February they cut the defenders at Martaban off from Brigade Headquarters at Thaton.[62] The Gurkhas' Commanding Officer, Lieutenant-Colonel H. A. Stevenson, realizing the position was hopeless, led a bayonet charge against the road-block: 'The withdrawal from Martaban and the subsequent march through difficult country of more than 50 miles in two days on little or no food was a telling ordeal, for some of us a foretaste of things to come.'[63] It later emerged that an order to withdraw had been sent but failed to arrive: the liaison officer was killed at the road-block, and two carriers and an antiquated BAF armoured car destroyed.[64] Smyth needed a tonic and on 9 February he received it in the form of Brigadier David Tennant Cowan, whose nickname 'Punch' derived from his resemblance to the belligerent old man on the cover of *Punch* magazine.[65] It was an unusual appointment, ostensibly to replace Jones at 16th Indian Brigade; Hutton must have been thinking of replacing Smyth with Cowan, but for the time being he would serve as his Brigadier General Staff (a position normally found only at higher headquarters), but effectively as his deputy. Cowan later recorded that Smyth was in a 'very nervous and jittery state; not at all the Smyth I knew'.[66]

During the night of 10 February, II/215th Infantry Regiment, crossed the Salween at Kuzeik and engaged 7th/10th Baluch deployed in a semicircle with their backs to the river without barbed wire or artillery support. After dark on 11 February the Japanese moved forward to make a silent assault, in which they specialized, their bayonets covered with mud to prevent them shining, but they failed to surprise the Baluchis and a stiff fight began soon after midnight. So effective was the resistance that 215th's regimental gun company was ordered to join the attack in the infantry role. Captain Suzuki Tadashi came across some tents.

> We advanced and stabbed a few men who were outside. When we entered a tent which looked like a combat headquarters I saw a wounded commander [Lieutenant-Colonel Jerry Dyer, whose jaw had been shattered by a bullet] sitting upright with several of his men. He signed to us to shoot him and died in a serene frame of mind. His attitude really was in keeping with the honour of a military man. I sincerely respected him and wished I might do the same.[67]

After four hours the Japanese began to get the upper hand and by 0800 organized resistance ceased; the survivors of this raw and inexperienced battalion, which had fought magnificently, made off in small parties. In all 7th/10th Baluch lost 289 killed (in bayonet fighting there is always a high proportion of killed to wounded, and the Japanese seldom hesitated to finish off the latter).[68] One such party, led by Captain Bruce Toothill, was cornered by yelling Japanese, and Toothill himself was severely wounded in the jaw in a shoot-out. He indicated to a Japanese soldier standing over him to finish him off but the soldier refused. He was subsequently well treated, his courageous resistance seemingly winning the respect of his captors, and spent the remainder of the war in Rangoon gaol.[69] The confusion caused by poor communications meant 46th Indian Brigade could not counter-attack effectively as ordered, and in any case 5th/17th Dogra Regiment was not sufficiently well trained to carry out a night advance and attack.[70]

Hutton was finding his responsibilities as Army Commander, Chief of General Staff at the Burmese War Office and *de facto* deputy theatre commander unbearable, and on 13 February he requested Wavell appoint a proper corps commander to conduct operations and a high-level liaison team to deal with the Chinese. He received no reply: Wavell was incapacitated after his fall, while Singapore fell two days later. So Hutton carried on as before, instructing Smyth to hold the Thaton–Duyinzeik line and not to retire on the Bilin without referring to AHQ – a mistake deriving from the continued failure to realize that the Japanese did not fight along roads like Western armies. The Japanese advanced rapidly with the as yet unengaged 214th Infantry Regiment leading 33rd Division across the Bilin river some 6 miles north of Bilin town, and 215th Regiment outflanking Duyinzeik to cross at Yinon. With 112th Regiment securing Moulmein, Headquarters 55th Division followed 143rd Regiment as it crossed the Bilin estuary and reached Taungzon on 19 February.[71]

Although reinforced by 48th Indian Brigade, Smyth now faced two Japanese divisions and neither 2nd Burma nor 16th Indian Brigade was in good shape. The Bilin presented no real obstacle and, although Hutton informed Wavell that he had every intention of fighting east of the Sittang, it might become necessary to withdraw, a prospect that caused great alarm to Dorman-Smith and his council in Rangoon. Another concern was the vast quantity of Chinese lend-lease stores piling the wharfs and warehouses in Rangoon. With the Chinese largely unable to move them, it seemed logical to employ at least some in the city's defence and Dorman-Smith in due course hinted at confiscation. After 150 lorries and some munitions were taken, the other stockpiles were impounded by American lend-lease officers until their fate could be agreed, but when the dispute came before

Chiang he carefully returned the perceived slight from Wavell by offering 20 machine-guns for Burma's defence.[72] Chiang, eager to play the international role, visited India in February to rally support, but Mahatma Gandhi swiftly put his true position in perspective. 'They will never treat us Orientals as equals', Gandhi said; 'why, they do not even admit your country to their talks.'[73]

For three days there was confused skirmishing along the Bilin. Between 16 and 18 February 214th Regiment tried to break the road-block to the north held by 2nd KOYLI on a front some 2,000 yards long, very thinly spread and short of ammunition, although this also affected the Japanese, who stressed the importance of saving it:

> Even the artillery tried to hit its target with only one shell. In contrast the British fired a barrage which was like ploughing the land with shells … Japanese weapons were inferior and their ammunition supply limited. From this first experience the Japanese realized that the only way to win was to attack the flanks or back of the British, where they could not develop their full strength, and to attack at night.[74]

Private W. Abbott of 2nd KOYLI endured a horrific journey to pass a message from his isolated company to Battalion Headquarters, during which he was shot by the Japanese and attacked by Burmese villagers. Eventually a message had to be dropped by air to order the company to retire.[75] When Smyth received reports on 18 February that 143rd Regiment threatened to outflank him to the south, he committed his last reserve, 4th/12th Frontier Force Regiment, who fought a stiff action on 16th Indian Brigade's left flank but failed to dislodge the Japanese. The next day Hutton visited Smyth and reluctantly gave permission to withdraw to the Sittang.

This would be a difficult move of 35 miles with Japanese air activity and both 16th and 48th Indian Brigades in contact; moving at night would make it doubly so. Ekin and Smyth disagreed on the method but Smyth insisted that he had reconnaissance troops to the north to cover his proposed plan. It seemed that help was on its way in the form of the fit and battle-hardened 7th Australian Division, then rounding the southern point of Ceylon, and in response to Dorman-Smith's urgent appeal for reinforcements, Churchill asked the Prime Minister of Australia, John Curtin, that they be sent to Rangoon. But Australia had been deeply shocked by Britain's lamentable defence of Singapore, including the loss of 8th Australian Division, and after the bombing of Darwin was looking to defend her own shores. Despite receiving unstinting support from Roosevelt, Curtin refused Churchill's appeals; Australia would never again sacrifice her interests for those of the mother country or empire.[76] Besides, they could not have saved Rangoon. Meanwhile the Viceroy of India, Lord Linlithgow, reacted violently to developments by cabling the Colonial Secretary, Leo Amery, that the failure was 'in great part due to lack of drive and inspiration from the top'. Churchill agreed, bitterly disappointed by Curtin's decision. He later wrote, 'if we could not send an army, we could at least send a man' and he relayed this sentiment to Wavell: 'If you concur with the Viceroy, we will send [Lieutenant-General the Hon. Sir Harold] Alexander at once.'[77]

# 4

## Disaster on the Sittang

> Betrayed by the country that bore us,
> Betrayed by the country we find,
> All the best men have gone before us
> And only the dull left behind.
> Stand to your glasses steady
> This world is a world full of lies,
> Here's a toast to the dead already
> And here's to the next man to die.
>
> Anon. *Calcutta Cholera Song*

IF THINGS SEEMED bad on the Bilin, they were about to get much worse. Although overshadowed by the fall of Singapore, the battle of the Sittang on 22/23 February ranks as a defining moment in the decline and fall of the British Empire.[1] Headquarters 17th Indian Division learned of its responsibility for the bridge on 14 February, before the battle on the Bilin, but only in the midst of retreat could it prepare the position.[2] During 20 February, as 16th and 48th Indian Brigades marched back to Kyaikto, tired but not despondent, 2nd Duke of Wellington's Regiment arrived direct from India via Rangoon, lacking transport but 'the freshest troops seen in those parts for several weeks'. James Lunt could not believe his old battalion was not sent to dig in around the Sittang bridgehead but was instead sent to Kyaikto and then ordered to retreat forty-eight hours later, by which time they had lost most of their weapons, all their kit and more than 300 officers and men.[3]

Kyaikto was the first stage of the withdrawal from the Bilin, some 15 miles across paddy fields and *chaungs*, whereafter conditions became worse: a single unsurfaced track pocked with bomb craters and barely wide enough for two vehicles to pass, with no provost to control the traffic and communications at all levels patchy at best. On either side was thick jungle, and there was no water. The first troops back from Kyaikto were 4th/12th Frontier Force Regiment, and the Malerkotla Sappers and Miners, an Indian State Forces unit, was to prepare the bridge for demolition. First

Burma Field Company had already been at work for a week bolting down sleepers next to the rail line to take road traffic, which as a rail bridge it could not do, and it was not yet ready by the evening of the 21st. Hutton had established a Line of Communications Area under Major-General Victor Wakeley to control Burma Army's communications from Rangoon to the Sittang, but he could only call on 2nd Burma Brigade for troops and Bourke (now reinstated) could only spare 3rd Burma Rifles, already down to just 300 men, together with a company of 2nd Dukes.

Meanwhile 16th and 46th Indian Brigades were still at Kyaikto and withdrawing towards the bridge early on 20 February. At 0830 the Japanese arrived and attacked the north-east of the defences; for the next forty-eight hours total confusion reigned. The retreating columns came under air attack, tragically from the RAF and AVG as well as the Japanese, and most of the Divisional Headquarters radio equipment was lost.[4] 'It is impossible to emphasize the effect these attacks had on the Indian troops', noted Lieutenant D. H. West. 'They had reached a stage where they could identify both our planes and the Japs and to be fired upon by planes bearing our markings completely shattered their convictions, the more so since the B[ritish] O[fficer]s were at a loss to give a satisfactory explanation.'[5] Night attacks by Japanese 'jitter parties' spread panic among the inexperienced troops who fired indiscriminately. This gave away their positions, cost them sleep and caused casualties among those trying to stop them; commanders had to impose tight discipline to guard against such panic.[6]

For Smyth, 22 February was a day of unmitigated disaster. At 0100 1st/4th Gurkhas were ordered to cross and guard against Japanese airborne assault from the west, taking the company of Dukes there under command. Smyth had by now arrived, and Brigadier Noël Hugh-Jones with Headquarters 48th Indian Brigade and transport was beginning to cross. Smyth ordered Hugh-Jones to take charge of the bridge defences; the staff officer from Army who brought the news of a parachute threat also informed Smyth that 7th Armoured Brigade with two regiments of light tanks had arrived at Rangoon, but would not be available for two or three days. There was no news of the Japanese. Smyth had placed FF2 to the north of the Kyaikto track to warn against outflanking, or so he thought. At 1430 the previous day it had been heavily engaged by 215th Regiment and withdrawn north-west, crossing the river by country boats and proceeding towards Pegu. No report of this contact ever reached Smyth. Sakurai had instructed 215th Regiment to go straight for the bridge and during the morning its 1st Battalion occupied 'Buddha Hill', which overlooked it. They then attempted to rush the nearby 'Pagoda Hill'.

Smyth was with a field ambulance just behind 3rd Burma Rifles on the east bank. Five minutes after he left, the Japanese burst into it screaming and yelling, bayoneting the wounded and capturing Smyth's senior medical officer, Colonel Kenneth Mackenzie. Had Smyth accepted the cigarette Mackenzie had offered him (he had just given up smoking), he might also have spent the next three and a half years in Rangoon gaol.[7] Soon afterwards Lieutenant West received orders to withdraw across the river only to find the road nose to tail with traffic, 'and a machine-gun opened fire on the bridgehead. I continued across and found that I was practically the last vehicle to get across as the driver of the vehicle behind me had been hit.'[8] But 4th/12th Frontier Force Regiment held firm on 'Pagoda Hill', although attempts to clear 'Buddha Hill' failed despite determined leadership from Captain S. H. J. F. 'Sam' Manekshaw before he was severely wounded. A second Japanese attack was held in the afternoon, but pressure was mounting all the time, and the Malerkotla Sappers were desperately trying to prepare the demolitions, completing two spans by 1800. All local boats had been collected by 24th Field Company, but unfortunately Smyth ordered their destruction, although three motor ferries on the east bank were already captured by the Japanese.[9]

Throughout the day 16th and 46th Indian Brigades withdrew towards the bridgehead and Mokpalin railway station, embroiled in a fierce and confused fight.[10] Some Japanese feigned surrender and Lieutenant-Colonel G. A. Ballinger of 1st/3rd Gurkhas was killed going forward to accept it. Other units were held up and had to bypass positions to reach the river.[11] The night was tense, with the British split into two groups, with little contact between or within them. At dawn on 23 February there was terrific weight of fire all around the bridge. Hugh-Jones conferred with the commanding officers of 1st/4th Gurkhas and 4th/12th Frontier Force Regiment, who told him the bridge should be blown as the troops could not resist a determined attack, and that all who could get across the river had done so. 'A terrible decision had to be made', wrote Hutton's Brigadier General Staff, H. L. 'Taffy' Davies. 'If he blew the bridge he sacrificed the bulk of his division. If he failed to blow the bridge and it was secured by the enemy, the way to Rangoon lay open with nothing interposing. General Smyth blew the bridge. In my opinion a heroic and inevitable decision.'[12] Brave it undoubtedly was, but its inevitability has been debated ever since. Hutton certainly did not regard it as inevitable, and nor did Wavell, but at 0530 on 23 February three colossal roars announced to all participants that one span was now in the river. Captain Bruce Kinloch of 1st/3rd Gurkhas recalled that, 'as the echoes died away there was complete silence. All firing ceased, and every living thing seemed to be holding its breath. Then the Japanese, like a troop of excited monkeys, broke into shrill chattering. Believing that everyone else had crossed over and abandoned us to our fate, we were filled with anger.'[13] But most of the division remained on the far bank.

Brigadier Jones of 16th Indian Brigade, now in command of the troops on the east bank, planned to hold his positions around Mokpalin until nightfall, but Japanese shelling and an air raid on to the massed brigade transport caused enormous damage. Fourth Burma Rifles broke, leaving a gap in the perimeter, and the rest were exhausted. It is the jaws of soldiers who have been in prolonged action one notices first; having been clenched for hours, they droop when relaxed, giving them a slightly idiotic look.[14] At 1430 Jones and Ekin decided they could hold no longer, and Jones gave orders for immediate withdrawal to the river. Those who got away by boat or swimming the river, swollen to 1½ miles wide by the incoming tide, owed much to those who continued to man the defences throughout that long, hot, thirsty day until nightfall: 2nd KOYLI, 3rd/7th Gurkhas, 5th/17th Dogras and 8th Burma Rifles, none more than 200 strong, many of whom were subsequently captured.[15] Most, however, made an attempt to cross the river either by swimming or by lashing together rafts. Sergeant Bill Crowther of the Dukes found himself manning a machine-gun with Bandsman Les Williams. When the ammunition ran out, Crowther threw the breech block into the river.

> I said: 'Follow it, Les.' To which he replied: 'Not me. I've to take my chances with the Japs. I can't swim.' I offered to take him but he wouldn't have it. So I shook hands with him, wished him the best, and dived in. I was born on the side of the Tyne (Newcastle) and spent my childhood days swimming in it, so the Sittang held no terror for me. Mind you, there were still some snipers and aircraft. How long I spent in that river I don't know – helping chaps to anything that floated.[16]

Ingenuity was widespread. Major S. F. Harvey-Williams of 3rd/7th Gurkhas saw many men with empty petrol cans and bamboo and helped to strap them on as flotation aids. They returned after a few strokes, tied them to their backs and set off again, making it across.[17] Lalbahadur Gurung of 1st/3rd Gurkhas saw the river's edge lined with fish killed by the blowing of the bridge.

> I saw a British officer who looked as if he was sitting down but he had sunk into the mud. He asked me my unit and I told him. I tried to pull him out but could not and he ordered us to go to an RV and have a meal with 1st/4th Gurkhas. I suppose he drowned in the mud, or maybe the Japanese got him first, I don't know.[18]

Major Jack Robinson, Corporal Fox and Lance-Corporal Roebuck of the Dukes swam the river at the broken span of the bridge and erected a lifeline across which some 400 men managed to cross, for which the major received a Military Cross (MC) and the two corporals the Military Medal (MM).[19]

Fortunately for the British, the Japanese virtually broke off the battle at nightfall, allowing more men to escape – albeit without weapons or equipment. But they faced other perils. Lieutenant-Colonel Basil Owen of 2nd Dukes was murdered while resting in a village on the west side of the Sittang, his head almost severed by a *dah* (a Burmese sword).[20] Lieutenant-Colonel Stevenson of 3rd/7th Gurkhas made his way back for twenty-three days through Japanese-held territory after surviving on five meals, being helped on the way by Tamil coolies and armed Karens, and walking the last eight days on bare feet, first to avoid trackers, then because they were so swollen.[21] Although it took the Japanese almost a fortnight to make a road from Kyaikto and bring forward bridging material, during which time 17th Indian Division reformed at Pegu, the Sittang disaster virtually destroyed the division as a fighting formation; 1st/4th Gurkhas and 4th/12th Frontier Force Regiment were virtually complete, but while 1st/9th Jats mustered 550 all ranks, 2nd KOYLI was down to 80 all ranks, 5th/17th Dogras had only 30, and of the division only 80 British officers, 68 VCOs and 3,335 men were assembled, most without weapons or transport.[22]

Hutton considered the decision to blow the bridge premature, possibly even unnecessary, and the withdrawal mismanaged, although he accepted that he might have made Smyth wait on the Bilin too long.[23] He criticized Smyth's failure to provide an adequate demolition guard and the positioning of Smyth's headquarters – 8 miles away at Abya, with only the civilian telephone for communication with the officer responsible for blowing the bridge. But although Smyth's radio was the most powerful in Burma at the time, it could not guarantee communications with Rangoon. Cowan disagreed with Hutton and wrote to Smyth years later: 'As a result of the Bilin delay we were doomed. We withdrew much too late, over a ghastly dirt track.'[24] Smyth attributed the delay to Hutton's refusal to allow any such move without his express permission. Hutton also thought that surely Smyth or Cowan should have remained at the bridge to ensure the division was safely across.[25] The responsibility on Hugh-Jones was colossal, and he agonized over it for many years before one day walking into the sea to drown. 'He was a Sittang casualty if ever there was one', Smyth wrote.[26]

Smyth was certainly not responsible for the unpreparedness of the bridge for wheeled transport; that responsibility fell to Burma Army, about which Smyth had written to Hutton over two weeks earlier.[27] But he was responsible for the failure to create a demolition guard, having sent back only 3rd Burma Rifles; Brigadier John Bourke protested strongly at this having little faith in their abilities. Only on the morning of the withdrawal was 4th/12th Frontier Force Regiment sent back, arriving exhausted, while the fresh 2nd Dukes was being sent forward to its ruin. So distant commanders – Wavell and Hutton – under pressure from both Governor and Stevenson, hindered by poor communications with a patently unfit divisional commander, combined to create a series of blunders.[28] The protagonists argued for years afterwards as to where the blame lay, but as Captain Attiqur Rahman of 4th/12th Frontier Force Regiment later wrote, Smyth was quite wrong 'to command when he was so ill. Everyone knows that he was a very brave soldier but unless a divisional commander, especially in the jungle, is 100 per cent fit, I think it is very unfair on his troops.'[29]

The disaster made Rangoon's evacuation inevitable. Like Wavell, still reeling after the fall of Singapore, Dorman-Smith was astounded by the turn of events. The War Cabinet and Chiefs of Staff seem to have underestimated the importance of Rangoon in keeping China in the war. A liaison officer from GHQ Middle East noted that as soon as Singapore ceased to be significant as a naval base, within a couple of weeks of the outbreak of war, 'the holding of Singapore became very much less important than the holding of Rangoon and Burma. Had this been appreciated it would not have been possible for troops to have been poured into Singapore at the expense of Burma, especially 18[th] Div[ision].'[30] Hutton later noted that a major contributory factor to the loss of Rangoon was 'the failure of the command in Burma to appreciate that the holding of Rangoon was fundamental to the effective protection of Upper Burma and the Burma Road to China'.[31] He also believed McLeod's most important contribution had been the preparation of the Rangoon Evacuation Scheme for a three-stage withdrawal and demolition. He never received a directive explicitly setting out the vital necessity of holding Rangoon, but whether this would have made a substantive difference is doubtful: better training, better equipment and control of the air might have.

On 20 February Hutton had implemented the second stage of the scheme, which caused immediate panic. Among the evacuees were most of the Women's Auxiliary Service (Burma) – WAS(B) – formed in January to perform clerical and cipher support duties in static headquarters of all three services.[32] It was, one noted, a 'grim night made more hideous by the shriek of drunken natives who were looting the houses and by the screams of lunatics and roving criminals, the gaols and asylums having let their inmates loose on the Town'.[33] Mi Mi Khaing was caught up by the compulsory sea evacuation of Europeans and selected Asians:

> I felt as though my heart would break against this awful machine which had suddenly made us so unimportant, and which did not care that I was a Burman amidst the crowd of foreign women it was evacuating, taking me from mother and sisters to whom I could not get news or explanation of my desertion ... a vast and inexpressible sadness settled upon me. Dawn had not yet broken, and only the glare from Kemmendine fires still lighted the sky. How sad, how black and empty each familiar house-face looked, with shut eyes and shuttered doors.[34]

Also evacuated was the American Muriel Degaa Upfill, who learned on reaching Calcutta that her New Zealand husband, 'Uppy', had been killed serving with the river patrol. Told shortly afterwards that she must leave India, she instead found a secretarial job with Colonel William 'Wild Bill' Donovan of the American Office of Strategic Services (OSS), and later worked with Mi Mi Khaing at the Ministry of Information.[35]

By 24 February Rangoon 'had become a dreary city of silence. Not a Burman was to be seen and all around were signs of previous looting and rioting.'[36] The police, mostly Indians, collapsed. Tony Mains's Field Security unit faced a mob of them looting the cloth market.[37] The Glosters equipped themselves as best they could from salvaged lend-lease motor transport and other equipment, including twelve mortars and two Italian Breda anti-aircraft guns with jeep wheels replacing those on the carriages, so that although weak in numbers, they were entirely mobile. The depot was transferred to Mandalay, where it was secure for the time being, and seventeen Russians were enlisted, all trained by the Shanghai Volunteer Force and speaking at least three languages; 'their initiative, courage and security mindedness' were their outstanding qualities. Private V. Phylatoff won the MM at his first action, and these 'fire eaters continually demanded to go on fighting patrols to contact the enemy and found our constant withdrawals very frustrating'.[38] Before the end of February a draft of thirteen officers arrived, but it 'could only be accounted a tragedy. Although they were brave and devoted, their inexperience meant that within a month, all but two were casualties.'[39]

Most RAF ground crews headed for Magwe, 'a very bare dry torrid place', according to Sergeant Ed Beable, 'situated very close to the home of the King Cobra snake'. Conditions were harsh, with ablutions from a canvas bucket and little food. 'Our breakfast was generally no more than half a soya bean sausage washed down with lashings of tea ... and the evening meal for weeks was tinned bully beef and whisky!' Days were spent waiting for the telephone to order 'Scramble!' and time passed playing card games, usually 'Acey Deucey'. 'This we learned from the AVG and it was played from dawn to dark.'[40] At Nyaunglebin, James Lunt noted streams of refugee traffic and large numbers of Indians and Chinese on foot.

> It was like a visitation of locusts. The bazaar was stripped clean, houses were broken into and looted, the roads were strewn with human ordure, and a large part of the town was set on fire. I happened to see Lady Dorman-Smith passing through in the Governor's Rolls, staring straight ahead, quite expressionless. Her world too was crashing around her.[41]

The final civilian evacuation was set for 1 March, and on 28 February Dorman-Smith held a last supper in Government House, attended only by his ADC and military liaison officer. Although disparagingly referred to by many as 'Dormant-Myth' and 'Dormouse-Smith', he was, according to Australian correspondent Wilfred Burchett, 'readily accessible and quick to act'.[42] Now it was too late: there was no iced consommé, sole, duckling or ice cream for the Governor's dinner, just some mutton from an old sheep of which Dorman-Smith recalled he had grown fond, and which would have been spared had there been anything else. The last evacuees of Government House vented their frustration by hurling billiard balls at the portraits of previous British governors of Burma. 'It was a massacre', said Dorman-Smith of the paintings.[43] But an empire ruled by prestige was also in tatters.

Before the Sittang disaster Wavell had been non-committal about the arrival of Alexander, preferring to defer any decision until he knew whether or not 7th Australian Division would land at Rangoon. Hutton's pessimistic if accurate appreciation of 18 February angered Wavell, but more so Hutton's action of the 21st, when only part of a convoy was landed at Rangoon, the balance carrying administrative personnel returned to Calcutta. Unfortunately this included mules for 15th and 28th Mountain Batteries, who now had to use motor vehicles, which made them road-bound and much reduced their mobility.[44] On 22 February Hutton was informed that he was to be replaced but to remain as Alexander's Chief of Staff – a most awkward position which he endured until he was replaced at his own request by Major-General John Winter, before returning to India in early April.[45] He was not given another active command. Churchill regarded Alexander as Britain's finest general. 'Confidence spread around him', he said, although opinions elsewhere were at best mixed.[46] Certainly he was incredibly cool under pressure, but his subsequent reputation does not rest on his time in Burma, to which he allotted only three pages in his memoirs.[47]

Hutton was not alone in his fall from grace, however. On 25 February Smyth wrote confidentially to Hutton requesting that he be granted the two months' sick leave recommended by his medical board. He received no reply. Hutton later claimed to have taken no part in Smyth's removal, indeed, not to have been consulted. But on 26 February he signalled GHQ(I) that Smyth's request indicated that 'he has lost confidence in his ability to command and should be relieved', proposing Cowan in his place. On the day of the Sittang disaster Wavell had been told to wind up ABDA Command in Java and resume his appointment as Commander-in-Chief India. He had throughout been hopelessly out of touch with the situation in Burma, bombarding Hutton with signals demanding offensive action. 'I admit quite frankly that I misjudged the situation', he later told Hutton, and he 'never expected the Japanese to get along as fast as he did, or in such strength'.[48] His ill-luck continued when, leaving Java on the 25th, his plane caught fire, but two days later he was back at his desk in New Delhi. Few generals have suffered such a succession of hammer blows as Wavell, who remained 'bloody but unbowed'; but there were more to come.[49] Wavell duly ordered that Cowan replace Smyth on 1 March and at Magwe, recalled Hutton, he expressed his displeasure at events with uncharacteristic venom, and 'stormed at me in front of the Governor, the AOC and a number of officers and civilians in a most excited way'.[50]

Blowing the bridge on the Sittang did not stop the Japanese, but they took the opportunity to regroup. Iida moved his headquarters to Kyaikto within forty-eight hours of Smyth abandoning it and decided to waste no time on the bridge but to move upstream to Kunzeik and elsewhere to ferry his men across instead. On 27 February he ordered 55th Division to begin crossing at Daik-u on 3 March and to block any interference by British or Chinese from the north, while 143rd Regiment would cross at Waw, turn south to encircle and destroy 17th Indian Division through Pegu followed by 112th Regiment, which would block the road to the south; 33rd Division would follow on after rest and reorganization and march due west through the densely wooded hills of the Pegu Yomas to the Rangoon–Prome highway, turn south and seize Rangoon. Iida impressed on Sakurai the need for speed before the British could bring in reinforcements.[51] Not that the outstanding Sakurai needed reminding. The British could find no answer to his aggressive encircling tactics.

However, in the short breathing space provided to Burma Army an administrative miracle took place, one that would enable them to continue the retreat for the next three months. It was Major-General

Goddard's drive, skill and willingness to cut through bureaucratic opposition by forcing the railways and the Irrawaddy Flotilla Company to face the harsh realities of war that ensured Burma Army still had petrol for its vehicles, ammunition, food and medical supplies with a major programme of back-loading supplies to Upper Burma before Rangoon was evacuated.[52] On 28 February 2nd Burma Brigade was transferred to 1st Burma Division coming down from the Shan States to cover the concentration of Chinese 5th Army at Toungoo. It had been given an almost impossible task, with battalions guarding 150 miles of the Thai border in thick jungle.[53] At Pegu 17th Indian Division reconstituted itself after a fashion, although many units had to amalgamate: 2nd KOYLI (about 200 strong) and 2nd Dukes (400) briefly formed the 'King's Own Dukes';[54] 1st/7th and 3rd/7th Gurkhas formed a single battalion, and 1st/3rd and 2nd/5th Royal Gurkhas also temporarily combined as 5th/3rd; 46th Indian Brigade was broken up, with its remaining soldiers and those of 3rd, 4th and 8th Burma Rifles joining 4th/12th Frontier Forces Regiment, but three British battalions arrived from internal security duties in India, fresh but only lightly equipped, as did 7th Armoured Brigade with American-made Stuart tanks. However, these were of little value in modern warfare, as they were lightly armoured and armed with only a 37mm gun and two .3-inch Browning machine-guns. They also had poor cross-country mobility in a land of jungle and paddy fields, whose *bunds* (clay-ridge enclosures) were baked hard and insurmountable.[55] But they were welcome nevertheless. Their first contact was made at the Waw canal on 2 March, when a troop of 2nd Royal Tank Regiment was engaged by a 75mm gun which knocked out two and damaged the third.[56]

Alexander arrived on 4 March and met Hutton and Dorman-Smith, the latter 'an unimpressive character' according to Alexander's ADC, Rupert Clarke, and 'clearly very dependent on Hutton'.[57] Alexander was a complete contrast to Hutton. He brought no great intellect to the post, but his imperturbable character was an undoubted boost to morale. Alexander cancelled Hutton's order for withdrawal until at least 63rd Indian Brigade and 1st Field Regiment, Indian Artillery (IA), had cleared the now deserted docks. Not that these reinforcements gave any cause for optimism. The standard of training was obviously far below that necessary. None of 1st/11th Sikh Regiment, including the officers, had even seen 2-inch mortars, anti-tank grenades or Bren guns before embarkation. As they approached Rangoon on 3 March, 'we were approaching a city of the dead! Not a sound came from the quay or the town behind but overhead a great covey of vultures floated lazily over the dead city.'[58]

The breakdown in order spread rapidly. Karens began to desert the Burma Military Police among rumours of clashes with Burmans in their delta villages.[59] And on the evening of the 5th the British suffered another serious misfortune. The command group of 63rd Indian Brigade were ambushed at a road-block while conducting a reconnaissance. Lieutenant-Colonel R. G. Leonard commanding 1st/10th Gurkhas recalled that, as they passed a tree,

> there was a harsh rattle of a light automatic. I felt as if a heavy draught horse had kicked me on the knees. I saw John Wickham and Ian slump towards each other and the carrier slithered to a stop. A moment later another burst followed the first and my left arm, by which I was bracing myself, was flung aside and I fell forward in time for my head to be missed by the third burst which, ricocheting off the back-plate filled the carrier with further splashes of lead.[60]

The Brigade Major, G. M. Fortreath, could see that Leonard 'was in a bad way as a number of bullets had passed through my arms and lodged in him. I was also wounded in the face. I did not realize at the time how lucky I was to be alive.'[61] With the carrier reduced to a shambles, Lieutenant Arthur Fearnley's tank of 2nd Royal Tank Regiment's escort troop lurched off the road and came to rest in a ditch. Seeing two Japanese approaching, Fearnley fired his revolver and ordered his corporal to fire the Browning. The corporal, unsighted, said 'What at, sir?' 'Never mind what at,' roared Fearnley, 'just fire the bloody thing!'

The corporal fired a few rounds before collapsing wounded in the chest. Fearnley discovered the driver was dead, and, unable to move him, had to sit in his lap to re-start the engine. They desperately tried to reverse out but were halted soon after by another block of two trucks end-to-end, which he managed to squeeze through after ramming them repeatedly. Although Fearnley was awarded an immediate MC, he felt an overwhelming sense of failure: Brigadier John Wickham and his three commanding officers had been killed or wounded before the brigade even got into action.[62] The following day Pegu was heavily bombed, then attacked by 143rd Regiment. Seventh Hussars, which had relieved 2nd Royal Tanks, were ambushed south of Pegu by Japanese 37mm anti-tank guns, in turn counter-attacked by the supporting 1st West Yorkshire Regiment company and overrun, killing most of the gunners. Soon afterwards the Hussars encountered three Japanese tanks, brought with difficulty from Thailand, and knocked them out.[63] A combined aid post was set up, served by the two regimental doctors and the 7th Hussars' chaplain, Revd Neville Metcalfe, who helped ferry wounded to Pegu hospital in his car when the only ambulance was destroyed, combining the duties of doctor, cook, orderly and priest among the carnage to earn a thoroughly deserved immediate DSO.[64] Following the 1942 campaign, the practice of decorating ambulances and hospitals with red crosses was abandoned since the Japanese regarded them simply as aiming points, which was undoubtedly the case at Pegu. A direct hit on the hospital from an aerial bomb provided a gruesome solution to the problem of disposal for some of the wounded. At midnight Alexander changed his mind and ordered that the Rangoon demolition plan be implemented and withdrawal to Prome begun the next day, with 17th Indian Division to retire to Hlegu. This they managed only with difficulty, in a running fight along the road.

At 0830 on 7 March 7th Hussars met a road-block, which they attacked, although after they got through it was closed again in front of 48th Indian Brigade. There was more confused fighting in which the Commanding Officer of 1st/7th Gurkhas was killed before a renewed attack alongside their affiliated regiment, 1st Cameronians, cleared it. A party of Japanese in a ditch were causing great trouble until Rifleman Whyte of the Gorbals and Lance-Naik Padam Sing Rai of Aisyalkarka in eastern Nepal attacked them, Whyte with a Bren-gun and Padam Sing by hurling grenades from a haversack. They slumped in the ditch and swapped cigarettes. 'Taught them bastards a lesson, Johnny', said Whyte. '*Thik Hai*,★ Johnny?' he asked. '*Thik Hai*, Jock', replied his friend.[65] But the brigade had become totally disorganized and many sub-units were now moving independently. Two companies of 1st/4th Gurkhas encountered a mounted platoon from 214th Regiment which chased after them. They lay down and shot several riders, the horses jumping them and disappearing into the trees. Thus, having faced the last cavalry 'charge' encountered by British troops, they continued.[66] Fortunately for 17th Indian Division, 55th Division had shot its bolt and, although followed by 112th Regiment, there was no further contact. The two formations would not meet again for seven weeks.

Meanwhile, Rangoon's air defence rested on a handful of weary fighter planes and their pilots, and with it the demolition of all remaining facilities that could be of any use to the enemy – a task ruthlessly carried out by 'last-ditchers' Mr Leslie Forster, a Shell-Mex engineer, and 23-year old Captain Walter Scott RE, who in one hour on Saturday 7 March destroyed £11 million worth of Burmah Oil Company property, sending a cloud of billowing

★ 'All right?'

smoke up to 23,000 feet before departing by launch down the Rangoon river to the *Heinrich Jensen*.[67] Meanwhile it was clear the RAF needed to be redeployed and Air Chief Marshal Sir Richard Peirse, AOC-in-C India, ordered Stevenson to reform 221 Group at Calcutta. Shortly afterwards some 3,000 airmen were withdrawn to India by air and Stevenson sent his remaining fighters – 3 Buffaloes, 4 Tomahawks and about 20 Hurricanes – to a rough landing-ground cut out of paddy fields at Zigon, some 120 miles to the north.

As a pall of smoke hung over the abandoned city, the advance guard set off towards Tharrawaddy but ran into a road-block at Taukkyan, held by III/214th Regiment. The first to encounter them were three carriers of 2nd Dukes under Captain J. A. A. Christison. He and four soldiers were killed and two of the carriers destroyed.[68] Attacks were launched on the road-block first by 1st Glosters and 1st West Yorks supported by B Squadron, 7th Hussars, then by 63rd Indian Brigade, but all to no avail.[69] The scene at Taukkyan was one 'of indescribable confusion and congestion', noted Captain Terence Dillon. The whole army in Burma, other than 1st Burma Division to the north, 'was concentrated within a two-mile stretch of the Prome Road, thousands of vehicles crammed into the plantations on either side'.[70] The villages either side of the road were practically all enclosed in woods and while these woods and villages entailed jungle fighting, noted Lieutenant-Colonel Charles Bagot commanding 1st Glosters, 'there was no jungle in Burma during the course of the campaign, which was comparable to some found in Assam ... or parts of Malaya. The snake-infested impenetrable jungles so freely talked about in connection with this Campaign were a myth.'[71] Nevertheless, the situation looked grim as Alexander made a plan for an all-out attack the following morning. If this plan failed, the alternative was even more desperate: the army was to split into parties of twelve and 'make their way to India independently'.[72] That night a Japanese attack on 2nd/13th Frontier Force Rifles reached Battalion Headquarters, killing the Commanding Officer and Adjutant. One Japanese officer attacked the chief clerk before being shot by Captain Rahim Khan, although the chief clerk's greatest fear was being shot by Khan, who only hit the Japanese with the sixth round from his revolver.[73] But it was the last straw for the exhausted Japanese. They had not expected the British to abandon Rangoon, and Sakurai was determined not to get involved in a fight that would slow its capture, and Colonel Sakuma Takanobu of 214th Regiment authorized the blocking force to break off contact after dark in order to continue the advance into Rangoon west of the Prome road.[74]

At first light on 8 March the British assembled to attack. The raw soldiers of 1st/11th Sikhs saw two mounted Japanese scouts and opened a wild, uncontrolled fire. When a platoon went forward, they were fired on and returned, 'like a troupe of dancing girls, laughing and chattering[;] they were obviously hysterical', recalled a regimental report. They 'were horribly untrained these recruits – they were horribly inexperienced these NCOs – and what of ourselves the Officers and VCOs? ... The men were bewildered, shaken, hungry and utterly weary.'[75] But in the confusion 7th Hussars found the road open, and the British poured northwards covering 28 miles and, by ferrying on motor transport, another 35 the next day.[76] The Japanese did not follow up and on 10 March the British were finally able to rest, greatly relieved, but not realizing that the Japanese had outrun their supplies and were dangerously short of ammunition. Iida was therefore determined to capture the port to ease this dangerous situation.[77] Sakurai was astonished to find Rangoon deserted, which may explain the single-mindedness displayed by the Japanese in a story (probably apocryphal, but popular at the time) of a British civilian left behind. As he hastened after the retreating army, his car broke down and while he was trying to fix it, a long column of Japanese troops approached, led by an officer on a white charger. As they drew near, the civilian doffed his hat and bowed and the officer saluted in return. After a seemingly interminable time the column passed and the civilian was able to start his car and speed off to catch up with Alexander's column.[78]

In fact, IGHQ in Tokyo had only authorized Headquarters Southern Army to capture the vital parts of Burma: Tenasserim and Rangoon, the inlet valve of the Burma Road. One reason was fear of Chinese intervention, for which 18th Division, then in Malaya, and 56th Division in Japan were in reserve; their availability depended on success in Malaya and shipping. With these aspects resolved, orders were issued on 4 March to capture Mandalay and occupy the rest of Burma, which Headquarters Southern Area forwarded on the 7th. In due course 15th Army issued its operation and administration orders on 15 March. The plan was to defeat the British and Chinese separately either side of the Pegu Yomas, and drive them from Burma for good.[79]

# 5

## Enter Slim

> He possessed above all generals of his time
> that calmness of courage in the midst of tumult,
> that serenity of mind in time of danger,
> which the English call cool-headedness...
>
> Voltaire on Marlborough

ALEXANDER WAS NOTHING if not cool, and he would need to be. Major Tony Mains saw him a few days after the evacuation of Rangoon, the 'most unruffled man in the whole set up ... sitting quite imperturbably in a Burmese house'.[1] Lieutenant Peter Collister's recollections of the following weeks were 'of digging trenches facing southwards and then suddenly hearing firing behind us to the north', but Sergeant George Ransome of 1st Glosters' Officers' Mess, 'preserved an urbane dignity and a comfortable surround in the best tradition of a regular battalion. We were not going to live like gypsies just because of a load of Japs.'[2] A. A. 'Archie' Donald, attached from the Burma Police, was admonished by Ransome:

> Do you know Sir, the last time you went out on one of your scouting expeditions you went out before breakfast and did not return to lunch ... that is not good enough Sir – one may be expected to die for one's King and country but to go without one's lunch is carrying war a bit too far.[3]

But for all Ransome's best efforts, conditions deteriorated. The battalion began the campaign 640 strong, with 87 attached followers* under the Quartermaster's control. As the retreat progressed, these eventually all disappeared into the flood of refugees.[4]

---

* Followers had characterized the Army in India for generations and performed duties usually carried out by soldiers in the British Army: cooks, armourers, bootmakers etc. Sweepers and bhistis (water carriers) were two of many grades of followers that also included malis (gardeners) and syces (grooms). Although greatly curtailed by the First World War, a large number of Public Followers (Non-Combatants Enrolled) still accompanied units on operations, most being on unit establishments and integral to it (A. N. McClenaghan, 'Followers', *Durbar: Journal of the Indian Military Historical Society*, vol. 19, no. 3 pp. 95–6).

With the sea and Arakan routes now closed, thousands more Indians fled north hoping to reach Assam, 900 miles away. Even for those lucky enough to travel by bullock cart, it was frightening; but for families, women with infants and carrying head loads of precious rice and cooking pots, the outlook must have been dreadful and for the first 200 miles the locals were openly hostile. By February 6,400 had reached Dimapur in Assam, and in March came another 9,000.[5] Marjorie Nickerson, who was married to an officer in the Burma Rifles, having reached Kalewa by steamer, joined a convoy of other women and children to walk to Tamu. 'My courage quailed', she wrote later as she saw the village swarming with dazed, scared and tattered refugees.

> I asked myself if it would be possible for our miserable company – for the lame woman at the head of our column, for the mother of those wailing babies that marched in front of me, for Alan [her small son] and me – to overcome this last obstacle to our freedom.[6]

South of Prome journalist George Rodger saw a makeshift toll gate where Burmans, some of them wearing police uniforms, were charging Indians a fee to pass. He drove them off with his gun.[7] Lieutenant Pat Carmichael saw what looked like bodies: three Tamil men and a woman slashed by *dahs*. Angered and sickened, his friends carried the bodies into the scrub, where 'we saw the bullock cart, its empty shafts in the air and the bodies of another woman and two children near it. They too had been slashed about the head and body.'[8] In February James Lunt noticed a beautiful Indian woman, 'striding along like a Rajput princess, her child clasped to her left hip ... her pleated dark red skirt swinging like a kilt at every stride. Bangles at her wrists and ankles tinkled as she passed, her kohl-rimmed eyes meeting mine for a brief moment.' Then, returning from Toungoo one evening through an endless stream of refugees, he saw bodies lying in the road.

> A bright red skirt caught my eye and we stopped the jeep. She lay there, her long black hair streaming out into a pool of fast congealing blood, her throat cut from ear to ear ... The bright red skirt had been pulled up above her waist in a final obscene gesture. The child, a little way apart, lay with its brains spilling on to the tarmac.[9]

On 10 March Headquarters Burma Army relocated to Maymyo, the summer capital of Burma. At 3,500 feet above sea-level it offered a pleasant break from the clamminess of Rangoon, 'like a slumbersome village in Kent or Connecticut'.[10] It was more European than Burmese in character, with a considerable Anglo-Burmese population, and while most of Burma was drab green with a brilliant blue sky, Maymyo presented a dazzling array of colour by way of its bluish surrounding hills, hibiscus flowers, yellow and red canna lilies and the 'tastiest strawberries in the land'.[11] Headquarters Upper Burma Area was already there; two military hospitals, a British infantry depot swelled with reinforcements and stragglers from the Sittang battle ('all last survivors report here', said a sardonic NCO), the Burma Rifles Depot and a 'Military Corrective Establishment' – a gaol designed to make life even harder than the front line. In the Club, over whisky and soda and iced beer, evacuated civil servants and assorted commercial civilians mingled with officers discharged from hospital, still bandaged or sick, to speculate wildly over what the future held.[12]

There was also Major Mike Calvert's misnamed Bush Warfare School, the real purpose of which was to teach guerrilla and sabotage techniques to stay-behind parties, including thirty Australian larrikins destined to employ these skills in New Guinea and Timor. With the official winding-up of the unit in early March, Calvert planned to lead his charges into action.[13] Meanwhile the Royal Marines in Colombo had asked for volunteers for 'special service of a hazardous nature' and Force 'Viper', a company-sized unit, had disembarked at Rangoon on 11 February. Originally destined to patrol the Gulf of Martaban in small boats, it soon found itself as a river flotilla operating inland assisting on various security tasks before eventually joining Calvert at Prome, to which he made his way from Maymyo.[14] Calvert and Major Duncan Johnston RM hatched a plan, vaguely informed Headquarters 17th Indian Division and then, after securing the steamer *Hastings*, headed down the Irrawaddy. At Henzada on 17 March Calvert harangued the population gathered in the square. He was halted mid-sentence by a voice in English shouting: 'Lay down your arms. You are surrounded.' Armed BIA men appeared and Calvert's throat dried completely, but not that of Corporal Maddox, who shouted 'Bollocks!' at the top of his voice, then let off a tommy-gun burst. Pandemonium ensued as the British scrambled back to the *Hastings* and the Royal Marines' boat *Rita*, pursued by a large party of Japanese as the bullet-ridden boats made off. The staff at Prome were not impressed, and Calvert returned to Maymyo to get drunk, only to find a brigadier sitting somewhat presumptuously on his desk. 'I glared at him and said: "Who are you?" He was quite calm and composed. "Wingate", he replied.'[15]

The day Burma Army relocated to Maymyo, Stilwell arrived at Chungking to discuss with Chiang the plan to train and equip thirty divisions. Chiang explained the situation in Burma and that Chinese forces should defend Toungoo while the British defended Mandalay, and next day he put Stilwell in command of the Chinese Expeditionary Force in Burma comprising three armies; 5th, 6th and 66th.[16] Almost immediately Stilwell got into a disagreement with the Generalissimo about strategy. He wanted 5th Army to remain at Toungoo while Chiang issued orders for some of its units to assist the defence of Mandalay. Chiang explained that 5th and 6th Armies were among China's best and that the expedition must at all costs be successful, urging extreme caution. But Stilwell's ambiguous position was highlighted when the commander of 5th Army, General Tu Lu-ming, explained to Dorman-Smith that Stilwell 'only thinks he is commanding. In fact he is doing no such thing ... We Chinese think that the only way to keep the Americans in the war is to give them a few commands on paper. They will not do much harm as long as we do the work.'[17] Stilwell was supposed to assist only in tactical planning and lacked the certificate of appointment from Chiang and the *kwan fung* issued to the commander of the CEF in Burma, General Lo Chin-ying. This was a seal two-inches by three with archaic Chinese characters which had to be stamped using vermilion ink on a field order to make it effective.[18]

Apart from his prickly personality and anti-British attitude, Stilwell's tendency to give primacy to military considerations above political ones did not make him an ideal theatre commander, especially in so tricky a theatre.[19] That Stilwell and Alexander should not get on at first was hardly surprising. Stilwell, the untidy, crotchety 'limey-hater', thought Alexander looked at him as if he had crawled from under a rock. Alexander, the impeccable Guardsman, was everything Stilwell despised most in the British. But they had far more in common than they realized, professional and dedicated to the cause as they both were, and Stilwell's diary recorded his softening attitude. From initial contempt by 22 March he noted 'this guy Alex is okay', and on 15 April that 'Alex calls me "Joe" now'.[20]

Chinese forces were not what the British were used to. To the occidental observer the age of Chinese soldiers was indeterminate; a 35-year-old might look eighteen and vice versa. They had no transport and carried everything they needed, up to 120 lb. per man. Most wore rope sandals but some were barefoot and, while the majority were stockily built and fit, about one third of their manpower were porters, many of them women or mere boys who carried equally heavy loads suspended on grass ropes 18 inches from the ground by thin bamboo poles.[21] O. D. Gallagher described them as the untidiest soldiers he had ever seen, including Spanish Republicans and Abyssinians, and all wore the same denim uniforms. 'There were no displays of badges of rank. I did not recognize a lieutenant-general when I saw him.'[22] However, Leland Stowe noted that they 'moved methodically and steadily about their tasks. Somehow you got a long forgotten feeling of confidence as you watched them.'[23] But they suffered terribly from malnutrition and disease. The normal daily ration was 25 oz. of rice (probably two or three years old) plus some pickled vegetables of little nutritional value. This was issued from communal pots, with the stronger getting more than the weak, and given there was no time to eat, it was bolted and ill-digested. When units moved, roads were lined with bodies. Epidemics of dysentery, typhus and smallpox were recurring, and neither officers nor men had any understanding of basic sanitation and hygiene or their connection with disease. Medical services were practically non-existent, though the idea of unlimited manpower was false. Recruiting was mainly by press-gang, but insatiable demand was incompatible with the needs of agriculture.[24]

To control 1st Burma and 17th Indian Divisions, Burma Corps (Burcorps) was formed. On 19 March its new commander took over: Lieutenant-General William Slim.[25] Born in 1891, the son of an unsuccessful Birmingham ironmonger, he won a grammar school scholarship. Hurried by his family's financial plight, he began as a trainee schoolteacher in a primary school in a desperately poor area, where he met the raw material of the British army in circumstances far removed from most senior officers of either war. The boys came from the roughest possible backgrounds, where drunkenness and violence were endemic, with discipline imposed through savage beatings. He soon learned that firmness and kindness worked wonders, but if he could reach day's end without a catastrophe it was a minor victory. In 1914 he was working as a clerk in an engineering works where the pay was better, although job satisfaction was minimal. Having devoured tales of Victorian military glory as a boy, and with war looming, he managed to enrol in Birmingham University Officers' Training Corps despite the fact he was not a student, and in August was commissioned in The Royal Warwickshire Regiment. Slim was that rarest of creatures, a natural soldier, and when severely wounded at Gallipoli and discharged as unfit for further service, overcame his wounds through strength of will and found his way back into service. Meanwhile, several events occurred that changed his life.

At Gallipoli, Slim had served besides 1st/6th Gurkhas and, charmed, was determined to join them. As a first step he obtained a regular commission with the West India Regiment, reputedly the only one where it was possible to live on one's pay, but never served with his new regiment; instead he joined another battalion of Royal Warwicks in Mesopotamia, where General Maude was rebuilding following the disaster of Kut-al-Amara in 1917. In 1919 he transferred to the Indian Army, and found his happy home in 1920 with 1st/6th Gurkhas. Career progress was painfully slow in the inter-war years, but he attended Quetta, the Indian Army Staff College, and taught at the British Staff College, Camberley, as the Indian Army representative, and studied at the Imperial Defence College before making lieutenant-colonel at the age of forty-seven. To make ends meet and to educate his children he took up writing under a pen-name, mostly short stories, and these reveal a keen insight into human nature and a dry sense of humour. In 1940 he was commanding 10th Indian Brigade in Eritrea and Sudan, where he was wounded in an air attack; the surgeon removed a large bullet and several pieces of Turkish ammunition carried since First World War days. But he was unsatisfied with his performance and considered himself fortunate to be given command of 10th Indian Division in June 1941, when its commander fell sick. This he led against the Vichy French in Syria and, learning quickly, he led it well.[26]

It was from this position that Slim was appointed to command Burcorps. Like Maude in Mesopotamia, he was set to revive the fortunes of a beaten army. At Maymyo, Alexander explained how he planned to salvage the situation: once relieved by the Chinese at Toungoo, 1st Burma Division would cross the Irrawaddy to join 17th Indian Division and 7th Armoured Brigade to form Burcorps. As the strain between Hutton and Smyth had demonstrated, personal relations between senior officers had serious implications for operations. 'By a trick of fate, for which I shall always be grateful,' wrote Slim later, 'Scott, Cowan and I all came from the 1st Battalion, 6th Gurkhas. We had served and lived together for twenty-odd years; we – and our wives – were the closest friends.'[27]

For troop reinforcement the British could bring in only 1st Royal Inniskilling Fusiliers, flown into Magwe between 8 and 13 March in American bombers. Allied fighters left Zigon on 12 March with the Hurricanes of 67 and 135 Squadrons flying to Akyab to form 'Akwing' with the Lysanders of 1 Squadron IAF, and 139 Squadron's Hudsons. The AVG and 17 Squadron flew to Magwe to form 'Burwing' with a few Lysanders from 28 Squadron and 9 Blenheims from 45 Squadron (after 113 Squadron's survivors had flown to Calcutta in early March). The AVG's 3rd Squadron arrived to relieve the 1st, but Squadron Leader Robert H. Neale refused to leave until ordered to do so directly by Chennault. But Chinese 6th Army, entering the Shan States, freed 13th Indian Brigade and 5th Army, moving down the Sittang valley, relieved 1st and 2nd Burma Brigades. Soon the Japanese were ready to resume their advance, having almost doubled their aircraft to 260 and more than doubled their troops. Terauchi held a commanders' conference at Daik-u to outline the next moves, the first being the capture of Toungoo. At the same time 55th Division, now reinforced by 18th Division from Singapore, would push Chinese 5th Army towards Mandalay with its back to the Irrawaddy, alongside the east bank of which 33rd Division – back in the fray after capturing Rangoon – would capture intact the oilfields at Yenangyaung, then cut off the retreat of British and Chinese forces west of Mandalay.[28]

At the end of February the Chinese passed through Meiktila, where Major Edward Cooke's 9th Burma Rifles were based. He noted 'their idea of total war was very complete; for instance they had no scruples about knocking down a church or any other fine building to improve their field of fire ... They had a mania for watches and bought or looted them in every town which they occupied.'[29] When Pat Carmichael reached the divisional baggage dump at Toungoo, he found the Chinese had been through it first and his lightweight engraved 12-bore was among the kit stolen: 'I was almost speechless with fury, not so much at the Chinese but at Division's failure to guard the dump.'[30] Their positions were to the east of the Rangoon–Mandalay railway, extending some 450 miles up the Thai border. When the Japanese attacked Pegu, they moved into central Burma, but by this point the position on the Irrawaddy front had become critical and they began digging in to the muddy fields around Toungoo during the second week of March.[31]

The relief of Scott's 1st Burma Division by the Chinese at Toungoo demonstrated their poverty: Scott's counterpart arrived in one of two staff cars the Chinese possessed, screeching to a halt with a cloud of steam from the bonnet. The driver, muttering darkly, delivered a blow to the engine with a spanner while the general and another officer stepped down – there were no doors. The general spoke no English and nor, apparently, did the second officer, supposedly the interpreter. But after regarding Scott's carefully prepared map suspiciously, he beamed and exclaimed 'Map!' He then produced a piece of rice paper about 3 inches square with some lines drawn on it. 'Very nice', said Scott weakly, noticing that his Intelligence Officer was on the verge of hysterics. Then he became aware of fire all around him – the Chinese method of putting the town in a state of defence was to burn most of it – and seeing flames within 100 yards of an ammunition dump, he decided the handover was complete and told his staff: 'Get out of it.'[32]

Chiang's chronic caution in hoarding resources against some future greater emergency further hindered Chinese effectiveness. Alexander asked General Tu what had happened to the field guns he had seen the day before, expertly dug in and camouflaged, and Tu said they had been withdrawn to safety. Thus discovering they would not be used in battle, Alexander asked what use they were. Tu replied that 5th Army was China's best, 'because it is the only one with any field guns, and I cannot afford to risk those guns. If I lose them the Fifth Army will no longer be our best.'[33] Although lacking artillery support and despite his unorthodox takeover, Major-General Tai An-lan, 200th Division's commander, was brave and resourceful. A detachment sent south to delay the Japanese was attacked on the night of 20/21 March by 143rd Regiment, vanguard of 55th Division, and fell back as 112th Regiment attacked Toungoo itself in overwhelming numbers on the 26th. Once more the Japanese sought the flanks of the position and when 55th Reconnaissance Regiment seized a vital bridge and attacked the Chinese flank guard on 28 March, they drove the Chinese into the town, where they fought with grim determination amid the burning buildings. Only next day were the Chinese forced to cut their way out, but they failed to demolish the bridge over the Sittang, which had been prepared for demolition by 1st Burma Division's engineers and which the Japanese captured intact: another disaster.[34] Iida was now in a position to occupy the Shan States via the Mawchi–Bawlake road, along which 56th Division under Lieutenant-General Watanabe Masao was soon directed, reinforced with 250 lorries, with the objective of Lashio to cut the Burma Road. It would prove the beginning of the end for Burma Army and its Chinese allies.

For the retreating Chinese there was little chance of the wounded receiving the care and attention that Allied troops expected. 'There were no stretcher parties or ambulances to take them back to the dressing station. They had to drag themselves along the road and they passed us without a whimper or a plea for help', recalled George Rodger. They were 'wandering wrecks of humanity battered and torn by a war that few of them knew why they were fighting. Only their stoic endurance drove them on, for with such loss of blood the strength of their bodies had already gone.'[35] Fortunately there was Dr Gordon Seagrave, a fourth-generation American medical missionary, and his twelve Shan nurses. His dressing station at Pyinmana was set in an attractive stucco house surrounded by purple bougainvillaea, but inside was a charnel house: the floor and unroofed porch were littered with Chinese wounded, men who died when the nurses' backs were turned, men who wanted to die. Dominating everything was Seagrave himself, constantly working through a week of sleepless nights, learning how to operate on two patients at once, administering chloroform at the same time as amputating a gangrenous limb.[36] Paul Geren, another American missionary from Judson College in Rangoon, who drove an ambulance and assisted Seagrave, recorded that:

The Chinese are callous to their own suffering. Their expectation is to suffer, and no evil thing comes as a surprise ... This splendid courage shows short on the other end in the same callousness to the sufferings of others. The Chinese soldiers do not jump to help a wounded man out of the ambulance, but wait to see what he can accomplish for himself.[37]

To the west, after a week in Rangoon 33rd Division began to advance on Prome on 16 March, reinforced with heavy artillery. Cowan had deployed a strong recce screen covering the central ridge of the Pegu Yomas called the Yomas Intelligence Service, comprising forest employees supported by BFF and BMP patrols and 1st Glosters, now the divisional reconnaissance battalion.[38] His problem was holding Prome long enough to back-load the vast stores accumulated there to Mandalay. The railway ended at Prome, so this had to be done by road and, without air cover, mostly at night. First Burma Division's baptism of fire at Pyuntaza saw mixed fortunes: 5th Burma Rifles broke *en bloc*, exposing 2nd/7th Rajput Regiment to Japanese counter-attack. To complete British misery, the Japanese established undisputed mastery of the air. On 21 March the RAF attacked their former installations at Mingaladon. 'Bunny' Stone recalled that diving 'at about 400 miles an hour, we were met by light flak, mainly from our old Bofors guns which the late owners had failed to destroy. The aerodrome appeared packed with aircraft, mainly fighters and Army Recce light bombers.'[39] As Canadian Pilot Officer Hedley 'Snooks' Everard looked down, he caught the bland, curious stare of a Japanese pilot being helped into his cockpit and swung round for a pass. 'By now the pilot had started his engine and was beginning to move towards the runway. With deadly purpose now, my bullets riddled the engine and cockpit. The aircraft slewed up on its nose as I passed overhead. I glimpsed the pilot slumped in his seat.'[40]

Following the fighters, Blenheims dropped 9,000 lb. of bombs in a very successful raid, but plans to repeat the effort were pre-empted. That afternoon and the following day five Japanese raids pummelled Magwe. There were only four casualties, of whom one died of his wounds; but the shrapnel caused havoc among the badly dispersed British planes, for which there were no spares.[41] When the last planes had gone, Flying Officer Kenneth Hemingway of 17 Squadron looked around at 'oil smoke, craters, scattered heaps of earth, dust and haze!' He returned to the mess and was told immediately to pack and take the eight remaining Hurricanes to Akyab.[42] Raids there soon forced evacuation to Chittagong: Burma Army was on its own. And the speed of this unprepared withdrawal as trucks full of RAF men rushed helter-skelter to Lashio did nothing for inter-service relations.[43] Such was the desperation of the situation that on the same day James Lunt saw his old friend Captain Sandy Sandeman, once of the Central India Horse, now leading a mounted column of BFF, mostly Sikhs:

> The curb chains jingling as they went, and the dust hanging over them in the still morning air. Behind them there lingered the smell of leather and sweating horses, and we were left with an unforgettable memory in a war which was waged mostly with machines. The Guides must have looked like that, I thought, as they scouted ahead of 'Bobs' on the way from Kabul to Kandahar.[44]

Sandeman went on to make history the following day, when he inadvertently bumped into a column of Japanese; drawing his sabre, he ordered his trumpeter to sound 'Charge!' – the final mounted charge in the long history of British cavalry, which cost him his life.[45]

Meanwhile Burcorps withdrew to Okpo and then, having blown the railway bridge at Paungde on 28 March, at Wavell's prompting Slim was ordered to attack and relieve the pressure on the Chinese at Toungoo. Cowan made a plan to retake Paungde and then Okpo while 33rd Division, unaware of British offensive plans, continued to advance in its favoured 'scorpion' formation with a regiment on either side of the main axis. Led by BIA elements, they were welcomed by locals – a pleasant change from China – and with RAF-free skies they could move in daylight. Thus II/215th Regiment crossed the Irrawaddy by ferry to seize Shwedaung on the evening of 28 March, a superb position for a rearguard or road-block just as Strike Force* cleared it heading south to Paungde.[46]

During the morning the BFF column covering Paungde had been heavily attacked, and 1st Glosters launched a two-company attack to relieve it.[47] Strike Force planned to attack the next day, but shortly before first light firing was heard to the east, where D Company, 1st Glosters, at Padigon were heavily attacked by 214th Regiment. When Brigadier J. H. Anstice arrived at 0700 hours to take command, a runner appeared to say D Company were surrounded and being bypassed to the west and north.[48] An attack cleared this block but by now I Company, 2nd Dukes, to the south was also under attack and needed reinforcing. With the block at Shwedaung now known to Headquarters 17th Indian Division, Cowan ordered Anstice to withdraw to Prome in the early afternoon via Shwedaung or Padigon, whichever seemed easiest. He chose Shwedaung.

Cowan ordered 16th and 63rd Indian Brigades to provide one battalion

---

* 7th Armoured Brigade less 2nd Royal Tank Regiment (divisional communications relied on its radios), and with 1st Glosters, 1st Cameronians and 2nd Dukes under command.

each to attack Shwedaung from the north, and during the afternoon of 29 March 4th/12th Frontier Force Regiment encountered some 1,200 BIA men a mile north of Shwedaung and hammered them; 60 were killed, 70 captured, 300 wounded and 350 deserted. The BIA never again attempted to intervene directly.[49] At last light Strike Force began its breakout attempt across paddy fields in bright moonlight. With 1st Glosters pinned down by heavy mortar and machine-gun fire, two troops of 7th Hussars supported by 1st West Yorks attempted to break through. One succeeded, but the second was intercepted and halted by Japanese armed with petrol bombs.[50] Lieutenant M. J. E. 'Kildare' Patteson was captured, tied to an overturned British ambulance and left to be killed by his own artillery. He heard the 25-pounders shoot and the whine of the shells. Leaning instinctively forward, either badly tied or cut free by a shell splinter, he kicked off the ties on his ankles and ran, hiding among a herd of stampeding heifers. After a night in the paddy he regained British lines at dawn. 'I was safe among friends! "Good Gawd! If it ain't Mr Patteson!" exclaimed a startled Cockney voice. My bonds were cut but it was a long time before I regained the use of my arms and legs, so stiff had they become.'[51]

Bagot spoke with Anstice to say his men were too few and too exhausted to break through, but Anstice insisted they try at 0200, and when this also failed, he planned to attack at dawn with his entire force. During the night Colonel Harada Munaji commanding 215th Regiment heavily reinforced Shwedaung, a large village of mostly two-storey wood and bamboo buildings but with some brick-built. As day broke, the British column was spread a mile south along the road – like most in Burma raised some 3 feet above the surrounding paddy – nose-to-tail and often double-banked. The Japanese made various attacks but were beaten off and during the morning six aircraft joined in, although two were shot down. But the problem remained of how to break through. The tanks were largely restricted to the road and vulnerable to mines and petrol bombs. The infantry were inexperienced, particularly in the art of picqueting a route to protect the vulnerable soft-skin vehicles. An attack at 0730 made no headway, with some tanks toppling over the embankment approaching the bridge, and the Japanese closed in again. To the north, 4th/12th Frontier Force Regiment and 2nd/13th Frontier Force Rifles supported by 2nd Royal Tank Regiment and 1st Indian Field Regiment also attacked but were equally unsuccessful.[52]

About midday, with the situation desperate, A and B Squadrons 7th Hussars and Headquarters Strike Force bypassed the village and broke clear, although they lost four tanks and numerous trucks and suffered many casualties. The guns of 414th Battery, Royal Horse Artillery, drove out like their forebears at Fuentes de Oñoro in Spain in 1811.[53] They were then sent north of Prome. C Squadron 7th Hussars, the infantry, gunners, sappers and most of the vehicles remained stuck south of the road-block. Lieutenant Peter Collister of 1st Glosters, twice wounded and in an ambulance whose driver had been shot, heard Major C. K. T. Faithfull, now commanding 2nd Duke's, call out that the men were to make their own way out. Then he lifted the flap at the back of the ambulance and said: 'Sorry chaps, but if any of you can manage to walk, do your best to save yourselves.' Collister and some others managed to clamber out and made an arduous escape via the river to Prome.[54] The majority of those escaping on foot managed to dodge the Japanese, but many seriously wounded were never seen again. Major Sato Misao met a wounded prisoner, shot through the abdomen.

> As I looked at him I saw a thin stream of tears coming from his eyes. I understood he was enduring his pain with all his might, his young pale face contorted. Ah! his attitude was really dignified ... while his life was ending. Unconsciously I cried and held his hands. I would never forget the last minutes of that young British soldier![55]

Total British casualties amounted to some 400 on what the 7th Hussars war diary called 'this useless venture'.[56]

Alexander's attempts to defend both Sittang and Irrawaddy valleys were doomed. 'At the time', wrote Hutton, 'I blamed Alex for these suicidal orders, and it was only later that I realized he was carrying out Wavell's orders.'[57] Nor did Wavell's determination to see offensive action do anything to help the Chinese in Toungoo, forced to abandon it the same day; furthermore it completely disrupted plans for the defence of Prome. A new plan issued early on 29 March laid stress on mobile counter-attack forces, although this was beyond the ability of the troops. Fortunately, perhaps, the growing crisis meant they did not have to try and implement it. That night III/215th Regiment attacked a party of Royal Marines operating on the west bank of the Irrawaddy, and at Padaung captured seventeen, left behind badly wounded. In a revolting display, presumably to demonstrate Japanese superiority in front of the villagers, the Marines were bayoneted to death hanging from trees, some by their ankles.[58] Meanwhile Strike Force limped back to Prome, held by 63rd Indian Brigade (now under Brigadier A. E. Barlow) with 48th Indian Brigade to the east and 16th Indian Brigade in the centre, with 7th Armoured Brigade providing the reserve. All the time the sappers were busy with demolitions, improving positions and tracks for the tanks to manoeuvre. On 31 March all units were ordered to send most of their vehicles back to Allanmyo to be replaced with a few bullock-carts and mules, supposedly to enable them to avoid encirclement at road-blocks. But bullock-carts are extremely slow.

That afternoon Wavell and Alexander visited Slim at Burcorps Head-quarters at Allanmyo. Wavell agreed that there was now no point in hold-ing Prome, but that as many stores as possible should be back-loaded before it was abandoned. A warning order was passed to 17th Indian Division but confusion reigned throughout, with units assigned to unfamiliar forma-tions and new commanders replacing casualties. At about 1900 on 1 April 215th Regiment commenced probing attacks and got among 5th/17th Dogras, which withdrew after some hours into Prome, and in the confu-sion at around 2100 Barlow ordered 63rd Indian Brigade to pull back from the town. Soon after midnight he was ordered to fall back and establish a position behind 16th Indian Brigade. This formation was not engaged during the night, but to the east 48th Indian Brigade set an ambush for 214th Regiment before being ordered to withdraw at 0400, which it did skilfully. Cowan now decided that Prome could not be recaptured and instead retired to Nawin Chaung to the north. The rearguard cleared this, and the bridge was blown at 1138 hours on 2 April.[59]

The next few days were extremely difficult for 17th Indian Division, withdrawing to Allanmyo in heat and dust with little water and under con-stant air attack. For eleven-year-old Stephen Brookes at his home 'Lindfield', in Maymyo, the war now arrived with a vengeance when a vis-itor called. Suddenly he heard a high-pitched scream.

> It came again and again, growing wilder, like the sound of an animal in agony ... Then I heard a voice.
> 'No ... No ... No ... Please God ... No ...'
> It was my mother – but I could not move ... she screamed again; 'Please God not Richard ... Please God, not Richard. Richard my son ... Richard ... Richard ... my son ... my son ...'
> This was no Anglo-Saxon lady discreetly weeping into a folded handker-chief. This was an Asian woman, distraught, broken, tearing at her clothes and hair in uncontrollable grief.[60]

Thus came news of the death of his eldest brother, serving with the BAF.

After the destruction of Magwe aerodrome Squadron Leader 'Bunny' Stone and 17 Squadron had retreated on Lashio, where the AVG contin-ued to operate with success, then along the Burma Road to Loiwing, where Stone saw a Japanese air raid jumped by the AVG. 'It was the best show from the stalls that I have ever witnessed.' The AVG claimed four-teen shot down, while one P.40 had a bullet hole in it.[61] Soon afterwards the squadron was ordered to Myitkyina to be flown over the Hump to India. On 4 April Dorman-Smith cabled Lord Halifax, British Ambassador in America, to ascertain how many American aircraft might be available to help evacuate refugees from Myitkyina. Pan-American Airways pilots joined the airlift in response to an appeal from Tenth Air Force, which had few pilots of its own at the time.[62] In total some 14,000 people, including 4,000 Indians, were flown out by American airmen; the fare was 280 rupees (£20 or $80), so a number of airmen made small fortunes.[63] But these people had an easy escape compared to most.

The Japanese switch into the Shan States compelled Alexander to change his plans. There was no point holding Prome with Toungoo lost, and it was imperative to cover the oilfields. He thus decided to hold a line, with Burcorps responsible for Minhla to Taungdwingyi, 5th Army at Pyinmana and 6th Army at Loikaw. Slim could not leave the west bank of the Irrawaddy exposed and had not enough troops to cover his frontage, and Alexander asked for Chinese help holding Taungdwingyi. A regiment was promised but never appeared: neither Chiang nor Stilwell had any faith in Slim's ability to hold the Japanese. Chiang communicated to Roosevelt that the British were not fighting hard enough, a view vehemently shared by Stilwell.[64] In any case, every plan Alexander made had to be scrapped almost immediately as the Japanese made the British jump. The lack of intelligence was now most keenly felt. Army Headquarters had no intelligence organization and although some elementary training was carried out, many men lacked confidence in themselves and their weapons. It would take a long time to gain, and in the meantime their inability to patrol made gathering information practically impossible.[65] The BFF columns formed for reconnaissance proved of little value, since their radios often failed. This combination of Japanese air supremacy, Burman hostility and the absence of intelligence enabled rumours to flourish, which was dreadful for morale. Fighting was taking place some 300 miles to the south, but the only transport was jeep, cart or train. Japanese planes and gangs of hostile Burmans roamed freely, and many towns and villages *en route* were already blazing.

Stilwell's attempts to control operations were also a nightmare. His headquarters, like Alexander's, was at Maymyo, several hours' flight away from Chiang at Chungking across some of the world's most forbidding terrain. For a man whose long experience was that Chinese generals could not be relied on, he faced constant frustration. 'Reluctance to attack', he commented, 'seemed to drench the spirit of the Chinese command beyond any measure of encouragement I could give.'[66] Stilwell arrived at Chungking on 1 April without notice, complaining about the commander of 22nd Division and that he intended to resign as Chief of Staff in order to concentrate on the training of the thirty divisions. Chiang sought to pacify him before he flew to Maymyo to meet Alexander and Slim on the 5th.[67]

After escaping what Sakurai had hoped would be a trap at Allanmyo, 17th Indian Division was in its new line by 8 April, with Burcorps stretching some 40 miles from the Irrawaddy to Taungdwingyi. The Japanese were reinforced with several new units, including heavy artillery and an engineer unit equipped with a selection of boats, some of them armoured.[68] Slim was also in the process of reorganizing and transferred three British battalions from 17th Indian to 1st Burma Division, although all now much reduced – 1st Cameronians could muster only 215 men. The Chinese were in the Sittang valley holding Pyinmana, and Slim asked Alexander to arrange for the Chinese to hold Taungdwingyi to release at least one brigade as a strike force. Stilwell and Tu agreed but no troops arrived, which left Burcorps stretched. It was now in Burma's dry zone, with little forest amid open undulating country, ideal for tanks. Slim hoped to fight a corps battle to stem the Japanese advance, but Alexander insisted that Taungdwingyi be held at all costs to support the Chinese in the Sittang valley. As a result, Slim had no spare troops to strike the Japanese flank and instead two divisional battles ensued.

On 9/10 April 214th and 215th regiments moved in lorries up the Allanmyo–Taungdwingyi road and brushed aside a British patrol. Here they parted company: 215th Regiment headed towards 48th Indian Brigade's position around Kokkogwa, covering the road to Magwe. After bumping an outpost of 2nd/5th Royal Gurkhas and following an exchange of mortar and artillery fire, I/215th Regiment was ordered to withdraw to Songon. II/215th attacked 1st/7th Gurkhas at 0430 but met strong resistance, including 2nd Battery, 1st Indian Field Regiment, firing over open sights.[69] But the fighting was not over, as many Japanese who had taken refuge in a deep dry nullah west of the village were attacked by 1st/4th Gurkhas supported by 2nd Royal Tanks. Only at Sonzu did the Japanese enjoy any success, isolating a company of 1st/3rd Gurkhas and inflicting heavy casualties before they broke out. But although sporadic fighting continued for two more nights, they had been beaten and I/215th Regiment had failed to collect its dead – shameful to the Japanese. They regarded the action at Kokkogwa as their one defeat of the campaign.[70]

However, the Japanese were never more dangerous than when there appeared to be a lull in the fighting. They regrouped with remarkable speed, moving by night and lying up by day, always seeking to outflank defensive positions. They would use any ruse to effect surprise; a patrol of 2nd/5th Royal Gurkhas mistook some Japanese for Chinese after being welcomed in English and were immediately taken prisoner. The Japanese handling of prisoners was often harsh, even sadistic; it all depended on the mood of the senior rank present. But at least they were the enemy; Burman villagers were another matter. With British rule crumbling, few had scruples about changing allegiance.[71] From the beginning the Japanese benefited from the tendency of Burman nationalists to disregard what the Chinese told them of the evils of their 'liberators'. Japan's alleged status as a fellow Buddhist country, combined with the fascination of military victory, led most to favour the Japanese over the British.[72] According to John Cady, the stunned Burmese took little part in the fighting and apart from Burman nationalists – particularly political *pongyis* and Thakins – were not actively hostile to the retreating British–Indian forces.[73] But British accounts repeatedly refer to Burman attacks on themselves and on refugees. One tank crew from 7th Hussars on outpost duty was approached by some villagers offering to sell chickens and eggs. But when bargaining began, three of them were cut down with *dahs* while the fourth managed to escape. In revenge, a company of 1st West Yorks sacked the village, killing everyone in sight, including some unfortunate Indian refugees caught in the middle.[74]

# 6

## Struggle on the plains

I love a lassie, a bonnie black Madrassi
She's as black as the coals in fuckin' 'ell
She's as black as fuckin' charcoal,
And she *saf karoes* her arsehole
With a *tora tunda pani*
From the well ...

British soldier's song

THE LOSS OF Rangoon led on 12 March to the abandonment of the Andaman Islands by 139 Squadron's Hudsons guarding the south-western approaches to the city. The Japanese arrived eleven days later and set up a flying-boat base, which the Hudsons attacked on 14 and 18 April from Akyab island, itself reinforced on 18 March with troops from India. However, heavy Japanese raids on 23 and 24 March led to collapse: desertion and arson were rife, morale dropped as malaria increased, and on 4 May Akyab was ignominiously abandoned.[1] More ominously, however, two powerful Japanese fleets under Vice-Admiral Kondo Nobutake prepared to thrust into the Indian Ocean to secure the reinforcement route to Burma, attack merchant shipping in the Bay of Bengal and spread panic among the Indian population. The main strike force under Vice-Admiral Nagumo Chuichi, including five of the six carriers involved at Pearl Harbor, rounded the southern tip of Sumatra on 2 April to attack Colombo and the Royal Navy base at Trincomalee in Ceylon.[2] However, there were no plans for invasion; the naval staff were in favour, but the army refused absolutely. The Japanese thus missed a golden opportunity for rich strategic gains: capturing Ceylon and Mauritius would have severed Allied sea contact with India and Persia, and there was little to prevent them.[3]

Appointed Commander-in-Chief Ceylon on 5 March, Admiral Sir Geoffrey Layton was aware of the threat through signals intelligence (sigint). Despite improving every aspect of Ceylon's defences on taking command, the aircraft available were heavily outnumbered by nearly 400 on the

Japanese carriers. Similarly, the defending naval forces under Admiral Sir James Somerville, who arrived to command Eastern Fleet on 26 March, were outclassed.[4] Force B's battleships looked impressive when assembled 80 miles south of Ceylon five days later but had not been fully modernized since the First World War and were acutely vulnerable to air attack; and the supporting carrier *Hermes*, with only twelve Swordfish, was equally unsuited to fleet operations. Force A also had serious limitations: many of its destroyers needed a refit, as did the cruisers *Dorsetshire* and *Cornwall*, which would have left the battleship *Warspite* and carriers *Indomitable* and *Formidable* vulnerable even if their aircraft had not already been hopelessly inadequate. The naturally aggressive Somerville never stood a chance of inflicting serious damage on Nagumo and, like so many commanders before him, he underestimated the Japanese.[5]

On 4 April Eastern Fleet was badly placed when a Catalina flying-boat reported the Japanese 350 miles away, heading straight for Ceylon.[6] Somerville's ships were taking on water and fuel at Addu Atoll but would, in any case, have been unable to prevent Nagumo's attack on Colombo next day. At around 0740 Leading Aircraftsman Bert Holt at Ratmalana airfield watched a large number of planes approaching from the sea.

> At the same time the phone rang – it was the RAF asking if we knew of any carriers sending off aircraft. I answered: 'Yes, Japs! Get your bods airborne!' I then ran outside, screaming as loud as possible: 'Scramble! Scramble!' ... The most vivid thing I remember then was a Sub Lieutenant, towel in hand and wearing only his black beard, belting out of the shower, heading for his flying gear.[7]

Hopelessly outnumbered, the defenders suffered heavily but the bombers did less damage than might have been expected, with 85 civilians killed and 77 wounded.[8] But the Royal Navy was less fortunate; Nagumo had 80 dive-bombers remaining and launched a concentrated attack that sank *Dorsetshire* and *Cornwall* within minutes as they steamed to rendezvous with Somerville's Force A.[9] Fortunately the Japanese did not follow up this success and Nagumo retired to the south-east while Somerville turned back south. Layton warned the Admiralty that Eastern Fleet stood in danger of 'immediate annihilation', and Somerville received permission to withdraw to East Africa.

Also on 5 April Vice-Admiral Ozawa Jisabura's force attacked Cocanada and Vizagapatam in north-eastern India, sinking sixteen merchantmen and causing the population to flee. The alarm spread to Madras on the strength of false air-raid warnings, but the Japanese failed to follow up their success, although on 6 April Japanese Army bombers sank the Royal Indian Navy's sloop *Indus* at Akyab, and over ten days submarines sank five merchantmen. Early on 7 April Ozawa turned back to Singapore while Nagumo prepared to attack Trincomalee on the 9th, inflicting heavy damage to port facilities and destroying the freighter *Sagaing*, reputedly loaded with copious amounts of whisky. The Japanese then spotted and attacked *Hermes* and her escorts barely 5 miles offshore.[10] Hit or narrowly missed by some forty bombs, she quickly sank, soon followed by HMAS *Vampire* and the tanker *British Sergeant*, Fleet Auxiliary *Athelstane* and corvette *Hollyhock*. Fortunately the Australian hospital ship *Vita* picked up some 600 survivors from *Vampire* and *Hermes*. In sad contrast, 11 Squadron's Blenheims managed only near misses on Nagumo's flagship *Akagi*, losing five in the process.[11]

The Bay of Bengal and Ceylon were completely at the mercy of the Japanese, but they abandoned them: Nagumo, entirely satisfied, ordered retirement to Singapore. Thus despite extensive damage, the Japanese failed to inflict a decisive defeat on the Royal Navy – although the latter did not return to Ceylon until 1943 – and they had given the US Navy a precious breathing space in which to build up its strength.[12] Following the battles of the Coral Sea in May and of Midway in June, Japanese carrier strength was practically destroyed: the initiative in the Pacific swung to the Americans and the threat to Ceylon was never renewed.[13] Meanwhile Roosevelt responded to Churchill's prompting and the American build-up of air power in India began in earnest, and Major-General Lewis Brereton's Tenth Air Force, originally intended as the basis for support for China, was allotted to the defence of India, much to Chiang's disgust – beginning operations with an ineffective raid on Rangoon.[14]

From the earliest stages of the British withdrawal Karen villages had been subject to attacks by Burmans, but among themselves the Burmans also had trouble. For the BIA's inevitably hasty recruitment led to a motley and undisciplined rabble, often criminal, officered only by untrained Thakins. Their main task was to appoint local governing committees in the wake of the Japanese advance.[15] All BIA officers operated under the ancient title of *Bo* (colonel), but few of these youths had government experience or even basic military training. One eyewitness at Zawgi described how in their new-found glory with newly taken wives, decked out in looted clothing and expensive jewellery, they were unprepared for inevitable popular rejection.[16] The military contingent of the BIA were expected to act as interpreters and guides or saboteurs and arsonists behind the lines, although there were some clashes with political *pongyis* among the most fanatical. Revolutionary Burman nationalists displayed genuine enthusiasm for Japanese triumphs, with slogans such as 'Burma for the Burmese' and 'Asia for the Asiatics'. At its height the BIA numbered around 30,000, mostly recruited through student groups by Thakins.[17] Thakin Nu described how they revived old songs, but the exultant mood was soon dissipated by the insulting behaviour of Japanese soldiers.[18] And the Japanese advance was so swift the BIA could not keep up and many regular administrators continued in place for some weeks before being elbowed aside. Lawlessness was soon rife; looting was followed by dacoity, while everywhere Burma burned as Japanese bombers ranged far and wide.

When George Rodger first saw Thazi, it was a 'sleepy little Burman village as colourful and gay as any. There were the usual picturesque little thatched or tin-roofed wooden houses and open fronted shops all covered by flowering creepers.' Doll-like children played in the road and bright-skirted girls 'strolled in twos and threes from shop to shop or stood gossiping in the doorways of their homes. Ox-carts lurched down the street with creaking unoiled axles, the drivers lolling under their wide bamboo hats, half asleep in the sun.' Now, the 'frail houses were flattened, rubble covered the street, trees stood stripped of their boughs and the shattered bodies of the villagers lay twitching in the dust.' Amid the raging fires screaming wounded desperately tried to crawl away.[19] Like that of Thazi, the bombing of Meiktila was as incomprehensible as it was indiscriminate. Near by Pat Carmichael watched helplessly as twenty-seven aircraft in three 'V's approached, 'the bombs swinging down into the town like a slow falling bead curtain, and the explosions reached us in a prolonged earth shaking rumble'. They drove to the now blazing bazaar, a shambles of stinking, burning corpses; Carmichael saw a Muslim bent in prayer and touched his back to say the planes had gone, but realized as he did so that the old man was dead. 'His only thought had been to seek Allah's mercy. Perhaps it had been granted him.' A badly wounded woman lay close by and his friend Tom Jones dragged a tin roof sheet over, 'and as we lifted her on to it he was muttering: "The bastards! The bastards!"' as they turned the railway station into a casualty one.

> A fair skinned Anglo-Burmese girl, six or seven years old and bare footed, in a simple frock, lay on her back relaxed in blissful oblivion, right arm stretched out palm upward, her head tilted the other way. The pretty little face was composed and she was quite unmarked. Looking down at her I was grateful she would have known nothing of the bomb which had blasted the life out of her small body.[20]

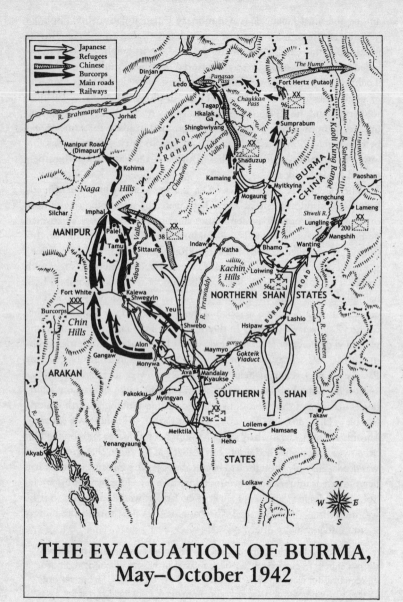

# THE EVACUATION OF BURMA,
## May–October 1942

The retreat continued. Burcorps would destroy and abandon the oilfields if pressed, with 1st Burma Division responsible for covering the withdrawal to India via Kalewa on the Chindwin and 17th Indian Division via Shwebo and Katha to cover the withdrawal via the Hukawng valley, north-west of Myitkyina (which means 'near the large river').[21] Alexander also proposed that 7th Armoured Brigade and one infantry brigade withdraw to China via the Burma Road with 6th Army, a prospect that horrified Brigadier Anstice and took no account of supplying the tanks with petrol; but Alexander never pretended to be a logistician.[22]

Yenangyaung, some 100 miles north-east of Meiktila, was an ugly mass of oil derricks that lit the night sky with burning gas – appropriate since its name meant 'smelly river'. The town itself lay on a succession of low rolling ridges with little vegetation except for one residential area of houses and bungalows with neat lawns and flower beds. By the time 17th Indian Division arrived it had been evacuated. The people had

> moved out in a hurry, abandoning their bungalows and their property. Beds that had been slept in had been left as they were, tables were laid with unfinished meals, clothes hung in cupboards and children's nurseries were still full of their books and toys. Yet there was no sign of panic or disarray; it was as if the owners had gone out for a moment and would shortly be back.[23]

Three unbridged *chaungs* flowed east–west into the Irrawaddy, the most significant being the Pin Chaung, several hundred yards wide but fordable in the dry season, forming the northern limit of the battlefield. The western edge was marked by the Irrawaddy itself, the eastern by the Taungdwingyi–Magwe–Yenangyaung road, and the southern by the Yin Chaung, an area of some 20 square miles. The troops were in a bad state, short of certain types of ammunition, vehicle spares and maps; 7th Armoured Brigade's tanks had long exceeded their track mileage and desperately needed an overhaul.[24] The Mountain Artillery's mules were beginning to suffer from poor feed and not enough of it. The big American mules normally needed 12 lb. of oats or at least maize per day, but even the latter had disappeared and they were reduced to paddy, which lacked essential nutrients for the hard work demanded of them. April is the hottest month in Burma and the troops were entering the most arid region of the country; in heat and dust the retreat was all the more dispiriting and difficult for troops now desperately short of water, a terrible problem especially for the wounded and animals.[25] Moreover, units that had been fighting for over two months had received no reinforcements. And as with all retreats, morale was steadily eroded while communications and control deteriorated; messages regularly failed to arrive and nobody knew with any accuracy where anybody else was.

The army was over-equipped with motor at the expense of animal transport, so that forces were tied to the main supply routes: yet transport remained wholly insufficient. Supply vehicles were lamentably few; hired and requisitioned vehicles were unreliable, and in any case only a proportion of units could be equipped from lend-lease as the heavy losses in Tenasserim and at the Sittang had to be made good. The rest were destroyed with the evacuation of Rangoon and further losses through bombing and at road-blocks. And with vast distances to be covered, maintenance difficulties meant many were lost to simple problems, with salvage practically non-existent. The only base facilities had been a civilian motor agency in Rangoon and the Lashio workshops of Watson & Son were taken over, but there were few trained personnel. Thousands of tons of supplies had been collected at Prome and local resources exploited to the full by the Army Purchasing Agency; in the last stages of the campaign these had been dispersed 'with commendable foresight' in depth on the Lashio–Mandalay railway. But considering that no plan had been made for the militarization of transport facilities it is amazing that as late as 22 April supplies were being dispatched along this line. Petrol, oil and lubricants were a source of unending anxiety; very few tankers were available and containers desperately short.[26]

Meanwhile, Japanese bombing reduced Mandalay to a burning, stinking shell on Good Friday, 6 April, destroying the railway station and hospital. The anti-aircraft guns at Fort Dufferin were wood and bamboo dummies, and once the Japanese realized this they bombed and strafed at will.[27] Maung Maung saw 'Mandalay, my home, die in great agony':

> I wandered dazed and sad through the burning city. The dead lay littered in the streets and some bodies were charred with burning. The roads along the royal palace moats were avenues of death. Men and cattle, the high and the lowly, the old and the young, all struck down and humbled together.[28]

George Rodger saw

> the carved stone figures of two elephants, cracked from the heat, still standing knee-deep in ashes, guarding the entrance to a temple which had gone. Every temple had gone; the bazaars and the shops had gone and the homes of 150,000 people; Mandalay itself had gone. What took a thousand years to build took but an hour to fall.[29]

Dead lay everywhere: men, women and children, bloated, festering and stinking, covered with millions of flies, while crows and kite-hawks circled overhead. It still burned when Stilwell arrived to confer five days later. Chiang, who arrived with Madame Chiang the same day, wrote to Churchill that in all his long experience 'I have seen nothing to compare with the deplorable unprepared state, confusion and degradation of the war area in Burma'.[30] From each town as it was reduced to charred ruin emerged those still living, although many were already condemned to death, carrying cholera and smallpox.

As a result of 215th Regiment's attack on 48th Indian Brigade, the latter was now isolated from 1st Burma Division and came back under command of 17th Indian Division. The orders they received to strike the Japanese advancing from the south while Kokkogwa was under attack were unrealistic for so inexperienced a formation, and they failed to make effective contact. Slim realized he must reorganize once more and directed 1st Burma Division back to the Yin Chaung. There was some water in this but behind it none whatever before the Pin Chaung 40 miles to the north. On 14 April 2nd KOYLI sent D Company to Thazi and then were ordered to move to Shabhinla. But before they reached it they were redirected to Myingun on the edge of the Irrawaddy, where they were to be joined by 1st Burma Brigade. They had been at Yenangyaung since the end of March: 'Except for minimum rations', recalled Lieutenant Gerald Fitzpatrick, 'we remained unprovisioned. No ammunition or equipment, no clothing and seemingly, no interest.' Within four hours of being informed they were to move forward to cover the withdrawal of Burcorps, they suffered fifty-nine desertions and a suicide, reducing strength from 220 to 160. Morale was on the verge of collapse. Information was sparse and inaccurate, command and control almost non-existent.[31] As Bruce Scott commented: 'You can only grasp at the shape of the antagonist before you, and then when you think you've solved the problem of his personality, he vanishes into thin air like a jinni.'[32]

On 15 April the oilfields were destroyed, blanketing the sky with an immense pall of smoke. The next morning the Japanese attacked the Yin Chaung positions. Rumours abounded that the Japanese were all around, including at Twingon to the north-east, and these proved true. The battle was another disaster for 1st Burma Division. At first, 5th Burma Rifles, now a mere shadow of a battalion, fought well but once the Japanese gained a foothold it disintegrated, forcing the rest of 1st Burma Brigade to retire across the Taungdwingyi–Magwe road, with 2nd Royal Tanks doing sterling work ferrying the exhausted infantry, collecting wounded and counter-attacking. They also provided the only effective radio communications, and without them 1st Burma Division would almost certainly not have got clear of Magwe. With it now lost, Slim ordered the rest of his precious 7th Armoured Brigade back through Yenangyaung across the Pin Chaung. The retreat of 1st Burma Division from Magwe was exhausting, in temperatures exceeding 100 °F (43 °C), covering 25 miles without a stop and no water on the way. Men and animals suffered dreadfully despite the best efforts of the Malerkota Field Company, who loaded 40-gallon drums of water from the Burmah Oil Company swimming-pool to set up water points as best they could. American correspondent Darrel Berrigan described the scene:

> Men, mules and horses were strung out across the dusty hills under a white blazing sun. They were collapsing dog-tired in the sand for a brief rest, then heaving themselves to their feet again and marching forward. Bearded, dust-caked men, with the sweat-salt dried white across their shirts, their water-bottles clacking dry against their hips.[33]

That night Yenangyaung power station was dynamited as the Japanese began to infiltrate the town.[34] Sakurai was following up with vigour, his men partly sustained by the 11th Disease Prevention and Water Supply Unit, which comprised some 200 men including seven doctors and a pharmacist equipped with water-purifying equipment and could utilize village wells and dig in *chaungs*.[35]

Slim tried to relieve the pressure on 1st Burma Division with attacks by 17th Indian Division but with little effect. Slim also asked for assistance from Chinese 38th Division,* reported to be moving into the battle area under Lieutenant-General Sun Li-jen. Speaking good American English, he was, said Slim, 'alert, energetic and direct', and would have made a good commander in any army.[36] Arthur Fearnley noted that, unlike most of his division, Sun's feet were not bare – he wore brown rubber-soled gym shoes, together with a white singlet, blue shorts and a sun helmet.[37] The Chinese had no artillery or tanks, and Slim immediately placed all he had under Sun's command. On 18 April they attacked Pin Chaung but made no progress against the strongly held block on the ford, although a company of 1st Inniskillings was taken prisoner after mistaking some Japanese for Chinese.[38] Once more the Japanese outflanked the position to the east held by 1st Burma Brigade now comprising 2nd KOYLI, 2nd/7th Rajputs and 1st, 5th, 7th and 12th Burma Rifles, although the last four units mustered fewer than a thousand men between them.[39] 'The whole area was darkened by a pall of smoke,' recalled Sergeant John 'Tim' Finnerty,

---

* 38th Division was raised from the 'Salt Guards' who originally guarded revenues from salt, a government monopoly, and were superior to most Chinese troops (Ho Y-c, *The Big Circle*, p. 3).

'stabbed in places by sheets of flame from burning plants and installations ... There was no shade, and the ground was dusty and hard, making it very difficult to dig deep enough to bury the dead.'[40] Scott realized his troops were nearing the end of their endurance; food amounted to cold bully beef and cheese on biscuits of granite hardness, said to be rich only in Vitamin W: 'W' for weevils.[41] Scott requested permission to break out that night after destroying his tanks and guns but Slim, speaking gently and courteously but firmly, insisted they hold on.[42] 'All right,' replied Scott, 'we'll hang on and do our best in the morning, but, for God's sake, Bill, make those Chinese attack.'[43]

They promised to do so at 1230 but their timekeeping was notoriously bad, and by early afternoon all communications with Scott had broken down, compelling him to try and break out whatever else happened. His tanks found a rough track leading to Pin Chaung about a mile upstream of the ford, hastily improved to take guns and lorries. A column personally marshalled by Scott began moving along it at 1400 hours under heavy fire. Once they reached the *chaung*, they found soft sand and had to abandon most of the vehicles and guns. 'Some horses and mules, maddened by the smell of water, broke loose to fall and roll in the *chaung*. Men collapsed at the *chaung*'s edge and buried their faces in the water, caring nothing but to assuage their terrible thirst.'[44] Shamefully, many seriously wounded were abandoned. An officer volunteered to return after dark to investigate and found every man had had his throat cut or had died by the bayonet. Pat Carmichael wrote bitterly of how the 'situation should have fallen to such a level that we had to abandon our wounded to the attentions of an enemy notorious for his savagery and brutality, must mark the last day of the Yenangyaung battle, as one of the blackest in the long history of British arms'.[45]

Eventually the Chinese attacked at 1500 with great spirit and took Twingon, releasing the Inniskillings captured the previous day and even fighting into Yenangyaung itself. Gerald Fitzpatrick had a panoramic view and was deeply impressed: a 'spectacular show of a superbly trained and drilled Chinese Army moving like clockwork, to the bugling and signalling of the boys and the calls of commanders'.[46] But Slim had to withdraw them before they became too embroiled. 'I had expected the Chinese soldier to be tough and brave', he later wrote. 'I was, I confess, surprised at how he responded to the stimulus of proper tank and artillery support, and at the aggressive spirit he had shown. I had never expected, either, to get a Chinese general of the calibre of Sun.'[47] Indeed, Chinese troops were far better than the British expected. But despite several tactical victories over superior forces, in the end they failed through lack of unified command. As General Ho Ying-chin noted, following the fall of Rangoon the British were operating west of the railway and the Chinese to the east, and 'Chinese forces could not be massed in time and their strength was therefore not fully utilized. As a result, the Chinese fought passively from beginning to end.'[48] Perhaps more significant was Chennault's observation that Stilwell's sacrifice of a Chinese offensive to save a few hundred British soldiers seemed to Chiang 'the sheerest sentimentality and incredible military callowness'. From then on Chiang had little faith in Stilwell's ability as a field commander, 'and his faith in Stilwell's personal integrity began to crumble'.[49] Not that Chennault got on well with his compatriot, seeing in his control of lend-lease supplies a block to his own grandiose visions of victory in China through air power alone.

Meanwhile, like secret ink suddenly becoming visible, the easternmost Japanese drives came into view.[50] Supported by 1st and 14th Tank Regiments, 18th and 55th Divisions moved with incredible speed through the Shan States, easily brushing aside 6th Army, which retired to Kentung to concentrate what was left of 49th and 93rd Divisions. Although the country was hilly and mostly forested, there were some fair roads between the Sittang and Salween rivers and the Japanese reached Mawchi, with its valuable wolfram mine, on 13 April.[51] Their speed completely disrupted the bold plan Slim made at Alexander's commanders' conference on 19 April, when the following day news arrived that Loikaw had fallen, completely scattering Chinese 55th Division and outflanking 96th Division, which was driven north of Pyinmana. Stilwell rushed the one and only Chinese armoured division from Lashio and after a desperate fight during 17–18 April it routed 33rd Division and helped save the British. But this left the right wing of the remaining Chinese forces unprotected and the Japanese were quick to react, also pushing in the left wing by occupying Taunggyi, capital of the Southern Shan States, on 20 April without a fight, leaving large petrol stocks to the Japanese, who by now had almost run out. When the Japanese arrived, Princess Sao Hearn Hkam had to restrain her small son Tiger from playing his favourite record, *God Save the King*.[52] Ten days earlier their bombers had turned it into a charnel house despite its lacking military targets or even a railway. Nurse Helen Rodriguez looked from the hospital window and saw burning buildings, topped by a pall of smoke. 'I realized the paradise I had known as Taunggyi had disappeared for ever.' The shell-shocked surgeon left Helen the responsibility of dealing with the wounded. She had to amputate a gangrenous leg, despite never having seen the procedure before; she defused a bomb with the aid of a magazine article, carried crippled patients to safety on her back and earned the George Medal (GM). She refused to leave the patients to the depredations of Chinese or Japanese. Injured by drunken Japanese soldiers, the lieutenant and doctor who took charge 'proved to me that one can never write off an entire nation as being composed of inhuman beasts. They treated me with generosity and consideration, and did their best to ensure that my work could continue uninterrupted.'[53]

Stilwell was forced to move 200th Division across from 5th Army to try and recapture this vital communications hub and personally led a Chinese company under intense fire, ordering it to stand firm until relieved, and he offered a reward of 50,000 R (rupees) if Taunggyi was taken by 5 o'clock. But his frantic efforts could achieve little: 'Are the Limeys going to run out on us?' he asked his diary on 20 April, 'Yes.'[54] Then, as if to prove him right and as if Alexander's burden was not heavy enough, next day Dorman-Smith announced he was handing over to him all civilian affairs because Alexander 'had shown himself quite excellent [in his] dealings with civilian officers and concerns'.[55]

Charles Braimer Jones helped a young wife pack.

> After a quick glance I said: 'You have far too much. Why on earth are you taking all those smart frocks and those hats? You are going on a jungle trip Pat; not to a tea party. Her reply was devastating in its feminine logic. 'My good man, we are ending our journey in Calcutta. Do you expect me to arrive there in jungle shorts and a topi?'[56]

But arriving there at all was becoming less simple. Arrangements for the evacuation of the many remaining dependants were now difficult, since the government had delayed issuing the order; the Army had advised this not to be done until the middle of April. A train packed with 700 left Mandalay on the 18th and took five days to reach Myitkyina, and on the 20th, 4,000 still awaited evacuation.[57]

Nevertheless the burden weighed heavily on Slim, who was 'feeling about as depressed as a man could'. He met a group of silent British and Chinese officers who looked at him. He recognized the anguish in their eyes, the need of reassurance from their commander:

> Sometimes he does not know what to say ... 'Well gentlemen,' I said, putting on what I hoped was a confident, cheerful expression, 'it might be worse!' One of the group ... replied with a single word: 'How?' I could cheerfully have murdered him, but instead I kept my temper. 'Oh,' I said, grinning, 'It might be raining!' Two hours later, it was ... Hard. As I crept under a truck for shelter I thought of that fellow and wished I HAD murdered him.[58]

Alexander and Slim began immediate plans to counter-attack with 17th Indian and Chinese 38th Divisions, as did Stilwell, while 1st Burma Division would retire to the area around Mount Popa (meaning 'Cobra' in Burmese) – an extinct volcano rising high out of the surrounding plain – to reorganize as best it could. Withdrawal provided only a brief respite, however. It was clear a line across north Burma could not be held indefinitely; the road from Assam could bring only 30 tons a day. It was no longer a question of retreat but of where to, while Wavell issued instructions to begin immediate planning for the reoccupation of Burma.[59]

The British were very jumpy now towards the Burman population, which they suspected of giving away their positions to the Japanese by burning hayricks or even houses, and of joining the fighting against them. Colonel Basil Amies at Burma Army Headquarters described how the Defence Platoon brought in a young Burman found with bits of telephone wire suspected of spying for the Japanese, and 'shortly after, I heard shots from a field over the hedge'. [60] *Pongyis* were treated with great suspicion. One told James Lunt he had been beaten up three times, twice by British soldiers and once by Indians, who threw him down a well that was fortunately dry. At Taungtha, Gerald Fitzpatrick rounded up twenty-seven Burmans apparently about to murder a group of Indian women refugees by burning them in a building. He ordered them to be shot and led the way in this action.[61] But many also helped the British: 2nd Lieutenant Ralph Tanner got separated from 2nd KOYLI south of Yenangyaung and was given food and shelter by villagers.[62]

At Mandalay on 22 April Major Duncan Johnston RM found most ships idle, being without crews, and those which were working at full stretch taking refugees to Myitkyina. With the water level in the rivers at its annual lowest, many of the boats would simply have to be destroyed.[63] Meanwhile the following day 4th/12th Frontier Force Regiment was guarding the bridgehead at Sagaing and was

> heavily bombed by the Japs but eventually the Division came through and once again we got clean away. It was in this area that we first faced the refugee problem. A continuous stream were coming through the whole time and cholera and smallpox were rife. Owing to the number of deaths on the road and the heat the stench was unbearable.[64]

On 25 April Alexander, Slim and Stilwell conferred at Kyaukse, some 30 miles south of Mandalay, where, according to Brian Montgomery, 'Slim dominated the scene, and made certain once and for all that no British or Indian troops would withdraw into China. Alexander gave me, at any rate,

the impression of being rattled. I think he needed Slim to help him com-
pete with Stilwell.'[65] Alexander announced that, with the monsoon
approaching, he had decided to quit Burma. If the normally ice-cool
Alexander was alarmed, it may have been due to Wavell's instructions:
above all to maintain close touch with the Chinese, to cover the
Kalewa–Tamu route back into India, to keep his force in being and to
retain as many points of re-entry into Burma for future offensive operations – incredibly difficult to resolve in the circumstances. But it was clear
that Burma could no longer be held and a withdrawal plan was agreed;
quickly implemented, this would deny Iida the decisive battle he hoped to
fight south of Mandalay.[66] It may have been an unpopular decision with
Stilwell but it saved Burma Army to fight another day. Their goal would
be Imphal in Assam or via the Hukawng valley to India. With the Japanese
streaming through the Shan States and closing on Meiktila, there was no
time to lose. Major-General Eric Goddard, unsung hero of the campaign,
had previously established an *ad hoc* administrative base at Mandalay. Now
he began back-loading to India via Yeu for the British, and Bhamo and
Myitkyina for the Chinese. Meanwhile 63rd Indian Brigade was to hold
Meiktila to cover 5th Army, where they inflicted a severe check on the lead
elements of 55th Division on 26 April. The same day, forced by the
Japanese entering Lashio, Dorman-Smith left Maymyo for Meiktila under
the false impression that Alexander would withdraw there.[67]

Stephen Brookes's father, a former army doctor now seventy years old,
was back in service in charge of the Medical Supply Depot at Fort Dufferin
in Mandalay. One morning he arrived home and bundled Stephen with his
mother, brother and sister into a three-ton lorry, and they set off for Lashio,
a wild and cosmopolitan hotbed of black market intrigue, 'the most interesting town in the whole of the Far East during those last months in
Burma', according to Wilfred Burchett.[68] Now it was gripped by anarchic
panic as civilians and Chinese troops struggled to escape. Stanley Short was
there four days before the Japanese arrived:

> Everybody's one aim seemed to be to get out of the place as fast as they pos-
> sibly could. Throughout the night streams of traffic poured out of the town
> towards the Burma Road and … we saw the chaos which had resulted from
> this mad, headlong, panic-stricken flight … Scattered broadcast over the
> steep embankment, lay debris of every description – beds, baths, mattresses,
> chairs, pictures, cooking pots, and all the other paraphernalia that goes to
> make up an Eastern home.[69]

The Brookes family pressed on to Wanting in China, where they stayed
with the Sawbwa of Mangshih, a Shan state on the Chinese side of the

border. Young Stephen's father wanted the family to fly to safety in India while he returned to continue the war, but his wife refused to leave him, and on 28 April they all headed back into Burma.[70]

Slim realized he must delay the Japanese south of Mandalay and directed most of 1st Burma Division to Monywa, while 17th Indian Division would hold south of Mandalay as long as possible. Increasingly order was breaking down. On returning to Maymyo he was astonished to find that a dump of petrol, vital for 7th Armoured Brigade, had been destroyed.[71] Mike Calvert had acquired some vehicles and was making his way north. He was astonished to see a group of fifty women and children cheerily wave from the road side, led by a 'very firm and decidedly grey-haired lady' of about sixty-five who 'had gathered the group together and kept them calm and orderly', and declared they were waiting to be collected on the promise of a colonel. 'This staggered me, for I knew the nearest British transport was miles away by now and heading for India, not Mandalay.' Calvert also knew that, although when he made the promise the colonel fully intended to keep it, he might well now be dead, and he offered the group a lift. She 'appeared to consider my offer, weighing the pros and cons. For her, there was a right and wrong way of doing things, no matter what the situation.' She finally agreed after Calvert promised to tell the colonel what had happened when he returned to collect them.[72]

Nevertheless, despite the inevitable confusion of retreat, Burcorps reached the west bank of the Irrawaddy and on 30 April blew the great Ava Bridge (where an attempted deception, Operation Error, appears to have failed completely), largely owing to the sharp check inflicted on 18th Division by 48th Indian Brigade on the 28/29th at Kyaukse.[73] Slim commented that the action at Kyaukse 'was a really brilliant example of rearguard work. It not only enabled the last of the Chinese to cross the Ava Bridge without molestation and gave us all a breathing space, but it inflicted heavy casualties on the enemy at extremely small cost to ourselves.'[74] Meanwhile 2nd Burma Brigade remained on the west bank of the Chindwin, forced to rely on bullock-carts for transport, although 'no British officer had the slightest idea how far or how fast a bullock cart would go, or how much it would carry'.[75] At Monywa the guard consisted of only 1st Glosters and the Royal Marines river patrol, while the town was crowded with refugees waiting for river transport to get to Kalewa. Yet Monywa was vital since it dominated the Chindwin and there was a rail connection with Yeu. Denial of it meant denial of retreat to India, but Slim admits an error of judgement here.[76] First Burma Division was marching towards it from the south, as there was not sufficient transport to lift them. Sakurai had driven 33rd

Division hard after Yenangyaung and had managed to get lorries across the Irrawaddy, to reach Monywa at around 1900 hours on 30 April, opening fire on it and capturing a steamer moored to the west bank. Slim thought the Japanese had captured the town and ordered stores to be abandoned and the wounded moved immediately to Shwegyin. Scott hurried to concentrate his division but on 1 May met a Japanese road-block interposed between his headquarters and the main body. His headquarters was scattered and retreated in confusion.[77] The first reinforcement to reach Monywa was 63rd Indian Brigade on 1 May, which arrived by rail from Sagaing, but, heavily engaged by Japanese artillery and mortars, 2nd/13th Frontier Force Rifles suffered 75 casualties in ten minutes.[78] They were joined by 13th Indian Brigade that night while Alexander and Stilwell had their final conference and agreed the situation was now drastically altered. Alexander and Sun both wanted 38th Division to remain under Slim's command, but Stilwell was reluctant. Winterton, the Chief of Staff, strongly advised Alexander to comply with Stilwell, but how then to save Sun's 'face'? Suddenly 'Alex's face lit up. "I know," he said, "I'll give him a British decoration."' and with scissors he cut the ribbon of the CBE from his chest and pinned it to Sun, 'who left us beaming all over his face', a gesture for which Alexander later received a stern rebuke from Buckingham Palace.[79]

That evening Scott ordered a two-brigade attack for next morning, which began with 13th Indian Brigade approaching from the east and 63rd Indian Brigade from the south, supported by 1st Burma Brigade. The Japanese had dug in strongly, but their air support found it hard to intervene between two closely engaged lines. Things seemed to be going well for the British when at 1700 a message purportedly from Alexander was received through an officer at 7th Armoured Brigade for 13th Indian Brigade to withdraw to Alon 6 miles to the north, an order later denied by both Alexander and Slim.[80] Both British and Indian official histories believe this was a false message passed by the Japanese using tanks captured at Shwedaung, and the fact that it was not queried can be explained only by the reliance now placed on 7th Armoured Brigade's tanks for communications within Burma Army.[81] Meanwhile 56th Division, racing up from the Shan States, seized the large suspension bridge over the Shweli at Namkhan when the demolition failed, apparently through faulty fuses.[82] This opened the way to Bhamo and thereafter Myitkyina. Lady Dorman-Smith was flown out on 2 May and the Governor, under direct orders from Churchill, followed two days later. Colin McPhedran saw him go. His brother Robert could hardly believe it. 'The Governor has got away safely and we, along with thousands of poor Indian refugees, are left behind!' he said, desolate. I did not feel abandoned as he did, I felt furious ... not only at those who had just been left behind, but at the system that treated everybody but the British as second-class citizens.[83]

The Japanese then secured the spectacular 825-feet high Gokteik via-duct, some 30 miles east of Maymyo between Mandalay and Lashio. Mike Calvert had been sent by Alexander to hold it at the end of April and then withdrawn about a week later, despite repeated requests to be allowed to destroy it. When Calvert met Alexander later, Alexander seemed pained that it had not been blown up, but explained that for political reasons he was unable to order its destruction. 'But he had wanted it blown up all the same and sent me there in the first place because he was told I was the most likely person to disobey orders!'[84] The Japanese pursued, but they were now as exhausted as the British, and by 4 May the majority of Burcorps had reached Yeu, ready for the long slog to Shwegyin. The following day, in accordance with their agreement of 13 December, the Thai Army began advancing towards the Shan States, and five days later they entered to occupy the area promised them by the Japanese. They soon took Kentung from Chinese 93rd Division, who withdrew into China, though desultory fighting continued between them throughout the war.[85]

# 7

## Retreat

The way here also was very wearisome through
dirt and shabbiness; nor was there on all this
ground so much as one inn or victualling house
wherein to refresh the feebler sort.

John Bunyan, *The Pilgrim's Progress*

ALEXANDER ORDERED SCOTT to hold Yeu until the Chinese were clear
of Shwebo. By 9 May, when Sakurai caught up with them, much of
Burma Army was west of the Chindwin, which left only Headquarters 17th
Indian Division, 7th Armoured Brigade and 48th Indian Brigade in a small
area called 'the Basin', an oval-shaped depression approached through a gorge
and fringed by almost vertical, jungle-topped cliffs.[1] Refugees were everywhere – some dying, some giving birth and all totally exhausted and hopeless. Over everything hung a retching stench of excrement, death and acrid
smoke from burning vehicles. In places vultures covered the trees, 'or were
in knots on the ground flopping lazily away from a corpse as we approached',
noted Pat Carmichael. 'In death some bodies had been twisted into curious
shapes by their acute terminal spasms.' The living were equally pitiful.

They walked in small family groups, father supporting the mother, an elder
son or daughter carrying the precious bag of rice on head or back. There
were few smaller ones now, but what children there were had distended bel-
lies supported on sticks of legs, and all them moved slowly, dragging along
with expressionless faces, eyes on the ground and bodies wasted to the bone.

He had to start shooting his precious mules. One driver was already
pleading: 'Sahib, let him be. I will stay with him and bring him on soon.
He will be all right. He is my friend. Do not shoot him.' But they could
not abandon mules to starve or be captured by Burmans or Japanese.

I told the driver to drop the lead rein and stand beside me. The poor beast
was dead beat and content to remain quite still. As I raised the rifle he was

looking straight at me, unblinking, and with the complete trust they always gave us. If anything, his steady gaze was rather quizzical, as if saying: 'What's he up to now?'

He fired and the mule collapsed with a thud. The driver dropped to his knees and embraced the animal's head, 'mewing to him. I put a hand under an arm and pulled him up. We walked off quickly to catch up the battery.'[2]

Similarly the Stuarts of 7th Armoured Brigade were on their last gasp and were thoroughly and methodically wrecked; engines drained of oil and run until they seized, wiring ripped out and radios and guns smashed.[3] Only one, belonging to 7th Hussars, escaped.★ As April dragged on, the Chindwin fleet of the Irrawaddy Flotilla Company had become more and more vital and ferried the remains of Burma Army across the river. John Morton, the manager, reached Katha on 3 May with the last few boats of his once proud fleet. 'Katha is a sight,' he told his diary, 'vessels anchored ten abreast and all deserted. The last train has gone, the town is evacuated. Parties are told off to sink every vessel ... to make for Manipur as best they can.' They worked all night sinking ships and paying wages before setting off for the Chindwin. Chief Engineer William Hutcheon had been commissioned into the Army for special duty. On 7 May he carried Alexander across the river, who came on to the 'flying bridge and had a yarn. Plenty of planes overhead and we are bombed – but he thanked me for a pleasant voyage!'[4]

Slim saw a woman dying of smallpox while her small son tried 'pathetically to feed her with milk from a tin a British soldier had given him'. A doctor managed to vaccinate the child but the mother died and he was placed with an Indian family.[5] Many British and Indians were still trailing behind the main force. Swimming in a tributary of the Chindwin still 200 miles from Kalewa, Mike Calvert met a Japanese officer and they fought hand-to-hand in the water. Eventually Calvert overcame his opponent, who floated down river 'like a ghastly yellow Ophelia'. Afterwards Calvert was violently sick.

> I had never felt so wretched before. I told myself this was war ... In fact this had been a fair fight. The Jap had asked for no quarter and would certainly have given none. I told myself all this but it did not help much ... I felt like a murderer that afternoon ... Even now, so many years afterwards, the memory of it is too clear and comes back to me too often.[6]

He reached Kalewa after being helped by Oriya coolies from Orissa in south-west Bengal. They had been threatened by the Japanese not to help

★ It returned to Burma in 1945 with 7th Light Cavalry. See p. 356 below.

the British, but insisted on helping Calvert's party with one stipulation: that they dress as women to hide their identities.

The defence of the Shwegyin 'Basin' fell to 1st/9th Jats and the last four Bofors of A Troop, 3rd Indian Light Anti-Aircraft Battery under Captain F. D. Webber. One deployed for air defence (and claimed two aircraft, taking the battery's total since Moulmein to twenty-two, plus three troop-carrying barges crammed with Japanese on the Irrawaddy) and the others in the ground role. At dawn on 10 May the Japanese attacked and established a toe-hold on the southern lip of the basin. They were counter-attacked by the Jats and 7th Gurkhas supported by the Bofors, now prodigious with the remaining ammunition. When the Japanese brought up a 70mm infantry gun, a duel over open sights saw the latter knocked over and its detachment killed.[7] Loading continued until early afternoon, when the steamer crews absolutely refused to make another trip. The only option was to make a night march towards Kalewa, and 2nd/5th Royal Gurkhas took up a fall-back position. 'So there we were', noted the war diary,

> a sitting target if the Japanese cared to follow up. We were surrounded by cliffs 300 feet high on two sides, difficult enough to climb by day, impossible to take against opposition by night. The 1st/3rd Gurkhas held the third side (Long Ridge) and on the fourth, to the east, ran back the road into Burma. On this road were several ammunition lorries burning furiously and lighting us up as we sat there. Small arms and mortar ammunition were exploding continuously ...[8]

The Jats and 7th Gurkhas withdrew at speed, covered by a frantic 20-minute Bofors barrage, pumping tracer shells into the gloaming. The last round fired by the last gun exploded in the barrel; the Number 1 reported, simply, 'Finished'. Then the gunners destroyed their pieces and followed the infantry on the night march to Kalewa.[9] The remaining flotilla party with every steamer capable of running now made for Sittaung, taking 48th Indian Brigade with them; there the remaining stern wheelers were scuttled. They then marched the 36 miles to Tamu, where they were greeted personally by Alexander. Chief Engineer Jack Murie won the MC for his work. Out of 650 units, 550 had been denied to the Japanese. From sleek, handsome paddle-steamers with teak decks and brass fittings to the flats that carried all the trade of Burma, soon all would be silted and irrecoverable, a sad end for the once proud flotilla.[10]

Throughout the campaign the Army medical services were stretched to the limit. After the fall of Rangoon, besides battle casualties (1,354 killed and 2,534 wounded) there was the constant fear of cholera among the floods of Indian refugees, and the medical staff were constantly fighting the cholera threat among the troops. Constant withdrawals meant much straggling, and the lack of provost staff was acutely felt.[11] Once more shortage of vehicles proved serious: two motor ambulance sections arrived without vehicles; one improvised section never had more than fifteen cars, all of which broke their half-shafts. Field ambulances arrived without transport and several Irrawaddy Flotilla craft had to be converted into hospital ships towards the end of March, and Japanese aircraft, for once, seem to have respected their red cross markings, as they did ambulance trains. Evacuation of sick and wounded to India was first carried out by air from Shwebo and then from Myitkyina, but lack of aircraft meant many casualties accumulated at hospitals.[12]

During the final eight weeks of the campaign, after the fall of Magwe, air action continued with bombers operating from Assam and the Calcutta area. In all some fifty-eight raids were flown in support for the army, although few (if any) soldiers noticed. No. 31 Squadron also continued transport operations, and eventually 8,616 personnel and some 2,600 wounded were evacuated by air.[13] Shwebo had been heavily bombed during the last week in April, forcing the abandonment of its airfield and leaving only Myitkyina for the evacuation of sick, wounded and European refugee families by air to India. This in turn was rendered unusable by an air raid on 6 May, which destroyed three out of five RAF Dakotas* as they were loading. A Japanese aeroplane flew over with a red flag, warning that the airfield would be bombed, and the passengers took cover, but twenty minutes later they got back in the planes.[14] When Colin McPhedran and his thirteen-year-old brother were refused a place, his sister and mother got off. As she did so, his mother 'picked up a young child who seemed to be holding its arms out to somebody on the plane and lifted the crying toddler into the hatchway'. As the overloaded plane started towards the runway it was strafed and bombed by two Japanese planes. 'We watched in horror as people fell out of the flaming wreck. There was nothing we could do but witness the slaughter.'[15] Major Edward Cooke of 9th Burma Rifles looked into a wrecked Dakota and saw

* The Dakota (C-47) was one of many military conversions of the commercial Douglas DC-3 airliner. Designed to carry heavy cargo with a strengthened floor and large cargo door cut into the port side, with a maximum speed of 220 mph, it could carry 9,028 lb. of goods or up to twenty-eight fully equipped troops.

Mrs Waddleworth had had her face blown away and must have died at once. Mrs Childers had what appeared to be a terrible chest wound as also had Major Homes. The doctors and stretcher-bearers took out those still living, then two more RAF planes carne in and took off more wounded. No more planes arrived.[16]

Now the 2,300 wounded not yet evacuated would also have to take the arduous tracks northwards.

When they originally discussed withdrawal plans on 25 April, it is doubtful the generals had any conception of the ordeal ahead. For decades India considered her eastern borders with equanimity; the threats were all to the north and west, and Burma seemed so secure that overland communications were unnecessary. Now, with the monsoon approaching, the dripping jungle would be infested with malaria, blackwater fever, typhus and the dreaded cholera. The roadless terrain across razor-backed mountains would defy the most enthusiastic engineer; only a few local trails threaded the hills and local tribesmen were too sparse to form a workforce. To the north lay the Hukawng valley, a vast overgrown forest intersected by numerous rivers draining into the Chindwin, which bisected the valley then forced its way through a narrow gorge to join the Irrawaddy south of Mandalay. This obstruction ensured the greater part of the Hukawng was flooded during the rains. It was fortunate that 1st Assam Regiment had been instructed to construct a bridle path from Ledo up to and beyond the Pangsao Pass at the northern end. Dropping areas were also selected and cleared for food drops onto otherwise inaccessible areas in readiness for RAF operations, although at this stage nobody on the staffs had any experience of them – everything was conducted by trial and error and the smallness of the areas meant only some 30 per cent landed on target.[17]

In February the Indian government had informed the Assam government that a mass exodus of Indian refugees was on the move, and most could be expected through Tamu. In March Major-General E. C. Wood was appointed 'Administrator-General' for Assam with almost unlimited powers to co-ordinate arrangements for the withdrawal, and construction of the road Wavell had ordered into Burma in December. Wood was appalled by what he found. There was, he reported, 'a desert' between India and Burma, with no provisions of any sort, and it was here that the Indian Tea Association (ITA) came to the rescue by organizing the labour necessary for the Manipur Project, as it became known, to build and stock a succession of refugee camps. On 3 March twelve men assembled at Dimapur (Manipur Road) with stores, transport and equipment. There a camp was established under Alexander Beattie, the Scottish manager of a large tea estate, and some 28,000 were working by the end of the month.[18] On the Burma side work began in February from Kalewa towards Tamu in the Kabaw valley, making extensive use of elephants normally employed by the Bombay Burmah Corporation in the teak forests, so that Mr Justice Harold Braund later wrote: 'It was an affair of "tea" to the rescue at one end and "teak" to the rescue at the other.'[19] Wood built a 54-mile road from Palel in eight weeks and organized a civilian transport shuttle service with some ninety lorries between Dimapur and Imphal, but when Alexander decided to evacuate the army on 26 April all facilities were turned over to the military, and civilians had to take their chances.[20] Two days later the road had reached Tamu, beyond which only jungle tracks ran through the malaria-infested Kabaw valley to Kalewa, 6 miles below which on the far bank of the Irrawaddy lay Shwegyin, in turn separated from Yeu by 120 miles of dense forest intersected by numerous unbridged *chaungs*. Now they were across the Chindwin, some soldiers asked: 'How do we get back to India?' 'You walk, mate', was the invariable answer, 'you walk or you die.'[21]

Marching was a chore in the best of circumstances, but with little food and water it was fearsome. The normal expletive-riddled talk that British soldiers use to relieve the monotony of hardship wasted precious breath, and halts became fewer and further between, since once halted it was increasingly difficult to get the men on their feet and moving again. The Indian and Gurkha soldiers, more stoical than the British, plodded on in total silence, but all races moved with the same mechanical gait. The lack of vitamin C in the diet caused many to suffer jungle sores. These started as pink patches, which reddened and suppurated and would not heal, and some men became covered in them. Among those waiting for the fugitives on the way to Imphal were 1st Seaforth Highlanders of 23rd Indian Division, whose quartermaster staff desperately issued tea and food and tried to dispose of the horrific residue of death wearing gas masks. With 63rd Indian Brigade as rearguard the main body marched through the Kabaw valley, 'probably the most harmless looking and yet the unhealthiest spot in Asia'.[22] It left Kalewa on 12 May and reached Tamu seven days later with personal equipment and double issue of small-arms ammunition but nothing else. On 12 May Army Headquarters left Tamu and the monsoon broke. At least it saved the Seaforths from having to deal with corpses, since they were washed away. But with the rains came more sickness; rates had remained low until mid-April, after which the strain began to tell; within a week of arriving at Imphal, to be put on half-rations without fresh clothing, bedding or mosquito nets, a quarter of 17th Indian Division were estimated to have gone down with malaria.[23] The heat was intense and insects abominable, but it was important to cover the 130 miles before the rains turned the dust to mud, and with careful staging, transport ferried the men wherever possible.[24]

On 20 May Burma Army and Burcorps were formally wound up and by the 28th practically all troops had crossed the border into India, bringing just 25 guns with them.[25] But the defeat had not degenerated into a complete rout, thanks largely to Slim, who watched the rearguard march into India.[26]

> All of them, British, Indian and Gurkha, were gaunt and ragged as scarecrows. Yet as they trudged behind their surviving officers in groups, pitifully small, they still carried their arms and kept their ranks, they were still recognizable as fighting units. They might look like scarecrows, but they looked like soldiers too.[27]

With them came the refugees. Brigadier Roger Ekin vividly remembered an Indian grandfather who staggered along on spindly legs with a wooden pole over his bony shoulders with a small bucket-like receptacle on each end – the classic Indian method of water carrying. In each bucket was a baby boy. The two mites eyed the world in silent, thumb-sucking bewilderment. They were the old man's grandchildren, he told Ekin, all that remained of his family that set out from Rangoon; the children's mother and father, along with their grandmother, uncle and aunt, had all perished on the way.[28] And so the longest retreat in British military history finally ended.

On reaching Imphal after a sixteen-day march from Myitkyina, Hamish Mackay of 4th Gurkhas saw an ITA refugee camp with a banner over the gateway that read, 'The Blennerhassetts Welcome You'. Mackay had been separated from his wife and child, but they arrived two days later.[29] When 2nd KOYLI reached Imphal on 19 May, it totalled 9 officers and 70 men. Gerald Fitzpatrick had gone from 158 to 112 lb.[30] The remnants of 1st Glosters went into camp north of Imphal, where 3,000 men were accommodated under conditions intended for 300. Unsurprisingly, it was 'uncomfortable, not only because it was raining hard ... but because we had no shelter or unsoiled ground on which to lie, thousands of people having previously occupied it, with surprisingly primitive ideas for soldiers, on the most elementary rules of sanitation'.[31] Having flown into Myitkyina on one of the last transports to arrive but unable to join the battalion, on 5 May Lieutenant J. A. Cumming and 2nd Lieutenant Peter Carr led a party of 70 men for seventeen days over 290 miles to join them at Imphal. 'I found it a great strain', wrote Carr, 'as I could never be anywhere but at the head of the column with an inadequate map and the little compass we bought in Bond Street on my last leave, and it saved us more than once.'[32]

When trains were finally available to move men back to India, from Dimapur to Ranchi, east of Calcutta, a journey taking three days across Assam, Bengal and into Bihar, they were as hellish as the march: there were no carriages, only steel trucks without bedding or medicines for the cholera, dysentery and malaria sufferers, and the death toll rose inexorably.[33] 'They were hell trains; no other description fits them', recalled Mike Calvert.

> There were no blankets and no food. We had cholera, dysentery, and malaria cases on the train but there were no medical or even toilet facilities. The lavatory accommodation consisted of ropes to which the user clung while hanging over the side of his truck ... We would have suffered more had it not been for the planters and their wives ... As we slowed or stopped at stations they threw us food and other supplies.[34]

On finally reaching India Pat Carmichael was put on a steamer down the Brahmaputra river, where a group of British women provided tea and sandwiches.

> It was a blissful moment. I took my empty cup and plate back to the tables and handed them to one of the women, telling her how grateful we were for their kindness. 'It is we who have to thank you. All of you', she said quietly, 'for what you have done for us.' Her grey eyes held mine as she spoke. 'Thanks all the same' I mumbled and turned away, confused by her sincerity and directness, and feeling a fraud.[35]

At Ranchi the apparently indifferent yet always immaculate staff became known as 'the gabardine swine'. Slim was most bitter concerning the reception given to his troops.[36]

However, there were reasons for the apparently harsh treatment received by the thousands of battle-weary, sick and exhausted men in no state to face monsoon downpours in leaky bamboo huts. First, once Alexander decided to cut his losses there was a strong element of *sauve qui peut* among officers and men, many of whom found their way back to India spreading alarm and conveying an impression of total breakdown in morale. Some units arrived tired but unbowed, while others lost all semblance of military discipline and fell apart.[37] Certainly Lieutenant-General Noel Irwin, commanding IV Corps responsible for the defence of north-east India, formed the very worst view of Burma Army as a result.[38] Second and most significantly, north-east India was totally undeveloped. The roads were poor, and the Assam–Bengal Railway, designed only to serve the tea plantations, was a bottleneck that drove men to despair, changing from broad to narrow gauge, after which there was only a single line. Congestion and chaos meant that by April Wavell was reporting to London that it took seven weeks to move a brigade from Ranchi to the Assam frontier, and in May, when 23rd Indian Division was moving from Calcutta to Dimapur, the railway buckled under the strain. A journey normally taking a single traveller twenty-five hours took 158th Field Regiment, Royal Artillery, no less than seventeen days. The concentration of the division was further hampered when a landslide washed away the line and bridges collapsed, so that one troop took seven days to move 40 miles, winching their guns every yard of the last 10 miles.[39] Meanwhile the medical services, already under colossal strain, were swamped, and the staff could only cope by back-loading as many sick as possible to India on the railway. Thus only essentials could be sent forward; there was simply no capacity for comforts.[40]

Stilwell's escape from Burma was as remarkable as any. At Shwebo on 1 May, having discovered Lo Cho-ying had stolen a train at gunpoint to try and escape to Myitkyina (he crashed it 25 miles on, blocking the line for two days), he parted from Alexander. Then two colonels, commander and executive officer of the newly formed Assam–Burma–China Ferry Command, which had begun operations ten days earlier, arrived in a C-47 and announced they had been sent to fly Stilwell out. He refused and sent his headquarters group instead before proceeding with his remaining staff 60 miles north to Wuntho. At the outset his party consisted of about 80 people, including Seagrave's unit, Chinese guards and various domestic staff, and it was joined by refugees of all races to total 114. He could retire either to India or via Myitkyina to Yunnan, but it was not until his convoy reached Indaw that he decided to turn west, taking a little used route to avoid the stream of refugees and Chinese. Stilwell controlled his party with meticulous thoroughness in an epic of its kind. 'By the time we get out of here,' he said, 'many of you will hate my guts but I'll tell you one thing: you'll all get out.' He was right on both counts. After setting out from Katha on 4 May they walked 140 miles, meeting a rogue elephant, ants, thorns, leeches, sores, blisters and infections, all under a blazing sun, to reach Imphal on 20 May, then by lorry and train to Tinsukia, whence they were flown to Delhi.[41] As his PR man said to Wilfred Burchett: 'Hell, that was a picnic excursion for him. He's just made of steel wire, rubber and concrete for guts.'[42] They were lucky to be led by so resolute and determined a man, although Chennault was scathing of his attitude.

If Stilwell had been a company, battalion or regimental commander whose primary responsibility was for the troops in his immediate command, his walkout would certainly have been commendable. But of a man with the tremendous burden of ranking American officer in Asia and Chief of Staff of the Chinese Republic, it was a startling exhibition of his ignorance or disregard for these larger responsibilities.[43]

Certainly the Chinese agreed; tens of thousands of their soldiers had been abandoned in northern Burma and thousands died. While Stilwell throughout the campaign managed to send reports to far-off Washington, he had not sent a single one to his immediate superior in Chungking.[44] Indeed, Chiang learned of Stilwell's retreat to India only through a personal message from Magruder, whereupon he commented, 'Stilwell deserted our troops and left for India without my permission'. From this time on he had little confidence in Stilwell.[45]

Sun Li-jen's 38th Division came out in good order on a route south of Stilwell and arrived in India between 25 and 30 May, although it felt the harsh effects of British racism: Irwin wanted to intern them until Wavell confirmed they were to be treated with respect.[46] The remains of 6th Army and 200th Division fought their way out to Yunnan; 22nd and 96th Divisions of 5th Army took diverging routes through northern Burma and were caught by the monsoon in the far north-west jungle, where they were kept alive only by air drops. The survivors of 22nd Division eventually reached Ledo in July and August, and 96th made their way over the mountains to China from Fort Hertz (Putao).[47] With them went Jack Barnard, who, having spent ten years as a forester with Steel Brothers and knowing the country well, had been hastily commissioned and posted to Noël Stevenson's Kachin Levies after just a few weeks training at Calvert's Bush Warfare School.[48] He arrived with two other officers at Myitkyina in early May, and retired with them towards Fort Hertz, where they met the Irish Catholic priest Father James Stuart at Sumprabum (meaning 'Mountain of Mists'), who stayed behind in the 'Triangle' and provided vital intelligence to the Allies, becoming known as the 'Fighting Father'.* While on a tour to raise volunteers they met Chinese 96th Division, or the 1,500-odd men left of it, as it retreated towards Fort Hertz. They decided to join their march to Yunnan across some of the most inhospitable terrain in the world, which involved back-aching climbs above the snow-line. At the frontier they crossed the raging Taron river by 'monkey bridge', on which a passenger was propelled down a twisted bamboo cable on a cane hoop 150 feet above

* See p. 139 below.

the torrent. It took 96th Division two days to cross and, if that were not daunting enough, beyond it a jagged series of snow-capped peaks 'soared regally above all the neighbouring summits, dwarfing them and appearing to touch the very heavens'. This was Gompa La – the Hump. They succeeded in crossing the 14,000 foot mountains to reach Kunming, although many Chinese did not: 'Their uniforms reduced to rags and tatters, their faces haggard and hopeless, their feet wrapped in sodden, blood-stained bandages ... weaving along mechanically, mouths agape, eyes glittering with incipient madness, their minds blank.'[49]

For thousands more stragglers and refugees the ordeal was far from over. For Arthur Bell Thompson (later to find renown as novelist Francis Clifford) the retreat began in early April, when his Karen company from 1st Burma Rifles found itself in danger of being overrun in the Shan States. As the Japanese drove towards Lashio, he decided on the 24th to make for Maymyo, but they encountered a lorry containing some British and Shans coming the other way, who informed him that the Japanese were already there. Accompanied by captains Eric McCrindle and Jimmy Nimmo, who would later return to lead guerrillas, Thompson, like so many others, made an astonishing journey to reach safety, first through Shan and Kachin country and then meeting the Sawbwa of Moneik and his English wife, who helped them on their way. On the Shweli river (the only one in Burma flowing north) they built rafts and enjoyed a magnificent sunset.

> The monsoon clouds were beginning to mass in the sky, and at sundown a vast red conflagration spread across the western horizon and mirrored itself kaleidoscopically in the shifting surface of the stream. The forests were dark scars along the base of the clouds, and here and there a lone palm tree reared its tufted head in a graceful silhouette.[50]

Marine William Doyle, although badly wounded in both ankles, also walked; from Myitkyina he headed north encountering many refugees, some Europeans but mostly Indians, and received much kindness from them. He also witnessed Burman brutality; at one point he found a young couple and their son lying face down in the dust, murdered and robbed for a few rupees. Much later he found a broken mirror in an abandoned house and 'could not recognize himself; his skin was almost black, hair long, and a beard growing unkempt and straggled. From walking into the sun, his eyes had sunk deeply into his head; they were bloodshot and yellow.'[51]

Also retreating to the north was Major Edward Cooke, who, separated from his unit on 8 May, with a few others managed to get hold of two cars. 'The road was choked with refugees driving bullock carts, ponies etc and also civilians driving motor cars; some of these civilians were under the impression they could motor the whole way to India, being quite unaware that the motor road finished at Sumprabum (132 miles from Myitkyina).'[52] In fact it finished at Milestone 102, some 40 miles from Sumprabum. On 1 May the Burma government signalled to Wood that 500 Europeans and 10,000 Indians were making for Ledo via the Hukawng and Pangsao Pass. All he could do was assemble mules, elephants and porters at Ledo. By 12 May the 'heart of the Hukawng was no more', noted R. H. Gribble. 'Its charm had gone leaving only a deadly nausea to the few who knew it before.'[53] On 14 May the Brookes family arrived to find hundreds of abandoned vehicles. India was still 300 miles away.[54] On 23 May Arthur Thompson's party met Father Welch, another Catholic missionary to the Kachins, who sent them on their way with a bottle of communion wine. But from now on the going became increasingly dangerous with the presence of Japanese patrols in the north.[55] Many refugees had encounters with the Japanese, but few civilians were mistreated. One Anglo-Indian exchanged cigarettes and chatted pleasantly with a senior Japanese officer who gave his party a written pass.[56]

At a river missionary Stanley Farrant Russell saw many drown trying to cross the rushing waters on a rope bridge; his party was fortunate enough to have an elephant to carry his party and many others across.[57] From the beginning of May Shingbwiyang ('the place of bamboo shoots'), an extremely primitive village devoid of food supplies, sanitation or elementary communal facilities, became the main junction for the floodtide of refugees taking the north-eastern route.[58] R. H. Gribble arrived on 17 May to find 'shortage of food, fear, exhaustion, and lack of sanitation had brought on considerable sickness among the refugees and there were tragedies to be seen on all sides. The sole idea of everyone in the camp was to get away from the filth and the corpses.'[59] On 26 May Cooke's party reached Shingbwiyang to find the RAF had been dropping rations. After seventeen days' continuous marching they allowed themselves a day's rest before pressing on. With frequent rain the trails deteriorated, slowing progress to funeral pace. At one village there were about a thousand starving refugees, including many women and children. Planes had dropped supplies the day before, but these had been looted by armed Punjabis and Sikhs of the BFF, who resold the rest to these starving wretches at colossal prices. Dozens of tins of bully beef lay around, opened and discarded by Hindus. Cooke's group used some to lay out a sign saying 'S.O.S. RICE'. When a plane began dropping rations, they managed to collect and distribute a fair amount to the women and, after taking a little themselves, set off again.[60]

Colin McPhedran with his mother, brother and sister, set out for the Hukawng. 'It was a wave of human movement, stretching as far as the eye could see. In front of us there were literally thousands of people; we brought up the rear.' Soon they were passing groups of dead, and the stench was heavy all around. 'One often reads of elephants choosing a single area as a final resting place, and here a similar scene seemed to be played out. Would it be that some humans were loath to leave their loved ones and in so doing gave up their own will to carry on?' Yet one body caught his attention, seemingly covered by a white sheet.

> As we stepped carefully around it, our movement appeared to disturb the shroud. Then we saw a cloud of white butterflies rise up with a whirring, humming sound, exposing the bloated, shiny corpse of an Indian refugee ... When we moved away, I looked back in amazement to see the cloud of white settling back on the corpse, a fitting veil for the deceased.[61]

The family plodded on through the rain up into the Patkoi range, seeing many more dead on the way.

There was still no sign of the organized camps they had heard about, and days of marching with no rest and poor food were beginning to take their toll. The numbers of dead were increasing rapidly. 'It looked as if the poor creatures struggling up the endless hills, getting weaker and weaker every day would come to a turn in the track expecting to find a summit and then still seeing the hill stretching away above them, just lay down and gave up trying', noted Cooke.[62] One morning Colin's mother could not find the strength to move. In frustration his brother Robert pulled at her hands but was too weak to raise her. She said the children must go on and bring help, and she gave her rings to Colin's sister, who, beyond words and beyond tears, gazed at her mother, her face stricken. Colin was shattered.

> I could not bear the thought of leaving her in the jungle ... I had reached the point in the trek when I would willingly have stayed with my mother and died with her ... She whispered, with words that have remained embedded in my mind, 'The world is full of good people ... I know you will find them and be well cared for, for the rest of your life. Son, you must walk on ... don't look back.'[63]

The Hukawng was a valley of death.

At each of the numerous river crossings people perished, unable to make the crossing or drowning in the attempt. 'The crossing at Namyang

Hka was about 150 yards wide', recalled R. H. Gribble, 'The temper of
the river was fierce, and the water tumbled and bellowed over the boul-
ders in an alarming manner.' It had to be crossed using a ropeway in water
4–5 feet deep, and keeping one's balance was very difficult.[64] Finally on 4
June Cooke's party reached the first camp, where cooked rice and hot tea
were dispensed to all. There was no accommodation, but at least camps
were now laid out at regular intervals.[65] Behind them the Brookes family
struggled on. In early August Arthur Thompson's party met two
American women Baptist missionaries and reached Fort Hertz, having
covered 925 miles in 109 days. They were finally flown out on the 26th,
by which time Thompson had been reduced in weight from 12 stone to
8.[66] One morning at the end of August Colin McPhedran awoke, 'overcome by a strange coldness'. The three children had rested huddled
together and Robert had died in the night. He tried to struggle on with
his sister.

> Ethel sank down as if to rest a moment. I moved on a short distance further,
> then I too let my body down into the ooze. I felt completely at peace. There
> was not a thought of food or water in my head. I just gently created a pocket
> in the mud that was comfortable and warm ... I observed, or perhaps I
> dreamed, a cloud of white butterflies floating down towards me. It was a
> comforting vision and I was not afraid.[67]

He awoke in a refugee camp at Ledo, saved by a Scottish tea planter. His
sister had also been rescued but had since died. Having started the journey
weighing 124 lb., he now weighed around 50. Marine William Doyle

> put one weary foot after the other, like an automaton, keeping going by his
> own momentum. When he stopped to rest, he had to force himself to get
> up. The temptation to lie there, even in the rain, was almost overwhelming,
> but he instinctively realized that if he could not overcome this yearning, he
> could lie there forever. He suffered hallucinations ... But when he looked
> again they had gone and the shining spears of rain hammering the great flat
> leaves of unknown plants emphasized his loneliness and fear.[68]

Then he saw a white tent and found a doctor – a real one – who gave him
quinine for his malaria and treated his torn feet as best he could. Another
day's limping march brought him to a road gang, and another to a tented
hospital, where he collapsed. He was then moved by stages, although not
without suffering from the pettiness of military administration – Royal
Marines were the Royal Navy's responsibility, and he was in the Army's
hands – to Calcutta.

Alexander Beattie, in charge of the refugee camp at Dimapur, died of typhoid in July. Harold Braund, who became Refugee Administrator at Imphal on 3 June, wrote: 'He had been at Dimapur from the beginning, and his utter steadiness and reliability throughout has been remarkable. Whatever else happened, we always knew ... that Beattie would still be there doing his work.' Nearly 150,000 refugees had passed through his camp, and with the onset of rain it had been inches deep in mud and conditions deteriorated dramatically. Yet Beattie had worked day and night, 'always with a kind word for the distressed, and a pocketful of sweets for the children. He did not spare himself for a moment, and I have met no one', continued Braund, 'who has not spoken of him in terms of admiration and affection. He never spared himself, and in the end I cannot doubt that he has given his life for the refugees he served.'[69] A medical report on the refugees noted 'complete exhaustion, physical and mental, with a disease superimposed, is the usual picture ... they suffer from bad nightmares and their delirium is a battle of rivers and crossings.'[70]

Clive North, superintendent at Shingbwiyang, struggled with a death rate of fifty per day. On 7 June the order came to close the route when the rains made it impossible to maintain the camps between Shingbwiyang and Ledo, and Wood issued strict instructions that no refugees were to be allowed to go beyond Shingbwiyang on the 16th, a decision that Stephen Brookes estimates led to the death of as many as 25,000 out of 45,000 refugees that passed through there. His family, having twice been robbed by marauding Chinese, arrived on 19 June and remained until October, surrounded by misery and death, including that of Major Brookes. But the rest of the family then made the final march of 128 miles aided by Naga porters.[71] Kachins, Garos, Phars, Khasis, Abors, Mishmis and Nagas all assisted with guiding and portering in the far north, where Ritchie Gardiner's party crossed the Chaukkan Pass, something that had never previously been done during the rainy season. They hired Kachin porters who demanded opium, which one member of the party managed to provide. As they climbed into the mountains the temperature dropped and once they reached the pass the Kachins left, so that everything they needed thereafter had to be carried by themselves. As June progressed conditions grew harsher and daily rations reduced to 4 oz. of (mouldy) rice, one (very mouldy) biscuit, a weak cup of Marmite and ½ oz. of cheese. But on 19 June they reached a village where some Mishmi tribesmen produced a note signed 'Gyles Mackrell', and after continuing on feet, now 'raw and inflamed all over including a large part of the soles', in boots 'literally on the point of falling off, they met a party of Gurkhas from the Assam Rifles and a camp by the Datha river organized by Mackrell. 'We still had a week's journey to reach civilization but it was with elephants and porters and *food*'. Mackrell, the local ITA liaison officer, had set out on 17 May and by 17 June had saved 101 people with his 'four and a half' elephants, bringing his last group over on 9 October.[72] Of the estimated million who fled, no accurate number of those who died *en route* has ever been recorded.[73]

# 8

## Plans

It is lack of this knowledge of the principles and practice of military movement and administration – the 'logistics' of war, some people call it – which puts what we call amateur strategists wrong, not the principles of strategy themselves, which can be apprehended in a very short time by any reasonable intelligence.

General Sir Archibald Wavell[1]

THE JAPANESE DID not penetrate as far as Tamu, even with patrols. When the British returned in November, a journalist described it as a 'city of the dead'. In reality no more than a village, it was strewn with hundreds of abandoned vehicles. J. H. Williams, known as 'Elephant Bill', confirmed the journalist's report: the vehicles were filled with grisly emaciated figures who had reached the village after the monsoon had broken and, unable to face the drenching mountains without food, sought shelter in the deserted cars. Among them was an ambulance. 'Four poor wretches had found shelter in it, and perhaps had even felt luckier than their neighbours in being able to lie down, at full length, on well-slung stretchers to die.'[2]

Japanese victory was devastatingly complete: British prestige had suffered another hammer blow, discrediting their concept of protecting, civilizing and supervising in Asia.[3] Maureen Baird-Murray was an eight-year-old Anglo-Burmese in the care of Italian nuns at Kalaw. When the Japanese arrived, the children were more excited than frightened, 'but there was always in the background the knowledge that at any moment everything could change at the whim of the occupying power. We learnt to look over our shoulders.' Later, the aunt of a friend appeared injured and bedraggled, having escaped on foot after her plane crashed leaving Myitkyina. The nuns nursed and sheltered her until one day the Japanese dragged her away. The Mother Superior reached out to show the nuns had not betrayed her, 'but one of the soldiers butted her away with his rifle as a warning. We felt the brave lady understood, as with bloody head held high she was marched away.'[4]

Within two weeks of the British evacuation of Rangoon, Suzuki had set up the Baho government under Thakin Tun Oke. By June, however, the BIA was ordered to take no further part in politics or government administration, although by this time they had already antagonized the Karens of the western delta and Salween districts, whom many zealous nationalists suspected of pro-British sympathies.[5] At Myaungya there was open strife, which resulted in the shooting of one Karen leader, Saw Pe Tha, and the taking of his English wife and family with other Karens into custody as hostages. The feud spread into the countryside, and for some weeks selected bands of hostages were shot, fanning the insurrection until mid-June, when the Japanese stamped it out.[6] This Japanese intervention was one of the few popular moves of their occupation. The BIA was assembled in Rangoon, ostensibly for re-equipping. It was, however, summarily disbanded, save for a select cadre of officers including Aung San, who was appointed major-general in charge of the new, more carefully selected, 4,000-man Burma Defence Army (BDA).[7]

For logistic support the Japanese would rely on railways. However, while the network north of the Irrawaddy was largely intact, the Ava Bridge was too big a demolition to repair during the war, and the destruction of the Irrawaddy Flotilla's boats created grave transport difficulties.[8] Already facing a shipping crisis, the Japanese deemed it essential to build a rail link to Burma from Bangkok. In March, 5th and 9th Railway Regiments and 1st Railway Materials Workshop – some 13,000 men – received preparatory orders, which were confirmed in June. As early as April the military authorities in Java, Sumatra and Singapore were marshalling prisoners of war northwards for numerous construction and labour tasks.[9] The first 3,000 from Changi gaol in Singapore began building base camps in July, and for fourteen months the railway was driven relentlessly through 260 miles of mountainous jungle in some of the most unhealthy climatic conditions in the world, linking Nong Pladuk in Thailand with the Moulmein–Ye railway in Burma. This was the scene of appalling suffering, in which prisoners of war (together with conscripted civilians) laboured for fourteen to sixteen hours a day with hopelessly inadequate rations and non-existent medical care under a rain of blows from fists, boots, sticks and whips, before returning at night to their pitiful camps, blood-stained, half-naked and starving, to dream of food.

Given their harsh military code, it is perhaps unsurprising that the Japanese 'had nothing but contempt for men whose disgraceful cowardice obeyed an order to become captive and still live'.[10] However, the treatment those men received was barbaric and inhuman. As the Australian medical officer Edward 'Weary' Dunlop noted in his diary: 'The state of health in these camps can only be regarded as an everlasting appalling disgrace.' [11] Rations never amounted to more than a couple of bowls of rice a day and perhaps some vegetable soup or stew; medical facilities were as if 'they had been flung back into the darkest of the Dark Ages when famine and pestilence stalked through the land'.[12] Conditions were exacerbated by the Japanese attitude that sickness was a result of lack of determination to be fit. Rations were cut for the sick because they supposedly needed less; it must have baffled the Japanese to watch prisoners feeding their sick first and tending them constantly. Perhaps no other act more clearly contrasted the differing outlooks than that sick Japanese applied to camp doctors for treatment. Yet everything had to be improvised: bandages from strips of cloth and even leaves, tin cans and other metal junk to create bowls and containers.[13]

In June the Japanese set up a military government under Iida with 300 officials from Japan. Iida, the son of a soldier who had enjoyed a brilliant career, proved an able administrator with a broad mind and cultivated personality.[14] While Japan proclaimed its Co-Prosperity Sphere as a 'family' of Asian nations with itself as 'father', it was in no sense a genuine liberation. The military administration – *Gunseikanbu* – directly controlled thirteen out of fifteen departments. Having cut Burma off from trade and commercial contacts with Britain, Japan failed to replace them, and the position of Burma as a front-line area came under special scrutiny in Tokyo.[15] The Total War Research Institute, headed by Tojo himself, recommended that the army should take full control of the country's economic and transportation facilities and that Co-Prosperity Sphere 'independence' be deferred longer than elsewhere. No liberal or communist agitation for self-determination would be tolerated. Indoctrination missions began and education programmes sent Burmese scholars to Japanese schools; some were selected from leading families and effectively held hostage.[16] U Hla Pe, Director of Press and Publicity under the occupation, later spoke of his fellow nationalist leaders being merely 'an executive commission' for the Japanese military authorities.[17] The Japanese plan to exploit nationalism proved contradictory and unworkable, based on the false premise of Japanese destiny and a racist sense of superiority no more realistic than the white rule it supplanted.[18] Iida had taken Ba Maw into voluntary custody at Maymyo in late May and asked him to head a new civil administration. Ba Maw's personal vanity and ambition along with his anti-British nationalism made him vulnerable to Japanese blandishments, although these traits later increased their difficulties in dealing with him. He agreed to head a government if independence were granted within the framework of the Co-Prosperity Sphere, and the government was installed on 1 August 1942.[19]

War had almost paralysed Burma. Rangoon, Mandalay and other towns were shattered; communications and oilfields were destroyed and the population totally disrupted, as were the economy and food distribution, particularly in Lower Burma. Cooking oil leapt in price by thirteen times, yet the country was left with 3 million tons of unsaleable rice in 1942, severely damaging future production. Cattle numbers were halved by disease and Japanese requisition while war contractors and Japanese business and manufacturing took over.[20] Most Burmese were soon disillusioned, and by early summer many were outspokenly anti-BIA and anti-Japanese: they said the British sucked blood but the Japanese went to the bone marrow.[21] Thereafter political interference led to the demoralization of virtually all routine administrative services. In Rangoon landless labourers were conscripted into 'civil units' and put to work sharpening bamboo stakes and clearing airstrips. By late 1944 they numbered 800,000, more than in any other area in South-East Asia, forming a *chwaytagyi* ('sweat army'), many of whom died on the Burma–Thailand Railway.[22] In the Shan States the Japanese first used the princes to help their administration, then undermined them with a youth organization.[23] Japanese commanders made the gross error of slapping the faces of village elders and even senior officials. That they treated their own underlings this way mattered not to the Burmese: such insults were unnecessary and uncalled for. Booted Japanese soldiers occupied *pongyi kyaungs*, used the sacred precincts for latrines and slaughtering purposes, and used their robes to bind the feet of horses – the Japanese regarded *pongyis* as spongers. Their forced inoculation programme at railway stations and road-blocks increased resentment further, but the depths of Burmese hatred were reserved, as in other occupied countries, for the *Kempeitai* (military police) and still more for their informers.[24]

Although their number in Burma never exceeded 540, the *Kempeitai* were ubiquitous and ruthless, employing spies and frequently torturing victims. Some Japanese officers acted as *agents provocateurs*, and hireling police were particularly dreaded. They were also key administrators of the *jugun ianfo* ('comfort women').[25] One reason leading Thakins joined Ba Maw's government was the protection it offered themselves and their friends from *Kempeitai* depredations. Many, including Ba Maw and other politicians, used them as a means to settle political scores, while many Burmans learned Japanese to ease communication with the authorities.[26] Unsurprisingly in such a climate, overt Japanese attempts to promote themselves failed lamentably. In October 1942 a United Pongyi Association to promote the Japanese programme and purge their enemies never got off the ground. Only among the Karens saved from Burman persecution in the immediate aftermath of invasion did the Japanese enjoy any favour. The most successful Japanese-sponsored organization was the apolitical East Asia Youth League, which included Indians, Karens, Mons and Shans, as well as Burmans, and concerned itself with constructive welfare matters.[27]

Meanwhile, denied access to Allied conferences and the Combined Chiefs of Staff committee, China's disenchantment deepened. China was a cornerstone of American policy, but her major concern was the Pacific campaign. She had no interest in restoring Britain's imperial position, while China was of no importance to the British, whose primary concern was the defence and security of India. Indeed Anglo-American differences, already more conspicuous than in Europe, increased with British dependency on US material support, further exacerbated by opinionated and cantankerous personalities. The meritocratic Americans, perplexed by British snobbery, were particularly swift to criticize and also quick to sympathize with the plight of Indians struggling under the Imperial yoke they despised; yet they were equally racist towards the 'wogs' while ignoring their own shabby treatment of African-American troops. These attitudes, intensified by the enervating heat of Asia, created misunderstandings of purpose and method.[28]

Stilwell was determined to fight back in Burma. On 25 May he told Associated Press in New Delhi: 'I claim we got a hell of a beating. We got run out of Burma and it is as humiliating as hell. I think we ought to find out what caused it, go back and retake it.'[29] With a plan approved by the Joint Chiefs of Staff in Washington he offered the Chinese High Command a training programme at Ramgarh, 200 miles west of Calcutta – previously a prisoner camp for 20,000 Italians – to provide weapons and training for a force of thirty Chinese divisions. Stilwell hoped to be free from political interference, except that he faced increasing complications. In early January 1942 the War Department had planned to establish Tenth Air Force in India to incorporate the AVG as 23rd Fighter Group. Chennault would come under not only its command but also under the Army representative (first Magruder, then Stilwell) and was deeply unhappy to lose so much authority.[30] Chennault, who loathed Stilwell, was messianic in his conviction that he could reverse the situation and ultimately win the war with air power alone: to begin with, he claimed he could do it with just 105 fighters, 30 medium and 12 heavy bombers.[31] On 20 June 1942 Ferrying Command had been renamed Air Transport Command (ATC) and on 21 October it took over responsibility for the Hump. Chiang particularly wanted supplies for Chennault's China Air Task Force but since Air Transport Command burned a gallon of fuel for every gallon delivered, and had to deliver 18 tons of supplies for every ton of bombs, Chennault's plan stalled. A cargo plane could carry 4 or 5 tons and hope to make a round trip in a day in good conditions, but operability was never above 60–70 per cent and losses were high.[32]

For the British before the fall of Mandalay, the importance of Burma in providing security to India's eastern border had never been assessed, and now she faced a grave threat to a border never previously threatened.[33] Yet Wavell's single eye rarely lost sight of the distant light of victory, having instructed the Joint Planning Staff to begin preparing an offensive to reoccupy Burma on 16 April. But the first study was unsatisfactory, and on 12 June Churchill signalled: 'All these minor operations are very nice but necessarily petty.'[34] He wanted the capture of Rangoon and Moulmein partly by fighting along the coast from Chittagong via Akyab, but mainly by an overseas expedition of forty or fifty thousand British troops, although this, he admitted, would be impossible if the Germans threw back the Russians in the Caucasus or the Middle East were lost.[35] With little support from Britain, India would have to fight the war alone; yet the financial system meant inappropriate peacetime methods severely hindered developing India as a war base. Communications were primitive in the extreme: the civil trunk telephone system was barely sufficient for peacetime needs. Transport links east of Calcutta needed developing to support large forces, and nothing could be accomplished until this was done. In June the appointment of 'Administrator-General' was abolished, and its responsibilities given to IV Corps; these included the Assam Line of Communications Area, which subsequently became 202nd Line of Communications Area, the boundaries of which roughly coincided with those of Assam.[36] Assam's 9 million population spoke 120 different languages, although most were Bengali-speaking Hindus in the Assam and Surma valleys. Most of the region was malarial, with cholera and smallpox not uncommon, along with dysentery and other stomach complaints. Thus the introduction of large numbers of men was bound to result in high sickness rates. Only rice and tea were exported and all other commodities (especially vegetables) produced only for local consumption; similarly, livestock was scarce.[37] Now the whole military administration of India, previously geared to the North-West Frontier, would have to be redirected to the north-east, while Churchill and Stilwell champed impatiently.[38]

In June, Stilwell reported to Chiang at Chungking. Chiang had sent a confidential message to his US representatives that was highly critical of Stilwell, but which urged them to allow time for introspection on the part of the US authorities, hoping they would recall him themselves.[39] Now supply problems came to a head, prompted by British defeat and the fall of Tobruk in Libya. In the ensuing panic the heavy bombers of Tenth Air Force together with ATC transports were despatched to Egypt. Chiang reacted angrily: every time Britain suffered a defeat, China lost equipment and supplies, and he presented the 'Three Demands' ultimatum, which threatened to liquidate the China theatre unless three American divisions arrived in India to restore communications through Burma with 500 combat aircraft to operate in China, and 5,000 tons a month to be delivered by ATC from August. Stilwell concentrated on the thirty-division plan: it was not yet apparent to him that Chiang was not really interested in such a force, lest it come under control of another leader or faction. But for Stilwell it formed the basis of the X-Y plan, with X Force invading from India and Y Force (or Yoke Force), trained and armed at Kunming in Yunnan, forming the other half of a double-pronged invasion. Stilwell offered the plan to Chiang as a way out of his ultimatum and felt the British would be pushed into it under pressure from Washington. Chiang accepted on 1 August, with two shrewd conditions: full British participation by land and sea, and adequate air support. But in reality the plan was considered unrealistic in China, Britain and America.[40]

Unknown to Stilwell, the reconquest of Burma, including Rangoon – code-named Anakim – was being considered by the British Chiefs of Staff and War Cabinet during July.[41] Besides an amphibious assault on Rangoon and Moulmein, it would also involve engaging the Japanese on the Assam front (Ravenous), to be carried out by IV Corps, and seizure of Akyab (Cannibal), for which five divisions and two in reserve were deemed necessary. But it had very low priority and depended on other theatres, especially the Middle East, and on Japan being drawn into war with the USSR. Wavell accepted the basic premise but doubted if November was a realistic start date. The slow build-up of forces, particularly air forces, meant it was never likely.[42] Between March and June 1942 the air force in India, under Air Marshal Sir Richard Peirse, grew from five squadrons to twenty-six. (It was planned to increase to fifty-two squadrons, but would only reach forty-two by February 1943.[43]) Furthermore, the attack on Rangoon required 29th Independent Brigade, then involved in occupying Madagascar. But shortage of aircraft, the need to allow 29th Brigade's beach parties and naval crews to recover at Durban from malaria, and ultimately lack of shipping – especially landing-craft, which were diverted to the Torch landings in North Africa on 8 November – led to first the postponement and then abandonment of this scheme, although planning for it continued deep into 1943.[44]

Besides, preparations for offensive operations were severely hampered by turmoil in India. In 1931 civil disobedience had resulted in the internment of 36,000 Congress Party followers, including Mahatma Gandhi, but four years later a new Government of India Act was passed, which made clear that independence would be a reality within a generation at most.[45] Following elections in 1937, eight out of eleven provinces returned Congress governments. Congress leaders were touchy and resentful, and, while loquacious in their opposition to fascism, doubted Britain's commitment to their own independence, clinging to the idea that Britain's difficulty was India's opportunity. They were furthermore profoundly ignorant about and uninterested in the Indian Army.[46] In 1940 and 1942 there were serious civil disturbances. With a Cabinet delegation which became known as the Cripps Mission, Britain made vague offers of complete independence at the end of the war and considerable immediate participation in government. But Congress was not appeased and in August Gandhi began the 'Quit India' campaign. In spite of the non-violence policy, well-planned attacks took place against India's communications system, destroying or seriously damaging 250 railway stations, although the staff stuck loyally to their posts, in some cases unto death. Communications with the front in Assam were cut for days at a time, seriously disrupting the reorganization programme. Eventually over 1,000 people died and some 60,000 were arrested: training, troop movements, stockpiling and airfield construction were all delayed as fifty-seven battalions, mostly Indian and including twenty-four from field formations under training, deployed on a large scale for the first time since 1857.[47]

K. S. Thimayya was a KCIO with 4th/19th Hyderabad Regiment; on seven occasions he managed to persuade mobs to disperse without resorting to shooting. At about this time the first rumours emerged of an *Azad Hind Fauj* or Indian National Army (INA), formed from among prisoners of war by the Japanese to help drive the British out of India.

> It was difficult for us, therefore, to view this action as anything but patriotic. If we accepted the INA men as patriots, however, then we who served the British must be traitors. This conflict was especially difficult for me because I heard my own brother had gone to the INA.[48]

Fortunately for the British, Japanese promises were so vague and reports from China so horrific that most Indians preferred to deal with the devil they knew. Recruiting was affected but Krishen Tewari, unsure if joining was the right thing, trained with a Dogra battalion. 'They were tremendously tough, tremendously disciplined. We admired them very much – they *charmed* us into joining the Army.'[49] And Thimayya noted that among Indian officers 'the consensus was that we should help the British to defeat the Axis powers and deal with the British afterwards.'[50]

In Ahmedabad on 10 August 2nd Royal Norfolk Regiment went to 'show the flag'. Although the large-scale demonstrations never became violent, they were certainly unpleasant. Second Lieutenant Dickie Davies recalled, 'they'd empty rubbish over you. Excreta wrapped up in a piece of newspaper was a good bomb!' Eventually the situation calmed down and when the battalion came to leave, Sergeant Fred Hazell noted, 'practically the whole population turned out and cheered us ... What started out looking like a pretty tricky operation ended up very friendly.'[51] But as Humphrey (later Lord) Trevelyan noted: 'In a large part of the country the political struggle hardly ruffled the surface until the end of British rule was in sight, when the machine began to run down and communal pressures could no longer be kept in check.'[52] And Peter Collister recalled:

> To the fighting army, and even to men on garrison duty, India was merely a background and a jumping off point for the Eastern Front. The impression given in books and films about the period that most British people, military or civilian, were obsessed with 'The India Question' is erroneous. Our chief sin was not hostility or, with some exceptions, even arrogance, but indifference.[53]

Most British conscripts had no interest in defending British rule. Clive Branson noted shortly after his arrival that 'the conditions were a howling disgrace. For this reason, and its reactions on our own immediate future (and present), the slogan among the British Other Ranks of "India for the Indians" is universally popular.'[54]

The air forces were little better served than the army, with hardly any airfields and few all-weather runways. A programme to construct 222 new airfields therefore received top priority and by the year's end no fewer than 150 were ready and RAF personnel and aircraft began to arrive, while expansion of the tiny Indian Air Force began. By the end of July US air forces totalled 812 officers and 8,350 men, while Tenth Air Force provided an administrative headquarters at Delhi and two tactical headquarters: one for air operations over Burma and the other for operations over China.[55] Roosevelt finally agreed to enlarge Tenth Air Force on 12 October and offered China other support, but he refused to send combat troops.[56] In November heavy bomber squadrons of 231 Group RAF began to arrive, equipped with B-24 Liberators. This type was produced in greater numbers than any other during the war – 18,500 – and Air Headquarters India was finally getting its share. In the war against Japanese supply lines its significance was demonstrated on the 26th, when eight Liberators raided an oil refinery and power plant in Bangkok, a return journey of 2,760 miles. Although it was unable as yet to make heavier raids, the Japanese noted that all the proposed Burma–Thailand railway was vulnerable, and most of it was not yet built. Furthermore, Bangkok was hit by twelve American Liberators on Boxing Day, and more were in action by the start of 1943, with Rangoon and Mandalay as principal targets. The USAAF's 7th Heavy Bombardment Group's 9th Squadron was returning from the Middle East, and 492nd and 493rd Squadrons were activated at Karachi and 436th Squadron added from Stateside. In September 341st Medium Bombardment Group (11th, 22nd, 490th and 491st Squadrons) was formed, flying B-25 Mitchells.[57] In February 1943 they began mining the ports, increasing the significance of the land-based alternative: the Japanese imported more prisoners and press-ganged labourers to increase the rate at which the railway was built. They also lured Malayan Tamils, former plantation workers whose economy had collapsed, with promises of pay and good rations. In reality, conditions during the monsoon were unbearable; death rates soon soared.[58]

Wavell did not communicate with Stilwell until September 1942.[59] They finally met on 18 October and saw Chiang's outline plans for reconquest of Burma from the north. They agreed their plans were in accord and it was only a matter of timing; they hoped to begin in February 1943, although the proposed build-up to fifty-two squadrons had slipped to the end of March. At a conference on 26 October Stilwell declared his aim of raising a full corps of 30,000 men and operating from a base at Ledo, down the Hukawng valley, along which he planned to build a road to reconnect with the old Burma Road near Bhamo, first to support his north Burma campaign then to supply China, following an old caravan route.[60] However, the British believed that even if the road could be built, it would absorb most of its capacity in maintenance. The Americans immediately accepted responsibility for the Ledo Road project.[61] Ledo was merely a coal-mining village which would have to be transformed, and the work would be a long, long slog, through a pass called 'Hellgate', over the Patkoi mountains towards the old Hukawng valley refugee trail.

Wavell wrote to the Chiefs of Staff that 'we must accept with good grace and willingness this American-Chinese co-operation in recapture of Burma', and later he wrote of his farouche ally, 'Stilwell is pretty close and does not give away much, but I like him and think him co-operative and genuine.'[62]

When Stilwell later discussed the plan with Chiang on 3 November, the Generalissimo agreed. But by now Wavell's force estimate for the reconquest had risen to ten divisions, plus an armoured division. Stilwell was playing the Chinese off against the British in an effort to persuade both to take part in the scheme, what he called 'sleeve-jerking'.

> Hell, I'm nothing but an errand boy. I run up to Chungking and jerk the Gimo's sleeve. I tell him to better be ready to move into Burma from the south ... the Chinese are going to lose a lot of face if the British do it alone. Then I fly down to India and jerk Archie's sleeve [and tell him] the Gimo is going to move down the Salween and you better get going too. You Limeys are going to have a hell of a time with the white man's burden if the Chinese have nerve enough to fight and you haven't.[63]

The British were very sensitive that the Chinese might regard America as senior partner in operations to reconquer Burma. But the desperate shipping shortage meant any build-up in India for offensive operations was bound to be slow. On 17 November Wavell reported to the Chiefs of Staff that amphibious operations to recapture Akyab looked increasingly unlikely, but the same aim might be achieved by advancing along the coast with 14th Indian Division, reinforced by British 6th Brigade. He was experiencing difficulties with Stilwell, who planned operations without reference to Wavell, 'and I think, without much reference to his staff here who seem to know little ... His senior staff officer here gives me the impression of being overawed by Stilwell and afraid of representing the true administrative picture.'[64] Wavell felt he was effectively communicating with Stilwell through Washington. Certainly Stilwell never showed any interest in administration or logistics, realities that constantly exercised Wavell's mind. Beyond the railhead at Dimapur everything had to go by road. To move the Chinese from Ramgarh to Ledo and sustain them would require 800 lorries and 200 tons a day over a 350-mile line of communication, which were not available; and there was, he maintained, no way of building a road to support Chinese operations during the monsoon. Then at an Anglo-American planning conference in New Delhi on 19 November the British declared plans in northern Burma must be postponed and the Akyab operation adopted instead.[65]

By December the north Burma offensive was fizzling out. Although they met on 17 and 20 December, when Stilwell insisted that a drive on Myitkyina was necessary because the economic situation in China demanded that the Ledo Road be opened, Wavell believed apart from a raiding force – a brigade of which was ready – significant forces could not be maintained. With 14th Indian Division struggling along the Arakan coast, the campaign was clearly as much about road-building as fighting. Chiang cabled Roosevelt on 28 December to urge the British to do more, and Roosevelt replied that he would urge Churchill at the Casablanca conference, which was due in early 1943. However, by early January 1943 Stilwell felt the British were reneging on promises for the reconquest of Burma that year, both military and naval, to support his plans with significant forces and secure the Bay of Bengal with Eastern Fleet. On 8 January Chiang formally declined to undertake it, since the Allies would not meet his conditions. As a result, Stilwell began to hate Chiang bitterly, while Churchill brushed aside Chiang's accusations of bad faith – relayed to him through Roosevelt – by saying he had not made promises as such.[66]

At Casablanca (14–24 January) the Americans were keen to see Anakim implemented to re-energize the Chinese, much preferable to deploying American troops. Marshall was not averse to blackmail, saying a situation might arise in the Pacific that would force the US to withdraw from commitments in Europe. The British replied that the landing-craft needed for the Rangoon operation would reduce her share of the invasion of Europe, but the American Chief of Naval Staff, Admiral Ernest J. King, offered to supply them from the Pacific, and Anakim was agreed with a target of date of 15 November 1943 and a final decision no later than July.[67] But events in Arakan were forcing Anakim into the background, making the reconquest of Burma seem to Churchill like 'munching a porcupine quill by quill'.[68] Roosevelt was beginning to agree, and suggested to Marshall it ought to be abandoned in favour of the second front in Europe; it also enabled him to transfer the burden in China to Chennault, and on 10 March 1943 Fourteenth Air Force was created for China, despite strong opposition from Marshall and the Chief of Air Forces, Lieutenant-General Henry H. 'Hap' Arnold.[69]

From the beginning Chennault complained of being starved of supplies by Stilwell while the latter pursued his Burma policy.[70] At Ramgarh, Stilwell wanted two divisions with support troops ready by February. Reinforcements came over the Hump, packed thirty or forty into a plane – naked since the Chinese thought it foolish to waste uniforms on men who would be issued new ones anyway. Several died of the cold, but most recovered quickly after an hour in the Indian sun.[71] By December 32,000 were in training. Chinese commanders were of the highest class, including Sun and Liao Yao-hsiang, a product of France's St Cyr Academy. Under their combined regime the Chinese soldiers, at first ragged, hungry and diseased, were transformed into efficient, confident units. But there were problems. Chinese and American concepts of command were at odds: the Americans regarded the Chinese as defensive-minded after seven years of war, while the Chinese regarded themselves as realists.[72] Unable to employ their normal training aids, ranging from films to Donald Duck comics, American instructors taught by example. 'Thank God we don't speak Chinese and we don't have interpreters', noted the programme's artillery director, Colonel G. W. Sliney. 'We demonstrate and they copy. They are the greatest mimics in the world and are learning very fast.'[73]

With his plans to invade north Burma scuppered, Stilwell concentrated on the thirty divisions for Y Force while work on the Ledo Road continued, despite huge labour problems caused by short contracts, language, caste, religion and different ration requirements.[74] The construction rate during good weather was ¾ mile per day, and forward units crossed the frontier on 28 February 1943 erecting a sign saying, 'Welcome to Burma! This way to Tokyo!' Returning along the refugee trail, Seagrave saw skeletons grouped at every waterhole and at the foot of every ascent, along with tattered clothing, civilian and military. British, Indian and Burmese clung to the bones.[75] But thereafter work slowed and only another 4 miles were completed by 11 May, when it was halted by the rains, which soon damaged the finished stretches, forcing backlog work. The newly arrived 330th Engineer General Service Regiment noted: 'It is impossible to exaggerate the difficulties which beset the 330th' as they struggled with washed-out bridges.[76]

In India military command was reorganized by the constitution of three armies to meet the threats of invasion from the south, north-west and north-east while a central command was established to relieve Army Commanders of internal security responsibilities. But the army as a whole was in disarray. Eastern Army (previously Eastern Command, with headquarters at Ranchi), now under Irwin, was also responsible for the internal security of Bihar, Bengal, Orrisa and Assam. In turn, IV Corps in Assam and XV Corps in Arakan had only the sketchiest communications and hundreds of miles of signals cable-line had to be laid to both.[77] In Assam IV Corps had the badly mauled 17th Indian Division and 23rd Indian Division not yet blooded; XV Corps under Slim from 2 June, with 14th and 26th Indian Divisions, was responsible for defending Bengal against seaborne invasion, while 70th Division (less a brigade group) and 50th Indian Tank Brigade were in reserve at Ranchi. But standards remained low. Second Lieutenant Dominic 'Nick' Neill recalled that his time at the Officer Training Centre at Bangalore 'was not up to standard, we did foot and bicycle drill, and trained in elementary tactics for the North-West Frontier. We trained with wooden machine-guns and wooden 2-inch mortars, we learnt very little indeed.' He was sent to 2nd Gurkha Rifles Depot and 'put in charge of recruit training. I knew nothing, my recruits knew nothing. My company commander had been a tea planter, and his military knowledge was very limited. We had no officer training and no language training.'[78] The *jawan* in a newly raised unit in 1942 was a boy under nineteen years old, suddenly removed from his village. He was barely literate and had to learn Urdu (many were Punjabi speakers). He was, recalled Charles MacFetridge,

> unbelievably uncomplicated and childlike. Many misfits and unfits were recruited; for instance drivers of vehicles were not found to be colour blind until suddenly confronted by the traffic lights in Calcutta! The period in the training centre was five months and the recruit had to be taught to wear boots – a painful ordeal for many. His keenness was astonishing and sustained him through these months of repetitive training, and then in his Battery with little or no equipment.[79]

The 1942 expansion programme had been set to raise four infantry divisions and one armoured division, but in the end only three infantry divisions – 23rd, 25th and 36th – were raised and the latter manned by British brigades in India. A division improvised for local defence of Calcutta had become 26th Indian Division in May. After the retreat the remnant of the Burma Rifles was collected. Many Kachins were told to make their way home with their rifles as best they could, to form the nucleus of Kachin resistance to the Japanese. The balance, having been offered the chance to return home, were posted into 2nd Burma Rifles under Lieutenant-Colonel Denis O'Callaghan, the only unit of the regiment to reach India in any way intact. The scattered remains of the BFF and BMP were formed into some five battalions and two garrison battalions of the new Burma Regiment.[80] The inquests following the defeat in Burma led to the realization that Indian formations were over-mechanized and road-bound. Seventeenth Indian and 1st Burma Divisions (redesignated 39th Indian Division) were reconstructed as light divisions, with only two brigades and largely animal transport.[81] Indeed 17th Indian Division went further and changed its divisional sign from a lightning streak – which Tokyo Rose, the English-language propagandist on Tokyo radio, had called yellow – to a black cat: one that became famous and is still used by the Indian Army.[82]

At the front things were no better. The Royal Indian Army Service

Corps (RIASC, known irreverently as the 'Rice-Corps') was responsible for transport and supply and expanded dramatically during the war. Captain David Atkins had no intention of giving up his cushy staff billet in Delhi, but by accidentally ordering ten times more rum than the army needed (although this would later prove useful) and sending the spare flour in India to Karachi in the north-west rather that to the north-east, he found his name with the Military Secretary for a change in employment. Having passed his Urdu exam and with the army desperately short of officers, at twenty-four and only two years after joining the Territorial Army, he was promoted major and told to raise a new General Purpose Transport (GPT) Company – 309th – one of eight raised in eight weeks. But when IV Corps sent forward more transport companies, each supposed to mount 100-lorry convoys, most could only manage twenty or fewer through appalling sickness rates, made worse by losses of one in twenty through crashes every time they covered the 120 miles from Dimapur; meanwhile food, munitions and clothing rotted in Dimapur's dumps while little arrived at Imphal. Malaria struck in September and drivers vanished or were straggling along the entire length of the road. Most front-line troops were eventually withdrawn from the malarial areas which formed hot spots; unfortunately Dimapur was one of these, and units stopping there were soon ravaged.[83]

Expansion was a massive and difficult undertaking. The Indian Corps of Signals needed technically trained men: the proportion of British to Indian was approximately 1:3 with a serious shortage of tradesmen, and not enough money was made available to encourage educated Indians to join, so this shortage persisted.[84] The Corps of Military Police (India) was formed in July 1942 and the Intelligence Corps (India) in November. An Indian Pioneer Corps was raised, amounting to some 400 companies with some 175,000 personnel and 1.5 million civilian labourers employed by the War Department, initially employed building myriad airfields and roads to Assam. On 3 April 1943 the Indian Army Medical Corps was formed by amalgamating the Indian Medical Service, Indian Medical Department and Indian Hospital Corps, and the Corps of Indian Electrical and Mechanical Engineers (IEME) came into being in May by taking staff from Indian Engineers, RIASC and Indian Army Ordnance Corps (IAOC) to take on the enormous tasks of equipment maintenance.[85] A Women's Auxiliary Corps (India) – WAC(I) – was formed in May 1942, with its first platoon from the WAS(B). By 1945, in a society that strictly limited women's roles, it had expanded to 1,160 officers and 8,900 women, demonstrating the peculiarities of Indian society: of every eight auxiliaries, one was

European, three Anglo-Indian, three Indian Christian and only one a non-Christian Indian.[86] Nor did they receive automatic respect. One British sergeant got twenty-eight days' field punishment for failing to salute a WAC(I) officer in Calcutta: 'Salute yer, by Christ,' he retorted, 'you say fuckin' Salaam to me.'[87]

# 9

# Donbaik

Women and children build up the only road
Where overhead the shells of death whine past
And cattle graze indifferent to the din.
I felt perhaps I'd understand at last
By clear observance of all that nature showed
'When life has gone, then where does death begin?'

Clive Branson[1]

V FORCE WAS CREATED in 1942 as a guerrilla and, more importantly, an intelligence organization by A. A. Donald, now a Lieutenant-Colonel. For a brief time there was some tension between the hill tribes and Anglo-Indian troops, but this soon dissipated and, supported by the Assam Rifles, V Force units became ubiquitous, sending out small patrols led by officers to collect information and set up agent networks in Japanese-controlled areas to provide tactical intelligence. In the Chin Hills area former forestry workers – Burmese-speaking British, Anglo-Indian, Anglo-Burmese, Anglo-Chin – were commissioned and sent back to collect information in an organization called Z Force, which probed ahead of army patrols with an escort of tribesmen.[2] Anthony Irwin was a V Force officer in Arakan, where the mongoloid Burmese Maugh were largely pro-Japanese, while Arakanese Mussulmen (descendants of Muslim coastal traders who settled the deltas and coasts) were strongly anti-Japanese and anti-Maugh. V Force operated chiefly among the latter, and Irwin would receive notes from up-country complete with bombing requests hidden in packets of cigarettes or pipe stems.[3] One of these read:

> Honourable Sir and Captain, last week I asked you to be bombing X – I give the position of the Japanese nicely. The bombing man comes and makes very bad bombings and kills many good publics. They kill my big son and his two wives and they kill my brother and many good publics. Please tell the

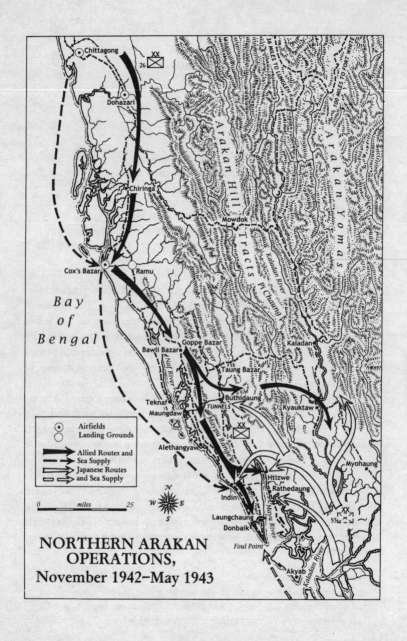

Chittagong

XX
26

Dohazari

Chiringa

Mowdok

*Arakan Hill*

36 MILES TO LUNGLEI

100 MILES TO FORT WHITE

*Arakan Yomas*

*Tracts*

*Kaladan R. Chaung*

Cox's Bazar

Ramu

*Bay*
*of*
*Bengal*

Goppe Bazar

Kaladan

Bawli Bazar

*Naf River*

*Kalapanzin River*

Taung Bazar

Buthidaung

Kyauktaw

Teknaf

TUNNELS

Maungdaw

*Mayu Range*

XX
14

Alethangyaw

Myohaung

Htizwe
Rathedaung

Indin

*Mayu River*

XX
55

Laungchaung
Donbaik

*Foul Point*

Akyab

*Kaladan River*

| | Airfields |
| | Landing Grounds |

➤ Allied Routes and
   Sea Supply
⇒ Japanese Routes
   and Sea Supply

0          miles          25

N
W ✦ E
S

# NORTHERN ARAKAN
# OPERATIONS,
## November 1942–May 1943

bombing man to come again, but now to bomb nicely. For which I ever
pray and successful British come quickly to ease the terrible sufferings of the
publics – Marlovi Haddi.[4]

As Irwin noted, there was no complaint about his grievous loss: no attempt
to deceive by saying no more bombs needed; just a mild reproach that the
airmen should 'bomb nicely'.

The Special Operations Executive (SOE⋆) mission in the Far East was
known as GS I(k) until 16 March 1944, when it adopted the title Force
136.[5] It aimed to provide long-range strategic and political intelligence
throughout South-East Asia, and to organize local resistance groups
against the Japanese. In the far north one of the Americans' first steps was
to set up an air warning system to protect the Dinjan area in connection
with 51st Fighter Group. KC8 comprised ten men with a V Force detachment of Assam Rifles and was one of seven such teams. Its intended location was Shingbwiyang, but when it was learned the Japanese were there
it instead set up at Hkalak Ga around 1 November 1942 and operated for
several months giving warning of Japanese air activity, including a major
attack on the Dinjan sector by forty-six Japanese planes, which was successfully intercepted and shot up. They also made friends with the Kachins
and Nagas but in March heard the Japanese were planning an attack and
in early April they moved out.[6] The OSS activated Detachment 101 on
14 April 1942 under Carl F. Eifler, an old acquaintance of Stilwell, which,
it was hoped, would help overcome Stilwell's scepticism of irregular operations: but at first they remained stalled in India until Stilwell gave him a
free hand, saying all he wanted to hear 'was "Booms" from the Burmese
jungle'.[7] The head of OSS, 'Wild Bill' Donovan, told Eifler his unit would
conduct a wide range of clandestine operations – espionage, sabotage,
escape and evasion, guerrilla warfare – and he recruited a small team of
specialists and trainers, but they learned only after they arrived in Karachi
that their principal area of operations would be Burma.[8] They moved to
Assam in October and deployed the first operational group in December
while seeking recruits in refugee camps in India. They also recruited
agents in Burma, including two Irish Catholic priests, Father James Stuart
and Father Denis MacAllindon, who became legendary within the organization.[9] Through these various groups by mid-1943 the Allies had a reasonable intelligence network. But they all regarded each other with some

⋆ A branch of the Political Warfare Directorate of the Ministry of Economic Warfare, with
headquarters in London and a branch office in Calcutta, it was for all practical purposes
autonomous of the military.

suspicion, while Regulars often dismissed them wholesale as 'skulduggery rackets'.[10]

On 17 September 1942 Wavell issued an operational directive to Irwin at Eastern Army to begin improving communications, with the aim of retaking Burma and opening the Burma Road as soon as possible; immediate objectives included Akyab island and upper Arakan, for which an all-weather road from Chittagong to Cox's Bazar was required, followed by steady infiltration down the Arakan coast.[11] Stretching from the Naf estuary on the borders of Chittagong to within some 90 miles of Cape Negrais, Arakan was highly malarial and infested with the most virulent type of mosquito. The hills and coastal strip were heavily intersected with *chaungs* and tidal creeks, often many miles long, and what few landing points these provided were heavily defended by the Japanese, there being no beaches between Akyab and Taungup. The coastal sector of paddy and mangrove swamp between the Bay of Bengal and the foothills of the Mayu range was up to 2 miles wide, narrowing to just a few hundred yards at Donbaik. The Mayu range itself rises to 2,000 feet and its steep, jungle-covered slopes provided a formidable barrier to movement in any direction. It dominated the Mayu valley, consisting of flat paddy and swamp, as did the Kaladan valley some 30 miles to the east. On the landward side of the range was the Upper Mayu or Kalapanzin valley, whose only motorable access to the coast was a disused railway track built in the 1890s to carry goods from Buthidaung inland from the little port of Maungdaw, featuring two tunnels that would become a battlefield. Slightly to the north was a pack-horse trail winding over Ngakyedauk Pass (soon universally anglicized to 'Okeydoke'). Annual rainfall of up to 200 inches made vast areas impassable, especially during monsoon, but also allowed country boats and *khishtis* to operate widely with regard to tides and flash-flooding.[12]

The original plans to recapture Akyab, code-named Nibble and Canny, involved 14th Indian Division under Major-General Wilfred Lloyd advancing along the Mayu peninsula combined with a seaborne landing by 6th Brigade from British 2nd Division, which had been trained and equipped for combined operations. But lack of naval units meant the latter was cancelled. Slim's XV Corps, protecting the Hooghly river with an improvised assortment of steamers armed with Maxim guns and other antiquated weaponry, was also responsible for support to the civil power and lines of communication, but Irwin ignored his headquarters entirely for the offensive.[13] The first ground move towards Arakan began with 1st/15th Punjab Regiment occupying the villages of Maungdaw and Buthidaung – linked by the only road in the entire region capable of taking mechanical transport – without opposition by 17 October 1942. Irwin strengthened 14th Indian Division before allowing it to proceed so that it now consisted of four brigades: 47th, 55th, 88th and 123rd Indian Infantry Brigades. For these communications relied on sea links between Cox's Bazar and Chittagong and a mixture of animal transport, sampans and a few 15 cwt. lorries beyond it. They were perhaps fortunate, therefore, to find Buthidaung and Maungdaw abandoned. The next stage would be Foul Point and Rathedaung, but now 6th Brigade arrived, not under command except for administration, now greatly complicated. Slowly the advance continued with only minor actions between forward patrols. By the end of the year 47th and 123rd Indian Brigades had occupied Rathedaung and Htizwe, and Eastern Army ordered a battalion to move into the Kaladan valley. But 14th Indian Division was now operating 150 miles from its railhead along an extremely tenuous cord, and when it paused the Japanese quickly moved companies to Laung Chaung and Donbaik to prevent further penetration, placing them in a better position with their rear support.[14] In December the Japanese responded as 112th Regiment of 55th Division was ordered to Arakan, reaching Akyab at the end of January hampered by the RAF.[15] But until then the only Japanese troops facing 14th Indian Division were two battalions of 33rd Division. Then, as Headquarters 14th Indian Division moved forward to Chittagong, 213th Regiment under Colonel Miyawaki Kosuke reacted with a counter-attack and drove the detachments out.[16] It was feared the Japanese would follow up but they did not, and preparations for the main advance continued. British uncertainty about Japanese plans was at least eased by V Force, which cultivated a remarkable network of local informers and contacts in most of the villages in Mayu as far as the Kaladan valley.[17]

Wavell and Irwin visited Lloyd on 12 January 1943 and stressed the importance of taking Donbaik, assuring him that tanks would be available. Slim objected to the proposal to use just one troop, pointing out that even on so narrow a frontage a regiment could operate, but he was overruled.[18] Slowly 47th Indian Brigade drew itself up in front of the Donbaik position. Finally on 18 January 1st Inniskillings and 1st/7th Rajputs, supported by one mountain and two field batteries with four carriers, attacked the Japanese positions; they made some progress around the village but were held up.[19] Next morning intense fighting continued in the village area and the carriers operating along the beach were disabled, except for that of Havildar Parkash Singh of 5th/8th Punjabis, who won a Victoria Cross (VC) by rescuing the wounded from two of them.[20] After failure by 47th

Indian Brigade, 55th Indian Brigade moved forward. On the afternoon of the 30th, 2nd/1st Punjabis occupied the Twin Knobs feature, outflanking the Japanese to the north and cutting their line of communication, while 1st/17th Dogras met strong resistance from a position called FDL★ Chaung.[21] On 1 February eight Valentine tanks belonging to 146th Regiment, Royal Armoured Corps (RAC), were deployed. Lieutenant P. Thornton's 11 Troop was seen disappearing into the *chaung*. There was noise of heavy fighting, followed by silence.[22] Attacks were repeated the next day and two prisoners taken – the first of the campaign – named Japanese PoWs No.1 and No.2.[23] By 3 February the situation had quietened, and while a reorganization took place 123rd Indian Brigade attacked at Rathedaung but was bloodily repulsed.[24] Under aerial attack the following day Lance-Corporal Fujida confided in his diary:

> We, while the bombs are falling act as though we were all dead – nobody says a word. It is only after the raid that there is laughing and chatter. Today is the last day of the year of the old calendar and in Japan there must be light and gaiety over new year's celebrations, but here in these dark holes in the ground how can we have any new year's spirit? Instead we pass the night listening to the sound of bombs.[25]

The attack at Donbaik was renewed on 18 February with strong artillery support, but although some men of 1st Inniskillings reached the *chaung*, it was again bloody and abortive.[26] Already the advance had reached its southernmost limit.

Communications remained a nightmare. Administration in war, as in peacetime, is the management of people and material, but with added complications; the physical environment and enemy efforts to make it as difficult as possible compound communications problems. If laying telephone line in jungle were not difficult enough already, all equipment had to be mule- or man-packed.[27] Radio equipment was sensitive to the humidity, which caused mould and fungus, destroying insulation, while atmospheric interference was particularly bad in April and May. Battery recharging was difficult, often done at the rear and batteries then brought forward to reduce engine sounds and raised demand for hand generators. Tropical proofing of equipment and waterproof boxes was essential, but not sufficiently available until 1944.[28] Road communications into the area were dreadful, with tracks fit for animal transport only while the Japanese relied on a simple and effective system based largely on impressed local and water transport. 'Sea trucks' were widely used, a loose term applied to ves-

★ Forward-Defended Locality

sels of many types and especially relied on in Burma. Many were sailing craft, often fitted with auxiliary engines and, because most of them sported lug-sails, known universally as 'luggers' to the Allies. Around 45 per cent of Japanese merchantmen in Burma were of this type.[29] At this stage British coastal forces were sparse: Headquarters Coastal Force at Trombay, near Bombay, had bases around the coast, the nearest one of which was Chittagong, from where some inshore craft operated – 'Wavell's Navy'. Officers were from the Royal Navy and Royal Indian Navy, with Indian ratings or drawn from the South African Naval Force, Royal Australian and Royal New Zealand Navies and the Burma RNVR. On 28 February they shot up a Japanese paddle-steamer and picked up five surprised survivors including a warrant officer, the start of a long campaign in the creeks and *chaungs*.[30]

As February drew to a close, Wavell was now completely out of touch with the situation but, under immense pressure to secure victory at practically any cost, demanded increased effort.[31] His exhortations only compounded existing problems as 26th Indian Division was ordered to Arakan and on the 24th 71st Indian Brigade relieved 55th at Donbaik while 47th deployed in the area astride the Mayu range to cover its flank. Thus command problems were piling up on Lloyd as 14th Indian Division now controlled five brigades with another *en route*, plus the Kaladan detachment and a 150-mile line of communications, not helped by Irwin's constant interference in detail. Early in March it became apparent the Japanese were building up in the Kaladan valley as 112th Regiment began to threaten the Indian forces in the Mayu peninsula and valley. Colonel Tanahashi Seizo, commanding 112th Regiment, proposed to Lieutenant-General Koga Takeshi of 55th Division, whose Headquarters was now at Akyab, that they should outflank and attack Rathedaung, and, in spite of the small number of troops available – there were still only six Japanese battalions in Arakan – Koga was determined to make the most of his opportunities. Tanahashi made his preparations with some reinforcements at the end of the month, and started forward on 7 March.[32] Japanese defensive tactics had been extremely aggressive, enabling them to defy a far stronger enemy and maintain their sense of superiority over Anglo-Indian forces. Furthermore, their operational ability to mix and match units from different formations according to task encouraged a tendency to exaggerate their numbers. Now, as the British prepared to batter at the block on the coast, they were once more ready to engage in their favoured offensive tactic of envelopment. At this stage of the war it was clear that the Japanese were better trained and seasoned than the Allies, especially war-raised Indian units.

'One could stare at the Jap line for hours on end with binoculars', noted a Jat Regiment officer, 'and scarcely see a thing move or a leaf displaced.'[33]

On 13 March they reacted quickly to the British withdrawal of the detachment in the Kaladan valley which exposed 55th Indian Brigade's flank, and heavy fighting broke out at Htizwe. Despite strong resistance by 2nd/1st Punjabis and 8th/6th Rajputana Rifles, the brigade was ordered to disengage on the night of 16/17th and to cross to the west of the Mayu river and thence to Buthidaung. This they did by the ferry, losing a large quantity of stores, equipment and mules in the process, but fortunately the Japanese were surprised by this and did not pursue closely. At about the same time Japanese parties infiltrated through the hills around Taungmaw, some 15 miles south of Buthidaung, and to an important defensive area on the road south of Rathedaung.[34] Flying Officer Gordon Conway of 136 Squadron recalled that the month 'was as exciting as the previous month as both sides fought to establish air superiority. We took part in several offensive sweeps and on other days were bust scrambling to interrupt Japanese raids designed to reduce our effectiveness.'[35] The airfields at Rani, Feni, Dohazzi and Chittagong were all attacked, and by the end of March 14th Indian Division was effectively deprived of air cover. It became clear to Eastern Army that Foul Point would not be reached and that landings on Akyab were no longer feasible: the Navy had quoted 15 March as the last date, beyond which it might not be possible to use landing craft. The Navy was also busy trying to intercept the small fishing boats used to supply the Japanese along the Mayu river. Major A. S. Turner of 8th (Sikh) Battalion, Indian Engineers, sent a locally recruited officer to accompany one such expedition as an interpreter. When this returned, the officer described how, while cruising the river, a small boat appeared making for the peninsula and he called to them in Urdu to stop. 'The Navy, perhaps by instinct, did not wait but opened up with all the guns firing', he continued. 'It was just as well they did so. The small boat rapidly sank, leaving four bodies dead or alive on the surface of the water. Two of the bodies wore Japanese uniforms and they were rapidly yanked out of the water.'[36]

Lloyd had seen his formation whittled away by battle casualties and sickness in two months and he wanted to adopt a defensive posture, aware that once the monsoon arrived he would have to withdraw, as there was no way of maintaining the division forward of Maungdaw and Buthidaung. Only 6th Brigade had not yet been used, but now a final attempt would be made to clear Donbaik. In early March III/213th Regiment at Donbaik was relieved by II/143rd, which had now reached Arakan. FDL Chaung was in a dry watercourse that ran into the sea 600 yards from the edge of the jungle, where the ground rose steeply. A secondary *chaung* ran off into the jungle some 200 yards from its edge, forming a triangle which the Japanese heavily fortified with bunkers and slit trenches, while inside the jungle the *chaung* formed a partial loop known as Shepherd's Crook behind their right flank, with two high points, North and South Knobs, in the jungle beyond. Some 200 yards behind this line was another, and behind that probably others, although the Japanese positions were easily identifiable. (Having been in place for some time, the leaves of their normally excellent camouflage had turned brown.)

Japanese bunkers were formidable in the extreme, built from logs and earth up to 5 feet thick and practically impenetrable: only direct hits on their loopholes could hope to cause any damage. Brigadier Ronnie Cavendish's 6th Brigade had been reinforced to six battalions, and his plan required 1st Royal Berkshire Regiment to demonstrate against the front of FDL Chaung while 1st Lincolnshire Regiment pushed south from the Twin Knobs.[37] Between these two movements 1st Royal Welch Fusiliers, advancing on an extremely narrow frontage in accordance with Irwin's direct instructions, would capture the triangle formed by the two *chaungs*. Two artillery regiments were in support of 1st Royal Welch, as was the Indian Field Broadcasting Unit (IFBU), a psychological operations unit that proved to have alternative uses.[38] Lieutenant-Colonel Humphrey Williams, a Territorial former schoolmaster commanding 1st Royal Welch, in turn planned to use three companies, which meant 'putting a very large number of men on top of a small piece of ground but this is the policy laid down by Irwin'. Both Williams and Cavendish wanted to make a 'silent' attack to achieve surprise but were overruled: artillery preparation was ordered by higher authority. The battalion rehearsed on a piece of ground laid out to resemble the position on which a propaganda film was to be made, to be shown at home in the event of victory, but Williams's confidence was not improved when he was made to waste 'a whole good morning having to go back to Indin (15 miles) to listen to a talk by Irwin. He spoke of the high importance of this attack and his desire to end the campaign on an "advancing note".'[39]

Although they moved forward on 13 March to a position north of Shepherd's Crook, they were made to wait for three days, harassed by mosquitoes and under sporadic mortar fire while engineer and other preparations continued.[40] 'What is war?' Corporal Fujida asked.

> A tragedy – the mutual infliction of human beings, the oppression of peoples – the use of civilization to get at each others throats. Will be at it again tonight – long live my motherland. Should I die – Mizue [his girl] you ought

to have chosen another man and been happy – look after mother – good-bye all.[41]

It was not until 18 March that a regiment of 25-pounders and one of 3.7-inch howitzers fired a barrage – with no apparent effect on the Japanese except to alert them – before, at 0540, the three forward companies rose from their slit trenches and dashed forward, into withering machine-gun fire.[42] Although they reached strongpoints Sugar 4 and Sugar 5, they could not breach them. To Fusilier W. C. Smith

> it was like a scene from Dante's Inferno – as screams and yells from the wounded and dying filled the air, even above the bombardment, and all the casualties seemed to be our own. We had feared the worst but this was sheer hell and we were unable to hit back at the enemy we could not see or get at.[43]

Then Lieutenant David Graves, son of the poet Robert Graves, sallied forth with Sergeant Jones 89 and Fusilier Jones 59. 'I saw Fusilier Jones going over the top firing a Bren gun from the hip,' recalled Colonel Williams in his diary, 'followed by David who bombed his way into a small trench about 15 yards further on. To my horror I saw a bomb being thrown at him but fortunately it landed short and he had already ducked.' Williams's attention was then diverted, and Graves sent Sergeant Jones back for more ammunition and further support. But the sergeant was wounded in the leg and when no support arrived, Graves himself went back to the jungle edge where he met Williams, and was last seen falling backwards as he was hit. His body was never recovered.[44]

Elsewhere, Company Sergeant Major Martin McClane of 2nd Durham Light Infantry discovered the ammunition his men were issued with, manufactured at Kirkee in India, was useless. He got down behind a Bren. 'One round fired and then the gun jammed solid. I went through all the drills, but nothing would work. I slung it aside in disgust.'[45] It was now clear that the Royal Welch could not break through and Cavendish, anxious that they should withstand counter-attack, sent them some reinforcements and gave orders for a night attack by 1st Royal Scots. Williams was also anxious about his positions since they would need to hold these to link up with the Jocks. Unsure of them, he now found a use for the IFBU, using their loudspeakers to give his orders in Welsh. Then at 0030 Major George Steer heard Scottish voices shouting, 'Come on you fuckers, get up!'[46] But the night attack was a failure: David Rissik of the Durhams 'was on watch at the time and heard the shouts as they charged across the short distance separating them from their objectives ... but it seemed a short while before it all died away.'[47] When finally withdrawn that night, 1st Royal Welch had lost 13 officers and 162 men. Slim paid tribute to them after the war.

> [They] stormed the position. They took it and were on top of those bunkers but they could not get inside them. They stood there until, I am afraid, most of them had been knocked out by the machine-guns and artillery. As a piece of sheer courage, I do not think it has very often been surpassed.[48]

Slim had been summoned by Irwin to report on the situation, an invidious task since he had no power and felt like a spy on Lloyd's performance. He rapidly concluded that Lloyd had too many brigades to command and saw the tell-tale signs of collapsing morale, so familiar from the previous year. He also condemned the repeated frontal assaults and forecast disaster. Irwin ignored him.[49]

By now Koga had his complete 55th Division in Arakan. As March drew to a close, the Japanese offensive plan – Operation 31 – developed in all sectors. Having taken Htizwe, they crossed the Mayu range to Indin, threatening the communications of 47th Indian and 6th Brigades, but received a bloody defeat.[50] Lloyd held a commanders' conference where he issued warning orders for withdrawal. However, permission for this move was not forthcoming from Eastern Army. Instead, Lloyd was relieved on 3 April by Irwin, who took direct command of the division, before appointing Major-General Clive Lomax of 26th Indian Division, whose 4th and 71st Indian Brigades were already in action. Japanese pressure was increasing, threatening the area west of the Mayu range, where many administrative units supporting the forward brigades, including many mule transport companies, were based. Retreat was ordered on 5 April but the Japanese cut the track behind 6th Brigade at Indin and broke into Brigade Headquarters, where they captured Cavendish, his Brigade Major and the GSO 3; the Brigade Intelligence Officer, Captain W. D. Rees, was wounded and survived only by feigning death. British shelling killed Cavendish, and some days later a Japanese soldier killed in an ambush was found wearing his socks.[51] Attacks by two battalions failed to break the road-block, and the brigade and its artillery were extracted only by driving along the beach at low water.[52]

On 14 April Slim as Commander XV Corps assumed operational (but not administrative) control of all the troops in Arakan and Chittagong. Fourteenth Indian Division had been struggling to control the large number of brigades and their supporting units assigned to it and, while it had managed to lay line for communications while ensconced at Donbaik and Rathedaung, this was cut so often during the retreat that commanders made much use of air transport just to keep in personal touch with subordinates.[53] V Force could no longer provide information, so intelligence on just where the Japanese were became sparse, although 28 Squadron RAF carried out continuous tactical reconnaissance in the teeth of strong Japanese air cover.[54] Nevertheless, it was clear to Slim that the Japanese advance was directed towards the Maungdaw–Buthidaung road carrying all supplies to the troops in the Mayu range. His troops were very tired; battle casualties had not been severe but were far outstripped by sick, especially from malaria – 1st Lincolns were losing 100 per week – and the road-building units were badly affected.[55] Reinforcements arrived untrained and unfit. Travelling by lorry, though covering long distances, was as fatiguing as moving on foot. Vast amounts of equipment had to be humped to and loaded; the permanent muscular strain of resisting the unending jolting and bumping; the dust, heat, and in many cases lorry sickness; the unloading, lumping of stores and digging of slit trenches, were almost invariably followed by a long march to take up tactical positions, involving more digging and patrolling. Added to this, the scarcity of water meant that only drinking water could be provided and troops seldom got the opportunity to wash for days on end.[56]

It was still not possible to build a road to all-weather standards and it was clear that, unless one was made, all five brigades would have to withdraw before the monsoon in May. Yet should the Maungdaw–Buthidaung road fall to the Japanese, they would be able to attack deep into the heart of the administrative area. Thus it was imperative that Slim should hold the road, the critical point of which lay in the region of the Tunnels, where it crossed the summit of the range. With 47th and 123rd Indian Brigades having left the area, he now had 4th Indian and 6th Brigades west of the Mayu range with 71st and 55th Indian Brigades to the east; the Tunnels area was held by 1st/15th Punjabis with 2nd/8th Punjabis at Maungdaw and with 36th Indian Brigade coming forward. But by 5 May the Japanese had cut the road despite repeated attempts by 36th Indian Brigade to dislodge them. Now all the troops east of the Tunnels in the Mayu range and at Buthidaung were cut off: a final withdrawal was inevitable and immediately carried out over the Ngakyedauk Pass.[57] In March Irwin had been determined to secure Maungdaw itself through the monsoon and 26th Indian Division was disposed for this purpose, reinforced by 23rd Brigade of British 70th Division, whose 14th Brigade also occupied Cox's Bazar. But Slim had to change this plan under the changed circumstances and Maungdaw was abandoned on 12 May, leaving behind much equipment and stores.[58] On seeing the situation reports, Churchill minuted: 'This campaign goes from bad to worse, and we are being completely outfought and out-manoeuvred by the Japanese. Luckily the small scale of the operations and the attraction of other events has prevented public opinion being directed upon this lamentable scene.'[59] The stock of the Anglo-Indian Army and Wavell's reputation with it had fallen to an all-time low, especially in the United States.

Once more Japanese success was down to their ability to manoeuvre in close country and their tenacity, since all their reports showed that they too suffered serious supply difficulties, and in direct action they often lost heavily.[60] In May, with Slim's common sense to restore the situation, the line to which he withdrew was virtually the same as that from which Lloyd had set off. Irwin's final shot was a signal that he would recommend Slim be removed from command of XV Corps, to which Slim remarked to his ADC: 'I suppose this means I've got the sack. I'll join the Home Guard in England. I wonder if I'll find Irwin there!' That same day, however, Irwin sent another signal: 'You're not sacked. I am.'[61] He had been replaced as GOC Eastern Army by General Sir George Giffard, with whom Slim soon developed an excellent working relationship.[62]

Battle casualties amounted to some 2,500 but were greatly exceeded by sick, especially malaria, with 7,500 cases.[63] Medical problems were complicated and intractable, but a great deal was learned, which would provide the beginnings of the system of disease prevention acknowledged as a key contributor to victory.[64] For every battle casualty suffered during the period of the 1943 monsoon, 120 men of Eastern Army were admitted to hospital sick.[65] One of the major achievements of the campaign was the management of one of the great diseases of the world: malaria. This involved not only prevention and treatment but also research by No. 1 Malaria Field Laboratory, based at Comilla. Measures included the development and issue of mosquito repellent and nets, but anti-malaria units were raised and later attached to army and each corps and division headquarters. The Malaria Forward Treatment Units (MFTU) could be set up like a field ambulance to treat patients and return them as soon as possible.[66] Mepacrine was issued, first in the autumn of 1943 and to all troops by 1 March 1945, and it was this that really won the battle against malaria, although at the price of turning the men's skin somewhat yellow.[67] The casualty ratio fell to 1:19 during 1944 and to 1:34 by 1945. As Brigadier Ian Milne said: 'It was really mepacrine, along with sulphaguanidine, which won us the medical war in Burma.'[68] Once in widespread use mepacrine had a dramatic effect, as did DDT, a powerful pesticide introduced in late 1944. In October 1944 2nd Division's weekly casualty rate fell from

250–400 per week to below 50 within six weeks of the drug's issue, and the incidence throughout Fourteenth Army in the first five months of 1945 was one fifth that of the same period during 1944. The main difficulty was ensuring that soldiers actually took it. Rumours that mepacrine led to impotence and sterility had to be combated and as the chief medical officer of 2nd Division, Colonel W. J. Officer, noted, the chief cause lay 'in the attitude and lack of experience among the senior officers in formations', many of whom had 'yet to appreciate the tactical effect of a first-class outbreak of Malaria during operations'.[69]

However, the first Arakan campaign had been a lamentable failure and the state of the troops could hardly have been worse, with a large number of self-inflicted wounds which the Indian officers and soldiers were reluctant to report. 'Desertions are reported as a matter of course', noted a post-operational report; 'why not self-inflicted wounds! Much more must be done to brand the deeds as shameful and men should be told that self-inflicted wounds will be reported and sent to their families.'[70] The Command Psychiatrist, Eastern Command, reported that 'no useful purpose would be served by counting psychiatric cases, for the whole of 14th Indian Division was for practical purposes a psychiatric casualty.'[71] The division saw no more active service. In June Lieutenant-General Kawabe Masakazu (or Shozo) reported that his men in Arakan 'now have a contempt for the Allied troops and generally a feeling exists that the superior numbers of the enemy are of little import as they merely indicate quantity without quality'. However, he went on to say, 'I personally realize this to be true of the past but I am convinced that the enemy will gradually dispose more highly trained troops against us as time goes on. An immediate improvement can be expected post-monsoon.'[72]

Part of the medical department's responsibility was the provision of suitable rations, and it remained critical of these throughout the campaign.[73] In the field rations were usually provided in composite 24-hour packs called 'compo'. This came in waxed cardboard boxes with a solid fuel 'Tommy cooker' and comprised tinned meat and vegetables (M & V), fruit, tea, sugar, condensed milk and hardtack biscuits. Tea was the most important item, while the biscuits 'were about 4-inch square and ½-inch thick', recalled Sergeant Fred Hazell. But 'you would have thought it was mild steel plate that you were trying to get your teeth into. You had to break them with the end of your bayonet.' As for the bully beef, it was usually soft and greasy in the hot humid conditions, usually made into a stew called 'burgoo'. Like everything else it varied in quality from batch to batch, and some brands were kept as a 'last resort' emergency ration, known as 'working mule' and containing inedible pieces believed to be harness. Occasional American rations provided a brief change but soon paled.[74] Generally the food had a 'preservative' flavour, not improved by solid fuel fumes. Gunner W. Johnson of the Royal Artillery 'hated the soya-link sausages; they were unappetizing, unfriable and jolly near uneatable too. How we existed I don't really know. Nobody had any spare fat on him.'[75] Major C. R. Jenkinson, while in Calcutta, handled a supply of American lend-lease soya-links. 'It was a nightmare. No one would eat them.' Eventually the Americans took back 2,000 tons and sent them to the Chinese, a terrible waste of transport by sea and air as they were shunted around the world.[76] Fortunately the rum ration was generous and cigarettes were usually plentiful, often sent out by well-wishers at home and some from private schools in England.[77] Indian troops ate twice a day; *roti* was at 1100 and *khana* at 1800. Their rations consisted of tinned milk, tea and sugar, flour (for making chapattis), dhal and spices. There were occasional fresh vegetables and tinned fish but often no meat, owing to the different customs of Hindus and Muslims.[78] Lieutenant John Hudson's Sikh engineer platoon at Imphal received meat, however, usually 'on the hoof', although animals roaming the lines became a nuisance. He was always relieved to get a movement order as goats would be rounded up and quickly slaughtered. 'For half a day everyone stuffed handfuls of hot dripping curried goat into their mouths with both hands and belched like foghorns. What we could not eat we could not keep and it was always gorge and go.'[79]

In June the Japanese withdrew their aircraft from their forward airfields, leaving the skies above Arakan to the RAF for sweeps over Akyab and 'rhubarbs',★ although this did not mean air superiority in the area: the battle was roughly a draw.[80] On 10 June six Hurricanes of 17 Squadron escorted Blenheims to Ramree Island, a flight of 3¾ hours. 'We strafed a Japanese occupied camp at the top of the island', recalled Monty Cotton, 'and a ship at the wharfs. Later we carried out another strafe at Thaitkido for the army and shot up Jap supply dumps.' On 12 June they strafed Sinho, and on the night of the 14th Cotton 'carried out a lone "rhubarb" from Donbaik to Buthidaung along the Mayu river and shot up the wharfs at Buthidaung for good measure'.[81] Flying was to continue throughout the monsoon, which imposed enormous strain on planes and crews, who also suffered from prickly heat and tinea. Private Dick Fiddament of 2nd Royal Norfolks described a problem that affected almost everyone:

★ Seek-and-destroy missions, usually along a line of communication.

Somebody with a hairy chest would get prickly heat and it could send you on the verge of bloody insanity. You shouldn't scratch, but you did scratch and it would bleed. Then it would become infected and all sore. You'd get it on your head, get it round your private parts – any part of your body.[82]

With the onset of the monsoon as the Japanese began constructing defences 26th Indian Division was ordered by Eastern Army to carry out aggressive patrolling. This they did, and on 19 June Lieutenant Bentley-Smith of 1st North Staffordshire Regiment was given the extremely difficult task of taking a Japanese prisoner. Wearing shirts outside *longyis* with no headdress or boots, and carrying tommy-guns inside umbrellas, his patrol followed some natives into a tailor's shop in Maungdaw. There they jumped some Japanese, killing two and coshing another, whom they took back.[83] On 8 July a company of 1st Lincolns raided Maungdaw and occupied it for five hours. The Japanese reacted by strengthening their defences in the coastal sector. By August Japanese activity in the western foothills of the Mayu range was increasing, and 26th Indian Division, which had been in the region since April, was relieved by 7th Indian Division, a process that took place steadily over two months to acclimatize the newcomers and allow them to gain experience through intensive patrolling. This was something the Japanese did not indulge in, and it helped the British and Indian forces enormously since it gave them confidence in one-to-one action, although by September the Japanese were beginning to add patrols to static defensive measures.[84]

# PART II
# STALEMATE

# 10

# Wingate

We are the sword he forged, eager and bright.
Tempered so cunningly, proudly bequeathed,
Tested, unbroken and keen for the fight,
Others must wield it before it is sheathed.

We are the torch he lit, blazing a trail,
Flaming through jungle land, shaming the sun,
Faith shall re-kindle it, no-one shall fail,
None shall turn back till the battle is won.

'Frolik', *Song of the Chindits*[1]

O N 20 MAY 1942 Wavell noted that he wanted 'someone with a mind not wedded to orthodoxy to plan a reconquest of Burma or operations against Japanese lines of communications as they advance towards India'.[2] When Mike Calvert met the strange brigadier sitting in his chair after his raid on Henzada, the name Wingate meant nothing to him. When Calvert pointed out it was *his* chair, Wingate moved aside at once.

> In spite of my unpleasant mood I was impressed. He showed no resentment at this somewhat disrespectful treatment by a major. He began talking quietly, asking questions about the showboat raid. And to my surprise they were the right sort of questions. Tired as I was I soon began to realize this was a man I could work for and follow.[3]

It was a common reaction to this truly extraordinary soldier. No other, except perhaps Montgomery, has generated such controversy. It is practically impossible to find a dispassionate judgement; he was either loathed or worshipped.

In reality he was sometimes right and sometimes wrong: Orde Charles Wingate's character was a blend of mysticism, passion and complete self-confidence tinged with darkest depression; he was obsessive, rude and overbearing. But as things stood, the scheme proposed by this 'broad-shouldered, uncouth, almost simian officer', as Major Bernard Fergusson noted, offered the only prospect of action.[4] In 1946 Fergusson wrote: 'Wingate would do any evil that good might come. He saw his object very clearly in front of him, and to achieve it he would spare no friend or enemy; he would lie; he would intrigue; he would bully, cajole and deceive. He was a hell of a great man and few people liked him.'[5] Summoned to India at Wavell's behest on 7 February 1942, he did little more than reconnoitre north Burma before the evacuation, but by this stage his ideas had developed into 'long-range penetration' (LRP). The aim was to 'maintain forces by air and direct them by wireless', because Wingate believed 'one fighting man at the heart of the enemy's military machine ... worth many hundreds in the forward battle areas'.[6] Not that Wingate invented air supply as is sometimes claimed: Giffard noted that Eastern Army could not have maintained its forward positions throughout 1943 without it.[7] Significantly, however, he did not believe hand-picked 'commandos' were necessary: it could be accomplished with ordinary soldiers if trained to the required mental and physical toughness.[8]

Until a year earlier 13th King's Regiment (Liverpool) had been on coastal defence duties in Essex.[9] They thought Wingate must be a freak, recalled Private Charles Aves. But most of them were impressed all the same – although by no means all. Like many soldiers, Aves was the conscript son of a First World War veteran who had been wounded and he had no intention of following his father's footsteps, subscribing to the motto 'Peace at Any Fucking Price'. But, he later recalled, Wingate 'exuded an aura of power. And yet he didn't speak in that manner, he spoke quietly and convincingly ... He realigned our perceptions of what was possible for ordinary people like ourselves ... He was a great man.'[10] And they 'were a good lot', wrote Fergusson, 'though they had some habits which might have driven me to drink; I could not cure them of being litter louts, nor could I make them properly silent; they would try honestly enough, and then forget. These things they learned in due course; and indeed they came more easily once across the Chindwin.'[11] The second unit in 77th Indian Infantry Brigade was 3rd/2nd Goorkhas,* men with an average eleven months' service and an average age under eighteen. Wingate detested the Indian Army – the only troops he would tolerate were Gurkhas – but 3rd/2nd were already raw when, shortly before setting out, they received a draft from 10th Gurkhas that was untrained even before LRP considerations. Nor were they well led, since 'there appeared to be a "glut" of offi-

* The spelling is peculiar to this regiment.

cers attached from different Gurkha regiments with no important positions in the column'.[12] By July the unit had already expanded to 26 British and 35 Gurkha officers with 1,289 Gurkha and 18 British soldiers and 20 followers, including a mule train of 9 British and 11 Gurkha officers and 485 men, plus RAF and signals detachments: all of which mixing reduced the unit's efficiency when it had to learn elaborate and complicated tactics.[13] And they disliked Wingate intensely. He rounded on Nick Neill, now an Animal Transport Officer, for not knowing the numbers of his mules branded only the day before. 'As far as my Gurkhas were concerned, Wingate showed no interest whatsoever – he certainly didn't ask what anyone's number was!'[14] John Masters, who later commanded a Chindit brigade, wrote: 'I believe Wingate lacked humanity. He thought in great terms, and worked for great ends, among great men. For that huge majority which is less than great he had little sympathy.'[15]

The brigade was organized into two groups and seven columns (numbered 1–8, less No. 6, which was broken up to replace casualties lost in training), each of about 400 men. Each column comprised three rifle platoons and a support platoon with two 3-inch mortars and two Vickers medium machine-guns, a mule transport platoon and RAF air liaison detachment. Also attached were a sabotage platoon of engineers and selected infantry and a platoon from 2nd Burma Rifles – reorganized as a reconnaissance unit in ten platoons, each 40 strong. It was they who formed the eyes and ears of the columns.[16] Wingate's concept of operations was for columns to march independently carrying a week's supplies, be resupplied by air drop and concentrate as required for specific tasks. Security would be provided by the difficulty the Japanese would have in finding the columns in the forests.

Training was certainly infused with Wingate's personality. Lieutenant Philip Stibbé, of a reinforcement draft from the Royal Sussex Regiment, recalled a 'constant stream of orders, pamphlets, information, encouragement and invective' from Brigade Headquarters. 'Everything was to be done at the double. Everyone must eat at least one raw onion a day. Only shorts should be worn when it was raining.'[17] The training was hard, particularly for men not used to such vigorous work. 'We did long marches', recalled Aves, 'all through the night. We had bad and inadequate food. The monsoon started. We were never dry, night or day. There were mud holes 4 or 5 feet deep.'[18] Not surprisingly, many went sick. Within weeks 70 per cent of the men were on, or trying to get on to, the sick list. 'Certain measures' were taken, wrote Wingate cryptically, and with the co-operation of the doctors the figure was reduced to less than 3 per cent by the end of training, though in the process Wingate fell foul of the medical staff.[19] All the doctors, according to Captain John Lawson, 'thought Wingate was mentally unstable. We couldn't write it down, of course, but we all agreed amongst ourselves. We couldn't understand why he was kept on.'[20] Another serious concern was the rations. They were living on what were supposed to be emergency rations for parachutists and commandos involved in short operations: 12 oz. of 'shakpura' – a hardtack biscuit of which Wingate was extremely fond, although another problem that perturbed him was the poor dental state of his men (fortunately they could be ground into porridge) – 2 oz. of cheese, 9 oz. of compressed almonds or raisins and 1 oz. of acid drops or chocolate, with tea, milk powder and sugar.[21] Wingate intended this should be supplemented by whatever could be purchased or hunted along the way, but purchase would mean entering Burmese villages, and that and hunting would both slow movement and impede security. Wingate also developed a partiality for buffalo milk and he was supplied by four animals kept at Brigade Headquarters.

Eventually over 200 men and many officers were sifted from the ranks of 13th King's and replaced by drafts from across India. 'We had toughened up considerably', recalled Sergeant Arthur Willshaw, a volunteer RAF radio operator. 'Flabby flesh had disappeared, chests had filled out, muscles developed where only outlines existed before and we began to glory in a new feeling of self-reliance that was so important in the coming task.'[22] But however physically hard, technically the training was not all that it should have been. Although Wingate ordered that non-swimmers* were to be taken in hand and taught to swim at least 50 yards, he seemingly did not ensure this was done. Nick Neill had received only rudimentary training before joining the brigade and hoped to get more. 'I did not. I was 21 years old and untrained in charge of 50 equally inept young Gurkhas ... We were badly trained, badly led, and the plans were over-optimistic.'[23] And the nature of the operation meant that casualties would have to be left behind if they could not walk, although this was not made apparent to all. Harold James, a nineteen-year-old subaltern posted in from 8th Gurkhas days before starting out, was not particularly perturbed, but did not realize the Gurkhas had not been told. It did nothing for morale when they were. Neill learned of this only as his column crossed the Chindwin.[24]

As 1942 drew to a close, Wingate held a final exercise and they prepared

* Many working-class Britons could not swim – the poorly funded state school system lacked swimming programmes. Also very few Gurkhas could swim. The only corps that encouraged it was the Royal Engineers, whose sappers received a small pay increase if they passed a test.

for their mission over Christmas. As they marched up the Manipur Road it rained often, and the staging camps were under water. It took nine nights to cover 120 miles to Imphal plain, where they stayed for twelve days, unsure as to what was causing the delay to the operation. Wavell – now Field Marshal – came to inspect them and after looking around they set-tled down with a bottle of whisky.[25] Belying his reputation for taciturnity, Wavell

> talked his head off. He seemed relaxed and spoke at length and amusingly of his early experiences in the Army as a subaltern. I think the atmosphere of our simple camp took him back to his young days before he had achieved high rank and taken on great responsibilities ... What he wanted was a yarn with the boys, and he got just that and no more with us in the jungle.[26]

However, Wavell's plans for an offensive by IV Corps had fizzled out, and he was considering cancelling the operation. Wingate pressed to be allowed to continue for six reasons: his theories needed to be tested; any delay might be bad for morale; he could discover whether the Burmese would co-operate in their liberation; his operation could hinder the Japanese drive on Fort Hertz; it would prevent Japanese infiltration across the Chindwin; and he could interrupt any Japanese plan for an offensive into Assam. Wavell agreed that he should go ahead as planned and also that 111th Indian Brigade be raised for future LRP operations.[27]

At Imphal, Wingate gave an interview to Alaric Jacob of the *Daily Express*. 'Most of my Chindits are not in their first youth, but married men between 28 and 35 ... If ordinary family men from Liverpool and Manchester can be trained for specialized jungle war behind enemy lines, then any fit man in the British Army can be trained to so the same.'[28] It was the first recorded use of the word Chindit, derived from *Chinthé* – the name of the mythical creatures that guarded Burmese pagodas – although at the time 77th Indian Brigade referred to themselves as 'Wingate's Circus'. Nor was Wingate at all pleased with the code name given to the operation by GHQ(I): Operation Longcloth.[29]

Setting off on 12 February 1943, Wingate knew he could not conceal his move for long. As a feint, 23rd Indian Division sent 6th/5th Mahratta Light Infantry to occupy Okkan, where they received heavy shelling five days later: 'Guy Fawkes visitation last night', according to the Commanding Officer.[30] Wingate himself sent a feint comprising Nos. 1 and 2 Columns of the Gurkha Group under Lieutenant-Colonel L. A. Alexander to cross the Chindwin south of his main body at Auktaung. He also sent Major John

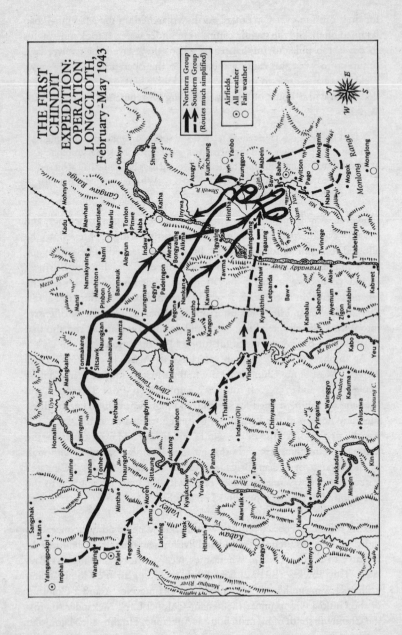

THE FIRST
CHINDIT
EXPEDITION:
OPERATION
LONGCLOTH,
February–May 1943

Northern Group
Southern Group
(Routes much simplified)

Airfields
⊙ All weather
○ Fair weather

Jeffries, Officer Commanding 142nd Independent Commando Company, wearing the insignia of a brigadier, with a small party still further south to inquire about Japanese positions and order rice and supplies for a large force. At Ta Nga, Jeffries requisitioned the house of the village headman, who was known to be pro-Japanese, and held ostentatious briefings with maps and loudly repeated place names. Both groups moved through Tamu without secrecy while the main body carefully moved cross-country at night.[31] But by the time they reached the Chindwin on the 16th they were already badly behind schedule and Wingate was agitated because an RAF supply drop, including letters from home, had fallen into Japanese hands, compromising security. Philip Stibbé was among those lectured on column discipline. Apart from the litter problem, mules (and men) were making far too much noise, and Wingate ordered the mules be given a sharp tap on the nostrils whenever they whinnied. This seemed to work, although Stibbé's own horse, Billy, just 'used to look at me reproachfully every time I beat him on the nose. He whinnied cheerfully to the end.'[32] By the third day there was much jettisoning of kit; the newly joined men clearly had no idea what to expect. 'One officer in particular', recalled Sergeant Tony Aubrey, 'had arranged himself like a Christmas tree in all its glory ... He was seen to offer a private soldier a resplendent silver-plated shaving mirror, but the Tommy replied, with real regret, "I'm sorry, sir, I'm afraid I won't be wanting that now."'[33] Everyone discarded their shaving kit, and consequently beards became a distinguishing feature.

Japanese forces in Burma reorganized so that 15th Army became Burma Area Army under Lieutenant-General Kawabe, with headquarters at Rangoon under Southern Army, based at Singapore.[34] On 18 March 1943 a new 15th Army was activated under Lieutenant-General Mutaguchi Renya at Maymyo, responsible for north and central Burma, whose formations included 18th Division (Myitkyina), 31st Division (Wuntho) and 56th Division (Maghshih), which faced the Chinese in Yunnan.[35] At 15th Army Headquarters it was at first thought the incursion was only a small reconnaissance unit that could be handled at a lower level. Nobody believed the British capable of launching large-scale operations and Japanese dispositions were entirely defensive, with small detachments holding a line Myitkyina–Kamaing–Kalewa and the main forces on the Shan plateau for training and recuperation.[36]

By the beginning of March the columns were approaching their objectives: Calvert's No. 3 Column amazed Wingate by calling him from as far east as the Wuntho mountains; Fergusson's No. 5 Column was nearing Bon Chaung gorge, where it would attack the railway, and No. 1 Column, its deception task completed, approached the railway from another direction. Meanwhile other columns were to divert attention from the railway by attacking small garrisons at Pinbon and Pinlebu when setbacks occurred. No. 4 Column under Major George Bromhead – a descendant of Gonville Bromhead, who won the VC at Rorke's Drift – was ambushed. 'Without warning, every possible type of weapon seemed to open up on us. Animals immediately started a panic and there was no holding them.' The battle raged for 2½ hours before the column dispersed.[37] They lost only 2 wounded and 3 missing but also lost over 30 of the pack animals, and, having collected about half his men, Bromhead found his radio was destroyed. The RAF 1082/83 radio weighed 240 lb. and needed three mules to carry it and its ancillary equipment. Without it to call for supply drops, Bromhead decided he had no option but to return to India; the remaining survivors marched north, almost 1,000 miles, to reach China. Wingate blamed this disaster on the disgraceful 'panic' by the mostly teenaged Gurkhas and praised Bromhead's 'judgement and courage throughout'. However, he was utterly damning of the failure of No. 2 Column of 3rd/2nd Goorkhas, who made the error of marching along a railway branch line in daylight, although their task was to act as a decoy for the other columns to the north and this was in response to an order from Brigade to march 'with all speed'. When they left their bivouac at 2200 on 2 March to attack the junction at Kyatthin, they were ambushed, and fought for almost two hours before dispersing. But as Nick Neill noted, the dispersal drill was bound to fail since no maps or compasses had been issued to the sections.[38] And while half managed to link up with Major George Dunlop's No. 1 Column, the other half under Major George Emmett, an Indian Army regular, headed towards India. Wingate denounced Emmett as 'unfit to command men'.[39]

For eighteen days after crossing the Chindwin Fergusson's No. 5 Column did not encounter any Japanese. After setting off to blow the railway line and bridge at Bon Chaung on the morning of 6 March, it soon ran into them and suffered five wounded, including Lieutenant John Kerr and his sergeant. These were left behind at a village with some silver rupees and whatever medicines could be spared. (All five were subsequently taken prisoner, but only Kerr survived torture and beatings in Rangoon Gaol.[40]) Also on 6 March Calvert's No. 3 Column attacked the railway, destroying three bridges, leaving numerous booby traps (usually 3-inch mortar bombs) and inflicting casualties on the Japanese for no loss. Afterwards, offering 2nd Lieutenant Harold James some chocolate, Calvert said it was his thirtieth birthday. 'How many people can say they celebrated their birthday by blowing up a bridge!'[41] The two columns then headed for a rendezvous at Tigyaing, where they marched openly into town. The Japanese had been dropping leaflets urging the 'Pitiable Anglo-Indian Soldiery' to surrender and the locals to apprehend these 'stragglers' and take them to Shwebo. Fergusson gathered men around him and read this pro- clamation out loud to show the townsfolk how they took it and was not disappointed. He also asked all those in the crowd who spoke English if they thought his men looked like stragglers and they laughed. With silver coins they could buy all manner of goods and amassed rations and cheroots.

Meanwhile the southern group was approaching, and Calvert and Fergusson told Wingate that if they crossed the Irrawaddy immediately they would be unopposed. He gave permission, although his hand had been forced by news that Alexander's No. 1 Column, which had been out of communications for some time, was already across. It was a risky decision since any withdrawal would now be over two major rivers which the Japanese would surely watch. Fergusson's column crossed by boat, but only just before the arrival of a large party of Japanese from the south.[42] Headquarters 15th Army believed the British had been destroyed along the railway line or had retreated, only for reports to arrive that they were cross- ing the Irrawaddy while, at about the same time, they learned their enemy was being supplied by air. Mutaguchi now ordered 18th and 56th Divisions to destroy the Chindits. Meanwhile, on his own initiative Colonel Koba Dai had already sent I/ and III/55th Infantry Regiment to intercept them.[43] Calvert's column was caught in a running fight and, despite pirating a group of Burmese vessels under sail, he was forced to abandon half of his mules and most of his supplies. Wingate himself crossed six days later with around 1,000 men and almost as many mules, at Hweibo, north of Tigyaing. He complained the men had made little progress at either boat-handling or swimming. 'The great majority could either not swim at all or were only capable of floundering a few yards', although he insisted no other brigade in India could have crossed the 1,000-yard river.[44] He planned to destroy the Gokteik Viaduct, but it was 100 miles to the south-east and the men were exhausted after a month on their short rations. Wingate realized, how- ever reluctantly, that he had gone too far, but they pushed on all the same. Fergusson's column was instrumental in getting a Japanese unit badly mauled by an RAF strike, while at the Nam Mit river Calvert staged a lethal ambush on a large Japanese patrol. 'We let fly with everything we had and a lot of Japs could never have known what hit them. It was one of the most one-sided actions I have ever fought in.'[45] They killed perhaps 100 but not without loss, as some later reports suggest. A few Japanese counter-attacked from a flank. 'A Gurkha rifleman fell back with a sigh before the rest of us rallied', recalled Harold James, then Havildar Tilbir Thapa 'screamed with pain as a Jap bayonet was thrust into his body. I fired and the Jap's face disappeared in a mask of blood.'[46] Fifty years on, his friend's scream would still haunt him. The Chindits' luck was running out. Mutaguchi ordered II/56th Regiment to the Shweli river and II/55th Regiment to Bhamo, and asked urgently for further assistance from Lieutenant-General Matsuyama of 56th Division, who sent II/146th Infantry Regiment to the lower Shweli as the noose tightened. With the latter and III/56th Infantry Regiment guarding the Shweli and I/55th Regiment along the west bank of the Irrawaddy, II/56th Regiment continued in pursuit.[47]

Wingate needed a major supply drop and he chose the area of Baw. It required a stiff fight to secure it, using Nos. 7 and 8 Columns, still ongoing when the drop came (including two signallers desperately needed by Brigade Headquarters). After dropping about 1½ days' rations the RAF decided they were feeding the enemy and flew off. Wingate was livid and took it out on a junior officer, whom he reduced to the ranks.[48] Then on 24 March Wingate was ordered to withdraw by Commander IV Corps, Lieutenant-General Geoffry Scoones, and he sent Lieutenant-Colonel Alexander's group a bizarre reference to Genesis XIX: 'Remember Lot's wife. Return not whence ye came. Seek thy salvation in the mountains.'[49] While Alexander and his officers pondered his meaning, Wingate issued orders for the retreat two days later, once more thwarting Calvert's desire to destroy Gokteik Viaduct before he could do so. Fergusson would always remember the scene at the final conference at Hehtin Chaung, 'the last reunion of a very happy band of officers, before setting out on the perilous homeward journey, which many of them did not survive'.[50] Wingate ordered the remaining columns to rendezvous east of the Irrawaddy and to cross it at Inywa. But Fergusson's column met some Japanese in a village and a firefight ensued. Most of the column made the rendezvous, apart from Fergusson himself and some 50 men. At Inywa, Wingate found the far bank defended by some 200 Japanese. He had to make a crossing in sufficient strength to attack them before they could react. Some twenty boats were located, with enough paddles for ten, and Wingate later complained that his men 'were floundering about'. As Major-General Sir Julian Thompson remarks, any commander with a free hand for six months to turn men who have completed basic training into competent soldiers has nobody else to blame if they do not reach his self-imposed standards. And it is difficult to see why river-crossing was not a major feature of training, given that he knew several rivers would have to be crossed.[51]

As the first platoon crossed they came under fire and suffered losses. The native boatmen deserted, and 1,000 men would take two days to cross the river even without enemy interference. Wingate reported later that he held a conference and decided to disperse, although Nick Neill's recollection was somewhat different. 'I saw a group led by Wingate in a huge solar topi and his enormous beard, his eyes staring. As he passed me, he shouted, "Disperse, disperse, get back to India." Those were his exact words. I thought the man had gone stark staring mad.'[52] They broke into small groups following a final supply drop. Rations on the return amounted to occasional chunks of buffalo meat, possibly python, and rice – endless rice. Every single time it was issued, recalled Calvert, one Cockney private said: '"Turned out rice again, ain't it?" It sounds flat and silly now, but at the time it never failed to raise a laugh.'[53]

The group already on the west bank soon dispersed, including Aves, who went in a party of twelve led by an officer wending from village to village, where they were well treated, with one exception; they left hurriedly and later heard a party ahead of them had been attacked by the Japanese there.[54] By no means all the dispersed groups had so straightforward a journey to safety. Thilbahadur Thapa of 3rd/2nd Goorkhas was in a group of six muleteers.

> One of them was my wife's elder brother. I had a compass. We found wood-apples and ate them. There was nothing else. Later we killed and ate deer. We lived off the land. We tried nettles but they made us piss many times during the night, always hot. We moved like that for three months. Sometimes we slept in trees and sometimes on the ground, where possible in caves.[55]

They were betrayed to the Japanese by Burmese villagers, one of whom killed Thilbahadur's brother-in-law with a *dah*. Major Ken Giles led 150 men of No. 7 Column to China and was flown back to India. Lieutenant Robin Painter had become separated from his column while leading a patrol and also decided to head out via China, which was closer than India. Led by a Burma Rifles guide, his party reached a Kachin village after eight days and bought food, but the following two weeks

> became a struggle to keep going and survive. My memories of this awful period are extremely vague. I remember a succession of agonizing marches through jungle and up and down very steep slopes by day and complete exhaustion felt in each bivouac – and especially I remember the fight against and the fear of sleep on those occasions when it was my turn for three hours on picquet duty.[56]

But the Karen, Kachin and Gurkha members of his party helped him to Lunglin, from where they flew back to India.

Without 2nd Burma Rifles the expedition would have been impossible. Wingate said: 'I have never had under my command in the Field as good a body of men.'[57] It was they who approached villages to buy provisions and, when this was not possible, showed their British and Gurkha comrades how to forage in the jungle. None deserted to return home: a lance-naik and rifleman isolated on the east bank of the Irrawaddy made their way over the difficult terrain and a great distance to Assam rather than return home. On another occasion when a rifleman met an old friend from his village, he told his officer: 'I am next door to my wife and family. I just want to send a message by this man to say that I am happy and in good health.'[58] Most marched to Fort Hertz, although Lieutenant-Colonel L. G. Wheeler was killed on the way.

One Gurkha got back to British lines clutching a map he swore had saved him. When he was eventually persuaded to show his precious possession, it turned out to be of the London Underground.[59] Wingate himself started out in a party of 42, having rested for seven days and slaughtered or turned loose the mules – heart-breaking for the muleteers, who invariably grew fond of them, but they had already suffered dreadfully and could go no further. The men, however, plodded on. 'There in that blue mist', Wingate told them, 'lies the Jordan.'[60] He reached the Chindwin three weeks later with 32, although another 5 reached India independently, most of those lost having to be left behind sick.[61] Harold James and his party reached the Chindwin on 14 April and were feasted by Sikhs of 1st Patiala Infantry. 'We ate, it seemed, through a mountain of rice and tawny, hot, delicious curry. Who was the first to admit defeat, I cannot remember. But certainly, as the youngest member, I continued for at least another plateful as the Sikhs watched in amazement and disbelief.'[62] Sergeant Tony Aubrey was rescued by 1st Seaforth Highlanders. 'They say the Jocks are hard and unsentimental. Are they hell! ... That patrol were fathers and mothers to us. They loaded us with cigarettes, took our packs and rifles from us, and all but carried us into the nearest British post.'[63] Most of the survivors found themselves in 19th Casualty Clearing Station under the benevolent eye of Matron Agnes McGeary, a deceptively petite and elegant, no-nonsense Scotswoman, known as Matron *Saf Karo* ('Make it Clean'), who had been decorated for bravery at Dunkirk and wheedled champagne from unlikely sources, which she fed to her patients.[64] Indeed, they were all now sick to varying degrees. Men would slip out of life – not merely consciousness – once between the clean sheets of a soft bed, so she ensured they got up and did errands before being gradually reintroduced to such luxury. However, few of the survivors were fit for further operations.

Many others were left behind: Lieutenant R. P. Wormell became separated from his column and headed for the Chindwin on a compass bearing. 'From this time onward I counted eight days before I was captured.' On a journey of 115 miles without food he was completely alone, except for two vultures that followed him for the last two days. 'They used to roost in the trees above me at night and started off at the same time as I did in the morning. I remember at the time it tickled my sense of humour.' He finally stumbled into a Japanese section, who saved his life, 'because I'd very nearly "had it" by this time.'[65] Philip Stibbé had been wounded and spent the rest of the war in Rangoon gaol, but not before his life was saved by Maung Tun, a Burma Rifleman who volunteered to stay with him and was tortured and killed by the Japanese for refusing to reveal Stibbé's whereabouts. 'I cannot put into words what I feel about this man', he later wrote.

> His utter unselfishness in volunteering to stay behind with me, his devotion in looking after me so well and, finally, his matchless courage in facing torment and death rather than betray me to the enemy – these are things I cannot trust myself to speak of even today. I can never be worthy of the sacrifice he made but, as long as I live, it shall always have the feeling that my life is not my own, and the memory of Maung Tun will inspire me to the end of my days.[66]

There had been about 450 battle casualties, and 120 Kachins and Shans were given permission to remain in their home areas, but of some 3,000 in his brigade who crossed the Chindwin only 2,182 returned, including 384 from 721 men of 13th King's, another 71 of whom survived captivity.

The achievements of the Chindits have long been debated. 'The strategic value of the operation', according to the Indian official history, 'was nil.'[67] Bernard Fergusson admitted not much tangible was achieved, and that what there was 'became distorted in the glare of publicity soon after our return. We blew up bits of a railway, which did not take long to repair [approximately four weeks]; we gathered some useful intelligence; we distracted the Japanese from some minor operations, and possibly some bigger ones ... we proved it was possible to maintain a force by supply dropping alone.'[68] The history of 2nd Goorkhas was far more blunt: 'Never have so many marched so far for so little.'[69] But with failure in Arakan, Longcloth took on new significance as propaganda. On 20 May the public relations people at GHQ(I) unveiled Wingate at a press conference: standing room only. British and American front pages splashed accounts of what Reuters called 'The British Ghost Army'. It was the same day that Alaric Jacob's piece using 'Chindit' appeared in the *Daily Express*, and the *Daily Mail* referred to Wingate as 'Clive of Burma'.[70]

Perhaps the publicity went to his head. Mike Calvert noted that Wingate's thinking was now significantly different: 'When Long Range Penetration is used again,' he said, 'it must be on the greatest scale possible and must lay an essential part in the re-conquest.'[71] Auchinleck, now Commander-in-Chief India, with Wavell having been made Viceroy, was more circumspect. LRP must be considered in proper perspective, he wrote. 'They are detachments from the main forces and their operations must be governed by the same principles as for all other detachments. They are of value if they contain superior forces away from the main effort, or if their operations, offensive or defensive, have an effect on the enemy's conduct of the main battle.' Bearing this in mind, he continued, they should be small and their commanders' actions clearly directed to support the main effort. Auchinleck had experience of special forces operations in the Middle East, where they had some success, but he stressed that they should not be allowed to grow too large or to become 'private armies' with their own strategic agenda.[72] However, Wingate had caught the attention of Churchill, and the prime minister was all too susceptible to such schemes.

Some of Wingate's supporters claim that he alone showed that the Japanese were beatable, but others had already noted the same thing. Ironically, given their propensity for practising bayonet fighting on prisoners, it was already known that the Japanese greatly feared the bayonet, and it was one of few tactics that would make them run.[73] Despite its being clear to all who took part that sickness would necessarily result in their being left behind with, hopefully, friendly villagers, the inability to evacuate casualties was recognized as a defect in LRP organization and remedied for future operations.[74] Certainly not all the lessons learned were correct ones. In his post-operation report Wingate noted that against advice from the Remount Directorate, the bullock company he raised proved effective. The eighty animals he purchased in the central provinces swam the Irrawaddy and carried loads on the east bank and provided walking rations; eventually they were all eaten. However, as No. 4 Column war diary noted, their maximum speed was 2 miles per hour and the bullock party always arrived in camp three or four hours after the rest. One night the column camped, awoke and prepared to leave, and the bullock party did not even arrive until two hours later.[75]

However, a very significant incident had occurred. A 31 Squadron

Dakota flown by Flying Officer Michael Vlasto evacuated 17 Chindit casualties after landing in a small clearing only 14 miles from a Japanese fighter airstrip.[76] He tried once and failed, recalled Major Walter Scott of No. 8 Column. Two days later he 'dropped a streamer telling me to mark out a strip with parachutes. He tried once and came round again, the second time he landed.'[77] Accompanying him was the *Life* photographer Bill Vandivert, who thus scooped a great story. 'Boy was I afraid!' said Vandivert afterwards. 'When I looked at the pilot after we cleared the trees there was a pool of sweat in Michael's lap. Was I glad to see those trees go by!' Vlasto got an immediate Distinguished Flying Cross (DFC), but more importantly the rescue proved it was possible to land large transport aircraft behind enemy lines and get away with it; Wingate was quick to note the significance.[78]

# 11

# Supremo

A commander-in-chief never finds himself at the beginning of an event – the position from which we always contemplate it ... Imperceptibly, moment by moment, an event takes shape in all its bearings, and at every instant of this uninterrupted, consecutive shaping of events the commander-in-chief is at the heart of a most complex play of intrigues, cares, contingencies, authorities, projects, councils, threats and deceits, and is continually obliged to reply to innumerable, always mutually contradictory questions.

Leo Tolstoy, *War and Peace*

TIDDIM WAS A small village at 5,500 feet and was the capital of the Northern Chin Hills.[1] 'That crazy road to Tiddim,' recalled a sapper officer, '180 miles away in the Chin Hills, zig zagging up cliffs, meandering through deep valleys, soaring again literally into the clouds. The making of this road was hardly a more wonderful feat than keeping it open against the spates, subsidence and the great landslides of the monsoon.'[2] The road was started in October 1942 to bring supplies into the Chin Hills, but the final 70 miles were manageable by mule and jeep only and had to be improved in Operation Navvy. 'Navvies we certainly were!' recorded Lance-Corporal C. Dent-Smith. Each man, from commanding officers down, was expected to shift 60 cubic feet of earth every day. The men of 1st West Yorks managed 56 cubic feet per man, 16 more than any other unit involved, which their Commanding Officer attributed to the high proportion of ex-miners in the ranks.[3]

The country was enormous: while Kalemyo was only 400 feet above sea level, Kennedy Peak towered to 8,871 feet. Headquarters IV Corps was at Imphal and the central front was separated from Arakan by the Lushai hills, where large forces could not operate owing to the total absence of communications. On the central front there were two distinct areas of operations, the Tiddim sector and the Tamu sector, held respectively by 63rd Indian Brigade of 17th Indian Division and 89th Indian Brigade of 20th Indian Division. Thus there was not a continuously manned front line but a series of strongpoints and outposts, and both sides depended for contact with the enemy on patrolling.[4] Things began to improve for 309th GPT Company when British NCO fitters arrived, who alone knew that a 'star' was a spanner (as in 'star-spangled banner'). They formed the front line until March 1943, when 17th Indian Division passed through them again, possible only once water supply to provide 69,000 gallons per day had been established by the sappers. Then throughout the period of Longcloth detachments served along the border, gaining practical patrol experience. During the 1943 monsoon dysentery was rife and the constant threat of cholera meant latrine inspections were commonplace, although the Indian troops found this absurd. One song roughly translated went, 'Every officer sahib enjoys looking at shit'.[5]

Most Allied troops instinctively disliked the jungle, partly because of the difficulty of movement and partly through mistrust of the unknown. 'They must be taught, with all sincerity, that the jungle is their best friend', recorded a post-operational report. 'It provides the best cover from ground and air. It offers the best concealed approaches.'[6] Night operations had also to be mastered. 'The night is one million reinforcements', ran a Japanese training slogan, and for all Slim's blaming 'civilization' for Allied inferiority in this respect, this overlooked long Japanese training in night movement and night vision.[7] In contrast, Anglo-Indian troops lacked stealth. 'Although we *do* want gangsters', one Gurkha officer complained, 'we also want cat-burglars and poachers, and every officer must combine the qualities of all three.'[8] Paramount in jungle fighting was the infantryman, and it was essential to develop the skills and qualities of this arm.[9] Prominent was 2nd/5th Royal Gurkhas, who, prompted by their brigade commander and former Commanding Officer, Brigadier Ronnie Cameron, developed the 'blitz' tactic that would become widely adopted.[10] Finding that fire and movement alone were not enough to cover the final yards of an assault once covering artillery and mortar fire had lifted, given Japanese skill in concealment and withholding their fire, they assaulted firing from the hip, shouting their battle cry *Ayo Gurkhali!* ('Here come the Gurkhas!'). Although the Allies had great respect for Japanese determination and willingness to fight to the death, they felt they could always win if fighting on equal terms.

After the road had been built down to Tiddim a Japanese incursion into the Chin Hills in May 1943 attacked No. 3 stockade east of Tiddim and the Kalemyo–Fort White* road. Having seized the stockade, however, the

---

* Named after Field Marshal Sir George White VC (1835–1912), who commanded Upper Burma Field Force 1886–9 and led an expedition to the Chin Hills. Fort White was nothing of the sort, being no more than a few huts and a telegraph station. The two stockades were survivors of four built to guard the mule track and telegraph route from Kalemyo.

Japanese merely fortified it, despite being only 16 miles from Kalemyo (the road was motorable for three-quarters of its length) but 200 miles from Imphal. By June the whole of 48th Indian Brigade was concentrated at Tiddim. At Basha Hill 2nd/5th Royal Gurkhas supported by 1st/4th Gurkhas tried the 'blitz' with partial success, after which it was practised assiduously and taught first to the rest of 17th Indian Division at the Jungle Warfare School at Mawflang.[11] Cameron was contemptuous of British troops and had demanded another Gurkha battalion to replace 1st Glosters. Instead, he received 9th Border Regiment, a war-raised battalion which with 10 jeeps (plus 21 from the RIASC), 9 ponies and 62 mules became the only 'light' battalion in the British Army, and one that soon proved its worth, so that Cameron called them his 'White Gurkhas'.[12] They soon became accustomed to mule transports and formed strong bonds with the animals, whose tough feet required no shoeing, and which, unlike horses, were happy on a mixed diet that might include young bamboo. They were stout-hearted creatures that responded to kindness, were steady under fire and seldom bolted.[13]

Battalions operating along the frontier covered wide frontages by patrols. One border action became celebrated when GHQ(I) published a report on it. Captain J. W. Arkell led two officers and forty men of 3rd/5th Royal Gurkhas, carrying seven days' light rations and minimum equipment, to mount an ambush and investigate a village headman reportedly co-operating with the Japanese. Within three days they lost an officer and eight men sent back injured and sick or carrying them. Then, after they had torched the headman's house, a party of Japanese approached. Arkell was beside the Bren gun as the lead Japanese, who had a dog on a bit of string, noticed the Japanese helmet brought from a previous patrol and laid as bait. He picked it up to show the four men behind him and as they gathered to look at it, Arkell tapped the Bren gunner on the shoulder. At 20 yards range

the smash of the bullets knocked the whole forward group away from us. I saw three crawling to the side after a long burst, but as I looked the gun chattered and they all went over. A single Jap stood in the centre of the nala and looked at us, his rifle held loosely and then rolled over backwards as if pushed as the tracer hit him. From my right I heard the crash of grenades and then a tommy-gun.[14]

Arkell's men withdrew but the surviving Japanese did not follow up. The patrol suffered two casualties but estimated they had killed seventeen. Now he had two stretcher cases, eight coolies, three prisoners, three extra rifles and lots of stuff from the raided village. He sent most of his group, which now resembled a Governor's safari more than a fighting patrol, back to base while planning to lay another ambush with ten men. But the Japanese were alert and he ended up playing a game of hide and seek instead, and lost one man missing. At one stage they avoided discovery by hiding up to their necks in a swamp, a typical tale of life along the Chindwin in 1943.[15]

The Chin Levies proved valuable information gatherers, although the fact that they were illiterate and able only to count to twenty made reports subject to exaggeration; also, although their numbers were swollen by numbers of former Burma Rifles and BFF men, they were poorly armed.[16] Similarly, although Gurkhali is basically a simple language, much meaning is conveyed by tone and inflection depending on context: *mathi* which means 'top' also means 'up'; *ooh mathi* might mean three feet up; *oooh mathi* a half mile up a hill, and *ooooh mathi* the top of a mountain. With a language involving such emphasis on tone and context, it might be difficult to pin down precisely where a patrol had seen the enemy.[17] With little wire for close protection, trenches and weapon pits were protected with *panjis*, sharpened bamboo stakes at about waist height. While the Chin Levies were mostly led by British officers, many of the Nagas were controlled by Ursula Graham Bower, an anthropologist and the only white person ever fully trusted by them. In 1937 she had been invited by a friend to Imphal, from where she visited the Nagas with the government doctor. Later she travelled the mountains alone, helping the sick, and soon became a Naga legend, regarded by some as the reincarnation of a goddess, although she believed this was built up as a 'propaganda myth'. During the retreat three Naga tribes asked her to take over the leadership and when V Force was formed she took command of some 800 square miles of mountains. She did all her own recruiting, although the only arms available were ninety muzzle-loaders.[18]

Meanwhile Hugh Seagrim had some interesting visitors at Payasedo. Corporal R. A. S. Pagani escaped the Burma–Thailand railway and, helped all the way by Karens, joined Seagrim. He then tried to reach India but was captured and spent the rest of the war in Rangoon gaol.[19] Saw Po Hla was a graduate who worked for the Irrawaddy Flotilla Company and served with 11th Burma Rifles until it was disbanded at Indaw in Upper Burma. The Japanese had occupied Indaw on 23 May 1942 and immediately began searching for former soldiers. Pursued by the *Kempeitai*, Po Hla eventually joined Seagrim, whom the Karens 'almost worshipped' and who, because he was very tall, was known to them as *Hpu Taw Kaw* ('Grandfather Longlegs'). Also joining Seagrim were Lieutenant Ba Gyaw, Captain Eric

McCrindle and Major Jimmy Nimmo, who had escaped Burma with Arthur Bell Thompson. In due course radio equipment was dropped, and from October 1943 they sent detailed reports on conditions and Japanese activity. It was through them that GHQ(I) first learned of disaffection within the BDA and details of the Japanese workshops at Insein, which were successfully raided by the RAF in December; they also advised against bombing the New Law Courts in Rangoon, a principal *Kempeitai* headquarters, because many captured Allied airmen were held in terrible conditions in its cells.[20]

On 22 January 1943 Tojo announced the aim of independence for Burma and the Philippines, and six days later he promised Burma independence within a year. On 11 March Ba Maw went to Tokyo to confer on details and was informed that a condition would be Burma's declaration of war on Britain and the USA.[21] Although far from convincing, Japan's offer stimulated Burmese collaboration, which was buttressed by the failure of the British to make any similar post-war offer. It was not helped, however, by Tojo's announcement of 4 July (without consulting the Burmese) that the easternmost Shan States of Kentung and Mongpan had been given to Thailand. Later that month Ba Maw and Thakin Nu went to Singapore, where they met Tojo and Subhas Chandra Bose, and it was made clear that 'independent' Burma would be the base for the proposed invasion of India by the Japanese and the INA – known to the Allies as Jiffs.* By June 1943 the Japanese Navy no longer threatened the Indian Ocean, and the invasion through the mountains of Assam and Manipur planned utilization of nationalist sentiment in India. This first saw the organization of the Indian Independence League (IIL), from the sizeable Indian population in Malaya and Burma and the INA from among the thousands of Indian troops captured in the early campaigns.[22]

At the first executive meeting of the IIL in Bangkok in June 1942, Captain Mohan Singh became commander of the INA and it was demanded that Subhas Chandra Bose be summoned from Berlin to lead them. Partly because of Tokyo's hesitation and difficulties in meeting the IIL's demands the opportunity to invade by sea slipped away. Soon the Indian camp in Singapore began to disintegrate and by December, when the Japanese finally proposed to move some 900 INA officers from Malaya to Burma in preparation for an invasion of India, Mohan Singh flatly refused

* Also as 'Jifs', supposedly standing for either 'Japanese-Indian Fighting Forces', or 'Japanese-Inspired Fifth-Columnists'.

to go unless Tokyo clarified once and for all the the future independent status of India, demanding full equality of Indian troops with the Japanese, custody of Indian property in occupied areas and non-interference in Indian political affairs. When Subhas Chandra's brother the IIL leader Rash Behari Bose took Tokyo's side, Singh threatened to dissolve the INA and was arrested, after which the INA ceased to be a realistic force.[23] Following this fiasco, the Japanese pushed Rash Behari Bose aside and sent for Subhas Chandra Bose, who arrived by submarine at Penang in June 1943. Chandra Bose had considerable difficulty in reigniting enthusiasm for the IIL, although he was able to raise 215 million rupees for the liberation of India (150 million from Burmese Indians alone). But his efforts to revive the INA as a fighting force turned to dust. The two divisions in Burma were a military joke, amounting to only around 6,000 men. In the 'March on Delhi' they were employed mainly as decoys, trying to persuade the Indian troops facing the Japanese to defect, much to the latter's amusement.[24]

Ba Maw complained about the overbearing attitude of the Japanese Army, and Tojo agreed to send civilian advisers to tone down their behaviour. The obvious need for Burmese help in this enterprise meant the military raised little objection to this move by Tokyo. On 1 August the military administration of Burma was officially dissolved and Burma's independence proclaimed, followed by Burma's declaration of war on Britain and the USA and the reading of the terms of alliance with Japan, which ensured Burma would provide every necessary assistance to the Japanese, who continued to administer the 'Hill Areas' (Shan, Karenni and Wa states, Arakan, Chin, Kachin and Naga Hills).[25]

Ba Maw took the title *Nainggandaw Adipadi* (the nearest translation in Burmese to *Führer*) and declared on the radio: 'Today, after more than fifty years of British occupation, Burma resumes her rightful place among the free and sovereign nations of the world.'[26] When Sao Hearn Hkam heard Ba Maw continue 'Now that independence has come to us out of this war, we must defend it in war', his voice sounded to her like that of a stranger, blurred by static.[27] In a sign of growing mistrust spreading throughout the country, Thakins had been overlooked, and two days later Ba Sein told Ba Maw: 'The people are starting to call it not "Burma's Independence" but "Ba Maw's independence".'[28] Indeed, despite nominal independence, Japanese control of Burmese political and economic administration remained real and effective.[29] Ba Maw's relations were far more cordial with Tokyo than with the local Japanese Army commanders, and he sent a procession of delegations to Japan.[30] Ba Maw rejected democratic methods and attempted to mobilize the country's manpower along fascist lines in ten functional categories, working in the closest possible co-operation with the Japanese Army under the slogan 'One Blood! One Voice! One Command!' But this adaptable, Westernized and essentially humane Burman lacked the genuine ruthlessness to play dictator.[31] And, lacking genuine political roots, his efforts to ingratiate himself with the religious authorities were unconvincing. At the same time the successful work of the East Asia Youth League's 600 branches in health, social and educational matters was an embarrassment to the government and won the gratitude of many people.[32] On 16 September 1943 the BDA was renamed the Burma National Army (BNA), although it was poorly recruited and suffered low morale, despite help through the East Asia Youth League. Most significantly, under new defence minister Aung San and his subordinate Ne Win the BNA developed distinctive Burmese traits. However, the Japanese habit of slapping Burmans who failed to salute meant it became increasingly anti-Japanese. Yet as the Burma Intelligence Bureau in India noted, when the British returned, they would be represented 'not as re-occupying British territory but as attacking and conquering a free people'.[33]

Meanwhile the strategy of the war in the Far East rested on a series of conferences, the first of which was Trident in Washington DC in May 1943. Churchill, keeping the political end in view, wished to bypass Burma in favour of operations leading to Singapore, 'the only prize that will restore British prestige in this region'.[34] In contrast, Roosevelt and the American military wanted China as a base for operations against Japan and subsequently as one of the four great post-war powers – something with no appeal for the British, who wanted to regain Hong Kong and were highly suspicious of China's claim to Tibet.[35] King and Marshall were both keen to open the land route to China, but the British Chiefs of Staff preferred the Hump, and Stilwell proved inarticulate proposing his case against both Churchill and Roosevelt's reluctance. Alan Brooke thought he 'disagreed with both of them and with himself as far as I could see!'[36] Chennault was called and he disagreed with Stilwell: the result was confusion. At one point Roosevelt asked Stilwell and Chennault for their opinion of Chiang: Stilwell called him 'a vacillating, tricky, undependable old scoundrel', while Chennault replied he was 'one of the two or three greatest military and political leaders in the world today'.[37] After another week's heated debate Roosevelt, supported by the British, decided to increase the Hump effort to 10,000 tons a month by September and Anakim was put aside, to be dusted off at each succeeding conference. The north Burma campaign was, however, saved and given a code name of its own: Saucy. On 21 May it was apparent to Brooke that Churchill had again lost confidence in Wavell and was considering him for the Indian viceroyalty, which he was having serious difficulty filling.[38] Stilwell had an audience with Churchill at which he complained about Wavell's defeatism and, to his surprise, Churchill agreed and announced he had already made up his mind to replace Wavell and his senior commanders.[39]

Wavell became Viceroy and was replaced as Commander-in-Chief by Auchinleck.[40] The failure of the Arakan operations led to searching inquiries into Indian Army capabilities, and on receiving these, the Deputy Commander-in-Chief, India, observed that over-expansion to meet Imperial needs had made for a second-class Indian Army. Leo Amery, the Secretary of State for India, noted the manpower of the martial classes had been exhausted and classes with no military background were now being recruited, a situation exacerbated by officers with little knowledge of the background or languages of their men, while deteriorating economic conditions meant further expansion would be dangerous and efforts should be directed to improving quality.[41] An Infantry Committee was formed under Major-General Reginald Savory, which in July recommended numerous improvements, including extended training and an end to 'milking' units. New establishments for reconnaissance, machine-gun and headquarters protection units were devised.[42] Churchill's criticisms of the Indian Army's size and efficiency reached a peak in August 1943 and had to be comprehensively rebuffed by Auchinleck.[43] Training organizations had been developing steadily, with specialist schools and training battalions becoming regimental centres. Between July and October 1943, 14th and 39th Indian Divisions were converted into training divisions, with establishments similar to conventional divisions but tasked to give drafts battle and jungle training before dispatch to front-line formations.[44] The two-month course in southern India was made as realistic as possible in order to teach 'jungle craft', which a training pamphlet defined as

> the ability of a soldier to live and fight in the jungle; to be able to move from point to point and arrive at his objective fit to fight; to use ground and vegetation to the best advantage; and be able to 'melt' into the jungle either by freezing or intelligent use of camouflage; to recognize and be able to use native foods; to possess ability to erect temporary shelters to ward off tropical downpours ... In short, the jungle is the home of the jungle fighter, and the sooner he learns to feel at home the better ... Above all the highest pitch of physical toughness is essential in all ranks, particularly officers, and the leadership of junior commanders must be confident, offensive and inspiring.[45]

Another pamphlet noted the jungle soldier 'must use his sense of smell. (It is a curious fact, but the Japanese soldier possesses a peculiar, unpleasant odour which is most persistent.)'[46] An 'operational' atmosphere was maintained throughout the course, with each phase tougher than the one before, but it was all good honest fun according to Peter Collister.

> We tramped, or rather hacked, our way through green jungle, where the tops of the trees grew so close together that the sky became an emerald green patchwork flecked with blue. Gaudy green, red and yellow parrots squawked noisily and monkeys swung disdainfully from branch to branch above us chattering with glee at the sight of our lumbering progress below.[47]

Meanwhile 116th Indian Brigade performed the same task for battalions posted from other duties. A battalion would spend four to six months with it before replacing a tired unit at the front, and 150th Indian Brigade joined it in this task in May 1944.[48]

Wingate's report on Longcloth was shown to Churchill by Leo Amery, who in turn dictated an excited memo saying, 'I consider Wingate should command the army against the Japanese in Burma. He is a man of genius and audacity and has rightly been discerned by all eyes as a figure quite above the ordinary level.'[49] But almost certainly his strategic astigmatism would have led to disaster, since he proposed to break up the army entirely to form LRP groups. Like many fanatical supporters of irregular warfare, he failed to understand the necessity of defeating the enemy's main body in battle, but his sense of divine purpose meant he believed he alone possessed the key to victory. Now Churchill ordered Wingate home, where he first met Brooke and demanded 'the cream of everything, the best officers, the best NCOs, the best equipment and a large air-lift'.[50] Churchill then interviewed him and was so impressed he decided to take him to the Quadrant conference at Quebec in August, to which he was leaving within the hour, peremptorily dismissing Wingate's protest of having only his tropical kit, and rebutting Wingate's complaint that he had not seen his wife by arranging for her to come too. Aboard the Queen Mary, Wingate outlined his proposals to the Chiefs of Staff, with Brooke noting that such operations 'would have to be backed up by the main advance, so as to make good what he had gained'.[51] In other words, the main force would have to support Wingate rather than vice versa. His ability to convince his superiors was one quality he shared with the man he is most compared to: T. E. Lawrence. In due course Marshall was so impressed he agreed to add an American unit with the code name Galahad, under Wingate's direction.[52]

Stilwell approved of the introduction of American combat troops, but

Japanese troops entering Rangoon railway station on 7 March 1942

Japanese troops fighting among the oil derricks of Yenangyaung

*Left:* In a country with few roads animal transport was often more flexible and effective than the mechanical variety, and watercourses often formed the best lines of communication

*Below:* The story of the Burma–Thailand Railway is one of appalling deprivation and cruelty on the part of the Japanese

Road- and airfield-building were tasks that required hundreds of thousands of labourers. Here Gurkha navigators are opening the road south, probably near Tiddim

The three-power conference in Cairo in November 1943, front row (*left to right*): Marshal Chiang Kai-shek, President Franklin D. Roosevelt, Winston Churchill

Air despatchers waiting to unload Christmas dinner. 'The soldier who depended upon air supply for beans, bullets, beer and shoelaces also depended upon the transports to bring him help when he needed it, to succour him when he was wounded, and to take him to India when he was granted leave.' (Joe G. Taylor, *Air Supply in the Burma Campaign*, p. 90)

Confident men of the Rajput Regiment wait to go on patrol near Ngakyedauk Pass

*Right:* Lack of transport facilities also made casualty evacuation very difficult, and the wounded, such as this Gurkha in Arakan, often had to be carried long distances before they could be treated or further evacuated

*Below:* Mud, glorious mud! Burma was a war of road-building, and the conditions in which the roads had to be made were often atrocious

*Above:* This horse is not keen to take part in Wingate's second expedition, Thursday, which apart from one brigade relied exclusively on air for transport and supply

*Left:* The Japanese were not well provided with artillery but, while visually unimpressive, the Model 92 70mm battalion gun was an excellent infantry support weapon

A ground crew rearms a Hurribomber before another mission. Burma saw the development of land–air warfare as a concept, and aircraft such as the Hurricane gave excellent service

This Lee tank of 3rd Carabiniers crossing a river at Imphal was obsolescent by European standards but gave excellent service in Fourteenth Army

The 2nd Division bath unit was an *ad hoc* arrangement run by Headquarters Administrative Branch. The Divisional engineers devised a water supply and heating system with REME modified vehicles

The aftermath of battle, as seen around the 'Scraggy' position during the battle of Imphal

was otherwise disgusted; he regarded Wingate as an 'exhibitionist'. At Quebec, while the Americans pressed for the Ledo Road to be completed in order to keep China in the war, Ambassador John Winant noted that Churchill was willing to see China collapse. Roosevelt was not prepared to contemplate this and Churchill proposed that a new South-East Asia Command (SEAC) should be established, separate from India, to settle some of the differences. Eventually Vice-Admiral Lord Louis Mountbatten, then Chief of Combined Operations, was chosen to be Supreme Allied Commander (SAC), with Stilwell as his deputy, while also retaining his other positions as American Commander of CBI and Chief of Staff to Chiang. Stilwell's responsibilities were now so complicated and tangled that 'no one then or since has been able to sort them into a logical pattern'.[53]

The American press credited Mountbatten as the most handsome senior officer either Britain or America could produce. At forty-three he was the youngest supreme commander since Napoleon; regal, dashing, brave and with a mystique of leadership, he was confident of his suitability for the job.[54] But his appointment came as a surprise. The post had been offered around behind the scenes, with Air Chief Marshal Sir Sholto Douglas and Admiral Sir Andrew Cunningham among those considered; but Cunningham declined what he thought 'an unattractive job'.[55] He and others dismissed Mountbatten, a substantive captain of middling seniority who had been acting vice-admiral for a year, but Mountbatten would prove well suited and he believed in Wingate, who would be, according to the Foreign Secretary's private secretary, Oliver Harvey, 'a good second'. His opinion that 'Mountbatten–Wingate is at least a refreshing contrast to Wavell–Auchinleck' was representative of the thinking in political circles.[56]

Mountbatten arrived to take up his post on 7 October 1943, only to find the various commanders-in-chief of land, sea and air were not formally under his command.[57] He was told by Irwin that he was taking over a hopeless situation, and that morale among the soldiers and airmen was so low it would take two years of rehabilitation.[58] In the middle of the month he visited the Joint Headquarters of Eastern Army and Eastern Air Command and offered Slim, then acting commander Eastern Army, command of the new Fourteenth Army.[59] As Slim's biographer Ronald Lewin noted: 'There can be no doubt that, from the end of 1943, the whole of the Far Eastern campaign revolved around the Mountbatten–Slim axis, and the contribution of the others, however great, was known and seen to be subsidiary.'[60] To many Americans SEAC stood for 'Saving England's Asian Colonies' or 'Supreme Example of Allied Confusion'.[61] When Stilwell first met Mountbatten, he accused Alexander of being a coward, of retreating the whole way and not fighting. Mountbatten pointed out that Stilwell had also retreated all the way and nobody had accused him of cowardice, which shut him up. Like most verbal bullies he was susceptible to a sharp reply.[62] Yet in his diary on 7 October Stilwell wrote, 'Louis is a good egg ... full of enthusiasm and also of disgust for inertia and conservatism.'[63] Praise indeed from 'Vinegar Joe'. Certainly Mountbatten did much to ease the distrust between British and Chinese, for example by immediately flying to Chungking to pay his respects to Chiang, whom he captivated.[64]

When SEAC was officially activated on 16 November, its tasks were defined as the capture of the Andaman Islands, an advance to Akyab, an advance in the central Front across the Chindwin, the capture of Mogaung –Myitkyina by Northern Area Combat Command (NCAC), the advance of Y force to Bhamo-Lashio, Chindit operations in support of NCAC and Y Force, and the airborne capture of Indaw, after which a division would be flown in to hold it pending the arrival of NCAC. However, at the Cairo conferences in November and December (Sextant) British and Americans continued to disagree about Burma; for Britain it was usually fourth in priority for assets after the UK, Mediterranean and Pacific. A 'war of the code words' ensued as various plans were bandied around. Churchill favoured Culverin, the assault on north Sumatra, which would bypass Burma and enable an attack on Singapore – the 'Torch' of the Indian Ocean, as he called it.[65] Mountbatten proposed a counter-attack in Burma (Champion), which Churchill eventually sold to Chiang, and a proposed assault on the Andaman Islands (Buccaneer), which the Americans strongly favoured since Chiang was demanding action to draw off the Japanese before he would commit in north Burma, and supposedly providing a springboard to Rangoon; but the British chiefs of staff were sceptical so it was never realistic. Throughout the plenary sessions the Chinese remained politely non-committal: three times Chiang was persuaded to support an advance into central Burma, but each time he qualified his agreement to the point of worthlessness.[66] Churchill, with his fixation on the 'soft underbelly' of Europe, preferred the large number of landing craft that would be required to be used in the eastern Mediterranean, and the American position was not helped by the excessive demands by Chiang for supplies over the Hump. Brooke believed that without far more air transport or landing craft than could yet be assembled in India offensive operations were unrealistic, and he did not believe the Allies would be in such a position until 1945.[67] Only with Roosevelt's personal intervention was Chiang finally persuaded to accept the SEAC plan and commit Y Force, only for the Generalissimo to change his mind shortly afterwards.[68]

Mountbatten wrote in his diary that Roosevelt, Churchill and the Combined Chiefs had 'been absolutely mad' by Chiang.[69] At the subsequent Tehran conference (Eureka) between 28 November and 1 December 1943 the invasion of Europe (Overlord) with its concomitant in the south of France (Anvil) was agreed. The latter immediately gave Churchill an excuse to cancel Buccaneer as he positively refused to do both, maintaining that the prospect of the USSR joining the war with Japan changed everything. This provoked fierce resistance from the American Chiefs of Staff, who expected Chiang to use this as an excuse to withhold Y Force and thus collapse the Burma campaign, without which both Marshall and King foresaw increased Japanese resistance in the Pacific. When news arrived that Sun's 38th Division was refusing to advance in the Hukawng valley in the face of unexpected Japanese resistance, it was seized on by the British as proof of Chinese unwillingness to fight, and on 5 December the two weeks of Cairo–Tehran came to a close with Roosevelt's laconic message to Churchill: 'Buccaneer is off'.[70] Although Buccaneer could never have been more than a gesture, the result was a deepening of China's mistrust of the West, while Western confidence in Chiang was badly damaged.[71] Back in Chungking, Stilwell found Chiang more obdurate than ever in resisting action, although he agreed to let X Force fight as planned and gave Stilwell full command in writing to use it as he saw fit; but he absolutely refused to allow Y Force to be used in Burma unless the British took the Andaman Islands or Rangoon or Moulmein.[72]

Back in India, Mountbatten realized the need to raise morale and instituted a theatre newspaper, *SEAC*, edited by Frank Owen with an ebullient leader headed 'Good Morning'.[73] He decided to visit the troops and ensured everything was stage-managed to convey spontaneity. A directive was issued with strict timings; he would meet first the officers, then the senior NCOs and finally the whole unit. The men would sit on the ground with their backs to the sun and he would drive up in a jeep and vault nimbly on to a previously carefully placed packing case, to deliver 'an absolutely first-class and apparently impromptu speech – simple, direct and genuinely inspiring. The men loved it.'[74] He began by noting that they were not merely the 'Forgotten Army' – 'nobody's ever *heard* of you'.* David Wilson

* The phrase 'Forgotten Army' may well have been coined by Stuart Emery, a *News Chronicle* war correspondent late in 1943, following a visit to 9th Border, but the idea had long held currency among the soldiers (J. Connell, *Auchineck*, p. 777: interview and correspondence with Ian Wilson). Another possible explanation is that the War Office first insisted the number of Slim's Army be kept secret lest the Japanese learn who they faced, and in the absence of a number someone coined the phrase (A. J. Barker, *The March on Delhi*, p. 49).

thought his visit was 'worth a month's leave ... I realized that although his brief, and what he said, was in essence the same to all, the way he said it was quite different in each case. Each man felt that he was speaking to him personally.'[75] The Indians and Gurkhas were especially enthusiastic, thinking it a great honour to be commanded by a cousin of the King-Emperor; especially the Mountain Artillery, who were gratified to have a new general ('admiral' meant nothing to them) called 'Lord Mountainbattery', an error their officers did nothing to dispel.[76] But not every unit was impressed; 2nd West Yorks thought the Supremo rather flashy; it was Slim that most of Fourteenth Army began to think of as 'Uncle Bill'. Slim had soon impressed his vision on Fourteenth Army, a vision that saw training, underpinned by sound principles and tactical method, as the key to success.[77] He also spent a third of his time visiting the troops, so it was Slim whom they saw as 'theirs, and they were his, linked in the brotherhood of battle'.[78]

Unfortunately for all concerned, command was not simplified but increasingly complicated. Wingate would be answerable to Slim as Commander of the new Fourteenth Army (while Eastern Army reverted to Eastern Command, taking over internal security duties); Slim in turn was under Giffard, now Commander 11th Army Group, whose other hat was Commander-in-Chief Allied Land Forces, South-East Asia (ALFSEA) – Mountbatten's senior soldier. On the other hand, Mountbatten's Chief of Staff, Lieutenant-General Sir Henry Pownall, detested Wingate, and he would also have to negotiate Stilwell's tricky antipathy. These tangled personalities were set in a sea of inter-service rivalries, and were further hampered by unhelpful or uninformed staff; moreover, Burma, with a barely formed industrial base in India to support it, remained last in the list for supplies and equipment. The service chiefs lacked trust in Mountbatten and he lacked trust in them, and all three maintained their own separate radio links with the Admiralty, War Office and Air Ministry in London: in particular, friction soon developed between Mountbatten and Somerville of Eastern Fleet, eighteen years his senior.[79] Mountbatten 'staggered them by saying that I understood that it was the custom to stop fighting during the monsoon in Burma, but that I was against this custom', and he hoped they would support him in maintaining the battle.[80] But he received support from Slim.

The increasing number of troops and labour engaged in road-building in turn increased the demand for rations and transport to move them. There were never enough transport companies to meet demand, and the Army had to impress vehicles belonging to Tea Gardens and other commercial concerns in Assam and Bengal. Petrol was another problem. Traffic

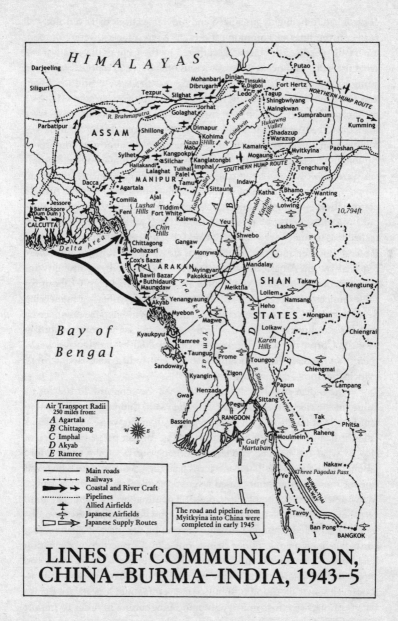

# LINES OF COMMUNICATION,
# CHINA–BURMA–INDIA, 1943–5

**Air Transport Radii**
250 miles from:
A  Agartala
B  Chittagong
C  Imphal
D  Akyab
E  Ramree

| | |
|---|---|
| —————— | Main roads |
| ┄┄┄┄ | Railways |
| ━▶━▶━▶ | Coastal and River Craft |
| ·············· | Pipelines |
| ✈ | Allied Airfields |
| ✈ | Japanese Airfields |
| ⊏▷ | Japanese Supply Routes |

The road and pipeline from
Myitkyina into China were
completed in early 1945

control had to be highly organized and provost sections deployed along all roads on the lines of communications. Driving offences were common, especially speeding, doubtless exacerbated by the feeling 'there's a war on, what the hell'. Americans were notorious offenders and especially resented being pulled up by British MPs. Shillong was the leave centre for Assam and Fourteenth Army, and this required special provost measures. It was a recognized brothel area, but the small number of MPs meant there were inadequate patrols and the incidence of VD was very high.[81] Burma was foremost an infantry war, but the engineers were almost as important. Building, widening and improving roads, and providing camps and hospitals were a colossal task, requiring vast amounts of equipment, labour and supplies, for which a chain of depots and sub-depots were created. Airfield construction was another enormous undertaking. The majority of those built were for transport aircraft and about 2,000 yards long. In 1943 it was realized a separate organization would be necessary, and the General Reserve Engineering Force (GREF) was created by GHQ(I) to build those required by the Americans while 202nd Area retained responsibility for those needed by troops in the Imphal area and Surma valley.[82] Labour for these projects was organized by the government's Military Engineering Services (MES), a vast organization set up to provide suitable engineering staff for attachment to the Royal Engineers, and came from the Indian Pioneer Corps, the Civil Pioneer Force recruited by provincial governments, and Indian Tea Association labour and Indian state labour units, principally from Travancore and Cochin.[83]

For the Indian population war transformed the economy. In late 1943 a failure of the rice crop, combined with the world shipping shortage, led to famine and at least a million deaths in Bengal, made worse since Burma's fall as it had been a major rice exporter. The British pegged the price of rice to what the bearers, coolies and other poor labourers could afford (about 30 Rs a month). The Americans paid their workers 300, which was fine for those getting it but caused severe price rises, making things worse. Many deserters rode the black market.[84] The situation was desperate until October, when Wavell took over as viceroy and began to address the problem. He signalled Churchill that it 'was one of the greatest disasters that has befallen any people under British rule and damage to our reputation here both among Indians and foreigners is incalculable'.[85] As the year's end approached, a failure of the wheat crop led Churchill to appeal in vain to Roosevelt for an allocation of shipping to avert famine. Instead, the British Chiefs of Staff cut their military shipping programme in order to import wheat from Australia.[86]

Even so, the effects were long-lasting: Captain Charles Evans travelled through Bihar and Bengal early the following year and

> saw the effects everywhere; emaciated women, men whose limbs were so thin I could make out the shape of every bone, families grubbing for scraps in heaps of cinders and rubbish. The children were the worst to see, their arms and legs spindly, their eyes hollow and their bellies big ... On the train we isolated ourselves from these wretched people; sepoys and British alike, we could not look at them as human; perhaps it was we who were not human.[87]

Trooper John Leyin's train stopped, and he saw two soldiers taunting a starving crowd with bacon fat – anathema to Muslims. 'Sickened, I could only wonder how any human being could possibly perpetrate such an unthinkable act. And these were British soldiers – not the "depraved" enemy, the Japanese.' Most of his companions were also disgusted but they said nothing, 'much to our shame. We should have done.'[88]

# 12

## The march on Delhi

The Jap holds out at Razabil
He's made a raid on Taung,
There's trouble on the Ngakyedauk
It seems he must be strong.

He's even tried for Briasco Bridge
The sky is full of Zeros.
His troops hold out on 731
Prepared to die like heroes.

Anon[1]

JAPANESE DETERMINATION TO complete the Burma–Thailand railway took an increasing toll of life, nowhere more than at 'Hell Fire Pass' and the bridge at Songkrai. During this 'speedo' period at the height of the monsoon, work continued for up to eighteen hours a day and cholera added to the horror. During the period October 1942–May 1943 there had been nine deaths among the 3,500 at Tamarkan camp, but from May it became a base hospital and the full horror of conditions further north became apparent. 'Parties of approximately 100 arrived nightly', wrote Lieutenant-Colonel Philip Toosey, the British commander. 'The sick were in appalling condition, approximately 75 per cent of the parties were stretcher cases and men frequently arrived dead ... During this time, we saw scenes of misery that will live for ever in the memories of all of us.'[2]

As early as 22 July 1942 Imperial General Headquarters had agreed to the study of a follow-up to the conquest of Burma with an invasion of Assam called Operation 21. This plan involved two divisions moving through the Hukawng valley, two taking Imphal and a fifth capturing Chittagong. It was dropped, however, after opposition from Mutaguchi (then commanding 18th Division), Lieutenant-General Yanagida Motozo, (of 33rd Division) and Iida.[3] In June, after recording the situation following the Arakan and Chindit operations, Kawabe concluded

> The situation on the frontiers may be regarded as satisfactory ... I am
> instructed to bear in mind that it is still the future intention of the Imperial
> War Council to invade India and that any operations I may undertake should
> be designed to further this intention by securing vital topographical features
> that are within my capacity, the improvement of communications and the
> extension of Japanese administration ...[4]

although he noted that without reinforcement, his ability to do this would
be strictly limited. However, Kawabe remained cautious and Terauchi's
later report made clear that Japanese overall intentions remained modest:
15th Army should neutralize the threat from Imphal/Kohima, no more.

Besides, Burma and India were the lowest priority after China and the
Pacific, and an invasion would be unlikely to receive support from Gandhi
and Nehru. Thus while the High Command certainly planned to cross the
border into Assam, and Bose may have cherished dreams of driving on
Delhi, even he questioned the wisdom of pressing further. He also insisted
that INA troops should lead since the Indian population would react unfavourably to a Japanese-led invasion.[5] But now as Commander of 15th
Army Mutaguchi seized the idea of an invasion of India with the passion
of a convert, pressing for the resumption of Operation 21, now christened
Operation U-Go ('C'). Having decided early in his career that the best
means to advancement was through membership of the political cliques
that pervaded the army, he chose poorly, joining the Cherry Society, the
main force behind the plot to seize Manchuria. After the failure of a coup
in 1930 by the Cherry Society he switched to the Imperial Way camp.

As a divisional commander, Mutaguchi, who had been a 'star' of the
conquest of Malaya and Singapore, resurrected this 'offensive-defence' to
a grandiose 'March on Delhi'.[6] He declared:

> I started off the Marco Polo Bridge Incident, which broadened out into the
> China Incident, and then expanded until it turned into the Great East Asia
> War. If I push into India now, by my own efforts, and can exercise a deci-
> sive influence on the Great East Asia War, I, who was the remote cause of
> the outbreak of this great war, will have justified myself in the eyes of the
> nation.[7]

When his Chief of Staff declined to support him, Mutaguchi replaced
him with the compliant Major-General Kunomura Momoyo. This
appointment, together with the effect of Longcloth, helped strengthen the
argument in favour of invasion, and in June Kawabe agreed.[8] The same
month Allied bombers began attacking Moulmein, and on 12 June they
bombed Thanbyuzayat, the Burma end of the railway from Thailand; three

Liberators bombed it again three days later, killing 17 prisoners and wounding 40 and forcing the Japanese to move the camps. Already the Japanese logistic strategy of land communications replacing maritime was being negated, while merchant shipping faced crisis: between March and June 1943 American submarines sank 147 Japanese merchant ships (600,000 tons or one-tenth of the pre-war total) just as plans were in hand to move from the strategic defensive to the offensive.[9]

Southern Army submitted a formal suggestion to Tokyo for offensive operations against India in July 1943 and requested reinforcement by 2nd and 54th Divisions, 24th Independent Mixed Brigade and logistical units, three months' ammunition for four divisions, and spares for 1,000 lorries. With Chandra Bose adding pressure, IGHQ approved the operation in August, although the detail was not yet agreed. Burma Area Army was less optimistic than Mutaguchi since transport and engineer assets were scarce.[10] Furthermore, there was dissent from subordinates. Mutaguchi and Lieutenant-General Sato Katoku of 31st Division were from opposing army factions and there was mutual deep distrust.[11] Sato was convinced Mutaguchi was using the offensive to further his own ambitions and was reluctant to see his men die for so vain a purpose. However, governed by the code of *shosho hikkin* ('implicit obedience to an imperial order'), he was, at least in public, supportive of his superior. But to avoid annihilation he tried to give his men the best chance of success, the essential element of which was supply. Yet the supply situation remained deeply unsatisfactory for offensive operations, and the planners had long given up hope of getting anything more than reinforcing units and war material to Burma. Southern Army planned to give Burma Area Army 140,000 tons for the Imphal operation, including 36,000 tons of ordnance supplies, 21,000 tons of motor transport supplies (with the rest to come from the Yenangyaung oilfields) and 63,000 tons of field supplies to supplement locally produced rice. With the railway incomplete, two-thirds were to be delivered by small coastal craft while the monsoon inhibited Allied air operations; the remainder would be sent by the railway once it was complete.[12]

On 25 October a railway 'opening-to-traffic' ceremony was held, which Ba Maw and Phibun were expected to attend, but Ba Maw was advised against it because a major Allied air attack was expected.[13] The railway was vulnerable to long-range bombers. It had sixty-three bridges more than 100 feet long, and shunting yards in Thailand and Thanbyuzayat were heavily attacked during early 1944. Before the offensive began it was due to provide 48,000 tons, but by the end of January less than half had arrived at Thanbyuzayat, whence it had to be laboriously ferried across the

Salween estuary and then the Sittang, also under constant air attack. Worse, much that did reach forward depots of the three divisions attacking Imphal was destroyed by Allied bombing.[14] With the transfer to China of most of 341st Medium Bombardment Group, 490th Squadron's Mitchells continued to attack bridges throughout the north, using the 'glip' technique: a combination of glide and skip.[15] The railway never delivered the 3,000 tons per day originally planned, or anything like it. According to Lieutenant-General Takaze Numata, Chief of Staff of Southern Army, its efficiency 'was marred by the defect in the hurried original construction.'[16] In fact, during the first six months of 1944 it struggled to move 400 tons per day, while bombing of other transport facilities continued.[17]

While some formations, including 54th Division, arrived by sea, others had to march along the unfinished railway. 'They were exhausted', noted one prisoner, 'and were driven even harder than we were. In addition to carrying full kit, arms and ammunition, they dragged little field guns, four or more to a battalion.'[18] An Australian fellow-prisoner noted with grim satisfaction tinged with pity, 'the ordeal of this Nippon cannon-fodder struggling to the front in such primitive conditions'.[19] Then with the railway's completion, loading and unloading complications meant it was only used for troop transport, and even then other means were necessary. Lieutenant-General Yamauchi Masafumi's 15th Division – whose badge, like that of 5th Indian Division, was a ball of fire – also had to switch from motor to animal transport and from field to mountain artillery, and abandoned its anti-tank guns because they were thought unnecessary at Imphal.[20] This was a serious misjudgement, and its artillery and one of its three infantry regiments as well as the most of its transport were still in Thailand when X-Day for the Imphal offensive came on 15 March 1944. And by the time its 21st Field Artillery Regiment joined it in early June, with the battle already effectively over, it had only twenty-seven rounds per gun.[21]

However, Mutaguchi's planning was well advanced: his main force of 31st and 33rd Divisions would move from the Kabaw valley towards the Sittaung–Palel–Imphal road, then towards the Imphal Plain itself, while 18th Division would occupy Tinsukia. But Mutaguchi was not satisfied with these objectives, and following a series of war games at Maymyo and Rangoon, IGHQ became more positive. On 7 January 1944 authorization arrived from Tokyo in the form of IGHQ Order No. 1776: 'For the defence of Burma, the Commander-in-Chief Southern Army shall destroy the enemy on that front at the appropriate juncture and occupy and secure a strategic zone in North-East India in the area of Imphal.'[22] Since a secure south-western flank was necessary and British intentions to launch a combined offensive had been heralded by naval bombardment of Ramree island in December 1943, the diversionary Operation Ha-Go ('Z') was planned as a diversion to U-Go, and 28th Army was activated in Arakan on 1 January 1944 with Sakurai (formerly of 33rd Division) taking command and Major-General Iwakuro Hideo as his Chief of Staff.[23] It comprised 2nd (later moved to central Burma and then Indo-China), 54th and 55th Divisions, plus 12th and 13th Naval Base Units and 105th Mixed Independent Brigade. The northern front was due to come under control of 33rd Army with 18th and 56th Divisions, which would form in April.[24]

When Lieutenant-General Naka Eitaro, Chief of Staff of Burma Area Army, visited 31st Division on 12 February 1944, Sato made him a parting gift of two peacocks and an elephant's tooth, urging a re-examination of the whole supply situation. Southern Army at Singapore and Burma Area Army both conceived of the Imphal operation as essentially defensive, but an advance as now ordered to Dimapur would be offensive.[25] His division having the longest approach march – over 1,000 miles – Sato also railed at Kunomura when the latter confirmed the final order and, to mollify him, Kunomura promised 250 tons of supplies before 25 March and 10 tons per week (7 of food) thereafter. This never arrived, although Sato foresaw this.[26] Before leaving the Chindwin he assembled his staff and addressed them over a glass of champagne: 'I'll take the opportunity, gentlemen, of making something quite clear to you. Miracles apart, everyone is likely to lose his life in this operation. It isn't simply a question of the enemy's bullets. You must be prepared for death by starvation in these mountain fastnesses.'[27]

The lack of supplies was, however, of less significance than might appear to Western military eyes. The Japanese officer seldom underestimated the endurance of his men: the Japanese soldier, with his effectively peasant background, was used to carrying up to 100 lb. of rice seedlings on his shoulders, so that portering heavy equipment and ammunition along jungle trails was not beyond him.[28] Now every man set off with a load 'so heavy', recalled Lieutenant Kameyama Shosaku, 'that once we sat down to rest we could not stand up by ourselves, we had to be pulled up by someone'. Nor were the requisitioned oxen much use. 'Burmese oxen were used to pull carts, not to carry heavy loads ... for oxen did not budge when they were tired. These ideas of our top brass proved to be wishful thinking which disregarded harsh reality.'[29] Indeed, Japanese intelligence services were so poor that much of their planning was based on such wishful thinking. At Burma Area Army the Chief of Intelligence was only a major (compared to a Brigadier at Fourteenth Army); nor was he called to give his opinion: Burma Area Army was interested only in identifying Allied formations.[30] Besides, one of his principal sources was news broadcasts on All-India Radio, which the British used for deception, so many titbits learned were false. And although the British were poor at concealing themselves or their dumps and much useful information might have been learned from aerial photography, Japanese photo-reconnaissance planes were twin-engined and cumbersome. Since they flew in steady straight lines to facilitate photography, British radar gave fair warning of their approach and, despite fighter escort, most were shot down.[31]

On the move, Japanese troops resembled a trail of ants, tending to walk individually rather than march, making their way to their destination directly with minimal fuss. Their water bottles were larger than Allied ones and worn on a strap over the shoulder so they could be reached while marching without interfering with other accoutrements – nor did march discipline preclude them from doing so. When they halted, they made themselves as comfortable as possible, at no stage worried by appearances, which were reserved for the parade ground. And unlike Western armies, they lived off the land. The principal ration was rice, compact and easily carried, usually in a type of stocking open at one end for pouring. In Burma and China, local food supplies were commandeered and where these were scarce, soldiers would shoot and fish, if necessary by a grenade thrown into a stream. They would collect firewood, perhaps *en route*, and when halted would cook individually or in small groups using their mess tins – there were no cooks as such, or field kitchens – with fish or meat skewered on bamboo.[32] But as they climbed into the mountains, this proved increasingly difficult as they become shrouded in freezing cloud. Senior Private Manabu Wada noted:

> Matches struck at this altitude went out immediately, so we could not light cooking fires or boil water. Our cattle and horses fell down the mountain-side, taking our provisions with them; the slopes were so steep we couldn't go down to retrieve anything ... But at last we reached the summit and could see, to the west beyond the boundless sea of clouds, Tibet and the Himalayas.[33]

During September much troop movement was reported by the Chin Levies and in October a battalion of 214th Regiment infiltrated into the area south of Tiddim; it took Falam on 7 November and Haka three days later, having already taken the pioneer camp 10 miles to the north. To counter this, 63rd Indian Brigade under Brigadier A. E. Cuming deployed

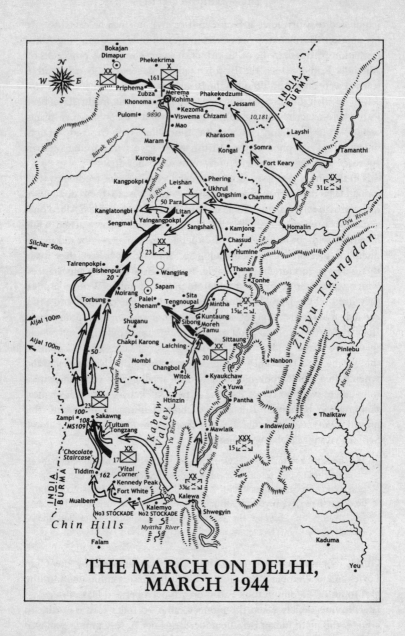

# THE MARCH ON DELHI,
# MARCH 1944

1st/4th Gurkhas along the Kennedy Peak–Dollaung track, while to the east 1st/3rd Gurkhas dug in at Fort White and 1st/10th Gurkhas picketed the Tiddim area itself. On 13 November Lieutenant Wynn Williams led two platoons of 1st/16th Punjabis to a track junction between Kennedy Peak and Fort White, where they encountered the Japanese in battalion strength. They held out for a night but when the Japanese realized their weakness and prepared to wipe them out, Williams ordered the survivors to charge and break out into the jungle. Only twelve escaped to tell the tale. The rest of the battalion, despite assistance from 1st/10th Gurkhas, were driven off two days later, and with communications cut, Fort White had to be abandoned.[34] On 28 November 1st/4th Gurkhas unsuccessfully counter-attacked the first position, defended in approximately company strength, and with 1st/3rd Gurkhas attacked Fort White itself on 15 December; but this too failed and 63rd Indian Brigade was withdrawn, with 48th Indian Brigade taking over the Kennedy Peak area.[35]

The recapture of Fort White remained an important objective, however, and with bitter experience of frontal attack 17th Indian Division decided to surround the position and starve the Japanese out. But although they erected a tight cordon with barbed wire, *panjis* and mines, the Japanese were able to cut their way out of the ring on the night of 12/13 January 1944. Although 17th Indian Division had failed in its plan to close in around Kalemyo, it had established ascendancy in patrolling against the Japanese and the Japanese had been unable to pin it down and prevent its later withdrawal northwards.[36] Meanwhile in the Tamu sector there was no front line at the beginning of November 1943, with only very lightly held outposts on both sides. The policy of Lieutenant-General Geoffry Scoones, Commander IV Corps, was to push towards the Chindwin and prepare for a thrust into central Burma with road-building and stockpiling of stores, a large dump being made at Moreh. On 7 November Major-General Douglas Gracey, commanding 20th Indian Division, laid down an aggressive patrols policy to maintain the initiative.[37] Covering the front was V Force. On 9 December a detachment reported that the Japanese had crossed the Chindwin, and that night their camp was attacked and destroyed by about 50 Japanese and 50 pro-Japanese Burmese levies. A similar raid was made on another camp on 23/24 December, but in both cases the Japanese returned to the east bank.[38]

Fourteenth Army's greatest problem had been to overcome the feeling of inferiority that defeat instilled between 1941 and 1943. This was achieved by developing individual superiority through patrolling and then extending this through minor operations that used only methods guaranteeing success.

But the time available for spiritual rebuilding was short between the closing down of Arakan operations in May 1943 and the opening rounds in February 1944. By that time the army looked much the same but was qualitatively of a different order.[39] By now firmly established in the Chin Hills, with a routine that revolved around patrolling, some units in 17th Indian Division had established bamboo messes and 9th Border had a bamboo chapel. This was testament to the engineers' road-building achievements during the previous year, and Christmas was celebrated by British and Indian units along the length of the road with extra goats, turkeys and even dancing girls brought from Imphal. Some areas remained healthier than others but, while some units had a good record, others suffered up to 90 per cent malaria.[40] Important tactical lessons had been learned: Japanese grenades were loud but ineffective and their 75mm guns were effective only within a 15-yard radius against men lying down; tree snipers were a menace and immediate counter-attacks very effective, but their tactics completely lacked subtlety and initiative.[41] Under accurate covering or blitz fire they kept their heads down and fired wildly and inaccurately in return. The Bren gun proved the mainstay of the blitz attack; if it stopped through casualties or lack of ammunition, the attack would fail and large amounts of ammunition were needed for it. Japanese morale was now better understood, particularly their dislike of air attack, so that it was now appreciated that 'fundamentally [the Japanese] has the same weaknesses as other nations'.[42]

As early as 19 November 11th Army Group warned Fourteenth Army of the possibility of a Japanese long-range penetration force cutting the Kohima-Imphal road and recommended the latter despatch a motorized battalion to Imphal, but it seems the suggestion went unheeded.[43] The Japanese occupied Mualbem on 8 January 1944, boasting to villagers they would soon invade India with a larger Indian army based at Kalemyo.[44] Mountbatten could see that Imphal and Kohima would soon be under siege, and if they fell so would Dimapur, creating a strategic disaster. He therefore sent his Deputy Chief of Staff, Major-General Albert Wedemeyer, to appeal to Arnold for the maximum possible number of transport aircraft.[45] Arnold agreed to create four combat cargo groups, each of 100 Dakotas or equivalent.[46] By 29 February it was not clear exactly what the Japanese intended but planning went on in case they attacked. With its airfields, hospitals and supply dumps, Imphal Plain was the key; its loss would be crippling. For Slim and Scoones the objective was simple: to hold Imphal Plain and destroy any enemy who attacked it. The problem for Slim was when exactly to call off his limited offensive plans and to ensure his divisions were not defeated piecemeal, especially 17th and 20th Indian

Divisions at Tiddim and in the Kabaw valley. He accepted this plan but left Scoones to decide the exact timing.[47]

At the beginning of March the only air presence at Imphal was two tactical reconnaissance (Tac R) squadrons, 1 Squadron IAF and 28 Squadron RAF.[48] For some weeks the RAF attacked the Japanese build-up. Squadron Leader Guy Hogan of 5 Squadron on Hurricanes reported they had quite good results flying night 'rhubarbs' to attack road transport until it suddenly dried up just before the siege began. It was clear the Japanese were moving up at night 'so I suggested we should go out at night, in periods of moonlight. It was absolute murder – convoys with their headlights full on etc, and we had a killing – flames going up all over the place.'[49] The air battle would be fought under 221 Group RAF, commanded by Air Vice-Marshal Stanley Vincent, with Headquarters established beside the main airstrip at Imphal, which like Palel was all-weather.[50] At Kangla, Tulihal, Wanjing and Sapam were fair-weather strips using Prefabricated Bituminous Surfacing (PBS or 'bithess' – hessian treated with bitumen) that proved excellent until the monsoon rains.[51] The RAF had established radar stations in the hills to provide early warning but these relied on line communications, since radio was so unreliable, and the withdrawal of 20th Indian Division removed this valuable system. But the arrival of Spitfires greatly helped the air balance and attacks by American Mustangs and Lightnings on Japanese forward airfields, which lacked an effective early warning system, forced them to withdraw to bases 500 miles away, near Rangoon.[52]

The first Japanese moves were begun by 33rd Division on 7 March, a week before the move of the main body on X-Day. They were spotted two days later by a lone Gurkha, separated from his patrol of 1st/10th Gurkhas, and reported by another patrol two days later. But Headquarters IV Corps discounted reports when air recce failed to confirm them.[53] Slim approved Scoones's plan of withdrawal to the plain but emphasized the order was not to be given until Scoones and the divisional commanders were certain the Japanese offensive had started in earnest. Giffard allotted the uncommitted 23rd LRP Brigade for use as a counter-penetration force and, with the Admin Box battle now over, Slim told Christison to move 5th Indian Division from Arakan by air; but there was a lack of urgency about the High Command. Scoones concentrated on his administrative plan for the withdrawal, setting up dumps along the Tiddim–Imphal road even as the Japanese, ever masters of concealment, were moving to cut off the escape route. Cowan's orders to attack towards Kalewa were not cancelled and, although he received a warning order from Scoones that 17th Indian

Division should withdraw as soon as the Japanese attacked and some units began to move back, five defensive boxes were organized around Tiddim to include divisional administration units. The fact that he did not know whether he was to stand and fight is demonstrated by the order that these should be stocked with ten days' rations, seven days' water and as much ammunition and petrol as possible.[54]

To the north, 20th Indian Division had similarly been deployed forward in the Kabaw valley and was surprised when a column under Major-General Yamamoto Tsunoro, commanding the infantry group of 33rd Division, came in behind it, heading for the airfield at Palel.[55] Gracey, like Cowan, was reluctant to abandon his careful preparations. On 20 January, following extensive patrolling, 1st Northamptonshire Regiment made an attack on a Japanese position at Kyaukchaw (showing that here at least the Japanese were well forward of the Chindwin), during which Lieutenant John Horwood won a posthumous VC after 'displaying remarkable endurance for 3 days and 2 nights':[56] this fighting confirmed that officer casualties were equally high among British units as among Indian and Gurkha ones, and that the Japanese also concentrated their fire on Bren gunners.[57]

The Japanese were certainly stirring. As early as 4 March a patrol of 14th/13th Frontier Force Rifles further south had been attacked by a strong Japanese force supported by tanks.[58] Dealing with these meant hurriedly learning to handle the newfangled Projectile Infantry Anti-Tanks (PIAT), still covered in packing grease. At least the Commanding Officer of 4th/10th Gurkhas had heard of them, even if he had not actually seen one.[59] By 14 March the Japanese had pushed as far as Witok, where a major battle took place between 213th Regiment, supported by tanks, and 100th Indian Brigade.[60] As the action progressed, six Lee tanks from 3rd Carabiniers came up to support the defenders, and during this confused action Gracey sent the code word 'Wellington' to signal immediate withdrawal to Tamu and the supply base at Moreh. They disengaged successfully, only to find on 17 March that the Japanese had got behind them, but they extricated themselves to reach Moreh two days later, although much equipment was lost.[61] 'The whole business is nothing to be proud of', recorded Lieutenant Anthony Bickersteth of 4th/10th Gurkhas in his diary.[62] But the division then sprang a clever ambush against the Japanese follow-up at a place called 'Charing Cross', where 3rd/8th Gurkhas and 9th/14th Punjabis, supported by a squadron of 3rd Carabiniers, inflicted serious losses, while some 20,000 support personnel, including 'Elephant Bill' Williams and his charges, withdrew to Imphal ahead of them.[63] But in a bitter message to Scoones, Gracey asked what was the point of building roads and a supply base at Moreh only to abandon them without a fight as his formation fell back slowly in front of 15th Division, to occupy a strong defensive position on the Shenam Saddle, 10 miles south-east of Palel. The last convoy of lorries left Moreh for Imphal just as one arrived loaded with petrol, so it appears Slim's plan was not clearly communicated at Corps level, though whether the fault lay with Corps or Army remains unclear.[64]

In early March, 23rd Indian Division under Major-General Ouvry Roberts was implementing a deception scheme called Amazon, which involved 1st Seaforths 'advancing' across the Chindwin on the night of 12/13 March with bogus radio traffic in support.[65] But it was a failure: the Japanese were long past caring. Within twenty-four hours came the order to retire to Imphal and the subsequent Tiddim Road battle caught 37th Indian Brigade engaged in an exercise – the fault, as higher command admitted, of not ordering withdrawal sooner.[66] Scoones gave the order on 13 March, although the timing is unclear.[67] To comply, Cowan faced a very difficult task, entailing moving 16,000 men, 2,500 vehicles and 3,500 mules along 150 miles through jungle-covered mountains against Japanese out-flanking moves. The Tiddim Road was strong enough to take two-way traffic of thousands of heavy military vehicles, and 17th Indian Division was rightly proud of the dominance it had established in the area. It was distributed between Tongzang, just over 110 miles south of Imphal, and Tiddim, some 40 miles further south. At Milestone (MS) 109 just north of Tongzang was the principal Line of Communication Base for the Tiddim Road. But now, instead of providing the basis for the proposed invasion of Burma, it witnessed a hurried and hard-fought withdrawal.

Yanagida's plan for 33rd Division to surround and destroy 17th Indian Division was a good one and came very close to success. It started well, with a three-pronged advance; one column made up the road from Tiddim to Fort White, while a second aimed for Singgel near MS 100 to set up the first of a series of road-blocks, and the third for the supply dump at MS 109. At MS 105 the Japanese took a dangerous position, which 2nd/5th Royal Gurkhas were tasked with clearing. Naik Sunbahadur Gurung won a posthumous Indian Order of Merit (IOM).[68] By now Scoones had a good idea of Japanese dispositions through V Force and realized the Japanese had stolen a march on him. He ordered two brigades from 23rd Indian Division, his only reserve, down the Tiddim Road, with orders to keep it open at all costs. Suddenly, the situation was critical; the Japanese offensive was at least two weeks earlier than anticipated. Fortunately Roberts had sent 37th Indian Brigade south twelve hours before receiving orders from IV Corps, suggesting that he thought Scoones was acting too slowly.[69] On 14 March, 17th Indian Division withdrew from positions covering a 15-mile arc around Tiddim. The Japanese were attacking a Jat Regiment company at MS 100, who received desperately needed support from 3rd/5th Royal Gurkhas, whom the Japanese attacked fiercely throughout the 17th, with both sides sustaining heavy losses before the Gurkhas slipped away quietly during the night.[70] They were soon ordered south to MS 109, where 17th Indian Division was held up launching repeated attacks against Japanese positions, with the latter dug in to block the road. But the Japanese were not having things all their own way; they were shaken to find themselves having to fight hard against enemies they contemptuously expected to crumble as in 1942.[71] But they did not, although MS 109 was now abandoned with seemingly no attempt to destroy stores. Lieutenant Peter Longmore of 129th Field Regiment RA 'liberated' an abandoned lorry of tinned peaches. His Commanding Officer said, 'Peter, your main job is to get that lorry through, and, by the way, see if you can match it with a load of Carnation milk.' This he achieved, together with a bulldozer, which the regiment prized highly.[72] As 9th Border passed through, they found the canteen stores, Field Supply Depot, ordnance and engineers stores were all looted without intervention by the divisional provost. The battalion rested for three days, brought looting under control and made a systematic issue.[73] The divisional engineers then blew the Kennedy Peak–Tiddim Road in several places with over 400 booby traps and delayed-action demolitions, including wrecking the water supply. The spectacle of Tiddim burning 'was a sight every man will remember', noted the RIASC history.[74] The Japanese took the dump on 18 March and wallowed in the spoils, roaring up and down the valley bottom in captured British jeeps, crazed by British rum. Large quantities of weapons were turned against their former owners. When the depot briefly changed hands again a week later, the mutilated and tortured bodies of two Indian soldiers were found among the ruins. But the diversion helped 17th Indian Division retire after blowing the bridge on the Manipur river on 26 March, at the same time handing out terrible punishment to the Japanese, especially 215th Regiment.[75] Following a series of difficult but well-fought actions 17th Indian Division was back on Imphal Plain by 5 April. After the battle Cowan disputed Scoones's report on the timing and details of his orders to move north, and in the official history the delay is blamed on Cowan. But Ian Lyall Grant shows this is false, and the withdrawal was well handled, surprising the Japanese in what proved to be one of the most critical battles of the Burma war.[76]

Meanwhile news of the assault reached Mountbatten, who was recovering from an eye injury. He discharged himself from hospital and flew to Slim's headquarters at Comilla on 14 March and learned of the desperate need for another 30 transport aircraft. Crucially, he received permission from Washington to divert 30 Hump aircraft to fly 5th Indian Division from Arakan, and to keep these for a month.[77] Over the next days he arranged this and it was during this period that he lost faith in Giffard, who had already been criticized for not moving up reinforcements as ordered on 5 March.[78] On 25 March Mountbatten appealed to the Combined Chiefs of Staff for another 70 transport aircraft but was refused permission to take these from the Hump, although he could keep those already taken until June. But four days later the Combined Chiefs sent 64 US and 15 RAF Dakotas from the Mediterranean.[79]

The move of 5th Indian Division under Major-General Harold Briggs, which deposited two brigades at Imphal and one at Dimapur between 17 and 27 March, was a masterpiece of improvisation.[80] It involved 758 sorties by 194 Squadron and 20 C-46s from the Hump.[81] 'These Daks were stacked up one behind the other', noted an observer,

> a quarter of a mile apart, touching down and those with troops were simply taxiing along and the soldiers rolling out and then the Dak was straight off again. Then the others came in on the other side of the runway with mules, guns, etc. ... It was the most magnificent piece of air transport I have ever seen. The logistics were unbelievable. They were literally coming in, rolling along and then taking off again back to Chittagong.[82]

Loading tables were issued and acted on for a highly complex move that would normally take months of planning and practice; prepared by Fourteenth Army in anticipation of such a contingency, they worked perfectly showing exactly which men, by rank and trade, would travel in which aircraft with which equipment so that in the event of a crash a unit would not be rendered *hors de combat* through loss of vital staff or stores. Nevertheless Private Aram, battalion tailor of 2nd West Yorks, managed to include among the essential equipment a full-sized treadle sewing machine, making the Quartermaster explode in wrath and order the bloody thing to be dug in immediately.[83] The only real hitch occurred regarding a vital tool for reassembling 25-pounders and urgently flown in by fighter, and one artillery regiment was dispersed to four airfields in Imphal.[84]

Mutaguchi hoped to deceive Slim by sending one battalion to move ostentatiously south-west towards Tamu, hoping to convey that all 15th Division was moving that way. In fact, most of the division was moving towards Sangshak while 31st Division was moving in three columns towards

Kohima. The British assumed the terrain to be so impenetrable that the Japanese could attack Kohima only in regimental strength rather than with the full division that subsequently did so, partly made possible by the 'road' between Humine and Kohima recently opened by Roberts of 23rd Indian Division. This led through the area of 50th Indian Parachute Brigade, responsible for the Ukhrul–Jessami area, excluding the Kohima–Imphal road and Kohima itself.[85]

Yukihiko Imai noted that it was cold and the rivers were full. Many horses and oxen were lost in ravines, and while the horses kept working to the last, the oxen were troublesome: 'When tired they would sit on the path and would not move a step though the soldiers beat them. As a last resort the troops had to set fire to their tails.'[86] The local Nagas were fiercely independent, clad in 'bright plaids, red and yellow lunghis [*longyis*], scarlet blankets on brown shoulders, head necklaces, elephant hair, ivory and polished brass bracelets on their arms, hornbill feathers in the hair, golden skin, page-boy haircuts, mongoloid hard. Their women were', according to John Colvin, 'magnetically attractive to some British soldiers.'[87] Of course, all women are magnetically attractive to *some* British soldiers, but it is nevertheless true that, despite eighty years of war and rebellion, the Nagas showed extraordinary loyalty to the British, happily acting as scouts, runners and porters. When the Japanese arrived in the area, they tried to win the Nagas over, to obtain rations and also enlist their help. But they brought a Congress Party flag, not realizing that the Nagas were deeply hostile to India (as they still are today), and worse, the INA behaved disgracefully: all cases of rape were later found to have been committed by them and not the Japanese. The only way they could persuade the locals to provide labour and guides was by hostage-taking. At the height of the crisis Ursula Graham Bower's staff asked to leave, and even she did not expect them to return. But within twenty-four hours they did so, having gone home, made their wills and given heirloom necklaces to their sons. '"After all," they asked, "what was the better thing? To desert and live, and hear our children curse us for the shame we put on them, or to die with you, and leave them proud of us for ever?"'[88]

On 18 February 1st Assam Regiment, commanded by Lieutenant-Colonel W. F. 'Bruno' Brown, arrived at Dimapur from training in the Brahmaputra valley. Brown received orders from IV Corps at Imphal to move to Kohima and then to establish defensive positions at Jessami, Kharasom and Phakekedzumi (commonly known as 'Phek' or 'Fake'). This was done by 27 February, and on 8 March came under command of 33-year-old Brigadier M. R. T. 'Tim' Hope-Thomson of 50th Indian

Parachute Brigade, which was also to hold Ukhrul and Sangshak.[89] With battle imminent, Hope-Thomson received hardly any information from IV Corps or 23rd Indian Division and continued training until 18 March. At next day's training conference came alarming news; a strong Japanese force was only 2 miles away. This was part of Sato's 31st Division, based on 58th Regiment under the infantry group commander Major-General Miyazaki Shigesaburo, although Sangshak was not in his operational zone at all and it remains a mystery to Japanese historians why he attacked the position.[90] The Parachutists, woefully short of transport, had only a troop from 158th Field Regiment RA and 15th Mountain Battery IA for artillery support, and that was at Litan, 30 miles to the rear.[91] Meanwhile 153rd Parachute Battalion was stranded at Kohima. Despite the evacuation of 30,000 non-essential personnel from Imphal to Dimapur, with much transport returning empty, Hope-Thomson was told there was none for his battalion. Eager to rejoin the brigade, they eventually reached Imphal but were unexpected and given no food, information or ammunition. After a long wait a few old lorries finally enabled about half to reach Sangshak in dribs and drabs. The following morning the lead company of 152nd Parachute Battalion was all but wiped out by III/58th Regiment. When the last survivors made a desperate charge in mid-morning, the Japanese saw a British officer, the last man on his feet, shoot himself, and 'felt deeply impressed by such a brave act'.[92] Hope-Thomson with one and a half parachute battalions, 4th/5th Mahrattas from 49th Indian Brigade and two companies of the Nepalese Kalibahadur Regiment, was ordered to dig in and fight to the last man and last round, without wire or digging tools.[93] The position at Sangshak measured roughly 800 yards by 300, a fairly bare hill which turned out to be the crater of an extinct volcano, made of obsidian and impossible to dig properly, with about twenty houses and an American mission church and, worse, virtually no water. Meanwhile at Litan, Headquarters 23rd Indian Division with half 153rd Parachute Battalion and some stragglers formed a defensive box and hoped for the best. Overlooked in all directions, it was indefensible, but Headquarters VI Corps insisted Litan also be held.

From 22 March Sangshak was as ready as it would ever be and the battle raged, with the Japanese making costly frontal assaults. 'We attacked every night from the 22nd to the 25th and every night many soldiers were killed', recalled Lieutenant Kameyama Shosaku. 'Despite that, we went forward.'[94] An air supply drop on 23 March was a failure, with most of it landing among the Japanese, but a captured map with the entire Japanese plan for Imphal and Kohima was found on a dead officer, and Captain L.

Allen, the Brigade Intelligence Officer, took on this extremely hazardous journey to Imphal; he repeated this 36-mile trip three times over the next three days. Yet no use was made of the information and his gallantry went unrewarded, despite Hope-Thomson's immediate citation.[95] After four days of confused fighting an order to withdraw arrived, giving a route and ending, 'Good luck. Our thoughts are with you.' As this was transmitted in clear, Hope-Thomson suspected a Japanese ruse, but verification followed this crass breach of security. He issued orders to destroy all documents and non-portable weapons and equipment. The wounded were dosed with morphine and abandoned (and most received good treatment). The retreat was not interfered with, as the Japanese were preparing a final assault.

Having borne the brunt of the fighting, 152nd Battalion lost 350 men; of 25 British officers, 18 were dead and only 2 remained unwounded.[96] 153rd Battalion with only three companies and a mortar section lost only a dozen, but the Mahrattas lost some 260 (100 were taken prisoner during the withdrawal). The brigade received no welcome whatever at IV Corps, where Scoones, whose inertia had almost lost 17th Indian Division, did not want to know about the fight that would help save Kohima, 'lost for the lack of a few rolls of barbed wire'.[97] Hope-Thomson was injured and concussed during the withdrawal and invalided home before he could make a full report on his brigade's destruction. Scurrilous comment regarding the brigade and its commander's performance began almost at once and persisted for decades before it was finally discredited.[98] The delay imposed was extremely costly to the Japanese; for many years after the war Sato dwelt bitterly on the lives, and time, wasted by Miyazaki's unnecessary encounter, which caused 16 per cent casualties and 'undoubtedly had an adverse effect upon the final operation at Kohima'.[99]

In the north, elements of Yamauchi's 15th Division skirting Sangshak reached Litan, 7 miles to the west and 16 miles north-east of Imphal, on 26 March, meeting 2nd/1st Punjabis from 5th Indian Division, also just arrived. Somewhat isolated, the Punjabis withdrew to Kameng, where 123rd Indian Brigade established a firm defensive position across a wide valley through which ran the Imphal–Ukhrul road. Yamauchi's advance had gone well, despite having to divert some infantry to Indaw to help deal with the Chindits. On 28 March his lead units cut the Imphal–Dimapur road at Kangpopki, and 58th and 60th Regiments established strong positions near Kanglatongbi and Mapao, enviously watching 120 lorries per hour passing along the road before they did so, and creating a major crisis for Slim and Scoones. But they were separated from Headquarters 15th

Division by high jungle peak and precipitous valleys. And they soon learned that victory would be neither swift nor easy. On 1 April an attack was launched by 80 men at Kameng, but only 8 returned, reporting the British had both tanks and flame-throwers.[100]

# 13

## Stilwell in the north

Is the Gateway to India at Bombay, really as beautiful as they say?

Don't rightly know, Ma'am. Did my part breaking point in the jungle heart;
Blasted the boulder, felled the trees, with red mud oòzin' around our knees,
Carved the guts from Patkai's side, dozed our trace, made it clean and wide,
Metalled and graded, dug and filled; we had the Ledo Road to build.

You've been gone two years this spring. Didn't you see a single thing?

Never saw much but the moon shine on a Burmese temple around
   Maingkwan.
And silver transports high in the sky, Thursday River and the swift Tanai,
And Hukawng Valley coming all green, those are the only things I've seen.
Did our job, though, like God willed: we had the Ledo Road to build.
                  Sergeant Smith Dawless, 'Conversation Piece'[1]

KNOWN AS 'OPERATION Vomit' and the 'Aluminum Trail' because of its line of wreckage, the Hump 'drove men mad', noted one history, 'sent them back to America wasted with tropical fevers and broken for the rest of their lives. Some boys called it the Skyway to Hell; it was certainly the most dangerous, terrifying, barbarous aerial transport run in the world.'[2] Banks of cumulus and cumulo-nimbus cloud, sometimes towering between 2,000 and 25,000 feet, could be deadly; the pilot would find himself tossed around like a pea on a drum, throwing the hapless machine on to a mountainside or sending it out of control. While combat crews looked down on them, the pilots delivered everything from specie to goats to engineering equipment to China; not that this all went to its intended end-users. There was deep mutual antipathy between Americans and Chinese: the Americans regarded the Chinese as 'hopeless, corrupt, thieving, sons-of-bitches';[3] they believed the 'slopeys' were not fighting and their efforts benefited only black marketeers. The Chinese found the Americans 'stupidly profligate, coarse, contemptuous, often brutal and easily corruptible'.[4] Indeed, Americans were not slow to share the spoils of corruption, with every item imaginable for sale in the black markets of Kunming. For most, CBI meant 'Confused Bastards in India', and discontent and frustration were rife.[5] Little surprise therefore, that to raise deliveries to 10,000 tons a month, as Trident demanded, was a struggle.

The most common aircraft was the C-47 (Dakota), an aeroplane 'born to fly', noted Otha C. Spencer. 'The C-47 takes off on its own. To fly in the air is not necessary – the C-47 flies by itself. You just tell it where to go and make it behave. To land the C-47 is another thing. You must force it to the ground – it wants to keep flying.' The C-46 (Curtiss Commando) – nicknamed 'Old Dumbo' after Disney's flying elephant, or the 'Pregnant Whale' – looked similar but was bigger and faster, with a higher ceiling. The C-87 was the cargo version of the B-24 Liberator; another variant, the C-109 tanker, which the pilots hated and called the 'Flying Coffin', carried a cargo of 100-octane fuel.[6] Morale among pilots based at Dinjan became a serious problem. They endured the worst conditions among Americans in theatre.[7] Japanese fighters were a menace and their airfields so well concealed, with aircraft hidden underground, that even Kachin scouts could not find them. The ATC operated homing stations, which at one point the Japanese mimicked, causing several crashes, although once discovered they went off air and the crashes stopped. But the weather was the biggest menace. Crews were rebellious and often bailed out if the engine missed just once or refused to fly if there was cloud. On 2 August 1943 CBS correspondent Eric Sevareid flew in a C-46 which lost an engine, and the twenty passengers and crew baled out over the Patkoi range, to be surrounded by half-naked spear- and *dah*-wielding tribesmen. 'Some instinct, born no doubt of the wild west novels of childhood, prompted me to step forward, raise my palm and say "How!"' As Sevareid and his companions made friends, a search-and-rescue plane dropped supplies and a radio, and they were later joined by three medics.[8]

Not that rescue was by any means certain. And as traffic increased, so did accidents: one for every 200 flights. The fall of Burma had forced the Hump to follow a more northerly route over mountains up to 20,000 feet, 'a land of desolation and terror – an airman's nightmare', according to Edmund Townsend of the Royal Australian Air Force.[9] Fort Hertz, in the extreme north of Burma, was originally occupied in September 1942 by a small detachment of Kachin levies who carried out many very successful operations, and were indeed so successful that the Japanese made a direct threat towards them. To counter this, 4th Burma Regiment was flown in at the end of November 1943 and soon afterwards the Americans agreed to maintain them by air. Command was then transferred in February 1944 to Stilwell. The isolated garrison maintained the only emergency landing ground on the route, for the jungles below held a special fear for the airmen: dark, silent, thickly matted with undergrowth and with very few trails.[10] The fate of those bailing out could be unbelievably gruesome: as they parachuted into tall trees, anything up to 150 feet high, the parachute caught in the branches. Suspended high up like puppets, often injured and unable to climb up or down, they faced a slow, agonizing death. Although not its primary mission, Detachment 101 rescued 125 ATC crew during 1943, but this was less than a third of those lost, the remainder of whom were killed or captured. In three years of operations ATC lost 468 aircraft; an average of 13 per month.[11] Escape and evasion were the responsibility of E Group, which taught survival techniques to aircrew. Lieutenant H. Erikson of 490th Bombardment Squadron parachuted into Naga territory and was guided back to British lines after being persuaded to leave his parachute behind, where its twenty-four panels of silk would clothe the entire village.[12] But ATC continued to expand and delivered an astonishing 13,000 tons in November 1943.

In his situation report for June 1943 Kawabe was sanguine about north Burma. The Chinese were being held with ease; the guerrillas north of Bhamo were a considerable nuisance, but it was 'not worth the extra effort necessary to deal with them'; and operations in the Hukawng valley had 'succeeded in driving a small wedge between the Chinese operating from Yunnan and my forces now finally threaten Fort Hertz'.[13] This would prove wildly optimistic; success for Stilwell's Ramgarh force – the Chinese Army in India (CAI), or *Chi Hui Pui* to the Chinese – would be measured on the battlefield advancing through north Burma more than 600 miles from their operational base in India.[14] Sun Li-jen said that the Chinese soldier 'has a tried and true record. Now he has been given a chance to prove what he can do when placed shoulder to shoulder with his ally and on equal terms with the enemy'. And Colonel Rothwell H. Brown declared Chinese troops 'the bravest soldiers I have ever seen'.[15] American objectives now included massive increases in aid to China, entailing vast works to improve communications along the Brahmaputra river, the Assam–Bengal railway, the Ledo Road and the fuel pipeline between Assam and Kunming via Fort Hertz.[16] Even air enthusiasts conceded these were vital for moving heavy equipment to China, although Auchinleck proved scarcely more enthusiastic than Wavell for the project, which Americans blamed on the 'no-can-do boys' at GHQ(I).[17] But, as Lieutenant-Colonel John E. Russell conceded, the transport system between Calcutta and Assam was 'the most fascinating and complex problem we have in the world'.[18] Towards the end of 1943 an American railroad unit with five railway-operating battalions under command arrived to take over the 805 miles of line between Parbatipur and Ledo, before formally taking over on 1 March 1944. They faced enormous problems, including lack of signals equipment and rolling stock.[19]

Although the Ledo Road progressed just 3 miles between May and August 1943, various engineer units now arrived, and Colonel Lewis A. Pick, who took over on 17 October and soon became known as 'Old Mud and Ruts', declared the road would be built – 'mud, rain and malaria be damned'.[20] Some 60 per cent of it was built by African-American units, whose morale was judged higher than that of white ones; also racial tensions among the many other nationalities represented were greater.[21] Pick organized a system of reliefs and rotations that ensured the road kept moving forward. Stilwell wanted the road to reach Shingbwiyang by 1 January, where Seagrave would establish a hospital, to which Pick agreed.[22] Aviation engineer battalions who normally built airfields found themselves on road-grading and gravelling tasks; 209th Combat Engineer Battalion operated a sawmill and on road maintenance, together with 12th Chinese Engineer Regiment and pipeline and forestry specialists. The road soon became known as 'Pick's Pike'.[23] Meanwhile as protection for Seagrave's hospital, a selected air defence unit, Battery E of 464th Anti-Aircraft Battalion, equipped with .5-inch Browning machine-guns, began a march into mountains that included 70 per cent gradients. Captain James R. Nagel recalled of one day's march that it 'was sheer will power that carried us through. I swore I was walking on "stumps", when we finally hit the crest. We made it in about seven hours, not quite a mile per hour. We could hardly move, but we had to, and did.'[24] Thus they became the first American combat unit to enter Burma, dispelling the oft repeated myth giving Galahad this honour.[25]

On 4 October the 5303rd Headquarters and Headquarters Company (Provisional) Combat Troops was activated.[26] Meanwhile Stilwell's deputy, in command of the Forward Echelon of Ramgarh Force, Brigadier-General Haydon L. Boatner, issued an operation order estimating enemy strength as being patrols of 40–50 BDA men with one or two Japanese NCOs attached. When Sun questioned this, Boatner replied nonchalantly, 'My dear fellow, you don't have to fight; just march in!'[27] When Sun demanded Boatner's removal because he felt Boatner seriously underestimated the strength of the Japanese in the Hukawng valley, Stilwell saw only a Chinese reluctance to attack, although Sun was subsequently proved right. But the episode generated further ill-feeling between Americans and Chinese. Stilwell returned to Chungking on 15 October to find the argument used as another basis for the Chinese to press for his recall until Mountbatten intervened to prevent it.[28] Stilwell was determined to reach Myitkyina, base of the northernmost Japanese garrison, before the monsoon. On 3 November Stilwell visited Pick at MS 50 and asked: 'When can you build me a jeep road to Shingbwiyang at Milestone 103?' Pick promised not a jeep track but a military highway carrying lorries by 1 January. Even Stilwell thought this too optimistic.[29] But engineer Lieutenant-Colonel William J. Savage recalled:

> it was comparatively easy to open up a mile or more of single-lane road with two or three dozers, in 24 hours time. With a little additional work this ... could be made into a dry-weather road for our trucks and other supply vehicles. Once an opening was made units could be established along the route to improve, widen, and surface.[30]

Progress was helped by using a dodgy clinometer. Pick was determined to keep grades to 10 per cent or less but, short of time and surveyors, most were 'eyeballed' (estimated). Several times Pick borrowed Lieutenant-Colonel Wright Hiatt's clinometer, which would not go higher than 11, to check grades where vehicles were clearly struggling, saying, 'Well, Hiatt, it's a bit steep, but we'll let it go.'[31] One such grade was at least 17 per cent, but the lead bulldozer reached Shingbwiyang on 27 December, four days ahead of schedule; the engineers had conquered the Patkois. But the longer the road became, the more troops were needed to maintain it, while men were also diverted to other duties, including combat, even before the monsoon brought its share of problems. At the same time the trans-Burma pipeline was under way and signals communications had to be established along the road's length.[32]

In December Stilwell went back into the jungle, where he would spend the next seven months apart from a couple of quick flights to Delhi and Chungking. Ignoring gibes that he was the best 'three-star company commander in the US Army' and about the 'platoon war in Burma', he was determined to open the road to China and believed only his personal leadership could drive the Chinese forward.[33] When Stilwell arrived in the Hukawng valley on 21 December 1943 with his offensive already a month late, he found the Japanese at Yubang Ga, the key to where the Ledo Road should cross the Tarung river, and Chinese 112th Regiment of 38th Division nearby already isolated and unable to advance or retreat, with relief attempts having already failed, while Sun and Boatner, Stilwell's

deputy and Chief of Staff of the Chinese Army in India, argued over supplies and artillery. He established Headquarters at Shingbwiyang, gave Sun
a roasting, dismissed the commander of 65th Regiment in 22nd Division,
and arranged for a co-ordinated attack, exhorting the troops that they must
succeed, which seemed to work: 'Where Stilwell went, something happened', noted Gordon Seagrave.[34] From 24 December it took a week of
intense fighting to clear the Japanese out of Yubang Ga, costing 38th
Division 315 killed and 429 wounded but providing the Chinese with their
first victory in Burma.[35]

On 31 December Stilwell went to Delhi to resolve his position in the
chain of command. Mountbatten wanted him to serve beside Slim under
Giffard, but Stilwell despised Giffard, believing him timid and inept.[36] (He
was nothing of the sort; honourable and kindly, he was also utterly competent, if slow and thorough. However, his instincts went against accepting
Mountbatten's inexperienced promptings, and clashes were inevitable.[37])
Stilwell flatly refused, citing his various other positions and giving a 'lesson
in the mobile offensive-defensive', according to Slim, resisting all reasoning
from Mountbatten until his air degenerated into 'a surly obstinacy that
showed him at his worst'. Then suddenly he announced his willingness to
fight under Slim until he reached Kamaing, knowing Slim would not hinder
him, and dismissing the latter's junior rank by declaring, 'I would fight under
a corporal as long as he would let me fight'.[38] In January Marshall wrote to
reassure Mountbatten that Stilwell would 'provide tremendous energy, courage and unlimited ingenuity and imagination to any aggressive proposals or
operations'.[39]

On 29 January 1944 the 5303rd changed its title, with 'Area Command'
replacing 'Combat Troops'. The rest of the title was then discarded to
become Northern Combat Area Command (NCAC) on 1 February.[40]
Opposing NCAC was 18th Division under Lieutenant-General Tanaka
Sinichi, among the toughest in the Japanese Army.[41] Stilwell's Chinese
comprised 22nd and 38th Divisions from Ramgarh, of about 12,000 men
each, and the two-regiment 30th Division, flown to India over the preceding months. He also had some 90 tanks in the American-Chinese 1st
Provisional Tank Group. In Yunnan Y Force comprised eleven weak and
as yet still static divisions. More significantly, the Allies now had air control, with implications not only for combat but also for casualty evacuation
and mobility. Supply formed the main bone of contention: sometimes
excessive Chinese demands were balanced by being left close to starvation
when airdrops were less than rigorously pursued. Stilwell made aircrews
live on the ground for a few days on spam and hot water. 'After the air boys

STALEMATE

learned what it was like down there,' Paul Jones recalled, 'they flew in every day, flew when you thought no one could, when clouds were on the tree tops.'[42]

Stilwell planned to take on 18th Division by mimicking the Japanese tactics of 1942 – enveloping them in packets and annihilating them. However, the Chinese proved reluctant to trap them entirely and face a fierce battle to the death, and preferred to form U-shaped ambushes to leave an escape route, following Sun Tzu's dictum that a surrounded enemy 'must have a way of escape'.[43] To overcome their feeling of military inferiority facing the Japanese, Stilwell ensured that his troops had overwhelming superiority in numbers; if a company was to be attacked, he assigned a regiment. 'He bullied, flattered and shamed, cajoled, bribed, goaded and pushed, rewarded with decorations, unit citations, press photos and every device of public relations.'[44] For his own information and purposes of command, American 'advisers' were attached to Chinese formations; although under strict orders to respect Chinese command decisions, they could influence them through the power to relay or veto supplies, and this was the means by which Stilwell ultimately exercised control. The system produced both quarrels and enduring friendships but was not really an effective means of command.

Stilwell's intelligence rested on Kachin guerrillas organized by Detachment 101, and this was not always effective.[45] In early 1944 Eifler was exhausted and replaced as Chief of Detachment 101 by William R. Peers. Operations now moved increasingly towards guerrilla activity, with some 2,500 in four areas of central north Burma in support of Stilwell and reinforced by American V Force personnel.[46] By late 1944 over 250 American officers and 750 men were involved. According to Roger Hilsman, one of some 50 US guerrilla commanders, there were over 10,000 guerrillas.[47] But while Detachment 101 may have had local successes, it spent too much time in counterproductive bickering with the British, so that William Langer, Chief of the Research and Analysis Division, later concluded: 'I believe the OSS as a whole had no important part in the war in the Pacific.'[48] Despite the extravagant claims made for its success, Detachment 101 was only really effective in one area – the creation of a retrospective aura of guerrilla expertise and invincibility – while British sponsorship of minorities similarly ensured the failure to assimilate them in post-war Burma.[49]

In January Mountbatten produced a revised plan called Axiom, which returned to the sea strategy via Malaya and Sumatra and would halt

Stilwell's drive in north Burma, which, given Chiang's refusal to commit Y Force, was declared impossible before the monsoon. Chiang's refusal was the cause of deep frustration. On 14 January Roosevelt telegraphed him to say that if Y Force could not be used, 'it would appear that we should avoid for the present the movement of critical materials to them ... and curtail the continuing build-up of stock piles in India'.[50] But the threat left both the Generalissimo and Y Force unmoved.

When Mountbatten despatched a high-powered delegation to London and Washington to persuade the Combined Chiefs of Staff to adopt Axiom, Stilwell sent one of his own to Washington 'to checkmate the limies'.[51] With his gimlet eye on Singapore and wary of becoming entangled in north Burma, Churchill 'liked Mountbatten's new plan'.[52] But Axiom also enjoyed favour among senior Americans; Mountbatten's delegation was led by Wedemeyer, a favourite of the Operations Planning Staff (OPD) at the US War Department and now impressing at SEAC, while Chennault also opposed Stilwell. Axiom would keep the British out of Burma for employment in Malaya and Sumatra once landing craft were available; Myitkyina would be abandoned in favour of expanding Hump capacity, a plan enthusiastically endorsed by Churchill but rejected by the American Joint Chiefs of Staff. However, all these arguments were ultimately futile since, as Barbara Tuchman notes, the March on Delhi committed the British to action.[53]

Meanwhile Stilwell was trying to trap and destroy the Japanese base in the Hukawng at Mainkwan. Throughout January he found the lack of aggression among the Chinese increasingly frustrating. The road and pipeline were progressing steadily, together with an airfield. 'Just a matter now of weather', wrote Stilwell on 1 February. 'God give us a few dry days and we can go.'[54] But God would not listen: although supposedly the 'dry' season, there had already been twelve rainy days in January and there would be eighteen in February and ten each in March and April, giving 175 inches of rain in this abnormal year. Stilwell hiked miles along forest trails to reach forward command posts and readily exposed himself to danger, but nothing he did could prevent another ambush failing to be closed and the Japanese escaping. On 19 February, following intense lobbying, he was reinforced by Galahad, released from SEAC to Stilwell's command under Brigadier-General Frank D. Merrill, who as Stilwell's operations officer in 1942 had planned the Ledo Road. Merrill was tall but 'by no means a rugged individual, being narrow of chest and rather thin', recalled his second-in-command, Colonel Charles Hunter.[55] On 1 January Galahad officially became 5307th Composite Regiment (Provisional), which was changed immediately to 5307th Composite Unit (Provisional) – 'sounds like a street address in Los Angeles', wrote one disgusted member, 2nd Lieutenant Charlton Ogburn Jr.[56] But as they marched, James Shepley of *Time–Life* remarked to Merrill that the unit's name had no appeal. 'I'm going to call your outfit "Merrill's Marauders".'[57] The name stuck: they had yet to see action, but as the only American infantry in theatre they received more and better press coverage than any similar-sized formation elsewhere. And, as one wrote home, 'my pack is on my back, my gun is oiled and loaded and as I walk in the shadow of death, I fear no son-of-a-bitch.'[58]

However, they were not all that they appeared. To form three battalion groups of 1,000 men each with jungle experience they were recruited from units in the south-west Pacific and Caribbean; one group from New Caledonia included many men already subject to malaria, while the 33rd Infantry Regiment in Trinidad was regarded as the dumping ground for the dross of the army. Many were volunteers only in so far as they would do almost anything to get out of Trinidad. One genuine volunteer was Phil Smart, serving with 1st Cavalry in Puerto Rico, 'enjoying the beautiful beaches, fiestas, girls and modern army quarters of that island paradise'. He volunteered because they were promised that if they survived the short but hazardous mission they would spend the rest of the war stateside, and thus out of homesickness, 'maybe mixed with a little guilt that after volunteering to fight the war we were instead enjoying the life of Riley while others were doing the job'.[59] But training in India revealed serious disciplinary problems, with 10 per cent going absent without leave and others shooting at cattle, chickens, even the feet of people just to see them 'dance'; they 'kept the military police busy, the neighbouring natives in a state of terror, and their own guardhouse full'.[60]

They were organized so that each battalion formed two columns along Chindit lines called combat teams, although not full combined arms groupings as the term meant to the US Army at the time. Their transport, like the Chindits, would be mule-based and at Ledo they received 700 new animals, although few of those appointed as 'mule-skinners' had any knowledge or experience of them and they had a hard time.[61] Thereafter they made a 130-mile march over the Naga range. Stilwell criticized their lack of speed (they took twenty-five days), in direct contrast to British advice that they conserve their energy whenever possible for the trials of Burma.[62] Stilwell immediately took Merrill and pointed at a map to Walawbum at the southern end of the Hukawng valley, saying, 'I want you to hit there on March 3'. As with all his directives, it was simple and to the point.[63] But rain hampered his plans. Until the road was surfaced with gravel, rain turned it into a thick gloop; even jeeps became bogged and lorries could only supply the road-builders, forcing the forward troops to rely on air supply that was also hindered by the rain. After another eight-day, 60-mile trek Galahad seized the road at Walawbum while a Chinese battalion of 88th Regiment marched independently 35 miles to Monsum, fighting numerous Japanese detachments on the way. The next day Galahad was heavily counter-attacked by Japanese 55th Regiment from the north.[64] The attack fell on 3rd Battalion, which, being mostly recruited from Pacific veterans, thought the other two battalions novices and referred to themselves as 'the Dead End Kids', after a popular film series. They fought off repeated Japanese attacks. 'Those little bastards must think we're amateurs at this jungle fighting stuff', remarked Lieutenant Victor J. Weingartner. 'Banzai charges might have terrified the civilians in Singapore, but they're nothing but good, moving target practice for us.'[65]

Meanwhile Japanese 56th Regiment tried to break their hold on the Kamaing road but ran into unexpected opposition, and the arrival of 1st Provisional Tank Group further dislocated Tanaka's plans. He was now convinced that he could not destroy Galahad as ordered, and instead withdrew using two roads as yet unknown to the Americans, who were now reinforced by a Chinese regiment from 38th Division. The battle continued for five more days – the first fought by Chinese and American troops together – and although the Japanese escaped once more, they lost 1,500 men, and were harassed all the way by Kachin guerrillas. One group under Lieutenant James Tilly claimed to have killed 150 and destroyed several supply dumps and lorries without loss to themselves.[66] But operating together caused problems. Despite American training, Chinese standards of sanitation remained lamentable and the Americans began to succumb to amoebic dysentery; only the very few who boiled all their drinking water avoided it. Their K-rations were also unsuitable, as Jack Girsham, an Anglo-Burmese guide, noted:

> Food is all-important in the jungle. The American soldiers didn't understand this at first. They watched the Kachin scouts and me picking mushrooms or tender bamboo shoots and catching fish we poisoned in the streams with roots and bark, and remained puzzled until they tried our diet. The Americans would eat rice and the stuff we ate whenever they could. They agreed that K-rations were too light for the rigours of jungle warfare.[67]

With the Japanese Arakan offensive now successfully wound up, Slim flew in to confer about launching Wingate's Thursday operation into the area south of NCAC's advance, and this commenced 5–11 March. Stilwell also received a visit from Mountbatten, with whom he was no longer on the best of terms, and whom he now referred to as a 'fatuous ass', among other insults.[68] But Mountbatten impressed the soldiers, who had no real idea why they were there.[69] One source of discord was Stilwell making press statements suggesting he was the only man in SEAC fighting a war, and Mountbatten was keen to redress the public relations balance – something very close to his heart, especially when it referred to himself.[70] And if the Americans felt they did not get due credit from the BBC and other British media for their part in the north Burma fighting, the Chinese felt exactly the same about them.[71] Mountbatten believed Stilwell had 'fire in his belly' but no understanding of global strategy or interest in administration, and that his unconcealed criticisms were unhelpful to teamwork; he wanted Stilwell eased out of SEAC to China and Wedemeyer to take over in Delhi. Escorted around the battlefield at Walawbum, he found the smell of corpses upsetting, and said sea battle was much cleaner; despite the outward friendliness, the fundamental difference in outlook between the two men and the countries they represented could not be hidden.[72] When the following day Mountbatten suffered a bamboo splinter in the eye, which was operated on by a distinguished eye specialist at 20th General Hospital, a rumour ran around the Americans that Uncle Joe had 'busted the Limey in the eye'.[73]

In the field Stilwell's spartan lifestyle in basha or tent made a strong impression on Chinese officers but not on Americans, and he often went unrecognized. One Marauder saw him in a jeep wearing his Chinese soldier's cap with a carbine across his knees and growled, 'Christ, a goddamn duck-hunter'.[74] 'Look at that poor old man', said an engineer; 'some draft boards will do anything.'[75] Later Dorn persuaded him the men wanted to see their Commanding General, that it gave them a thrill and something to write home about, and after thinking it over he wore his rank insignia.[76] Stilwell handed out cigarettes wherever possible and 'paid special attention to the people at the bottom', according to one Chinese officer, attaching particular importance to casualty evacuation; he had Calcutta's Imperial Hotel (where American SEAC staff lived) stripped of fans for 20th General Hospital at Ledo. The efforts of American medical staff, from evacuation to base staff, reduced the death rate from wounds, normally limitless in the Chinese army, to 3.5 per cent, giving the soldiers new-found confidence; consequently the soldiers would crowd around him, wanting to talk to 'our Commander'.[77]

However, with the opening of the Japanese offensive, the threat to his communications should the enemy cut the Bengal–Assam Railway, and the resulting drawing-off of supply planes to support the Imphal front, Stilwell realized the essential need for a second front on the Salween and signalled Marshall that Chiang must be made to commit Y Force. At the same time Mountbatten pleaded with both Roosevelt and Churchill to make personal appeals to the Generalissimo, but in reply to the President, Chiang said China was too weak to undertake a major campaign while threatened by Communists to the north and Japanese on the Yangtze.[78] Stilwell pressed on: Galahad's second task involved splitting, with 1st Battalion as advance guard ahead of Chinese 113th Regiment moving to Shaduzup, while the 2nd and 3rd Battalions made a wider movement to strike the Kamaing road further south at Inkangahtawng, some 20 miles from Kamaing – a march of some 80 miles.[79] On 15 March Chinese 22nd Division, supported by 1st Provisional Tank Group, began attacking towards Jambu Bum. But over the next two weeks the tanks and infantry kept getting separated and the attacks stalled; the infantry lacked confidence in the armour, whose numbers the Japanese steadily eroded as they counter-attacked repeatedly. Stilwell was unaware of these difficulties and assumed all was going well.[80] His health was suffering and deep lines had replaced the hard, healthy look around eyes and mouth, but despite a liver complaint he refused to be hospitalized. Although news from the Chindwin front was bad, he would say 'if the Japs are behind us, we are also behind them'.[81] As 1st Battalion were struggling toward Shaduzup, skirmishing all the way, Stilwell berated their speed. On 23 and 24 March they hacked a trail throughout the jungle, moving only 5 miles but ensuring security. Finally they launched their attack on 28 March, achieving complete surprise. Counter-attack was, however, inevitable, and it came with artillery support. During a brief lull after fierce shelling 'a voice of exasperation was heard in the darkness, controlled but distinct. "Where the hell are the other five thousand three hundred and six composite units?"'[82]

Meanwhile the other two battalions made a similarly gruelling march, joined by 300 Kachin guerrillas. Approaching their objective, they received urgent orders from Merrill, under pressure from Stilwell, to attack Inkangahtawng immediately because it was feared the Japanese were withdrawing. But 2nd and 3rd Battalions were now separated, as the former was providing flank protection. 'This was disturbing news', wrote Colonel Charles Hunter after the war. 'Our air photos had failed to arrive; there would be no time for reconnaissance ... In addition, the Mogaung river was between us and the road. We did not know the location of the fords, or even whether or not the river was fordable at this time of year', although the Kachin scouts assured him it was.[83] Therefore on 23 March 3rd

Battalion moved swiftly forward, drove in some Japanese patrols and waded the river, to be halted by increasing opposition some 300 yards east of the Kamaing road. But the situation was extremely dangerous: the three American battalions were isolated and incapable of immediate mutual support, and Tanaka was not slow to react. On 24 March Hunter sent patrols to contact Chinese 113th Regiment, supposedly moving towards his road-block at Inkangahtawng from Shaduzup, while a fighting patrol of 2nd Battalion approached Inkangahtawng village but was repulsed. Just as they reached the battalion perimeter the Japanese attacked, and throughout the day they probed the position. Pressure increased and ammunition ran short, forcing an eastward withdrawal across difficult terrain, with rain so heavy that holes had to be cut in the bottom of the litters so the dozen wounded would not be covered in water. On 26 March 2nd and 3rd Battalions both moved towards Nphum Ga, receiving a badly needed supply drop *en route*. The astonishing beauty of the country did not go entirely unappreciated by the sweating GIs. 'The minority of us who openly enjoyed it', noted Lieutenant John B. George, '(as apart from the conventional majority who called all military combat terrain hell holes) would shake our heads in awe, pausing at a turn in the hillside trail or while fording the crystal clear water to let the vista imprint our memories.'[84] But the Japanese followed on their heels, skirmishing with the rear and flank guards until they reached Nphum Ga on 28 March; after seven weeks in the jungle Galahad had crossed 100 rivers and streams, fought a heavy action and then withdrawn in contact, and they were nearing exhaustion.

Now 2nd Battalion were forced on to a position on a sharp thin ridge at the end of a mass of hills, with 3rd Battalion holding an airstrip at Hsamshingyang, 5 miles north. Following them was a strong force under Colonel Maruyama Fusayasu, comprising 114th Regimental Head-quarters, 1/114th Regiment and 1/35th Regiment with four field guns. Their orders were not to outflank the Americans, as the latter thought, but to push them away from the flank of 18th Division.[85] The first probing attack began at around 1600 on 28 March but, familiar with Japanese tactics, the Marauders held their fire to conceal their positions.[86] Soon afterwards, George reported to Hunter, who listened

> with an appearance of utter, smiling calm, for which I gave him my utter, unsmiling admiration. He was sitting in his lean-to, shirtless, cross-legged with a map on the ground before him. After I'd given him these terse facts and the news that the battalion probably was now fully besieged, he paused for a moment and then asked, 'What do you think we should do?'

George suggested moving north and Hunter nodded, 'but much in the way of a professor, waiting for a not-too-bright student to talk himself out … Finally he stopped smiling, let a out a short breath that seemed the opposite of agreement or approval, and said, "Yes, George. That's one way to do it. But we're going to hold that hilltop."'[87]

On 27 March Stilwell visited Chungking, where he was promised two more divisions. On returning three days later he found Merrill, long a sufferer from heart trouble, had been evacuated and the weather continued wet. Meanwhile Maruyama ordered a powerful attack on Nphum Ga on 29 March, from which day Hunter was in effective command of Galahad. On 30 March the Japanese fiercely attacked the eastern end of 2nd Battalion's perimeter, previously ignored, and conditions deteriorated. Some 75 out of 200 transport animals had been killed by shelling and their carcasses were beginning to rot. But things would get worse: the following day the battalion was surrounded and effectively under siege, with every man now called to the defences.[88] While Maruyama shelled 2nd Battalion's position, he sent a strong patrol towards the airstrip to prevent support coming from 3rd Battalion. The water situation inside the perimeter gave most cause for concern. 'We were drinking muddy, and I mean muddy, water', recorded the battalion diary for 1 April. 'Nothing else to be had. Even seen fellas taking water from a pool where dead mules lie.'[89] They fought off two infantry attacks that day and more the next. But two 75mm howitzers arrived at Hsamshingyang, sent by Merrill, who never formally relinquished command, and manned by detachments assembled from former members of 98th Field Artillery Battalion from New Guinea, and these were soon supporting 2nd Battalion. They needed it; by the end of 3 April wounded were dying for lack of water. Most of the men had dysentery and other stomach disorders.[90] Unaware of Galahad's plight, Stilwell met Slim and Mountbatten at Jorhat and offered to send back 38th Division if it would help stem the Japanese tide, but Slim directed him to continue towards Myitkyina, confident of stopping the Japanese.[91] The same day Chinese 14th and 50th Divisions began airlifting; they were flown to Assam in a record eight days for preparation to move to staging areas in the Hukawng valley. Also that day Roosevelt signalled Chiang to urge him to use Y Force, saying it was inconceivable that with their American equipment they could not advance 'against the Japanese 56th Division in its present depleted strength. To me the time is ripe.'[92]

Meanwhile Hunter decided it was necessary to fight through to 2nd Battalion and ordered in all patrols. The morning of 4 April was devoted to preparation, but the attack had to be delayed until 1600. At 1530 a demonstration was staged, which drew off Japanese mortar fire. But the attack made little progress before dark or on the next day, as the Japanese defended each successive position with their usual tenacity. These attacks did not prevent continued attacks on 2nd Battalion's perimeter, which came close to being breached on 4 and 5 April. But the defenders antici-pated them thanks to Sergeant Roy Matsumoto, a Japanese-American who

> would sneak out every night to listen to the Japanese and find out where they would attack next. If he had ever been caught, I hate to think what they would have done to him. We set up our automatic weapons where they would attack. One day they were to attack in two waves. The first wave came out but the second wave was hesitant. Roy jumped up and yelled 'attack' in Japanese and on they came. He saved the battalion.[93]

On 5 April the Japanese held off but shelled the perimeter. Slowly 3rd Battalion fought its way forward, gaining yards at a time along the trail to Nphum Ga. On 6 April they made 500 yards; on 7 April a few more, but now they were reinforced by 1st Battalion, which had spent four days hacking through unmapped jungle to join them. On 8 April Hunter planned an all-out attack to lift the siege and it went as planned but with limited success, costing 25 casualties. But the following day, Easter Sunday, to the delight of all concerned, the Japanese had gone, departing in haste as abandoned equipment testified.[94] There was no pursuit. The Marauders were utterly exhausted; the battle at Nphum Ga cost 52 dead and 163 wounded, and among them an alarmingly high proportion caused by friendly fire or carelessness, indicating extreme fatigue to add to growing sickness.[95] They would get no sympathy from Stilwell, although the arri-val of Chinese troops at least allowed them two weeks' rest and reorgan-ization.

Convinced that Sun and Liao were dragging their feet on orders from Chungking, Stilwell got Marshall to agree that, unless Y Force moved, its lend-lease supplies should be stopped. On 14 April the Chinese agreed to cross the Salween, but immediately showed signs of delaying. 'My God, repeat, God,' Stilwell radioed to Dorn, Chief of Staff of Y Force, 'so that begins again. Do not shoot yourself before notifying me three days in advance.'[96] Nevertheless, the dash for Myitkyina could begin, and on 21 April Stilwell decided to make a secret penetration of the mountains. This was kept secret from SEAC as well as from the Japanese, since he feared their gloating should he fail: Mountbatten had responded to urging from the Joint Chiefs to seize north Burma on 14 April that the plan was 'unsound and should not be attempted'.[97] Stilwell wanted to seize the airstrip, which would then permit reinforcements and supplies to be flown in to take the town, and despite Kachin warnings that the steep Kumon mountains could not be crossed by pack animals except in dry weather, he was determined to try. Although the Chinese troops selected were not from Sun's or Liao's commands, he decided he could not rely on them without an American vanguard. Galahad was ordered to lead the way despite being reduced to 1,400 men through exhaustion and disease: although their officers declared them fit, the men – dazed and confused – thought otherwise. They had covered 300 miles through dense, dripping jungle, struggling with their mules and waiting anxiously for airdrops, eating cold K-rations and sleeping on wet ground, getting closer with every weary step to a menacing enemy. During this march 3rd Battalion lost twenty-three mules over precipices, and rain beat down incessantly. 'Hour after hour, day after day, week after week of being continually soaked to the skin,' recalled Lieutenant Logan Weston, 'accompanied by the ever present cacophony of the rain beating on the jungle canopy overhead – it was like nothing I ever experienced before.'[98] Charlton Ogburn recalled it was the sense of 'danger above everything' that strained the nerves, made worse by feeling unappreciated while Stilwell lavished reward and recognition on the Chinese. Perhaps some praise might have encouraged them, but Stilwell shared Pershing's puritanical outlook that Americans should fight without needing 'to be patted on the back or have their hands held', and at no stage during either training or operations did he even visit them; consequently the men came to hate him.[99]

Stilwell knew he was asking more than was reasonable but told Merrill he had no option. On 28 April the 1,400 Americans, 4,000 Chinese and 600 Kachin Rangers set out; at the same time, seemingly by magic, Sun and Liao moved forward in a renewed effort towards Kamaing, possibly released as Chiang was encouraged by the relief of Kohima. Rain cursed their every step as they struggled to make 4 or 5 miles a day, sometimes crawling or cutting steps in the muddy slopes, while losing half their pack mules to exhaustion or falls into deep gorges.[100] The task force was to signal the troop carriers when they believed themselves within forty-eight hours of the objective and Stilwell pushed on to chase up Sun and Liao's Chinese while waiting in suspense for the signal. He pushed the Marauders, too, and they were angry. They plodded on, making their feelings known:

This was positively to be the last effort asked of us. We had it from General Merrill himself that when we had gained our objective we would be returned at once to India, given a party to cause taxpayers a shudder, installed in a well-appointed rest camp, and given furloughs. It was this prospect more than anything else that gave the 5307th the resolution to surmount the obstacles that lay before us on the trail to Myitkyina.[101]

# 14

# The Admin Box

Last night I felt the moving active quality in the star-grown sky and
the dark night and the silent watchful land – and there seemed to be
a marvellous depth and freedom as well as danger and secrecy in it all.
When you see Orion you are looking with my eyes. And the Plough
tilts down on us both.

Alun Lewis[1]

IN OCTOBER 1943 the Japanese planned a major air raid on Calcutta, A few
light raids had been made in December 1942, but Calcutta was well
defended and this would be the first in a year. It would be carried out by 7th
Air Brigade in two waves, the second being Imperial Japanese Navy aircraft in
the first joint attack on an Allied target. Following diversionary raids on airfields around Chittagong, Agartala and Silchar, the attack on 5 December was
a success, destroying or badly damaging nine Hurricanes and a Spitfire and hitting Kiddapore docks, although damage was only slight. But the Japanese had
achieved surprise and enjoyed some luck, forcing the RAF onto the defensive.[2]

However, Japanese air tactics were generally poor, preoccupied with
attacking landing grounds while neglecting lines of communication. Pilot
shortage was exacerbated by their honour code, which caused unnecessary
loss of skilled, experienced air crew, and they remained reluctant to fit
armour or even make use of cloud. Furthermore, they received no instruction in blind landing and lacked air-to-ground communications. In early
1944, 5th Air Division in Burma and Thailand had 370 aircraft (plus 50
naval aircraft) against 719 Allied machines in north-east India, whose steadily improving types included Spitfire Vs and VIIIs from October 1943.[3]
Unable to dogfight the manoeuvrable Japanese planes effectively, they
adopted the dive-and-zoom tactic, maximizing their superior speed and
firepower, and enjoyed increasing success.[4]

But the major air event of the month was the reorganization of Allied
forces with the creation of SEAC. In contrast to the emasculation of his

campaign plan at Cairo, Mountbatten persuaded Arnold to agree to the formation of Allied Air Command, South-East Asia, under Peirse. Peirse's American second-in-command, Major-General George E. Stratemeyer, would control Eastern Air Command (EAC), including Tenth Air Force, and become Allied Air Commander for Burma, although these arrangements were strongly contested by Stilwell, who continued to hold Air Transport Command.[5] On 15 December Troop Carrier Command formed, incorporating 443rd Group USAAF and 177 Transport Wing RAF under Brigadier-General William D. Old.[6] On 18 December 3rd Tactical Air Force (TAF) was formed, incorporating 5320th Air Defense Wing USAAF at Dinjan with 221 and 224 Groups RAF at Imphal and Chittagong. On the army side came air supply companies, of which five were operating by the end of 1943, requiring special signals arrangements to connect forward headquarters and delivery airfields with supply agencies and base airfields. The final form of air supply organization included an air element – the Anglo-American Combat Cargo Task Force under the American Brigadier-General Frederick W. Evans – and an army element, Combined Army Air Transport Organization (CAATO), with headquarters and a number of rear and forward air maintenance organizations to handle supplies at base or forward airfields and drop zones respectively.[7]

On 1 November XV Corps assumed operational control of Arakan under Lieutenant-General Philip Christison comprising 5th and 7th Indian and 81st (West African) Divisions, which had arrived in India in August.[8] Throughout 1942 it had been suggested that West African troops with cross-country mobility provided by their porter transport might be effective in Burma, and in January 1943 Headquarters West Africa was asked to prepare two divisions.[9] In July, 81st (West African) Division sailed for the Far East, followed in May 1944 by 82nd.★ On his way to India with them A. J. Humphreys was entertained at Durban by the 'Lady in White' – Perla Siedle Gibson, a professional concert soprano – singing her favourite *Land of Hope and Glory* 'until her voice failed to reach us'.[10] Troop ships were dreary affairs on which the men, if not incapacitated with seasickness, 'lay

★ The divisional sign of the 81st was a spider. Gizzo (Anase) the spider is a traditional hero of Ashanti folklore; his outstanding quality is subtlety, using his wits to outsmart repeatedly those who would harm him. That of 82nd was two crossed spears passing through a headpad, symbolizing 'Through carriers we fight'. It recognized the importance of the Auxiliary Groups, who carried heavy loads by head in the traditional African manner, enabling the division to move over country non-African divisions could not even contemplate (A. Haywood and F. A. S. Clarke, *The History of the Royal West African Frontier Force*, pp. 376, 428).

on deck all day, drinking tea at two pence a pint', recalled medic Len Thornton. 'We were all sunburnt and very bored.'[11] The food deteriorated as the voyage progressed, so that skin diseases became rife. The limited film stock was soon exhausted and, in any case, liable to constant ribald interruption during love scenes or ironic cheering at American war efforts.

There was also the constant menace from German and Japanese submarines and, although the vast majority got through, the sinking of the SS *Khedive Ismail* was one of the worst maritime disasters in British history, and a closely guarded secret during the war. She was attacked by *I-27*, a 2,000-ton Japanese submarine, near the Maldives on 12 February 1944. Hit by two torpedoes, she sank in two minutes.[12] Only 260 of the 1,297 passengers and crew were saved (only 113 of 787 askaris of 301st Field Regiment, East African Artillery survived), including just 9 out of 86 women, most of whom were below decks at a concert party. One eyewitness account especially haunts: a nurse scrambling through her cabin porthole was trapped half-out by her hips, her agony mercifully cut short when she was engulfed after only a few seconds. Escorts brought the sub to the surface with depth charges and kept the crew from reaching her 5.5-inch deck gun with cannon fire, then eventually sank her with torpedoes.[13]

In India, Aziz Brimah of 5th Gold Coast Regiment recalled the rumours surrounding the Africans' arrival.

'They are cannibals! They chop [eat] people! They have tails!' So when we went to bathe in the streams, people asked us to take our pants off – our blue PT pants – in case they would be frightened by our tails! Then the British authorities began to spread the story: 'We are bringing in the Africans. When they catch you, they will chop you alive.' This was the best way they had of putting fear in the Japanese.[14]

Early in October 1943 Major-General C. G. Woolner was given the task of getting 81st (West African) Division – less 3rd (West African) Brigade, which was with Wingate – into the Kaladan valley to protect XV Corps' flank.[15] This involved a 70-mile march through the wildest country imaginable.[16] Woolner chose to build a jeep track over precipitous jungle-clad hills to Satpaung on the upper Kaladan, cut by hand without heavy equipment, which became known as 'West African Way'. In the meantime supplies were paddled upstream by native boatmen along the Sangu river to Mowdok, held by 5th/9th Jats.[17] Shortly after Christmas the real advance began: a sweating, straining march over terrible terrain in debilitating heat. Realizing the Africans posed a threat to 28th Army communications, Sakurai reinforced Myohaung and formed Koba Force (of regimental size) under Colonel Koba Hiroshi to defend the valley.[18]

Meanwhile 5th and 7th Indian Divisions began their advance, Operation Cudgel, clearing the Teknaf peninsula in November and securing Letwedet Chaung by Christmas. Captain Anthony Brett-James saw Arakanese working on the Mayu road. 'The tiny boys laughed as they scampered to and fro with their tins of pool water, while their fathers and elder brothers worked spasmodically in the shade of wide wicker hats. Even the women aided this work, and added a brighter swirl of colour with their gay dresses that even constant dust did not fade.'[19] The march along the 110 mile road took five days. 'During the day the sun blazed down, interrupted by intermittent heavy showers', recalled Major John Shipster. 'During the night it rained steadily. The surface of the road was of soft, wet, sticky clay, badly broken up by military vehicles. Our boots and legs were soon caked knee-high with mud and frequent halts had to be made to let everyone scrape and hack it off.'[20]

As the new year turned, Japanese fighter sweeps formed up just south of the front line, recalled Gordon Conway, 'well inside their own territory, frequently turning further away as we set out to intercept. Our problem was lack of numbers [224 Group had ten squadrons of all types] ... on 15 January we met them in equal strength and had a field day.' Five days later the Japanese suffered a heavy defeat and relaxed into non-activity until their offensive started, which 5th Air Division fully supported.[21] Meanwhile ground operations continued. A platoon of 1st/11th Sikhs was sent to mask a Japanese OP on Point 1600 and seize it if possible, which it did. They then fought off violent counter-attacks, after which the position was surrounded, preventing resupply. Asked by radio how long they could hold out the platoon commander replied: 'Without food for six more days; without ammunition, as long as you like; we have bayonets.' It was no idle boast, as the Sikhs would later prove repeatedly, but it was unnecessary as a company of 4th/14th Punjabis relieved them two days later.[22] The first engagement of 161st Indian Brigade was Operation Jericho to take Point 124. Fourth/7th Rajputs found themselves pinned and attacked continuously for six days, with the Japanese abandoning the position only on 7 January.[23] Raymond Street was a company runner in January 1944. It was a hazardous job, but he preferred the independence.

> I was happier on my own, making my own decisions. I felt safer. I took messages and laid and repaired lines of communication, sometimes cutting those of the enemy. I carried a little book which the officers had to sign when they received a message ... Many a time the Signals Officer would shout for the C Company runner and my heart would sink ... Then I started moving down the track off the hill, to the paddy-fields below, passing by bunkers

and trenches, with someone saying 'Alright Streety', to give moral support in some small way.[24]

Operations were launched by 89th Indian Brigade against Cain and Abel on 20 January, first by 2nd King's Own Scottish Borderers, followed by 4th/1st Gurkhas, then taken over by 33rd Indian Brigade while 89th prepared for operations with 25th Dragoons – equipped with Lee medium tanks – thus ensuring that Major-General Frank Messervy had a spare brigade available when the Japanese launched their main throw.[25] The first attempt to secure Razabil fortress began on 26 January, but the infantry of 123rd and 161st Indian Brigades, supported by 16 heavy and 12 medium bombers, 24 Vengeance dive-bombers and tanks from 25th Dragoons, did not get very far forward and the Japanese soon counter-attacked.[26] Two days later all vegetation had been removed, revealing four bunkers, but attacks still failed and on the 31st were called off. The infantry had clearly been misled as to the effectiveness of the bombardment.[27] It was here that the INA had its first contact but to its surprise, when they advanced shouting *Jai Hind!* ('Victory to India'), their compatriots shot at them.[28]

When he took command of Fourteenth Army, Slim evolved a new method for coping with the infiltration tactics of the Japanese. Appreciating that in a theatre with few troops to cover vast expanses of difficult and often dense country it would always be possible to turn a defensive position, he planned to establish pivots of manoeuvre well stocked and capable of withstanding immense pressure. By placing these formations in those areas that the enemy would need to attack in order to open a line of communication for his own advance, he wanted those forward to stand firm and act as anvils against which mobile forces could be deployed to destroy the enemy, rather than attempting to hold ground.[29] 'Mountbatten later claimed he was the originator of these tactics', wrote the Commander of XV Corps, Lieutenant-General Philip Christison in his unpublished memoirs. 'What he had done was to endorse them and make them possible.'[30] In fact, it would be Christison's battle, supported by Slim, who instructed his chief administrative officer, Major-General A. H. J. Snelling – known to the men as 'Grocer Alf' – to be prepared to maintain those forward formations by air at any time and to step up such preparations. Army reorganization saw 5th and 7th Indian Divisions' artillery put on a 'jungle' footing. They would have one conventional regiment of towed 25-pounders, a jeep-drawn field regiment equipped with 3.7-inch howitzers and 3-inch mortars, a mountain regiment of mule-borne 3.7s, and a combined anti-aircraft/anti-tank regiment. All guns were to defend themselves, with infantry not being sited to do so. Working with XV Corps was 'C' Flight of the newly formed 656th Air Observation Post Squadron.[31] Another significant addition was a deception unit called 55th Observation Squadron, under command of Captain Lubeck, a Czech, with British and Sikh troops who could simulate everything from a tank squadron moving forward to a battalion attack and once 'attacked' Kyaukit down the Kaladan river with fire-ships. Lubeck's favourite expression was, 'Eff you give me a ball of string and some fuse I will arr-range.'[32]

Christison continued preparations for XV Corps to assault Buthidaung in February of 1944. Fourteenth Army suspected an offensive in Arakan but had no idea of its scope or direction, although it was believed that it would probably attempt to outflank XV Corps. Operation Ha-Go would be carried out by 55th Division, commanded by Lieutenant-General Hanaya Tadashi.[33] Keeping one battalion in reserve, Hanaya divided his division into columns named after their commanders – Koba, Yoshida and Doi – with Major-General Sakurai Tokutaro, commander of the divisional infantry group, leading the main effort.[34] The aim was to infiltrate and encircle 7th Indian Division, and then drive the neighbouring 5th Indian Division into the sea.

When he first took over 7th Indian Division, Messervy foresaw 'that our brigades and the Japanese regiments will become interposed with one another like the layers of a Neapolitan sandwich. Our tactics will then be quite straightforward. We will fight back towards our own people and in doing so will destroy the Japs between us.'[35] On 3 February Sakurai Column began moving through 114th Indian Brigade's outposts, and only its rearguard was detected and dispersed. Steadily they made their way across the Kalapanzin river and established contact with elements of 89th Indian Brigade. On 4 February contact was made by a number of units across the front with Japanese infiltration parties; a column heading for Goppe Pass collided head-on with an RIASC mule column whose Pathans bravely stood their ground, turning them away. In Christison's opinion, it was crucial to the forthcoming battle since had they crossed the Goppe they could have threatened Headquarters 5th Indian Division and Headquarters XV Corps at Bawli Bazaar, defended only by Indian Army pensioners, where stragglers 'wandered in all that day, soaked and weary, many of them wounded and drooping, with a mixture of bewilderment, fear and relief at escaping from the early morning ordeal'.[36]

Slim warned Snelling to prepare to put the air supply plan into effect. As the 5th progressed, attacks against 89th Indian Brigade intensified until it became obvious a much larger Japanese force was involved than anticipated,

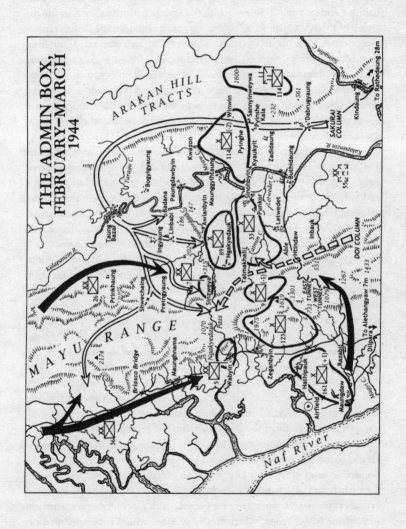

THE ADMIN BOX,
FEBRUARY–MARCH
1944

and Slim put 26th Indian Division under XV Corps command and mobilized other reserves.[37] With satisfaction at the progress made by Sakurai,
Hanaya set the Doi Column moving on 5 February to join the attack on the
British centred around Sinzweya, the abandoned Burmese village in the
centre of the XV Corps area.[38] Next day the situation for the British rapidly
deteriorated. Fifth Indian Division's administrative area was raided, and from
then on all convoys required escort and routes patrolling. As the fighting
approached Headquarters 7th Indian Division at about 0530, a battalion-
sized Japanese force penetrated the widely separated posts, and screams and
shouts were heard in the car park outside the signal centre. 'Suddenly, out
of the dark, misty night, a long line of figures could be discerned approaching the main defences', recalled Lieutenant-Colonel Pat Hobson. 'There was
no doubt who they were and fire was opened ... the advance wavered, came
to a halt and then swiftly withdrew – the wounded and dead being dragged
away.'[39] Messervy and the divisional staff withdrew and the fighting continued throughout the morning. At about 1030, with the Japanese threatening
to occupy higher ground, and with Messervy and his staff already gone,
Brigadier A. F. 'Tim' Hely, the Commander Royal Artillery, decided to
evacuate: a dangerous operation, but the jungle helped conceal movement.[40]
Messervy instructed his units to concentrate as best they could and, split into
small parties, the signallers made their way to the Admin Box at Sinzweya.
This was a flat area of dried-up paddy fields some 1200 yards square, surrounded by low wooded hills. It comprised 7th Indian Division's rear echelon and the basis of XV Corps Forward Maintenance Area under the
command of the corps's 36th Light Anti-Aircraft Regiment RA.[41] In the
middle was a low hillock some 150 feet high, covered in rough scrub. On
this was stacked ammunition and it thus became known, unsurprisingly, as
Ammunition Hill. Further east lay a second conspicuous hill, called Artillery
Hill.[42] Besides ammunition the Box contained an assortment of petrol and
supply dumps, a hospital, officers' shop, mule company and other administrative units due to form the supply core for the projected offensive.

Without communications to Messervy, Christison assumed the worst –
Headquarters 7th Indian Division had presumably been overrun – and he
decided to send 5th Indian Division's 9th Indian Brigade to Sinzweya. In
the early hours of 6 February Brigadier Geoffrey Evans, newly appointed
brigade commander, was traversing Ngakyedauk Pass to his new formation
west of the Mayu range, which in dry weather would have presented no
problem. But after two or three hours of heavy tropical rainfall it had
turned into a morass of mud, and his carrier slipped and slithered in the
mire. It was not easy for traffic negotiating its mass of twists, turns and hair-

pins, clinging grimly to the contours, often at a gradient of 1:8 or more and with signs saying, 'Sweat made the road, carelessness will break it'. Traffic was one-way: eastwards in the morning, westwards in the afternoon, always in low gear and strictly controlled by the Military Police. Any breakdowns had to be towed or pushed up, or tipped over the edge and abandoned.[43] 'It was an awe-inspiring, nerve-wracking drive round endless hairpins,' wrote Lieutenant-Colonel Geoffrey Armstrong, 'of precipitous drops if one looked down and it gave many of us recurrent nightmares for weeks afterwards.'[44] At 1000 on the 7th, Evans received the order from Christison to take over the Admin Box 'and hold it at all costs'; somewhat bemused, he made for Sinzweya, and instructed 9th Indian Brigade to join him as soon as possible.[45]

Half a mile from Sinzweya the carrier baulked at an uphill slope and Evans continued on foot, reaching the Admin Box at 1130. Slim told Christison that the Japanese could probably maintain a force of about a regiment in the rear of XV Corps, but only for a limited period and they would be hoping to force a British withdrawal. It was imperative, therefore, that both 5th and 7th Indian Divisions stand firm until reserves could arrive: 26th Indian Division was due that day and 36th Division in around another week to ten days. In the meantime he would maintain air supply.[46] Indeed, air would prove critical with Beaufighters, Wellingtons and Vultee Vengeance dive-bombers providing ground support, while Spitfires protected the vulnerable transports dropping supplies.[47] But on 8 February Dakotas of 31 and 62 Squadrons were jumped by Japanese Oscars, which shot down one, forced another to crash-land and disrupted the drops of the rest. With the success of the 'stand and fight' policy depending on the badly shaken crews, Old personally led a flight into the battle area to deliver badly needed ammunition despite heavy ground fire. His own plane was hit and holed but the mission was completed, and next day 31 Squadron flew sixteen sorties (although seven failed through the presence of enemy fighters or ground fire). The supply battle was hotting up. Fortunately Spitfires from 81 Squadron also arrived to add their weight, and on 10 February 62 Squadron made thirty-six drops, 194 made eight day and twelve night drops, and 31 Squadron made four, while RAF Wellingtons and USAAF Liberators bombed Japanese airfields near Rangoon. By the middle of the month Japanese air units were forced to withdraw.[48]

The Box, meanwhile, became a nest of headquarters. Messervy and some staff managed to reach Headquarters 25th Dragoons to tell the Commanding Officer, Lieutenant-Colonel H. R. C. Frink, 'Frinkie, I've lost my Division.'[49] After revival with char and whisky he spoke with his scattered commanders via the Dragoons' wireless, instructing Evans to continue commanding the garrison, and re-established Divisional Headquarters south of Ammunition Hill, joined by Headquarters 9th Indian Brigade, with Headquarters 89th Indian Brigade just south of the Ngakyedauk Road. Most of the defending units were administrative with two infantry companies of 4th/8th Gurkhas and three of 2nd West Yorks; 25th Dragoons operated from two harbours protected by 3rd/4th Bombay Grenadiers, with two batteries of 6th Medium and a troop of 8th Heavy Anti-Aircraft Regiments RA.[50] Evans told unit commanders their job was to stay put and keep the Japanese out. They faced a stark choice – fight or be captured, with its attendant horrors – and he instituted a prize for the sector that killed the most Japanese in the previous twenty-four hours. Morale among the men was low: rain and mud made movement a nightmare; trucks and carriers bogged and mules had to be cajoled and driven; while men clung to the dripping branches of trees in ragged, disheartened groups. Evans's blunt and bullying manner was justified in the circumstances but was perhaps mistaken with his senior officers. He had an almighty row with Frink, only smoothed by sending Major Hugh Ley as liaison officer. Evans believed the tanks were so important that he decided to share Ley's slit trench, where he met his match. Ley's soldier servant was Trooper John Evans, a gentleman's gentleman in civilian life, who disliked the army and its ways and refused to allow it, or the close proximity of hand-to-hand fighting, to affect his standards. Trooper Evans duly informed Brigadier Evans that, if the latter wanted a mug of hot tea after morning stand-to, he would do well to remember that he was a guest in the major's trench. It is believed Brigadier gave Trooper no further cause for complaint.[51]

During the night of 7 February a Japanese attack on the eastern entrance of the Box was driven off by tank fire from 25th Dragoons and a counter-attack by 2nd West Yorks. Suddenly there were screams and desperate cries for help. 'Good God!' Brigadier Evans heard someone say, 'They've got into the hospital!'[52] Fortunately most of the wounded had already been evacuated from the lightly defended Main Dressing Station (MDS), owing to earlier shelling. But the Japanese found those remaining, stole what drugs they wanted and threw the rest away, then inflicted on the wounded a truly hideous ordeal. They bound and beat them, kept them without food or water, and shot those who cried out. Next morning they murdered both patients and medical staff. When 2nd West Yorks finally managed to clear the area on 9 February, they discovered the bodies of thirty-one patients and four doctors, with only three survivors.[53] The ferocity of the Japanese demonstrated an inhumanity that both strengthened the immediate resolve of the defenders and helped inspire Anglo-Indian forces to kill the Japanese without mercy.

On 8 February 123rd Indian Brigade was ordered to clear Ngakyedauk Pass. This entailed a long series of battles over the next twelve days, usually on a company frontage.[34] The Japanese manhandled mountain guns into a position with good views over the area. 'Tim' Hely noted the extraordinary mobility of these mule- or man-packed weapons.

> They would lie up silently watching British troops. The first day the British soldiers would keep under cover ... the third day they'd be full of confidence and hanging their washing out on the hill – and that would be the day the Japs would let fly with their gun. Those two rounds would kill 20 or 30 men. All too often five or six rounds fired by a hidden Jap gun would do more damage than a huge barrage fired by our massed artillery.[55]

They fired on Ammunition Hill until a counter-attack drove them off, but it took until the evening to douse the fires and control the explosions.[56] Later a column was observed moving along a nullah running beneath the West Yorks' administrative headquarters, under Regimental Sergeant-Major Jim Maloney, who waited before pouring a devastating fire into the Japanese below, killing 110. A Japanese officer managed to scramble up the bank, slashing with his sword at the orderly room sergeant, who caught the blow on his rifle, and together with his corporal bayoneted the samurai. The contents of packs revealed that many of the Japanese had taken part in the attack on the hospital but, better still, a marked map revealed plans for the next few days and how far behind schedule the Japanese already were. It also showed that the ambush position was a Japanese rendezvous, whose poor communications and slavish adherence to orders led to regular repetitions of the incident over the coming days until the stench became unbearable and the site was bulldozed.[57]

The revelation of the ambitious Japanese plan showed that British offensive plans could not effectively begin before the monsoon, and allowed the release of formations earmarked for those operations to strengthen positions, particularly in the Imphal plain. This was in itself of enormous significance to later battles, and demonstrated to Slim the need to attack wherever possible to exploit the Japanese miscarriage.[58] The Box perimeter, now continuously held, settled into a routine of stand-tos, shelling, patrolling and Japanese attacks while artillery and armour switched to counter each new threat. Most of the attacks were conducted at night. Previously they had subjected the inexperienced and nervous troops to shouted orders or screams for help in English and Urdu to provoke a reaction, but the technique was now familiar, and the use of passwords including the letter 'l', which the Japanese invariably pronounced as an 'r', overcame this. 'Midway through the siege', wrote Scott Gilmore, an American subaltern in 4th/8th Gurkhas,

> my platoon was subjected to an all-out assault. It was not a soothing experience. In the morning there were sixteen bodies lying neatly in a wedge formation in front of our position ... One marvels at the bravery of these men so far from their homes charging desperately and suicidally with sword and bayonet straight into our fire.[59]

Their principal failings were, however, more fundamental. Attacks were unco-ordinated around the perimeter and regularly ran over the same ground, resulting in yet heavier casualties. With ten days to complete the operation – always optimistic given that in order to infiltrate British lines, they were moving with light scales of equipment and minimal supplies – it soon became clear that, despite their fanatical courage, in a stand-up fight the Japanese were poor battle practitioners and the confidence of all within the defence grew.[60]

On the night of 11/12 February II/ and III/143rd Battalions arrived to join the attacks, and 25th Dragoons and 2nd West Yorks were repeatedly called to eject parties of enemy who succeeded in digging in between the perimeter defence posts. Unfortunately for Evans, casualties were mounting and the two 2nd West Yorks companies forming his reserve were seriously depleted. Messervy decided, if possible, to bring 89th Indian Brigade into the Box. Seventh/2nd Punjab Regiment managed to reach Sinzweya the following night, and Brigade Headquarters with 2nd King's Own Scottish Borderers entered on 15/16 February to take over the eastern half.[61] On the 13th Messervy told Christison the position was desperate, but Christison urged him to hold on and directed Lomax's 26th Indian Division to try and effect a relief. Although this was unsuccessful, a few 1st Lincolns led by Major Charles Ferguson Hoey broke in; Ferguson Hoey died of his wounds but received a VC.[62] Having intercepted a wireless order on the afternoon of 14 February, the defenders were prepared when Sakurai launched a night raid with three battalions. The Japanese attacked at 2220 amid much yelling and shouting and, held up against the wire and illuminated in the lurid glare of star shells, were torn apart by guns, tanks and small arms. The Japanese did, however, succeed in pushing a company of 2nd West Yorks from a height known as C Company Hill. This greatly worried Evans, since it put them in view of the new hospital and within 300 yards of his own headquarters. It was retaken by A Company, 2nd West

Yorks, under Major Chris O'Hara, supported by ten tanks of 25th Dragoons. As the infantry approached the objective, O'Hara signalled the tanks with a Very light and the gunners switched from high explosive to armour-piercing solid shot, to enable the Yorkshiremen to advance just 15 yards behind the covering fire. At a second signal the tank fire ceased, and they went in with the bayonet to recover the position.[63]

By now two brigades of 26th Indian Division had concentrated in the neighbouring Kalapanzin valley and, despite the dense jungle and steep slopes, contact was established with 4th Indian Brigade. But Sakurai was suffering too. His strength went from 2,190 on 11 February to 400 by the 21st. From the 15th onwards serious supply problems forced deferment of subsequent assaults, first from the 19th to the 20th, then again to the 22nd. The mountain guns had no more ammunition and the men were foraging with their helmets for unhulled rice. Positions to the front of 33rd and 114th Indian Brigades were found abandoned, which suggested the Japanese were contemplating a general withdrawal. On the 19th Christison ordered patrols southwards to exploit any such intention, planning an all-out effort to destroy the remaining enemy within his area. By the time the order had been issued, however, both brigades found parties of Japanese dug in and clearly not retiring, to cover the extraction of Sakurai Column. On 21 February, 2nd/1st Punjabis of 123rd Indian Brigade finally cleared Point 1070, which commanded a view of the entire Admin Box area.[64] On the 22nd a fanatical attack was launched by a tiny number of Japanese towards Headquarters 7th Indian Division. The attack orders found on a body gave the battalion strength as 3 officers and 73 men. Christison was now confident he could soon clear his land communications, and issued orders for the continuation of his original plans to attack the Buthidaung position. On the 23rd Lieutenant Johnson of 25th Dragoons led the tank troop that relieved the Box. At one point he dismounted and, extrapolating back from the scar on his tank, located the anti-tank gun that caused it, calmly remounted and destroyed it. Thus 89th Indian Brigade secured Ngakyedauk Pass and evacuated 500 casualties from Sinzweya. By now the MDS was overflowing, with flies everywhere and dysentery starting to take its toll. 'And all over the Box the sickly smell of putrefying human and animal flesh hung heavily in the stifling air, which got stronger and revoltingly stronger.'[65]

The next day Hanaya abandoned Ha-Go. Tanahashi of 112th Regiment had, in fact, ordered a withdrawal two days previously. He had broken wireless silence to tell Sakurai, 'I regret doing this, but am determined to do it; there is no alternative.'[66] 'We had run out of our food, and had not eaten for the past two days', recalled Lance-Corporal Sakano Toshiyuki; 'it was very difficult to go down the mountain carrying stretchers when we were so exhausted and hungry. The line of stretchers was a miserable sight of defeated men.'[67] Although A. J. Barker comments that 'the battle was not of the magnitude which the fuss at Delhi suggested it was', since three divisions backed by air power had defeated an attack one third their strength, the Japanese left 5,000 dead on the field; more importantly, the Admin Box was a psychological turning point, a real boost for morale since as Slim noted, Anglo–Indian forces had decisively defeated a major Japanese attack for the first time and proved themselves 'man for man, the masters of the best the Japanese could bring against them ... It was a victory, a victory about which there could be no argument and its effect, not only on the troops engaged but on the whole Fourteenth Army, was immense.'[68] It proved that there was an answer to Japanese infiltration and encirclement tactics, invariably successful until that point.[69] The vital difference was air drop. Everything necessary arrived by this means: food, fuel, ammunition, medical supplies, cigarettes and rum – even new spectacles for Messervy, who lost his and complained that lack of them hampered his chances during his evening game of liar dice.* Hundreds of essential spare parts were also dropped; two days after 136th Field Regiment RA indented by wireless for a breech mechanism cartridge extractor for the A1 gun, the part landed in the very gun pit.[70]

On 24 February Messervy instructed that the Cudgel offensive should resume. The next day large numbers of small Japanese parties were intercepted moving south, which suggested a *sauve-qui-peut* order had been issued. But that day as his tank was negotiating 'Tattenham Corner', Trooper J. McKnight heard a loud clang, indicating the tank he was driving had been hit by a solid anti-tank round. A few seconds later another sent debris flying across his periscope.

> My earphones seemed to leap from my head, Arthur Bears (the loader) yelled into his microphone as loud as he could, 'Branson is dead'. With my ears still ringing from the message, and concentrating on driving the tank through a very hostile situation, I couldn't comprehend what I had just heard. Branson had just been speaking to me.[71]

Clive Branson, poet, artist and sergeant in 25th Dragoons had been killed; his command periscope had taken a direct hit and been blown into his head.

* Liar dice – using five dice marked with the nine to Ace of each suit – was the Burma theatre game, since the little ivory poker dice were weatherproof, portable and visible even in poor lighty (J. Hudson, *Sunset in the East*, p. 49).

'How it must have affected the crew', wondered John Leyin as later they sadly took his body from the tank for burial. 'Indeed, I tremble as I write this.' Branson was a conscript like the rest of them but, at thirty-six, much older and something of a father figure. 'I looked down at Sergeant Branson, his eyes half-closed in death and wondered ... just what did I know.'[72]

Woolner had been ordered to press on to Kyauktaw and, when the Admin Box battle started, to press on faster, which he did with only two battalions led by 11th (East African) Scouts and with all his administrative units, guns and tail immediately behind.[73] Message bags were dropped in lieu of radio communications, weighted and with two coloured streamers, which proved popular with the Africans, who used them to decorate their tents.[74] Air supply provided the men an opportunity to indulge their love of brilliant colour, and they 'stitched themselves with some startling pieces of underwear from parachute silk', noted Captain David Cookson. 'They were so proud of these distinctive garments that disciplinary measures had to be taken to make them keep their trousers on and prevent them revealing our positions by vivid flashes of lingerie.'[75] Parachutes had other uses; warm as blankets and soft as a mattress, they provided excellent insulation to bunker walls and roofs.[76] Lieutenant John Hamilton noted the Africans 'adapted well to the trying and arduous conditions of the Arakan with patience, endurance, and seldom-failing good humour'.[77] But Kofi Genfi of 7th Gold Coast thought otherwise:

> To be in the Burma jungle is the hell ... The monsoon rains – oh dear, dear, dear! It rains: it rains. You are soaked; you don't undress. You dry off when the rain stops. For three weeks you are not taking off your top dress, you are not taking off your shoe ... oh! Woe betide you when you take off your shoe! The foot will be very white, as a pig's trotter. And – it – will – stink! ... up to a mile away! Oh, dear, dear, dear![78]

'Rivers were our nightmares', noted Major Charles Bowen of 5th Gold Coast. Contrary to the canoe-paddling impression of Africans given by movies,

> the average African is *not* river conscious – on the contrary, at the first sight of deep water his senses appear to desert him utterly and he falls into a sort of trance ... His shoulders must be twisted in just the right direction, till eventually he is sat in the boat clutching its sides and on his face all the misery of a soapy dog in a bath.[79]

But the men's acute senses and excellent bush skills made them very effective. One platoon commander leading his men along a jungle path heard a metallic click like a weapon being cocked. 'Sah', said his sergeant in the pidgin that was the West African's lingua franca, 'I savvy dis palaver. One small bushbird make dis talk, it never be mortal man', which brought gales of laughter from the men.[80]

They advanced 70 miles down the Kaladan in four weeks. The whole campaign was characterized by ambushes and short sharp actions as the Japanese continually tried to work their way around the flanks. Slim believed Hanaya had not been deflected from the Admin Box by pressure from the Kaladan, but this was untrue.[81] On 24 February Christison met Woolner and issued orders both to control the valley and strike south-west at the same time, but with only two brigades this was an extremely dangerous and difficult manoeuvre, somewhat akin to doing the splits. A confirmatory order arrived three days later that Kyauktaw must not fall, which left six battalions with only light artillery support to prevent approximately five of Japanese attacking his rear 40 miles away, despite the addition of 7th/16th Punjabis, who were in any case, restricted to the north.[82] As 28th Army received reinforcements from 2nd Division and the INA, Koba ordered 55th Reconnaissance Regiment to attack Kyauktaw while he took a strong force around the flank. As Woolner's scattered force advanced, the East African Scouts reported the Japanese movement and Woolner sent 1st Gambia Regiment across the Kaladan to their assistance. V Force provided valuable information but was sometimes criticized for being too late or exaggerating Japanese strength; but this was often due to the Japanese propensity for splitting into tiny packets spread far and wide. 'One might meet a patrol, foraging party or OP. Odd soldiers had the habit of appearing on every known track, often without any apparent reason.'[83] At Pagoda Hill the Japanese attacked the Gambians and after three days drove them off, threatening the whole divisional position. Woolner was forced to withdraw, and the motor transport and heavy equipment so laboriously brought down 'West African Way' was now an embarrassment and had to return in what Christison regarded as a 'disaster' for which the West Africans were never really forgiven. Despite 7th Gold Coast giving III/111th Regiment a mauling at Kyingri loop, the campaign ended in disappointment.[84]

Following the Admin Box battle 5th Indian Division resumed Cudgel with the task of securing Razabil on 29 February with 9th and 161st Indian Brigades, with 3rd/2nd Punjabis and 3rd/9th Jats under command respectively. After preliminary moves secured Point 731, the attack resumed on 11 March against only light opposition as the Japanese fought a rearguard action toward the Tunnels. Naik Nand Singh of 1st/11th Sikhs won the VC for taking three trenches despite being wounded, before his platoon cleared the position, while 123rd Indian Brigade took the Wrencat position.[85] Control of the forward area was now transferred to 25th Indian Division and 36th Division as 26th Indian Division was brought up, and 44th (Royal Marines) Commando raided Alethangyaw on the coast to prevent Japanese reinforcements moving north during the main attack on the Maungdaw–Buthidaung road.[86]

On 13 March an attack was made on Point 551, an 800 yard long precipitous T-shaped ridge that dominated the Maungdaw–Buthidaung road. Second/13th Frontier Force Rifles was supported in this assault by 26th Indian Division's artillery plus two medium regiments and two batteries from 36th Division, one squadron from 149th RAC, one from 25th Dragoons and a machine-gun battalion. At 0800 all four companies attacked but made only small gains. Together with 4th Indian Brigade more attacks were launched, with Vengeances flying in support, but nothing would dislodge the defenders.[87] At the Tunnels the enemy was subjected to shelling and dive-bombing for three days before being attacked at dawn on 26 March by 72nd Brigade. D Company 6th South Wales Borderers attacked a spur which became known as Tredegar Hill after five men from the town died on its slopes. On 4 April a Sherman tank came up and fired into the tunnel mouth with spectacular effect; bodies and debris were blown out of the far end, with fires and explosions continuing for hours afterwards as an ammunition dump went up.[88] Another attack was launched on 15 April against Point 551, which once more was held up. But with the monsoon approaching Akyab could not now be taken, and Sakurai could see no point in clinging to the summit. On 17 April he instructed Hanaya to prepare to withdraw. It was finally taken by 1st/8th Gurkhas and 2nd/7th Rajputs on 4 May.[89] Captain David Gardiner of 2nd/13th Frontier Force Rifles was bitter: 'The ridge in front of my positions is called Gurkha Ridge and 551 is called Rajput Hill. We're just the 2/13 FF Rifles who've lost almost 350 men and several bloody fine officers in this "soften us up" process.'[90] But following their disappointment in the Kaladan valley, 81st (West African) Division enjoyed a measure of success during April after transferring west across the mountains into the Kalapanzin valley to protect XV Corps' immediate left flank, while a task group called 'Hubforce' including 1st Gambia covered the Kaladan. David Cookson noted:

They had volunteered to fight for the British, and if the British sent them to a wilderness, that was a sufficient reason. They squatted down in their trenches, polished the leather charms they wore next to their skin, prayed to Allah for his protection, and good-humouredly got on with the job.[91]

The fighting continued into June before the final withdrawal as the monsoon took over, with 1st Gambia earning a unique battle honour: 'Mowdok'.[92]

# 15

# Thursday

We are the path he made through the unknown,
Straight as a spear at the enemy thrust,
Never again shall we struggle alone,
We are his legacy, we are his trust.

We are the flag he raised, bloody and torn,
We are his dagger that leaps to the kill,
Strong in our hearts is his courage reborn,
He is our leader, the conqueror, still.

*Song of the Chindits*

NOT CONTENT WITH securing a private army, Wingate soon had a private air force. 'Hap' Arnold was so horrified at Wingate's account of abandoning wounded during Longcloth that he agreed to provide aircraft for casualty evacuation.[1] Initially Arnold kept it quiet from the rest of the recently opened Pentagon, seeing an opportunity to expand and exploit air power. He put Colonel Phil Cochran in command (with Colonel John Alison as his deputy) of what was called 'Project 9' and 'Project CA281' – supposedly after the hotel room where Cochran and Alison met to plan. Cochran was a straight-talking Pennsylvanian, known in USAAF circles as the model for Flip Corkin, an extremely popular comic strip character whose creator had been at school with him.[2] But he had earned his place as hero with a DFC, Croix de Guerre and Silver Star in North Africa.

In August 1943 Arnold sent Cochran to London to confer with Wingate. Their first meeting was inauspicious, recalled Cochran, as Wingate 'mixed everything up with scholarship and the history of war', and a 'gurgling defect of speech' so that, 'I didn't know what he was talking about'. But the following day Cochran suddenly realized Wingate controlled his guerrilla columns in much the same way that fighter planes were controlled from the ground, and 'there was something very deep about him ... When I left I was beginning to assimilate some of the flame about this guy Wingate.'[3]

Back in the States, Cochran secured not only 100 short take-off and landing (STOL) L-1 Vigilant and L-5 Sentinel aircraft for casualty evacuation, but also 30 Mustang fighters, 20 Mitchell bombers, 20 C-47 and 12 UC-64 Norseman transports, with 150 Waco cargo- and troop-carrying gliders with 50 more to come ('I don't want those guys to walk', Arnold had said), and 6 new fangled Sikorski YR-4 helicopters – the first ever used in operations – following a heated argument with the Navy, who also wanted them. Project Nine was renamed 5318th Provisional Unit (Air) in late 1943, then No. 1 Air Commando Group and finally 1st Air Commando Group on 29 March.[4] Although equivalent to a regular wing (normally some 2,000 men), it was to be entirely air transportable and thus just 87 officers and 436 men.[5] However, it was only mandated for ninety days and Wingate would still require considerable support from 221 Group RAF in the Imphal plain, where 31 and 194 Squadrons had Dakotas, and 84 Squadron's Vengeance dive-bombers in the Surma valley.[6]

On returning from London, Wingate found the staff in Delhi distinctly unenthusiastic and threatened to go direct to Churchill. Turning to his new Chief of Staff, Derek Tulloch, he asked, 'Do you think I was too bloody?' Tulloch replied, 'No – we were getting absolutely nowhere. It was the only thing to do.' By this action Wingate 'virtually declared war on the entire staff of GHQ India.'[7] Certainly GHQ(I) was in no hurry to provide the necessary staff, but in October Wingate received the experienced and battle-proven 70th Division – which had led the break-out from Tobruk in November 1941, comprising first-class units. Major-General G. W. Symes of 70th Divison was understandably upset to see it dissolved in favour of a junior involved in operations of dubious value, but his support for the concept ensured a correspondingly good effect throughout the ranks.[8] In his diary he wrote, 'Wingate, although possessing boundless self-confidence, is lacking in administrative and organization knowledge, and knowing it, has an inferiority complex on the matter.'[9] More importantly over the next six months, Wingate remained unaware of changed strategic circumstances. Having been told at Quebec that he would support IV and XV Corps's attacks, he expected these plans to remain set in stone. And despite the limited operational remit, he indulged in grandiose scheming to force his superiors to acknowledge his force was no less than a corps of two divisions – certainly it absorbed the resources.[10] Originally only three brigades would deploy, to be relieved by the other three; eventually five were used, with Slim using 23rd Brigade on the flank of the Kohima battle. With Zionist enthusiasm Wingate wanted to call his formation 'Gideon Force', but this was too clearly linked with him for security and so it became Special Force, then 3rd Indian Division, to cover its LRP purpose.

However, the reordering of strategic priorities at the Cairo conference threatened the entire north Burma offensive and Wingate's part in it. Chiang was sulking and Stilwell disgusted that No.1 Air Commando – nicknamed 'Cochran's Flying Circus'* – had been assigned to support the despised British. British commanders were also envious, and Cochran urged Arnold to draft a letter insisting the Air Commando was in India to support Wingate and no other.[11] Furthermore, with evidence of a Japanese offensive brewing, LRP operations to disrupt them seemed to offer alternative employment for Special Force, and Wingate developed the idea of Strongholds which led him to demand another four battalions in addition to the twenty-three he had already.[12] This idea was very different from guerrilla columns roaming rear areas: convinced by Cochran and Alison that gliders could fly in engineers and bulldozers capable of producing working airstrips, and that undamaged gliders were recoverable, he wanted each 'demesne', as he called them, to enclose a wide area and to include shops and cultivated fields.[13] He even planned to fly 70th Division's dance band, whose signature tune was the current favourite *Praise the Lord and Pass the Ammunition*, both as morale booster and for propaganda effect.[14]

A successful exercise convinced Mountbatten, but Slim and the RAF, who would be required to commit much of their strength, were reluctant, and Wingate's overbearing manner won him few friends. As his best friend Derek Tulloch saw it: 'Conservatism in the armed forces has always striven to stifle "nonconformity" and there were many officers of both services in India in 1943 who honestly thought that Wingate's plan of putting a force of corps strength behind enemy lines and maintaining it by air was suicidal and impossible to achieve.'[15] But only operational success could prove the theory. Meanwhile in training Wingate emphasized watermanship and issued American K-rations – preferred to British 'light scale' hard-tack biscuits and bully beef.[16] 'Breakfast offered a fruit bar, a 4 oz. tin of bacon and egg hash, a small packet of biscuits, and packet of coffee powder', recalled Captain Paddy Dobney. 'However, the British soldier does not like coffee, and this had to be supplemented by tea, powdered milk and sugar.'[17] Dinner included processed cheese and biscuits; supper was meatloaf and more biscuits, with chocolate and soup powder. But these rations were only designed to sustain assault troops for short periods, and offered few more calories than the rations carried on the first expedition. Fergusson,

---

* Also known affectionately by the Chindits as 'Cochran's Young Ladies' (P. R. Boyle and J. R. Wood, *Jungle, Jungle Little Chindit*, p. 97).

when offered command of a brigade, said he would not take troops into Burma on the starvation diet of the first jaunt and Wingate promised better; when Fergusson saw the K-ration, he realized Wingate had lied to him. He tendered his resignation but was persuaded to withdraw it by Mountbatten.[18] Another lie of Wingate's was that Cochran's airmen would provide flying artillery: as a gunner he should have known this was hogwash for, however dedicated and skilled the pilots, they could simply not provide the accuracy or flexibility of guns.[19]

However, most Chindits had unshakeable faith in their commander. Lieutenant J. R. Sealy met Wingate on numerous occasions. 'There was no charisma – but most certainly there was something really compelling about him. An uncanny feeling that what he said was right and that what he intended to do would inevitably be done.'[20] One of the most important lessons taught in training was unpredictability: constant vigilance and deception, feint and bluff.[21] In the months preceding the operation numerous plans had been touted and cancelled. Wingate wrote a stinging note on 5 January 1944, stating that Giffard 'is opposed to taking any of the action proposed by the Supreme Commander to support LRP operations, and no such action is in fact being taken'.[22] He followed up with a memorandum four days later. The original plan as agreed in Quebec was, he said, for three LRP brigades to enter the area of Japanese interior communications bounded by Wuntho–Lashio–Bhamo–Ranmauk and create a situation that could be exploited by the forces advancing on the Chindwin and to open the Burma Road from Myitkyina. The new plan was essentially the same, except that the failure of the Yunnan offensive meant a Kachin rebellion was no longer on the cards and there was also no plan to advance in IV Corps area, making it an unsupported raid on Japanese communications. He was prepared to go ahead with the existing plan or else see his force disbanded, but not for it to remain idle.

Still Wingate pestered Slim to release 26th Indian Division to him and to immobilize 50th Indian Parachute Brigade and release its resources to him but Slim resisted, despite Wingate's appealing directly to Mountbatten. On 19 January he was told he could have the extra four battalions, but five days later Slim changed his mind and wrote to Mountbatten urging the operation be cancelled. Since Wingate refused Indian Troops, 3rd (West African) Brigade was eventually selected to garrison the landing grounds and 3rd/9th Gurkhas and some field and anti-aircraft guns would join 77th Brigade.[23] Wingate wrote again to Mountbatten on 27 January to say it was on. Further letters shot back and forth with ludicrous demands, which Mountbatten's penchant for the 'heroic, the eccentric and the larger-than-life' tolerated.[24] Finally Wingate was given three tasks: to assist Stilwell's advance on Myitkyina; to create favourable conditions for Y Force to cross the Salween; and to inflict maximum loss on the Japanese in north Burma. To achieve this he was to dominate the 'Railway Corridor' between Shwebo and Myitkyina – the main supply route of the Japanese opposing Stilwell in the Hukawng valley – the road between Myitkyina and Bhamo, and Indaw. He chose four landing zones named Piccadilly, Chowringhee, Broadway and Templecombe – to fly in four brigades (Fergusson's 16th would march in), but crucially, having rejected parachuting, zones were chosen to take gliders. Among the first men in would be the American 900th Airborne Engineer Company to clear landing strips to accept Dakotas. Consequently they were a long way from the objectives. Each brigade would then maintain a stronghold which Wingate hoped the Japanese would attack while 'floater' columns operated around them.[25]

Meanwhile on the Imphal plain Cochran's men established two airfields at Hailakandi and Lalaghat. Besides landing strips, bamboo accommodation and service buildings were erected, and air and ground crews worked stripped to the waist alongside native labour and elephants. When Old paid a visit, he was not pleased by the slovenly state, which included many beards. He told Cochran to smarten them up, which Cochran relayed as follows: 'Look, Sports, the beards and attempts at beards are not appreciated by visitors. Since we can't explain to all strangers that the fuzz is a gag, we must avoid their reporting that we are unshaven (regulations say shave) by appearing like Saturday night in Jersey ... Ain't it awful?'[26] They trained hard, although not without mishap. A glider crash killed seven, but Captain Bill Taylor, commanding the glider pilots, received a message from the Chindits: 'Please be assured that we will go with your boys, any place, any time, any where.' These last words became the official motto of No. 1 Air Commando.[27]

Fergusson's brigade set out on 5 February with heavy loads, made heavier by torrential rain. They covered between 9 and 35 miles a day across slimy hills over 5,000 feet high through bamboo and teak on permanently short rations.[28] Captain James Dell noted it took all day to climb a mountain. 'The sappers had cut steps in zig-zags, but they crumbled before half the column had passed. In places the slope was so steep the mules had to be unloaded and their loads passed up by hand.'[29] Bill Cooper of 2nd Queen's Regiment recalled the draining routine. 'Jungle extended on both sides of the track – the same view mile after mile – as we slogged on. Ten minutes halt [every hour], trek, halt, trek. At last we were able to stop for the night, take our packs off and flop down, we were all so exhausted.'[30]

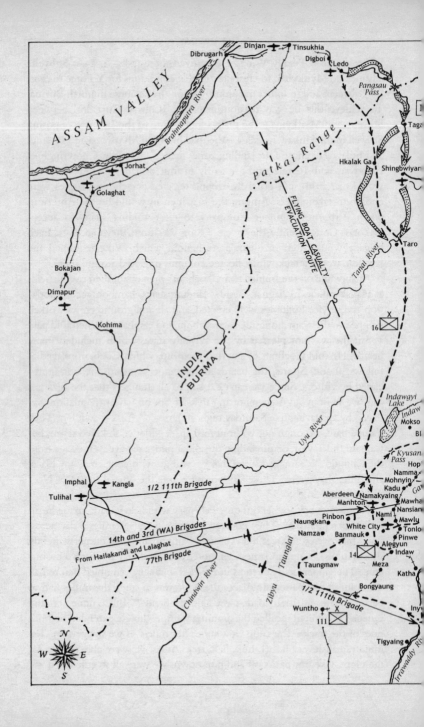

ASSAM VALLEY

Brahmaputra River

Dibrugarh
Dinjan
Tinsukhia
Digboi
Ledo
Pangsau Pass
Taga

Patkai Range

Jorhat
Golaghat

Hkalak Ga
Shingbwiyan

FLYING BOAT
CASUALTY
EVACUATION
ROUTE

Tanai River

Taro

Bokajan

Dimapur

Kohima

16

INDIA
BURMA

Indawgyi
Lake
Indaw
Mokso
Bl

Uyu River

Kyusan Pass
Hop

Imphal
Kangla
1/2 111th Brigade
Namma
Mohnyin
Kadu
Namkyaing
Gav

Tulihal
Aberdeen
Manhton
Mawha
Nansian

14th and 3rd (WA) Brigades
Naungkan
Pinbon
Nami
Mawly

Namza
White City
Tonlo

From Hailakandi and Lalaghat
Banmauk
Pinwe

77th Brigade
Alegyun
14
Indaw

Chindwin River
Zibyu
Taunglai
Taungmaw
Meza
Katha

Bongyaung

1/2 111th Brigade
Iny

Wuntho
111

N
W    E
S
Tigyaing

Irrawaddy Ri

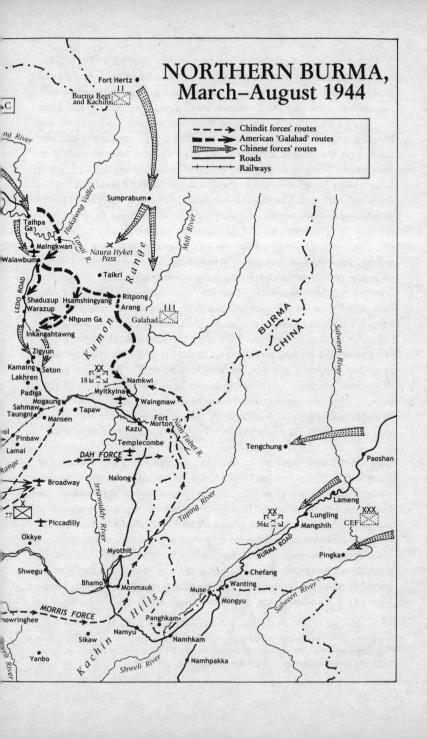

# NORTHERN BURMA,
# March–August 1944

| | |
|---|---|
| – – – ➤ | Chindit forces' routes |
| ━━ ➤ | American 'Galahad' routes |
| ▓▓▓ ➤ | Chinese forces' routes |
| ──── | Roads |
| ┼┼┼┼ | Railways |

Fort Hertz

Burma Regt and Kachins

C

ng River

Sumprabum

Hukawng Valley

Taihpa Ga

Maingkwan

Walawbum

Tanai R.

Naura Hyket Pass

Taikri

Mali River

LEDO ROAD

Shaduzup

Hsamshingyang

Ritpong

Warazup

Arang

Nhpum Ga

Galahad

Inkangahtawng

Kumon Range

BURMA

CHINA

Salween River

Zigyun

Kamaing

Seton

Lakhren

18 XX

Namkwi

Padiga

Mogaung

Myitkyina

Sahmaw

Taungni

Mansen

Tapaw

Waingmaw

Fort Morton

ol

Pinbaw

Kazu

Nam Tabet R.

Tengchung

Paoshan

Lamai

Templecombe

ange

Broadway

DAH FORCE

Nalong

Irrawaddy River

Lameng

77 X

Piccadilly

56 XX

Lungling

Mangshih

CEF XXX

Okkye

Myothit

Taping River

Pingka

Shwegu

Bhamo

Monmauk

Muse

BURMA ROAD

Chefang

Wanting

Mongyu

Salween River

MORRIS FORCE

howringhee

Panghkam

Namyu

Namhkam

Sikaw

Kachin Hills

Namhpakka

Yanbo

Shweli River

li River

STALEMATE

They crossed the Chindwin around the beginning of March but still had another 150 miles to reach Indaw – nearer 400 in real terms.[31] At the same time 1st Indian Brigade simulated a river crossing far to the south, which appeared to provoke a lively reaction, until it was eventually realized that this was part of the Japanese offensive.[32] Meanwhile Cochran's aircraft attacked widely dispersed targets, particularly Mandalay, caught Japanese fighters on the ground at Shwebo and cut telephone lines by trailing an arrestor-like hook: one Mustang returned to base dragging a telegraph pole.[33] On 3 March Wingate wrote that with six LRP brigades, a second divisional staff would be needed, constituting an Army Corps of LRP. 'I shall ~~use maximum pressure~~ expect [Wingate's correction] to obtain it.'[34] Such plotting suggests he had little interest in conforming to strategic direction. Slim disliked 'private armies' intensely, but once approved, nobody supported Thursday more whole-heartedly than Slim, who wrote, 'Wingate and I agreed better than most people expected'.[35] D-Day was fixed for Sunday 5 March, H-Hour for 1700, and a galaxy of senior officers gathered to see Wingate off. But Wingate had forbidden air reconnaissance, to avoid alerting the Japanese: a ridiculous order showing total misunderstanding of air recce.[36] So when Cochran landed a light aircraft at 1630 with a photograph showing Broadway and Chowringhee were clear, but Piccadilly was not, he exploded in rage.[37] When he calmed down, still believing that operational security had been breached, he consulted Calvert, who said he was willing to use Broadway alone; and when Wingate reminded Slim – in distinctly insolent tones – that the final decision was his, Slim did not waver, and the first Dakota moved off at 1812.[38]

Some mules were reluctant to emplane, recalled Revd Donald Mackay, padre with 1st Cameronians.* 'We coaxed, we pulled, we pushed (warily), we beat, we kicked – all in vain, till finally, by a mighty united effort, we twisted him up the ramp and Bismillah! – he went!'[39] The mule's reluctance was justified: at Broadway the gliders hit furrows made by logs dragged to the river by elephants during the monsoon – the apparent blocking had been routine logging. Gliders lost their wheels so they could not be cleared, and successive gliders crashed into them or into the surrounding trees. 'At times the rending, tearing, crunching sound of wings and fuselages being torn apart was quite deafening', recalled Calvert, 'then all

* An effort had been made to de-voice mules for Thursday; a total of 547 horses, 3,134 mules and 250 bullocks being on Special Force strength (J. Clabby, *History of The Royal Army Veterinary Corps 1919–1961*, pp. 124–6; 'Major Douglas Witherington', in D. Twiston Davies (ed.), *The Daily Telegraph Book of Military Obituaries*, pp. 402–6).

would be quiet for a moment until the cries of the wounded men arose from the wrecks.'[40] Lieutenant Christopher Rooke's first task was to help with an amputation, 'a badly mangled arm, of a soldier who had come in. [The doctor] had no anaesthetics and I remember I had to hold the arm while he operated. The man was only semi-conscious and he kept calling for his mother. The operation had to be performed under candlelight.' Rooke was sent to find blood plasma, but by the time he returned the patient had died.[41] Calvert had to decide what signal to send: 'Pork Sausage', the cookhouse favourite, for success, or 'Soya-Link', its loathed substitute, for failure. Reluctantly, he sent the latter.

Of 62 gliders that left Lalaghat, 350 men arrived unharmed in 35; casualties amounted to 30 killed and a similar number wounded. Eight gliders were recalled on receiving 'Soya-Link'. Many had been overloaded by the troops, and eight crash-landed in India, the remainder landing inside Burma, which at least spread confusion among the Japanese – one even landed near Headquarters 15th Division at Pinlebu.[42] About half of these men managed to return to Assam and join the expedition later; only 66 did not return. But in the meantime Calvert grew more confident. A smart latecomer wearing a monocle marched in with his men in step. '"Major Shuttleworth and thirty men of the 1st Battalion, the Lancashire Fusiliers, reporting for orders, sir." What a welcome sight and sound that was, a real slice of military order and discipline after a night of confusion and disaster.'[43] He sent 'Pork Sausage', much to Wingate's delight.

The following day 900th Airborne Engineer Company cleared the wreckage from the runway, and Major Andy Rebori led 12 little L-5s in to evacuate the wounded.[44] That night another sixty-five Dakota sorties brought in 900 men plus stores and mules while defences were prepared. Fortunately there was still no sign of the enemy.[45] On D+2 Air Marshal John Baldwin, AOC-in-C of 3rd TAF, hitched a ride on Group Captain George Donaldson's Dakota, forcing the navigator to stand. Then Alison appeared, 'and said "Okay if I join you fellas?" He squatted on the floor and promptly went to sleep – within kicking distance of a mule!' recalled Donaldson. 'I was very touched by this gesture, which so naturally epitomized the solidarity and confidence which had developed between our American allies and ourselves.'[46] Between 5 and 11 March No.1 Air Commando and the 177 Wing RAF flew 579 Dakota sorties, landing 9,000 men, 1,300 animals and 250 tons of stores without a single loss to enemy action – a remarkable feat by any standards.[47] One night Colonel Matsumura Hiroshi of 60th Regiment in 15th Division, due to attack Imphal, was woken by the throbbing sound of aircraft. He and his men peered up into the bright moonlight and could not help but be impressed by the formations of aircraft. 'But what are they making for behind our lines?'[48]

Soon 111th Brigade under Brigadier W. D. A. 'Joe' Lentaigne had flown into Chowringhee and Broadway, where a hospital was set up. By 7 March three British battalions were firm in Broadway, and 3rd/6th Gurkhas arrived that night 'As the aircraft became airborne there were exclamations of surprise and noses were pressed against the small windows, but before long everyone was asleep.'[49] The airstrip was efficient enough to base six Spitfires from 81 Squadron there, making Cochran feel he had been bounced off his own field. He thought Wingate complicit until he was disabused of this notion after confronting him. But despite surprising some Japanese aircraft raiding Broadway, early warning was insufficient and they were forced to leave, although the airfield remained secure enough for amenities including a dispensary, a small garden and even a chicken farm to be established.[50] Meanwhile No. 1 Air Commando attacked Japanese airfields, catching aircraft on the ground, claiming over 30 destroyed and stopping only when dense clouds of smoke from burning aviation fuel blotted out the targets.

On 11 March Wingate issued a stirring Order of the Day warning that 'the enemy will react with violence'.[51] However, the Japanese reaction was less than perhaps Thursday's planners hoped. Certainly Mutaguchi was unfazed, regarding it as a 'mouse in a bag'.[52] Nevertheless, the immediate effect was to delay the forward move of Headquarters 15th Army, jeopardizing liaison with the divisional commanders and inhibiting transport of supplies towards Imphal, since it not only cut the lines of communication to 15th and 31st Divisions (and of 18th Division to the north) but also prevented the scheduled movement of vehicles from Indaw–Homalin to the Shwebo–Kalewa road. Some elements of 15th Division had to be committed against it, as was 53rd Division, the only available reserve, and much of 5th Air Division. However, the absorption of massive air power in its support also meant that crossing the Chindwin and the initial phases of the battle were carried out with little interference from the air.[53]

Meanwhile Calvert set off to establish a block on the railway. The route involved crossing the 3,000-feet Gangaw range and the slow but deep Kawkke Chaung, and it took six days to reach the railway at Henu, where they shot up two infantry companies Mutaguchi had assembled to send to Indaw.[54] On 18 March the Japanese who had penetrated the position of Major Ron Degg's 80 Column of 1st South Staffordshire Regiment were seen on a small hill near the railway. Realizing swift action was needed, and with a company of 3rd/6th Gurkhas to cover them, Calvert ordered the South Staffords to charge, which, reluctantly at first, they did. A few shots came back, but then the Japanese leapt out and charged back, something which was 'certainly not going according to the military rule books'. They clashed in an area some 50 yards square on the hilltop, and the air

> was filled with the sound of steel crashing against steel, the screams and curses of wounded men, the sharp crack of revolver and rifle shots, the eerie whine of stray bullets and the sickening crunch of breaking bones. Everyone slashed and bashed at the enemy with any weapon that came to hand, yelling and shouting as they did so. In Europe the cold steel part of it would have been restricted to bayonets; out here there was more variety, with Japanese officers wielding their huge swords and the Gurkhas doing sterling work with the kukri.[55]

It was medieval in its savagery. Norman Durant saw his friend Lieutenant George Cairns struggling on the ground. 'I saw George break free and picking up a rifle and bayonet stab the Japanese again and again like a mad man. It was only when I got near that I saw he himself already had been bayoneted twice in the side and that his left arm was hanging on by a few strips of muscle.'[56] Calvert and others saw Cairns almost lose his arm to a sword stroke, then shoot his assailant before picking up the sword and leading on his men.

The small bloody battle of Pagoda Hill was won, albeit at a price – 23 killed, including Cairns, who died of his terrible wounds and was eventually awarded a VC, and 64 wounded[57] – and they counted 42 Japanese dead on the position, had killed and wounded many more, and were elated by victory. The ground won became a new base, called White City because of the parachutes that came to drape the surrounding trees, including a large drop of defence stores and ammunition on 18 March that took a week to collect. A battery of 25-pounders and two troops of anti-aircraft guns were landed, but fire support relied heavily on Cochran's fliers.[58] When signalling proved difficult at night, Major R. C. Pringle was ordered to try and use the railway signalling system and found it connected to the Japanese telephone network. Stilwell sent two Nisei (Japanese-Americans) to listen and interpret and for ten days they gleaned useful information before the Japanese cottoned on; connecting a Brigade Headquarters directly to the enemy's telephone exchange remains one of the more unusual feats of military signalling.[59]

Once the Japanese realized they were dealing with more than a few airborne companies, III/114th Regiment was sent towards Henu from near Mandalay, then II/51st Regiment to take over from the two companies mauled by Calvert at Pagoda Hill. They had an encounter with a Chindit column on their way to attack White City on 21 March.[60] Fighting continued for two days but then the Japanese retired to Mawlu. Meanwhile Fergusson's men plodded onwards, first to set up a base at Taungle, then to support Calvert, before Wingate changed his mind and told Fergusson to seize Indaw, although by now his columns were not well placed and his men exhausted. Wingate arrived by light aircraft to confer and also moved his base 2 miles. This was Aberdeen, into which he proposed to fly 14th Brigade. However, these plans were changed when Wingate returned to Comilla to confer with Slim, who said he needed 14th Brigade 60 miles south-west of Aberdeen to disrupt Japanese communications now that they were attacking Imphal. Wingate also argued with Mountbatten over a press release stating Fourteenth Army had launched a successful airborne operation without mentioning the Chindits or the Air Commando. Mountbatten replied that Wingate's missives 'made me realize how you have achieved such amazing success in getting yourself disliked by people who are only too ready to be on your side'.[61]

It took some time for Burma Area Army to react to the Chindits, with their attention held by the 'March on Delhi', and while Kawabe ordered Major-General Hayashi Yoshihide of 24th Independent Mixed Brigade to clear the railway and provided a division's worth of troops, Calvert strengthened his position. Unfortunately the change of plan regarding 14th Brigade had not reached Fergusson, who thus needlessly attacked Indaw, which the Japanese had reinforced by 21 March. With Fergusson unable to concentrate his dispersed columns the attack was a failure as they blundered into Japanese outposts.[62] One column of 45th Reconnaissance Regiment was fired on by one of 2nd Leicestershire Regiment, revealing the poor fire discipline and training of some of the new Chindits.[63] Another column from 2nd Leicesters captured one of the two airfields, but were then ordered back as part of a general withdrawal to Aberdeen, which was falsely reported as being under heavy Japanese attack. In fact, both 14th and 3rd (West African) Brigades were arriving. On 24 March Wingate visited Calvert and told him he had signalled Churchill to say that, given another three squadrons of Dakotas, he could take all of north Burma.[64] Then he set off for a conference at Imphal, but his Mitchell never arrived.

The news that Wingate had been killed in an air crash struck everyone immensely hard. 'Who will look after us now?' wondered Captain Richard Rhodes-James. 'Our master was gone and we, his masterpiece, were now ownerless.'[65] For Captain Rodney Tatchell 'the bottom had fallen out of the campaign.'[66] Yet it had barely started. Partly on Tulloch's recommendation and partly on seniority, Slim appointed Lentaigne as replacement, although few would argue that the death of their inspirational leader knocked some of the bounce out of Special Force. In effect, Lentaigne was not so much in command of the Chindits as there to advise, exhort or chide them as necessary – by signal – and they saw little of him.[67] At Jorhat on 3 April Slim came under pressure to divert the Chindits south to disrupt Mutaguchi's communications, but from 6 April the Japanese flung themselves at White City for five days, and bombardments increased in intensity. Mike Calvert remembered 'lying in my dug-out and giving way to uncontrollable fits of shivering, brought on partly by fear and partly by frustration'.[68] Private William Merchant recalled: 'There were hundreds of Japanese bodies hanging on the wire ... The Japs were very brave but stupid – they'd attack the same place every night. They came across the paddy banging and shouting.'[69] As Thursday developed into a major operation and the possibility of a co-ordinated offensive with Stilwell developed, the long-planned formation of 33rd Army under Lieutenant-General Honda Masaki was accelerated, with organization orders issued on 8 April, to include 24th Mixed Independent Brigade, 18th and 56th Divisions with 53rd Division – *en route* from northern Malaya – coming under command on 24 April. Its mission was defined as operations against X and Y Forces and Special Force.[70]

No. 1 Air Commando flew in support of 14th, 16th and 111th Brigades. They could be directed to any spot at 2½ hours notice but were most effective at White City, which they were accustomed to, now reinforced by 3rd (West African) Brigade.[71] James Shaw was a forty-year-old sergeant, one of around forty British NCOs serving with 12th Nigeria Regiment. His orderly, Zaki, was a Munchi from an isolated northern tribe. 'As is usual with his tribe, his teeth were filed to points like a dog's, and the skin of his face stood up in bumps and ridges. It had been cut in infancy with a knife, another playful Munchi habit.'[72] They found the entire area pitted with craters and all vegetation destroyed. The filth of war was everywhere – half-eaten tins of food and spent cartridge cases – while the latrines were mere holes in the ground and every night stores of every description descended by parachute. For columns operating outside the bases a map reference would be signalled to Air Base, and a large 'L' made on the ground with either flares or fires at night or smoke by day. When the aircraft was about 10 miles away, the signal fire would be lit and the pilot would confirm the position by radio or Very flares, recalled Flight Sergeant Albert Friend: 'they lit a triangle of fires, then we dropped almost adjacent to the fires.'[73] Those on the ground 'always knew whether the crew were our own or

American, The RAF would only listen, but the Yanks enlivened the proceedings with wisecracks.'[74] Parachuted loads might land in the drop zone or up to a quarter of a mile off, if wind or a bad approach pushed the pilot off his correct course and altitude. The aircraft would circle and each time along the long arm of the L drop several parachutes; the men below quickly dragged away the supplies to break them down for issue. Only fragile loads were parachuted. Most, such as clothing, mule-feed and barbed wire, was 'free-dropped'.[75] Lieutenant Rooke found it 'quite nerve-wracking when you heard a twang of the barbed wire no more than 15 yards away from you, particularly as they used to bounce up again and go dong, dong, dong as they repeatedly jumped … one person was killed by a bale of hay landing on him.'[76]

On 11 April the Japanese were 'buzzing like angry bees' around 111th Brigade, now commanded by John Masters, formerly the Brigade Major.[77] One Gurkha Bren gun team engaged them from a flank and were fired at in their turn by a Japanese machine-gun. The No. 1 got a burst in the face and neck, which killed him instantly. 'But he did not die where he lay, behind the gun. He rolled over to his right, away from the gun, his left hand coming up in death to tap the No. 2 on the shoulder in the signal that means *Take over.*' Masters knew the seventeen-year-old No. 1 and was close to tears when he heard the tale.[78] The last Japanese attack on White City came on 17 April, led by Hayashi on a white horse, who was killed as his men penetrated the defences. Lieutenant Durant had a grandstand view commanding the South Staffords' machine-gun platoon as they 'mowed down a number of Japs attacking from the north', before a Nigerian counter-attack accounted for the survivors. When the Japanese withdrew, one was left behind in a trench being heavily grenaded. Rather than surrender, he charged. 'A West African dropped his rifle, picked up a wooden box containing twelve grenades and batted him over the head – end of "suicide Joe".'[79] The defence owed much to the field guns flown in to the airstrip beside the railway and to the bold and skilful support of Cochran's fighter-bombers. Desmond Whyte, a medical officer, noted the risks Cochran's men took. An L-1 landed and the pilot, seeing his casualties, said

'I'll take two.' We pointed out that the plane could take only one passenger plus pilot, the patient being almost literally wound around the pilot's waist, not even a stretcher or medical attendant being feasible. Saying 'We can't leave these dying men here', he loaded up and sped across the open paddy, hitting the trees at the far end. A white-vested figure pushed itself out of the wreckage saying, 'Ah shit, I ought to be shot.' I said, 'We will if we don't scarper.'[80]

On 21 April the world's first operational helicopter sortie took place when 2nd Lieutenant Carter Harman flew a rescue following the crash of an L-1.[81]

Also inserted near by was Dah Force, led by Lieutenant-Colonel D. C. Herring, a Burma Rifles officer tasked with raising Kachin guerrillas, while SOE also had operatives in the area, none of whose operations was properly co-ordinated.[82] On the Bhamo road near the China/Burma border, Morrisforce – based on 4th/9th Gurkhas – with three independent columns, demolished the bridge on the Taiping river but was forced to withdraw into the hills. Major Peter Cane met some Shan Chinese and bought their crop of rice and tea, although one man seemed unhappy with his generous payment. 'The reason for this soon became apparent. The ten pounds of tea may have been highly priced at Rs 8/-, but not so the contents of the false bottom of his basket, which contained opium valued at Rs 10,000/ – I'm afraid we didn't pay for it as Mike Busk's Burma Police instincts forbade it.' They carried it for a long time before sending it to India for medical use.[83] Later they had some success against Japanese camps along the Bhamo road that might have strangled the last lifeline to Myitkyina, but Headquarters Special Force in Assam refused them the necessary air support, and Japanese reinforcements arrived, forcing them to withdraw.[84]

After attacking Kyaungle and destroying stores dumps, 111th Brigade was ordered to join 16th Brigade at Aberdeen and form a block as 77th Brigade had done at White City; orders that Masters did not like because they negated the Chindits' great strength: jungle mobility.[85] However, the orders originated not from Lentaigne but from Slim, acceding to Stilwell on 23 April. They were then ordered to move north to establish a new block at 'Blackpool' on the road and railway between Hopin and Pinbaw with support from 14th Brigade, which, having flown in and demolished the rail bridge at Bonyaung, was moving towards Indaw. With Wingate now gone, rumours abounded. All agreed that White City could be held in the dry season, but the monsoon was another matter. Air supply was always tricky, but bad weather made it practically impossible. A captured diary revealed one Japanese attitude: 'British prisoners say they will win with their big material resources and superior arms. They are bastards, but to some extent I admire them.'[86] Wingate had promised that each brigade would operate for no more than ninety days, and although Fergusson's 16th Brigade were pulled out shortly after this limit, the others were already very tired, and the sick list was increasing daily. Every Chindit suffered malaria at some point, but only acute cases were evacuated. Some were left hidden while their column completed its task, as happened to ten men outside White City. The next evening they were found by a Japanese patrol, who had 'five minutes bayonet practice before their supper. Only one man escaped and when he staggered into the Namaan observation post, his reason had nearly gone.' He had somehow hidden under a dead comrade's body 'while Japanese soldiers had laughed round their fires and sentries strolled among the dead'.[87] The behaviour of the Japanese, 'the hobgoblins of the Burma forest, remained beyond the grasp of our imagination', noted Major Charles Carfrae of 7th Nigeria. 'We didn't hate them; they were too strange, too alien to hate. At the time we hardly thought of them as men.'[88]

With bis command crumbling, Lentaigne tried to invoke Wingate's special relationship with Churchill to shore it up. In a message to Mountbatten he requested that the prime minister be informed that 'Operation conceived by Wingate successfully completed, but lack of follow-up troops makes withdrawal inevitable'.[89] But Mountbatten had no intention of allowing Lentaigne a direct line to Churchill. On instructions from Mountbatten, Lentaigne and Slim visited Stilwell on 1 May and agreed that Special Force would come under the latter's command, at a date to be specified.[90] Consequently Lentaigne decided to abandon Aberdeen, Broadway and White City and to reinforce Blackpool with 3rd/9th Gurkhas and 1st King's (Liverpool) from 77th Brigade, the rest of which with 3rd (West African) Brigade would protect its east and west flanks.[91] The various positions in Blackpool were nicknamed after cricket fielding positions – Cover Point, Midwicket and the Deep – after a friend assured Masters that familiar names gave comfort and familiarity in foreign fields.[92] With only II/146th Regiment in the area, Japanese attacks were sporadic to begin with, but they soon intensified once 53rd Division arrived under Major-General Takeda, which was now closing in on Blackpool.[93] But unlike White City, Blackpool lacked the 30-yard deep belts of wire, mines and bunkers roofed with railway sleepers. And although it cut the railway line, it could not dominate the road, along which the Japanese could pour these reinforcements. After creating an airstrip on which a couple of C-47s crashed, and centralizing the brigade's mortars to bring fire on any threatened corner of the perimeter, a sustained and heavy Japanese attack came on 2nd King's Own Royal Regiment in the Deep.

> The actions of the next five nights defy description or reasonable analysis. At the north-west corner of the block, round the Deep, a furious battle raged from dusk till an hour or two before dawn, fought at ten yards range with Brens, grenades, rifles, tommy guns ... to the left of the attacking Japanese, and in full view of them, C-47s landed with glaring headlights on the by now brilliantly lighted strip.[94]

Between the airstrip and the Japanese, Masters had no troops and the far side of the strip was only lightly protected, but the Japanese never changed their point of attack and always attacked head on. But Revd W. H. Miller, the padre, noted how fatigue and sickness dulled performance and the numbers of self-inflicted injuries rose.[95]

On 10 May James Shaw's column prepared to walk out of White City after booby-trapping everything that could not be removed and making careful displays of normality. They were soon among steep valleys and thick bamboo, which 'we crashed through with a shocking noise as mules slid and loads swayed ... Sweat poured from us, and we cursed the tendrils and treacherous roots that tore at our feet and almost hurled us headlong. The animals suffered dumbly, far more than we yet realized.'[96] On 17 May, 2nd King's Own were forced out of the Deep. Masters replaced them with 1st Cameronians as they came back into reserve. Fortunately 1st King's (Liverpool) and 3rd/9th Gurkhas arrived, who, having been spared most of the long marches, were fit and at full strength. Scott Leathart's Gurkhas took over from a British unit, and Leathart found a soldier looking out over the valley. 'He took no notice of me when I jumped in beside him', he recalled, and when he then tapped him on the shoulder,

> he rolled over sideways, stiff with *rigor mortis*. There was no sign of wounds and I never discovered how he died. But finding him like that, with none of his officers or comrades having even noticed his absence, was a chilling experience and one which typified the atmosphere in that ghastly place.[97]

However, the elements were as much an enemy as the Japanese. With the weather seriously affecting air operations, 1st Air Commando was replaced by Tenth Air Force on 20 May. By the end of April, Cochran noted, the fighter pilots were 'getting sick with extreme fatigue ... we had harder work than ever in winding up the job, and wore ourselves out, were ourselves ill.'[98] On the ground things were worse with the rains rendering airstrips unserviceable and thus preventing casualty evacuation. 'We were all to see once robust men waste away to skin and bone, and to fall exhausted from sickness and weariness,' recalled Lieutenant-Colonel P. H. Graves-Morris, 'to die before they could be evacuated.'[99]

# 16

## Kohima: the siege

Whence Thou Persistent vision I perceive
These thrice times daily with mine eyes?
How did strange alchemies conceive
Thy content's formula, thy size?

What Witch's Cauldron, Den of Vices,
Devil's Kitchen, Orient Spices,
Serpent's fangs, and poisonous potions,
What magic spell of mystic motions
Blended in unearthly brew,
Produced a Rissole, such as you?

Anon, *Odious Ode to a Soya Link*[1]


IT WAS LUCKY for Slim and Stilwell that when Mutaguchi instructed Sato to take Dimapur, Kawabe made him rescind the order on the grounds that it was not 'within the strategic objectives of the 15th Army'.[2] However, Sato never saw the slightest chance of 31st Division being able to attack Dimapur; supply shortages, particularly of ammunition, rendered it impossible. But Imphal was expected to fall very quickly after the first attack and then, with supplies and reinforcements sent up from 15th and 33rd Divisions, 31st Division could go for the railway.[3]

Unlike Imphal, Kohima was not deliberately chosen as a battlefield by the British; but whoever controlled Kohima Ridge controlled the Dimapur–Imphal road, which looped around it.[4] Kohima sits at 5,000 feet above sea-level and is dominated by mountains up to twice that height: It was a cool hill station, the civil administrative centre for the area, now turned into a base camp including 53rd Indian General Hospital, 57th Reinforcement Camp and supply and workshop facilities. These were laid out on various hills below the village around which the road looped, and gave them their names, dotted with *bashas* – windowless bamboo huts with space between the walls and roof that served as stores and workshops. To

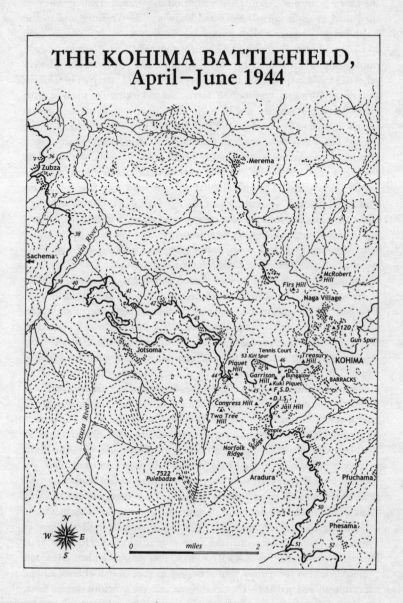

# THE KOHIMA BATTLEFIELD,
## April–June 1944

Merema

Zubza

Sachema

Dzuza River

McRobert
Hill

Firs Hill

Naga Village

▲5120

Gun Spur

Jotsoma

Tennis Court

IGH Spur

Treasury
Hill

KOHIMA

Piquet
Hill

DC's
Bungalow

Garrison
Hill

Kuki Piquet

BARRACKS

F.S.D.

Congress Hill

D.I.S.

Two Tree
Hill

Jail Hill

Pimple

Norfolk
Ridge

G.P.T. Ridge

7522
Pulebadze

Aradura

Pfuchama

Phesama

Dzuza River

N
W — E
S

0       miles       2

the west was the wooden fort that withstood an eighteen-day siege in 1879, now used as government offices and known as the Treasury, and to the north lay the straggling Naga township.

Colonel Hugh Richards had commanded 3rd (West African) Brigade until Wingate discovered he was fifty years old. He was immediately relieved as Wingate decreed nobody over forty could take part in Chindit operations (Wingate was himself forty). After kicking his heels at 11th Army Group, Richards was sent via IV Corps to command Kohima Garrison with orders to deny the area Jessami–Kharasom–Kohima to the enemy, but when he arrived on 22 March he found Kohima in chaos.[5] Instead of 1st Assam Regiment he found only elements of the Indian Pioneer Corps and RIASC: supply depots, field bakeries, even a cattle-conducting section.[6] The only combatants were some men from 3rd Assam Rifles, the Shere Regiment (raw troops from the Royal Nepalese Army), two companies of 1st Burma Regiment and various detachments, including convalescents.[7] With little time to prepare, he immediately set about evacuating transport and stores, and digging and stocking defensive positions, all of which continued until the last minute.[8]

Initially Richards was under the command of Major-General R. P. L. Ranking at 202nd Area, which included both Kohima and the railhead at Dimapur, which with its score of stone monuments like enormous button mushrooms was known to the British as 'Prick Park'.[9] This administrative formation was concerned with the minutiae of discipline, reports and returns, and with the manning and running of reinforcement and rest camps.[10] Its main concern were the dumps at Dimapur, some 11 miles long and at least a mile wide. But Richards soon found that troops came and went without reference to him, and the size of the Box and the number of troops available to man it were therefore almost impossible to compute.[11] He needed barbed wire but an administrative order prohibited its use in the Naga hills. His delight at the arrival of 2nd West Yorks was short-lived as they were almost immediately despatched elsewhere, and then 4th Queen's Own Royal West Kent Regiment of 161st Indian Brigade arrived from Dimapur, only to be ordered to return. Their movement order of 25 March had anticipated this confusion; it was code-named 'Shytehawk'.[12]

Ranking had initially ordered 161st Indian Brigade under Brigadier Frederick 'Daddy' Warren to take over command of the Kohima area. But the commander of XXXIII Corps, Lieutenant-General Montagu Stopford, whose formation Slim arranged to take overall control of the area, instead ordered it to Dimapur to defend the precious dumps from anticipated Japanese infiltration, an order that Slim endorsed.[13] Unaware that Sato's objective was limited to Kohima, Slim's instinct gave way to Stopford's hard logic, and he agreed to this plan, though it caused much bitterness: both Richards and Warren saw the danger of the Japanese taking Kohima, enabling them to cut communications between Dimapur and Imphal. At the same time the Deputy Commissioner at Kohima, Charles Pawsey, who had served with the Nagas for twenty-two years, believed they were being abandoned by the Army to the depredations of the Japanese. When Ranking explained that an RAF report suggested the Japanese were outflanking Kohima to make for Dimapur, Pawsey scoffed: 'If the Japanese were there, then my Nagas would have told me so!' Indeed, Richards came to realize that the Nagas regarded Pawsey 'as their father who would solve all their troubles', and that information from them via Pawsey was always accurate.[14]

Meanwhile, Japanese 138th Regiment attacked 1st Assam Regiment at Jessami on 28 March and were beaten off. The Adjutant described the second day's fighting:

> Apart from another heavy attack in the morning, we had a comparatively quiet day. We took full advantage of this to brew hot tea. We assumed, and quite rightly, that the Jap was licking his wounds and bringing up reinforcements, for towards evening he opened fire with his beastly little battalion gun (nick-named the 'Whizz-bang') but did little damage on this occasion.[15]

That same day Richards raised the 'last man' order with Warren and Ranking when they arrived at Kohima, and Warren hastily arranged to withdraw all the forces east of Kohima.[16] But communications were parlous and the orders only reached the garrison at Phek, where Lieutenant John Corlett, doubtful that messages dropped from the air had reached the rest of the battalion, took the hazardous mission of passing this personally to Jessami: just as well since every minute's delay increased that the chances the action truly would be a 'last man, last round' struggle. The Japanese, aware of the intention to withdraw through having indeed captured messages dropped from the air, renewed their efforts to destroy the garrison. The situation rapidly deteriorated and the withdrawal became ragged and disorganized, although most managed to get away.[17]

Unfortunately, the rescinding of the 'last man, last round' order never reached A Company at Kharasom. With the approaching Japanese far too strong to be stopped by a single company, its young Glaswegian commander, Captain Jock Young, summoned his platoon commanders and ordered them to break out for Kohima. 'Since my orders are to fight to the last man,' he announced, 'I will *be* the last man.' Later, another Assam

Regiment officer heard from a jemadar in tears who saw Young 'standing on the firestep of his bunker, stacking tommy-gun magazines on the parapet, piling quantities of hand grenades around him and passing a Bren gun to a wounded sepoy who had dragged himself to Young's bunker'.[18] Nagas later reported that the Japanese attacked at dawn; there were explosions and firing, followed by silence. The battalion was split in two; 260 joined the Kohima garrison while the others reached the Dimapur road behind 161st Indian Brigade.

On 1 April 2nd Division began to arrive at Dimapur. 'The whole place is one big flap', wrote Captain Arthur Swinson of Headquarters 5th Brigade. Base staff were 'digging and wiring themselves in their offices, and gangs of pioneers are putting slit trenches around the Rest Camp Transport with wild-eyed Indian drivers speeding north along the Bokajan road with barely six inches between the trucks'.[19] Headquarters XXXIII Corps was opened at Jorhat on the 2nd, and Stopford assumed command of all troops in the Assam and Surma valleys. At a conference next day Slim told him to reinforce Kohima 'as soon as he could without endangering the safety of Dimapur'.[20] On 4 April Stopford felt strong enough to return 161st Indian Brigade to Kohima. Led by the Royal West Kents, they set off with the men considering calling themselves 'The Duke of York's Own', after the nursery rhyme.[21]

The Kentish men were commanded by Lieutenant-Colonel John Laverty, 'a "bloody-minded" Irishman of immense courage, of great strength of character and possessed of inflexible stubbornness' and known as 'Texan Dan'. 'He looked something like a cowboy, with his broad-brimmed Gurkha hat straight on his small head, his uniform hanging untidily from his skinny body, his face both kind and sad, as cowboys' faces are.'[22] A Territorial battalion of the 'Dirty Half Hundred',* after service in France in 1940 it was badly handled at the battle of Alam Halfa in the Western Desert in 1942 and more recently in Arakan, where it suffered heavy casualties: 63 dead, 146 wounded and 2 missing, although 92 of the wounded had rejoined.[23] It had since been made up with drafts from other regiments, including one just two days previously that had originally been destined for the South Wales Borderers, now posted to B Company. But it retained the essential character created by local bonds, and fulfilled

---

* There are various explanations for the Royal West Kents' nickname, the most common being that it referred to their blackened faces at the battle of Vimiero in 1808, and the black facings of their redcoats, although in this they were not unique. The 'half hundred' refers to the 1st Battalion's having originally been the 50th Regiment of Foot.

Auchinleck's alleged preference for Territorials as 'more enterprising, less hidebound' than Regulars.[24]

They arrived on 5 April, shortly before Kohima was surrounded by the Japanese, together with 20th Mountain Battery, an engineer detachment from 2nd Field Company and another from 75th Indian Field Ambulance, including the 'Tactical Doctor', Lieutenant-Colonel John Young, who arrived the following day and would prove invaluable.[25] Warren realized there was insufficient room on Kohima Ridge for his entire brigade and deployed the remainder around Jotsoma, some 2½ miles to the north-west, although most of 1st/1st Punjabis had deployed to Tuphema on 28 March to patrol to the north and north-east. When they made contact with Japanese 58th Regiment on 30 March, the situation along the length of the Kohima–Imphal road deteriorated so quickly that they were ordered back to Mao Songsang, then steadily withdrew to join the rest of the brigade at Jotsoma on 6 April.[26] This box proved one of the decisive factors in the subsequent battle, since it enabled 24th Mountain Regiment to provide artillery support to the garrison throughout the siege.[27] All through 6 April they arrived around two road junctions nicknamed 'Lancaster Gate' and 'Paternoster Row', while 2nd Mountain Battery exchanged fire with Japanese gunners, who quickly took their guns out of action, probably knowing that they did not have the ammunition to engage in duels. Shortly afterwards Major John Nettlefield noted 'an elephant carrying what our binoculars seemed to indicate was another mountain gun ... ambling along the Bokojan track. Our first round landed very close and the elephant was seen to charge, apparently out of control, into the nearby cover. We followed up with a few more rounds for luck – we were sorry about the elephant, but it was war.'[28]

As they arrived, 4th Royal West Kents met some non-combatants Richards was evacuating, who claimed the Japanese were already attacking Kohima. Leaving their transport, they went forward on foot carrying only light-scale equipment: the Japanese immediately shelled the convoy, destroying much of the warmer clothing and blankets, although some cooking equipment was saved.[29] Richards waited to welcome Laverty but recalled that it was not a happy meeting: 'Laverty merely asked, "Where's Kuki Piquet?" I told him and he went off without speaking further.'[30] Laverty placed A Company as a central reserve on Garrison Hill (also known as Summer House Hill, or Dog to the Japanese), B Company on the eastern side of Kuki Piquet (Monkey), C Company on DIS (Detail Issue Depot) Hill (Horse) and D Company on FSD (Field Supply Depot) Hill (Ox). Although his Battalion Headquarters was close to that of

Richards and Major Richard Yeo's 20th Battery Command Post, Laverty was contemptuous of both Richards and many of the garrison troops, and worked directly to Warren, who also ignored Richards.[31] Soon after 4th Royal West Kents moved on to the position, the garrison's solitary 25-pounder was knocked out after firing one round – Japanese artillery observers had the entire area well covered. Thus it was never possible to fire 20th Battery's 3.7-inch howitzers from the cramped and observed space of the perimeter, and ultimately two had to be abandoned. The inadequate and poorly protected medical arrangements were also rapidly apparent. On his arrival John Young began organizing the centralization of medical stores for the garrison and digging trenches for the wounded.[32]

At 1700 Richards heard a Naga report that the Japanese were approaching from the south. This was a battalion-sized advance guard of 58th Regiment, under Major-General Miyazaki Shigesaburo.[33] Miyazaki rode a horse with his pet monkey Chibi ('Tich') on his shoulder. He had received his little friend as a present from the headman of Mao Songsang, whose villagers also presented five pigs, ten chickens and a hundred eggs for his men.[34] As night fell, GPT Ridge to the south was attacked and its demoralized composite garrison fled into the hills rather than the reduced perimeter. More worryingly, this loss included the main water supply, leaving the garrison perilously short.[35] At around 0400 on 6 April, 58th and 138th Regiments closed in, first infiltrating the Naga village to the north and capturing many defenders when these paraded for breakfast. They also discovered sacks of enough rice and salt for two years under Treasury Hill, and managed to secure some three months' worth before the RAF bombed the rest. The endurance of the ordinary Japanese soldier was just as well for Sato: after crossing the Chindwin on 15 March 31st Division received no ration supplies of any kind and they were beginning to forage – although strict disciplinary supervision meant it was reasonably successful, at least to begin with.[36]

The Japanese stormed Jail Hill (Goat) to the south, thus reducing Kohima to a triangular perimeter measuring some 700 by 900 by 1100 yards. Now their guns and mortars could be sure of targets over open sights, and thus it was fortunate for the defenders that their ammunition supply was limited. Their effectiveness was, however, immediate: some composite companies fell apart and the behaviour of some base personnel in the perimeter justified Laverty's contempt. One, who became known as 'the man in the hole', spent the entire siege cowering in a deepening trench but was left there by Laverty, out of sight.[37] Others ran from one supposed safe point to another, serving only to draw sniper fire, but the garrison was rein-

forced by A Company, 4th/7th Rajputs. Already the Advanced Dressing
Station (ADS) was overflowing and Young received Richards's permission
to evacuate 80 walking wounded and 100 Indian non-combatants, which
was accomplished that night in a seven-hour journey led a by Naga guide
under escort by a Rajput platoon.[38] But the Japanese responded by closing
the gap in their lines, and soon the ADS was full once more. Lieutenant
Kameyama Shosaku addressed his men shortly before they went into battle:
'Keep your heads, keep cool. If you want to find out just how cool you are
feeling, put your hands in your trousers and feel your penis – if it is hanging down it is good.' But when the lieutenant tested his own advice,

> it was shrunk up so hard I could hardly grasp it. More than 30 soldiers did
> the same thing, then looked at me curiously, but I kept a poker-face. I said,
> 'Well mine's down all right. If yours is shrunk up, it's because you're scared.'
> Then a young soldier said to me, 'Sir, I can't find mine at all. What's hap-
> pening to it?' With this everyone burst out laughing and I knew I had got
> the confidence of the men.[39]

By nightfall only eighteen of those thirty young Japanese were still alive.

After the failure of their first daylight attack, the Japanese reverted to the
scare tactics and tricks that had previously served them so well against
Anglo-Indian troops during darkness. On the night of 6/7 April 58th
Regiment attacked 4th Royal West Kents' C Company on DIS Hill. They
began creeping close to the British lines to cry urgently, 'Hey! Johnny, let
me through, let me through. The Japs are after me, they're going to get
me!' Then they would start shouting from all directions, hoping to receive
an answer that would give away British positions. When this failed, they
resorted to sniping in the hope of provoking a reaction, which, while
extremely nerve-wracking for the defenders, also failed to draw a response.
When the Japanese did attack,

> the top of the bank was a crowd of seething, cursing, sweating men in close
> combat, killing, maiming, wounding. Then the defenders became slowly
> aware that there were fewer of the enemy up against them, until there was
> only one here, who had been left behind, or another there, more deter-
> mined than his comrades.

The end of the fighting left only 'silence in the darkness, except for the
groans of the wounded and the rustling of the bushes as the last defeated
Jap made his way back through the jungle where he had come from'.[40] By
morning, after four such attacks, both the company commander and his
successor had been wounded and the company had suffered 40 casualties.
Laverty ordered D Company to counter-attack.

Since over a third of their number were sick or wounded, Indian sappers were pressed into service as infantrymen to assist them. Immediately they began, two Japanese machine-guns engaged them from the flank and men started falling; the attack shuddered to a halt, pinned to a slope. Undeterred, Lance-Corporal John Harman – the burly nineteen-year-old son of the owner of Lundy Island – advanced, almost casually, and bombed a bunker from which machine-gun fire was coming, before reappearing with the Japanese machine-gun over his head. His platoon then went forward and cleared the remaining enemy from the bashas. Although the position was not finally cleared until the following day, one of 58th Regiment's battalion commanders described this as 'a crushing defeat'.[41] Nevertheless, by 8 April 138th Regiment had completed Kohima's encirclement to the north and attacked Hospital Ridge opposite the DC's Bungalow, making small gains against the Assam Rifles, although driven off by counter-attack the following day. But then an intense Japanese attack drove the defenders in this area, consisting of British and Gurkhas from the reinforcement unit and Dick Yeo's Sikh gunners, out of the bungalow and on to the tennis court above.[42] Richards stabilized the line with an Assam Regiment platoon and one of 1st/7th Gurkhas. Laverty also responded by ordering his A Company from reserve and his mortar platoon to switch fire from Jail Hill to the Bungalow. On 9 April the Japanese renewed their suicidal assault on DIS Hill, resisted by C and D Companies and a platoon of Rajputs. Lance-Corporal Harman charged a trench filled with Japanese, fighting like a man possessed. Officially he shot four and bayoneted a fifth, but it is possible he killed ten.[43] He emerged quite casually, but was hit by a machine-gun burst in the base of the spine, and although he was brought into the British lines, he knew that he was dying and refused aid. 'I've got to go', he said. 'It was worth it – I got the lot.' He was awarded a posthumous VC.[44] Laverty could no longer hold his perimeter and shortened it by withdrawing the now combined C/D Company to FSD Hill, abandoning DIS Hill to the Japanese.

The strain of the siege was recorded by Corporal Harold Norman, whose diary noted his rations for Wednesday 12 April:

> For breakfast (0800 hrs) we had Hard Biscuits, 1 Sausage, Baked Beans, 1/2 cup of cold tea. We were mortared all day ... For Tiffin (1230 hrs) we had Hard Biscuits, Salmon, Jam, No Tea. For Dinner (1800 hrs) we had 'Bully' Beef, Fried Tomatoes, Tea (1/2 cup, Cold), We managed to get a p[acket] of Australian coffee biscuits (Guest's) and a few tins of pears and milk.[45]

Conditions were appalling: dead lay in close proximity everywhere and with human faeces and acrid cordite made a horrific stench. Escape through sleep was precious and rare (that night Corporal Norman managed 3½ hours), and water was always scarce. When a tropical downpour brought some respite, it was short-lived; it soon soaked to the bone and chilled to the marrow. Ray Street described the routine that settled over the garrison:

> We got barrages twice a day, one at first light and another at evening 'stand to' or just getting dark. We would hear him putting mortar bombs down the mortar barrel, mostly in groups of seven, and we would watch the barrage creep up the hill till it was our turn. Then we got down flat in the bottom of our slit trench.[46]

Captain Tom Coath later described the siege as 'a private's battle, and our success was mainly due to the very high morale and steadiness of the NCOs and men'. But the soldiers were equally full of praise for their officers from Laverty down, including their padre, Captain Revd Roy Randolph, a gentle ascetic who hated war. But the Royal West Kents also thought highly of Pawsey, who had chosen to remain with his Nagas, and Richards, whom they encouraged on his daily visits, often under sniper fire, by cheering 'Come on, Sir, you're winning!'[47]

Sergeant Richard Spencer was a signaller who had been delivering batteries when the Japanese cut the road: a visit due to last a few hours lasted a month. At one point a Japanese soldier jumped into his slit trench.

> We stared at each other in complete amazement before we began to fight, but in that confined space there was no room to even use a knife. Desperate, I put my hands round his neck and applied as much pressure as I could muster. Eventually he lay quite still; he had stopped breathing. I had never killed any one before, least of all with my bare hands. It was an experience that continued to haunt me for many years after the war.

Spencer spent the next five days crouched in his hole, using dead Japanese as sandbags, before being joined by a Royal West Kent soldier. 'I told him to face the rear so that each of us was guarding the other. By now I was completely exhausted, not only from lack of sleep but also from lack of food and water.' He lost consciousness.

> Then a mortar bomb must have exploded just in front of the two bodies behind which we were sheltering. The explosion brought me to my senses almost at once. I nudged my companion of just a few hours but to my horror found that his jungle green battledress was covered in blood. He had been stabbed in the back – either by knife or bayonet. While I slept the Japanese had overrun our position and must have thought I was already dead, and passed on.[48]

The scattered components of the defence were so effectively pinned down by fire that any movement, certainly in daylight, was extremely hazardous, and all were only very vaguely aware what the situation was. Artillery support was of crucial importance, not only because it inflicted casualties but also because of the boost it gave the defenders' morale.[49] The accuracy of 24th Mountain Regiment's fire was such that, although the front lines were often no more than 30 yards apart, no shells landed inside the perimeter.[50] While the garrison had to eat, sleep, shit, piss, fight and die in their slit trenches, conditions were little better for the attackers. Hiraku Masao, quartermaster of III/58th Regiment, was trying to feed the men attacking the ridge: 'My unit with fifteen men cooked rice and boiled water for drinking all night after sunset. We put two rice balls in a mess kit and water in a canteen per person, and carried them to the front line. They ate them, breaking them into small pieces.' But there was little to go with the rice. 'We purchased pigs from a village about 20 miles away and collected wild edible grasses from the field which were boiled with salt and put in the mess tins.'[51]

Meanwhile 161st Indian Brigade at Jotsoma was itself cut off from Dimapur by elements of 138th Regiment with orders to prevent reinforcements reaching Kohima. This occurred on 8 April, when linesmen checking communications found the road cut near Zubza, only 36 miles from Dimapur. A detachment of 1st/1st Punjabis tried to clear the road the following day but was repulsed.[52] Lead elements of 2nd Division were ready to advance from its concentration area at Bokajan on 9 April, led by 5th Brigade under Brigadier Victor Hawkins. Unfortunately 2nd Division were not well organized, with lavish mechanical transport for European conditions, unsuited to the mountains; only 6th Brigade had seen action in theatre in Arakan, while most training had been for amphibious rather than jungle operations.[53] Now the first 400 mules for 5th Brigade arrived with their Pathan handlers, together with a Royal Engineers bulldozer that soon proved invaluable and elicited repeated requests to borrow it.[54] Stopford ordered the divisional commander, Major-General John Grover, to take over operational control from Ranking the following day.[55] He also ordered Hawkins to move immediately, and by midday on 11 April 7th Worcestershire Regiment engaged a strongly entrenched Japanese force on a precipitous position around MS 37½ called Bunker Hill, which resisted fiercely for three days.[56]

The divisional artillery consisted of three assault field regiments, comprising one self-propelled battery with Priests, one of 25-pounders and one of six 3.7-inch howitzers. The Priests, being totally unsuited to the mountainous jungle terrain, were replaced with 25-pounders and the 3.7 battery made up to eight guns that could be easily replaced with 25-pounders once more open country was reached. There was no corps artillery at this point, but two 5.5-inch guns were available at Dimapur, manned by scratch detachments from 4th Field Regiment RA from 5th Indian Division, temporarily separated from its formation.[57] Grover wanted to use tanks but the two squadrons of 149th RAC allotted to him had not yet arrived at Dimapur. However, Lieutenant R. H. K. Wait had five spare Lees belonging to 150th RAC, engaged at Imphal, and with scratch crews he reached Zubza with three of them on 13 April. The Japanese, realizing the threat these beasts represented, tried to break into his harbour area that night with anti-tank mines: the first attack was beaten off and the second annihilated.

Sergeant Fred Hazell's 18 Platoon from 2nd Royal Norfolks was escorting the tanks and suffered three wounded.

> One of them had been wounded in France, during the retreat to Dunkirk he got shot in the backside. As he passed me on his stretcher he sort of sat up, beamed at me and said, 'I've been shot in the arse again!' I wondered if it was his custom to stick his arse in the air to get it shot at.[58]

The next morning Wait's tanks and the bayonets of 1st Cameron Highlanders attacked Bunker Hill from the rear following twenty minutes' intense artillery preparation. Company Sergeant-Major Cook of C Company killed a Japanese officer with his own sword and then several others, earning the Distinguished Conduct Medal (DCM).[59] But although they had broken through to Warren at Jotsoma, two bridges needed replacing before transport could use the road, which had to be constantly patrolled. As sappers worked to clear the route, Captain Swinson saw them sorting through the detritus of war, including piles of photographs, 'with great curiosity, bursting with laughter when they found a "filthy" one … There were soldiers' pay-books too, surprisingly like ours in character. One sapper, seeing a figure entered in red, exclaimed: "My God, the little bugger's in debt!"'[60]

Resupply of the beleaguered garrison was essential, but the only way was by air. This started on 13 April, with disappointing results. The Japanese shot holes through the water containers and the ammunition was 3.7-inch for the mountain guns – useless to the defenders, who desperately needed grenades and 3-inch mortar ammunition – which, combined with a particularly bad day's fighting, earned the day the title 'Black 13th'. The vulnerable transport aircraft had to fly along the valley and were thus exposed to a barrage of small-arms fire.[61] Flight Sergeant J. V. Bell of 31 Squadron recalled: 'often we would end up about 250 feet over the hills, with the Japs shooting at us. All I could see was a mass of faces looking up at us. I could not see the type of weapons, only the flame from the guns.'[62] Sometimes drops fell accurately; sometimes, despairing men watched the enemy receive the blessing of heaven, what the Japanese called 'Churchill's rations'. One flight dropped mortar ammunition outside the perimeter, although it eventually reached its destination: the Japanese had captured British mortars. Later drinking water was dropped in motor-car inner-tubes, and the water situation improved marginally when a pipe fed by a spring was found on the road north-west of the box, although this could be observed from Japanese positions and so was used only during darkness.[63]

On 14 April Richards issued an emotional Special Order of the Day, praising all ranks for their efforts and promising relief soon. But they knew they could not hold out much longer. Everywhere Richards and Laverty struggled to stretch dwindling resources; sub-units were amalgamated and rotated through the worst sectors as well as possible. One of these was the tennis court of the DC's bungalow. Nightly the Japanese formed up on the terrace below to assault across it; repeating this action can only be described as stupid. 'We held the Tennis Court against desperate attacks for five days', recalled B Company commander, Major John Winstanley. 'We held because I had instant contact by radio with the guns and the Japs never seemed to learn how to surprise us. They used to shout in English, as they formed up, "give up". So we knew when an attack was coming in.'[64] British guns and mortars would cut them apart even before they began to charge into the fire of Bren guns and grenades, now plentiful; a few grenades might be thrown in return, but the tennis court would be left with another layer of bloated, festering bodies to feed the millions of flies that rose with the sun.

The wounded could not be evacuated and all suffered enormously. Corporal Norman was on water fatigue during the night of 14 April:

> On the way to the water pipe we had to pass through the hospital and it was a most terrifying and heart-breaking experience. We kept falling over dead bodies which were black and decaying ... As we passed through the Hospital the smell was overpowering. Col[onel] Young had designed a large pit, covered by a tarpaulin which he used as an operating theatre, but hundreds of wounded were lying in open pits and this area was continually being mortared and shelled day and night and the wounded were sometimes getting wounded a second and third time and being killed.[65]

The exhausted Royal West Kents above the tennis court desperately needed relief: in the early hours of 15 April two platoons of 3rd Assam Rifles and one of 1st Assam Regiment under Major Albert Calistan took over this sector and repelled a number of attacks.[66]

On 16 April with 5th Brigade at Jotsoma, 161st Indian Brigade with 1st Royal Welch Fusiliers under command advanced aiming to relieve Kohima.[67] Grover saw Warren was worried about his right flank and wanted to modify his plan once more. Although Warren appreciated the severe plight of the garrison, Grover was wary of the threat posed to the Dimapur road by Japanese artillery on the Merema ridge, and, unaware of the severe plight of the garrison, having received a misleading message that it was 'firm and in good heart', decided the final operation to break through should be postponed to 17 April.[68] Dissension among Japanese commanders contributed as much to their defeat as determined British assault. On 17 April Mutaguchi instructed Sato to send three infantry battalions and a mountain artillery battalion in captured British lorries to join the Imphal battle, which he insisted must be captured by the 29th, the Emperor's birthday.[69] But heavily engaged and with no supplies, Sato saw this was impossible. Besides, he was not prepared to sacrifice his men's lives for Mutaguchi's glory. He first ignored the order and then, when it was repeated on 20 April, declared it impossible to comply with.[70] That day Lieutenant J. A. C. Carbonell of 1st Camerons shot dead a Japanese sergeant-major carrying a copy of Mutaguchi's order, which was finally cancelled on 29 April.[71] Slim was very disparaging of Sato's efforts, and even instructed the RAF to avoid bombing his headquarters, but Sato of all Mutaguchi's subordinates came closest to achieving his objectives, and was 'neither stupid nor unenterprising'.[72]

Significantly, British commanders were all criticized by their superiors for being too slow: Grover by Stopford, Warren and Hawkins by Grover, and Hawkins's lead battalion commander by Hawkins – until he saw the ground.[73] All were considered tardy by the garrison, but the terrain made it practically impossible to operate on divisional, brigade or even battalion frontages, which explains not only British problems but also why it proved so difficult for the Japanese to make numerical superiority count during the siege: often company attacks were all that was possible. Grover's plan as it stood was already wildly optimistic, given the nature of the ground, and as Hawkins of 5th Brigade noted, there was 'very little artillery support, if any ... we were to try and do everything by "infiltration" methods'.[74] What Grover could not understand was the savagery of the assaults now launched against the garrison. On the night of 16/17 April a concentrated attack on

FSD Hill, well supported by artillery fire, finally showed that the Japanese had learned some lessons from their abortive operations thus far. They charged 'shouting Wasshoi! Wasshoi! (Rush forward!)', recalled Lieutenant Kameyama. 'The enemy was startled by this dashing cry and fled towards Kuki Piquet along the ridge. We chased them and captured FSD as well as Kuki Piquet.'[75] Despite counter-attacks led by Major Naveen Rawlley, FSD Hill had finally fallen. Next morning 6th Brigade took over the Jotsoma box to enable 161st Indian Brigade to open the road to Kohima, but the Japanese countered by occupying other hills in their path and attacking 4th/7th Rajputs, inflicting heavy casualties.[76] The next night the Japanese tried again at Kuki Piquet, where the defenders were swamped by sheer weight of numbers and few escaped. Among those who perished was Company Sergeant-Major W. Haines, who had been blinded early in the fighting but who, with the aid of a soldier guide, had stayed behind to encourage his mates with his voice.

When Richards emerged from his command post on 18 April, it seemed the end was near; across a wasteland in which every tree and building had been utterly shattered the perimeter had shrunk to within 100 yards of Garrison Headquarters, and even closer to the ADS, where 600 wounded lay in constant peril amid the stench of stale sweat, blood and rotting flesh. 'Many of the wounded, I feel sure,' thought Major Donald Easten of D Company, 'died in the last few days because they had given up hope.'[77] Now only Garrison Hill remained and, although fighting was obviously approaching from Jotsoma, the chances of relief did not seem high. A panic broke out among Indian support troops, and for an hour there was uproar, 'a shambles of wailing wounded, struggling stretcher-bearers, stampeding, fear-struck men in tattered uniforms, a hellish babble of terror and dismay', until order was restored.[78]

Then came the sound of 25-pounder and 5.5-inch shells screaming in to explode on Japanese positions, followed by Hurricane fighter–bombers (Hurribombers) roaring in to bomb and strafe. Looking through binoculars, Richards could make out Lees crawling along the Dimapur road, followed by tracked carriers and lorries. Although the column was held up for an hour at MS 45, they fought their way through and at noon 1st/1st Punjabis arrived to take over Piquet Hill, where Jemadar Mohammed Rafiq, whose three section commanders were killed early in the action, led his platoon to clear out the Japanese, who left behind 16 dead; Rafiq was awarded the MC. Next day the Punjabis attacked Kuki Piquet, but the Japanese were resolute and the two assault companies lost 9 dead and 43 wounded.[79] Meanwhile a company of 4th/7th Rajputs had been driven off

Terrace Hill commanding the road into Kohima, and the task of retaking it fell to 2nd Durham Light Infantry.[80]

On the morning of 20 April 1st Royal Berkshires relieved 4th Royal West Kents. Major John Nettlefield noted: 'When we first saw Kohima it was beautifully fresh and green – an attractive town perched on the hills.' Now 'the place stank. The ground everywhere was ploughed up with shell-fire and human remains lay rotting as the battle raged over them. Flies swarmed everywhere and multiplied with incredible speed. Men retched as they dug in ... the stink hung in the air and permeated one's clothes and hair.'[81] Already most rifle companies in 2nd Division were reduced, some to as few as 30 men, while the Kentish men were 'too tired for humour, they just wanted to get out, back to a good meal and then sleep, sleep, and more sleep.'[82] Brigadier Hawkins noted that 'we, 5th Brigade, prepared a meal for them (at Zubza) as they came through ... They were in great heart in spite of the terrible time they had had; and they were a sight for the gods! Long beards of all hues, and their clothes fit only for scarecrows. They were a grand battalion.'[83]

Of 444 men who had marched in, 61 had been killed and 138 seriously wounded; most of the remainder were injured in some way and would normally be considered unfit for duty. First Assam Regiment suffered 15 dead and 21 wounded, and the rest of the garrison some 600 casualties. Richards waited until the remnants of his original garrison had departed before following two days later.[84] While nineteen British and Indian regiments would earn the battle honour 'Kohima', only the Royal West Kents and Assam Regiment were awarded the honour 'Defence of Kohima'. As John Colvin says, 'Kohima really was the turning point of the Burma campaign' and but for 4th Royal West Kents, whose motto was *Invicta* – 'Unconquered' – the siege would not have lasted beyond the first couple of days: 'without much food, always short of water, in continual close combat against an incomprehensible and brutal enemy, thousands of miles from home or any of its joys, the band of Kentish and Welsh men held the pass.'[85] The siege was over, but the battle was about to begin.

# 17

# Imphal

I early learned that a battle has many faces and all of them are false. The falsehood on the one hand, consists of the untruth born in the heat of battle itself – the contradictory reports, the wrong information, the doubtful rumours that shake the conviction of even the most hardened commander; and on the other hand, it consists of the lying legend about a battle that arises after it is over. No one ever knows what happened.

Jack Belden[1]

WAITING BEFORE THE battle, unaware of the ordeal ahead, signals Captain Richard 'Tug' Wilson noted:

Perhaps it was providential that we were not too well informed; stouter hearts than ours might have quailed at the prospects had the future been foreseeable. So there we were, me and my worthy subalterns, drivers, clerks, orderlies, cooks, the faithful bhisties and goodness knows why, the section shoemaker, right in the fairway, or as Sandy observed later, in the orchestra stalls.[2]

Imphal was an extremely untidy battle, in no conventional form such as Alamein, lasting from the end of March until mid-June, during which hundreds of chance encounters, ambushes, frontal attacks and desperate defences occurred that cannot be charted, and never will be.[3] Mountbatten described it as swaying 'across great stretches of wild country; one day its focal point was a hill named on no map, the next a miserable, unpronounceable village a hundred miles away. Columns, brigades, divisions marched and counter-marched, met in bloody clashes, and reeled apart, weaving a confused pattern hard to unravel.'[4]

Shortly after Christmas 1943 a visitor who spent the holiday with friends at Imphal described the area as idyllic – like Shangri-La – with a wonderful climate, beautiful scenery and happy smiling people, amid wonderful flora, flights of wild fowl and streams teeming with fish. Administratively Manipur was a Native State, and the nearest outpost of British India was at Cachar in Assam. In May the monsoon turns paths to mud and ricefields into small lakes; apart from the western foothills, which are treeless, the country is wooded with deep ravines covered with peach trees, oak scrub, teak, wild banana and feathery bamboo; purple irises, white jasmine and gold and maroon marigolds flowered; snipe, geese and ducks thronged Logtak Lake; and in the woods deer, flying foxes, elephants, tiger and leopards were joined by kraits, cobras and hamadryads, while every type of insect thrived.[5] In peacetime food was plentiful and money scarce: now wages rose from 4 annas to 5 rupees per day and rice from 1½ to 40 or even 60 rupees a maund (80 lb.). The villagers had at least a year's supply, so were not afraid of running short, but other commodity prices shot up too. The Hindus objected to the killing of cattle and drove them away to prevent their being taken to feed the army; sheep and goats were kept at Imphal instead, for which there was plenty of rice straw, and a further 18,000 tons of vegetables were cultivated.[6] And when the Japanese arrived, hundreds headed for Imphal with all their earthly possessions. Soon much of the area closely resembled the battlefields of the Somme.[7] Nevertheless, throughout the siege Imphal's Golden Market remained thronged with Manipuri women, 'who came there to sell, buy and gossip over bowls of *zhu* [native rice liquor] and *biris*. Here they discussed with considerable heat, local politics as well as the course of the current war which by now had become their own.'[8]

On 26 March Slim ordered the creation of the Lushai Brigade, formed two days later with the task of blocking routes through the Lushai area of the Chin Hills, covering some 180 miles south of the Silchar track and operating directly under Fourteenth Army.[9] As the Japanese closed in, IV Corps were effectively cut off by land on 30 March, when 31st Division reached the Imphal–Kohima road. For the next thirteen weeks they would have to rely exclusively on air for supply, reinforcement and casualty evacuation. A conference of air and military staff agreed to keep the garrison going by this means, entailing 500 tons a day or more than 150 plane loads, amounting to up to five sorties per day for the air crew. At the same time they flew out as many non-essential personnel as possible. On the plain more squadrons were deployed: army and RAF units alike prepared defensive 'boxes', each given a code name, and all had to muck in by digging trenches and standing guard.[10] Facing them, 5th Air Division had four fighter and four bomber *sentais* (regiments).[11] Slim's plan was for IV Corps to defeat the Japanese on the perimeter of the Imphal Plain, with XXXIII Corps taking over the Kohima battle from 3 April; the next day IV Corps was able to concentrate on its task with the four divisions to hand – 5th,

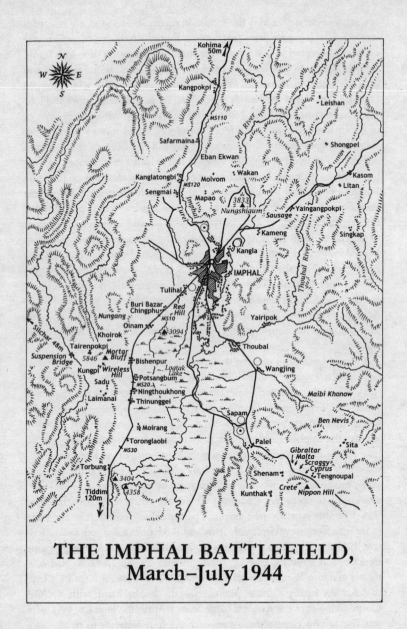

# THE IMPHAL BATTLEFIELD,
## March–July 1944

17th, 20th and 23rd Indian Divisions – now concentrated on the plain and 254th Indian Tank Brigade. The part played by this brigade with two British regiments of Lees and an Indian regiment of Stuarts cannot be over-emphasized. The few Japanese tanks available were in no way comparable, but failure to break through at Donbaik in 1943 had led several officers at GHQ(I) to overreact and claim gloomily that armour would be no use in Burma. This resulted, as Brigadier Reginald Scoones noted, in few infantry battalions training with tanks 'or knowing their capabilities, all of which had to be learned on the battlefield'. Consequently 254th was the only brigade being used which allowed for no reserve, which with consistent demand for tank support meant both tanks and crews were 'heavily flogged'.[12]

Scoones planned that while 17th and 20th Indian Divisions held the ring, 5th and 23rd would hunt down 15th Division north-east in the direction of Litan and Ukhrul. But then came the unwelcome surprise that 31st Division was advancing in strength on Kohima, where earlier estimates suggested no more than a regiment would do so.[13] The defensive system relied on a series of 'boxes', often formed by combat support and administrative units. Lion Box was largely defended by engineer and RIASC units, with a couple of platoons of 2nd West Yorks and two troops of 3rd Carabiniers. So confident were the Japanese that on one officer's body were found visiting cards printed in English, giving the address as New Delhi.[14] On 29 March the Japanese cut the line of communication north of Imphal at MS 118 near Kanglatongbi, 'but not before the Provost TCP [Traffic Control Point] had warned Headquarters IV Corps at Imphal and had been able to turn back convoys converging from Kohima'.[15] On 4 and 5 April the first attacks were made by 15th Division against 123rd Indian Brigade's positions by 51st Regiment, while 60th Regiment probed south towards the large stores dump, where staff of 221st Advance Ordnance Depot repeatedly foiled Japanese infiltration attacks from 5 April until Good Friday, staying at their posts for three days under continuous and heavy fire in what the IAOC history calls 'the undying glory' of Kanglatongbi.[16] Most of the stores were rescued by 9th Indian Brigade, but the Japanese eventually took the dump and sent a patrol to destroy the water-pumping station. They wrecked the valves and believed they had cut off Imphal's water supply. Fortunately, however, the night watchman had slipped away before the Japanese arrived, and fearing reprimand for deserting his post, merely switched to the reserve system, which functioned for the rest of the siege. This was the prelude to one of the biggest and most significant battles on the front: for the commanding heights of Numshingum,* an uneven ridge over 3 miles long where several peaks dominated the plain 1,500 feet below, only 5 miles from Headquarters IV Corps at Imphal, where Scoones spent what little free time he had in the cultivation of orchids. Although of stern demeanour, Scoones took pains over the soldiers' welfare. When after some weeks of siege constant bully-beef began to pall on the British troops, he took pains to get some tinned steak and kidney pudding brought in to vary the diet. Visiting an artillery unit, he asked a gunner busy with his midday meal how it was. 'It's not too bad,' replied the soldier, 'as long as you lace it with a bit of bully.'[17]

The defence of this feature switched to 9th Indian Brigade and 3rd/9th Jats, who sweated up the steep hills to reach the summit on 6 April but were attacked by 51st Regiment before they had time to dig in or lay wire. With heavy casualties they were forced off the top, during which action Jemadar Abdul Hafiz became the first Muslim to win the VC during the war, but the following day the battalion counter-attacked and retook the feature.[18] Yamauchi retaliated with stronger forces and on 11 April drove the Jats off once more. The next day a major conference was held at Headquarters 5th Indian Division, where it was decided that 1st/17th Dogras would attack, supported by B Squadron 3rd Carabiners, the divisional artillery, two squadrons of Vengeance dive-bombers and one of Hurricanes.

The air attack began at 1030 next day, followed twenty minutes later by the artillery, as the infantry and tanks deployed in full view of both sides. By 1130 two companies and six tanks had almost reached the summit. The steep incline meant the Lees could not depress their guns to engage the Japanese bunkers, and the commanders had to lean high above them to get a view. When some Japanese ran to attack them with mines, they drove them off with pistols and grenades, but within minutes of reaching the crest all the tank commanders were killed or seriously wounded. At this point Squadron Sergeant-Major Craddock took command, backed by Subedars Ranbir Singh and Tiru Ram of the Dogras, and using sign language they swept the Japanese away.[19] Climbing to seemingly impossible heights to support the infantry had a powerful morale effect on both sides. The British armour had predicted its task and trained accordingly on hill-climbing. When Colonel Omoto Kimio, Commander of 51st Regiment, heard from his veterinary officer they were crunching over the bodies of

---

* Also Nunshingum, Nungshingum and Nungshigum: I have chosen the easiest for pronounciation.

his men, he exclaimed: 'Don't be a fool! How could they? Give me those glasses!' He saw the final tank assault and exclaimed in tears, 'We're done for! That's it!'[20]

Defeat at Numshingum had a profound effect on 15th Division; if 51st Regiment withdrew, it would seriously endanger 60th Regiment's position holding the Kohima road to the north-west.[21] Already a sick man, Yamauchi was devastated by the losses and the realization that he had no answer to tanks, but with 51st Regiment reduced to a miserable remnant he chose to withdraw. However, he still had units scattered around Kanglatongbi and they could watch the daily procession of transport aircraft bringing in their precious loads. Once Numshingum was secure, 5th Indian Division cleared Mapao spur, running north from Scoones' Headquarters, which also offered excellent panoramic views of the plain. First Indian Brigade from 23rd Indian Division tried to outflank the Japanese and capture Yamauchi's Headquarters at Khasom. Following a long march and with air support they drove out the Japanese garrison, to be followed up by 37th Indian Brigade driving north from Kameng to clear the road to their position.[22] At this point the Japanese were giving ground, but soon afterwards 23rd Indian Division had to relieve 20th Indian Division on the Shenam ridge some 25 miles to the south, and the area became the responsibility of 5th Indian Division, although reinforcements arrived on 18 April, when 89th Indian Brigade (from 7th Indian Division) arrived to replace 161st Indian Brigade fighting at Kohima.[23] For many weeks 5th Indian Division patrolled and fought around Mapao in an attempt to defeat the Japanese holding the road to Kohima at Sengmai and Kanglatongbi.

On 25 April three Dakotas were shot down, although during April over 6,000 sorties were flown by the Allies and over 1,000 tons of bombs dropped.[24] Hurribombers carried two 250-pound bombs on each sortie, so a great many were needed, flown in by Wellingtons of 94 and 205 Squadrons. They had 11-second fuses, so the Hurricanes could drop them from as low as 50 feet and they would dig into the Japanese bunkers before exploding.[25] Losses during dive-bombing operations were minimal: the greatest threat came from anti-aircraft machine-guns since the Japanese had been unable to bring any heavier air defence weapons with them.[26] But Japanese bunkers were so truly formidable that two Gurkhas watching a display of air and artillery firepower directed against some remained unimpressed. 'Like popcorn', said one. 'More like goats farting', replied the other.[27] Meanwhile, 4th/5th Mahrattas held a feature called 'Sausage' some 2,000 feet above the plain, barely 40 feet away from III/151st Regiment.

They were host to an IFBU on 4/5 May.[28] A Japanese prisoner made a bad speech, after which he complained he had not had enough time to prepare. The following day he made what the translators agreed was an excellent speech, though the Mahrattas disagreed, since it merely provoked a fusillade of mortar bombs on to B Company.[29] Three days later the Mahrattas and the rest of 49th Indian Brigade attacked along the ridge and 5th/6th Rajputana Rifles seized the Pinnacle, but operations had to be curtailed to enable 23rd Indian Division to redeploy.[30]

Around the Shenam Saddle 20th Indian Division was fighting its own isolated battle covering the vital Palel airfield, but Gracey had only two brigades to cover his large frontage of several hundred square miles of broken hilly country. Shenam Saddle was a long, uneven ridge running roughly east–west, with hills of varying height rising from it, each of them given names by the soldiers who fought there, with a metalled road on the Allied side over the Shenam Pass to Imphal. Gracey's troops held the high ground for observation and patrolled vigorously to prevent Japanese penetration, although the first major clash came on 1 April, when 2nd Border, having captured part of Nippon Hill, were driven off, whereupon the Japanese dug in like moles right under the summit. 'By Christ them little bastards can dig', noted a sergeant. 'They're underground before our blokes have stopped spitting on their bloody hands.'[31] Many of the forward posts were no more than 20 yards from the enemy. On 3 and 4 April 4th/10th Gurkhas put in two company attacks which failed to budge the Japanese. In support Sowar Jot Ram of 7th Light Cavalry described going into action for the first time.

> I wish I could see more. I wish I were a gunner instead of having to sit on this [radio] set. I have to pass a more difficult test, and am only a grade 3 operator, and that addle-headed Munshi Ram firing the gun is the dunce of a dozen villages, but is a grade 2 gunner mech ... There is a flash in front of my eyes. I cannot see even in front. It must be Japs coming. I open fire with the lap-gun. There is smoke in the tank. I get a kick in the back of the head. My ears are scorched with shameful abuse on the intercom. 'By the tail of your grandmother who most assuredly swung from the trees in the jungle, if you fire at nothing again I will pistol you myself' ... The Jemadar Sahib certainly gets his tongue round some wicked abuse.[32]

The Japanese were only dislodged a week later by 1st Devonshire Regiment with strong air support but at high cost to both sides, as the Japanese counter-attacked throughout the night.[33] The Devons then handed over to 9th/12th Frontier Force Regiment, who held it for a week under constant attack, with Yamamoto driving 213th Regiment until they finally took it.[34] Gracey decided the road to Tamu was not essential and left the Japanese to fortify themselves there until July.

Thus was the pattern of the battle established. 'Every night', noted John Hudson, 'there was a disturbance of some sort. Out in the forward positions or back in my bunker on Sapper Hill I sprang awake to the urgent whisper in my ear. *Sahib! Sahib! Dusman agaya!* (Enemy attack, Sir!) I did not know whether it was a jitter raid, a full attack on our position, on another box near by or a false alarm.'[35] Both sides had time to construct bunkers and well-sited supporting trenches until soon the entire area became a shambles reminiscent of the Western Front during the First World War. Artillery played a significant role and the hillsides were stripped of vegetation, while dead bodies lodged in inaccessible places where they rotted. 'Shenam Ridge soon began to smell with that sweet sickly horrifying aroma of death!'[36] Near Tengnoupal village 1st Devons now faced a wave of Japanese attacks on Crete, Cyprus and Scraggy, which pushed them back at appalling cost.[37] Signals Captain Robin Painter found himself at 1st Devons' RAP, 'thickly packed with wounded soldiers ... many close to death'. Writing fifty years later, the 'memory is still vivid and, above all else, [I can] recall the grey-green pallor of those shocked and badly injured men and their quiet, stoic acceptance of the situation. There was no complaint.'[38] Meanwhile at Sita Ridge, Captain R. S. Noronha's company of 4th/3rd Madras Regiment held an isolated position for sixteen days, wired and mined in but overlooked on three sides by jungle-clad hills, before finally being relieved by A Company of 3rd/1st Gurkhas after a winding 18-mile approach march.[39] That night the Japanese attacked but were held off. On 23 April after a two-day bombardment 213th Regiment attacked 3rd/1st Gurkhas on Crete West, capturing four bunkers, but then were driven off.[40] Now the Gandhi Brigade (2nd Regiment, 1st Division) of the INA made its appearance; having previously been used only as guides and porters, they had insisted. On the night of 2/3 May they launched an attack that went disastrously wrong, and thereafter many were found wandering about looking for Allied units to surrender to.[41] The probably apocryphal story soon emerged of an INA propagandist shouting 'We'll be in Delhi in ten days', to which a *jawan* recently returned from leave replied, 'not on Indian ruddy railways you won't.'[42] In the first week of May 1st Devons were once more on Crete West. Again the Japanese attacked fiercely, well supported by artillery; again they were bloodily repulsed.[43]

On 1 May Mountbatten signalled the Combined Chiefs of Staff that he faced a stark choice. He could either return his transport aircraft as ordered;

the Chindits would have to withdraw, Stilwell retreat and IV Corps evacuate Imphal, leaving their guns, heavy equipment and stores behind – in effect that the front would collapse with all the ramifications that entailed. Or he could hang on to them until the road was open and Imphal was relieved. He received no immediate reply and the battle continued.[44] Early in May Mountbatten tried to persuade Giffard to retire on medical grounds, 'but he is such a straight and upright old gentleman' he refused the subterfuge. Having already obtained Brooke's permission if necessary, he sacked Giffard. 'The trouble is we all like him', wrote Mountbatten, but he was 'non-aggressive, a non-co-operator, and unwilling to recognize me as the one responsible for the Burma campaign'.[45] Giffard's loss was deeply regretted by Slim, who nevertheless apparently expected to be appointed to his position. But none of those involved in the appointment, from Churchill and Brooke down, considered Slim for the post and Mountbatten was faced with the embarrassing task of asking Giffard to stay on while his successor was appointed, which Giffard did without demur.

Meanwhile on 4 May Scoones signalled Slim that if road access were not reopened by mid-June the situation would be critical. Slim was visiting Stilwell and did not receive this until the following day, by which time he had received a signal from Peirse saying that transport aircraft on loan from the Middle East must be returned by 8 May. Keeping his cool in the face of this threat and supported by Baldwin, he signalled Giffard and Air Headquarters SEAC, forcibly explaining the disastrous consequences that withdrawal of these 79 aircraft must have. Giffard immediately saw Mountbatten and supported Slim. Mountbatten agreed the aircraft should be retained, ordering they were not to be released without his permission and taking full personal responsibility.[46] Churchill warmed to this gesture, signalling: 'Let nothing go from the battle you need for victory. I will not accept denial of this from any quarter, and will back you to the full.'[47]

Slim's priority was not the relief of Imphal but the destruction of 15th Army, and Mountbatten backed him.[48] Yamamoto wanted a breakthrough at Shenam, and at midnight on 10 May the Japanese made another desperate attempt against 2nd Border and 4th/1st Gurkhas on Scraggy; their first waves died on the wire, forming crossing points for those following, and the lead trenches were taken. So great was the pressure that the Gurkhas' Commanding Officer ordered artillery down upon his own positions to relieve the pressure.[49] Scraggy was the most bitterly contested hill on Shenam Saddle, with trenches sometimes only 10 yards apart. Sergeant Wallace Hodson of 114th Field Regiment RA won a DCM when the mortar ammunition in his pit caught fire and he continued firing his mortar while throwing the ammunition out of the pit.[50] Slim and Scoones realized the strain on 20th Indian Division, and between 13 and 16 May 23rd Indian Division relieved them. On 20 May the Japanese strongly attacked 3rd/10th Gurkhas and 5th/6th Rajputana Rifles but were repulsed, with over 100 dead.[51]

A hero of this battle was Neil Gilliam of the American Field Service (AFS). He found the big Chevrolet ambulances too cumbersome and with REME help converted jeeps to take two stretchers. In one of the most violent battles around Gibraltar, following the death of a medical officer, he stayed with the unit and organized the RAP and evacuated the wounded.[52] On 23/24 May came the battle of Gibraltar. This involved 37th Indian Brigade, reinforced with 1st Seaforths, 5th/6th Rajputana Rifles and tanks. But they were overlooked from Nippon Hill, and the move was under constant fire of all kinds. If the Japanese were suffering from ammunition shortages, it did not prevent 250 shells landing on Malta in a single day, or 100 on Gibraltar in a single hour, with constant mortar fire and jitter raids ensuring that those in the forward trenches had no sleep or rest and had to be relieved frequently, sometimes twice a week.[53] By 24 May the Japanese had a precarious hold on Gibraltar, and a force had infiltrated behind the defended localities which Major Dinesh 'Danny' Misra of 5th/6th Rajputana Rifles called 'Lone Tree Hill'. Misra was to take two companies and clear it. He asked the RAF Liaison Officer to arrange dummy air strikes after the real one and, while this happened, they got onto the hill without firing as darkness approached, then faced repeated counter-attacks, the last one coming hand-to-hand. 'At such a time you feel detachment and absolute hatred', recalled Misra.

> I am not a man who could kill anyone, not even a fly; but at that moment your one aim in life is to kill him. I felt myself change – I become a demon, I swear, I scream. The Muslims shout their battle-cry; the Rajputs cry, '*Jai Mata!* Victory to the Mother!' and the Jats shout the war cry of Hanuman the monkey-god. The Japanese, too – they were shouting '*Banzai!*' and wielding their samurai swords.[54]

They subsequently received a congratulatory message from Slim renaming Lone Tree Hill as 'Rajputana Hill'.

During this time 1st Indian Brigade made a wide sweep north of Shenam Saddle to clear a position to the north known as Ben Nevis. To bring forward heavy weapons to help clear it posed enormous problems now that monsoon rains had set in, turning the tracks to glutinous mud. But four 25-pounders were brought forward to support the attack. This with strong air support was a success for 1st/16th Punjabis and 1st Patiala Infantry, and confirmed that, contrary to impressions gained around Scraggy and Gibraltar, the Japanese had no more reserves or supplies to maintain their pressure, although they did attempt to retake Ben Nevis four days later, when they were driven off.[55] A long lull at Scraggy eventually ended on 9 June, when the Japanese made a final, futile effort. With the news now dominated by the D-Day landings in Normandy, John Hudson noted:

> Press reporters never reached our besieged positions and any stories that were printed, after heavy censorship, were bland, late and inaccurate ... We were important to our own kinsfolk and nobody else, but when a bullet struck home we were just as dead as the lads in Europe and we were glad they could not see the conditions we had to endure.[56]

Many were equally scathing when they first heard about the striking of a new medal – the 'Burma Star' – especially when it was discovered it would also be issued to base troops around Calcutta. It was christened the 'Calcutta Star', to be awarded for 'Gluttony beyond the call of duty' and 'For standing firm in the Howringhee brothels'.[57]

Some of the fiercest fighting took place in the south-west corner, where 33rd Division (which Scoones called his *bête noire*) had followed up the drive from Tiddim by hooking round to cut the Imphal–Silchar track.[58] From Imphal a reasonably motorable road led south-west some 15 miles to Bishenpur, whence the Silchar track branched off across the hills to the west.[59] On the night of 14/15 April the Japanese attacked towards Bishenpur, at the same time launching a mission to destroy the 300-foot suspension bridge over the hills to Tairenpokpi on the track that would cut Imphal's last land line of communication.[60] In early May they established themselves around the village of Ningthoukhong, where elements of 214th and 215th Regiments encountered 32nd Indian Brigade from 20th Indian Division, reinforcing 17th Indian Division, and a fierce battle developed.

Point 5846, held by 1st Northamptons, and Wireless Hill, initially held by four platoons of 7th/10th Baluch before being reinforced by 3rd/8th Gurkhas, was repeatedly attacked by 215th Regiment over several days, cutting them off all round.[61] On 13 April 150th RAC were supporting 1st Northants on Wireless Hill when the Japanese attacked. Sergeant C. C. Cusworth's troop drove up the hill with headlights blazing, forcing the attackers to flee. 'Daylight revealed the full horror of the situation', recalled Cusworth. 'Some had literally to be prised apart, having died in a frenzied grip on each other; some still lived with frightful wounds, arms or legs blown off, by grenades dropped in the trench; some with terrible bayonet or knife wounds.'[62] Gurkhas in such fighting, recalled Lieutenant Donald Day of 1st/4th Gurkhas, 'prefer the kukri to the bayonet, they can cut a man in half with it. A standard blow is cross-cut to the shoulder. They cut off heads. It is a terrifying weapon, and used in the hand of a Gurkha is lethal.'[63]

Japanese attacks continued for eight or nine days, fought off with the tanks using canister. A major attack on 3rd/8th Gurkhas was fought off on 16 April.[64] On 27 April Cusworth's troop was committed to clearing the Japanese from a hill covering the Silchar track. The infantry reached the top, but the last 20 feet were too steep for the tanks and they could not remain. One had already been lost in a side-slip and rolled some distance down the slope, although the crew got out unhurt. As the remaining two tanks returned down the track, the Japanese threatened to overwhelm the Northamptons at the top, who had put their wounded in the lee of a bank at one side of the track. The tanks naturally swung clear of this to avoid them but the outer edge of the track gave way.[65] Sergeant Cusworth yelled into the intercom for the crew to hold on,

> and then we were gone, with a rumbling crash, we seemed to be bouncing like a great ball, and the loose equipment in the tank seemed to go past me two or three times and I felt my arms would be torn from their sockets, wrapped as they were round the breech of the 37mm gun.[66]

Amazingly, nobody was seriously injured and after a pause they got out, carefully removing breech blocks and firing pins. Then, taking a Browning machine-gun with a ground mounting and grenades, they joined the infantry and helped to defeat the Japanese attackers. Cusworth was awarded an immediate MM.

Below them the rest of 32nd Indian Brigade was fighting the battle of Potsangbam village – 'Pots-and-Pans' to the troops – during another desperate attempt by 33rd Division to destroy 17th Indian Division around Bishenpur. On 6 May A Company 9th/14th Punjabis, while patrolling carefully into the village itself, surprised two Japanese 47mm gun detachments brewing tea, killed them and captured the guns. The action soon developed into a fierce battle involving artillery and tanks, and the Japanese were driven off. This enabled the captured weapons, which included a 70mm infantry gun, to be taken back, providing valuable technical intelligence.[67] This was the prelude to a long drawn-out and intense battle for Potsangbam itself, where the Japanese were strongly entrenched with carefully sited anti-tank guns amid paddy and deep water-filled ditches that proved serious obstacles for tanks. In their first serious attack the Punjabis lost 40 dead and 100 wounded. On 14 May 9th Border and 1st/10th Gurkhas attacked supported by three tanks, during which Major R. A. Cooper won the MC.[68] With 32nd Indian Brigade now heavily engaged along the Silchar Track, 63rd Indian Brigade took over while the Divisional support battalion, 1st West Yorks, was sent forward of the village on the Ningthoukhong road, a waterlogged position that they held for several weeks during May as the battle wheeled around them. Unable to dig in properly and under all kinds of fire, when the monsoon set in they began to lose men to foot rot, another echo of the Western Front.[69]

Meanwhile at the end of April artillery had been concentrated in a 'Gunner Box' north of where the Silchar track joins the Tiddim Road. Although it provided certain advantages, it also drew counter-battery fire and air attack, causing some losses, and in May even infantry raids which the gunners had to fight off.[70] The front slowly stabilized amid the marsh and paddy. When the Japanese failed to carry all before them, their senior commanders tended to squabble among themselves. Colonel Sakuma Takanobu of 214th Regiment had set out in early March with over 4,000 men but could now muster fewer than 1,000; yet he was severely reprimanded for failing to advance. Senior officers had little idea of conditions at the front, and when Mutaguchi arrived on 22 April at Yanagida's Headquarters 33rd Division, demanding to know what was happening and having brought twenty geisha girls to install in Imphal, he was highly critical of Yanagida and announced he would take over, then ordered an immediate attack by the thoroughly depleted 214th Regiment. Yanagida sulked in his tent while his staff failed to support him, and Mutaguchi secretly told 33rd Division's Chief of Staff, Colonel Murada, to overrule Yanagida if necessary, as he would soon be replaced. By now the water situation on Wireless Hill had become critical and work parties had to fetch it from a point 1,000 feet below, protected by sniper Private (later Sergeant) E. P. 'Ted' Kelly DCM, who watched the track day after day even after being wounded, and was credited with 23 Japanese victims. On 30 April the road was opened, and 1st Northamptons received supplies and were able to evacuate wounded.[71] But 33rd Division was still exerting strong pressure on 17th Indian Division, and 32nd Indian Brigade in particular, which relied strongly on its artillery especially around the Silchar Track and Point 5846.

Once the position had stabilized somewhat, Cowan decided to counterattack southwards with 48th Indian Brigade parallel to the Tiddim road and cut off the Japanese supply line, then advance with 63rd Indian Brigade to crush the Japanese. After setting off in early May, 2nd/5th and 1st/7th

Gurkhas made a wide sweep past Logtak Lake to reach Torbung on the 16th; there they set up an ambush and destroyed some tanks and several lorry convoys of precious supplies.[72] (Japanese shell shortage was not helped by a dummy artillery position which attracted 100 rounds.[73]) Soon 33rd Division was reacting violently to the threat to their lifeline and the Gurkhas were subjected to fierce attacks, while simultaneously 63rd Indian Brigade's attempts to advance southwards were held up in the absence of armour and artillery support. This created a dilemma at Torbung, which was dangerously isolated. The Gurkhas had to form a defensive box and fight their way north, making a wide detour of Ningthoukhong to reach the division's main position. Thus Cowan's plan had failed.[74]

Major-General Tanaka Nobuo, who replaced Yanagida on 13 May, said: 'Our death-defying infantry expects certain victory when it penetrates the enemy fortress ... Regard death as lighter than a feather ... expect that the Division will be almost annihilated ... the infantry group is in high spirits and afire with valour. All officers and men fight courageously.' But in private he noted: 'The officers and men look dreadful. They've let their hair and beards grow and look like wild men of the mountains.'[75] He ordered 214th Regiment to make a flanking attack across the Silchar track to Nungang, just west of Buri Bazar, and assault Imphal with two battalions; while 215th Regiment would capture Bishenpur to link up. Sakuma, despite objecting that 215th Regiment had already repeatedly failed at Bishenpur and that 214th Regiment risked isolation, set off on 16 May on a four-day march in monsoon rain which turned streams into raging torrents that swept men away. Despite his doubts, 215th Regiment's attack supported by elements of 213th Regiment which had slipped past Potsangbam, caught Headquarters 32nd Indian Brigade and the Gunner Box by surprise on 20 May. In pitch darkness and driving rain the main assault fell on 9th/14th Punjabis and 3rd Carabiniers, and by daybreak over 100 Japanese had dug in with machine-guns and mortars north-east of Bishenpur village. The battle was complicated by the presence of 300 mules from 63rd Indian Brigade's 'B' Echelon, tethered east of the main road in an undefendable area that subsequently became the main battlefield, which the Japanese began to use as cover from the heavy fire of all kinds that they were subjected to. Headquarters 17th Indian Division was invested at the same time 7 miles north-east of Bishenpur and 63rd Indian Brigade needed supply from 32nd Indian Brigade's small reserves, while the majority of casualties could not be evacuated to Imphal and had to be treated at 32nd Indian Brigade's ADS.[76] All this amid a stench of disintegrating bodies so powerful that men had to be issued with field-dressings soaked in eucalyptus to cover nose and mouth to stop them vomiting. When the defenders were finally overcome, 320 Japanese bodies besides the mules were found and had to be buried by bulldozer in a pit covered with tons of lime.[77] On 25 May two small groups, including some sick and wounded, with no thought of returning to base, attacked the Gunner Box but were trapped in a nullah. Tom Dolan of the AFS wrote in his diary: 'Brought up tanks and Bofors to blast them. Like a cricket match. Spectators all around cheering, half of them in front of the attacking infantry. When all over, they all just surged in for souvenirs.'[78]

Sakuma had meanwhile reached Nungang and prepared to cut the Bishenpur–Imphal road at the hamlet of Chingphu, which just happened to be where Cowan had established Headquarters 17th Indian Division, now attacked by a company of 214th Regiment. Hasty reinforcements were called in from corps reserve and 20th Indian Division as the battle developed amid the usual confusion. Even after their difficult march the Japanese once more set up an effective defensive position and determinedly threw back every attack. Cowan brought up a scratch force under 50th Indian Parachute Brigade, now recovered from Sangshak, which fought for five days, mostly hand-to-hand, on Red Hill; but neither side made much progress.[79] Units ran out of ammunition and carriers bringing up more became bogged in paddy fields. But the Japanese position was more desperate still and on 30 May they withdrew, leaving many bodies and a few prisoners in the final stages of shock, illness and exhaustion.[80] Both 214th and 215th Regiments had been effectively wiped out at Bishenpur; when Sakuma received reinforcements, they were not a fresh battalion but 250 motley sick and wounded, some 100 of whom were killed by an artillery strike before reaching him.[81]

Meanwhile, having been relieved on Shenam after its hard fight there, 20th Indian Division had been moved into the line to the north near Yangapopki. In June a two-brigade attack was planned to destroy the remains of 15th Division and hopefully to cut the line of retreat of 31st Division at Kohima. It entailed a long approach march by 80th Indian Brigade, which set off on 7 June, hacking through thick jungle, up and up steep slopes, clinging to branches and driving on reluctant mules across streams now swollen and torrid with monsoon rain. As it did so, 100th Indian Brigade, which was also to take part, had first to repel Yamauchi's last desperate fling of 15th Division as Mutaguchi bombarded him with absurd orders such as 'Seize Imphal!' 'Seize the airfields!' Although whittled to almost nothing, his units attacked once more with vigorous determination and one party reached within a few hundred yards of Brigade Headquarters, where it hung on for two days before being driven out.

Around Bishenpur, Tanaka persisted with aggressive tactics; on 7 June he sent 154th Regiment of 54th Division, recently arrived from Arakan, to mount a strong attack on Ningthoukhong, held by 1st West Yorks, whose lead platoon took the brunt. Sergeant Victor Turner took them on with grenades, five times returning for more before being cut down, but the Japanese withdrew. He received a posthumous VC.[82] On 9 June 3rd/3rd Gurkhas were attacked on Scraggy.[83] Tim Carew's A Company had 'acquired' a 3rd Carabiniers trooper; no one knew how he got there and everyone was too busy to inquire. For a week he occupied slit trenches and went on long arduous patrols, queueing patiently for rice and chapattis with the Gurkhas and shortly before he departed he requested, in all seriousness, to transfer.[84] Once more Neil Gilliam distinguished himself, 'tireless in his efforts – at times climbing the hill with a stretcher on his shoulder, and at times creeping inside bunkers looking for wounded and digging them out'.[85] He was recommended for the VC but as an American non-combatant was ineligible, although to the satisfaction of all he received the GM. Yet Tanaka refused to give up on the Silchar track and sent 151st Regiment from 53rd Division, which had recently been facing Calvert at Mawlu, in an attack from the west. But everywhere they were blasted by the firepower of artillery, tanks and air and took staggering losses. On 18 June 2nd/19th Hyderabad Regiment made an abortive attack on Maibi Khonow, which cost over 100 casualties including 38 dead.[86] Sakuma's 214th Regiment put in yet another attack on Mortar Bluff near Point 5846 on 24 and 25 June, which Subedar Netrabahadur Thapa set out to retake with his platoon, but were eventually overrun in the night. Netrabahadur and Naik Agansing Rai of 2nd/5th Royal Gurkhas won VCs.[87] As Slim put it: 'Whatever one thinks of the military wisdom of his pursuing a hopeless object, there can be no question of the supreme courage and hardihood of the Japanese soldiers who made the attempts. I knew of no army that could have equalled them.'[88] But even these men had their limits.

In the north as well the Japanese refused to give up the Kanglatongbi road-block. Scoones was worried by the approaching monsoon and fixed 21 May as crucial: with 155,000 men and 11,000 animals to feed, the requirement for air supply was colossal, greatly exceeding what could be managed. He set 5th Indian Division to make a major effort to clear the road-blocks and Mapao ridge, started by 89th Indian Brigade on 11 May with 1st/11th

Sikhs attacking Eban Ekwan supported by 7th Light Cavalry, then taken up by 123rd Indian Brigade on 15 May, when 3rd/2nd Punjabis and 1st/17th Dogras attacked, later joined by 2nd Suffolks – a battle that went on until the 21st.[89] On 20 May, 9th Indian Brigade made a concerted attack on a position that had defied it for weeks on the great hill mass of Molvom, known as the 'Hump', supported by Hurribombers and massed artillery. But it failed and still the Japanese resisted. Behind, the sappers built jeep tracks to permit resupply and casualty evacuation as well as water cisterns and pumping stations, while being in constant demand to repair bridges and tracks and remove booby traps and other obstacles. The sappers of 323rd Field Park Company IE were asked to create an effective charge for dealing with Japanese bunkers, with portability essential. Eventually these 'backroom boys' created one from sheet iron, ghee tins and local stocks of plastic explosive, which was not at all plastic and had to be kneaded like dough, giving the 'bakers' violent headaches.[90]

Although it was clear to those Japanese at the front that no progress was being made and there was little prospect for success, a combination of remoteness from battlefield realities and wishful thinking on the part of Burma Area Army and Southern Army kept the offensive going until defeat turned into disaster. On 21 May Kawabe decided he must see the situation for himself and set off for the front; he met Yanagida after leaving Kalewa on the 31st.[91] On 6 June he had a formal meeting with Mutaguchi, who informed him of Yamauchi's replacement in command by Lieutenant-General Shibata Uichi and pleaded for reinforcements. However, Mutaguchi could not bring himself to say that U-Go had failed, although Kawabe suspected he wanted to.[92] That evening Kawabe said; 'I'm going back to Rangoon with confidence in you, and with peace of mind.' Four days later Mutaguchi finally recognized his gamble had failed. He recommended to Kawabe that his army should withdraw to a line from the Yu river to Tiddim, although Kawabe refused to sanction this until he in turn had permission from Terauchi, commanding Southern Army at Singapore – acknowledgement of which did not arrive until 4 July.[93] Kawabe reached Maymyo on 9 June and sent a factual report to IGHQ but did not seek authority to cancel the offensive. However, on reaching Rangoon he found a pile of signals hoping for success and urging patience, and was left with no choice but to order a fight to the finish.[94]

However, nothing would dislodge the Japanese, so Briggs decided to by-pass the Hump and Molvom and to drive 9th and 123rd Indian Brigades up the Kohima Road. Thus on 6 June they began another long and pain-

ful advance in incredible conditions. They drove the Japanese out of a succession of strongly held positions – 'Zebra', 'Pip', 'Squeak' and 'Wilfred' –
with support from 7th Light Cavalry and 3rd Carabiniers. On 7 June 2nd
Suffolks attacked 'Isaac', losing 9 dead and 30 wounded, but failed to take
it until the following day.[95] Jats, Punjabis and West Yorks each took up the
lead against more quaintly named objectives: 'Eye', 'Button', 'Carter' and
'Liver'. The latter proved especially stubborn and, as it was holding up the
entire division, Briggs decided to send 3rd/14th Punjabis on a wide detour
to the west to get behind it while 3rd/2nd Punjabis and 1st/17th Dogras
went on an even wider detour and 3rd/9th Jats continued to press to the
front. They began with a two-company advance that made some progress
but, despite heavy artillery support, were unable to take the crest. Then on
20 June patrols discovered it had been abandoned.[96]

On 22 June the road from Kohima was finally opened. For the beleaguered defenders it was not a moment too soon, yet still the Japanese
fought on. In 17th Indian Division the depleted West Yorks were replaced,
but the Japanese pressed on with tank support, now against 48th Indian
Brigade. The Gurkhas had been issued with PIATs and Rifleman Ganju
Lama, despite being wounded three times, destroyed the lead two. Having
recently been awarded the MM, he now received a VC.[97] Not even in July
did the Japanese finally abandon their defiant, if futile, efforts. Yamamoto
scraped together everyone he could for one last tilt towards Palel and, when
this failed, on 3 July he sent a *kirilomitai* (commando raid) of 13 men that
eluded the RAF Regiment guards and planted limpet mines on two
Hurricanes of 113 and three Spitfires of 152 Squadrons, and on two
Harvard communications aircraft. To make the point they also broke into
the office of 113's Commanding Officer and shat on his desk, an exploit
summed up by Group Captain Henry Goddard, who announced 'the
damage incurred is commensurate with the missile employed'.[98] Realizing
there was no hope of 31st Division joining the battle at Imphal, Mutaguchi
knew his gamble had failed. After an exchange of signals with Kawabe in
which the latter – prostrate with dysentery – confirmed that only the
offensive was acceptable, Mutaguchi ordered a renewal of the offensive by
15th and 31st Divisions. Nothing happened. The buttons on his control
panel were no longer connected. On 8 July Mutaguchi finally ordered his
battered formations east of the Chindwin and slowly, painfully, 15th Army
began to withdraw, its nightmare far from over.[99]

# 18

## Kohima: the battle

When the light comes down over Burma
And the velvet shadows unfold
The depths of the pillared forest
And the air grows still and cold;
Lay you down to slumber,
And ere you fall asleep,
Hark to the sigh of the treetops
And the myriad crickets' cheep.
Softly dream, young soldier,
Of life and its sweeter fruits ...

But always hang on to your rifle
And never get out of your boots.

Anon, *Nocturne*[1]

'IT BECAME NECESSARY to double while moving from one place to another and one instinctively adopted a crouching attitude', noted Lieutenant-Colonel Wilbur Bickford of 1st Royal Berkshire's soon after their arrival. This became known to the troops as the 'Kohima crouch'.[2] Lifting the siege of Kohima was an important success, yet who made a 'desperate bid' for Kohima − Japanese or British − was a moot point. The British never admitted losing it while barely retaining a quarter of the area and the road to Imphal was well and truly cut; but reporters were forbidden from using such terms.[3]

Now lifting the siege of Imphal was critical and Slim sent 23rd LRP Brigade, withheld from Thursday, from Dimapur to harass Japanese communications through the Naga Hills. Starting on 10 April, it gradually worked its way towards Phek on a broad front over the next three months. The enemy was less of a danger than the climate. Although racked by malaria, dysentery, heatstroke and jaundice, its effect on Japanese communications in what they considered 'friendly' country was considerable.[4] Not that the Nagas were friendly to the Japanese, who talked politics rather than deliver rice, salt and silver like the British.[5] At Phek, W. A. Wilcox was alarmed by Nagas carrying something from a bamboo pole, hanging 'like a trussed pig, jolting and swaying ... a Japanese, dead, his head cloven – a member of a party that had robbed the village of rice and pigs, found alone sick with dysentery and malaria.' The British paid (in salt) for Japanese equipment: 1 lb. for a rifle, 7 lb. for a machine-gun, and 14 lb. for an officer's head.[6]

Meanwhile Miyazaki's efforts to take Garrison Hill were now directed against 2nd Durhams. As Lieutenant Pat Rome discussed Teesdale with his friend Roger Stock – soon to be killed – their opponents were cutting hair and nails to make memorial packages and writing final letters home: 'Dear father and mother, what is life like in Japan now? Soon I shall be going to a faraway place. For some time I'll not be able to send any news, but don't worry, there's no need!' Captain Yoshifuku looked at the photograph of his eldest son proudly showing off a 'top of the class badge' after his first year in school. 'So you're top of the class,' he wrote in reply, 'you've done well. Even when Daddy's not there, keep it up!' How else does one say: 'I am going to die now'?[7] Early on 22 April Grover ordered 6th Brigade to attack the DC's Bungalow., occupy FSD Hill and clear the high ground to the right of the road forward of Jotsoma, known as 'Shrewsbury'. Urged by Stopford, he also sent 161st Indian Brigade back to Zubza and brought forward 4th Brigade to Jotsoma for future operations. But neither attack made any ground, despite tank support. The tanks could not negotiate the steep drive to the bungalow although, Grover noted, a single tank from the DC's Bungalow could dominate any position: the problem was how to get one there. Many attempts would be made, at the cost of numerous lives, before the problem was solved.[8]

Before despatching 138th Regiment to Imphal, Sato wanted to make a last attack on the perimeter before British reinforcements made it impregnable. Three companies from 58th Regiment attacked 1st Royal Berkshires in the DC's Bungalow area while a battalion of 138th Regiment came in against 2nd Durhams from Kuki Piquet, forcing two companies to withdraw – under constant sniper fire. As Captain Sean Kelly recalled:

> Every now and then there would be a crack and nearly always a groan or cry for help and the stretcher-bearers would rush forward, kneel where the man had been hit, dress him, and carry him off! What cold-blooded courage! It's nothing to charge in hot blood, but to kneel and do your job where a man has just been hit, and where you must be hit too, if another comes, is the bravest thing I know.[9]

When Hawkins reported that 5th Brigade was established below the road to Merema, Grover instructed him to create a road-block about a mile north of the Naga village: another unorthodox operation, although without air drops the brigade was almost out of rations. A request was made for 250 Naga porters, who arrived where Arthur Swinson 'turned to see Nagas tumbling off the bonnets of jeeps, leaping out of trucks, degorging from ambulances and any vehicle that would give them a lift'. When the interpreter arrived, Swinson sorrowfully 'found myself thinking that this wasn't war; that if this was the best system the Division had to supply its troops once off the roads, it had better pack up and go home'. But his fears were misplaced. 'Later, Brigade came on happily to say that the Nagas had reached them in two hours instead of the estimated four.'[10]

On 24 April Stopford urged Grover to press on: 5th Brigade must move south on Kohima while 4th Brigade executed a right hook around the back of Pulebadze, cutting the Imphal road below Aradura Spur 2 miles south of Kohima, led by 143rd Special Service Company.[11] This difficult move would take four days across mountains even the Nagas were sceptical about crossing. Everything had to be carried. Fred Hazell saw Naga 'men, women, young lads and even young girls carrying ammunition and water. There was young girls with a box of ammunition on their head tripping along quite gaily. We were staggering under our packs!'[12] Nagas, 'merry, gentle, courageous and apparently tireless', also proved admirable stretcher-bearers, carrying wounded three times as fast as British or Indian bearers and frequently declining any recompense beyond tea and a cigarette – preferably Player's rather than Woodbines.[13]

As 5th Brigade continued towards Kohima from Merema more slowly than Hawkins intended, the column split in two and Hawkins hoped commanders would keep moving and reach the right positions. During 25 April they continued, although a large hill remained to their front that would require a set-piece attack. On 26 April the first air resupply arrived and they also received another Naga-borne delivery, including medical supplies and those essentials of war, rifle-cleaning flannelette and oil.[14] For Sato very few supplies arrived: Sergeant-Major Imanishi set off with 270 head of cattle but reached Divisional Headquarters with only 14. 'The remainder are dead, worn out on the journey or fell down into the valley', he said.[15] While it was true that the Japanese could live on very little – food in the form of bamboo shoots and game was for emergencies[16] – they suffered beri-beri, dysentery and malaria (there was little quinine and if a man was struck by both together he would die within three days). Also the wet made equipment mouldy and disintegrate. But ammunition proved the biggest problem. Although attempts were made to bring it forward, the amounts were insignificant (each of the 17 mountain guns began the battle with 150 rounds and about another 30 rounds per gun were brought forward).[17]

Slim was also demanding ammunition, especially artillery ammunition, but little arrived at the front and it soon ran out for the 3.7s altogether, making the infantry's task much, much harder.[18] So the battle continued, with battalions making ground slowly in their sectors: on 27 April, 1st Camerons cleared the hill that separated them from their objective at the road junction and 5th Brigade was reinforced with a troop of Lees from 149th RAC and one of Stuarts from 45th Cavalry.[19] At 0830 on 28 April a dozen Japanese Oscar fighters unexpectedly attacked Zubza, surprising everyone grown accustomed to every aircraft being friendly. Although largely ineffective, the attack highlighted the risk of using a single road to support five brigades plus divisional and corps troops. Were the Japanese to make a concentrated effort to disrupt this thread of communication by air action, maintenance of the forward troops would become practically impossible.[20]

Lieutenant-Colonel Jock McNaught commanding 2nd Dorset Regiment also decided tank support was necessary, and on 28 April a Royal Engineer bulldozer driver tried to haul a Lee up the steep slope towards the Bungalow. Acting with incredible coolness, the sapper first made a track and then dismounted to make an adjustment; but the tank went into reverse by mistake and pulled the dozer back down the slope on to itself. Two days later another attempt was made with a Stuart, but this was knocked out by a 37mm anti-tank gun. The Dorsets' difficulties were partly their own fault: the Japanese were hidden by a thick screen of trees, and only when 4th/7th Rajputs moved into the Garrison Hill perimeter and began cutting them down to reinforce their dug-outs did McNaught suddenly see 'a sight which stirred me as much as Cortes must have been excited at his first view of the Pacific – I could see the District [sic] Commissioner's bungalow!'[21] The Deputy Commissioner's tennis court was fought over for sixteen bloody days before finally being cleared by the Dorsets. Each Japanese foxhole or bunker was systematically destroyed, with no mercy shown.[22] However, the Japanese still held the high ground on three sides, so that taking each bunker was fraught with danger. These strong points could even withstand direct hits from a Lee's 75mm main armament, and with only two 5.5-inch guns and little ammunition on the entire front the only other way to damage them was with a pole charge (25 lb. of explosive fitted to the end of a long stick) or grenades through loopholes; but each bunker was sited for mutual support from its neighbours, so that applying these was extremely danger-ous.[23]

Hawkins ordered 1/8th Lancashire Fusiliers towards the next hill to his brigade's south, Firs Hill. They advanced on 28 April straight into trouble. John McCann later recalled that his platoon suddenly found itself before the main defences, which erupted in machine-gun, rifle and grenade fire:

> I emptied my magazine into the bushes and threw myself to the ground. As I did so, I caught a glimpse of the one man still on his feet. Major Pearse, body vibrating as he fired from the hip, was surging forward, visible to me only from the waist upwards and calling; 'Come on C Company.' I would never see him again, and it was the end of our attempt to capture Firs Hill.[24]

Meanwhile 4th Brigade struggled across the mountains in pouring rain with only gas capes for protection and unable to light fires, so that 'the heat, the humidity, the altitude and the slope of almost every foot of ground, combine to knock the hell out of the stoutest constitution', noted 21-year-old Lieutenant Sam Horner.

> You gasp for air which doesn't seem to come, you drag your legs upwards till they seem reduced to the strength of matchsticks, you wipe the salt sweat out of your eyes. Then you feel your heart pounding so violently you think it must burst its cage; it sounds as loud as a drum, even above the swearing and cursing going on around you ... All you can think of is the next stop.[25]

On 29 April Grover announced a change of plan. With transport aircraft short and Stopford demanding action, 4th Brigade would attack GPT Ridge instead of securing Aradura Spur: a march of 7 miles on the map, but 7 miles of almost impossible terrain.

The following day 1st Royal Welch were ferried forward to relieve the Durhams. 'Space was so limited ... It was almost impossible to dig anywhere without uncovering either a grave or a latrine.'[26] Water was still rationed to a pint per man per day, but thanks to the RAF this later increased to three pints, all reserved for 'brewing up'.[27] The tracks from Zubza had rapidly deteriorated and the Pathans were no longer leading their mules but driv-ing them like cattle, often to slither and slide, crash into tress and split their bamboo 'carriers', spilling their loads into the valley below.[28] On the eve-ning of 2 May the Japanese shelled 2nd Dorsets with a 75mm gun at 300 yards range. Geoffrey White confessed to a large lump in the throat as he watched the 28 survivors of his old company which began the battle 100-odd strong, approaching Battalion Headquarters the following morning, 'blackened and red-eyed'.[29] Elsewhere progress was slow. On 1 May, after another climb so difficult that engineers had to cut steps and make rope lines for the men to pull themselves up, 4th Brigade reached the ridge above Aradura and GPT Ridge, and the next day they descended, crossed the Aradura valley and climbed the spur directly above GPT Ridge. They reported to Divisional Headquarters that 2nd Royal Norfolks were on Oaks Hill while 1st Royal Scots occupied Pavilion Hill, where they were attacked by a strong Japanese patrol on 2 May.[30] Clearly the Japanese were in greater strength on this flank than previously thought, which was confirmed when 4th/1st Gurkhas of 33rd Indian Brigade, newly arrived on Two Tree Hill, ambushed another Japanese patrol from 124th Regiment not formerly known to be on this flank. Grover was glad that 4th Brigade's plan had been changed, since they might otherwise have been cut off had they proceeded south of Aradura Spur, as originally intended.

On 3 May final preparations were made for the attack. At 5th Brigade the biggest headache was providing gym shoes to enable a silent approach. Eventually the senior ordnance officer at Dimapur collected 3,000 pairs amid threats from the operations staff to cancel the attack.[31] Brigadier Willie Goschen, Commander 4th Brigade, took a 22-man patrol to try and ascertain exactly where they were. 'We could see absolutely bugger all', recalled the Intelligence Officer, Captain John Howard.[32] At first light on 4 May the advance began but almost immediately met resistance and many casualties fell in the undergrowth, where it was difficult for the stretcher-bearers to find them. The Commanding Officer of 99th Field Regiment RA was hit, and later hit again and killed while being evacuated.[33] But the column dared not slow down and many men were left. The men's fire discipline meant they would not open fire without a target. Lieutenant-Colonel Robert Scott of 2nd Royal Norfolks ordered his men to do so and when one replied: 'But, sir, we can't see the target!' he hurled imprecations followed by a string of grenades at the source of fire. From then on every Japanese burst was similarly met. The Norfolks stormed GPT Ridge without bothering to call the artillery support prepared for them, although few remained standing and unwounded. On the left they slightly overshot their objective and came under fire from a bunker complex soon to be known as 'Norfolk Bunker', which dominated any direct casualty evacuation route (except the most tortuous) down to Jotsoma, trapping the many wounded at the RAP. The Medical Officer, Captain John Mather, crawled repeatedly into no man's land to recover the wounded.[34] Scott was inspirational. He took a glancing blow across the scalp and shook his fist at the Japanese lines, shouting. 'The biggest bloke on the damn position and you couldn't get him! If you were in my bloody battalion, I'd take your proficiency pay away!'[35]

On the other flank 5th Brigade buried their boots at dusk on 4 May and put on gym shoes, sorted roughly into sizes. While 7th Worcesters picqueted the tracks running down from Firs Hill, 1st Camerons and 1/8th Lancashire Fusiliers advanced on Point 5120, including Church Knoll and Hunter's Hill. Stealthily they bypassed numerous Japanese positions. Word finally reached Hawkins at 0500 that the Camerons had secured their objectives of the eastern knolls of Naga Village, and he decided to push on with 1/8th Lancashire Fusiliers at once. Tense though the advance was, there was only a small skirmish before they too were on their objectives.[36] The Japanese counter-attacked and retook some of the most westerly positions, which would later prove troublesome. But 1st Camerons still held positions on the west of the village and on 5 May began sending patrols towards Treasury Hill.[37] Simultaneous to the flank attacks by 4th and 5th Brigades, 6th Brigade attacked in the centre while 2nd Dorsets carried on their epic 'battle of the tennis court' trying to bring a Lee forward with limited success. It was unable to depress its main armament enough to hit Japanese positions, but repeat attempts were made on 5 and 6 May, having to evade a newly dug but incomplete anti-tank trench.[38] Meanwhile 2nd Durhams supported by tanks went around the rear of FSD, where they began systematically subduing bunkers. Their Commanding Officer was among those killed, and the companies on DIS and FSD were soon in trouble.[39] The former moved towards Kuki Piquet, believing this had been captured by 1st Royal Welch, but their attack had failed. Repeated efforts all ran into torrents of fire. Somehow a platoon commanded by Lieutenant Eric Ogburn made a lodgement on FSD which was reinforced after dark, harassed by snipers but supported by tanks.[40] Meanwhile the Japanese put in a strong attack on the Camerons and Lancashire Fusiliers around Naga Village, costing the Camerons 38 casualties and putting the British in some disarray. But amid the confusion of the night and despite losing one position, the Camerons were still in place by morning and Hawkins ordered 7th Worcesters to come forward.[41]

Next morning it was apparent that 2nd Royal Norfolks' position was compromised by the 'Norfolk Bunker'. Late on 5 May Captain Jack Randle led a recce patrol in advance of a raid to try and deal with it.[42] On 6th Brigade's front the situation was serious: 1st Royal Berkshires and 2nd Durhams were so depleted that they had to amalgamate and were reinforced by 4th/7th Rajputs from 161st Indian Brigade, which struggled to bring up supplies. Another attack was put in on Kuki Piquet by two companies of 1st Royal Welch, but they achieved practically nothing. They had lost 189 casualties, including 18 officers, and the Japanese remained as strongly entrenched as ever.[43] Grover's assertion that he could not renew the attack on Jail Hill before the 9th was unacceptable to Stopford, who sent forward the remainder of 33rd Indian Brigade for an attack on the 7th and visited Grover personally. It was the beginning of a breakdown in relations between them. Stopford insisted the Japanese must be given no respite; the attack on Jail Hill must happen on the 7th, with another on Treasury Hill – also by 33rd Brigade – two days later. He also announced that Slim was sending Messervy with Headquarters 7th Indian Division to take over 33rd Indian Brigade together with 23rd Brigade, still operating to the left of 2nd Division; the Lushai Brigade and 268th Lorried Indian Brigade would also be allotted to him, enabling the battle to be fought on a two-division front. This was welcome news to Grover, since it relieved him of some of the strain of having the corps staff on his neck.[44]

When they took over positions at Kuki Piquet, Captain F. T. Burnett, Intelligence Officer of 268th Indian Brigade, with a war-time commission in the Indian Army, came across British troops for the first time. 'The British were confident, self-assured, and assumed an inherent superiority, which contrasted with the quiet diffidence of the Indian "Jawan". I felt that part of this assurance derived from the fact that they were better informed than their Indian counterparts'. Indian troops did receive their own paper, *Fauji Akhbar*, but it arrived belatedly and gave only general war news. The close relationship Burnett felt existed between officers and men derived from the *man–bap* nature of the relationship, more 'mother–father' than officerly, and including the old Mughal custom of the durbar ceremony, a parade at which any sepoy could petition, make a plea or ask a question.[45] Indians were often treated shabbily by British superiors. On receiving a GSO III appointment at Fourteenth Army, Captain M. 'Bosco' Nair of 16th Light Cavalry was sent back to Delhi; Auchinleck and Slim had to sort it out and the latter sent letters to Commanding Officers and GSO Is to ensure such incidents did not recur.[46] That night men of 1st/1st Punjabis and 4th/1st Gurkhas reached 4th Brigade, bringing rations forward and evacuating wounded. Initially the Punjabis resented acting as 'coolies for British troops', until they saw the numbers of Japanese dead lying around. They carried the wounded with great care – never letting go or overturning them – and the British were filled with admiration. It was 2nd Division's first encounter with Indian troops and, as Grover noted, 'No British troops could have done that job.'[47]

Early on 6 May Jack Randle led his raid. Almost immediately he was hit at least twice but refused to go down. Sergeant Bert 'Winkie' Fitt managed to deal with one bunker: 'I managed to get a grenade in, pushed it in through the slit and after four seconds "WHHOOFF" it went up.' But he was too late to assist Randle 20 yards away, who had been hit again. 'As he was going down he threw his grenade into the bunker and he sealed the bunker entrance with his own body. So that nobody could shoot from it. But he had in fact got the occupants – killed them.'[48] But the Japanese position extended much further and was covered from Jail Hill. Clearly three platoons would not be enough. Randle was awarded a posthumous VC and Fitt a DCM, although as Captain John Howard noted, had Fitt been killed instead of Randle, it would have been the other way around: 'they were in it together'.[49]

Although the siege had been lifted three weeks before, water was still too scarce to permit washing. Torn battledress was smeared in mud, blood and excrement, and everyone stank. A bath unit was set up at Zubza for those fortunate enough to get the chance to use it, where men could luxuriate, singing their lungs out.[50] A canteen was also established where men could buy toiletries, chocolate and cigarettes. Staff Captain Swinson was still inundated with paperwork: an inquiry regarding the loan of three tables in October 1942; why wasn't Private Smith writing to his wife (dead for three weeks); divorce papers in respect of Private Brown returned (one deletion not initialled); two men from Coventry wanted to broadcast home. Attempts to reduce this bumf, including leaving it in the open, never seemed successful. That attached to mules seemed inviolate while mule-loads of rum or other essentials were always accident-prone, and paper arrived in astonishing quantities: sometimes twenty mule-loads per day. This included newspapers, usually hopelessly out of date, but officer subscribers of *The Times* crossword continued to enjoy their hobby, although the solution might arrive before the puzzle.[51] In this respect *SEAC* 'was an absolute boon to us', recalled Fred Clarke, bringing precious news from home,

> a little of what was happening in the rest of the world, items of sport and a few articles to raise a smile. It also brought details of the misfortunes of Jane [a popular cartoon character], someone who was very close to serving men and still raises a gleam in our eyes.[52]

It also made a substitute for the letters, which rarely reached the front lines and, when they did so, were often weeks late.

Soon after dawn on 7 May 4th/1st Gurkhas with a company of 1st Royal Scots attempted to clear the remaining bunkers on GPT Ridge. The Commanding Officer was hit as soon as he emerged from the Royal

Norfolks' trenches, and Brigadier Goschen was killed by a sniper when he rushed forward to help his orderly, who was hit trying to help the Gurkhas' CO.[53] The advance of 1st Queen's against Jail Hill began at 1130 after heavy artillery preparation, but the Gurkhas' failure left them exposed and, despite some local successes, they had to withdraw.[54] This set-back marked probably the bitterest time of the battle for the British: after thirty-four days of horror the Japanese still held the main bastions of their position, and no amount of high-explosive seemed able to shift them. Despite their own dreadful suffering and privations, absence of food and ammunition, the fire pouring from Japanese bunkers was as merciless as ever.[55] Yet the British were often astonished by how few men held individual positions. The secret of their effectiveness was their reliance on mutual supports; bunkers were sited to fight to the flank rather than the front. This required a high standard of training and discipline; Anglo-Indian troops preferred to fight to their front, each man responsible for his own protection. They eschewed overhead cover, preferring the free use of their weapons, while Japanese bunkers enabled them to bring mortar fire down on their own positions. Japanese mortars were the counterpart of German machine-guns, and time and again they prevented British and Indian troops from digging in.

Grover now decided that 100th Anti-Tank/Anti-Aircraft Regiment RA should dismantle a 6-pounder and send it up to clear the bunkers on GPT ridge one by one. But this would need a new track and a gun pit built by sappers and the earliest start for this operation was 11 May. Stopford, in conference with Slim, agreed to this and also began planning operations for Messervy's 7th Indian Division to the south.[56] At 2200 on 10 May, 1st Queen's and 4th/15th Punjabis began their approach march. Major Tony 'Raj' Fowler, translated a passage from *King John* into Urdu, which he said had a tremendous effect on the men: 'Come the three corners of the world in arms and we shall shock them. Nought shall make us rue.'[57] At 0500 to the stirring sounds of *dhools* and *sharanais* (drums and pipes) playing *The Wounded Heart*, the Punjabis dashed forward carrying their religious books with them, and with Jat and Sikh war cries – *Bol Ghanaye lal ki Jaii* and *Sut Sri Akal* – rising above them. But they were soon pinned down, digging with whatever they could lay hands on. By midday A Company was reduced to 25 men and C Company to no more than half strength.[58] A detailed account of the attack by 4th/15th Punjabis concluded that it would never be complete

without mention of the followers of the battalion. Sweepers brought ammunition under fire to forward companies ... Bhisties and sweepers carried
wounded back from the RAP to the ADS. Forward companies were always
supplied with hot tea and food. No words can ever express the devotion to
duty and gallantry shown by the followers of the battalion.[59]

At 1800 hours 4th/1st Gurkhas advanced in support of 1st Queen's on Jail
Hill and made a little more ground. Only 1st/1st Punjabis enjoyed any
luck, finding Pimple Hill unoccupied.

A miserable night brought heavy rain, and morning brought little respite. However, tank support was now forthcoming and this transformed
the situation, blasting bunkers at point-blank range with the Japanese
streaming away to be cut down by the Vickers machine-guns of 2nd
Manchester Regiment.[60] However, not all went well for the British: following the mortal wounding of Goschen's replacement the previous day,
Hawkins was wounded, hit in the hand and the scrotum, fortunately without serious damage. There was a lesson to be learned, he told David
Wilson, 'waving goodbye with his bandaged flipper; "Never scratch your
balls in the face of the enemy!"'[61] Once more Robert Scott found himself
temporarily commanding the brigade, despite having been wounded several times himself.[62] But before 1st Royal Scots could be brought forward
to deal with 'Norfolk Bunker' patrols on 13 May revealed the Japanese had
withdrawn. Their own limit of endurance had been reached. Major Arthur
Marment of 4th/15th Punjab Regiment recorded: 'The Japs were either
dead, buried, or had packed up ... it had been a wonderful show. All was
quiet and someone thrust a bacon sandwich into my hand. I have eaten a
lot of bacon since men, but no bacon sandwich has ever tasted quite so
good again.' That night he entertained his company with the story of the
three little pigs, which he translated into Urdu.[63]

While the main offensive had been taking place around them, 2nd
Dorsets had been somewhat neglected, although the battle for the tennis
court had never died down.[64] Now the sappers managed to bulldoze a track
up Hospital Spur, enabling a Lee to be brought up: a difficult task on
sodden ground up a steep gradient. After much slithering and spewing of
mud from the tracks it took a place of honour near the cookhouse – a
'dragon, which was to help us annihilate the stubborn defenders of the
bungalow on the morrow', recalled Major Geoffrey White, who with Jock
McNaught was so excited that they 'recklessly squandered half a mug of
water each on a shave!'[65] At 1000 on 13 May it went in, and soon some 50
Japanese were seen running into the nullahs below, pursued all the way by
fire and then by the infantry, clearing every bunker and hole methodically

into the night to leave another 60 bodies.[66] A few days later Richard Sharp, BBC war correspondent, broadcast home one of the few graphic descriptions of the fighting in Assam to reach Britain: 'Now all that's left is the litter of war – piles of biscuits, dead Japs with flies, heaps of Jap ammunition, broken rifles, silver from the District Commissioner's bungalow. And among it, most incongruous of all, there's a man cleaning a pair of boots, another boiling tea ...'[67]

Sato knew the crisis approached and signalled Mutaguchi for permission to withdraw. Mutaguchi peremptorily refused, saying Imphal would fall within ten days. Sato had no option other than to obey and, although his left flank had been turned and his centre driven in, his position was still on high ground from Point 5120 in the north down to Aradura Spur. The British had to hope the Japanese would have less time to dig their formidable bunkers. The few remaining Japanese positions on GPT and Treasury were cleared on the night of 14 May, and 4th/1st Gurkhas decided to make themselves at home. 'Our Mess on Treasury caused great interest to all visitors,' noted the regimental historian, 'as it was almost completely underground ... even the rain – which had a bad habit of pouring in through the earth roof – could not take away the look of luxury and splendour which the piano gave the Mess.' Unfortunately the mortar officer's persistent harassment of the Japanese provoked retaliation and a round hit the Mess roof, damaging the piano 'whose dulcet tones no longer graced those barbaric hills'.[68]

On 15 May a new brigadier, rejoicing in the name Michael Alston-Roberts-West, took over 5th Brigade. His first task was the capture Church Knoll and Hunter's Hill, where the Japanese had dug in in their usual thorough manner, and the new brigadier's appreciation to Grover was pessimistic. No additional troops were available and it was decided to try and infiltrate 1st Camerons on to the positions at night. To begin with, this went well but as soon as the Japanese were alerted a Naga hut was set alight, which left no option but withdrawal. Next morning Grover sent for West and it was agreed to use tanks, which were winched up to 5th Brigade's perimeter two days later, and on 18 May the RAF struck the enemy's forward positions with Hurribombers. The following day another air strike was planned but eventually cancelled owing to low cloud, and at 0830 the artillery opened fire, plastering the targets before 7th Worcesters attacked. But by 1500 it was clear that neither hill would fall and Grover cancelled the attack. Attempts to work tanks to the flank were fruitless; what Grover needed was medium artillery but there was none. His only consolation was a prisoner from 58th Regiment, who volunteered that he had 'reached the limit of endurance'. His company was reduced to 40 men under command of an NCO, and all they had to eat was rice and salt; the shelling was terrible and caused many casualties. But nobody expected a flood of prisoners to follow him.[69]

While Messervy's attack was failing on the left, Grover was preparing another drive towards Aradura Spur on the right. Frontal attacks would be made by 1st Royal Scots and 2nd Royal Norfolks while 6th Brigade, supported by 1st Burma Regiment, attacked GPT Ridge. Brigadier J. D. Shapland's plan for 6th Brigade involved an advance of 2,000 yards and a climb of 2,000 feet and would involve passing 1st Royal Berkshires through a box formed by 1st Burma to the first bound, where they would dig in, with 1st Royal Welch to continue the advance and 2nd Durhams (now reduced to a headquarters and two rifle companies) in reserve. The infantry commanding officers did not like this plan, but Shapland, previously Commander Royal Artillery of the division, insisted this 'stepping-up' procedure was normal for gunners, and there was no reason why it should not work for infantry.[70] The advance began on 27 May and proved a shambles. The rear of 1st Royal Berkshires' column had barely cleared the defensive box when some half an hour later 1st Royal Welch's attack was abandoned and 1st Royal Berkshires and 2nd Durhams dug in where they were; next day they were ordered to withdraw.[71] Meanwhile 4th Brigade also attacked, with 1st Royal Scots swiftly getting on to the objective. Lieutenant-Colonel Peter Saunders, temporarily commanding the brigade, ordered 2nd Royal Norfolks to disengage, move around to the Jocks and attack again from the left. Scott led two weak companies forward, shouting at the top of his voice and hurling grenades. This demonic, fantastic warrior was, however, not invulnerable and was wounded. Protesting loudly, he was carried away, once threatening a doctor with court martial 'for evacuating me against orders'. (He protested all the way to Dimapur but he had seen his last day's fighting.) Another attack had failed.[72]

After a night of skirmishing against enemy in unknown strength, 6th Brigade's advance resumed at 1000 next day. Both 4th and 6th Brigade's attacks had failed, but things were no better on the left flank; 4th/15th Punjabis were thrown back with heavy loss – a total of 7 British and 11 Indian officers and 443 men killed, wounded and missing – but not a yard of ground had been captured.[73] John Shipster's company from 7th/2nd Punjabis went to reinforce them:

I have never seen such devastation in my life. The former buildings were unrecognizable and the trees were gaunt skeletons, from which hung gaudy parachute canopies. In some places, ammunition boxes swayed below the parachutes in the breeze. What struck me most was the stench of dead bodies, many of which had been lying there for three weeks.[74]

The flies were so thick that corpses were 'almost buried by them. I, for one,' noted Major Martin Lowry, 'have eaten several of the largest filthy-looking bluebottles, having settled on a bully-beef sandwich between hand and mouth.'[75] Not all sandwiches were so unpleasantly presented. Arthur Marment was at 33rd Indian Brigade Headquarters when Brigadier F. J. Loftus Tottenham asked his orderly to bring some sandwiches for the staff. Half an hour later the orderly appeared hopping and skipping in and out of the shell-holes and presented the sandwiches: not only were the crusts seen to have been cut off, but the plate was a china one with the regimental crest on it.[76]

These failures deeply worried Stopford, Grover and Messervy. Behind formidable Japanese defences lay magnificent positions to site further ones. Although Mountbatten had persuaded the Americans to allow him to retain the 79 transport aircraft until 15 June, IV Corps at Imphal had been on short rations for some time and reserves were exhausted. Yet as so often happens when the moment of crisis arrives, something tips the balance. Derek Horsford had just taken command of 4th/1st Gurkhas, at just twenty-seven years old, when Loftus Tottenham ordered his battalion to take a hand against Church Knoll. Loath to repeat frontal assaults, he offered an alternative, which the brigadier accepted, saying: 'It had bloody well better work.' For three nights the battalion patrolled carefully to plot the Japanese positions as thoroughly and accurately as possible, while Horsford worked on a plan that involved infiltration followed by assault. By 29 May, the day after 4th/15th Punjabis' third abortive assault on the feature, everything was ready. After leaving their positions on Treasury Hill at 1945, one company silently occupied a position known as 'False Crest', then another moved on to 'Nose', leaving 'Basha' to be assaulted, with the lead company advancing barely 50 yards behind the barrage. As the Gurkhas approached, the tanks switched between high-explosive and armour-piercing solid shot just 10 yards in front of the leading riflemen, who wore white towels on their backs so the tankies could see them. The defenders were found huddled in the shelter of their bunkers and dealt with by grenade, bayonet and kukri; the rest fled. It was a complete success, with just 12 men lightly wounded, and the Gurkhas dug in.[77]

The continuous pressure persuaded Sato on 30 May to withdraw his battered remnants, alone if necessary. Mutaguchi urged him to hang on for another ten days, but Sato signalled back, 'no supplies and men wounded and sick'.[78] As one lieutenant of the 58th Infantry Regiment recorded:

> Even the invalids and the wounded were driven to the front to help supply manpower. Even those with broken legs in splints were herded into battle, malaria cases too. I have seen these going forward with yellow faces, the fever still in their bodies. I saw one man, whose shoulder had been shattered by a bullet, stagger forward to the front. Some of the wounded who were over 40 fondly hoped that they would be sent home, but even they were sent forward.[79]

Sato sent a further signal on 31 May to 15th Army: 'Our swords are broken and our arrows gone. Shedding bitter tears, I now leave Kohima.'[80]

Stopford realized that the success of 33rd Indian Brigade on Hunter's Hill and Church Knoll meant the infantry could advance through the Assam Barracks area to attack three features on a ridge about a mile from Kohima that now formed the centre of the Japanese line – Dyer Hill, Pimple and Big Tree Hill – which Stopford hoped would force the Japanese to abandon Aradura Spur. Patrols from 114th and 268th Indian Brigades reported Big Tree Hill and Dyer Hill unoccupied on 3 June; lead elements of 2nd Dorsets found all three features occupied but Dyer Hill was abandoned the following morning. An attack on the Pimple on 4 June was repulsed, but 1st Camerons took the lead and cleared it. The following morning a fall-scale assault against Big Tree Hill cleared the position by 1130. On 6 June news arrived of the Normandy landings. 'What a place to be told this news!' wrote Arthur Swinson.

> The sunlight was streaming across the mountains, stretched west and south as far as the eyes could see ... Great, green, untamed country, almost as unaware of man's presence on the earth as the day God created it. I gazed for a moment, then thought of Normandy and the men fighting that vital battle there ... Other people must have felt like this too, as all the troops have been coming up to our signallers asking 'How's it going? How are they doing in France?'[81]

During the night patrols from 1/8th Lancashire Fusiliers found Aradura Spur abandoned, and by evening Headquarters 4th Brigade was established 3 miles south of Phesema. The 64-day battle was over, although it would take another fifteen days to open the road all the way to Imphal and the pursuit of Sato's broken division was not going to be easy: it left over 3,000 dead at Kohima and some 4,000 of the survivors were wounded. The rearguard was led by the tough little Miyazaki with some 750 men of 124th

Regiment. Every time they blew a bridge or culvert and covered it with fire they were able to halt 2nd Division's progress, and all the time rain fell continuously. Stopford goaded Grover to press on and Grover goaded his brigadiers. The pursuit finally got under way again on 17 June, when the lead elements crossed the ridge at Mao Songsang. Next day an armoured column rushed 13 miles to a blown bridge at Maram as the plight of the retreating Japanese became apparent: corpses littered the route. Sato was trying to evacuate some 1,500 stretcher cases, and all were half-starved and exhausted. When Kunomura arrived to see Sato, he declared himself astonished at the headlong retreat. Heated exchanges followed in which Sato declared that the failure of 15th Army to supply his division released him from obligation to carry out its orders. Miyazaki fought on, but with diminishing effect.[82] The position at Mazam was to have been held for ten days, but 7th Worcesters reduced it in hours. By nightfall on 19 June the vanguard was at MS 80 and the following evening it was at MS 88. On 22 June the vanguard reached MS 108. Sean Kelly noted that the tanks spotted some movement and

> began to brass it up properly. Soon they stopped. A plaintive message relayed through many sets had reached them: we were brassing up the advanced elements of 5th Indian Division of the beleaguered IV Corps. Imphal was relieved. We sat alone in the sunshine and smoked and ate. Soon the staff cars came pouring both ways. The road was open, It was a lovely day.[83]

# PART III
# VICTORY

# 19

# Monsoon

Eck dum, eck dum, the monsoon's come
The basha walls are drawn,
When strong men mutter, grim and glum,
'We'll all be drowned by dawn.'

Eck dum, eck dum, the monsoon's come
No use to sigh and sob!
Just fill the mugs with char, old pal,
And talk about demob.

Anon, *Monsoon*[1]

ONCE 'GENERAL RAIN' and 'General Mud' took command in early May 1944, it added to the strain on men and the deterioration of equipment, especially radios and instruments: nothing was immune and metal could acquire an appreciable thickening of rust overnight, while in twenty-four hours leather work was covered in mildew.[2] Everything steamed and went green, clothes rotted and men's fingers turned white and wrinkled, while nearly everyone suffered dysentery, diarrhoea and from mosquito bites and sores. 'Clothing, bedding, accommodation all became very damp with no chance of drying out', said Gunner W. Johnson. 'Food, if a fire could be kept going, tasted musty, cigarettes became soggy and tended to disintegrate, stamps and envelopes simply stuck together.'[3] At 4,000 feet the troops were submerged in rain or cloud for weeks on end; visibility was reduced to 100 yards and trenches collapsed, but the fighting did not stop.

The RAMC had serious difficulty evacuating casualties throughout the campaign, and had to adjust their plans constantly as the battle ebbed and flowed. The Japanese treated their badly wounded as practically dead. Small wonder that a Gurkha NCO on burial detail had to be restrained from shooting a Japanese 'corpse' that was clearly still breathing. When reprimanded, he replied: 'But Sahib, we can't bury him alive!'[4] British arrangements were often improvised, including using sampans as ambulances in Arakan; but shortage of jeeps meant mules and coolies often carried stretchers all the way to the field hospitals. John Shipster in Arakan was wounded early in 1944 by mortar fragments and took sixteen days to reach Chittagong, but he was relatively lucky. The first part of the journey was on a stretcher in an ambulance jeep to an improvised airstrip, from where Dakota aircraft were evacuating large numbers of casualties to different hospitals in India.[5]

At Imphal, Len Thornton worked in 41st Indian General Hospital's operating theatre, which was

> like a butcher's shop and every case needed major surgery; arms off, legs off, sometimes both; bayonet wounds, bullet wounds, horrendous burns and lots of head injuries. It went on and on, every day and every night. We never knew what to expect … we were all feeling the strain of this non-stop onslaught and even our instruments were beginning to wear out.[6]

Nevertheless, 90 per cent of the wounded recovered; disease was more deadly. During the fighting 66th Indian General Hospital arrived to deal with scrub typhus, caused by mites that sat on the tips of grass waiting to seize on animal or man. One casualty was Major R. A. Adams of 1st/11th Sikhs, who heard he had been awarded the MC two days before succumbing to it.[7] Martha Davies was a nurse who dealt with malaria, cholera and battle casualties, but typhus was the worst. 'Nothing in the medicine list did any good, I could only try aspirin to keep the temperature down. What was required was real bedside nursing day after day.' Following the siege some known areas were marked 'Typhus: Keep you Arse Off the Grass'.[8]

The singer Vera Lynn had wanted to visit Fourteenth Army for some time and eventually set off on 23 March 1944 by flying-boat (her first ever flight) via Gibraltar, Cairo, Bombay and Calcutta, where she visited a hospital and learned the importance of direct contact, being asked constantly, 'how are things at home?' From Chittagong she proceeded to perform at every stop along the Arakan Road. The men adored her. Thomas Hankin 'was not the only one with tears in my eyes, with joy and hope'. She sang in torrential rain, doing encore after encore. 'The officer in charge of entertainment was forced to intervene because I'm sure she would have sung until she was exhausted.'[9] She would never forget visiting five hospitals in one day, as well as giving afternoon and evening shows. On one occasion, when suddenly sickened by the smell of gangrene, disinfectant and the utter sense of desolation, she sat down on the nearest bed feeling weary, ill and futile. She asked for a glass of water. Someone said gently: 'We've no drinking water, but there's some lemonade if you'd like it.'[10]

Also popular were 'Gert' and 'Daisy', a Cockney gossip act, although Mountbatten's friend Noel Coward was less well received, especially with the Americans. He was not surprised, he said; only the RAF appreciated his shows.[11]

For the soldiers the constant strain was the hardest thing to bear; severe physical pressure under constant downpour and on pitiful rations, with the psychological effect of constantly losing, through one means or another, old friends with whom one had trained and lived, sometimes for years. The wounded knew there was little chance of their getting right back to 'Blighty' – home. That would require a serious incapacitating wound, and wounds or sickness had to be quite severe even to entail evacuation to India, while death always loomed large. The dead soon rotted and the smell brought swarms of flies. 'A dead soldier in that heat turned black and bloated in a day,' recalled John Hudson, 'his skin shiny tight with gases, heaving in a metallic armour of greeny-blue flies and white maggots … Even now a bluebottle fills me with loathing and I could never go fishing with maggots for bait.'[12] But maggots had their uses. Sergeant William Robinson was evacuated from Kohima on a stretcher:

> My leg was bad by this stage, putrefying. Eventually when I got down to the bottom the medical officer looked at it and said, 'Well you owe your life to these!' I said, 'What's that?' And I was maggoty – they'd cleaned it … I was most upset, the appearance of it. I didn't want it as my leg was so horrific. I thought, 'If you've got to take it off, take it off – I don't want that!' That's as bad as I felt.[13]

Leeches, looking like animated shiny black matchsticks, could detect the approach of human bodies at several yards and move rapidly towards their next meal in a determined base-over-apex rush. An anti-coagulant helped them swell to several times their normal size. Bugler Bert May noted: 'If we got leeches on us we never pulled them off, because the head stayed in the flesh and that made a very, very nasty ulcer. So you used to get a lighted cigarette, stick it in its tail and "bonk" he used to pop off. You'd see blood, it would still be coming out.'[14] There were other hazards to contend with. Albert Satterthwaite of 9th Border went to the latrine,

> and there was a chap already there, he seemed a bit agitated and kept look-ing down. In the end he said 'look at this'. He had a tapeworm about 4 or 5 inches hanging down from his behind. We had been told about tapeworms and warned they had not to be broken, or they may cause an infection in the bowels. So I told him to leave it alone and dashed off to find a medical orderly. The orderly got the worm out intact; it was about 25 inches long.

It was lucky it was taken out whole, there was no room for modesty in the jungle![15]

Foot rot was also endemic, especially during the monsoon, and could develop into trench foot, despite the application of vast quantities of foot powder.[16]

The more fortunate reached one of eleven Forward Area Hospitals in Fourteenth Army, manned by Queen Alexandra's Imperial Military Nursing Service (QAIMNS) and Red Cross Voluntary Aid Detachment (VAD) supported by Australian, Canadian, New Zealand and Indian nurses. Tensions existed between QAs and VADs, and the latter felt pressure to prove their worth, which they did as casualties increased.[17] Living conditions varied considerably, often consisting of mud-floored bashas. Patients might be any nationality but the best was regarded as the Indian, who was considered child-like when sick and showed more gratitude for all that was done than any others.[18] Marian Robertson was a VAD, a 'nurse' on the British side of her hospital, but on the Indian side QAs were 'Burra Sister Sahibs' and VADs 'Chota Sister Sahibs' (senior and junior).[19] The West Africans were also very appreciative, regarding the nurses as a cross between magician and kindly relative. Much credit for the expansion of medical facilities must go to Mountbatten, but also to Slim and Giffard.[20] Another vital part in the medical chain was provided by the AFS, seen throughout the theatre, of whom a high-ranking medical officer complained: 'The only fault I can find with them is that they want to go too far forward.'[21] They were volunteers from all walks of life; some had failed the stringent US Army medical, but many were Quakers. Captain Leslie Beswick met an AFS driver 'calmly reading Gone with the Wind as he waited for his services to be required, whilst shells were landing round the next bend in the road. He was the sort of conscientious objector one could respect.'[22]

One task for officers was to censor outgoing mail. Edward L. Fischer with Galahad found most letters dull, some disturbing, but others beautiful.[23] Peter Collister 'learned to skim over the personal parts without taking much in, looking for military terms. They were mostly letters of good domestic men, anxious to get on with winning the war and getting home.'[24] The most difficult and demoralizing duty an officer had to perform was writing letters to the next of kin of those killed,

> particularly the wives. The more one knew a man, the worse it was, and on all our 'rest' periods this was the first thing to be done. No words could ever express what one really felt: the man was brave, he was a first-class soldier

... but what could it mean to a wife thousands of miles away? Nothing, absolutely nothing. Her husband was gone; how he behaved in battle didn't matter; the fact was he was gone and she would never see him again. For us, his friends, it was bad enough, for his wife it must have been awful.[25]

While the Allies set great store by the men's welfare, the Japanese were lucky even to get mail. They might receive none for a year and then get a bundle of comfort letters dated three months earlier from children, telling them to cheer up *Heitai San* ('Dear Soldier'). But they got no family mail. Some received six-month-old mail just before the surrender, making clear that their people in Japan had received nothing from Burma.[26] Nothing is more important to soldiers than mail from home, but it was sporadic and erratic, and it did not always bring joy.[27] Ted Maslen-Jones was sharing a tent with a 2nd Division doctor who received a letter from his fiancée saying she could no longer wait, 'the sort of letter that many men receive, but in this situation it was so much worse. Even references to "having a good time" were bad enough. The senders had no idea what they were doing and it would, in most cases, have been better to say nothing.' The following morning the doctor shot himself.[28] 'The Forgotten Army? The Forgotten War? The Forgotten Loved One?'[29] Loneliness was amplified during the immense jungle night, everything sealed while a continuous rain fell as the stink of dead teak – almost indistinguishable from the stink of dead men – rose from the soil. A soldier emerging from his hole felt as rough as he looked, with sunken grey eyes and crusted beard, wet battle-dress and muddy, mouldy equipment.

Tea – the eternal army tea – brought some life to the eyes, as the face slowly cleared.[30] At Pinbaw the water in 2nd Royal Welch Fusiliers' trenches became quite warm. 'A shout – "The Char's up!" – answered from a slit trench – "Bring it over here, Dai, I don't want to leave this water to get cold."'[31] Tea was often brewed centrally in dixies with several tins of condensed milk and sugar. Company Sergeant-Major John Edwards of 2nd Welch Regiment recalled the best cup of tea 'I had ever tasted' was strained through the cook's sock, which he put back on when the brew was over.[32] Otherwise brewing tea was an essential section chore; the cry was, 'when in doubt, brew up', recalled Lieutenant A. W. Munn.

> Each section's blackened biscuit tin was filled and boiled up on fires kindled in the bottom of the section's weapon-pit. Each man would then dangle his piece of mosquito net, holding his tea leaves, into the boiling water until it appeared to be the acceptable colour. The bags of tea leaves were then removed for use another time or until they were not producing any more

colour, when the netting bags would be replaced with fresh supplies of tea. This well used 'Burma brew' technique may well have been the forerunner of modern tea-bags![33]

The resulting evil concoction was always generously sweetened, often with wild cane sugar when supplies ran out, and the frequent and ritualistic brewing of tea became the only activity in an animal-like existence that even vaguely recalled civilization.

Reinforcements arrived. Rest areas were organized by divisions on a battalion basis, and certain other organizations such as Toc H set up accommodation for leave personnel. 'The vast majority were used to their 48 hours of leave in civilized conditions with cinemas, dances, shops etc. Here, there was none of that; a mobile cinema, two pints of beer, a few extra cigarettes and no bullets flying was about the best most men had in a rear area.'[34] Nancy 'Bubbles' Clayton served with the WAS(B) in battledress that made her 'look like a corpulent teddy-bear'. Chief Commandant Ninian Taylor's 250 girls ran fifty-six teams throughout SEAC, serving all the major formations with canteens, selling buns to majors and bacon sandwiches to other ranks, 'who are much friendlier and funnier on the whole'.[35] The greatest desire was for reading matter. 'A tattered paperback was more valuable than gold dust', recalled John Hudson; money was of no real value but a book might be read over and over again. One day he dropped a book off the back of his jeep and on the return journey was stopped by a tankie, who returned it. 'If I had dropped a one thousand rupee note it would not have mattered, but what selfless integrity to return a book!'[36] Soldiers also took great interest in war news from elsewhere whenever available and in war situation maps wherever these were shown: the growing American air raids on the Japanese mainland caught their imagination. But they were pessimistic about their chances of getting leave before operational requirements led to its cancellation, and they grumbled about the long term that had to be served overseas before repatriation. Five years in peacetime India and five years in the gruelling conditions of wartime Assam/Burma were very different matters. They felt strongly that this should be reduced to three years, in line with the RAF (a long-standing complaint among many soldiers). Nor had they ever heard a reasonable justification as to why they had to serve so long overseas compared to the Americans. Still, their families could benefit from their enforced absence: Brooke Bond India and Lipton would send tea at very reasonable cost to any address in the United Kingdom (although duty had to be paid to Eire).[37]

After the Imphal–Kohima battles the lucky ones got leave back in India, although some units got only one two-week period (with two weeks for travel) in four or five years overseas. But leave was not properly organized until August 1944, when facilities were established, especially in the hill stations in the Himalayan foothills – Darjeeling, Dalhousie and Simla, among others – and arrangements were made for the troops to go to Calcutta. There was good food and beer, cinema shows and concert parties.[38] Ray Street recalled: 'Most of us went to Firpo's Hotel as it was said to be the place to go ... large long room with rows of tables and chairs in typical English style with snowy white tablecloths ... and we settled down to a meal of duck with green peas and potatoes, washed down with a few bottles of ice cold beer.'[39] Flight Sergeant Dick White noted the 'blood-stains' on the sidewalk made by the betel-nut chewing Calcuttans. 'We didn't spend every night at Firpo's; the AFI (Auxiliary Forces Institute) always had an attractive bar – more attractive than some of the armed-forces characters you met there – and ran dances most nights; well-played rhythmic dance music, and a good selection of young ladies [mostly Anglo-Indians] keen to ease the hardships of suffering aircrew by dancing with them.'[40] John Shipster got to Calcutta following the Kohima campaign. But in contrast he noted

the total lack of female companionship. The reasons for this were varied and understandable ... In wartime Britain there were thousands of women in the Armed Forces: in India there were only a few British nurses and a sprinkling of welfare workers. In the 5½ years I was overseas I hardly ever entered a private house, British or Indian; our social habitat was the clubs and messes. I had a great deal of sympathy for the problems of British other ranks in India.[41]

Soldiers were paid a pittance and could only afford the cheapest forms of entertainment, their preferences being booze and women of the 'looser' variety.

Mutual resentment surfaced between British and Americans. Otha C. Spencer noted that his American countrymen gave occasional grudging respect to the British because they always did their best against the enemy, but 'it was to hell with the other Allies'.[42] Ironically, most Brits would say the same in reverse. Anti-American sentiment stemmed from their late entry into the war and their scornful attitude to other nation's efforts, recalled John Hill of 2nd Royal Berkshires.

Stories of men losing their wives and girlfriends to American forces in Britain, and films of gum-chewing, jiving, laconic groups of American

soldiers and airmen, no doubt fed us the wrong messages. The huge
American war effort and the sacrifice in men, both in Europe and across the
Pacific, was no less than ours.[43]

But the received impression was often that the war was a purely American
affair. Private G. Coulthard of 10th Glosters saw an Errol Flynn film at
Poona. 'Bloody clever bastards in Hollywood, it hadn't really begun, so he
won the war for us before we started. Inside the cinema everyone cheered
as he won the war. "Fucking hoorah!" yelled Eddie. "Now we can all fuck
off back home." That got even more cheers than the film.'[44] Scuffles
between British and Americans were not infrequent, with the British
resenting the extra purchasing power of the Americans. Allan Barrett of
2nd Survey Regiment RA thought Calcutta was 'very Americanized ...
most magazines were American, shops and bazaars sell badges, bracelets
and rings with the US flag, and after film shows the US national anthem
is played in full, followed by one hastily played verse of ours, usually as
everyone is rushing to leave'.[45]

Scott Gilmore went to Bombay because the Taj Mahal hotel was better
than the 'ratty' Grand in Calcutta; the extra three days' travel each way did
not affect his two-week leave allowance, and 'sitting in an Indian train was
not such a terrible fate. The bunks were luxurious after hard ground; the
food was marginally better than, certainly different from, Fourteenth Army
rations; the heat was no worse; responsibilities nil. Above all, no one was
likely to shoot at us.'[46] Bombay was a long way from the war, although a
curfew and other measures provided a reminder. But there were numerous
places to relax, including dancing until midnight at the Taj for the officers.
Non-commissioned ranks attended Green's next door, where 'the scene
was more raucous, most nights brawls erupted into the street. Squads of
tough military police separated the bloody, drunken combatants and
hauled them off to the cooler.' After curfew, a popular haunt among officers was Madame André's,

> a bordello with the decorum and class of a girls' finishing school ... a con-
> genial atmosphere surrounded by a spectrum of young ladies, Chinese,
> Punjabi, French, English, Lebanese, and many other in-between pleasing
> blends. All were gowned and perfumed as for a hunt ball. One British major,
> posted to Bombay to be in charge of the docks, found the atmosphere so
> congenial that he took up permanent residence.'[47]

In India, Gunner Harry Barrowclough made the error of going along for
a ride in a Dakota loaded with baskets of vegetables.

MONSOON

I asked one of the soldiers what all the baskets of spuds were for. One of the soldiers replied: 'We are dropping them over Burma to the soldiers fighting at the frontline, they call us "kickers" in this trade and the reward is a shilling extra a day danger money.' 'Danger money, why? Is it dangerous?' I replied. 'Well between shells and mortar fire, and dodging the close knit mountains, it is a bit.' All I could say was 'Bloody hell!'[48]

Over the target area they lined up the baskets three high and one man lay on his back kicking them into space through the open doorway, but it took ten runs over the area, circling amid the mountains. A typical day's work might involve three sorties totalling 8–10 hours, flying. A typical load might be 7,000 lb. of rice in sacks delivered from 50 feet. Other trips might be to a forward airstrip under mortar fire, before returning with wounded.[49]

Among the complications of supplying Fourteenth Army were its thirty different ration scales plus a dozen for animals, with normal, composite, hard and light scales. Thus while the Indian Pioneer Corps drew normal Indian rations, the Indian States' Labour units drew extra rice but less of other items; the Dhotiyal and Assam Porter Corps had their own scale, which differed from that of the Indian Tea Association. Meat was difficult to supply because the length of communications meant livestock succumbing to the climate before it could arrive. Similarly fresh fruit and vegetables perished and only later were frozen stocks available as air supply increased.[50] The demand for parachutes was such that silk was scarce and Slim's staff, with the help of Calcutta jute merchants, using 400 powered sewing machines specially supplied from Britain by Mountbatten, produced a cheaper version called a 'parajute' for dropping stores and equipment. By this mean guns, jeeps, petrol, livestock and stores of every kind were delivered safely. Nevertheless, most units at Imphal suffered severe food shortages, which became progressively worse as ration scales were cut. The most unfortunate had to subsist on hard biscuits and jam. Water was also scarce, especially high in the surrounding hills, and men became unimaginably filthy.[51]

On the Imphal plain progressive ration reduction took its toll: they were reduced by a seventh on 12 April; petrol was rationed using work tickets and 25-pounder ammunition was restricted to 6 rounds per gun per day, apart from corps-approved tasks (similarly for other heavy weapons). But the hardest restriction for most men was cigarettes, at 30 per man per week.[52] And these were usually of poor quality. 'V' cigarettes were notoriously bad (reputedly made of dung); 'Cape-to-Cairo' were 'at best foul tasting and at worst damp, mildewed and unsmokeable'.[53] But when 'Lions' were issued they prompted an angry letter to a forces newspaper:

317

They now have the audacity to issue even worse cigarettes than Vs to fellows who are doing the scrapping, to fellows not within miles of a canteen who cannot even buy other cigarettes. A man who is suffering the hardships and privations of the front line should be given the best his country can give.[54]

Americans had better cigarettes and, to the British, always seemed to have more generous rations; but Edgar D. Crumpacker of 4th Combat Cargo recalled, 'we were supposed to be self-sustaining, and we never had good living conditions ... all we got in the way of army supplies were C-rations which were pretty bad.' Much of their work involved flying British rations from New Zealand – tinned fruit, cheese, bacon – and they carefully loaded 50 lb. baskets of eggs 'without cracking one!' The British became aware of pilfering, 'said to be of crisis proportions. We felt we should be allowed to eat as well as they did since we were hauling the food for them. The problem was particularly acute when it came to handling fancy foods, wines and liquors which they claimed was for hospital patients ... we suspected they were actually going to privileged officers.'[55] But the daily ration was down to 3,500 calories by mid-May, below 3,000 by the beginning of June and only 2,750 by mid-June, pitifully low for troops fighting in the monsoon. Once the road was reopened on 22 June the effect on rations was quickly felt; fresh meat and vegetables were issued within days and full rations restored by early July.[56] Meanwhile, the airlift – Operation Stamina – had carried 12,000 reinforcements and 21,600 tons of supplies, including 423 tons of sugar, 919 tons of food grain and 1,303 tons for animals, 7,000 gallons of rum, 27,000 eggs (for hospitals), 12,000 mailbags, 835,000 gallons of fuel and lubricants and 43,745,760 cigarettes, as well as bringing in 5th Indian Division and evacuating 10,000 casualties and non-essential personnel.[57]

Among the notable successes in the air had been the shooting down of Master Sergeant Igarishi Kisaku of 50th *Sentai*. Between December 1943 and June 1944 he had shot down sixteen Allied fighters (including four probables) and three Dakotas.[58] By June 1944 Japanese air strength in Burma had been reduced to 125, while total Allied losses in the previous six months were 230; but these had been made good.[59] The Americans had long had doubts about the wisdom of integrating air command, owing to conflicting objectives, and on 20 June EAC was reorganized into Strategic Air Force (SAF), 3rd TAF, Tenth Air Force, the Photographic Reconnaissance Unit and 293 Wing.[60] To keep aircraft flying, work in the Recovery and Salvage Units continued at night under lamps, but it was almost impossible to maintain a complete black-out and this attracted sniping, albeit long-range and largely ineffective. One airman whose father had been at the siege of Ladysmith in 1900 said wet horse-blankets would stop stray rounds. They tested the principle and found that, except at relatively short range, it worked, and then rigged up all they could find. When Scoones visited a few days later he demanded the meaning of this unmilitary, multi-coloured display and, on learning the reason, ordered the blankets to be taken down and a Bofors gun brought up. That night everyone took cover and switched on the lights. The Bofors engaged the flashes and ended the sniping for good.[61]

In modern warfare it was the Allied ability to keep men and equipment in order that gave them the edge. One of the most important weapons in their inventory was the bulldozer, allowing other heavy equipment to proceed and greatly assisting the sappers who spent the monsoon constantly trying to maintain roads, bridges and culverts.[62] But the jeep earned men's affection. Lieutenant-Colonel G. P. Chapman regarded the vehicles as

> curious things ... They are described as 14 H.P., Four-Wheel Drive, Open Runabouts, but they are universally known as Jeeps or Mice. They are miraculous. They go anywhere, stand up to anything, require the minimum of attention, and with their narrow track (4' 7") and short wheel base, they are manoeuvrable to a degree. Also, and most important, they will carry nearly half a ton or pull a field gun.[63]

'The Jeep is like a good pony: like a duck; a rat; like a person with a good, strong heart and like everything that will not admit defeat but tries again', wrote Gerald Hanley.[64] 'It does everything', noted another war correspondent, Ernie Pyle, in 1945. 'It goes everywhere. It is as faithful as a dog, and as strong as a mule, and as agile as a goat ... The Jeep is a divine instrument of military locomotion.'[65] In the monsoon it gave mobility through mud that had men and mules floundering.

In June 1944 Slim complained about the lack of intelligence from Burma.[66] With 28 Squadron RAF and the IAF providing tactical air reconnaissance, No. 3 Photographic Reconnaissance Unit now provided excellent strategic photographic coverage.[67] But although signals intelligence was available, it was not as comprehensive as in Europe, and Slim relied more heavily on human intelligence.[68] Yet Z Force only operated some 60 miles inside Burma and Force 136 was very limited, with little on the lines of communication.[69] And a wounded officer sent back from south-east of Imphal offered a word of warning:

Watch these so-called V Force fellows. Everyone now says he is in the V
Force – some have British rifles and equipment, others have adopted Jap
style complete with Jap rifle – some are V Force, some just rogues. As an
instance, a complaint from a villager that men were stealing eggs – on investigation, it was found the local V Force 'wallah' had been stealing the eggs,
selling them to the sepoys, and then reporting to the villagers that the men
had been stealing them.[70]

While initially there was a degree of co-operation between Detachment
101 and Force 136, rivalry and distrust spread following the formation of
SEAC. OSS gradually took over the Kachin areas in the north, while Force
136 fought to maintain a monopoly on the Karens.[71] By late 1944 it was
not enjoying much success in Burma, lacking as it did the support of the
Burmese. Commanding the Burma section of Force 136 was Ritchie
Gardiner. It maintained two divisions in Burma: one west of the Sittang,
working chiefly through Thakin Soe's Communist guerrillas, the other on
the east working through Karens and Shans. Terence O'Brien, a former
flight commander with 357 Squadron, RAF which flew many clandestine
missions, noted these operations were wasteful of resources and lives amid
much duplication of effort. Also engaged in clandestine operations was the
Inter-Services Liaison Department (the Indian title of MI6, the Secret
Intelligence Service), D Division (the deception branch), E Group (escape
and evasion) and the Psychological Warfare Department (PWD – dealing
with psychological operations).[72]

By now D Division controlled a network of agents and double-agents.[73]
Operation Backhand was an attempt to plant a double-agent, a volunteer
Punjabi officer, supposedly keen to join the INA, on the Japanese; but this
proved all too subtle for the *Kempeitai*. They accepted the suitcase radio he
brought with him as proof of his identity but threw it away, seeing no
reason for him to contact the enemy. Instead they put him to work in the
propaganda department in Rangoon.[74] Another abortive deception plan
was Operation Corpse, a Far East version of Operation Mincemeat – The
Man Who Never Was – in which a body carrying false documents was
planted on the enemy. Unlike the fictitious Major Martin, who played a
crucial role in persuading the Germans that the Allies did not intend to
attack Sicily in July 1943, this operation was a total failure: 'he not only
never was, he never did.' Indeed, with the Japanese paying little heed to
their intelligence staffs, there was little evidence of success for any D
Division schemes, which often ran into difficulties where they conflicted
with real plans.[75]

That the tide of war was going against the Japanese had not escaped the

Burmese. In August 1944 a conference was held at the BNA's model battalion in Pegu and established the Anti-Fascist Organization (AFO), the first political coalition in Burma's history, which included the Communists and other mass parties. Its leaders were convinced that success in an anti-Japanese uprising would come only if everyone worked together, but difficulties existed through the almost total lack of representation of the various ethnic minority groups and their continued support for the British, who saw them not only as more reliable anti-Japanese allies but also as a counter-weight to the Burmese national liberation movement.[76] British policy was utterly conservative: Churchill envisaged a pre-war colonial system, with only minor changes, once Japan was defeated, and while prepared to co-operate with the resistance to oust the Japanese, the government-in-exile at Simla remained deeply hostile to it. Dorman-Smith wanted to withhold self-government for seven years after Japan's defeat, but what seemed reactionary to most Burmese was anathema to Churchill, who accused Dorman-Smith of wanting 'to give away the Empire'.[77]

SEAC was significant because it was independent of the Indian government and it included a Civil Affairs Service, Burma – CAS(B) – under Major-General C. F. B. Pearce, former Commissioner for the Shan States, under 11th Army Group. Mountbatten was realistic enough to see good relations with resistance leaders as beneficial, although establishing them through Force 136 proved difficult. When the AFO formed, Force 136 sought to recruit them while CAS(B) wanted them arrested as collaborators.[78] On 9 September 1944 a Force 136 meeting was held at Meerut, at which it was agreed that fourteen specialist sections – code-named 'Jedburgh' teams – which had proved effective in Europe organizing sabotage, should be employed in Burma.[79] These teams underwent jungle training in Ceylon, which John Bowen recalled dreamily:

> Every tree, every creeper, every leaf had its message. We could interpret jungle sounds; we could identify jungle smells. We developed the quivering awareness of the beasts and reptiles of the jungle, for were we not sharing this tangled luxuriance with wild elephants, rhinoceroses, man-eating tigers, buffaloes, deer, monkeys, cobras, chameleons and hamadryads twelve to fifteen feet long?[80]

Meanwhile 23rd LRP Brigade finally emerged from the jungle at Phek, then proceeded to Ukhrul. Captain P. P. S. Brownless of 44 Column recalled their total exhaustion as they struggled through thick mud past a continual line of Japanese corpses:

The extreme misery of this march is impossible to describe. The incessant rain, the monotonous drips from the trees ... We had been sodden for weeks, were covered with mud, and we stank. Hollow-eyed, wasted, hungry, and yet incapable of eating more than a minute meal, we talked of nothing else but food.[81]

They had marched 337 miles, climbed 62,900 feet and descended 60,700; 56 Column had marched 341 miles, climbed 65,400 feet and descended 63,900; the two Essex Regiment columns had lost 47 dead and 42 wounded, and practically all the rest were sick.

With the remnants of 15th and 33rd Divisions gathering around Ukhrul, Giffard directed Slim to clear them away. Major Patrick Nepean of 1st Devons recalled: 'There was no bread for six weeks, matches became more valuable than gold and some troops smoked toilet paper as cigarettes became non-existent. By the end, our clothes were practically falling off ... No mail was received or sent.'[82] At night, when quiet was essential, Major Harry Smith of 4th Royal West Kents heard muffled curses from his B Company signallers' trench. 'I demanded angrily in a stage whisper what the hell was going on. "Very sorry, sir" came the reply, "but there's a bleeding snake in our wireless set!" There was too – a banded krait (black, yellow and red striped), one of the deadliest killers.'[83] The march to Ukhrul was incredibly difficult, recalled John Shipster of 7th/2nd Punjabis:

> Every foot of progress had to be hacked out of trailing vines, creepers and spongy-leaved bushes. Giant teak trees, rising through the dense under-growth, shut out the light. The column marched steadily and slowly through the dim twilight under a thick canopy of green. No sound broke the silence other than the patter of raindrops ... Torrential rain fell periodically; mist swathed and swirled in the valleys and around the towering peaks. In the bottom of the valleys swollen streams raged unabated, the noise of which could be heard thousands of feet above.[84]

By the end of the march troops and mules were in a poor condition. Diarrhoea was rife and many subsisted on a diet of rum and hot tinned milk, which was all they could keep down.

By 1 July Slim had completed the encirclement of Ukhrul, where a dour battle ensued in the rain. Many Japanese wounded were abandoned, and in more than one hospital the patients were found shot through the head; in another they grinned bonily, having been picked clean by red ants. Total Japanese losses were 54,000 out of 84,000 men committed, with most of the survivors wounded, sick and malnourished.[85] And it was not only the men that suffered from sickness. Surra, which affected mules, was cut from

17 per cent of Allied animal strength in 1942 to 2 per cent in 1944–5 through improvements in animal management and a drug called nagonol. In contrast, the Japanese could not control it in areas where it was prevalent, and during the follow-up large numbers of Japanese mules were found uninjured but dead, probably of Surra.[86] Their welfare was the responsibility of veterinary officers who would regularly inspect and report on the state of the animals and the grain situation; either *dana* – mixed barley and unhusked rice dropped in 200 lb. sacks – or *bhoosa* – dried grass, chopped straw and chaff.[87] Without them the country to be crossed in monsoon conditions would otherwise have been described as impassable. Steep ascents followed by descents into deep valleys under flood, repeated *ad nauseam*. Lieutenant-Colonel Lewis Pugh described his brigade marching 'slowly and painfully on, digging its way up hills step by step, and sliding down the muddy slopes. Six mountain ranges had to be crossed, each entailing an ascent and descent of more than four thousand feet in under ten miles.'[88] Ahead the Japanese left a trail of bodies in their wake as many committed suicide. Naga tribesmen began to collect prisoners too sick to move, noted Pugh, 'filthy skeletons, raving, weeping and gibbering in their madness, the ultimate resistance of their minds broken by the unspeakable hardships to which their bodies had been subjected'.[89]

On 4 July Stopford informed Grover at Maram that he was to be replaced by Major-General C. G. G. Nicholson, a harsh example of the immutable law of the British Army: if two commanders cannot work together, the junior one must go. But it was a shock to 2nd Division, who regarded Grover as 'their general'.[90] In Tokyo the worsening strategic situation compelled Tojo to resign as Prime Minister and Chief of the Army General Staff, and at one point Terauchi was put forward as successor. But General Koiso Kuniaki became prime minister and Terauchi remained in post at Southern Army.[91] Sato, on the other hand, was dismissed from 31st Division on 7 July. In a farewell speech to his staff he said: 'I ask the forgiveness of those who lie dead at Kohima because of my poor talent. Though my body is parted from them, I shall always remain with them in spirit. Nothing can separate those of us who were tried in the fire at Kohima.'[92] Sato was not the only senior casualty: on 30 August Mutaguchi was finally relieved and replaced by Lieutenant-General Katamura Shihachi from 54th Division, who was in turn replaced by Miyazaki. Kawabe was replaced as commander at Burma Area Army by Lieutenant-General Kimura Heitaro (or Hoyotaro), a flexible, shrewd and skilful strategist from the Ordnance Administration Headquarters in Tokyo.[93] Tanaka was appointed Chief of Staff, his dogged resilience despite defeat in the north being appreciated; it was believed their combined skills would help solidify the Japanese position in Burma.[94]

Of 65,000 men who had crossed the Chindwin in March the Japanese lost 30,000 killed and 23,000 wounded; only 600 allowed themselves to be taken prisoner, and 17,000 pack animals also perished while not a single heavy weapon was brought back to Burma. A further 15,000 casualties were inflicted on the 50,000 support and administrative personnel of 15th Army. In contrast, Fourteenth Army lost a total of 24,000 in Arakan, Imphal and Kohima, many of whom recovered.[95] War correspondent Marayama Shizuo noted that at Kohima, 'we were starved and then crushed ... we and the enemy were close together for over 50 days and could watch each other's movements, but while they got food, we starved.'[96] It was true that the Japanese had fought without reinforcement, without air or armour support, with inadequate artillery or ammunition supply or rations from across the Chindwin.[97] But this was the same complaint of the once triumphant Germans in Italy and north-west Europe. Sato blamed the stupidity of Mutaguchi: in defeat, both Germans and Japanese blamed their deficiencies rather than give credit to the bravery and drive of the enemy that was defeating them.[98] But in such appalling conditions it was barely possible to keep the advance going. After the Japanese had been expelled from Ukhrul, 23rd Indian Division led the way to Tamu, at the head of the Kabaw valley, after which 11th (East African) Division took the lead while most Indian troops were withdrawn to India. The Africans were ready to move by the end of July. The Askari rapidly gained confidence and excelled in 'killer' patrols, silently stalking Japanese sentries. This had a profound effect on the morale of the Japanese, who believed the Askari ate their enemies, an idea that particularly appalled them since how then could they join their ancestors?

# 20

## Myitkyina and Mogaung

> ... a spry
> Small ghostly figure will be seen along
> The Ledo Road – his campaign hat awry –
> Roaring in his jeep down toward Mogaung,
>   ... and we shall say
> 'You see? He never really went away.'
>
> Anon, *Salute*[1]

O N 4 MAY came a phase shift in American strategy when the Joint Chiefs of Staff confirmed their intention of landing on the Philippines, Formosa and the Chinese coast which, wrote Admiral Ernest J. King optimistically, would enable the use of 'Chinese manpower as the ultimate land force in defeating the Japanese on the continent of Asia'.[2] The Army was thinking more in terms of bases for heavy bombers. Either way, it marked a silent divergence within the Anglo-American alliance, with American effort directed through the Pacific with Stilwell's spearhead in support, increasingly ignoring the imperial periphery, although SEAC would continue as before. This was marked the day before by a directive to Stilwell that Myitkyina was to be his primary goal, independent of SEAC, in order to develop communications with China in support of the Pacific effort.[3]

Tanaka had been told to hold Kamaing indefinitely and, once the Chindits had been cleared off his line of communications, he expected to be reinforced with 53rd Division in order to launch a counter-attack to recover all the ground lost.[4] That would naturally depend on success at Imphal but, with the offensive stalled, he received only two battalions from other formations while Burma Area Army wavered over where to deploy 53rd Division. Tanaka therefore relied on the monsoon to provide some cover in front of Myitkyina, while the Chinese-American forces pushed slowly forward. On 4 May Liao's 22nd Division took Inkangahtawng, and Galahad and the Chinese pressed on: Ritpong, a Japanese-held village, was surrounded and taken after a sharp fight *en route*; a combat team commander, Lieutenant-Colonel Henry L. Kinnison, and several men died of typhus, and two combat teams out of rations had to stop at prearranged clearings to await airdrops.[5] But on 14 May Colonel Charles Hunter's combat team sent the 48-hour signal and prepared to attack as Kachin scouts reported no more than 700 Japanese in the area.[6]

At 1000 on 17 May the attack was launched by 150th Regiment of 50th Division while Galahad's 1st Battalion took a nearby ferry on the Irrawaddy. Surprise was total and the airstrip secured by 1050, but Hunter wanted to be certain the position was secure before sending the final success signal, and there was an agonizing four-hour wait for Stilwell before it came.[7] With a 'Whoops!' in his diary he ordered in reinforcements: 'Will this burn up the limies!'[8] Mountbatten was outraged at not having been informed and Churchill wanted an explanation of how 'the Americans by a brilliant feat of arms have landed us in Myitkyina'.[9] Soon after, Mountbatten issued a generous Order of the Day and Wedemeyer flew in to see at first hand Stilwell's triumph, but Stilwell's anti-British hubris soon saw all goodwill evaporating. Everyone at NCAC expected the town to fall soon after the airstrip, and he refused the offer of the fresh and full-strength 36th Division so that Chinese-American forces could take it.[10] Believing the town was held by only 350 Japanese, he sent in 150th Regiment, but the Chinese fell back at dusk when they came under sniper fire and shot themselves up badly, while Tenth Air Force delivered a company of 879th Engineer Aviation Battalion and two troops of 69th Light Anti-Aircraft Regiment RA instead of the food and infantry reinforcements ordered.[11] Major J. F. F. Barnes, Stilwell's British liaison officer, noted the poor staff work in his headquarters with 'a lamentable lack of co-ordination between the various branches'; the intelligence branch was perhaps the most useless: it persistently underestimated Japanese strength, was 'inclined to take their information at face value and did not appear to sift it sufficiently'.[12]

Next day Stilwell and no fewer than twelve reporters arrived, to be greeted by a joyous Merrill, ready to take command. But 150th Regiment's second attack ended in the same confusion. The Marauders, sustained only by the belief they would be flown out to Ledo once the airstrip was taken, were summoned to make another effort as the two combat teams in the forest struggled in suffering jungle sores and dysentery, many not having eaten for several days. Merrill called them 'a pitiful but splendid sight', before suffering another heart attack on 19 May and being evacuated.[13] Captain Chan Won-Loy, a Chinese-American officer, noted that Stilwell's staff knew the Marauders were 'a physically spent force whose effective strength was about half what had been when they hit the trail out of Ledo back in February'.[14] When they heard Myitkyina had fallen, Masters and Lentaigne met with Stilwell, but only the airstrip had fallen. On 19 May Stilwell took command of Special Force. Masters asked when the town might fall and Stilwell replied 'Soon.' Lentaigne was soon infuriated with Stilwell's staff. 'He's difficult enough,' he burst out, 'but they're impossible. There's one chap who keeps whispering in Stilwell's ear that the Chindits do nothing but march away from the enemy and drink tea, by Jove, eh what?'[15] However, only on 25 May was air support provided to Blackpool, while most efforts were now directed to 77th Brigade's attempts to reduce Mogaung.[16]

Now, having wasted Galahad, Stilwell's misanthropy was at its worst, and he told Lentaigne the Chindits were a 'bunch of lily-livered Limey popinjays'. The 'popinjays' in Blackpool were so exhausted that to John Masters everyone seemed to move like sleepwalkers in slow motion.

A Cameronian lieutenant fell headfirst into a weapon pit and two Japanese soldiers five yards away leaned weakly on their rifles and laughed; while the officer struggled to his feet, slowly, and trudged up the slope the shells fell slowly and burst with long slow detonations and the men collapsed slowly to the ground, blood flowing in gentle gouts into the mud.[17]

Finally Masters had no option but to withdraw from the block, a manoeuvre carried out with skill. 'A soldier of the King's Own limped by, looked up at me and said, "We did our best didn't we sir?" ... A Cameronian lay near the ridge top, near death from many wounds. "Gi' me a Bren," he whispered to his lieutenant. "Leave me. I'll take a dozen wi' me."'[18] After seventeen days and beaten, they left Blackpool, but the Japanese did not pursue.

'Any man trying frantically to retrieve a mistake is a menace', noted Terence O'Brien, 'and Stilwell's claim to have captured Myitkyina was such a mistake.'[19] While spurning 36th Division, Stilwell was prepared to use Special Force to support the capture of Myitkyina by maintaining the railway block, and when he heard Blackpool had been abandoned he was livid. Rounding on Lentaigne, he threw in his face Wingate's assertion that strongholds could be held in the monsoon; Lentaigne had to explain the difference between a block and a stronghold. Consequently Morrisforce was ordered to attack villages east of the Irrawaddy opposite Myitkyina and 77th Brigade to attack Mogaung; 14th Brigade, having covered the reorganization of 111th Brigade was to protect the southern half of Lake Indawgyi with 3rd (West African) Brigade, and 111th Brigade the northern half.[20] Morrisforce spent the next month attacking well dug-in and

supported Japanese positions, with no heavy weapon support. 'Eight times
in all we carried out such attacks by the direct order of the Commanding
General Myitkyina Task Force [Boatner]', recalled Peter Cane. Boatner
was as much hated as Stilwell. 'Usually there was no advance warning and
we were merely ordered to "Attack regardless". Regardless of what, we
weren't told: Japs? Support fire? Country? Time? Casualties? Anything? ...
it was heartbreaking to see men being killed by the avoidable mistakes and
misdirection of the higher command.'[21]

Retiring from Blackpool, a British column passed James Shaw's
Africans, plodding wearily along, great packs upon bent shoulders and in
bearded faces sunken eyes. 'They looked like very old men, and not a
dozen raised their heads to look at us. We didn't speak to them – it seemed
as though the effort of replying would have been too much.'[22] At Lake
Indawgyi four days after leaving Blackpool, Sunderland flying boats from
230 Squadron – named 'Gert' and 'Daisy' after the two music-hall characters – arrived to evacuate 537 seriously wounded and sick over thirty-two
days.[23] When in the middle of June the Sunderlands were no longer available, a fleet of ten 'Dreadnoughts' or river craft – essentially large rafts –
were built at Mamonkai (renamed 'Plymouth').[24] Now the three padres
with the brigade – one Church of England, one Presbyterian and one
Roman Catholic – asked to hold a service of thanksgiving, which Masters
curtly refused: they had been defeated, and he would only allow a service
of intercession for the fallen. At the four points of the compass pairs of
Cameronian sentries knelt.★ The senior padre asked him to say a few
words, and he looked at the sea of a thousand faces and muttered a few
words of thanks for their courage and discipline.[25]

When supplies arrived, they included a bundle of some eighty letters
for James Shaw. While in Nigeria he had written a letter of thanks to a
school from which they had received a gift of cigarettes, 'and before I realized what was happening I was in correspondence with no less than twelve
schools in all corners of Britain ... how I blessed the idea now!' The letters had two things in common: little about the war, and affection for a
strange man the children had never seen: ' "My favourite dinner is stew and
jam tart. Would you like some?" "We shoved snow down the girls' necks

★ The Cameronians were descended from the Covenanters who were proscribed and per-
secuted during the 17th century by the government and church, but met in defiance on
moorland and heath, always putting out sentries. Every recruit was issued with a Bible until
the regiment was disbanded in 1968, and they took no chances even now, 8,000 miles and
300 years away.

last week. Are you sweating or shivering?" "We are glad you sent us the picture cards. Our Daddy was killed."' As Shaw recalled, these simple, loving letters 'helped to preserve my sanity during this ghastly period'.[26]

Mountbatten sent Slim to mediate as Stilwell and Lentaigne argued fiercely over Myitkyina. Then orders came for 14th, 111th and 3rd (West African) Brigades to move north and operate west of Mogaung. On 9 and 10 June they set off through marshy mud with large and vicious striped mosquitoes, biting flies and leeches for company, and, weighed down by kit, developed the 'Chindit stoop'.[27] Four days later they found some emaciated Japanese, long dead, with others killed by the vanguard, in some dilapidated huts identified on the map as Lakhren. The following day the BBC reported 3rd Indian Division had captured an important communication centre. Years later, veterans would discuss the railways and nightclubs of teeming Lakhren. 'A poor joke, but as anyone who has been there will know, wretched conditions have the same effect on bad jokes as starvation has on bad food.'[28] With the rains now truly upon them – up to 4 inches per day – the mules struggled. Many Chindits regarded their mules as heroes; nevertheless many mules became 'water shy' and had to be unloaded at river crossings, and their stores carried across on improvised rafts. Padre Miller remembered that when a mule slipped over the Khudside

> it was a giant of a West African who picked it up and set it down upon the path again. When there were steps to be hewn out of the steep and slippery mountain-sides, the West African was there. When the sick and wounded were so exhausted that they could only sink down by the track, it was the West African who bore them to safety on his strong wide shoulders. When men were dying from hunger, a West African would be the first to share his rations.[29]

Once across, they would plod slowly onwards, 'for the mud was like gum. Skidding down and crawling the banks of *chaungs*, we cursed Burma, the war, and the Japs to hell and back.'[30]

By now the Japanese had gathered reinforcements from all around and within two weeks had 5,000 men at Myitkyina beginning another suicidally desperate defence. Supply was complicated by having to feed 8,000 of the original 10,000 inhabitants at a refugee camp so that June dragged on with transports flying in with zero visibility, seeming to 'smell their way to their field'.[31] Galahad was shot, as Stilwell himself admitted, and by now they had grown to hate him. 'That bastard ain't no American', commented one Marauder as he flew out towards the end. 'He was born in his God-damn Myitkyina, and I hope he dies there.'[32] The sick were being evacuated at a rate of 75–100 per day, but he would not let them withdraw. The last of them fell asleep under fire trying to hold a Japanese counter-attack, and their commander, Lieutenant George A. McGee, fainted three times. When Stilwell arrived to investigate, one bitterly noted, 'I had him in my rifle sights. I coulda squeezed one off and no one woulda known it wasn't a Jap that got the son of a bitch.'[33] Phyllis Braidwood Dolloff, who served as a recreational director in China and Burma, would later recall the distinct difference between men of the air corps and the infantry. With the latter, 'one could almost reach out and touch their loneliness'.[34]

Throughout June rations were short while the Japanese mortared the airstrip. Stilwell tried different commanders as Merrill's replacement but mostly relied on Boatner, appointed on 1 June to command Myitkyina Task Force.[35] Two battalions of engineers were brought in from the road, but while brave in defence their infantry skills were practically non-existent in attack. But even patrol actions could be costly: Private First Class (Pfc) George C. Presterly of the engineers won a posthumous Distinguished Service Cross (DSC) when his patrol attacked an enemy strongpoint.[36] Two replacement battalions for Galahad also arrived direct from the USA; for lack of better designation they were called New Galahad. Richard F. Bates landed at Myitkyina on 4 June 1944.

> We did not know each other, other than the men who had traveled together in our immediate compartment on the ship. We had not trained together for one day since being thrown together at Fort Meade. We had not had one session of exercise and conditioning in more than six weeks since we had left Missouri. Some of our personnel were not fit for strenuous walking; some were not infantry trained. We had not been assigned to the various positions that were needed to operate a fighting unit.[37]

Fortunately there was a leavening of experienced NCOs from 5th, 14th and 33rd Infantry Regiments – regulars from Panama, where they had been protecting the canal, and with jungle experience. But they were still extremely raw and many ran under fire. 'They are in many cases simply terrified of the Japs', reported Boatner.[38] Stilwell demanded more from everyone and, stung by the idea that Americans were not up to the task, ordered Galahad convalescents back to the front; men suffering dysentery were given a sulphaguanamide pill and returned, an order that proved Stilwell, to Charlton Ogburn, 'bloodless and utterly cold-hearted, without a drop of human kindness'.[39] Sun had bounded forward, leading his men in a month of aggressive fighting to capture Kamaing on 16 June, and Stilwell sent back for Brigadier-General Theodore F. Wessels to command ground operations. 'Boatner looked very tired', noted Captain

Chan.[40] On 26 June, following another bout of malaria, he handed over to Wessels.

Meanwhile Stilwell ordered 77th Brigade to attack Mogaung. The Chindits soon came to hate him as his own men did. By now clothing

> was caked with red mud, and equipment beginning to rot. Much of it was held together with lengths of parachute cord. Hats were green with mildew, and the boot laces normally carried around the crown were being used to suspend wrist watches from the neck. Every watch-strap had fallen to pieces. And the queue awaiting medical treatment was longer than ever.[41]

But, as Calvert recalled, here were the Chindits, 'the guerrillas, the mobile marauders who were at the enemy's throat one minute and away the next looking for another target ... exhausted after three months behind the enemy lines, depleted in numbers by wounds, sickness and death, and with orders from a bitchy American general to take Mogaung'. But Calvert was also the first to admit they would never have come anywhere near success had it not been for the US airmen who supplied them with food and ammunition, bombed the Japanese guns and flew out their wounded from a soggy landing strip in a state 'to give any flier nightmares after one landing and take-off. But some of those chaps did it several times a day.'[42] The Japanese garrison was at least a regiment (from 53rd Division), reinforced by Headquarters III/128th Regiment with support troops. Even the hospital's patients were armed with grenades.[43] The battle began on the night of 6/7 June, the only possible approach being along a narrow causeway since flooding barred any flanking movement with clinging stinking mud, sometimes waist-deep; attack took the form of a series of short rushes, with 1st South Staffords leading the way. Lieutenant Norman Durant wrote to his parents:

> We pushed on slowly all day clearing villages and copses of small parties of Japs until in the late afternoon we reached the road about 400 yards from the bridge. The [3rd/6th] Gurkhas then passed through and put in a magnificent attack through thick creepers and deep mud against well dug-in Jap positions, clearing the bridge just before dark.[44]

They fought their way forward slowly, but by 13 June 77th Brigade had been reduced to 550 men and Mogaung further reinforced with II/128th and I/151st Regiments.[45]

On 18 June the Chindits were relieved by Chinese 114th Regiment, who were reluctant to attack frontally. Mogaung had almost fallen, but could they find the strength for one last push? In the early hours of 23 June a heavy mortar barrage was fired and 77th Brigade attacked at first light, 'probably the greatest day' in 3rd/6th Gurkhas' history, during which twenty-year-old Captain Michael Allmand and Rifleman Tulbahadur Pun won the VC.[46] Captain Allmand was mortally wounded charging a machine-gun post. Chhabe Tapa was with Tulbahadur, and his account of the action differs greatly from the official one.

> I told him I would give him covering fire on the Japanese position that had two L[ight machine-guns] that fired left and right at the same time. Talbahadur was not seen by the Japanese who were about 200 yards away. At the same time as my [mortar] bombs hit the position Talbahadur aimed [his Bren] at the smoke above the Japanese position and, quite by chance, killed the Japanese in it. The position was destroyed. Small arms fire continued from both sides but at no time did anyone close with the enemy for hand-to-hand or kukri fighting.[47]

Meanwhile both 1st Lancashire Fusiliers and 1st South Staffords suffered heavily as they attacked the railway rest-house, but they took it. On 26 June 3rd/6th Gurkhas advanced cautiously to find the Japanese had finally had enough and withdrawn.[48] Stilwell then announced to the world that the Chinese had taken Mogaung, although they had suffered only 30 casualties compared to 77th Brigade's 950 since 17 May. Calvert signalled that, as the Chinese had taken Mogaung, 77th Brigade would take umbrage, and later recalled that 'Stilwell's son who was his intelligence officer said, "They've taken a village called Um-bra-gay which we can't find on the map".'[49]

Calvert baulked at the idea his brigade might be sent to continue fighting at Myitkyina, and there was talk of a possible court martial. But when he met Stilwell soon afterwards, Stilwell said, 'You send some very strong signals, Calvert'. He replied, '"You should see the ones my brigade major won't let me send", which made "Vinegar Joe" roar with laughter. "I have much the same trouble with my own staff officers when I draft signals to Washington", he said.'[50] The Japanese withdrew south; Lentaigne ordered 14th Brigade to take Taungni and Namphadaung; 3rd (West African) Brigade to take Hill 60 – a key point *en route* to Sahmaw named after a position on the Ypres salient during the First World War – and 111th Brigade to take Point 2171, a strongly held feature north of Taungni. These latter operations lasted until 5 July, with the utterly exhausted and malaria-ridden British, African and Gurkha troops forcing themselves up the jungle-clad hills against Japanese log-topped bunkers.[51] Finally it fell to Major Jim Blaker's company of 3rd/9th Gurkhas. Bill Towill, Battalion Intelligence Officer, saw Blaker hit in the midriff by machine-gun fire.

The impact stopped him dead in his tracks and flung him staggering backwards against a tree. He had been hit badly and as his legs buckled under him, he slowly sank to the ground, his back still against the tree trunk, all the while cheering his men on as, inspired by his selfless leadership, they charged past him to capture the hilltop.[52]

He was posthumously awarded the fourth Chindit VC of the campaign.

The siege of Myitkyina continued, but as early as 24 June signs appeared that the Japanese were preparing to withdraw, with reports from escaped locals of morale problems, suicides and raft-building.[53] On 30 June Mountbatten told Stilwell to evacuate the remains of 77th and 111th Brigades, accusing him of keeping them in action far too long. The Chinese-American force continued to squeeze Myitkyina, and on 12 July an air strike by 39 Mitchells was delivered but mostly fell among the assault troops. At best only yards were gained each day.[54] Finally on 17 July, after a bitter series of signals, John Masters' demand for medical examination of 111th Brigade was agreed to. Over three days all 2,200 men were examined, of whom those judged fit for service in any theatre amounted to 118. Masters added his own name to the list and ordered the unfit to Kamaing, where Force Headquarters staff would take over. He then asked, with bitter sarcasm, for orders from Stilwell for the remainder of his brigade. Stilwell sent them: 111th Company, as he now called it, would guard a Chinese artillery battery. When they arrived at their new task, the friendly but puzzled American liaison officer said that they did not, really, need guarding much. 'I wasn't going to let the Chinese get away with that nonsense', wrote Masters. 'When a major of Chinese artillery gets a brigade commander of the Regular Indian Army assigned to protect him, he's damn well going to be protected.' They dug positions; when begged to leave, they dug deeper. After ten days someone tired of this nonsense and 111th Company was permitted to leave Burma. Masters 'scrambled into a C-47 and, not knowing or caring where it was going, fell asleep'.[55]

Early in July 72nd Brigade finally led 36th Division, under Major-General Francis Wogan Festing, into Myitkyina to move down to Katha along the 'Railway Corridor', leading some 145 miles down a road (in deplorable condition) but with a railway along its length. Thus the division was able to use its jeeps for transport converted with railway wheels.[56] Consisting of just 29th and 72nd Brigades, 36th Division operated on an extremely light scale, with American air supply and artillery support initially by three Chinese batteries. Having recently acted as marines, 'now they were to be carried to the battlefield in American aircraft! And supported by Chinese gunners! What next?'[57] Nevertheless, to fly in the entire division and make good this transport would take two months, although it eventually achieved a daily lift of 8,000 ton-miles.[58] But despite their defeat the Japanese remained in strength in Burma and their Ichi-Go offensive, aimed at capturing Chennault's airfields in China, was about to begin. Advised by Stilwell and supported by Mountbatten, Roosevelt urged Chiang to order Y Force across the Salween, which he resisted. Against this background, Mountbatten flew to London in early August to discuss the next stage of the campaign, which would involve an advance by Fourteenth Army across the Chindwin in a plan called Capital and, if possible, Dracula: the recapture of Rangoon by air- and seaborne assault. At a final staff conference on 9 August Mountbatten's plans were approved, although Dracula depended on the early defeat of Germany.[59]

Mountbatten was dissatisfied with Delhi and in the middle of 1944 moved his headquarters to Kandy on Ceylon, which soon became renowned for elegance and luxury, from which he ventured in a transport aircraft called *Mercury*, modified to his own specifications as a flying wireless and cipher station.[60] More importantly, the size of the staff ballooned ridiculously to reach 7,000, and Brooke drew the line at another lieutenant-general to represent Mountbatten in Delhi when Giffard or Peirse could do so.[61] On 30 July Stilwell left Burma for Kandy, where he was to deputize for Mountbatten while the latter was in London. One purpose of the visit was to have Stilwell replaced as Deputy SAC, although Stilwell was entirely sanguine about it. Spurning the staff car, he demanded a jeep and with what appeared a petty show of disdain drove up to Kandy wth one leg hanging over the side. At 1545 on 3 August news arrived that Myitkyina had finally fallen, after seventy-eight days.[62] The splendour and luxury of Kandy compared to Burma were 'sleek, smart and prosperous', according to public relations officer Ralph Arnold, but even he found 'something wrong with Headquarters at Kandy ... I was always half asleep.'[63] Stilwell, with no interest in planning or logistics, made no effort to conceal his boredom, only relieved by news of his promotion to General.[64] His disdain was heartily reciprocated. 'All my senior staff, British and American,' wrote Mountbatten, 'reported to me on my return that he had been quite incapable of taking charge or giving any useful directions at Theatre level.'[65]

Also promoted General was Major-General Mizukami Genzu, the commander tasked with personally defending Myitkyina 'unto death' – an unusual order even for the Japanese, who normally expected such orders to state a specific time or 'to the last man' – which permitted the remnants of the garrison to withdraw. On the first night the walking wounded crossed the river singing the popular soldier song *Shina No Yoru* ('China

Nights'), with the regimental records, flags and the garrison's sixty-three 'comfort women'.[66] While Mizukami and his headquarters stopped on an island in mid-stream, still technically within the town limits, the remaining troops left on the second and third nights. Mizukami then atoned for failing the emperor by committing suicide.[67] Galahad had lost 272 Americans dead and 955 wounded and 980 through sicknesss; the Chinese counted 972 dead and 3,184, wounded; while the Japanese had 790 dead and 1,180 wounded. It was effectively the end of Galahad, although as the Marauders they had received more publicity than any similar sized formation and, even as they were disintegrating, their reputation was never higher.[68] Charlton Ogburn heard

> with amusement of a group of rear-echelon types in New Delhi who, one day on a street corner, desisted from their congenital pastime of deriding the British to bait a Japanese-American enlisted man standing by himself. The object of this attention merely made a quarter turn, bringing into view the 5307th's well-known shoulder patch. And that was that.[69]

And the scandal of their treatment would continue to boil long afterwards.[70] But it was not yet the end of the Chindits: on 11 August. 7th Leicesters fought their way into Taungni;[71] the final objective for 14th Brigade was Point 1497, north-west of Namphadaung. After a 10-mile approach march by 2nd York and Lancaster Regiment and a day of confused fighting, the Japanese withdrew, allowing 36th Division to take Namphadaung itself.[72]

Overlooking Sahmaw, dominated by the iron chimney of its sugar factory, 3rd (West African) Brigade was relieved by 36th Division and, since his nephew was serving with them, James Shaw was given permission to go and look for him. The men of 36th Division stared at him. 'I hadn't had a haircut for over three months, and my hat was pushed up in a dome above the black beard. My trousers were rolled up above the knees and my green denims were plastered with rich, brown … mud.' The adjutant of 9th Royal Sussex Regiment gaped before sending for Colour-Sergeant Jones, who appeared and stood looking, uncertainly. '"What's up, Tom?" I asked quietly. "Don't you know your Uncle Jim?" His stare of incredulity changed to one of recognition. "Why – you old bastard", he stammered. "Uncle to you", I sternly corrected him.'[73]

Hill 60 fell to 9th Royal Sussex and 6th South Wales Borderers.[74] A diary found on the Japanese commander read:

> Owing to constant mortar and artillery fire, the mountain-top is bare of all foliage, giving us no concealment. Most of us are now delirious with lack

of sleep and deaf with the thunderous bombing. Some are shell-shocked and in a daze. Our valuable food supply is being bombed away daily. From this date we have nothing to eat. We are just existing by drinking river water. It is obvious that the men are literally falling from exhaustion ... Sergeant Kinoshita and Corporal Yamada contracted beri-beri. As long as there is a drop of blood in us, we will not give up.[75]

Shaw's Nigerians were taken by jeep-train to Myitkyina and flown out to Assam. Fewer than half remained and just six of the original forty or so Europeans. Meanwhile the Japanese counter-attacked 72nd Brigade, and 9th Royal Sussex fought a ten-day action at Thaikwagon before being relieved by 2nd East Lancashire Regiment on 25 August.[76]

Once the Chindits were evacuated, efforts were made to rebuild them, but in February 1945, with Fourteenth Army across the Irrawaddy, they were disbanded. Mike Calvert was utterly dismayed to hear the news of their disbandment, although Mountbatten later wrote to him to say, 'I only agreed to it because by that time the whole Army was Chindit-minded.'[77] Their sacrifices were enormous by any standards, and de-briefs show the men were deeply unhappy with the military and medical care they received: they were especially bitter over conditions in Blackpool; reinforcements were inadequate and poorly trained; the campaign was far too long – had it finished before the monsoon many deaths from disease would have been avoided; and K-rations were almost unbearable after three months.

The little round tins of meat, the cellophane packets, began to exasperate us, until we longed for plain food that was not wrapped up, hygienically prepared and guaranteed to contain all the necessary vitamins ... The troops weakened through unsuitable rations and the process was accelerated by the fact that they could not make themselves eat all that was provided ... Malnutrition grew apace, stealthily but really.[78]

The psychiatric reports 'make unhappy reading'.[79] But given that mepacrine was available and the principles of sanitation well understood, Michael Hickey's assertion that the high sick rate was due to poor training and discipline has merit, and he blames Wingate's belief in the power of mind over matter, which 'placed a low value on preventive medicine'.[80] Medical failings were extremely serious despite the sterling efforts of medical officers. Wingate insisted on far fewer medical staff than his senior doctor recommended. Column 16 had to rely on an RAMC corporal for six weeks, and men were afraid to report sick for fear of being declared wasters and of being left behind. In any case, few were confident of being evacuated if they did. Typhus laid many low, but their friends were afraid to visit the dying.[81]

Derek Tulloch has tried to show that Thursday was a major reason for the Japanese failure at Imphal.[82] Rather, it was against 18th Division's communications that the Chindits had most effect; they did not affect 15th Army or the main battle at Kohima/Imphal, and few Japanese troops were actually diverted from the 'March on Delhi', although it did affect their subsequent transport and supply.[83] Furthermore, had Imphal fallen, it would have been Special Force that was cut off without hope of restitution, the official Japanese view being that they 'greatly affected [33rd] Army operations and eventually led to the total abandonment of North Burma'.[84] Undoubtedly Chindit action around White City and Mogaung helped Stilwell push forward the Ledo Road, not that they received any gratitude. Rather, Stilwell's incredible attitude – British soldiers were 'pig-fuckers'[85] – led him positively to foment bitterness. He sent a favourite staff officer to tell the Chindits they were yellow, a job the man relished so much that Calvert took to standing with him on the fixed lines of Japanese machine-guns, hoping. The Marauders themselves regarded Stilwell's staff as 'stuffed baboons'. Charlton Ogburn knew the man, and wrote to John Masters after the war, that he 'had not realized that his qualities had transcended national boundaries to such an extent'.[86]

Alec Harper, who commanded 3rd/9th Gurkhas, although massively inspired by his experiences, later concluded that their greatest contribution was to demonstrate the efficacy – and limitations – of British troops supplied only by air in tropical jungle, while from the Japanese he learned how to construct bunkers and never to surrender.[87] But war demands a return, and after a certain point the Chindits no longer provided a return. Trained for mobile operations, they became embroiled in static fighting for which they were not properly armed, and received massively more generous air support than any normal corps could hope for, at enormous expense.[88] And most of their time was spent marching rather than fighting. As Julian Thompson has noted, it was really air-mobile warfare before the advent of effective medium- and heavy-lift helicopters. Yet they were, in fact, less mobile than the Japanese.[89] Writing after the war, Slim found it necessary 'to give an idea which after all the newspaper blah [sic] was the effect of [Wingate's] operations. Compared with those of a normal corps they were painfully slight.'[90] Nevertheless, the private tributes showed the impression Wingate had made. Both Churchill and Slim spoke of 'genius', whatever that may be, and Mountbatten 'loved his wild enthusiasm and it will be very difficult for me to try and formulate it from above'.[91]

In eastern Burma Y Force, now renamed the Chinese Expeditionary Force (CEF), under General Wei Li-huang, had moved painfully forward on 11 April to begin inching its way over 10,000 foot mountains towards the Salween. The campaign was one of astonishing exertion and endurance by the troops overlaid with caution from above, exemplified by the matter of replacements. The CEF went into action accompanied by American liaison officers and medical teams 115,000 men short of its official complement; 95,000 men had been promised by the spring but by May only 23,000 had arrived and then they stopped coming.[92] But they crossed the Salween, 60 feet deep and full of whirlpools, on 11 May 1944 and 32,000 men crossed the river on the first day – an achievement that, according to one senior Chinese officer, they had never managed in a thousand years of occupation. They were clear of the gorge and into the cloud-covered mountains before the Japanese knew about it, and they captured Japanese strongholds deep in the fastnesses of the Kaolikung mountains. An American officer wrote: 'The ruggedness of these mountains is incredible, and it is doubtful whether any people other than the Chinese could have successfully traversed them, particularly with the stubborn Japanese defending fanatically at every possible strategic point.'[93] But once more the results proved disappointing to the Americans as, although the CEF took Lungling on 10 June, they were driven out again by a 56th Division counter-attack.[94] And in China itself the situation was rapidly deteriorating as the Japanese began their Ichi-Go offensive to capture Fourteenth Air Force's airfields.

To keep the Burma Road closed and maintain the initiative in the area, Kawabe ordered Honda's 33rd Army to be prepared to take the offensive on the Salween front; to relieve him of responsibility for Mogaung, 53rd Division was transferred to 15th Army and on 12 July he told 28th Army to release 2nd Division to Honda.[95] The fear in Washington, in the face of the success of the Ichi-Go offensive and Chinese passivity, was that the Japanese Army there might continue to resist even after the defeat of the home islands. The Joint Chiefs responded by proposing to put Stilwell in command of the Chinese armed forces. It would also answer the official demand now emanating from London that he be removed from SEAC.[96] Meanwhile, for every ton of supplies flown to China, three tons had to be moved through Assam; following the capture of Myitkyina and the reopening of the southern Hump route to add to the northern one, tonnage carried was greater than that by the Burma Road.[97] With Japanese pressure mounting as a result of Ichi-Go, Chiang issued an ultimatum in

August that the Ramgarh divisions must attack towards Bhamo to take the pressure off the Chinese at Lungling, or he would recall the CEF across the Salween to protect Kunming. Stilwell was furious and raged mightily in his diary, but Tengchung was attacked by Chinese 36th, 116th, 130th and 198th Divisions while a simultaneous attack was launched against Sungshan, held by around 1,500 Japanese.[98]

Chinese casualties mounted throughout August, but the end came for the Japanese when the 42 remaining defenders were blown to pieces by a 6,000-lb. mine dug under their bunker on 20 August. Tengchung, a city said to have been old even when Marco Polo visited it fell four days later.[99] Its walls were 35–40 feet high, 60 feet thick at the base and 8 feet at the top. For weeks the Chinese pounded it with artillery and mortars, but it was Fourteenth Air Force that blew huge holes in it. Li Shi Fu remembered: 'A lot of Chinese infantrymen had died trying to scale the walls of the old city with ladders and other objects. We suffered a lot of dead. But once the walls were smashed and we could fight our way inside, the Japanese troops began to pull out quickly.' Further on they found Japanese defenders chained to their positions. 'We were amazed! *Amazed*! Chained to the battlefield! What kind of an enemy had we been fighting?'[100]

With Kawabe's replacement by Kimura and failure in north Burma, IGHQ considered abandoning Burma altogether, but rejected this as endangering the chain of defences from the Andamans through Sumatra. On 3 September Honda opened his offensive but 2nd Division soon ran into difficulties south and south-east of Lungling with 56th Division also held up, and by the 7th there was stalemate as the Chinese occupied Sungshan, the 'Gibraltar' of the Burma Road, on a high peak criss-crossed with trenches, dotted with pillboxes and blockhouses, and with a network of tunnels linking the principal defence points: a result of Chinese courage, American know-how and fierce air support from the Tenth and Fourteenth Air Forces.[101] On 19 September Terauchi issued a directive requiring Kimura to ensure the security of southern Burma at all costs, with the severing of communications with China as secondary. Kimura then ordered Honda to secure a line from Lashio to Mandalay and protect the right flank of 15th Army, which in turn would hold the Irrawaddy from Mandalay to Pakkoku; 28th Army would hold the Yenangyaung oilfields, Arakan coast and Rangoon delta.[102]

Now besides the threat of collapse in east China came Chiang's refusal to take any further part in breaking his own blockade, and on 16 September Marshall presented Roosevelt with a strongly worded note, which the

President signed because he was either past caring about Chiang's dignity or paid little attention to the text – amounting to the same thing. The language was harsh and blunt – Stilwell should be placed in command of all Chinese forces – and Stilwell took great delight in delivering it personally.[103] 'The harpoon hit the little bugger right in the solar plexus and went right through him', he wrote.[104] But Chiang knew he could not accept without courting his own demise, and insisted that he had lost faith in Stilwell and his military judgement; furthermore, it was the Burma campaign that drained resources, leaving China vulnerable to the Japanese offensive. This was forwarded on 11 October, and eight days later Roosevelt agreed.[105] Stilwell was recalled and CBI split in two, with Wedemeyer succeeding him as Chief of Staff to Chiang and Commander American Forces in China, and Lieutenant-General Daniel Sultan taking over Burma–India and Lieutenant-General Raymond A. Wheeler becoming Deputy SAC.[106] Thus ended the command crisis, and within forty-eight hours Stilwell was on his way home.[107]

While Western historians blamed Nationalist incompetence for the eventual Communist triumph in China, and justified this view through Stilwell's story, Chinese writers unsurprisingly take a different view.[108] Immediately after his return Stilwell produced a massive report which, even when heavily edited, ran to over 700 pages. He was informed that if he wanted it officially published he would have to tone down the unstinting criticism of Chiang and the British, and when he refused, he effectively ensured its suppression.[109] The fact is Stilwell was quarrelsome by nature. He knew that, militarily, he was relegated to a backwater in Burma, yet he talked and behaved as though he was 'Burma'.

# 21

# Pursuit

Sole, Sole, Sole
We don't know where we're going,
But we're going away;
Sole, Sole, Sole
Perhaps we are going to Kenya,
We are sorry we are leaving home.
But it is war. Time of trouble.
Sole, Sole, Sole
Young men are going away to war.
We go to defend Kenya and Africa,
Because the enemy is near.
Sole, Sole, Sole
Time of trouble.

Nyasu askari marching song[1]

FOLLOWING THE OCTAGON conference at Quebec in September 1944 the Combined Chiefs of Staff approved two plans: Dracula, an amphibious assault on Rangoon with a target date of 15 March 1945;[2] and Capital, the conquest of north and central Burma – planning for which Slim started in July. With Slim not wishing to lose the fruits of victory, Capital would include the capture of Rangoon overland, and was christened 'Sob' – 'Sea or Bust'.[3] At the end of 1944 major changes in senior appointments were made. Although he had been dismissed in May, Giffard was still awaiting his replacement in October. To many, including Mountbatten's Chief of Staff, Henry Pownall, the only one man for the job was Lieutenant-General Sir Oliver Leese, who commanded XXX Corps during the battle of Alamein and subsequently Eighth Army in Italy. Pownall duly pressed for the appointment with Brooke, but it was not until 14 September that Churchill finally agreed, and not until 24 October that Leese was informed by Churchill of his new appointment. He set off for the Far East on 1 November and arrived at New Delhi a week later, then left for Colombo, where he met Mountbatten, who invited him to a ball. Mountbatten drove them in a small Austin and as they entered the ballroom the band struck up 'Happy Birthday to You'. A very pretty Wren walked across the ballroom and kissed Mountbatten *avec empressement*. Later Leese wrote to his wife:

> They were at extreme pains to explain that it did not often happen! But I doubt that. It was gay and full of life – full enough of drink – and very odd. Most girls were U's [Mountbatten's] and other secretaries and they seemed to spend their time sitting on the arms of U and others' chairs. It all seemed a pity somehow, as it gives the Playboy atmosphere, in terrible contrast to those from the battle.[4]

Once back in Britain, Giffard dined with Brooke, who thought most of the credit for the Burma success was due to Giffard. He blamed Pownall, who was frail and needed replacing, and after various suggestions were made, including Slim, the bold and energetic Lieutenant-General Frederick 'Boy' Browning was appointed; he arrived in mid-December.[5]

On 12 November 1944 Leese became Commander-in-Chief, Allied Land Forces South East Asia (ALFSEA), and three days later he moved to his Headquarters at Barrackpore, where he met Slim and Christison, who would no longer come under Slim, freeing the latter to concentrate on the invasion of central Burma. 'I got a good impression of Slim,' wrote Leese to his wife, 'though I think he bellyaches. He was slightly defensive about the Indian Army, the difficulties of Burma and the need to understand how to fight the Japs ... He is very proud of his Army, and well he may be. I think he is sound in his tactics.'[6] Slim was also uneasy about Giffard's replacement, especially when Leese introduced former Eighth Army staff which, Slim wrote, 'had a good deal of desert sand in its shoes and was rather inclined to push Eighth Army down our throats'.[7] Although superficially relations were cordial, when Leese's liaison officer found himself in conversation with Slim shortly after his arrival, he was taken aback when Slim barked at him: 'Well, what do you think of Fourteenth Army?' Before he could reply Slim answered his own question: 'I think it's a damn good Army!' His sharp tone suggested some people thought otherwise.[8]

Slim's concentration on central Burma also enabled him to make a change. Scoones had borne the brunt at Imphal and, after taking his corps to Ranchi for a rest, returned in October to prepare for the new campaign. Throughout Imphal he had been steady, 'far-sighted' Slim called him, but slow. For the offensive, Slim needed someone dashing and aggressive and when Scoones was offered the job of Commander-in-

Chief Central Command in India he promoted former cavalryman Frank Messervy for the charge that would cut the Japanese in two.[9] Meanwhile Somerville was replaced by Admiral Sir Bruce Fraser and then, when Fraser went to the Pacific, by Vice-Admiral Sir Arthur Power; and Air Marshal Sir Guy Garrod replaced Peirse.[10] Peirse had led criticism of Giffard, especially his lack of understanding of air and his opposition to new ideas, but his protracted affair with Lady Auchinleck had become an open scandal, and neglecting his duties while cavorting with her in Kashmir lost him the respect of his officers, so he had to go.[11] Garrod reigned only briefly, as he was due to be succeeded by Air Chief Marshal Sir Trafford Leigh-Mallory, but Leigh-Mallory's plane crashed in the French Alps on 14 November. In due course Air Chief Marshal Keith Park took over, but not until 25 February 1945, so Garrod was responsible for the planning of air support for the offensive.[12] Slim's immediate counterpart at 221 Group was Vincent and they formed a joint headquarters. When 3rd TAF disbanded in December 1944, it left the two groups to work direct with the ground forces overseen by EAC, which had a total of 627 RAF aircraft in December 1944, rising to 772 by the following March. The USAAF had 691 and 748 respectively.[13] Many experienced pilots arrived from Europe, including Battle of Britain ace Squadron Leader James 'Ginger' Lacey, who joined 17 Squadron.[14] Many RAF squadrons re-equipped with P-47 'Thunderbolts', which were often used as dive-bombers in the ground support role. Additional airstrips were needed, adding further to the Royal Engineers' list of tasks, while mobile signals units had to be created. Although the RAF Regiment had defended the Imphal airstrips, it had been short of numbers. Now it was strengthened and reorganized.[15]

In the north, Capital would see NCAC seize north Burma through Kalewa and Lashio to protect Fourteenth Army's flank while the Chinese would cross to the central plain. NCAC would be in position by February 1945 and would also thus protect the air supply route and enable the Ledo Road to be driven through, led once more by American troops. Where replacements, equipment and mules were brought in, marked 'M & R' for 'Merrill's and Replacements', the GIs corrupted this to 'Mars', which became the code name of the new formation.[16] 5332nd Brigade (Provisional) was formed, comprising 475th Infantry Regiment, largely from Galahad and New Galahad veterans, 124th Cavalry Regiment (Special) – formerly of the Texas National Guard and now serving as infantry, and 612th and 613th Artillery Battalions (Pack) with mule-borne 75mm howitzers. The brigade was activated in India on 26 July 1944 and in Mid-August began training at Camp Robert W. Landis – named in honour of the first Marauder casualty – 10 miles north of Myitkyina. On 31 October Brigadier-General John P. Willey assumed command.[17] Stilwell addressed the 475th and, sensing his talk was not going well, asked what was wrong. A sergeant told him bluntly: no promotion; no USO shows; only canned food; no regular mail. Soon afterwards these complaints were addressed and before returning to action the men got beer (five cases each arrived in one go), movies – a different one each night – and shows such as Ann Sheridan's troops of entertainers, which included a beautiful female contortionist who dominated conversation for the rest of the men's time in Burma.[18]

With IV Corps resting at Imphal, XXXIII Corps would initially control the advance led by 5th Indian Division along the Tiddim Road to destroy 33rd Division with 11th (East African) Division advancing along the Tamu Road to destroy the remnants of 15th and 31st Divisions, whereafter the two thrusts would converge on Kalemyo. Slim told the Africans that he was sure 'that really good troops would be able to move and fight even in the appalling conditions of the monsoon'.[19] Thereafter the winding Tiddim Road would be abandoned as a supply route in favour of the Kabaw valley and air supply. Christison summoned a high-level conference in October 1944 to state that XV Corps, now under Leese's command at ALFSEA, would start in early December. On 8 November Mountbatten issued a directive that Arakan was to be cleared and Akyab captured by amphibious assault by the end of January (Operations Romulus and Talon).[20] This would involve an attack down the Mayu peninsula with 25th Indian and two West African divisions, one brigade being supplied entirely from the sea, and by 27 November plans were complete for a continuous series of combined operations under a headquarters comprising naval Force W under Rear-Admiral Bernard Martin, and XV Corps and 224 Group RAF under Air Vice-Marshal the Earl of Bandon – known as the 'Abandoned Earl'[21] – with a specially equipped cruiser, HMS *Phoebe*, as headquarters ship. The seizure of Akyab was of considerable importance since this would secure the Kaladan estuary, enabling support to be given to the West African division driving down it, and more vital still, would provide a springboard for future operations, not only of XV Corps in Arakan but also for supporting Fourteenth Army in the Irrawaddy valley by providing a Rear Airfield Maintenance Organization, part of the CAATO under Brigadier J. A. Dawson.[22] This was essential, given that packing took hundreds of man-hours than road transport and was far more expensive in terms of fuel, parachutes and flying hours, a fact illustrated

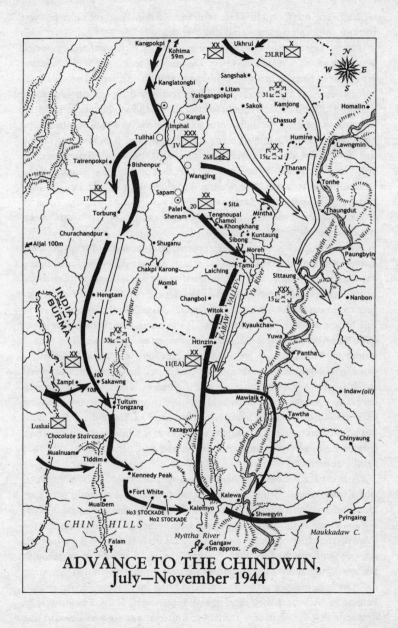

# ADVANCE TO THE CHINDWIN,
## July—November 1944

when a note was found in a box of rations saying, 'Stop eating so fast you bastards, we can't pack the stuff quick enough.'[23]

For the Japanese the concept of driving into China and holding Burma as a flank guard was now reversed. Despite the success of Ichi-Go it was now clear to Kimura that simply holding on in Burma would be very difficult. As early as 2 July Southern Army had issued Operation Order 101 that the British should be fought west of the Chindwin but eliminating the advance on India; as their fortunes declined, this was outdated by September and in October Burma Area Army defined its aims as securing the line Lashio–Mandalay–Yenangyaung and Rangoon.[24] The major difficulty in their reduced state was how to defend the long length of the Irrawaddy, up to 1,000 yards wide and studded with islands. For this they chose to distribute 15th Army's depleted forces along some 250 miles of riverbank, what Iwakuro called 'the line of change of the hearts of the Burmese people'.[25]

Kimura desperately needed reinforcements and supplies for his depleted armies, and with the post-monsoon season of 1944 Allied air forces began concentrating on Burma's communications system, including the railways. It little mattered if these received only intermittent attention if other targets to forward Japanese formations were also attacked, since the lack of side routes was an inherent weakness. If the marshalling yards at Bangkok, Pegu and Mandalay were put out of action, or two successive of its many vulnerable bridges – 126 were over 100 feet long and 176 over 40 feet – this also isolated rolling stock, which could then be destroyed, and forced the Japanese to transfer stores around the breaks, a time-consuming process. The Japanese were particularly sensitive to attacks on Rangoon and it became one of the most heavily fortified areas of South-East Asia, with heavy anti-aircraft and searchlight defences at vital points and the larger part of Japanese fighter strength concentrated at Mingaladon and other nearby airfields.[26]

By late 1944 Burma Area Army's supply situation was extremely grave, and Kimura received the last reinforcing formation he would get: 49th Division. Southern Army had available 60,000 reinforcements for his existing under-strength formations, along with weapons and ammunition for three divisions, 45,000 tons of supplies, 500 lorries and 2,000 pack animals: the problem was getting them to him. Barely a trickle came through Rangoon, the approaches to which were now regularly mined. Shipping losses in 1944 reached 2.3 million tons and large ships went no farther than Penang in Malaya, if they even passed Singapore.[27] Tokyo's plight was so desperate that the number of twelve- to fourteen-year-olds involved in war work rose from 700,000 in October 1944 to over 1¼ million by February 1945.[28] By October 1944 some 30,000 reinforcements arrived by sea, using 60 coastal vessels operated by No. 38 Harbour Unit at Rangoon, but ironically some troops were rapidly withdrawn again to shore other sections of the crumbling Imperial dam.[29] The Liberator force of 231 Group RAF with US 7th and 12th Bombardment Groups came under overall control of Headquarters SAF, whose job was now to support Slim in his task of reoccupying Burma, with the primary targets being forward supply dumps, airfields and the transport system, including the Burma–Thailand railway.[30] When Mountbatten decreed that operations would continue throughout the monsoon this included strategic air operations, although some thunderstorms were quite capable of destroying an aircraft even as large as a Liberator.[31] Meanwhile, Wing Commander James Blackburn of 159 Squadron RAF, by experimenting with cruise control and extra fuel tanks, had increased the bomb-loads of his Liberators from 3,000 to 8,000 lb. at the maximum range of 1,100 miles.[32] And since March they had been supported by Beaufighters from 27 Squadron (later joined by torpedo-equipped Beaufighters of 47 Squadron to form an anti-shipping force) and 177 Squadron, whose 20mm cannon and machine-guns were ideal for attacking locomotives and rolling stock, and which were nicknamed 'Whispering Death' by the Japanese.[33] A third squadron, with rocket-firing aircraft, arrived in January 1945 that could deal with engines in protective sheds. However, with the diversion of US 7th Bombardment Group to transporting fuel to China in January 1944, the railway was still able to double its effectiveness between July and the end of 1944, raising tonnage delivered from 70,000 to 113,000.[34]

SAF operations in 1944 and 1945 were to interdict the entire Japanese transport system in South-East Asia to reduce their military power in Burma.[35] Makeson railway workshops near Bangkok were attacked at night, but most attacks on targets in Burma were in daylight, usually in formation from around 6–8,000 feet, although attacks on the Burma–Thailand railway were made individually in turn from 300 feet, using bombs with eleven-second delay fuses to allow the planes to escape. 'The major problem was persuading the bomb to stick on impact', recalled Squadron Leader Reg 'Lucky' Jordan,

> and it took a while to become proficient in the art. The instinctive approach of putting the aircraft practically on top of the target at a few feet, before releasing the bomb, merely brought gasps of astonishment from the rear gunner at the sight of the bomb bouncing along in pursuit of him: initially achieving heights well above his turret, as we sped away, hugging the ground to evade the defences.[36]

When, at the end of October 1944, 7th Bombardment Group returned from Hump duties, it began to attack the railway once more, and early in 1945 improvements in technique, beginning with a shallow-dive, improved effectiveness enormously.[37] In late 1944 the AZON, or 'azimuth only' bomb arrived. Fitted with a gyro and solenoids in the tail fin, it was the progenitor of modern 'smart' munitions. Dropped from 15,000 feet, it could be steered left or right 2–3,000 feet by radio signals. Whenever a target defied destruction, 493rd Squadron would take it on with AZONs. Between the end of 1944 and June 1945 the bridges at Tamarkan were subject to seven major attacks and several were damaged, although not without cost.[38] Fortunately the Japanese rarely sent their fighters after them, preferring to operate from airfields out of the daylight radius of Allied bombers for fear of attack. Nevertheless, there was often heavy anti-aircraft fire, and 34 British and 29 US bombers were lost between January 1944 and the war's end. But at no stage did the strategic railroad live up to its planners' expectations.[39]

The most important anti-shipping operation on the approaches to Rangoon took place on the evening of 9 September 1944, when 211 Squadron's Beaufighters located thirteen small vessels and accompanying escorts. Then 177 Squadron were ordered to attack the same target the next morning and 211 Squadron in the evening. Flight Lieutenant Atholl Sutherland Brown arrived off an island in the Gulf of Martaban 'to find one coastal freighter stationary at sea. Attacks were made *en passant* to try to sink it but we continued round the lee of the island where six or seven ships were moored or beached.' They attacked, but it was hard to tell how effectively, although it was believed seven or eight ships had been destroyed or seriously damaged.[40] Kimura stated emphatically and more than once that the Burma campaign had been for him a war of supply. The most important effect of Allied bombing was the crippling of his supply system. His transport could move only at night, hampering its efficiency, and while air attack affected morale, this was not nearly so important as his supplies.[41] Desperate for information on Anglo-Indian troops movements, the Japanese sent a Dinah reconnaissance aircraft over Imphal on 24 September. It was met by a Spitfire and destroyed near Pinlebu, and the following day the anticipated repeat operation was chased by Spitfires from 155 Squadron. 'It blew up!' reported Flight Sergeant Lunnon-Wood on landing. 'Just like the films – little bits – poof!'[42]

Known as the Rhino Division because of its divisional sign, 11th (East African) Division came from lands where, in the 1940s, 'such things as clocks, pills, telephones, engines, bullets, antiseptics, dynamite and electricity, pressure-gauges for tyres, compasses, dial-sights, maps, keys, boots, cigarettes, mosquito-nets and prophylactics were to enter their lives as new and strange things'.[43] On replacing 23rd Indian Division at the beginning of August 1944, they found Tamu in utter chaos; over 550 Japanese bodies unburied in the streets to keep the hygiene squads busy, with a gruesome method of disposal: a Japanese helmet filled with flame-thrower fuel and poured over the corpses, to leave a trail that, once lit, consumed the body in a hissing flame. Another 100 diseased and starving were taken alive. 'The living Japanese were even more terrible to look at than the dead,' noted the war correspondent Gerald Hanley, 'for they walked as mockeries of their prostrate comrades, like animated cadavers.'[44]

After Imphal, Major James Nicholson noted, 'the number of Japanese prisoners taken and the amount of other intelligence obtained rose from a meagre trickle on the way to Imphal to a steadily increasing flow as the advance southward from Imphal gathered momentum'.[45] Because their creed refused to accept the concept of surrender, Japanese prisoners were never taught how to behave if captured and, rare though they remained, they often proved valuable sources of information.[46] However, the lack of linguists – one translator and one interrogator per division – hindered rapid intelligence-gathering and many documents had to be flown out to India.[47] With the advance beginning, the Burma Intelligence Corps, formed from Burmese and Anglo-Burmese personnel, would play an increasingly important role, comprising ten platoons attached to divisional and other formation headquarters.[48] Gerald Hanley watched an interrogation. The interrogating lieutenant gave the prisoner a cigarette and a mug of tea and said: 'He is going to break down shortly and cry, they nearly all do. It's damn strange.' After a few questions while the prisoner drank his tea, he 'suddenly gripped his head in his hands and began to weep brokenly, drawing long sobbing breaths and in such a manner that his whole body shook violently'. The lieutenant explained he was crying because he remembered how he had been deserted by his officers. Unable to go any further, he had been abandoned with a grenade but had been too afraid to kill himself.[49]

To most British this attitude of wilful self-destruction was sub-human and they felt no compunction about helping the enemy on their way. But seeing the wretched state of Japanese stragglers affected John Hudson. 'After respecting their awesome invincibility for so long, looking down at our prisoners with yellow diarrhoea trickling down their trembling shanks, my hatred turned to compassion. Starvation, disease, rain, jungle and the "vaulting ambition which o'erleaps itself" had brought them to this.'[50] Lieutenant John Nunneley agreed: 'I was discovering that it is one thing to kill in the heat of battle and another to see a man dying from wounds, disease, and starvation who might have been saved, perhaps by one's own actions.'[51] But not all were sympathetic: Home Kanir of the Indian Pioneer Corps, who had himself been captured by the Japanese, saw six of them crucified, tortured and mutilated by African troops in reprisal for similar atrocities committed by them.[52]

At Sittaung the pathetic remnants of 15th and 31st Divisions waited to cross the Chindwin under British air attack, and piles of maggot-infested corpses, some already picked clean, were indistinguishable from heaps of earth. When the planes flew off, vultures took their place in the sky. Manabu Wada was one of the few survivors.

> I remember how we longed for a place, any place at all, where we could take shelter and rest. Once we found a tent in the jungle. But inside it were the bodies of some nurses. We had never imagined there would be female victims, especially so far over the Kohima mountains. Why, we asked ourselves, had the regiment not taken the nurses to a place of safety?[53]

With three comrades he built a raft to float down the Chindwin. One man was lost in the strong currents and only desperate determination to survive saw the others through their ordeal. Some years later a Burman told how he watched groups of Japanese straggling through his village, how after scrounging food they would squat in circles and talk. He noticed that, if a certain word was uttered, the conversation would break off into silence. Only later did he learn that the word was not Japanese, but an Assamese place name: Kohima.[54]

Only the Yamamoto detachment maintained any cohesion to resist the advance.[55] The East Africans fought their first action in which 11th King's African Rifles (KAR) attacked a position: one askari was killed and fifteen wounded, but also killed was Major R. Fulton, which shocked the askari. Although wearing black face cream to hide his identity – essential since a white face was the signal for sustained and accurate Japanese fire – he had been conspicuous by his leadership. A Wakamba tribesman asked why his officers had to go in front to be killed. He thought they should just indicate enemy positions, then get out of the way until the askari dealt with them. That way, he said, they would still have their officers.[56] The Africans' great physical strength and keen senses made them excellent at patrol work while the 'defence-and-delay' tactics they encountered in the Kabaw valley never varied: mutually supporting bunkers would be encountered, blasted by air strikes, then assaulted under cover of artillery fire.[57] Mutili Musoma from Machakos in Kenya was serving with 302nd Field Regiment, EAA.

The Japanese was hard trained. He can't accept to surrender. When he sees that he's unable to manage anything more, he simply burns his rifle and ammunitions; and after that he accept you to kill him. But he can't accept to be arrested. If he refused to go and try and resist, we simply took out the panga and killed him. Cut his head off.[58]

On 8 September 26th KAR became the first troops across the Chindwin. An attack was made on Leik Ridge on 10 October, then patrolling and small-scale actions continued, although finally clearing Leik Hill on 22 October proved the East Africans' fiercest engagement of the war, costing 4th KAR 19 dead and 102 wounded.[59] Four days after Leik Hill 22nd KAR attacked at Kantha. 'I couldn't see them', Lieutenant-Colonel K. H. Collen wrote to his wife afterwards. 'But I could hear them whooping and yelling "Sokolai, sokolai, Yao-oo-oo", the Nyasa war cry.'[60] John Nunneley's young orderly Tomasi wanted to accompany him on patrols, but Nunneley always refused since he was very inexperienced, having received only rudimentary training in Ceylon. Finally he relented, but they were separated during a firefight across a *chaung*. Wounded, Nunneley managed to get back and went to the main track. 'Tomasi saw me, joy and relief written all over his face. Leaping to his feet he started to cross the track towards me. He had taken just five paces when the Japanese machine-gunner covering the approach to the *chaung* fired a long, long burst.'[61]

South-west of the Kabaw valley 5th Indian Division led the pursuit along the Tiddim Road, greatly assisted by the Lushai Brigade harassing the flanks of the retreating Japanese.[62] Staff Sergeant Nishiji Yasumasa recalled: 'We called the road "Human Remains Highway". What happened was beyond the bounds of acceptable human behaviour. It was a vision of hell.'[63] Japanese delaying tactics were always the same, and the means of dealing with them was also always the same. A crater would be found beyond which the lead infantry would come under fire and would have to be filled or covered using a Valentine bridgelayer, while air strikes would break up the blocking position to allow tanks from 3rd Carabiniers forward to support them.[64] Some losses were keenly felt. On 19 September Major Ghulam Qadir of 1st/17th Dogras was killed, an officer so gallant and efficient that the battalion history was moved to recall he was a Pathan in a Hindu battalion, and 'the Dogras would have followed him anywhere … he was thought of very highly by all ranks. His was an amiable, and attractive personality with a natural sense of humour, essentially a soldier and an absolutely first-class one at that.'[65]

That same month 1st/1st Punjabis found an elephant standing sadly on a hilltop near MS 116, swathed in cloud and with a little bell fastened round its neck. It was escorted to Brigade Headquarters, where Brigadier Warren's orderly, who had experience as a *mahout*, was entrusted with its care. A large '68' was painted on its back for recognition purposes just like a vehicle's tailboard, and it was employed taking the brigade's laundry down to the river with its hide as a scrubbing board. For a slit trench the elephant was provided with a shelter previously dug into a bank for a 3-ton lorry, and to this it wisely retired at the first sound of gunfire. 'For all its docility and wisdom, the elephant possessed a terrible voice, that was likened to someone tearing up strips of corrugated iron.' When the battalion advanced once more, the elephant went back to Imphal with three soldiers on its back, scaring the wits out a mule-train belonging to 2nd West Yorks in the process. It was last heard of in the stables of the Maharajah of Cooch Behar.[66]

'Tiddim Road Ted' was a Japanese corpse on one knee leaning with one arm against a pile of cut wood, left as a marker so that people would define a spot as so many hundred yards before or beyond him.[67] On the road Anthony Brett-James found postcards showing domestic scenes, humorous cartoons or bird paintings. 'It seemed so incongruous that these fantastical, boasting and often barbaric enemies should scrawl home to their families on such peaceful and civilized postcards, a contrast of ugliness and beauty, of mass brutality and tender thoughts.'[68] At the front Naik Sher Khan of 4th/14th Punjabis led a night recce to see if the Japanese still occupied Point 689. Some time after midnight grenades were heard, but it was not until near dawn that Khan's three companions returned to battalion lines, saying Khan was ahead of them when the firing started. The three withdrew and waited for him. 'Poor Sher Khan', they told their company commander, Major Peter Gadsdon. 'He did not come, and we are afraid he has been killed.' At dawn when everyone stood-to, they saw Sher Khan trudge up the valley. 'Well, sahib,' he explained,

> we did as you said and set off to climb Point 689. Getting near the top we walked into an enemy position. They started firing but it was not very straight. I crawled under a bush and hid. They threw some grenades and then came out and ran about shouting 'yah yah'. I stayed and they gave up after a time and went back to their trenches. An hour before dawn I heard them move off, talking at the tops of their voices.[69]

He had followed them and was able to report the hill clear of enemy except for this standing patrol part-way down the slope at night.

Under constant pressure the Japanese evacuated Tiddim on the night of 6 October, allowing the capture of Fort White and Kennedy Peak, where the Lee tank No. 25711 of 4 Troop, C Squadron, 3rd Carabiniers, commanded by Lieutenant C. W. Bell and driven by Trooper M. L. Connolly, created a tank altitude record by reaching the top.[70]

An attack on 25 October saw Subedar Ram Sarup Singh of 2nd/1st Punjabis earn a posthumous VC. His citation describes how, despite already being wounded in both legs, when the Japanese put in a strong counter-attack with three waves of twenty men approaching from a flank, he 'led a charge against the advancing enemy, bayoneting four himself and checking them. He abused the enemy and encouraged his own men throughout. He was badly wounded in the thigh and fell down, but got up and ignoring his wound again went for the Japanese, shouting encouragement to his men. He bayoneted another Japanese and shot another, but was mortally wounded by a burst of medium machine gun fire in the chest and neck. With his last breath he shouted to his platoon havildar, "I am dying, but you carry on and finish the devils." '[71] At the end of October the way to Tiddim took Charles Evans and 7th IMFTU over 'the Chocolate Staircase', an astonishing piece of engineering climbing 3,000 feet in 7 zigzagging miles. 'There were fourteen hairpin bends in the first two miles and the whole track up to just under 5,000 feet was carved out of a clayey soil the colour of milk chocolate.' On reaching Tiddim, a village of some fifty houses a few miles further on, he saw white crosses and Japanese skulls perched on sticks, which were

> as much a part of the scene as the roadmenders and the statuesque Nagas and Chins; they were as familiar as the dropping zones with their discarded baskets and parachutes, as the burst sacks of flour and the supply planes droning overhead. There were cooking fires, piles of chapattis and the smells of curry; there was everywhere a feeling of pressing on, of being 'in it'.[72]

Of XXXIII Corps's average weekly strength of 88,500 between July and November about half were maintained forward of Imphal in pursuit of the Japanese. Total casualties amounted to 50,300, but only 47 of these were killed in action. More than half of the 47,000 sick had to be evacuated to India, and even with mepacrine there were 20,000 malaria cases.[73] Sickness was a problem throughout the Japanese Army in Burma, with never enough medicines for suppressive treatment of malaria. In September 1944 53rd Division was down from 16,000 to 2,600.[74]

Arguments continued to rage within SEAC and OPD in Washington about the merits of the Ledo Road project, but it proved a success, delighting Pick with the tonnages carried. With the fall of Myitkyina he had pushed on. The final advance began as, after a three-month lull in the north, fighting was rejoined when Chinese 22nd Division and 475th Regiment moved forward in late October, throughout November and into December. Thirty-eighth Division, heavily supported by Tenth Air Force, battered at the gates of Bhamo, whose 1,200-man garrison had orders to hold until mid-January.[75] On 6 December a 1,150-foot pontoon bridge crossed the Irrawaddy; this was later replaced by a 1,300-foot aluminium floating bridge of 25 tons capacity.[76] Sergeant John R, McDowell, field correspondent of *CBI Roundup* newspaper, travelled the road, noting improvements as new fills and cuts eliminated bad curves, layer on layer of crushed rock and gravel improved the surface and steel replaced the wood of myriad bridges.[77]

On 6 December 475th Regiment received orders to relieve the Chinese around the village of Tonkwa, but before they could do so, the Japanese drove the Chinese north, where they dug in around Mo-hlaing on the 9th. Once more the Chinese-American force faced 18th Division, now commanded by Lieutenant-General Naka Eitaro, who was alarmed by Chinese movement towards Tonkwa, which he reinforced with 55th and 56th Regiments. The Americans took over an excellent defensive position which the Japanese abortively attacked on 13 and 14 December. Skirmishing and patrolling continued, but by Christmas the Japanese had disappeared. Having broken Chinese codes, they knew that 22nd Division was being withdrawn to China and no major offensive was planned for the area, and they pulled out to concentrate on the defence of Mandalay.[78] The blocking of a Japanese relief force for Bhamo by Chinese 30th Division also led to its early evacuation on 14 December, and only 50 miles now separated X Force from Y Force. Although the Japanese were still covering the Burma Road, their purpose was to defend against any attack towards Mandalay. The withdrawal of 18th Division and relative quiet in the Bhamo area led Sultan to modify his plan and he directed 36th Division, now at the southern end of the 'Railway Corridor', to move east of the Irrawaddy and then south-east to cut the old Burma Road in the Kyaukem–Hspiaw area, well south of Lashio, and Chinese 50th Division would take the town itself while Mars Task Force would cut it near Ho-si.[79] On the night of 6/7 January the most tragic storm on the Hump's history claimed seven aircraft and thirty-one crew when a Siberian cold front met warm air from the Bay of Bengal, but the newly formed Chinese First Army cleared the Shweli valley and its lead regiment of 30th Division moved through it, meeting little opposition as 33rd Army withdrew, and on 20 January they made contact with their brethren from Yunnan.[80]

'Dear Mrs Tremlett', wrote Lieutenant-Colonel J. F. Snow of 1st Devons, waiting to move forward, to the Regimental Comforts Fund who had knitting parties in most Devonshire towns and villages.

> The cigarettes are gradually arriving and could not have arrived at a more opportune moment ... Being British manufacture they are fully appreciated and every man has been told they are from Devon. The socks have not turned up yet but will be most welcome. Colour doesn't matter a bit, 1,000 pairs will enable me to issue three pairs a man (full scale) and I reckon that 500 a month for maintenance will just nicely cover our requirements.[81]

On 9 November Major-General Pearce of CAS(B) made a radio speech to the Burmese people and had pamphlets dropped that ended by announcing, 'the era of face-slapping is over'.[82] After more skirmishing with elements of 33rd Division Kalemyo was occupied on 14 November. Slim ordered IV Corps to cross the Chindwin and capture Pinlebu, and Scoones in turn sent 268th Indian Brigade across at Sittaung, followed by 19th Indian Division. On returning to Burma, Major E. E. Spink of 1st/11th Sikhs recalled the last time they had been along the Kabaw valley in Tamu, retreating.

> Now, nearly three years later, we are on the same road again, but this time with a difference – tanks, guns, lorries pour down the road in a steady stream – moving south! The continuous buzz of aeroplanes speeding on their way many and nefarious missions is entirely ours! We are on the same road, with a difference, for we are tried and trusted veterans of war and we are moving south! Jubilantly we shall go back to avenge our gallant comrades who are no more ... We shall keep faith with those who died.[83]

In the Railway Corridor 29th Brigade had taken over the lead from 72nd and met less opposition, while alongside 36th Division Chinese 50th and 22nd Divisions had also advanced, with the latter reaching the Irrawaddy unopposed on 3 November. On 9 November 72nd Brigade took the lead once more and at Pinwe, with 1st Royal Scots Fusiliers under command, another tough action was fought which dragged on for three weeks.[84] They were later joined by 26th Indian Brigade as they approached Katha, near the end of the Railway Corridor. Katha, recalled 9th Royal Sussex's A Company diary as they took up positions near the Irrawaddy, 'is a lovely spot'. 'There is lots of furniture in the houses and everyone has a bed of sorts. The company helped clean out a Church and a Toc H canteen. The only bad feature of the town is the number of mangy dogs.'[85]

Lieutenant John Henslow's sappers 'blasted, bulldozed and built bridges, then replaced the bridges with stronger bridges, blasted more hillside away and bulldozed more earth away to accommodate larger vehicles'. But while he noted it was a great engineering achievement, Henslow was troubled by 'the memory of the burnt-out Japanese tanks along the route. They had somehow done the same thing before us in the opposite direction. They had to get their transport over the same features without building a motor-way to do it'.[86] However, it was not the terrain that caused their abandon-ment but the monsoon, RAF and disease; vehicles go nowhere without fuel or when broken down, and simply moving along a route is not suffi-cient. In November and December 19th Indian Division IEME repaired 723 vehicles and the recovery company recovered 195, so the division reached Onbauk having lost only 29 out of 2,794, including 47 repaired Japanese vehicles added.[87]

Kalewa was captured on 28 November with 7th Light Cavalry in sup-port of the East Africans. One tank that 7th Light Cavalry brought to Burma had been the only one to leave in 1942: a Stuart with its turret removed that now served as Lieutenant-Colonel Jack Barlow's command tank, *The Curse of Scotland*.[88] Nearby, Captain J. C. S. James of 254th Indian Tank Brigade IEME saw another tank unit parked in a field.

> But after a few minutes I noticed the complete lack of activity in the area
> of the vehicles and I got out to look more closely at this unusual unit. There,
> in the early morning sunshine, parked in neat rows in the long grass of an
> overgrown paddy-field was apparently a complete regiment of abandoned
> Stuart tanks. The grass and growth around them made it clear they had not
> been moved for many months.[89]

It was 2nd Royal Tank Regiment, who had avoided fire in the destruction of their tanks in 1942 so as not to give away their position. Having motored on tracks all the way from Imphal, 7th Light Cavalry's running gear was worn out and James spent an extraordinary week stripping the Stuarts of tracks, sprockets and engines in a great cannibalization exercise that ena-bled 7th Light Cavalry to continue for another 700 miles.

Meanwhile the troops behind the front line were engaged in road build-ing, supervised by engineer and pioneer officers in what 'must be the most soul-destroying job in the world for convicts, prisoners of war and men doing detention'. All units and all ranks were involved and 'even now', wrote Major John Hill forty-five years later, 'I remember how glad I was when the job was finished. Sweaty, filthy with dust, blistered and tired, we needed the daily quick wash in "our" stream flowing nearby and all the sleep we could get during the 16 days of our navvying.'[90] Roads were also built by cantilevering sections of track from cliff-faces, while five new Bailey bridges were built on a 5-mile stretch in twenty-three days. 'Elephant' Bill Williams and his charges helped fell trees, build bridges and clear space for airstrips laid out every 50 miles and brought timber for 500 river barges built at Kalewa.[91]

Behind them a monotonous march began in search of the Japanese; 2nd Division covered 200 miles in twenty-two days (of thirty-one days over the Chindwin twenty-six were spent marching, covering 400 miles).[92] At Mawlaik, 30 miles north of Kalewa, 20th Indian Division crossed the Chindwin between 2 and 5 December on two rafts, christened by 1st Northamptons 'Horrible Charlie' and 'Stinking Henry'.[93] On 10 December Mountbatten was deeply annoyed when Wedemeyer tele-graphed him shortly after arriving in Chungking to say the Japanese from Yochow to Liuchow threatened the Hump terminal at Kunming and to ask for two Chinese divisions, three combat cargo squadrons, two troop carriers squadrons and heavy bombers. Having so recently been Deputy Chief of Staff to Mountbatten, Wedemeyer was fully aware of theatre requirements but now his priorities were different. Mountbatten reluc-tantly agreed, appreciating that China must be kept in the war; but this meant cancelling the airborne element of Capital and would slow the advance of both Fourteenth Army and NCAC, and the noise of the air-craft engines as they departed 'was the first intimation anyone in Fourteenth Army had of the administrative crisis now bursting upon us', wrote Slim.[94] Twentieth Indian Division were followed over the Sittaung bridgehead by 19th Indian Division, which made for Pinlebu and Pinbon with its commander, Major-General T. W. 'Pete' Rees, relishing Slim's instructions to take risks for the sake of speed; they crossed the Zibyu hills, making their road as they went, and linked up eight days later with 36th Division to unite NCAC's and Fourteenth Army's fronts.[95]

For the crossing a 'Chindwin Navy' was formed, with two wooden gun-boats mounting a Bofors and two Oerlikon cannons and two pairs of Browning machine-guns. They were built at Kalewa and named *Pamela*, after Mountbatten's youngest daughter, and *Una*, after Slim's. Thus Slim became the only general to have designed, built, christened, launched and commis-sioned ships for the Royal Navy. Their task was to protect the Inland Waterways Transport's lighters, barges and launches, built by Fourteenth Army's Chief Engineer, Brigadier Bill Hasted, who felled forests to create them and for which outboard motors were flown in. The IEME recovered MV *Ontario*, patched, caulked and repainted her.[96] In due course IWT craft car-ried some 38,000 tons of stores.[97] The task of establishing a firm bridgehead across the Chindwin was accomplished by the East Africans clearing a series of Japanese positions along either side of Myittha river gorge on 2 December after recce by the Sea Reconnaissance Unit (SRU).[98] As the bridgehead was expanded, bridging equipment for what, at 1,154 feet, would be the longest floating bridge in the world was assembled and constructed in sections on the Myittha and floated down to the Chindwin and completed in just twenty-eight working hours between 7 and 10 December.[99] On 14 December Slim and the three corps commanders who had made possible the deployment for the reconquest of Burma – Scoones, Stopford and Christison – were knighted in a ceremony at Imphal by Wavell, Viceroy of India, by special permission of the king.[100]

Kimura had chosen not to make a major stand on the Shwebo plain between the Chindwin and the Irrawaddy, and it was the Anglo-Indian forces that were now at the end of tenuous supply lines as they debouched from the jungle towards the hot dusty plain. The Japanese could deploy some five divisions – all seriously understrength – and other formations against them, but if before the Japanese had been supermen, now Slim's Tommies and Jawans had 'seen them run. They had smashed for ever the legend of the invincibility of the Japanese Army. Neither our men nor the Japanese soldier himself believed it any longer.'[101]

# 22

# Arakan

I was walking down the street the other day.
When I chanced to hear a certain lady say:
'Why isn't he in khaki, or a suit of navy blue,
Fighting for his country like the other fellows do?'

I turned around, and this is what I said:
'Now lady look I've only got one leg.
On two legs I'd be firmer,
But the other one's out in Burma.'

Anon, White Feather[1]

THE 1944 MONSOON was especially hard. Roads were glutinous and impassable, bridges washed out, and some areas so malarial that even mepacrine could not control it. As Christison travelled his corps area, relaxed and genial, he somehow contrived to compile a bird-watching guide, *The Birds of Arakan*. Although large-scale operations were suspended, unlike in previous years the war had continued all along the front as patrol activity intensified. In the light of disaster at Imphal and Kohima, Burma Area Army issued defensive orders to 28th Army on 12 July and ordered all spare transport to join 33rd Army.[2] In Arakan 3rd/2nd Goorkhas received a warning order to prepare for a special operation: the capture of Point 1433. With the support of the divisional artillery and RAF the attack went in before dawn on 8 September, but it took five days of bitter fighting and reinforcements from 14th/10th Baluch and 17th/5th Mahrattas finally to secure this valuable ridge.[3]

Concentrating first in the Kalapanzin valley, 82nd (West African) Division was in due course to replace 81st in the Kaladan valley, and 26th Indian Division would also be withdrawn for rest. But the initial operations would fall once more to 81st. Major-General F. J. Loftus Tottenham took over 81st (West African) Division on 24 August 1944 and found it seriously short of NCOs since no British reinforcements had arrived: he therefore had to promote Africans, who proved entirely satisfactory. 'The British Army', he declared, 'had behaved blimpishly in failing to develop African leadership in peace time.'[4] Having brought their transport into the valley the first time to no purpose, for the second campaign the division operated on an entirely headload basis, and a rash advance was to be avoided in favour of successive bounds.

On 1 October it began to move back down the Kaladan. The Japanese held Mowdok stubbornly and the jeep track of the previous year had deteriorated completely, so it was decided to go in southward across steep and almost trackless terrain.[5] The only fire support available was in the form of 41st Mortar Regiment with two batteries, later joined by two batteries from 30th Indian Mountain Regiment.[6] As Peter Jeffreys commanding 5th (West African) Brigade noted, 'the supporting weapon that we infantry soldiers loved was the 3-inch mortar. It was easy to control, simple to maintain and fire, very mobile and manned by devoted teams of brave, adventurous gunners.'[7] The Africans cleared Mowdok on the 18th, removing the last Japanese troops from Indian soil, after which they continued to the end of the month in three columns to drive back Japanese outposts – once more they faced 55th Reconnaissance Regiment – as far as the Pi Chaung. By 3 December they were firmly established on the line Kyingri–Kwangyaung–Orama.[8] A captured Japanese diary read:

> The enemy soldiers are not from Britain but from Africa. Because of their belief they are not afraid to die, so even if their comrades have fallen they keep advancing as if nothing happened. They have excellent physique and are very brave, so fighting against these soldiers is somewhat troublesome.[9]

Lieutenant-Colonel C. E. B. Walwyn of 4th Nigeria Regiment challenged Lieutenant-Colonel Philip van Straubanzee's 1st Sierra Leone Regiment to a limited overs cricket match, played to the accompaniment of ranging mortars and small-arms fire in the distance. Batting first, Straubanzee's XI made 157 for 7, thanks largely to a fine 88 by Lieutenant L. C. Smith, then dismissed the Sierra Leone XI for 109 to win by 48 runs. The Japanese then counter-attacked some hours after stumps were drawn with heavy artillery support, which considering the divisional plan was to deceive them by demonstration, 'was surely a classic example of very good deception!'[10]

On 15 December the Japanese launched a strong attack with artillery support against 6th (West African) Brigade. Private Kweku Pong, number two on a Bren, was wounded and separated from his section. Well armed with twelve magazines, he engaged the Japanese with short bursts for hours as they searched for him, until he eventually lost consciousness from loss of blood. Havildar Umrao Singh's gun section of 30th Mountain Regiment was supporting the brigade when it was overrun and his officer badly wounded. With two other men he defended the position with rifles, bayonets and grenades until they were rushed and he defended it by swinging a rammer until borne down and bayoneted. The Japanese were eventually driven off when both men were found; Singh was awarded a VC and Pong an MM. Slim never changed his view that Africans would be 'lost' without British guidance; but he probably never heard of Kweku Pong, who found himself alone, badly wounded in the middle of the night with Japanese rampaging through the bush around him and a battle going on behind. No white man was there to tell him what to do, no African NCO nor any other African for that matter. Nobody would have blamed him for lying doggo, but instead he showed considerable courage and good tactical sense. For this action 5th Gold Coast Regiment was awarded the unique honour 'Tinma'.[11]

Before beginning its advance along the coast, 25th Indian Division implemented a deception plan threatening coastal landings, and 51st Indian Brigade,* which was to remain covering the base area, had to seize some important features blocking 81st (West African) Division. This it started on 20 November. Two days later Sepoy Bhanderi Ram of 16th/10th Baluch won the VC at the 'Office', and by the end of the month corps engineers had complete routes through the Tunnels.[12] On 3 December 53rd Indian Brigade attacked the Inbauk position to clear the tracks that would support the divisional advance and, with preliminaries complete, the stage was set for the long awaited final offensive.[13] Beginning on 12 December the advance led by 26th Indian Division was carried out in bounds, with units leap-frogging each other and the pace set by the speed at which the sappers could repair or construct routes to support the following vehicles. At Taung Bazaar, 7th Indian Field Regiment discovered several bundles of Japanese currency, which delighted its Madrasi gunners, who could play cards for hundreds or even thousands of the worthless units rather than their own annas.[14] The second phase of the advance began following a deceptive patrols programme on 19 December by outflanking Tinma towards a position known as 'West Down', from which the Japanese could threaten the Africans' concentration area. Therefore a saturation air attack

* This was the first all Indian formation to have all Indian Commanding Officers: Lieutenant-Colonel K. S. 'Timmy' Thimayya (8th/19th Hyderabad), Lieutenant-Colonel S. P. P. Thorat (2nd/2nd Punjabis) and Lieutenant-Colonel L. P. 'Bogy' Sen (16th/10th Baluch).

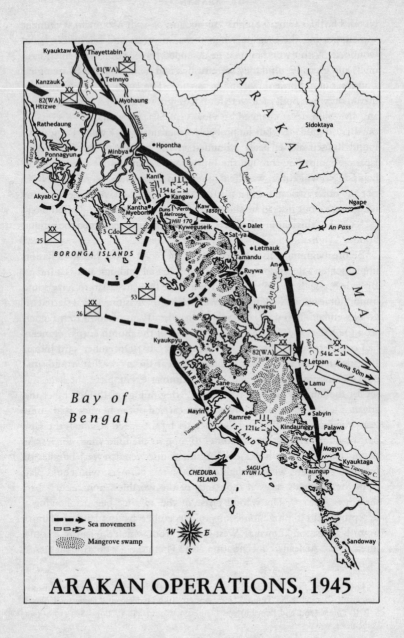

# ARAKAN OPERATIONS, 1945

was laid on for three days, with 240 fighter-bomber and 213 light bomber sorties – the latter mostly by USAAF planes – dropping over 500,000 lb. of bombs and 1,200 gallons of a terrible new weapon: napalm. During the night of 21/22 December 6th Oxfordshire and Buckinghamshire Light Infantry made a night march of over 20 miles to seize Donbaik of dread memory, which fell unopposed. Only now were the remains found of the Valentine tanks and crews lost two years earlier.[15]

After serving in Persia, Alister McCrae, formerly of the Irrawaddy Flotilla Company, had returned to Chittagong in January 1944. 'I had to ask myself if ten years of living and working in Burma had cast a spell on me,' he later wondered, 'that I was infatuated by so much that Burma gave all of us who came from the West; the beauty of the land and the water-ways, the tinkle of the temple bells, the language with its quaint and intri-guing terms of speech.'[16] Now as Lieutenant-Colonel, Indian Engineers, he was to command the Inland Water Transport Group. Chittagong was supply base for Arakan operations, and McCrae's group was responsible for lightering and coastal steamers running south of Cox's Bazar, and the advance on Akyab would rely heavily on water transport. During the cam-paign Coastal Force destroyed hundreds of boats to prevent Japanese re-supply, killing some 300 and capturing another 20.[17] To support the coastal move McCrae and his Marine Staff Officer, Captain Stewart Knowles – a Hooghly pilot in civilian life – decided to use locally built Landing Craft Maintenance (LCMs) and some 600 country boats of various types. However, strong cross-currents were discovered on the proposed supply beaches and McCrae set off to recce with a Sikh escort. 'On that beauti-ful morning, with the apparently calm blue sea of the Bay of Bengal stretching to the horizon, it was hard to imagine a problem existed.' But one did: Knowles in a motor boat could get no closer than 300 yards. McCrae promised something would be done, although he had no idea what. Fortunately, he was saved by the arrival of DUKWs ('ducks') – amphibious wheeled vehicles – which could operate on the shore and in the currents, and supply was restored.[18]

Throughout the 'Chaung War' the army tended to view all areas marked on maps in blue as navigable by HM ships, and most ran aground at some point or other. HMIS *Narbada* inquired of a motor launch on the mud, 'Are you a dredger?' The ML made no reply but got its own back a few days later when the roles were reversed, signalling 'Welcome to the Dredgers' Union'.[19] Meanwhile inland, beginning on 14 December, 53rd Indian Brigade and 82nd (West African) Division pushed through Buthidaung and secured 'Vital Corner', enabling the Kalapanzin river to be opened for supply with some of the boats McCrae had assembled. In a campaign dominated by supply problems the transportation of these boats to Buthidaung was a great achievement. Several miles of rope were used securing them, and some were so large they cleared the Tunnels with only inches to spare.[20] As 53rd Indian Brigade advanced along the axis of the river the Africans cleared strong resistance at Kindaung village and crossed the Saingdin *chaung*. Thereafter they met further company-strength delaying positions but opened up the Kalapanzin plain. By the end of December, 25th Indian Division had advanced to the tip of the Mayu peninsula. Local resistance forces were represented by the Arakan Defence Army, to which Force 136 sent liaison officers in December. On 1 January they rose, killed their Japanese instructors and went underground, becoming the Patriotic Army of Burma – Arakan Division. Over two months' operations they rendered useful service, attacking Japanese outposts and providing valuable intelligence.[21] The Japanese withdrew and the two West African divisions made contact on 4 January.

The original plan for capturing Akyab island involved 26th Indian Division and 3rd Commando Brigade, supported by HMS *Queen Elizabeth* (a battleship with 15-inch guns unused since 1915), three 6-inch cruisers and other ships; 10 Mitchell and 5 Liberator squadrons; and 21 assorted fighter squadrons. The tentative D-Day was 18 February.[22] However, Romulus had proceeded ahead of expectations, and intelligence suggested very few Japanese were left on the island. A new plan, 'Lightning', was hastily drafted to assault Akyab on 3 January, which Christison maintained Mountbatten did everything possible to forestall, since the photo-opportunity of a full-scale combined operation in the full glare of publicity was too good to pass up.[23] But a recce aeroplane reported the locals showing no anxiety and on 2 January messages were dropped in Urdu and Burmese asking them to sit on the ground if the island was still occupied or stand with their hands in the air if not. Captain Jimmy Jarrett of 'C' Flight, 656 AOP Squadron, then landed to a rousing reception and found the Japanese had quit on 31 December, although nobody believed him until a senior officer flew in to confirm it. It was agreed that 25th Indian Division should land without the accompanying bombardment and the island was occupied next day.[24] Not that the landing went smoothly. The beachhead was seized by 42nd (Royal Marines) Commando and the second wave was due to land on an adjacent beach, but a signalling error put them down behind the first wave, with the tide now at its lowest ebb. When 44th (Royal Marines) Commando left their landing craft, knee-deep gooey mud claimed boots and socks. Some fought on individually; others formed rugby scrums and when these collapsed, took several minutes to untangle themselves, their equipment covered in thick ooze.[25] Lieutenant-Commander J. M. Ramsay RAN from HMAS *Ramsay* became the first Allied officer to enter Akyab town, where he raised a Union flag.[26] It was, according to another Australian, journalist Roy McKie, an SABU – a self-adjusting balls-up. Akyab was 'a wilderness. Trees grew inside wrecked buildings. Vines covered roofs. Signboards hung on rusty nails in empty streets.'[27]

Rapid progress called for rapid thinking, and XV Corps had to move quickly to block Japanese lines of retreat. Consequently on 6 January 9th York and Lancasters moved by boat to establish a block on the Yo river at Ponnagyun, where it discovered the Japanese remained in strength.[28] Supported by 4th/18th Royal Garwhal Rifles, they fought a sharp action at Yongon when the Japanese attempted to withdraw through the hills on 11/12 January and were relieved by 81st (West African) Division on the 18th.[29] That day 53rd Indian Brigade's other battalion, 7th/16th Punjabis, formed a block position at Kyeyebin, past which the Japanese had to fight to escape. Major R. A. K. Patterson later recalled that the enemy attacking force appeared to be 150 strong. They attacked three times between 2400 and 0600 and

> with bayonets flashing in the moonlight and shouts of 'Banzai', they advanced again and again to within 20 yards of the positions, endeavouring to form up for the assault. LMGs were switched from one flank to the other, wherever the threat arose, and broke up the enemy attacks with overwhelming automatic fire, grenading and 2-inch mortaring.[30]

The Punjabis later counted over 100 bodies, having themselves lost 4 wounded and 2 dead, including Lance-Naik Sher Shah, who, despite being badly wounded, repeatedly went forward to attack the Japanese from the flank and was awarded a posthumous VC.

Meanwhile the Japanese had not opposed 82nd (West African) Division's crossing the Htizwe–Kanzauk track into the Kaladan valley and rapid advance to relieve 81st. The new commander of 82nd (West African) Division was Major-General Hugh Stockwell.[31] A tough former Commando who had served with 4th Nigeria during the 1930s, he found it 'rather a luxury organization', with indifferent British NCOs that he sent back as first-line reinforcements to Fourteenth Army. He also sacked a number of commanding officers and picked out a regimental sergeant-major from 3rd Nigeria who had fought for the Germans in West Africa during the First World War. 'He stayed with me as a pesonal RSM for a year and a half. He advised me on the Africans and through him I could find out what they thought of their British officers. He was tremendous.'[32] The 81st had been in action for over a year and was to return to India to take part in the invasion of Malaya. Meanwhile Mountbatten ordered a landing by 25th Indian Division and 3rd Commando Brigade on the peninsula to cut the main Japanese line of communication while 26th Indian Division pressed on to take Ramree island. The Myebon landing – Operation Passport – was hurriedly planned and executed on 12 January. The assault beach had been found blocked by a large row of wooden stakes which would hole landing craft, but a naval Combined Operations Pilotage Party (COPP) planted delayed charges on these the night before to create gaps, which were cleared without difficulty.[33] Some opposition was met on the beach but the supporting bombardment cleared this. Thereafter it stiffened – every hill was defended – and the Commandos had a tough fight to capture Pagoda Hill and Myebon village. The following day, with tanks from 19th Lancers, they pushed on up the peninsula with artillery support from Z craft (landing craft each mounting a troop of 25-pounders).[34] Follow-on troops in the form of 3rd/2nd Goorkhas from 74th Indian Brigade took Point 262 on 17 January and fought off a series of counter-attacks, and subsequent patrolling revealed the Japanese had completely gone four days later.[35]

Christison's aim was now to form an anvil position at Kangaw to smash the Japanese with the hammer of 82nd (West African) Division. Having had only four days' rest, 3rd Commando Brigade would land and secure a bridgehead, including Hill 170, whereupon 51st Indian Brigade from Akyab would pass through and secure the block around Kangaw. But first, tired of 'shrewd orderlies who became expert at intrigue', Lieutenant-Colonel K. S. Thimayya commanding 8th/19th Hyderabad requested the biggest bonehead in the unit as his batman. The subedar-major produced Ram Singh, a young Jat: 'Sahib', he assured Thimayya, 'here is a man of vast stupidity. He is a veritable monument to ignorance.' From then on Ram Singh ministered to his commander's needs, although Thimayya wondered how 'a human being could have such low-voltage cerebration and still remain mobile. Yet to this day Ram Singh regards me as slightly half-witted; he really believes that I manage to keep going only by the benefit of his ministrations.'[36] The landing operation took place at 1300 on 22 January and achieved complete tactical surprise. Realizing the danger they were being put in, the Japanese reacted violently and began a series of counter-attacks against the Commandos throughout the night, but with 51st Indian Brigade supported by a troop from 19th Lancers concentrating in the bridgehead and 16th/10th Baluch relieving one of the Commandos they made no progress. At 0300 on 28 January, 8th/19th Hyderabad attempted to seize the Duns feature but ran into fierce opposition, losing 19 dead and 61 wounded, but 16th/10th Baluch later succeeded in securing the Kangaw hills and a foothold on Melrose to reach a false crest before the Japanese again counter-attacked. During the day they fired some 800 shells on the bridgehead, the heaviest artillery concentration fired by the Japanese in Burma.[37]

It was now clear the Japanese were in greater strength than anticipated along the Kangaw Road. Second/2nd Punjabis was now ordered to secure the 'Melrose' feature and 16th/10th Baluch to take Kangaw village. The former attacked covered by a smoke screen, but the last 50 feet below the crest were, in the words of the official history, 'a mad charge up the slope culminating in bitter hand-to-hand fighting. The Japanese asked for no quarter and gave none, and in this desperate struggle it must be said they fought magnificently'.[38] Around 100 Japanese dead were counted, while the attackers suffered 80 casualties, most of them wounded. Thereafter came the inevitable counter-attacks with heavy artillery support, but the following day the village was secured and with it the road cut. 'The battle of Melrose was', according to the Punjabis' Commanding Officer, Lieutenant-Colonel S. P. P. Thorat, 'an acid test of our calibre – we fought the Jap on equal terms with the odds perhaps in his favour and we beat him – and beat him we shall whenever we come to grips.'[39] On 13 February 8th/19th Hyderabad attacked 'Perth'. Before devising a plan Thimayya called one of his bravest naiks, Jagmal, to lead a patrol. Jagmal replied he knew of no such thing as a patrol, and wanted instead to take the hill. Thimayya watched Jagmal and twenty men creep forward, then spring into action. Jagmal led assaults on three successive posts before collapsing through loss of blood from his wounds. As he was carried to the RAP, Thimayya went to him, 'still hysterical with delight at having captured the famous hill', as he pointed to it saying, 'I took it – I made the Japs run.'[40] Later 25 Japanese dead were counted around the position, and Jagmal and his platoon commander, Subedar Mata Din, were awarded the IOM.[41]

Meanwhile 82nd (West African) Division had relieved 81st in the Myohaung area and had begun to drive rapidly south.[42] The Japanese defenders now faced being encircled, and a withdrawal plan involved capturing Hill 170, thus splitting the wasp-like Allied bridgehead and opening the road. This attack began on 31 January with a heavy artillery bombardment, before 154th Regiment launched what proved the most desperate counter-attack of the campaign. An engineer assault party managed to set fire to one Sherman and blow the tracks off another, but the third remained unharmed and with its supporting platoon of 2nd/4th Bombay Grenadiers destroyed the assault party. The fighting was intense all over the the hill and Lieutenant George Knowland of 1st Commando won the VC, though it cost him his life, while the divisional artillery and combined mortars wrought havoc among some 300 attackers in their mangrove swamp forming-up place.[43] Corporal H. 'Harry' Winch of 1st Commando was there.

> I remember, I remember ... On the lee side of the Hill was a small pool from which we drew our water supply. In the bushes nearby we found the body of a Burmese girl. We buried her and a few days later the body of a baby was also found. The innocent were also being killed in the battle.[44]

During the night 7th/16th Punjabis moved on to Hill 170 and in the morning carried out a sweep of the mangrove swamp: for two days the Japanese put up astonishing resistance amid bayonet and grenade work, and by 2 February 700 bodies were counted around the small hill.[45]

The fighting continued, although less intense, for another two weeks as the rest of 25th Indian Division came into action, but while the Japanese were no longer in a position to mount a major threat to the bridgehead, local counter-attacks continued. They also continued to hold out stubbornly on the hill features they still held in order to contain the Allies as long as possible and withdraw their artillery. The battle eventually lasted twenty-two days and cost the Japanese some 2,000 men, 15 large and 12 small armed water-craft and much equipment. Allied casualties were 210 killed and 760 wounded. But exploitation was limited because of transport difficulties in the beachhead: no water supply had been found and 4,000 gallons had to be brought in each day by LCM; wheeled vehicles were unusable and most mules soon became casualties, so that supply and casualty evacuation relied on manpower, but the Indian Pioneer Corps were insufficient in number and had to be supplemented from the infantry. Both 58th and 61st Indian Field Ambulances and No. 1 Indian Bearer Company earned the admiration of all involved.[46]

Immediately Akyab had been captured, Christison had turned his attention to Ramree, 70 miles to the south-east, together with neighbouring Cheduba, and to clearing the surrounding islets. Ramree – some 50 miles long and 15 miles wide – was an important port for coastal shipping, providing sheltered anchorage for large ships. From it further operations could be developed along the coast and supplies flown inland.[47] The task of landing was allotted to the 71st Indian Brigade Group of 26th Indian Division with 2nd/7th Rajputs and A Squadron, 146th RAC under command. Considerable intelligence had been gathered on the garrison by an OSS detachment and the Special Boat Section (SBS), which showed it to consist of two battalions of 121st Regiment from 54th Division – some 1,800 men – and strong resistance was expected, so a considerable naval bombardment group was assembled in support. Early on 21 January the naval bombardment group opened fire. Christison and the other Force Commanders were watching through field glasses from the bridge of HMS *Queen Elizabeth* in her first engagement since the Dardanelles in 1915. 'Some shells fell on a marsh behind the Jap defences, and I saw a number of duck spring up. "Duck", I shouted. "The Royal Navy never ducks", said the Admiral.'[48] With her second salvo *Queen Elizabeth* scored a direct hit on the Japanese ammunition depot. The assault craft reached the objective at Kyaukpyu at 0933, having lost one landing craft and a motor launch to mines, but the two lead companies of 1st Lincolns got ashore with little opposition, and what little resistance there was rapidly withdrew so that contact had been lost by evening. First/18th Royal Garwhal Rifles and 5th/1st Punjabis also landed without trouble and took their objectives.[49]

The following morning 71st Indian Brigade handed over the beachhead to 4th Indian Brigade and began advancing first on Minbyin and Kyaupyauk, both found clear of Japanese on 23 January. Over the next two days they advanced to the Yanbauk Chaung, which the Japanese defended strongly.[50] On 26 and 27 January 5th/1st Punjabis made unsuccessful attempts to form a bridgehead but were forced to withdraw. Meanwhile Cheduba island had been taken and cleared by a force from 36th Indian Brigade. The natives were very friendly and a party was held where the Royal Marines provided the music of 'Yes, We Have No Bananas'.[51] On 30 January Sagu Kyun island was also taken without opposition, and 8th/13th Frontier Force Rifles then moved across to the southern tip of Ramree by 4 February. Meanwhile, despite strong naval and artillery support, 71st Indian Brigade was still held up at Yanbauk Chaung. The plan to approach Ramree town was thus changed so that most of 71st Indian Brigade would by-pass the *chaung* to the north-east and 36th Indian Brigade would launch a series of nuisance raids before striking from 8th/13th Frontier Force Rifles' beachhead in the south.[52]

This first involved 1st Lincolns and 1st/18th Royal Garwhal Rifles in several small but vicious battles to secure objectives called Point 233, 'Bear' and 'Banana', supported by Lees from 146th RAC, in which the protecting infantry of 2nd/4th Bombay Grenadiers suffered heavily but kept their charges safe.[53] On 5 February the Garwhalis attacked 'Banana' for a second time, having been only partially successful thus far, and were again pushed back, but in so doing the main Japanese counter-attack was smashed by the tanks and gunfire from 160th Field Regiment RA.[54] On 6 February 5th/1st Punjabis found 'Banana' unoccupied while 1st Lincolns took Point 233 and Namudwe village. The road beyond was heavily mined and booby-trapped, but they advanced steadily towards Ramree town while the Engineers tried to clear the route behind them. It was now possible for 4th Indian Brigade to cross Yanbauk Chaung and follow up the Japanese to Ledaung Chaung. On 8 February 1st Lincoln's patrols found the Japanese holding bunkers around Ramree town, but they were soon forced to withdraw.[55] In fact, despite snipers and mines, organized opposition had largely collapsed. On 11 February an effort was made to evacuate the Japanese garrison with 40 powered craft from Taungup, but 36 were sunk *en route* to Ramree and the others on their return with all personnel on board, in return for which HMS *Pathfinder* suffered slight damage.[56] The rest of the month was spent clearing the remnants and driving the survivors into the swamps and *chaungs* where an estimated 900 Japanese soldiers were killed by crocodiles trying to escape! At this point a XV Corps planning conference agreed that 82nd (West African) Division should proceed towards An, supplied by air until the road from Tamandu was clear, while 26th Indian Division would land a brigade at Letpan, some 35 miles southeast of Ruywa.[57]

By early February Fourteenth Army was progressing much faster than SEAC had anticipated 'straining its logistical support, while large all-weather airstrips were being constructed on Akyab and at Kyaukpyu on Ramree. The importance of these to air supply of Fourteenth Army cannot be overemphasized, since it meant supplies could be shipped direct from Calcutta and other ports rather than via the tortuous overland route via the Imphal Plain. It was therefore decided to send whatever formations XV Corps could spare back to India and 25th Indian Division was chosen, to be followed by 26th. Equally 3rd Commando Brigade needed a rest, as did 50th Indian Tank Brigade, which in any case was widely dispersed and of only limited value given the nature of the country.[58] While Ramree was being cleared and the Kangaw battle fought, 82nd (West African) Division had made good progress, reaching An. Now Christison's instructions to take the corps up to the monsoon in late April were to clear Japanese from the coastal strip of Taungup, Sandoway and Gwa and to contain those forces in the An area, held by elements of 54th Division, now much depleted. They would defend the An and Taungup passes, neither of which had an all-weather road, and if the monsoon broke before these objectives were secure, the consequences were potentially catastrophic.[59]

The new plan would see an assault landing by 53rd Indian Brigade at Ruywa, after which 2nd (West African) Brigade would pass through, followed by 74th Indian Brigade, which would exploit north to Tamandu and trap the large body of Japanese troops known to be there. Before D-Day a deception plan involving a British and two Indian sloops and motor launches manned by British, Indian and South African crews supported by Z craft and fighter-bombers would hold Japanese attention in Tamandu by engaging a series of targets in the area.[60] At 1030 on 16 February the landings took place: 9th York and Lancaster were unopposed and were quickly followed by 17th/5th Mahrattas, who secured the high ground which was their objective. The next day the rest of the brigade landed and a company of Mahrattas occupied Ruywa village, where they captured a Japanese captain in a lorry that drove into their lines, who confirmed the landing had achieved complete surprise. Only on 20 February did a reaction set in, with attacks on a feature called 'Alps'; but long-range shelling of the beach made another one necessary nearer to Ruywa and not under observation.[61]

By 22 February 2nd (West African) Brigade was passing through the beachhead, and three days later it had advanced some 4 miles to the east, where the track petered out, while 74th Indian Brigade arrived. By 28 February 14th/10th Baluch of 74th Indian Brigade had reached Dokekan, where they encountered a Japanese defensive screen and confused fighting continued until 4 March, when Japanese resistance faded. However, the success of Fourteenth Army in central Burma meant air supply resources had to be concentrated there, and Leese reduced XV Corps's supply lift from 130 tons per day to 30 tons, and later to 15, forcing 82nd (West African) Division to alter its axis to be supplied by road or water. It was thus imperative that Tamandu be captured and a Forward Maintenance Area be established, and Christison ordered it captured by 4 March.

When 3rd/2nd Goorkhas could not persuade the Japanese to relinquish the 'Alp' area, it was decided in view of their small numbers to bypass them. A feint by 14th/10th Baluch enabled 6th Ox and Bucks to cross the Me Chaung, forcing the Japanese to abandon their line – a noteworthy exploit against a good defensive position – and at first light, supported by a troop of 19th Lancers, they moved northwards.[62] By nightfall the sappers had bridged the *chaung* and by late evening on 4 March, 3rd/2nd Goorkhas secured the 'Snowdon' objective and, when counter-attacked, Rifleman Bahn Bhagra Gurung won the VC: 25th Division's fourth in four months.[63] The Tamandu–An road ran north-east over the ridge of which 'Snowdon' was part, and further west on 5 March 7th/16th Punjab attacked 'Pig', which they took by a silent attack at bayonet point, approaching from an unexpected angle to achieve complete surprise. Later that evening, however, when also ordered to take 'Whistle' and 'Strong' while still holding 'Pig', they suffered heavily, including both company commanders and all platoon commanders. In all they suffered over 100 casualties during the day.[64]

On 10 March another attempt was made to take 'Strong' while 5th Nigeria, under command of 74th Indian Brigade, completed an outflanking move to cut the road. Speed was of the essence since 25th Indian Division was to be withdrawn to Akyab by the end of the month, but the Tamandu area had to be cleared. Therefore 74th Indian Brigade came under 82nd (West African) Division and a direct assault was planned for 11 March. Fortunately a dawn patrol discovered the Japanese had already abandoned it.[65] Two days later 4th Indian Brigade landed near Letpan, and a road-block was established on 15 March by 2nd/13th Frontier Force Rifles to prevent the escape of five Japanese tankettes; and while exploiting to the south, supported by 146th RAC, Lieutenant Claude Raymond RE won the VC with 2nd/7th Rajputs.[66] By 30 March 22nd (East African) Brigade had reached Letpan and 4th Indian Brigade was reorganizing to attack Taungup when the High Command decided to relieve 26th Indian Division, including 4th Indian Brigade, and return it to India. In the meantime, however, it continued vigorous patrolling. On 3 April, 2nd Green Howards captured Hill 370, north of Taungup.

The battalion's campaign is dismissed in a few lines by the regimental history, which describes it as three months losing men to the Japanese and disease without fighting a major engagement. The Burma campaign brought them 'much discomfort, some casualties, but little glory'.[67] But that was not how it seemed to Lieutenant Jim Allan, whose D Company spent six days and seven nights on Hill 370, being reduced from 87 men to 22. A mortar bomb landed at his feet but failed to explode; a grenade landed 10 feet away, injuring two men and bruising his shoulder; nine rounds from a machine-gun burst struck his rifle; and the Indian artillery observer had already run past him when a Japanese came at him, whom he killed firing from the hip. Finding himself suddenly completely alone, he turned and ran. 'As I did so, I found my back was arching as I anticipated the bullets which would soon hit it. Suddenly, I was flaming angry and I stopped, turned, and slowly walked backwards.' He stopped by a tree and sheltered, 'wondering what I could possibly do. In my first battle I had suffered the disgrace of being driven off my position and there was nothing I could do.'[68]

In fact, he joined a Sikh company of 2nd/13th Frontier Force Rifles, which retook the hill with tank fire support.

> Because of the narrowness of the approach the leading Sikhs inevitably became casualties but those following leapt over their bodies to meet a surprisingly large number of Japanese still alive on the position. The defenders suffered the disadvantage of having to climb out of their trenches to meet the Sikhs and most of them never made it.

The Sikhs lost five dead and four wounded in this action. Allan then found the bodies of his men and had the appalling task of recovering the dog-tags from their swollen bodies before they were collected and buried by the pioneers. That troops sometimes failed is often ignored by regimental histories, but Jim Allan did not blame them.

> They had for weeks been in contact with the enemy, being under great stress under most unpleasant conditions. Any physical effort in the heat and humidity of the Arakan at this time of year was extremely enervating and this, added to the loss of sleep and inadequate food, took its cumulative toll and eventually, the men, being human, cracked. *I* did and I had only a few days of the strain.[69]

After an air strike on 15 April patrols entered the town itself. The relief of the brigade was completed shortly afterwards. For the rest of April and into May, 82nd (West African) Division kept pressing hard on the withdrawing Japanese, and on 15th May it reached Gwa, thus claiming to have rid the Arakan of Japanese for good.[70] With Rangoon having fallen to Allied air and sea forces, Sakurai planned to move across the Irrawaddy into the shelter of the Pegu Yomas, but Fourteenth Army had broken through more quickly than expected and 54th Division's move out of Arakan was slow, forcing it to fight across the Irrawaddy at Kama and a rearguard action at Paukkaung before reaching the shelter of the Pegu Yomas hills.[71]

# 23

## Across the Irrawaddy

By the old Moulmein Pagoda, lookin' lazy at the sea,
There's a Burma girl a-settin', and I know she thinks o'me;
For the wind is in the palm-trees, and the temple-bells they say:
'Come you back, you British Soldier; come you back to Mandalay!'
Come you back to Mandalay,
Where the old Flotilla lay;
Can't you 'ear their paddles chunkin' from Rangoon to Mandalay?
On the road to Mandalay,
Where the flyin'-fishes play,
An' the dawn comes up like thunder outer China 'cross the Bay!
Rudyard Kipling, *Mandalay*

MOUNTBATTEN FACED SERIOUS difficulties co-ordinating ground operations with a spontaneous uprising against the Japanese. British efforts to foment rebellion had not been very successful. In February 1944 the Japanese had set about tracking down the British agents operating among the Karens. McCrindle and Nimmo were both killed and in order to stop the savage reprisals that the *Kempeitai* were instituting against the Karens, Hugh Seagrim gave himself up and was slung into the Rangoon Ritz – a single-storey structure in the centre of a courtyard surrounded by the high buildings of the New Law Courts.[1]

After November 1943, when some forty prisoners were killed in an American air raid, captured aircrew were sent there as punishment for attacking civilian targets and mixed with dacoits, murderers and lepers in cells 9 feet by 12, shared by between five and nine people. They saw no sun and were given minimal food and water and practically no medical treatment. Of 57 incarcerated in the first six months, 23 died of disease and beatings. In July 1944 they were all moved to Rangoon Gaol, where many spent up to five months in solitary confinement and many more died.[2] Finally in January 1945 they were moved into the main compound, allowed fresh air and to talk to each other. One American airman counted fifty lice on two square inches of his blanket. Arthur Sharpe, a Beaufighter pilot, described how the other inmates were intrigued by Seagrim and his repeated interrogation.

> He refused to call the Japs 'master' and persisted in making cheeky remarks to them. He had us laughing all the time. When the Japs said 'No talking' he would ignore them. They would hit him on the head with their clubs and he'd start talking again. He laughed a lot, kept very fit with exercise and was never sick.[3]

Subsequently Seagrim and many Karen leaders were shot, but they had sown seeds that would bear bitter fruit for the Japanese. Seagrim had pleaded for the lives of his fellow accused and was awarded a posthumous George Cross.[4] Perhaps he was lucky; the crew of one RAF Liberator were tortured and beheaded by the *Kempeitai* in Pegu district in February 1945.[5]

As early as spring 1944 the BNA was preparing to fight the occupiers once they were on the run. The first stirrings of resistance in June were promptly crushed by the *Kempeitai*, but the organization of the AFO with the East Asia Youth League (renamed the All Burma Youth League) as a constituent member signalled the beginning of serious attempts to throw off Japanese control. The prime architects of this movement were Aung San and Than Tun. Following a speech on 1 August 1944, when Aung San noted Burma's independence was on paper only, the AFO manifesto, entitled *Drive Away the Fascist Japanese Marauders*, was secretly published and distributed. Ba Maw was aware of this development, but despite his own implacable opposition to a British return, he refused to betray it to the Japanese.[6] In November Colin Mackenzie, Head of Force 136, had decided to start arming the BNA without consulting CAS(B), who only discovered this in February, when a major controversy erupted, and on the 15th CAS(B) persuaded Leese to announce the AFO would not be armed or employed. But Mackenzie and John G. Coughlin, Head of OSS at SEAC, persuaded Mountbatten to overrule Leese on the 27th, and Mountbatten agreed since he needed all the help he could get for the drive on Rangoon.[7] In the same month Ba Maw visited Japan to urge the authorities to evacuate Burma and spare the country further destruction and suffering: the Japanese demanded continued military co-operation.[8] Ba Maw was acceptable to them because of his fascist and anti-British leanings, but his personal pride and nationalist spirit prevented him being merely a puppet. He persistently tried to evade Japanese limitations imposed on him, although only in spring 1945 did he finally dare legislate on important economic matters without first gaining Japanese approval.[9]

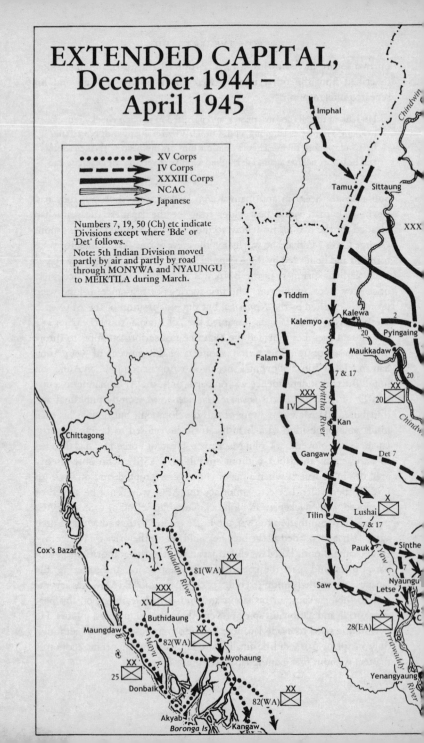

# EXTENDED CAPITAL,
## December 1944 – April 1945

Legend:
- XV Corps
- IV Corps
- XXXIII Corps
- NCAC
- Japanese

Numbers 7, 19, 50 (Ch) etc indicate Divisions except where 'Bde' or 'Det' follows.

Note: 5th Indian Division moved partly by air and partly by road through MONYWA and NYAUNGU to MEIKTILA during March.

Imphal

Chindwin

Tamu

Sittaung

XXX

Tiddim

Kalewa

Kalemyo

2

20

Pyingaing

Maukkadaw

Falam

20

7 & 17

Myittha River

20

XXX

IV

Kan

Chindwin

Chittagong

Gangaw

Det 7

Tilin

Lushai

X

7 & 17

Cox's Bazar

Kaladan River

Pauk

Sinthe

Yaw C.

7

81(WA)

XX

Saw

Nyaungu

Letse

XXX

XV

Buthidaung

XX

28(EA)

X

Maungdaw

82(WA)

Mayu R.

Myohaung

Irrawaddy River

C

25

XX

Yenangyaung

Donbaik

82(WA)

XX

Akyab

Boronga Is

Kangaw

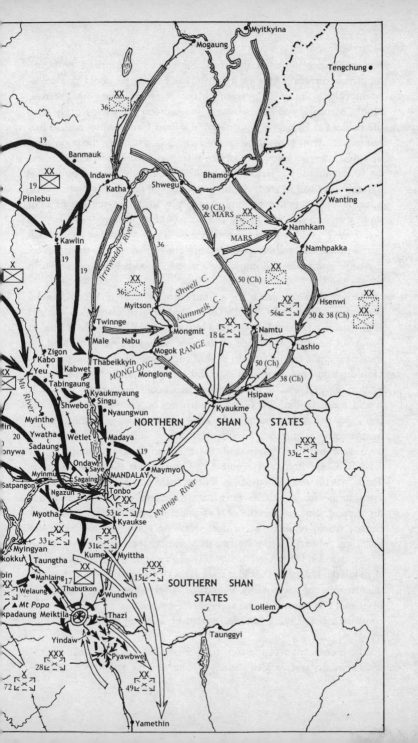

For an advance into central Burma, Slim faced two massive problems: supply and surprise. Once the monsoon had broken, he would have colossal difficulty maintaining his force with no communications other than air supply. Mandalay and Meiktila were 500 and 600 miles respectively from the railhead at Dimapur. Slim noted in a Press Club lecture in 1946 that Fourteenth Army now had a ration strength of 750,000 – the population of a great city – scattered over an area as large as Poland and with the poorest communications. 'Before we could get on with our real business – fighting – we had to feed, clothe, house, and all the time we were doing it, equip, doctor, police, pay and transport by road, ship, rail and air all of those men. All that and jungle too!' It would mean improvisation. 'No boats? We'll build 'em! No vegetables, we'll grow 'em! No eggs? Duck farms! ... Malaria, we'll stop it! Medium guns bursting? Saw three feet off the barrel and go on shooting! Their motto, "God helps those who help themselves."'[10]

With bridgeheads across the Chindwin now secured, Slim devised a daring plan: Extended Capital. Rees's rapid progress made Slim wonder at the Japanese failure to try and stop him west of the Irrawaddy. If Kimura could not be trapped this side of the river, as he originally intended, he must be trapped on the far side. If Slim could grab Meiktila, the communications nodal point for both 15th and 33rd Armies, they would have to fight to regain it, and he was confident they could be decisively beaten. It would mean sending IV Corps down the Gangaw valley to cross the Irrawaddy at Pakokku, while at the same time convincing Kimura that his main effort was directed towards Mandalay, involving a reorganization with 19th Indian Division and 268th Indian Brigade coming under XXXIII Corps from 26 December.[11] The road was all-weather as far as Tamu, but the next 112 miles to Kalewa were not. He therefore improvised, using bithess, suitable for roads with careful preparation on bone-dry ground. Nor was this the only engineering problem: an advance into Burma would require 145 bridges, totalling 8,500 feet in length not including culverts.[12] From Kalewa to Mandalay (190 miles) the road was fair-weather and thereafter it was all-weather, but since he planned to abandon the Kalemyo–Pakokku track once IV Corps had passed through, maintenance of that corps would be river-borne from Kalewa to Myingon. For immediate use and casualty evacuation, each corps would construct airstrips every 50 miles, a relatively easy feat in dry, open country.[13]

The modification of the plan to take not just central Burma but the whole country was decided entirely by Slim and his staff without consultation with Leese, who was only informed after Messervy and Stopford had received their initial orders.[14] Slim requested further resources, principally 17th Indian Division, from Mountbatten, confident 'of attaining the object', which was 'the destruction or expulsion of all Japanese forces in Burma before the 1945 monsoon'.[15] Mountbatten approved, subject to uninterrupted air supply, but Germany's continued resistance caused the cancellation of Dracula. Fortunately Arnold supported it and when, on 3 February, Mountbatten received a new directive urging the liberation of Burma as soon as possible, to be followed by that of Malaya, he secured another 145 transport aircraft (40 of which were to be used by his civil affairs chief, Air Marshal Sir Philip Joubert de la Ferté, for feeding the civil population). Without this additional support Extended Capital could not have succeeded.[16]

The *tour de force* of deceptions against the Japanese would aid the crossing of the Irrawaddy. Slim's intention behind the plan, known as Cloak, was to conceal the main crossing until the last possible moment by persuading the Japanese to believe that the force preparing to move down the Gangaw valley to cross the river near Pakokku and seize Meiktila – IV Corps – was merely making a feint to distract attention from the attack on Mandalay by XXXIII Corps from the north.[17] D Division had double-agents in India, but their communications with Rangoon were so unreliable it was decided to rely on radio and physical means.[18] Until now Fourteenth Army's commanders had been reluctant to use any but the simplest signals deceptions, but now they were enthusiastic even to the detriment of operational communications, and three schemes were adopted. Pippin covered the withdrawal of 5th Indian and 11th (East African) Divisions;[19] Stencil created a dummy IV Corps Headquarters that appeared to control formations under XXXIII Corps; and Cloak was designed to give a false impression of the forces operating – that the forcing of the Irrawaddy would take place away from the real main effort, and that any movement the Japanese saw in the Gangaw valley was itself only a diversion.[20] There is no doubt the speed the advance into central Burma achieved was in no small measure due to this deception scheme, which also used political channels, displays and deception devices dropped by Mosquitos and Beaufighters; there were also fake drops to fake agents.[21]

While these plans were being developed, 20th Indian Division fought its way down the east bank of the Irrawaddy, opposed at Budalin and Monywa by 213th Regiment. Budalin was cleared on 9 January and, following up to Monywa, 32nd Indian Brigade occupied the town on the 22nd after heavy air strikes by almost 200 aircraft between 18 and 20

January had wrecked the place.[22] The division also took Myinmu and linked up with 19th Indian Division, already across the Irrawaddy.[23] From Shwebo, 19th Indian Division had turned east to the Irrawaddy and prepared to cross at two places north of Mandalay: Kyaukmyaung, 40 miles north of the city, and Thabeikkyin, 15 miles upstream, supported by 254th Indian Tank Brigade. On 11 January 62nd Indian Brigade failed to cross in country boats at Kyaukmyaung but, after shifting their crossing point, they succeeded on the night of 12/13 February 1945 in engineer assault boats. Over the next two nights 98th Indian Brigade established its bridgehead and 64th Indian Brigade, the last to leave the Shwebo area, made its crossing on 16 and 17 January.[24] The Japanese believed that 19th Indian Division was part of IV Corps and that its crossings were bridgeheads for that formation, and they counter-attacked fiercely in some of the bitterest fighting of the entire campaign.

An important feature was Pear Hill, which rose some 800 feet above the barren plain, found abandoned by Captain Frederick Rowley of 5th/10th Baluch, and subsequently subject to intense artillery fire and counter-attack.[25] The Japanese were further confused by the movement of 36th Division, which appeared to suggest a joint offensive between Fourteenth Army and NCAC. Unfortunately, the weakening of the latter by the withdrawal of two Chinese divisions enabled the Japanese to concentrate both 15th and 53rd Divisions supported by tanks against 19th Indian Division before it had consolidated its bridgehead, although each numbered only around 4,500 men.[26] And there remained Japanese on the west bank at Kabwet. Here the Machine-Gun Battalion, 11th Sikhs found themselves cut off and had to be reinforced by 2nd Royal Berkshires. On 25 January Rees directed 98th Indian Brigade against it. 'Frogs croaking, the chirping of cicadas and the rustling noises which are common features of dusk in the East, provided a subdued background to our silent progress through the bamboo thickets and low thorny shrubs', noted John Hill, as his company prepared to attack at Kabwet. Facing them was I/51st Regiment, amounting to just 200 men, whose positions were finally reduced by 30 January to a single thick-walled pagoda.[27]

From the north came news on 22 January of the meeting of Y Force and NCAC, and the Ledo Road was cut through to join the old Burma Road at Bhamo and opened for traffic on the 25th. 'We have broken the siege of China', proclaimed Chiang. 'Let me name this road after General Joseph Stilwell in memory of his distinctive contribution and of the signal part which the Allied and Chinese forces under his direction played in the Burma campaign and in the building of the road.'[28] With spectacular bridges now crossing the Taping and Shweli rivers, it was by any standards a phenomenal achievement of military engineering through terrain widely considered 'impossible' and in climatic conditions that could hardly have been more difficult. For all his faults, Stilwell's drive and determination had made it happen, and he thoroughly deserved the accolade, although within a few months the road would be redundant.[29] Nor did the completion of the Stilwell Road mean the end of Hump operations. In July 1945 a record 71,042 tons of supplies were flown over, but this rapidly tailed off and the route was officially closed in November.[30] Haulage operations officially started on 1 February with 58 truck companies assembled under three group and 11 battalion headquarters (of which 52 and 9 respectively were African-American) and a further 7 engineer aviation battalions (4 of them African-American), 2 dump truck companies (both African-American), 2 light pontoon companies (1 African-American), 1 engineer construction battalion, 2 engineer combat battalions, an engineer maintenance company, a heavy shop company and a forestry company.[31] One African-American soldier, Private Clyde Blue, was contemptuous: 'Allow me to give credit where it is due – the CBI war in *my* area was one big, lousy joke … If what I've read about war in books or seen in the movies is war, then either they are lying or they certainly weren't having a real war in my area.'[32]

Mars Task Force to the south was having a real war, however. Although there was little fighting at this time, there was much hard marching, in mountains rather than lowland swamp and jungles – as tough as anything that faced the Marauders. Along one steep hillside Mule No. 34, Troop K, 124th Cavalry, was on a narrow ledge which suddenly gave way beneath him.

> On a slope of a good 60 degrees, there was no hope for a footing as gravity took its natural course, and Number Thirty-Four rolled, not easily nor gently, but head over heels with increasing momentum for 150 feet until he jammed between two trees. The topload jolted lose. The chests burst open. Records and supplies littered the path the mule had battered through the jungle.[33]

His handler and two companions slid down to assess the damage and cut the straps holding the load. The mule tumbled another 30 feet to the valley floor. Then, to everyone's amazement he rolled over, gained his footing and started munching bamboo.

The Americans reached the Ho-si valley on 19 January and began occupying a number of mountaintop positions overlooking the Nam

Baw river. They had cut 56th Division's communications and here would fight their last battles of the campaign. First it was necessary to assault Loi Kang ridge, made worse by the Americans being out of food. The Japanese 4th Regiment were supported by 150mm guns, which had greater range and punch than the American pack howitzers. Throughout the next three days a pattern was established of American patrols, ambushes and booby traps by day, and Japanese attacks and shelling by night. To the north Chinese 114th Regiment also put a block on the Burma Road, which the Japanese attacked for five consecutive nights, inflicting horrific casualties, although they were in fact in the process of withdrawal, which supported Willey's doubts about placing Mars Task Force above the road rather than on it. As January drew to a close this process of small-scale actions continued in the hills.[34] Pfc Peter J. Faggion remembered 27 January in particular.

> The Japanese were retaliating with much fury and pinpoint accuracy this day. It crossed my mind at the time that one of those Whizz Bangs had my name on it. This skirmish continued for about one-half hour and they were coming in very close. There was earth/dust flying in the air and I recall seeing my foxhole's walls cracking and crumbling all around from the concussion.[35]

On 2 February Lieutenant Jack L. Knight – one of thirteen original National Guard inductees in his Troop F from Mineral Wells, Texas – led an attack up a 400-foot hill. After killing two Japanese he reached the crest and, standing fully exposed, called to his men, 'There's nothing up here. Come on!' As they dug in under heavy mortar and shell fire Knight discovered a bunker, which he grenaded, and then another; his troop had somehow got inside a horseshoe defensive position. Wounded in the face by grenade splinters and out of carbine ammunition, he nevertheless organized another attack. Wounded again by a grenade, his brother and platoon sergeant, Curtis, rushed to his aid but was cut down. Calling to his men to get his brother out of the line of fire, Jack rose and attacked a sixth Japanese bunker. But he was hit again and this time did not rise. He was awarded a posthumous Medal of Honor, the only infantry award in the China–Burma–India theatre.[36] In the same action Pfc Anthony Whittaker won a posthumous DSC, but by now the Japanese had had enough, and two days later they were gone. For Mars Task Force the campaign was over, and in March they redeployed to China: they had lost 122 dead, 938 wounded and 1 missing.[37]

In early 1945 36th Division crossed the Irrawaddy to form three bridgeheads. Their first contact was in January 1945.[38] The only Indian unit in 36th Division was 30th Field Company IE, commanded by Bob Swaine, who, according to its only Indian officer, Lieutenant R. M. Rau, 'was a fine old gentleman. (He was about 30 but he looked old to us.) With a fine sense of "Divide and Rule", he gave me the Punjabi Mussulman platoon, knowing I was a Hindu. To this day I remember with pride the loyalty these men gave me.'[39] Indian sappers were renowned for their ability to improvise, and orders given in Burma generally ended with, '*Aur sab chiz bamboo karangi*' ('Everything will be made of bamboo').[40] The first crossing failed, leaving a company of 2nd Buffs on the far bank with all its officers dead. A newly arrived Indian sapper subaltern, M. R. Rajwade, won the MC for organizing the company's defence and evacuating the wounded. The divisional commander ordered another attempt upstream. On 14 February 9th Royal Sussex, reinforced by a company of 6th South Wales Borderers, repelled strong counter-attacks, during which time the Borderers' mortars fired 3,000 rounds in four hours with two of their six barrels being cooled in the river at any one time.[41] Rau led a recce, only to find himself stranded on the far bank among 9th Royal Sussex Regiment with all his boats damaged.

> I jumped into a trench with a couple of Tommies. I was not exactly welcome, but we soon became friends. The Japs were all around shouting orders, and put in a couple of Banzai attacks. I fired my revolver half a dozen times at nothing in particular. There was nothing but bully-beef to eat [taboo for Hindus], and after surviving on water for two days, my will-power ran out. All my inhibitions disappeared as I gobbled up the stuff, and the Tommies solemnly shook my hand.[42]

On his fourth day in the trench the crossing was made good. Three days later the Japanese attacked No. 1 bridgehead at Myitson, where 2nd Buffs, 2nd/8th Punjabis and 1st/19th Hyderabad Regiment succeeded in fighting them off. No. 2 was ordered to be evacuated, abandoning heavy equipment, but the Japanese had failed and withdrew south.

In early January 2nd and 20th Indian Divisions moved on Yeu and Monywa against minimal resistance. Yeu was cleared on 2 January and 2nd Division crossed the Mu river, which separated it from Shwebo, the next day and were forcing their way into Shwebo within a week. They were not, however, the first into the town; 5th/10th Baluch of 19th Indian Division had attacked from the east on 7 January.[43] Far to the west what became known as the 'Chindwin Steeplechase' had now begun. Before IV Corps began its 328-mile trek, Messervy having taken over on 8

December, the road south had to be improved. Most of 7th Indian Division was still at Kohima and the divisional engineers were taken by motor transport on 19 December to Kalemyo, where they were joined by an Army Group Royal Engineers (AGRE) to begin work, while 114th Indian Brigade followed on foot and 28th (East African) Brigade was ferried in stages towards Gangaw as part of the deception plan.[44] The move to Pakokku along the Myittha valley was a logistic triumph: a one-way traffic system ensured tank transporters edging around the precipice did not meet others coming in the opposite direction, and at some points gradients were such that tanks had to tow their own transporters.[45] Lieutenant-Colonel Geoffrey Armstrong was among them.

> Bumping through the dust on every track to the river and beyond, were every kind of weapon and vehicle, guns, tanks, transporters, lorries, jeeps, bulldozers and sapper contrivances, mules, horses and even elephant 'bridging' teams, all on the move. Airstrips came into being overnight, and overhead went the bombers, fighters, 'bully' bombers [Dakotas] and light inter-comm planes.[46]

After the Lushai Brigade had cleared Gangaw with the aid of 'earthquakes' (air strikes carefully targeted with coloured smoke laid by the artillery), 28th (East African) Brigade, which had been in the area for some time, assumed advance guard duties with 136th Field Regiment RA in support.[47]

Life was not without its pleasures. 'Much has been written on the horrors of Burma warfare, of rains and leeches and snakes, of unseen enemies and deadly ambushes', noted the *4/8th Gurkha Rifles News Chronicle*.

> This time we experienced none of these things. The Burma hills in January are cool and fresh, and when in the sunset the hillsides turn to all the greens and browns of an English woodland in autumn, their beauty is unsurpassed ... Who can convey on paper the charm of the little pagodas, standing in clusters large and small, guarded on their hill tops by the chinthes, and with their tinkling, silver-voiced wind bells that never stay silent? How clean the villages are, so unlike those of India, where the sanitary arrangements are nil and a circus of hawks wheel above. The livestock seemed in first-class condition, small sleek cattle and poultry that would rival the pride of English farmyards. It was indeed delightful to trek through in those January days.'[48]

By and large the locals were reserved; some had provided Japanese coolie labour and most had been called upon to supply food. Norman Hiscox, a Royal Artillery signaller, 'soon realized we would have to settle for almost complete indifference from the Burmese in most of the towns and villages that we captured'.[49] Some villages remained empty while the troops passed through, their inhabitants having had enough of soldiers; others turned out to greet them with smiles, bearing gifts of fruit. Among the troops there were mixed feelings towards the Burmese. Those of 17th Indian Division no longer trusted them, yet many British soldiers and airmen had been sheltered by them. The Burmese, on the other hand, dreaded the return of the Indians to Burma. As a civil affairs officer told Gerald Hanley: 'They will put the screw on again, and the people are really afraid of them.'[50]

'Many soldiers found the Burmese willing to barter and very business-minded. They would not accept paper money, but while they asked high prices in coinage', noted J. Dewar McLintock:

> A bright clean safety pin would go as far as ten rupees, and I got a very good fat chicken for one small brass one. We had had great difficulty in restraining the troops from 'flogging' various items of their smalls, such as pants, socks etc. – which were commanding good value in foodstuffs and cigars. Such items, in fact, would buy almost anything in a Burmese village.[51]

They marched throughout January, with each day following the same routine. The troops would step off at night and march until early afternoon – their destination selected for water and a flat space for dropping supplies. 'We came to love the sight of those overworked Dakotas labouring in across the hills', recalled Scott Gilmore. 'In the fine weather of the Burmese winter they always found us.' Thus the first task would be to lay out a drop zone and defensive positions. Although a surprise attack by the Japanese was considered unlikely, nobody was taking any chances: 'The sweat had hardly dried from a rifleman's back before he began digging. March, dig, eat and sleep. A simple life perhaps.'[52] Night involved sentry duties, entailing two hours on and two off, a tiring routine but one recognized as very necessary. John Shipster recalled an unusual example of the local fauna that provided interest and merriment:

> Every evening we would take shelter in some relatively pleasant area, often near a small stream or river. Invariably just before the sun went down we would hear the unmistakable cry of the 'Fuck U' bird. Starting with a robust cry of 'Fuck U' it would continue its repetitious performance in diminuendo until the final cry just faded away in the evening air. The bird was always heard and never seen.

One evening this performance disrupted the Commanding Officer's conference and so annoyed him that he offered a prize of 15 rupees (about £1) for the identification of the tormentor. The *Jawans* were delighted at any chance for games or competitions, and the culprit was soon revealed to be not a bird at all, but a large lizard that produced a strange noise from the dewlaps under its throat.[53]

As they proceeded southwards, Slim gave Messervy a further instruction on 17 January: having taken Pakokku, IV Corps was to seize Meiktila. Messervy realized that, once in the dry central plain, watering of the many animals would cause problems, but mechanical transport and armour would be well served by the conditions. He therefore proposed to keep the MT currently on loan and to reorganize 17th Indian Division to two motorized and one air-transportable brigade, which Slim accepted. This began on 22 January and was complete by the end of the month. At the same time representatives of 1st and 2nd Air Commandos attended the corps conference on the 26th and agreed to provide 50 Mustangs and 7 Mitchells, plus 50 Thunderbolts from mid-February, while the whole of 221 Group was free to support Fourteenth Army and XXXIII Corps.[54] While these plans were formed, 20th Indian Division approached the Irrawaddy. Stopford wanted 2nd Division to attack Mandalay from the north-west and 19th and 20th Divisions from the north. Throughout January, 19th Indian Division was involved in continuous fighting to extend and consolidate its bridgeheads, which were counter-attacked by 15th and 53rd Divisions (weak though they already were), and at Kabwet, while 2nd Division was out of contact until the 21st. Intelligence on Japanese intentions remained sketchy at best; in fact, most of 15th Army were in their allotted posts along the Irrawaddy, although construction of defensive positions had been much slower than expected.[55] By 1 February the forward troops of Fourteenth Army were in sight of the Irrawaddy, with two Japanese enclaves on the west bank, at Pakokku and Samaing, to be attacked by 7th Indian and 2nd Divisions respectively.

Hampering the defence was the withdrawal by Southern Army of 5th Air Division to Thailand.[56] Slim held the initiative, screened by the mighty river and with complete air superiority. He planned to begin with a thrust by 19th Indian Division from the Kyaukmyaung bridgehead, followed by a crossing in the Myinmu area by 20th Indian Division to make as great a show of force as possible, after which 7th Indian Division would cross at Nyaungu as unobtrusively as possible. Here the Irrawaddy was at its narrowest and gave access to rivers leading east and south; it was defended by the INA's 2nd Division and was 15th Army's weak point, due to be transferred to 28th Army, although this did not happen before the Allied attack.[57] Then following a build-up the Meiktila strike force would launch itself by way of Taungtha.

Kimura had covered the most obvious crossing-points with a powerful counter-attack force ready to fall on any lodgement. Therefore Messervy also planned a considerable deception programme that included the simulation of a crossing at Seikpyu, 40 miles downstream, opposite the important town of Chauk using 28th (East African) Brigade and a dummy parachute drop involving Paragons (dummy parachutists that fired battle simulators on landing) and a marked map showing Yenangyaung as the objective. Simultaneously a small feint would be made at Pagan by 1st/11th Sikhs, to cross if possible.[58] The Africans had a difficult task; the country was open and they would have to dig for water, while the brigade had to cover the frontage of a division with only one field battery in support. They advanced in two columns and encountered scattered opposition before arriving in front of Seikpyu in the evening of 8 February. Following reconnaissance by the SRU, the demonstration began on the night 12/13th with sappers crossing the river south of Seikpyu, where they laid several explosive charges timed to go off at dawn.[59] Artillery, mortar and machine-gun fire were laid on in the north, and they were so successful in simulating a major crossing that Japanese reinforcements rushed towards them and counter-attacked for the next month, during which 71st KAR particularly distinguished themselves.[60]

In the north 19th Indian Division began its breakout on 11 February. By 20 February it found the Japanese had long since given up trying to contain it, and Rees exhorted them, 'on to Mandalay'.[61] Gracey's plan for 20th Indian Division's crossing was to begin thirty-six hours before 7th Indian Division. At Satpangon, 2nd Border of 100th Indian Brigade began crossing as darkness fell on 12 February, followed by 14th/13th Frontier Force Rifles at 0400. By nightfall on the 13th the bridgehead was 2,500 yards wide and 1,000 yards deep. The subsidiary crossing of 32nd Indian Brigade ran into difficulties, however, with many boats of 1st Northamptons swept away or overturned.[62] The next few days saw the Japanese desperately trying to prevent the two brigades linking up, mostly falling on 14th/13th, which suffered 169 casualties at Kanlan Ywathit.[63] Jemadar Prakash Singh was wounded repeatedly, first in both ankles, then in both legs above the knees and then again in the right leg and finally the chest. Throughout the action he fought with 2-inch mortar and Bren gun, then began redistributing ammunition and exhorting his men. When the Japanese threatened to overrun his platoon's position, he shouted the Dogra war-cry so loudly that the others took it up and drove the enemy off. When his Commanding Officer arrived, Prakash Singh told him not to worry, he could look after himself, and died shortly afterwards at 0230 on 17 February. He was awarded a posthumous VC.[64]

It took three weeks of bitter fighting for 20th Indian Division to establish its bridgehead, during which elements of thirteen Japanese battalions belonging to four divisions were identified against it. At Satpangon, Corporal Andrews was leading the point section across a bund, recalled Lieutenant K. W. Cooper of 2nd Border.

> A machine-gun clattered, piercing the silence like a needle through a blanket. Andrews knelt down slowly, then rolled forward on his face. The man next to him — and the regulation five paces distant — spun round like a top and flopped in a heap beside Andrews. Two other men — the Bren gun team — dropped into a fold in the ground and fired one burst before the traversing Japanese gun found them.[65]

All night the battle raged around the village until, near dawn, they heard cheering, explosions and a bugle, followed by a crackle of small-arms fire.[66]

The crossing by 7th Indian Division on 14 February was a massive engineer undertaking, involving ten field companies, two field park companies, a bridging company and an engineer battalion.* All three groups of Sappers and Miners were represented, creating tremendous competition, and each raft flew its own 'house flag' while a control tower housed the 'Clerk of the Course of the Irrawaddy Regatta', recalled Major M. B. 'Bill' Adams. 'The scene may well have resembled Margate-on-Sea on a Bank Holiday.'[67] But there was a change of plan: Messervy and Geoffrey Evans (now commanding 7th Indian Division) were overconfident, and instead of 4th/15th Punjabis, who had trained for days with the Sappers, the prestige of going over was to be given to British troops. Lieutenant-Colonel T. W. M. Mitchell of 2nd South Lancashire Regiment was given only three days to prepare and none to rehearse his men, since Evans had to delay the operation when the boats arrived in dreadful condition.[68] Messervy spoke to them the night before the assault. Acknowledging that they had been kept in the dark for security reasons, he believed there would be little opposition, but

> I hope you are going to have an unopposed crossing — in fact a kind of Blackpool boating trip ... and so confident am I over your coming success that I have already prepared a signal to General Slim. I will read it to you: 'Great day for Lancashire. George (Brigadier Collingwood) safely over Beecher's Brook. Race going splendidly.'[69]

A disaster was in the offing. The Punjabis knew the boat handlers and could communicate with them in Urdu, but 2nd South Lancs could not. John Henslow recalled:

---

* Engineer battalions were peculiar to Indian formations, provided on the basis of one per division as corps troops. They were combatant units, including 16 LMGs and 16 anti-tank rifles or later PIATs.

The night was filled with muffled curses. 'Move up you bastard', 'Not f'ing likely, you've got a bloody Bren gun. It's your place up front.' 'Well budge up then.' 'Not bloody likely – I'm not going to be the silly fucker up front.' And so it went on.[70]

The first company managed to cross, but at first light the INA defenders retaliated and the assault dissolved into a shambles as boats circled in the river following each other. Colonel Mitchell's boat was so tightly packed that the artillery officer, killed beside him, 'had not fallen down and on two different occasions I felt his body move as bursts of light machine-gun fire hit him. Most of the other boats within voice control were in the same way.'[71] Mitchell managed to get back to Brigade Headquarters, where he was told another battalion would reinforce his isolated C Company. Major Denis Sheil-Small watched from the bank as a

> sense of horror gripped me as those lads, with whom we had laughed and joked a few hours previously, continued to drop under the hail of bullets. The drifting craft, draped with the bodies of the dead, trailing their lifeless limbs in the turning currents, presented an awesome sight as the cries of the wounded carried to our ears across the water.[72]

Henslow, unable to locate any officers, asked a sergeant why they were heading away and not going in. 'We are the reserve company, sir', he was told. Fortunately they returned to their start point, where 4th/15th Punjabis, the second wave, were waiting. Now, with precise movements and supported by air, armour and artillery, they went in successfully to relieve the isolated South Lancs company.[73]

At Pagan – the ancient capital of Burma between the ninth and thirteenth centuries, when Buddhism was first brought to the country – 1st/11th Sikhs crossed the river more easily and encountered 'Pagoda City'. They found hundreds of pagodas in varying stages of decay populated by surrendering Jifs.[74] Now merely a village 'choked with its own holiness', it seemed that no house could 'squeeze between the serried ranks of pagodas, which for lack of space have filled the country for miles around. Little pagodas, big ones, square ones, round ones, pagodas of mellow brick, huge white and gold masses, a fairyland of towers and pinnacles, dancing in the magic of the warm evening sun.'[75] Nyaungu was finally secured and cleared by 16 February after some tunnels the Japanese were using were discovered by 1st Burma Regiment. Eventually, when all forms of bombardment including napalm failed to shift the defenders, the tunnels were sealed up.[76]

Through no fault of its own 2nd Division could not move forward as quickly as it wished. After the capture of Yeu and Shwebo, Stopford had to restrain his corps, 400 miles from its railhead and with 19th Indian Division entirely on air supply despite a new group of airfields being available on the Shwebo plain.[77] Once 268th Indian Brigade had taken over Sagaing, 2nd Division had a 15-mile frontage to select its crossing point, but in an area where the river was between 2,000 and 4,000 yards wide– far wider than in 19th Indian Division's sector – and shortage of assault boats meant it could not begin until 20th Indian Division had largely completed its operation. Every conceivable deception would be needed to persuade the Japanese the thrust would come in the south-east corner of the river, through the Sagaing hills, and 5th Brigade, tasked to carry out the initial assault further east, would have to seem very thin on the ground. Sentries were therefore disguised as natives pounding maize.[78] In a *Daily Herald* report of 2nd Division's crossing of 24 February Arthur Helliwell named 7th Worcesters and was critical of the state of the boats, suggesting either an oversight or a very liberal view taken by the censor as, 'suddenly when we were in midstream, there was a single vicious crack, followed by a sound like tearing calico, as machine-guns opened up. Someone shouted "They've seen us! Paddle like hell, boys!" And from the Colonel's boat came a cool crisp order, "Start up the outboards."' But while the men fiddled and swore, nothing happened and they continued paddling wildly as the bullets cracked past.

> Two thudded into the boat and I felt a gush of water against my legs. To right and left of us other boats were sinking under the men as they paddled. The Commanding Officer's boat had sunk too and the water ahead was dotted with bobbing heads    One youngster threw up his hands and shouted, 'For God's sake save me,' as we drifted past, but we were helpless. Other drowning men were clinging to our boat, and soon it was obvious that with so many boats sunk we would never hope to force a landing.[79]

And so they turned back, cursing the boats, which were five years old and rotten. Seventeen were sunk, although 1st Camerons and 1st Royal Welch later made it across.[80] Second Dorsets were then sent 5,000 yards across country to Myittha to cross behind the Camerons and open the bridgehead. Thereafter the bridgeheads were expanded with air support making use of napalm.[81] Fourteenth Army was across the Irrawaddy and ready to break out. The crossings, with their complex logistic and engineering problems, constitute a campaign within a campaign: in five weeks Slim with meticulous planning had put two corps across one of the world's widest rivers in a feat that rivalled any in history.[82]

# 24

## Mandalay and Meiktila

Out there in the jungle, down by Mandalay,
A few forgotten soldiers slowly fight their way,
They dream of the girls they left back home,
And soon they hope to cross the foam
To see their land and loved ones,
Never more to roam.

Some of them are repat, some are time expired,
Longing for their troopship, and their fireside.
They often talk of Burmese plains,
Of dust and heat, and monsoon rains,
Of roads that lead to heaven,
And tracks that lead to hell.
　　Anon., *Down by Mandalay* (to the tune of *Lili Marlene*)[1]

WHEN IT CROSSED the Irrawaddy, 19th Indian Division was supposed to draw the enemy north of Mandalay, but Rees wanted to capture the city. His plan involved attacking on a two-brigade front with the aim of drawing the Japanese on to 64th Indian Brigade on the motor road on his left flank. This would ease the way for his main drive down tracks on the right by his other two brigades, which would leap-frog south, where the Irrawaddy would protect his flank led by a mobile column called Stiletto, based on the divisional recce battalion, 1st/15th Punjabis with C Squadron 7th Light Cavalry and a troop of Lees from 150th RAC. The latter were protected by 3rd/4th Bombay Grenadiers, and despite

> the almost complete inability of the men of 150th Regiment and these brave Jats to understand a word of each other's language, they established between them that odd lingo by means of which British and Indian troops have conversed for so long. With this lingo was created also an unbreakable confidence in each other's abilities and friendship, which eased the hardest tasks.[2]

Starting on 6 March, the feint on the left proved successful and the right soon made progress, allowing Rees to slip his reserves into the main attack, which soon turned into an all-out advance. 'We rumbled down the cattle tracks in the heavy dust', recalled John Masters, who had joined 19th Indian Division as GSO 1.

> We passed the 25-pounder[s] of the artillery, bounding and roaring in a score of clearings, hurling shells far ahead into yet another village ... Infantry, trudging along the sides of the road, plastered with dust and sweat ... The light hung sullen and dark overall, smoke rose in vast writhing pillars from a dozen burning villages, and spread to make a gloomy roof above us. Every village held some Japanese, every Japanese fought to the death, but they were becoming less, and less organized.[3]

After three days they reached Madaya, half-way to Mandalay. As they approached the city, Rees decided to capture Maymyo as well and detached 62nd Indian Brigade under its former Chindit commander, 'Jumbo' Wilson, across country to do so, with 2nd Welch leading the way and soon clearing it.[4] On this excursion Robin Painter met a private of The Cameronians left behind in 1942 who had 'gone native' and married a local girl. The villagers had sheltered him whenever the Japanese came. 'He had virtually become a Shan tribesman. He probably stayed on there for the rest of his life.'[5]

On 8 March 19th Indian Division could see Mandalay Hill, rising 1,000 feet above the plain, but they had to spend another two days under its baleful shadow, approaching the city under accurate fire from Japanese artillery on any movement, especially by vehicles. On the night of 10/11 March 98th Indian Brigade fought their way up its flank to the summit, from which they could look down on the city. Then began the gruesome campaign of extermination of the defenders among the temples of one of the most sacred places in the Buddhist faith. 'All the while the infantry fought in the brick rubble of the burning city, among corpses of children and dead dogs and the universal sheets of corrugated iron.'[6]

The defenders – 67th Regiment on Mandalay Hill, 60th Regiment to west and south and Headquarters 15th Division in Fort Dufferin – had orders to resist to the last – orders that were largely futile since, as Kimura admitted later, 'the only reason it was held at all was for its prestige value'.[7] The Commanding Officer of 4th/4th Gurkhas knew Mandalay Hill intimately from before the war, and begged for the privilege of leading the attack on it where the Japanese had dug in around the hundreds of golden-topped pagodas around the sides and crest of the hill; his men scaled it from the north-east, supported by 150th RAC and 'Twidle Force' of 2nd Royal Berkshires under its second-in-command, Major Bob Twidle.[8] When the latter was held up by snipers, a Sikh machine-gun was firing at a Japanese position.

> The No. 1 on the gun, firing, was shot stone dead through the head from the enemy position. Without hesitating, the No. 2 by his side pushed No. 1 away, laid an aim and fired, silencing the Japanese position; for cool courage that takes some beating. That was their standard of training and discipline: No. 1 is killed, 'Fall out No. 1, carry on No. 2!' – exactly as in parade-ground drill for the Vickers machine-gun.[9]

The defenders were finally eliminated from their tunnels by barrels of burning tar and oil, and the hill cleared by 13 March.[10] The main Japanese depots were at Tonbo, some 10 miles south-east, and desperate measures had been made to move them away, but there was simply not enough transport. Throughout 1945 the Beaufighters of 901 Wing had severely disrupted Japanese transport. The climax came in March, when 177 Squadron flew 137 sorties, 26 of them at night, for a total of 708 hours – believed to be a record for Beaufighters in the theatre. They damaged 15 locomotives, destroyed 25 motor transport vehicles and damaged 31, another destroyed or damaged 41 powered river or sea-going craft and 63 river craft, and they ignited pipelines three times.[11]

Both 2nd and 20th Indian Divisions were also involved in the capture of Mandalay, the former marching east from its bridgehead on 26 February. Gracey's 20th Indian Division would advance to Gyo while holding the Myinmu bridgehead, while 2nd Division moved on Myintha and 268th Indian Brigade secured the northern end of the Ava Bridge. Gracey's plan was for a breakout to the east in a 50-mile drive east to Kyaukse, some 25 miles south of Mandalay. On 5 March Charles Evans was posted as MO to 1st Devons, who had been under fire for seven days and whose own MO had been unable to continue. Soon the advance began and all stability of lines ceased as they moved from village to village. There was no obvious front line and patrols were needed to clear surrounding villages; laagers at night had always to be defended from all directions. Each day involved marching, the infantryman's

> sweaty tramp … relieved by ten-minute halts, sallies of grim wit and, very occasionally, pleasing encounters with villagers. At last, usually before noon, he reaches a clump of palms or a village, throws off his pack and sets about brewing up. Someone shouts 'Char's up!' and he pours the sweet, milky tea into his dried-up gullet, sore and stiff with dust and heat. Out come the picks and shovels and the digging of trenches and fox-holes begins.[12]

By 15 March both divisions were advancing together when it became known that 18th Division had withdrawn from the northern front, by-passed Mandalay and was concentrating in IV Corps's area. To assist the latter, Stopford ordered Gracey to send a strong column south towards Meiktila and 2nd Division to co-operate with Rees at Mandalay.[13]

The armour's difficulties were highlighted by a report from 3rd Carabiniers. The Japanese liked to fight in villages in beautifully concealed positions that were never revealed by shooting too early. With numerous buildings surrounded by trees, often set alight by artillery fire and providing smoke, this was not ideal tank country; nor could the infantry go in alone unsupported. The only way forward was for the tanks to shoot up everything in sight since, fortunately, the Japanese had few anti-tank weapons and most of them were ineffective. Their best was the mine but these were laid obviously, unmethodically and often incorrectly fused.[14] Advancing through Tabetswe, 1st Royal Welch intercepted a telephone message (meaning that a curious fusilier probably wandered into the station master's office and picked up the phone, after which an interpreter was summoned). From this 99th Field Regiment RA were able to shell a train at Paleik station, the fire being helpfully adjusted for the guns by the Japanese, who said down the phone that the shells were landing near the Pagoda, clearly marked on the map some 200 yards away. When Paleik was entered not long afterwards, the train and two other locomotives were found abandoned.[15]

With distances along the lines of communication steadily increasing, 'we appreciated the work of the American pilots of the little L-5 aircraft even more at this stage', recalled gunner Captain Tony Bell.[16] Captain John Lawson, Medical Officer with 1st Camerons, had been sure that what made evacuation possible was the aeroplane, particularly the American L-5, which could hedge-hop and whose pilots were 'amazing'. He also had immense respect for the RASC ambulance drivers, who, while notoriously bad walkers, 'make up for this by pushing their vehicles up to incredible places to save the RAMC carrying their patients farther than necessary. This habit plus always carrying tea, sugar and milk made them universally popular.'[17] Meanwhile Rees turned his attention to Fort Dufferin.[18] This formidable bastion was square in layout, with walls 2,500-yard long, battlemented similar to early Norman style, and fashioned 'nine yards high' by order of King Mindon in 1857. These surrounded it on four sides, behind which a great earth bank reaching the top from a base 20 feet thick added solid strength to already formidable workmanship. Along each wall at intervals, ten bastions with curiously carved roofs (known to the

Burmese as *pyathat*) rose tapering skywards, while entrances comprised three gates of sheet steel protected by a baffle wall in front. Some 25–30 yards in front of the wall was a 75-yard wide moat filled with water, crossed by two railway bridges and five road bridges. Beyond the moat the town extended east, west and south with now ruined blocks.[19]

After Thunderbolts bombed it and 5.5-inch guns pounded its walls, 8th/12th Frontier Force Rifles and 1st/6th Gurkhas probed the approaches but were held up. The first attack on the fort on 18 March was called Operation Duffy and would involve stealth. This, however, failed.[20] Next RAF bombing and gunfire opened another seventeen breaches in the walls, more than the defenders could cover, but Rees wanted to avoid the stalemate of Myitkyina and, remembering a culvert beneath the moat, prepared to send an assault unit behind a Burmese guide. But following another air attack on 20 March a party of civilian hostages emerged under a white flag and a Union flag to announce the Japanese had withdrawn the night before, also using a drain under the moat. Captain Frederick Rowley's 5th/10th Baluch were among the first to enter.

> We were going gingerly when we heard and saw a figure about 50 yards away. As it got closer, it didn't look like a Japanese. I shouted a challenge, and he turned out to be an American from Shwebo [airstrip] who had just driven in in his jeep looking for souvenirs. He said: 'The gates were open. I'm on holiday, on leave.'[21]

The Divisional Provost was swiftly on hand to prevent looting and was kept busy with a stream of visiting 'brass'. On 21 March Vincent flew Slim as his passenger in an L-5 to land at the racecourse for a triumphal entry into Mandalay.[22] Vincent wrote that Mountbatten and Leese 'were both "hurt" that we had done the triumphal entry and not they. It was apparently resented that those who were actually responsible had taken the credit.'[23] The same day 2nd Division managed belatedly to get in on the act; Brigadier West of 5th Brigade had been told to link with his neighbour of 19th Indian Division and escorted by a troop from 3rd Carabiniers drove through the shambles of the city.[24] Maurice Maybury, with CAS(B), arrived in Mandalay three days after its capture to find it in a sad state of ruin.

> The damage caused by the Japanese air raids of 1942 had never been repaired and had been added to by the concentrated bombing of the past few months. Yet in the midst of these ruins there were still people living, making such shelter as they could from the shattered materials around them.[25]

On 22 March three of Charles Evans's stretcher-bearers were killed by a shell, probably a 25-pounder. Always a close-knit group,

> Young, Herford and Scully usually went about together and they had two particular friends at the RAP, Macey and Stevens. The two were so broken by the news that I knew that for a while I could make no use of them. 'Why can't they stop?' cried Stevens, 'God! Why can't they stop?' I hardly knew the three dead men but ... their deaths shook me too. Stoffles, the usually cheerful water corporal with the peacock feather in his hat sat on the ground with his head in his hands, saying, 'I can't stop thinking about them.'[26]

At least 19th Indian Division enjoyed a brief interlude of peace. Rees and his officers were entertained by a troupe of Burmese dancers. 'The clown clowned,' wrote John Masters, 'the incredibly delicate and fine-boned girls, so tightly sheathed in silver and gold dresses that it seemed impossible they could move, writhed and gesticulated to the whine of *saing waing* and the rattle of bamboo clappers, their faces as white as death under the masks of rice powder.'[27] J. Dewar McLintock also encountered a Burmese band in a village.

> The music started with a strange impact on the jungle night, as though someone had suddenly turned on a queer, tortured, hysterical radio at full volume. The first impression that it was hideous, however, gave way to one that it was merely unusual. Then in but a moment, it became clear that there was an enchantment, an irresistible quality of intoxication, about this most unusual combination of sounds.[28]

All was set for the armoured drive on Meiktila, headed by 255th Indian Tank Brigade, which had trained hard during the winter of 1944/5 with 17th Indian Division, the Royal Deccan Horse with 48th Indian Brigade and Probyn's Horse with 63rd Indian Brigade, and they crossed into the Nyaungu bridgehead on 17 February.[29] On the approach it had been planned to use transporters, but heavy going and hundreds of bends on bad mountain roads forced them to do 200 miles on tracks so that hardly one did not need new bogies, idlers or sprockets welding. All these spare parts had to come by air.[30] With 116th RAC detached to support 7th Indian Division, the column set off on the 80-mile drive towards Meiktila on 21 February. Now, in thick country with the tanks 'closed down', they were deaf and blind, so the squadrons of Probyn's Horse and the Royal Deccan Horse were escorted by infantry of 4th/4th Bombay Grenadiers. The 'Grinders' would communicate with the tank crews via telephones on the backs of the tanks and protect them from suicide attacks and in the night laagers, when the tanks' machine-guns, firing on fixed lines, helped to protect them. Each tank's 'Grinders' effectively became part of the crew, even helping with daily maintenance.[31] At Oyin on 22 February Probyn's met resistance from 16th Regiment of 2nd Division, a mud bank and cactus hedge providing cover for snipers with tall trees between the houses. The tanks could not advance, so 6th/7th Rajputs went forward to clear the village.[32] Lieutenant-Colonel Miles Smeeton, commanding Probyn's Horse, described how first one then another Japanese soldier would spring from fox-holes or undergrowth to try and detonate explosives against their tanks, with faces 'twisted in frantic determination':

> If in harvest time I had seen a rabbit, shaken out of a corn stook, turn sud-denly on its pursuers ... I couldn't have been more surprised than I was at the sudden appearance of these Japanese soldiers, with their anguished look of determination and despair, pitting their puny strength against such tremen-dous force. Their desperate courage was something ... we saw with amaze-ment, admiration, and pity too ... If a British Regiment had fought against such odds as they had fought, the story would live forever in their history.[33]

The battle cost the Rajputs 70 casualties, including a company com-mander and a tank commander shot through the head; but 200 Japanese were killed. Yet in every way Japanese tactics and fighting abilities were below the standards of 1944. Immediate counter-attacks never material-ized; they were reduced to battered automatons sitting stubbornly in their bunkers with little support, simply waiting to die.[34] Lone charges by sword-wielding officers were never going to stop tanks, and suicide assaults were, in fact, quite rare; others took to hiding in holes armed with aircraft bombs to be detonated when a tank passed over. They made little effort to defend themselves when found by infantry, 'only peered up [and] seemed to say to themselves, "A man! I'm waiting for a tank," and again bow their heads, in which position they were shot'.[35] Significantly, the unit the Rajputs defeated had no radio, so news of their destruction did not reach Meiktila that night, although leaflets warning of imminent bombing were dropped on the town.

The following day Meiktila was bombed and that night Japanese staff cars arrived for an important conference the following day at which various counter strikes were discussed. While they did so, the drive towards them continued and reached Taungtha, 43 miles away. Slowly reports of the approaching Anglo-Indian force trickled back, queried by the rear-echelon officers that comprised the garrison. The scepticism was shared by Headquarters 33rd and 53rd Divisions and at 15th Army. The Japanese were caught short, as Slim had been at Kohima, but they did not know it, as arguments raged about the strength of the incursion. The town garrison with its airfields included 52nd and 84th Airfield Battalions and 36th Anti-Aircraft Battalion but no front-line combat troops and was the site of 107th Lines of Communications Hospital. Most of its personnel were transport troops, so Major-General Kasuya of 2nd Field Transport Headquarters took command. On 26 February the Royal Deccan Horse reached Thabukton airfield, 15 miles north of the town, and after the divisional sappers had prepared it, 99th Indian Brigade were flown in by 2 March.[36] On 27 February 16th Light Cavalry's armoured cars met strong opposition 8 miles out, but 9th Border executed a left hook with A Squadron of Probyn's Horse with an air strike, and 80 Japanese were killed. The same day Colonel Tsuji Masanobu urged Katamura at 15th Army to put everything into Meiktila's defence; Burma Area Army insisted he keep to his objective of defending the Irrawaddy, but I/ and II/168th Regiment from 49th Division began concentrating at Kyaukse nevertheless. Communications were now so bad that it took up to five days for a signal to reach Burma Area Army. There little importance was attached to intelligence and the chief intelligence staff officer, only a major without direct access to Kimura, was never called to give his opinion, and interested only in identifying Allied formations.[37] But Katamura would not be fazed. He pressed on with his 'Plan for the Battle of Meiktila' while at Burma Area Army arguments raged: Kimura supported Katamura, while Tanaka passionately advocated sticking to the original plan defending the Irrawaddy line.[38]

Watching Fourteenth Army advance, Mountbatten could not accept this was the way to re-conquer Burma; his instructions to Slim remained vague – he was to occupy north Burma. The opening of the Ledo Road ought to have freed resources for further operations, but instead Chiang had lost interest. And since the Japanese offensive threatening Kunming had already caused Wedemeyer to withdraw two divisions and air support from Burma, Wedemeyer, now viewing Asian strategy through his new spectacles, wanted to shift the emphasis to China, a view readily endorsed by Chiang.[39] While 36th Division was marching to relieve 19th Indian Division, the aircraft needed for Meiktila would have to supply them and Kimura could transfer troops south: unpalatable facts that Slim learned only after the tanks began their march on Meiktila. In March Mountbatten flew to Chungking to try and persuade Chiang to relent, but Chiang insisted that no Chinese troops could operate south of Mandalay. Fortunately the success of Fourteenth Army meant this was no serious loss, especially after Mandalay's fall, and a personal message from Churchill to Marshall emphasizing the need for Slim to keep his aircraft until after the fall of Rangoon was accepted. But he had only until May to achieve this, and could not afford to get stranded between Meiktila and Rangoon.[40]

Meiktila was a lovely place between two lakes, with elegant red-brick buildings and pleasant villas, set among bird-filled trees with a view of Mount Popa; but in March and April the heat is intense and the lakes shallow. The hard red soil made digging arduous and, as Mandalay saw a medieval siege, so Meiktila saw a desert battle. But Slim saw only formidable defences as he flew in with Messervy to Thabukton.[41] He had invested too much into this plan to leave it to Cowan, who thus had both the Army and his Corps Commander breathing down his neck. The town's defences were reported as strong on the western side but Cowan had to take it since its airfields were essential, and so 63rd Indian Brigade put in an attack, although it was not pressed, and formed a road-block to the south-west. The main assault came from 48th Indian Brigade supported by two tank regiments from the east and north-east, and in the face of fierce resistance it took two days, hard fighting on 1 and 2 March to clear the town. Every bunker was defended to the last, the Shermans methodically engaging them with high explosive and solid shot until the infantry could get in and bomb them. Slim was right up front watching the battle, far closer than he should have been, and a tank firing solid shot sent 'overs' in his direction, forcing himself, Messervy and the American general whose bomber had brought him to Meiktila to throw themselves to the ground.[42] Jaharman Sunwar of 1st/7th Gurkhas took part in the battle: 'Our troops came from all sides and the Japanese became flustered. At one cross-roads we had machine-guns on fixed lines and the Japanese came in crowds. We slaughtered them and their corpses were like grains of rice spread out to dry. A dozer buried them.'[43] One particularly stubborn bunker was consigned to oblivion by a turretless tank from the Royal Deccan Horse's Light Aid Detachment (LAD), machine-gun bullets spattering in vain against its inexorable bulldozer blade.[44]

Several more days followed to extend the captured area, keep the airfield out of artillery range and secure neighbouring villages. On 2 March Naik Fazal Din of 7th/10th Baluch was run through the body by a Japanese officer's sword. He then grabbed the sword and killed the officer with it, then another Japanese soldier and assisted a sepoy to kill a third before staggering to platoon headquarters, where he collapsed and died before reaching the RAP.[45] He was awarded a posthumous VC, as was Lieutenant William Weston the following day with 1st West Yorks. Kasuya felt he could ask no more of his surviving men and ordered them to break out east for Thazi.[46] But as they did so reinforcements were arriving from all directions and the roles would be reversed, while 2nd Lieutenant Imahara Kanichi of 2nd Field Transport Headquarters was bitter at the order: 'They say we were routed, all the units who were in Meiktila, and that we did nothing. That's very hard to take ... even the sick fought to the death, and the survivors should see to it that it goes down in history.'[47] The battle was over, but now the Japanese reacted and the siege was about to begin.

On 20 February a depleted 18th Division was sent north-east of Maymyo to take part in the battle of the Irrawaddy bend. A week later it was ordered to Meiktila and moved using its transport of sixty lorries and eighty from an army transport unit as far as Myitta, where it continued on its own resources from 3 March, by which time Meiktila had fallen. Taking 119th Regiment from 53rd Division and 214th Regiment from 33rd Division under command plus a unit of heavy artillery and 14th Tank Regiment, it was ordered first to trap the Allied force and then to destroy it in conjunction with 49th Division.[48] Cowan chose not to wait for them but instead adopted an aggressive defence with fixed company posts and mobile groups at six points around South Lake, where single companies with mortars and machine-guns were placed in static defence; three from 99th Indian Brigade, one each from 48th and 63rd Indian Brigades and one from the Divisional Headquarters battalion, 6th/7th Rajputs. On 6 March five powerful columns swept out of town along the roads radiating towards Mahlaing, Zayetkon, Pyawbwe, Thazi and Wundwin and between 7 and 10 March patrol actions took place, after which the Japanese began to occupy the area north of the sluice and Kyigon in order to attack the central area based on the 'golden pagoda'. In one of these actions George MacDonald Fraser summed up his emotions as

> a continuous nervous excitement ... shot through with ocassional flashes of rage, terror, elation, relief and amazement. So far as I have seen, most men are like that, by and large, although there are exceptions. A few really enjoy it; I've seen them (and I won't say they're deranged, because even the most balanced man has moments of satisfaction in battle which are indistinguishable from enjoyment, short lived though they may be).[49]

On 11 March one of the bloodiest actions of the siege was fought when 1/56th Regiment and an anti-tank battalion fought against tanks some 4 miles west of Meiktila. Captain Sobha Chand of 4th/4th Bombay Grenadiers found his D Company up against stronger opposition than was anticipated. Having recently done a mortar course and with the radio working for once, Chand persuaded the Commanding Officer, Lieutenant-Colonel S. C. H. Tighe, to lay on a shoot, which he would direct. The battalion mortars plastered the village but Captain Chand was disappointed, having lost one of his platoons in the dark. Colonel Tighe told him to have a drink and wait and see. The next morning revealed 27 Japanese dead, a captured anti-tank gun and detachment and his lost platoon safe and sound.[50]

Meanwhile Naka planned to encircle the town from the north and west, but two vigorous night attacks failed and the Japanese shifted their centre of gravity eastwards. On the night of 15/16 March two battalions of 55th Regiment dug in within 100 yards of the airfield perimeter but were driven off by 1st Sikh Light Infantry, although they continued to shell the airstrip.[51] Flight Lieutenant Brian Stanbridge of 31 Squadron recalled flying into Meiktila to evacuate casualties. 'The strip was taken over every night by the Japanese and retaken every morning by our troops. It was under constant mortar fire which caused the loss of several aircraft while unloading. Our turnarounds were the quickest ever.'[52] It was tricky for the defenders who were trying to cover the fly-in of 9th Indian Brigade from 5th Indian Division, and when Brigade Headquarters arrived with 3rd/2nd Punjabis on one of fifty-four American sorties that day, they were perturbed by the battle going on around them. 'Get out quick, for God's sake', yelled the pilots as they landed, who then stopped to take photos of Japanese corpses near the aircraft before taking off again. Only one Dakota was hit.[53]

On 16 March the Japanese reinforced their main infantry positions around Kandaingbauk with anti-tank guns and knocked out some tanks. Tanaka, Chief of Staff of Burma Area Army, arrived at Honda's headquarters to inform him he was to take command of 18th and 49th Divisions, which had been operating in isolation of each other, and to regain Meiktila. He felt it hopeless, given the situation on the Irrawaddy, but two days later began planning a combined attack from north-east with 18th Division and from south-east with 49th. Their artillery under Colonel Uga Takeshi was especially well handled during the battle, as Captain Jack Scollen of 'B' Flight, 656 AOP Squadron, noted:

> The Japs shelled us steadily for two and a half hours, keeping us in our slit trenches the whole time ... One shell missed a trench in which one of our men was sheltering by no more than a yard. His kit was riddled with splinters and he had a lot of earth thrown over him but he was quite unhurt. After crouching, bent up, in my trench for what seemed hours, I grew stiff, sore, very bad-tempered and madly hungry too.[54]

Cowan was also bad-tempered. He and Slim had served together in 1st/6th Gurkhas and his son had joined their old battalion, where Slim spoke to him. Now Cowan learned that the young man had died of wounds sustained at Mandalay; he sacked the experienced Brigadier J. A. Salomons of 9th Indian Brigade and had sharp disagreements with his tank commanders.[55]

Defending Meiktila between 'battles' involved offensive patrols and 'routine chores', involving clearing areas and laying ambushes. 'The disinclination of the Japanese for surrender', noted Major Patrick Davis,

> deprived us of an important source of information about them. Without live bodies to question, Brigade vented a continuous moan for documents. To satisfy Brigade someone had to kill Japanese. This the forward companies did with some success. There was a steady flow of badges, flags, notebooks, pay books, identity discs, maps and diaries taken from the bodies of the dead.[56]

Among the more bizarre trophies was a Japanese colonel's head removed by a Gurkha NCO and hung near a bunker. Men came from wide about to stare at it, many having never seen a Japanese, alive or dead. Increasingly desperate, the Japanese tried to mount one last attack in strength on 20 March by 55th Regiment, supported by tanks, but they were broken up by heavy artillery and mortar fire before they could start.

Following one more determined effort against 48th Indian Brigade's perimeter next day, which left another 195 bodies behind, the order came to retire to Thazi on the night of 22 March and the artillery fired off its remaining ammunition.[57] They estimated they had inflicted 300 casualties on the Anglo-Indians and knocked out 22 tanks but failed to identify any of the formations facing them. They were sure that the rolling open countryside suited Allied armour, artillery and air power while 18th Division was 'pitch-forked' into the battle with practically no preparation in an attempt to restore the situation quickly.[58] Now Tanaka authorized the withdrawal of 33rd Army – to cover 15th Army's retreat. The latter was now in total disarray and streaming away from the Irrawaddy towards the safety of the Shan Hills and Toungoo. Later at Kalaw the convent girls

> were surprised by the appearance of a new type of Japanese soldier who sometimes ventured into our compound when it was dark. For the most part on crutches and maimed, some with bandages on their heads or arms in slings, they would beg for water or rice, extending a metal container and slinking off into the darkness afterwards. Somehow they gave us to understand that all the hospitals had been closed. Leaving the wounded and ill soldiers to fend for themselves as best they could.[59]

The military role of the BNA was small but significant. By late 1944 its 11,000 men were restricted to training and communications duties until October, when they began to assemble near Rangoon. Preparations for the AFO rising took place throughout February and March with Force 136 liaison.[60] On 17 March the BNA left for the 'Front' at Toungoo–Pyinmana following a farewell parade and a march through streets lined with people 'who whispered prayers or openly wept'.[61] The fighting around Meiktila was falling badly behind schedule if Fourteenth Army were to reach Rangoon before the monsoon broke – failure to do so could mean forcing withdrawal since it would be impossible to supply them overland from India. On 26 March Leese recommended that the plan for amphibious assault discarded in February should be revived. Thus the decision of the Burmese to fall on the Japanese on 27 March was strategically important and timely.[62] Only when the families of Than Tun and Aung San disappeared did the Japanese get an inkling of what was abroad, but by then it was too late: next day came reports that their former allies had struck the Japanese in the rear. Significantly, Aung San made no move against Captain Takahashi Hachiro, his adviser and constant companion. When Takahashi asked Aung San what sort of deal he had struck with the British, Aung San replied: 'Ideally, what we want is total independence for Burma. If that's not possible, then we shall accept being a self-governing dominion, and we're negotiating on that basis now. But if neither of these things prove acceptable, I shall fight the British to the bitter end.'[63] Burmese co-operation also helped in the Northern Shan States, where the Chinese were refusing to cut off the Japanese retreat route at Loilem as requested by the British.[64]

Gracey's 20th Indian Division was moving south towards Meiktila in an effort to finish off 33rd Army, killing some 3,000 Japanese and capturing 50 guns. Captain William Pennington was an artillery forward observation officer, and near Kyaukse directed that rare and phenomenal thing a corps shoot, involving all the guns in range from the entire corps on a large body of Japanese troops spotted in the open.

> I was not sure how many guns were allocated to the target but it looked as if the entire British Army was responding. Through my binoculars I could see our enemies' bodies being flayed and flung into the air by the tremendous power of the bombardment, limbs torn apart and scattered as if to the four corners of the earth.[65]

The infantry then advanced to deal with what little resistance was left. When Japanese packs were captured they often contained severed fingers and toes, and in one case 'a whole gangrenous hand wrapped in a Japanese flag'. It shocked the British.

> We had learnt that as long as some part of the body could be taken home for burial in Japan, Shinto beliefs decreed that eternal rest would then be found. These grisly relics were destined to be carried thousands of miles. To us, their comradely loyalty seemed barbaric but only served to remind us that we were up against a ruthlessly dedicated enemy – if we needed such a reminder![66]

Gracey organized a flying column under Barlow of 7th Light Cavalry to drive 70 miles to Wundwin, some 17 miles north-east of Meiktila.[67] Lieutenant Reginald 'Rex' Wait of 18th (Self-Propelled) Field Regiment RA recalled:

> We broke out of the bridgehead and drove as fast as possible southward into enemy territory. During the day there was no enemy traffic on the roads, no doubt because of our Air Force. Each night we would settle down at a cross-roads to ambush any Japanese vehicles that might come along. Japanese supply lorries would drive unsuspectingly towards us, often using full head-lights, until all hell suddenly broke loose.[68]

When Barcol made contact with 17th Indian Division, Gracey directed him towards Kune, where he drove 300 Japanese into the hills, killing 100; by the end of March the area from Mandalay south to Wundwin was in XXXIII Corps's hands and the two corps were ready to begin driving for Rangoon.

Desperate now, Kimura looked to 28th Army in its Arakan fastness to attack the Nyaungu bridgehead and block IV Corps around the Yenangyaung oilfields and along the lower Irrawaddy. Sakurai, who had little regard for Kimura or Burma Area Army, had long expected to have to save its bacon, and had begun constructing defences around Mount Popa in October 1944. This 500-foot volcanic knoll dominates the plain around it and offered excellent defensive positions first garrisoned by 112th Regiment and a battalion of 5th Heavy Artillery Regiment from Tenasserim, with a mobile reserve of three battalions from 55th Division and artillery and engineers under Major-General Nagazawa Kanichi to hold the south-west of the Irrawaddy delta around Shinbu. But these forces were dissipated under huge pressure from Arakan, and attempts to pinch out the Nyaungu bridgehead foundered at Letse, while 7th Indian Division took Kyaukpadaung, and at Myingun, Lieutenant Karamjit Singh Judge was awarded a posthumous VC for a prolonged display of outstanding bravery together with Naik Gian Singh, both of 4th/15th Punjabis.[69] The threat from Mount Popa proved short-lived as, now garrisoned by 2nd INA Division, 5th Brigade took it after a three-day aerial bombardment which persuaded the Japanese to retire and the INA to surrender in droves.[70] Not that they found this easy, as 2nd Dorsets discovered after capturing the INA Divisional Headquarters, and from 'some of their Part II orders (written in English), the number of admissions to hospital with sword slashes showed clearly those who had been unfortunate enough to be discovered'.[71]

From Meiktila to Rangoon is 338 miles via Pyinmana or 441 miles via Taungtha. Slim was sure the Japanese were not strong enough to defend both routes, and on 30 March 17th Indian Division began to drive south from Meiktila. Honda planned to block IV Corps at Pyawbwe with 18th and 49th Divisions as the battered remnants of 31st and 33rd Divisions of 15th Army were pouring into the Shan Hills while 53rd Division retreated through Taungtha to Yanaung, just west of Pywabwe, pursued by 7th Indian Division.[72] Cowan directed 99th Indian Brigade first to Thazi, then south to Pyawbwe, and 63rd Indian Brigade to bypass it to the west and come up from the south-west: precisely the sort of pincer of which the Japanese were once so fond. But to add spice he sent Claudcol, a powerful column under Brigadier Claud Pert, to drive through the villages west of Pyawbwe and cut between it and Yamethin, thus surrounding it. Claudcol, with two squadrons of Probyn's Horse, two of 16th Light Cavalry, 4th/4th Bombay Grenadiers and 6th/7th Rajputs with gunners and sappers, set off on 4 April. First it struck Yindaw, held by 1,000 men from 49th Division and after three days' fierce resistance, which cost the Rajputs two company commanders, Pert decided to bypass it.[73] On 8 April it cleared Yanaung, catching the exhausted remnants of 53rd Division – already shorn of their artillery, apart from two anti-tank guns and two battalion guns – before they could organize their defence. Claudcol made short work of them, killing 230 and destroying the anti-tank guns, as Honda ordered them south to Sinthe Chaung, where he expected them to make a stand with 49th Division at Thatkon. Claudcol drove on to Ywadan, killing 200 more Japanese and taking 4 guns, then sent a detachment south to Yamethin and began driving north towards Pyawbwe.[74] Having already destroyed one column of the reinforcements Honda was desperately summoning from Yamethin, Probyn's Horse were withdrawing into laager when they heard the distinctive sound of Japanese tanks coming south from the town. They scrambled into the nearest tanks, the gunner's place in Smeeton's mount being taken by Lieutenant Bahadur Singh (who soon after became Maharajah of Bundi). 'As the lead tank came round the bend', recalled Smeeton, 'I leaned forward and touched Bahadur Singh's shoulder. A dagger of flames shot from the barrel of his gun, the enemy tank glowed redly, and immediately with a great belch of flame blew up.'[75] A second tank tried to escape the line of Shermans but was caught, while a third reversed at top speed, crashed into a river bed and overturned. The rest withdrew quickly, only to be destroyed the following day, along with fifty-three lorries and cars trying to escape.

The Pathans of John Randle's B Company 7th/10th Baluch attacked Point 900; 'the men were screaming and had a wolfish look with bare teeth. I tried to take a few prisoners but my Subedar said "it's no good, you're wasting your breath" ... about an hour later you suddenly get a feeling of melancholy.'[76] With 48th and 99th Indian Brigades now battering the north of the town, although the infantry were suffering heavily in the process and Naik Lachhiman Pun and C. H. M. Harkabir of 1st/3rd Gurkhas won posthumous IOMs, 63rd Indian Brigade secured the west on 10 April and the Japanese withdrew next day.[77] Honda's headquarters escaped by sheer luck, situated in a village 1,000 yards south of the town. Seeing the approach of Claudcol, they scattered in all directions while Honda sat in a hole writing his will. Signals intercept was regularly locating headquarters positions, but 33rd Army's radio communications had ceased or Pert would not have broken off what he believed a minor action to head for Pyawbwe. Honda used liaison officers to control his scattered formations, and Tsuji watched one disappear into the gunsmoke to deliver a message to 18th Division, disguised in *longyis* and looking for all the world like two Burmans escaping the noise of battle. By 14 April 33rd Army amounted to just 8,000 men in total, with a sprinkling of mountain guns and three 150mm howitzers.[78] Slim described the battle of Pyawbwe as one of the most decisive of the war, being the last proper defensive position between Meiktila and the sea: 'It shattered Honda's army, but it did more – it settled the fate of Rangoon.'[79] Honda's plan was a desperate attempt to delay Messervy until the monsoon arrived. Slim had another 312 miles to go and at best four weeks to do it.

# 25

# Rangoon

The Army camp is in fields covered in frost.
I think of the old days when the poet sang:
'So clear and limpid in the autumn air.'
Tonight the moon is shining peacefully ...
Citadels I have destroyed and captured castles
My body has suffered a thousand pains
Yet here I am miraculously alive
The thoughts of parents and friends upon me ...

Japanese Soldiers' Marching Song[1]

MOUNTBATTEN'S GAZE WENT far beyond Burma, with a plan to seize Phuket as a stepping-stone on to the Kra isthmus – coined Operation Roger by a wag on his planning staff with schoolboy humour and a poor grasp of Thai pronunciation – to be followed by Zipper on the west coast of Malaya, and Mailfist, the recapture of Singapore. Mountbatten's timetable was extremely tight and Rangoon *had* to be secure some time in May.[2] With lack of resources and army opposition making Dracula uncertain, he was told overland columns might reach the city by mid-April but, in fact, everyone doubted this.[3] Thus even with Fourteenth Army's momentum sustained, Slim agreed with Leese on 19 March that a seaborne assault on Rangoon should be mounted as insurance against the monsoon, and three days later a conference at Monywa considered the delay caused by the withdrawal of transport aircraft.[4] The greater part of air supply still fell to the Americans, who flew 75 per cent of 88,500 tons in March and 70 per cent of 80,000 tons in April, but there was enormous pressure to divert them elsewhere and air forces remained hugely significant.[5] Fourteenth Army's reliance on air was so complete that Slim regarded Extended Capital as a joint land–air campaign in which the two were equal partners, and could rightly claim to have made a distinctive contribution towards a new kind of warfare.[6]

On 2 April orders were issued to mount a modified Dracula against

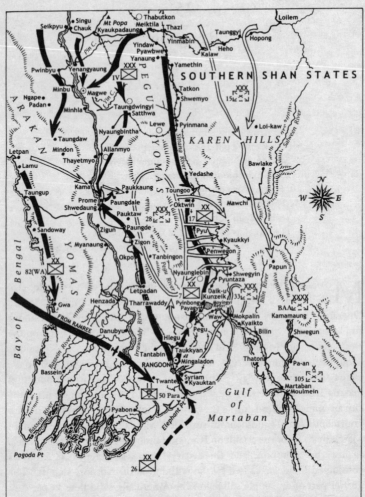

# THE FALL OF RANGOON AND
# THE BREAKOUT OF 28th ARMY,
## May—August 1945

Rangoon, involving a seaborne division and airborne battalion by 5 May at the latest.[7] Mountbatten told Leese that Fourteenth Army must first secure sufficient airfields to provide cover for it, fearing possible heavy casualties otherwise, and wanted Toungoo and Pyinmana.[8] Starting on 5 April, 5th Indian Division advanced from Meiktila and they fought a stiff action at Yamethin then into Pyinmana, once more almost killing or capturing Honda.[9] The use of tanks in the armoured car role had been exasperating. When A Squadron 3rd Carabiniers rejoined the regiment after leading 4th Indian Brigade for four days, they had done 140 miles and expended another 50 engine hours. There were not above a dozen Japs to show for this. The Squadron 2i/c complained 'we were not even chasing hares, we were chasing air'.[10] Now the pursuit was usually led by the Daimler armoured cars of Prince Albert Victor's Own and 16th Light Cavalry, showing true light cavalry spirit in raiding far afield.[11] The former was first into Prome, while 8th Light Cavalry arrived at Monywa on 29 March and served to the end of the campaign.[12] As their cars burst down the road towards Rangoon past bloated Japanese corpses, Fourteenth Army represented an India that was taking possession of her own future. 'The feats of valour, privation, endurance and the capacity to fight even for their foreign master', wrote Anil Chandra, 'was the inheritance of the Indian Army flowing down decade after decade.'[13] It had grown to stand now on the verge of independence, 'proud, and incredibly generous to us, on these final battlefields of the Burmese plain', thought John Masters. It was all summed up in the voice of an Indian colonel of artillery who, 'bending close to an English colonel over a map, straightened and said with a smile, "OK, George. Thanks. I've got it. We'll take over all tasks at 1800. What about a beer?"'[14] The IAF started the war with just half a squadron but finished with nine, having been built up for reconnaissance and army co-operation. On 12 March 1945 it was granted the honorific 'Royal'.[15]

Toungoo was 69 miles further south and entrusted to 123rd Indian Brigade. Kimura had hoped 15th Army would emerge from mountain tracks to the east to cover 33rd Army but they never arrived as, with Slim's order on 13 April, the Karens rose to stop them. In early 1945 Force 136 attempted fifty secret operations, thirty-eight of which were successful.[16] Its most spectacularly successful military operations were Nation and Character. The former inflicted an estimated 4,000 casualties on the Japanese for the loss of only around 70 guerrillas.[17] Among those who had parachuted back into Burma in February 1945 was Bill Nimmo, brother of Jimmy, and Kan Choke, who had also escaped in 1942 with Arthur Bell

Thompson. They dropped in the Karen Hills as part of Character, in which some 12,000 Karen levies were armed to attack the Japanese.[18] Dalbahadur Khati was one of 75 men from each of 1st, 2nd and 9th Gurkhas who served on these operations, during which time they were supplied by air. 'One three-week period we had nothing and so lived on jungle produce, tapioca, yams, bamboo shoots and sweet potato but no salt. We were very hungry.'[19] Dick Rubinstein was another operative.

> We took about 100 weapons, which we distributed at once. We received more a night or two later. We laid ambushes, doing pin-prick operations on Japanese moving south, sometimes on the roads, sometimes on tracks. If the parties were big enough we brought down an air strike on them. If they were small we dealt with them ourselves. We were quite successful.[20]

As 15th Division tried to move south in a race with IV Corps for Toungoo they were repeatedly ambushed. More importantly, they failed to reach Toungoo on time and were soundly beaten by 5th Indian Division.[21] The Karenni were passed by Fourteenth Army within three weeks but continued to operate against Japanese in the hills into July. Many other small detachments operated all over Burma. Stopford of XXXIII Corps concluded the Karens inflicted in the region of 10,000 casualties, more than the regular army.[22]

In 123rd Indian Brigade 7th York and Lancaster had replaced 2nd Suffolk Regiment. Captain Leslie Beswick later recalled an orders group. When the Brigade Commander asked for questions, 'The first was "What about repatriation?" He looked towards me and the CO of the Indian Field Ambulance next to me, raised his eyebrows and said, "The battalion will be repatriated from Rangoon *when* we have captured it." '[23] Hilda Corpe had married a Burmese before the war, much against her parents' wishes, and when the Japanese first arrived hid in a monastery until she was discovered by the *Kempeitai* and interned. Although not tortured herself, she did witness it.[24] Released in late 1944 on the responsibility of Thakin Nu, a friend of her husband's, she found her home was the local *Kempeitai* headquarters and she had to make careful conversation with its commander. In April the Japanese suddenly left and British soldiers appeared.

> My heart was beating so fast I was speechless. My hands trembled so that I could scarcely unlock the door. At last they were inside the house. I clung to them sobbing; I did not care. Relief, joy, and pride in their wonderful achievement made my tears flow the faster ... I was free. Only those who have endured captivity can know what that means.[25]

In XXXIII Corps area 32nd Indian Brigade of 20th Indian Division continued to move south, led by 150th RAC, and reached Magwe on 19 April, joining with 268th Indian Brigade west of Mount Popa to cut off the Japanese.[26] Already hard pressed in Arakan, and far from threatening IV Corps, Sakurai found himself on the verge of being surrounded. But the supply situation was so acute and reinforcements so scarce that it was decided to fly 2nd and 36th Divisions out to India. Transferred by air to Mandalay, 36th Division fought their last action in Burma at Myittha Gorge and the Indian battalions of 36th exchanged with the British battalions of 20th Indian Division, leaving only Indian formations to Messervy for his southward advance from Meiktila.[27] 'The dash down the road was exhilarating', recalled Harry Smith. 'We had little hard fighting and the enemy were in complete disarray and losing cohesion all the time.'[28]

Ploughing on, 5th Indian Division overran 1st INA Division – 150 officers and 3,000 men – at Pyu and put them to work repairing the Toungoo airfields, then pushed on 20 miles to Penwegon, where 17th Indian Division took up the running on 25 April.[29] They were now faced by the dregs of Rangoon's garrison organized as 105th Independent Mixed Brigade from administrative, airfield and anti-aircraft units, including many civilians given uniforms and rifles, under Major-General Matsuo Hideji. He created a forward unit from a marine transport battalion, NCO school, railway staff, anti-aircraft batteries and 138th Independent Battalion (from 24th Independent Mixed Brigade), a force with sufficient engineering knowledge to make an effective stand against armour, which it did on 27 April at the deceptively quiet village of Pyinbyongi. A Royal Deccan Horse Sherman bulldozer was blown up, and later at Payagale another tank had its engine blown clean out of it by an aerial bomb, and the crew had to be rescued by the supporting infantry as the Japanese closed in. They lost two others, and suicide attacks continued through the afternoon.[30]

Between Meiktila and Rangoon 255th Indian Tank Brigade encountered nine blown bridges and one prepared for demolition but captured intact. Valentine bridge-layers were employed three times and Japanese tanks met on several occasions, usually as static pill-boxes or occasionally driven at night at the perimeter, where they were destroyed. In total the brigade suffered 37 dead and 79 wounded and lost 26 Shermans written off.[31] With only two tank brigades, Fourteenth Army made great demands on the armour, and in what until now had been a predominantly infantry war, armoured commanders were aware of a feeling that tankies were always harping on about the need for time off for maintenance, a problem exacerbated by the tanks being old, with few replacements available. But lack of previous combined arms training meant infantry commanders failed to understand that, just as horsed cavalry once needed time for rest, feeding, watering and grooming if horses (and therefore the cavalry arm) were to retain their effectiveness, so did tank crews if mechanical problems were to be avoided.[32] The offensive with mobile operations caused serious problems for IEME as divisional and corps 'tails' became increasingly stretched over dreadful roads, further hampered by small parties of retreating Japanese. Recovery in the far rear areas was largely non-existent, and anything that could not be repaired further forward had usually to be written off. This meant hanging on to everything, even when it should have been condemned. At one point Sherman final drive failures were occurring at an alarming rate and the brigade moved forward leaving the workshops to bring repairable tanks forward the 160 miles to their destination, which, with only one serviceable final drive among six tanks, they did one at a time. Similar arrangements had to be made for engines, since without such improvisation tanks would have to be abandoned without replacement. Air supply caused unusual problems: when no tackle capable of unloading Sherman engines was available at a landing strip, a forklift had to be flown in while nine transports carrying nine engines sat grounded for thirty-six hours. Many bridges in Burma were of low classification, so tanks could not be taken across on transporters but had to be repaired in situ or winched across, and a shortage of 4×4 vehicles also hindered movement.[33]

Sent to locate a crashed L-5, another L-5 from No. 3 Repair and Salvage Unit found it easily enough, but had to turn back when their own aircraft developed engine trouble. Returning two days later, they found the site had been stripped bare by the locals, an increasingly regular occurrence, although what value the parts had and who the locals hoped to flog them to, escaped the RAF men.[34] Scott Gilmore described meeting Burmese villagers

> driving creaking ox carts along tracks in the open country inland. They regarded us apprehensively. Nor could we be sure that they were not informers to the Japanese. The older women sitting on their haunches smoking large cheroots, neither veiled their faces nor scurried out of sight, as would have been the case in rural India, [and] one did not blame the village maidens for showing some shy unease in the presence of our fierce, slant-eyed Mongolians [Gurkhas] bristling with arms.[35]

Charles Evans, now with 114th Field Regiment RA, discussed 'non-fraternization' with his Commanding Officer, who 'said, "It's hopeless with the British soldier if there are children about, I mean, look at 'em Doc".' They were in a village where a truck was halted on the road with children all over it. 'In central Burma we had lots of the little beggars about – quiet smiling and attractive, with brown faces, almond eyes, chubby bodies, jet-black hair.'[36]

Seventeenth Indian Division reached Pegu on 29 April. Three brigades crossed the Pegu river and the Japanese held both banks. During the 30th the infantry splashed through the mud to clear the east bank in a series of dogfights while the Japanese blew the bridges. But reckless parties of Indian troops probed for crossings, and A Company 4th/12th Frontier Force Regiment under Major Amrit Singh rushed across, when Singh found that a single girder of the southernmost bridge was crossable in single file. He arranged a demonstration to distract Japanese attention and an artillery barrage for cover and a platoon crawled across in ones and twos. Despite some casualties, the platoon commander led a bayonet charge that broke into the Japanese position. The Japanese reacted violently, preventing reinforcements arriving before dark, when another platoon got across, and these held off a number of counter attacks until with a final burst of fire the Japanese slipped away at first light.[37] Cowan was desperately keen to enter Rangoon: five of his battalions had been among those driven from Burma in 1942. But the following day torrential rain struck Pegu. The monsoon had arrived two weeks early.[38]

Tamura Masataro was Third Secretary at the Japanese Embassy in Rangoon. On 21 April he agreed with the Consul-General that the Burmese government and Japanese civilians should evacuate the city and called on a senior staff officer at Burma Area Army. The officer said the British would be stopped, but Tamura pointed out the only possible point to do so was the Sittang, just 50 miles away. The staff officer had no answer except to say that at the last moment the *Kamikaze* would blow.* Ba Maw held his final Cabinet meeting on 22 April and evacuation was agreed, but Ba Maw and Japanese civilians were not the only ones to leave for Moulmein on the 23rd. Despite being ordered to hold Rangoon to the death, Kimura ignominiously abandoned the city – a decision apparently taken on 22 April, although no orders were issued for two days. Rangoon had suffered heavily from Allied bombing raids in early 1945; the water supply had also been wrecked, with none available since 22 March; and there was no transport, electricity or sewerage. Kimura later declared he was 'astounded by the complete ignorance of the actual situation shown by the staff of Southern Army'.[39]

* The *Kamikaze* ('Divine Wind') was a typhoon that saved Japan from invasion by the Chinese under Kublai Khan in the thirteenth century.

The inmates of Rangoon gaol were divided into 'fit to march' and 'unfit to march', with the former departing on 25 April towards Pegu, then along a single railway track towards Waw. Four days later the senior officer, Brigadier Hobson, was called out to speak with the commandant. Half an hour later Hobson shouted out, 'We are free! We are free!' The guards had simply disappeared. But they were caught in no man's land before the advancing Fourteenth Army, and fashioned a Union flag from cloth provided by friendly villagers and set a haystack on fire. 'Suddenly', recalled Denis Gudgeon, 'all hell was let loose. I cowered behind a mango tree while three Indian Air Force Hurricanes ground strafed us. Each plane made three passes and I was lucky to escape with bullet grazes to my right ankle and knee.' Brigadier Hobson, less fortunate, was the only man killed. 'Poor Hobson! Could anything be more poignant?' wrote Colonel Mackenzie. 'He was destroyed by his own side, after the years he had suffered at the hands of the enemy.'[40] Later Major Lutz, an American PoW Mustang pilot, made contact with the British and they were officially liberated by 1st West Yorks.[41]

Swarms of refugees were subject to air attack, including the puppet governments of India and Burma. Chandra Bose seems to have shown more concern for the fate of the Burmese capital than Ba Maw, leaving 5,000 INA men to keep order until the British arrived. 'Indeed, the scramble to get out was humiliating for all of us', recalled Tamura. While the general and his staff flew to Moulmein, the diplomatic and government staff had to walk most of the way along rain-sodden paths in rough country. Matsuo, commanding the Rangoon Defence Force, was furious when nobody told him of the evacuation, and the supply depots were abandoned without being destroyed.[42] The last Japanese troops left Rangoon on 29 April. The remaining emaciated inmates of the gaol disarmed the few INA guards and fortified it for their own protection against Burmese marauders. It was as well Slim had accepted that Dracula might beat Extended Capital to Rangoon. One of the main problems involved in the landing was the short time available for preparation and the situation within 50th Indian Parachute Brigade, so that only a composite battalion group was available and had to be dropped by 38 US aircraft with no experience of parachutists. However, the first lift landed on target on 1 May and advanced without opposition, but unfortunately they got ahead of schedule and were bombed by the SAF despite being some 3,000 yards from the objective at Elephant Point, suffering 40 casualties in the lead company. The second lift arrived and was briefly held up by a Japanese bunker, then rained on for three days while the whole area was inundated by a spring tide to a depth of 3 feet.[43]

On 2 May Mosquito pilot Wing Commander A. E. Saunders of 110 Squadron spotted a message on the central gaol roof: 'JAPS GONE! EXTRACT DIGIT!' (the second phrase written after a bombing). He landed at Mingaladon airfield, where he suffered a small prang and blown tyre on the pockmarked runway, and walked into town.[44] Having visited the gaol and assured himself the message was true, he took a sampan down river to meet the troops advancing towards it, as 26th Indian Division had now bypassed the parachutists to land unopposed and secure the city, covered by Vice-Admiral H. T. C. Walker's 3rd Battle Squadron from Trincomalee in Ceylon with battleships HMS *Queen Elizabeth* and the Free French *Richelieu*, two escort carriers, four cruisers and six destroyers.[45] Lieutenant Glyn Evans RN was one of the first ashore 'and saw no-one, not even a dog. What we did see was a mass of paper money lying in heaps outside a blown-up door to a bank.'[46] Lieutenant Sydney Pickford of 1st/8th Gurkhas went to the ice factory to take the surrender of the INA troops there.

> As I turned to move up the jetty, I found my way barred by a very old
> Chinaman (with a beard down to his waist) who was kneeling with his hands
> clasped in the attitude of prayer. Tears were running down his face. 'Oh,
> thank God you are back, Sir Thank God the British are back. Now we can
> live again.' I was lost for words.[47]

Sub-Lieutenant Russell Spurr RINVR, a PR officer and his padre friend Pat Magee saw a group of soldiers in Japanese uniforms, then realized they were Indians. A smiling Sikh major approached. '"Delightful to see you chaps", he said, "We couldn't wait to get this surrender business over." The men crowded around him and murmured their cheerful approval.' But when Spurr explained he could not accept, Magee chipped in: '"But we'll accept a drink." "By Jove, that's a jolly good idea", said the Sikh major', and they returned to the INA mess, where the subalterns crowded round for news. '"Pink gin suit you?" inquired the Sikh major. He handed me two glasses. Men who had lately been our enemies snapped to attention as the major called, "Gentlemen. The King–Emperor!"'[48] Later that day torrential rain fell once more, confirming the arrival of the dreaded monsoon.

So Rangoon fell without a shot, although Slim could not have foreseen this – Kimura's abandonment surprised his own officers – and on 6 May 1st Lincolns from 26th Indian Division met 1st/7th Gurkhas at Hlegu, just 27 miles north of the city, where law and order had effectively broken down and took some time to restore.[49] Yet the *Kamikaze* had come: the monsoon was two weeks early and Fourteenth Army bogged down, on half-rations and with the roads cut to pieces, but there were no Japanese left in the Delta to take advantage of it. In nine months' continuous fighting from 6 August, Slim took his army, including tanks and heavy equipment, across 1,000 miles of largely undeveloped country, crossed two wide rivers and inflicted a decisive defeat on the most resolute of enemies. His achievements should be judged by the scarcity of resources, and this is the measure of his greatness.[50] Always at the bottom of the Allied global list of priorities, lack of assets was overcome by improvisation such as the use of bithess and the IWT Service, and by cunning and deception in planning to create surprise. If he was not a great battle commander (he admitted to Roy McKie that it was his fault Kohima was so thinly defended), he more than made up for it at Meiktila – the master-stroke, according to Kimura.[51] And he was a great leader. 'He understood men', wrote the Australian McKie. 'He spoke their language as he moved among them, from forward positions to training bases. He had the richest of common-sense, a dour soldier's humour and a simple earthy wisdom. Wherever he moved he lifted morale. He was the finest of Englishmen.'[52]

On 3 May at Kandy, Mountbatten, recovering from a bout of dysentery, was told by Leese that Slim was tired and that, with little experience of combined operations, he would be inappropriate to command Zipper. He therefore proposed to Mountbatten to offer him command of the new Twelfth Army, which would garrison Burma. Mountbatten disagreed and, according to Browning, who was present, made clear to Leese that Slim might be 'sounded out' but that there was no indication that Mountbatten had lost confidence in him.[53] Instead, Leese sent a private signal to Brooke seeking approval of his proposals, to which he received a non-committal reply, and a senior staff officer, Major-General George Walsh, a man renowned for a lack of tact, to explore the possibility of Slim relinquishing command. Slim was outraged and demanded that, if the Commander-in-Chief had lost confidence in him, he should have the courtesy to discuss it with him face to face. Leese arranged to visit Slim at Meiktila on 7 May but on 6 May told Christison he was to be commander of Fourteenth Army in Slim's place.[54] He then told Slim of this *fait accompli* and offered him command of Twelfth Army, which Slim refused as an insult, saying he would rather resign and return to the United Kingdom: although Leese denied it was his intention, Slim considered himself sacked. Brooke was astonished at this, as was the whole of Fourteenth Army, who regarded Leese, the Guardsman, as something of a fop.[55]

Jim Allan met Leese, who asked each man how long he had been out east and replied to each with 'Good show!' Allan did not take to a man 'who clearly did not bother to listen to what we said'.[56] Shortly before leaving the Meiktila area, John Hill was summoned to meet Leese along with several others who had recently been decorated. 'Although an eminent soldier, he seemed to me, probably unintentionally, to be slightly supercilious and haughty ... he was so very different in approach and in dress from the down-to-earth, dour, tough Slim – a soldier's general every step of the way.'[57] To Anthony Brett-James, Slim appeared a homely general: 'In his jaw was carved the resolution of an army, in his stern eyes and tight mouth resided the determination and unremitting courage of a great force. His manner held much of the bulldog, gruff and to the point, believing in every one of us, and as proud of the Fourteenth Army as we were.'[58] Slim was 'the only man I've ever seen who had a force that came out of him', wrote George MacDonald Fraser; 'he spoke of what his army had done, it was always "you", not even "we" and never "I".'[59] They trusted him. But although Slim liked to give the impression of a blunt, simple fighting soldier, he was also subtle, articulate and extremely clever.

Slim was, unsurprisingly, stunned, and wrote on 14 May:

> It was a bit of a jar as I thought 14th Army had done rather well. However, he is the man to decide. I had to sack a number of chaps in my time, and those I liked best were the ones who did not squeal. I have applied for my bowler [hat – i.e., to retire] and am awaiting the result.[60]

But Brigadier J. S. 'Tubby' Lethbridge, who went to console Slim, was told bluntly: 'This happened to me once before, and I bloody well took the job of the man that sacked me. I'll bloody well do it again.'[61] On the same day Mountbatten learned from Brooke what Leese had done and sent for him immediately, telling him he had acted without authority and to reverse the changes forthwith. Reluctant to dismiss a second Commander-in-Chief, Brooke gave him no option. Mountbatten felt obliged to remove Leese in mid-June, replacing him at ALFSEA with Slim in July, by which time Slim was on leave, while Stopford stepped up to replace Slim and General Sir Miles Dempsey arrived to command Twelfth Army.[62]

On the night of 12/13 May the Japanese launched desperate night attacks against the northern point of the ridge being held by 4th/8th Gurkhas, during which battle Rifleman Lachhiman Gurung was awarded the VC.[63] Aung San arrived at Meiktila on 16 May to confer with Slim, who was impressed by his honesty: 'I could do business with Aung San', he said.[64] On 28 May Twelfth Army, based at Judson College in Rangoon, was formed from XXXIII Corps, which disbanded, while Fourteenth Army was withdrawn to India to prepare for the invasion of Malaya.[65]

Mountbatten prompted that the BNA be formally accepted as an ally at a meeting on 30 May. Nevertheless, most British troops regarded the BNA with deep suspicion as mere dacoits. 'The average BNA member is the most unmitigated thug that can be imagined', recorded Lieutenant-Colonel John Ashton in a post-operational report.

> Before the war dacoits abounded and kept the gaols full up. Now they have been released from their life sentences by the Jap, but armed to the teeth by us, and thus provided with the prospects of loot beyond the dreams of avarice ... Far too well I am afraid the future administration of this area will discover.[66]

And the BNA's contribution to the Allied victory was nugatory compared with that of the minorities, who were scathing of Mountbatten's acceptance of Aung San's choice of 'Burmese Patriotic Forces' (BPF) for the BNA's new title (although they were known as Local Burmese Forces to the British until 29 June).[67]

With 28th Army holed up in the Pegu Yomas, and with 15th and 33rd Armies scattered east of the Rangoon–Mandalay road or retreating through the Shan Hills towards Tenasserim, 24th Independent Mixed Brigade attempted to protect the coasts between Moulmein and Tavoy, where the Burma–Thai railway emerged. At Toungoo a new and grandiosely named formation, Army Group Phoenix, was established with 56th Division and elements of 15th Division and 15th Army to block the Mawli road and the Salween against 19th Indian Division, while the main body of 55th Division was transferred to Indo-China, where Ho Chi Minh was installed in Cao Bang province, fed by OSS weapons.[68] All these moves made no sense if the objective was that Burma be held at all costs. Thailand remained quiet, but the *Kempeitai* were not fooled. Despite the technical state of war with the Allies, many sections of the Thai élite had liaised with the British and Americans from the outset. Indeed, Phibun himself tried to make contact and turned a blind eye to anti-Japanese resistance activity, even at the highest level of the administration, and, with the Allies preparing to invade Malaya and Thailand from Burma, Thailand was *de jure* an enemy but *de facto* an ally.[69]

Japanese forces were now in total disarray. Private Aida Yuji was with a lieutenant charged with collecting stragglers at a rendezvous point, where many were dying of disease. He was shocked to be awakened by the sound of Burmese villagers raiding the corpses, smashing open the heads with rocks to steal the teeth, even of those not yet dead.[70] As the British tried

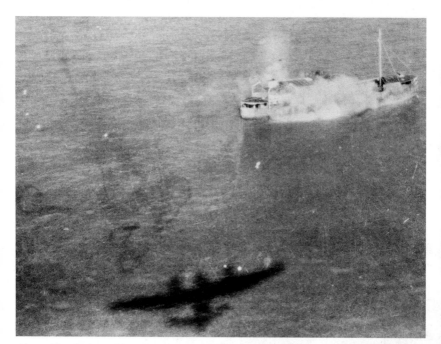

*Above:* The shadow of an RAF Beaufighter is thrown on the sea as it attacks a Japanese merchant vessel off Elephant Point, near Rangoon, July 1944. Cannon shells are to be seen bursting along the ship's hull

*Right:* Men of 2nd Durham Light Infantry from 2nd Division meet the Sikh crew of a Stuart tank from 7th Light Cavalry on the Kohima–Imphal road, 22 June 1944

*Left:* An American 75mm pack howitzer pounds the Myitkyina garrison, surrounded by nine hours' worth of empty cases. Note that its normal wheels with pneumatic tyres have been replaced with local wooden ones

*Below:* Improvisation was the watchword in Burma where transport posed the greatest problems. Here Jeeps have been modified for use by 36th Division in the 'Railway Corridor' by the addition of rail wheels

Air attack on a bridge. The bomb bursts are caused by the aircraft that have gone in ahead of this RAF Liberator

On 14 December 1944, by special permission of King George VI, Slim was knighted in a ceremony at Imphal by Wavell, Viceroy of India, with Mountbatten looking on

*Left:* The divisional badge of 82nd (West African) Division was two crossed spears passing through a head-pad, symbolizing 'Through carriers we fight'. It recognized the importance of the auxiliary groups who carried heavy loads by head in traditional African manner

*Below:* Opportunities for relaxation were rare but often included sport. A cricket match also provided the basis for one of the more unusual deception schemes of the war

At 1,154 feet the bridge across the Chindwin at Kalewa was the longest floating bridge in the world

Landing craft with troops wading ashore to capture Akyab

*Above:* River transport had been the lifeblood of Burma, but the effective destruction of the Irrawaddy Flotilla Company in 1942 meant that trade ground to a halt. When the Allies returned in early 1945 the IEME found MV *Ontario* beached with 300 tons of silt in her

*Left:* A young Burmese guerrilla armed with a Sten submachine-gun

A 5.5-inch gun of 134th Medium Regiment RA engages Fort Dufferin over open sights. The gun barrel has been shortened here in an effort to extend the gun's life

A Stinson L-5 communications aircraft used by 615 Squadron RAF comes in to land at a sandy airstrip on the Arakan front on 29 March 1945. The L-5 evacuated many hundreds of casualties from front-line positions as well as serving (as here) as a communications plane

*Left:* A dead Japanese soldier in the bottom of a pit after waiting for an Allied tank to roll over it, when he would detonate the aerial bomb between his knees

*Below:* Japanese officers surrender their swords. Until the 1930s it was said Tokyo sword makers were a dying profession, but by 1940 business was booming

to establish a cordon on the Pegu Yomas in which 28th Army was seeking refuge, 33rd Army was to defend the east bank of the Sittang and harass the British along the Mandalay–Rangoon road, and also to provide supplies along 28th Army's expected breakout route.[71] The Pegu Yomas, running 75 miles north–south and 30 miles east–west, were not high but they were densely wooded. Sakurai's overriding problem would be crossing the Sittang, and he divided Operation Mai into four phases: concentration, preparation, breakout across the Sittang plain and river, and reconstruction in the Bilin area. Once they reached the Pegu Yomas, the 27,000 men of 28th Army had to train for the breakout on 20 July, to be known as X-Day. Since so many of the personnel were nurses, oil technicians or civilians, special river-crossing units were formed and since all training manuals had been lost, Army Headquarters condensed field service instructions into a song called 'Break through the Enemy' which translated literally (without metre or rhythm) went:

> To break through the enemy is not difficult
> You can find a way out of difficulties if you forget self-desires and
>     lingering affections. Become thoroughly imbued with the spirit to die
>     a heroic and honourable death.
> Armed with a thorough understanding of Imperial Rescripts, a strong
>     *esprit de corps* and an indomitable spirit, advance in high spirits.[72]

When 54th Division had broken off contact at Paukkaung on 17 June, they had had to abandon the remainder of their heavy equipment, including all guns over 75mm calibre. Rations were already short, amounting to just 400g of rice per day, and foraging was difficult in the sparsely populated Yomas; bamboo shoots were mixed with edible grasses and whatever fish and game could be found, including snakes, snails and lizards. Suffering from salt deficiency and with clothing and boots disintegrating in the monsoon rain, despair set in among men unable to light cooking fires. As they moved to their concentration points on the eastern side of the range, the number of suicides increased and the hills reverberated with grenades detonating.[73]

With 50,000 Japanese still in Burma and these 'yellow vermin' making for Thailand, Park instituted 'a Jap-killing competition between squadrons and wings'.[74] For Twelfth Army administrative difficulties remained enormous, with vehicles having completed 10–16,000 miles, usually in country without proper roads, so that all needed servicing desperately. The mules had also marched every step from Imphal, always in sodden saddlery carrying soaked and gruelling loads; they and their drivers led a miserable life.[75] And there was not only the army to supply. At Kalaw on 8 June Maureen Baird-Murray and her little friends saw movement at the bottom of the hill and watched in fascination, as crawling towards them came

> men not with yellow faces, but bright brick-red ones. Certain that they were British, we threw caution to the winds and beckoned the soldiers on, unable to stop jumping up and down with excitement … How we stared at them, noting the differences in uniform and colouring, and their strange English voices, so long unheard. Now for the first time and to our complete surprise and delight we heard that the war in Europe was over.

The soldiers promised to return the following day and did so with food. 'From now on they called every day, loaded with all kinds of food in tins, packets and sacks, food we hadn't seen for years such as bacon, butter, margarine, bully beef, sausages, even toothpaste and soap, but best of all sweets and chocolates.'[76]

In the low-lying marshy ground 7th Indian Division was attacked as it drew up to the Sittang on 3 July by 53rd Division – some 2,000 men – towards Myittha, and 18th Division launched 1,000 men towards Nyaungkashe and Abya, putting 4th/8th Gurkhas under great pressure so that every man in the RAP was killed or wounded. As Lieutenant Farrow of 1st/11th Sikhs noted: 'Never, perhaps has the term "fluid" been more aptly applied to operations.'[77] The brigadier in temporary command of the division ordered a withdrawal, which was completed along a corridor provided by 4th/15th Punjabis, but the Japanese also withdrew, having taken heavy losses.[78] Eighteenth Division's attempts to launch guerrilla attacks were no more successful.[79] John Randle's Pathan company of 7th/10th Baluch blocked one exit, at the same time escorting an experimental mortar unit portered by elephants. Randle soon discovered that elephants consume vast quantities of greenery, and within a couple of days the well-camouflaged position was eaten bare and obvious. The elephants also produced vast amounts of dung,

> which in the hot monsoon conditions attracted equally vast numbers of flies and a hefty 'pong'. The Indian soldier, for religious and cultural reasons, was very averse to handling any sort of excrement. The company sweeper insisted that he had been enlisted to deal with human excrement, not elephant, and in any case he could not be expected to dig it down because any hole soon filled up with monsoon water.

Eventually Randle persuaded his Pathans to shift the dung on the grounds that they had shifted mule dung earlier in the war, and an elephant was sort of a big mule.[80]

The breakout began during the night of 20/21 July and continued at maximum intensity for four days, after which it declined as the broken Japanese forces reached and crossed the Sittang river. The Japanese had learned that the British were destroying all the country boats on the river and prepared to build rafts as 28th Army made for an area known as the 'Sittang Bend'.[81] It was largely a gunners battle: infantry patrols would locate the enemy and immediately call for artillery and air support. Airburst was used to good effect, as borne out by Japanese reports.[82] The reason was that crucial translation of captured documents had revealed the movement orders of the Shinbu Detachment, and by inference, 28th Army. With its brigades strung out along the Sittang – 17th Indian Division alone covered a 74-mile front – IV Corps could not hope to block every exit from the Yomas or every crossing point of the river, but it could cover them with fire while BPF forces would attack any that made it across. Major-General W. A. Crowther, the new GOC 17th Indian Division, planned accordingly.[83] At Maunggyi, Havildar Bharat Singh of 1st/19th Hyderabad led his platoon into the attack, where they killed 115 Japanese, by now so weak and exhausted they were barely able to resist.[84]

As the Japanese poured out of the Pegu Yomas, John Masters received an intelligence report from Force 136 saying that at a given time and map reference four captured jeeps, five captured British lorries of 1941 vintage and forty-three Japanese lorries had been observed. These vehicles contained: 'of Engineers – 23 privates, 4 corporals, 2 sergeants, 1 captain (probably Captain Shimeyoki Masatsu); of Artillery – 78 gunners, 23 corporals, 9 sergeants, 4 lieutenants, 1 captain, 1 major (probably Major Banzai Hideki) ...' It was the most detailed intelligence report Masters had ever seen, and nobody was inclined to believe it at first, until he remembered a man from the Chindits called John Hedley had joined Force 136, and recognized his work. He could imagine Hedley peering into the backs of lorries and opening sacks.[85] Aubrey Trofimov was operating with Team Mongoose South when he learned that some Karen levies were fighting to stop some Japanese crossing the Shwegyin river, a tributary of the Sittang. They held a section 2 miles long and dug in.

> The Japs would come out at dawn or sometimes just before dark, and they would come out in masses, some staying on the banks firing at us. They built rafts of bamboo. It got to such point that the odds were a bit against us. We called the RAF who were very effective, so we found out later.[86]

One morning in July Randle was shaving and enjoying his morning char at his company redoubt, centred on a cockroach-infested rice mill on the Rangoon–Pegu–Toungoo road, when he heard much laughter and Pushtu wisecracking. His orderly reported with a broad grin that a patrol had intercepted a group of 'comfort girls'. Not keen on Pathan leg-pulling so early in the morning, he investigated and found six clean, tidy and cheerful girls and reported to Battalion Headquarters. Eventually, while the Pathans enjoyed chatting them up, a party of Military Police arrived to escort the girls away. That evening Randle discussed the unusual events of the day over dinner with his redoubtable second-in-command, Subedar Moghal Baz MC, who commented that the day had, indeed, been unique. 'How so Subedar Sahib?' Randle asked. 'In all my service,' replied the Subedar, who had seen much hard fighting in Waziristan and the North-West Frontier besides Burma, 'I have never seen either women or military police in a front-line position. Today we have had both.'[87]

In July Twelfth Army killed 11,500 Japanese for the loss of 96 killed.[88] Japanese prisoners were kept stripped to their shorts in a cage of bamboo poles by the Sittang, where every so often men would come to stare at them

> as if they were some form of nocturnal animal. Up on the banks was posted a Bren gunner with a slate watching the Sittang roll by. A number of Japanese were trying to cross it and being swept down, some dead, some floating and playing dead, some clinging to flotsam. Each received a burst, and a resulting cry or a convulsion was recorded with a tick on the slate.[89]

Although the Japanese tried to avoid contact where possible to avoid further casualties, they still only expected to evacuate a third of their strength. Yet by 5 August 17th Indian Division had counted 4,500 bodies and taken 500 prisoners. Bodies had been counted floating down the Sittang at a rate of 200 per day during daylight hours alone (not included in the total). Many areas where the guns had caught large numbers of the enemy had not been visited. Only 7,000 managed to reach the camps of Tenasserim and they were wracked with malaria and dysentery, their feet swollen by beriberi. The rest were cut down by Twelfth Army or drowned in the Sittang, from where their bodies floated out into the Gulf of Martaban. Yet Sakurai and Iwakuro both declared the army's 'bold determination to seek life in the midst of death and break defiantly through the enemy' a success.[90] In Thailand, Allied prisoners witnessed the state of returning Japanese wounded, and many were deeply moved despite their own harsh treatment. 'They were in a shocking state', wrote Ernest Gordon; 'I have never seen men filthier. The uniforms were encrusted with mud, blood and excrement. Their wounds, sorely inflamed and full of pus, crawled with maggots.'[91]

# 26

# Return

> They say there's a troopship just leaving Bombay,
> Bound for Old Blighty's shore.
> Heavily laden with time-expired men,
> Bound for the land they adore.
> There's many a soldier just finishing his time,
> There's many a twerp signing on.
> You'll get no promotion, this side of the ocean.
> So cheer up my lads, bless 'em all.
>   Jimmy Hughes, Frank Lake and Al Stillman, *Bless 'em All*

O N 6 AUGUST, as the last remnants of the diseased and starving 28th Army reached the relative safety of the east bank of the Sittang, an atomic bomb was dropped on Hiroshima; three days later another was dropped on Nagasaki. This act has remained contentious ever since, not least among former Allied servicemen.[1] 'I am glad the bomb confined my war,' wrote Patrick Davis, 'for after one campaign I wanted no more of it.'[2] J. Francis Clifford, a twenty-year-old private, was the only survivor of a quintet conscripted together.

> Towards the end I was becoming more and more depressed. I was fed up with being a survivor. Fictional heroes survive violent death time after time and still come up smiling ready to go through it all again; it is not so, you get burned out inside, then you have had enough.[3]

It was not the atomic bombs alone that convinced Japan to surrender; in Mountbatten's opinion they were only an excuse to surrender without loss of face.[4] The decisive factor was the USSR's declaration of war and rapid sweep through Manchuria, an event the Soviets brought forward in an attempt to forestall the Americans. The Supreme War Council debated fiercely whether to accede to the Allies' demand for unconditional surrender: it took Hirohito's personal intervention to secure agreement. In Saigon, Terauchi was still determined to fight on, and only the arrival of

Prince Chichibu persuaded him to accept the Imperial will. Terauchi had ordered the deaths of all prisoners once the invasion of South-East Asia proper began, planned for 6 September, and the timing of the atomic bombs was thus crucial to their survival: equally the apocalyptic nature of the atomic weapon allowed Japanese forces to withdraw with honour from a war that might otherwise have been fought to a bitter end.[5]

In Burma itself there were great difficulties in establishing communications for surrender, especially with an army that shunned the entire concept. Stopford in Rangoon first heard of the possibility on 11 August and ordered Twelfth Army to suspend active operations on the 15th.[6] Isolated parties of Japanese wandering eastwards knew nothing of it, however, and Stopford's intelligence had a better knowledge of Japanese dispositions than Kimura did. Fittingly, a unit of 17th Indian Division made the first contact; on 22 August a patrol of 6th/15th Punjabis met a group of eight Japanese who offered to surrender, and a meeting was arranged for two days later at Abya.[7] Lieutenant-Colonel Brian Montgomery (brother of the Field Marshal) was commanding 6th/7th Rajputs and sent to the Salween to accept the surrender of 33rd Army. General Honda was most co-operative and everything went ahead in perfect discipline.[8] Meanwhile, having reached Martaban on 18 August, Sakurai was still trying to contact his scattered remnants through *Gunshi* – peace envoys – permitted by the British to try and bring them in. Japanese officers were brought from Bangkok with copies of the Imperial Surrender edict and, knowing full well how these might be received, the text continued:

> This is not a hoax by the British. The army is sending continuing reconnaissance flights, but there is to be no more bombing over the entire front. The fact that you cannot hear it any more will seem very strange, but it is proof that the war is at an end. It is imperative that you trust this order, dismissing all doubt from your minds.[9]

On 23 August Headquarters 33rd Army broadcast a signal: 'According to a broadcast from the BBC in London on 22 August, 200 Japanese troops who have not heard of the surrender of the Japanese Army in Burma are in conflict with British forces on the move south through Shwegyin down the east bank of the Sittang.' It was astonishing for a hostile army in the field to discover what was happening on its own doorstep through the BBC, but typical of the situation of the broken Japanese armies in August 1945.[10] The *Gunshi* were escorted by BPF parties. Dr Maung Maung did this for a fortnight, watching while the soldiers stood rigid, rapt. At the end they would crumble to the ground, weeping, and tear the earth with frantic hands. Some would attempt *Hara Kiri*, and it took an effort on the part of the major to stop them. One lieutenant was fast. He just crumbled in a heap, pulled off the pin of his grenade and blew himself up before our eyes.[11]

Some groups were still groping their way eastwards in September. In Rangoon a victory parade was held for which new uniforms and medal ribbons were flown in especially from Calcutta.[12]

Within weeks the process of recovery of prisoners of war and internees (RAPWI) was under way. On 27 August Japanese delegates at Rangoon signed a preliminary agreement ordering local Japanese commanders to assist and obey British commanders of reoccupation forces. The first five RAF Dakotas landed at Bangkok the following day to fly the first batches of prisoners to India, and then home.[13] On 5 September 5th Indian Division landed with a small British RAPWI team and mass evacuation began, happening so quickly that by the time Australian and Indian teams arrived, many of their compatriots had already been sent home, although the many thousands of native labourers were less well cared for.[14] Many prisoners had kept secret diaries (and risked their lives doing so) and since the war dozens of accounts have been published.[15] H. Robert Charles, a Marine aboard USS *Houston* when she was sunk after the battle of the Java Sea on 1 March 1942, was taken first to Singapore and then to inland from Moulmein at the end of October to work on the railway. For the following fourteen months his hero was Dr Henri Hekking, a Dutchman who kept many men alive long after they would have perished from amoebic dysentery, malarial fevers, beriberi or pellagra.[16] Of approximately 61,000 Dutch, British, Australian and American prisoners forced to work on the railway, some 13,000 (21 per cent) died. Of 270,000 Asians no fewer than 90,000 died, a figure that amounted to one death for every sleeper laid on the railway. Thanks to Dr Hekking's skill his group suffered only 7 per cent mortality. But completion of the railway was not the end of their ordeal.

With the war's end Lady Mountbatten visited Kanburi, where the Americans told her that were it not for Dr Hekking they would be dead. She asked to be presented to Hekking.

> Poor Doc ... There was the wife of the Supreme Allied Commander of South-East Asia, shaking his hand, thanking him for the splendid job he had done, smiling in her royal benevolent fashion, and there was Doc looking down, suddenly realizing all he had on was a pair of skivvy shorts. But then, considering the shape the prisoners were in, so skinny and all, it's doubtful she even noticed.[17]

The railway remains contentious to this day. Abe Hiroshi was a 2nd lieutenant in 5th Railway Regiment:

> That movie, *Bridge on the River Kwai*, is complete fiction ... That wasn't the
> way it was. Our unit specialized in building bridges and only borrowed pris-
> oner labour from a prison-camp unit. We'd go there and ask, 'Can we have
> three hundred workers today?' The guard unit would then provide prison-
> ers and guards for them.[18]

Many of the guards came for Korea, which provided some 187,000 men
to the Imperial Japanese Army. But they were denied status and restricted
to menial and labouring tasks, while subject to the same brutal discipline,
as well as racial and verbal abuse. This they passed on to the prisoners, who
worked 'at bayonet point and under the bamboo rod, and [who] risked
their lives continually seeking for an opportunity to sabotage the bridge'.[19]
The Burma–Thailand railway was not the worst example of Japanese treatment of prisoners; nor was it the best. Its notoriety stemmed largely from
its scale, for it involved a third of a million people of remarkably hetero-
geneous background set to achieve a military purpose in total disregard of
the cost in human life and suffering. But this was a consequence of the
Japanese purpose, not an end in itself, as the Rape of Nanking had been.
Although there were many instances of individual cruelty, what most characterized the Japanese approach was neglect and maladministration. Camp
staff varied enormously, from hard but fair to venal and corrupt, and some
were undoubtedly sadistic, but by no means all.[20]

Screening of the Japanese for war criminals was a laborious and pains-
taking process; eventually some 1,700 were sent to Singapore for trial.
Among those arraigned was Abe, who had been conspicuous in his failure
to prevent the worst excesses of his subordinates. At his trial one of his
chief accusers was Cyril Wild, the liaison officer at the Songkrai Camp. 'I
saw his face every day', Abe recalled after the war, since it was to him that
Wild made his appeals, always saying that using prisoners of war for this
work was against the Geneva Convention.

> I told him, 'I have been ordered to build a bridge using you people. You're
> here to help. You will follow orders.' I didn't know anything about the
> Geneva Convention, except that something like it existed ... The rail unit
> had a regimental commander, battalion commanders and company com-
> manders. I was just a second lieutenant at the time, in command of a pla-
> toon. But I was the only officer Wild knew in 5th Railway Regiment ... I
> really didn't do anything wrong. It was my fate to go there. I just worked
> there.

Yet over three thousand men had died at Songkrai, and Abe was among those sentenced to death, although this was later commuted to fifteen years' imprisonment. For many years afterwards the Changi Club met once a year. 'We always end up talking about war-criminal issues like "Victor's justice". I think it's pretty damn selfish. We can't solve anything just by saying the victors tried the defeated. We first have to talk about the wrongs we committed.'[21]

In contrast to their behaviour during the war, after the surrender the Japanese willingly obeyed British orders, noted Captain Derek Ballance. 'They were so good, and so kind, and so obliging, and you would snap your fingers, anything you wanted, they would do it.'[22] Captain Rau's 30th Field Company IE was sent to Thailand to build a railway branch line with 5th Railway Regiment under command:

> They showed me special consideration as the only Asian officer in the Indian Engineers there ... it was difficult to believe these were the same men [who built the 'Death Railway'] working with us, so disciplined and obedient. The scene at the railway station when we departed was unbelievable. Half the female population was on the platform in tears waving farewell to their boy-friends. One resourceful lady turned up in Malaya later claiming that the Education Havildar was the father of her son ... Siam had been a very enjoyable sojourn for everyone.[23]

Following the surrender some 70,000 Japanese Surrendered Personnel (JSPs) remained in Burma and were employed on reconstruction tasks. In June 1946, over a three-week period, fourteen liberty ships repatriated about half. 'My parents were so happy to see me', recalled Lieutenant Yoshino Suichiro.[24] But not until March 1947 did repatriation of the rest begin, known as Operation Nipoff, finally ending in June.

The most noticeable result of the war in the East was the rise of nationalism throughout the region, among all peoples: winners, losers and spectators.[25] Subhas Chandra Bose went with the Japanese to Bangkok and was killed in an air crash on Formosa on 18 August 1945. Undoubtedly Bose was a man passionately committed to the cause of his country's freedom, but the INA showed a singular determination to surrender and were not well met by their loyal comrades; orders had to be given to provide them with a kinder welcome.[26] Although militarily insignificant, the INA made most impact after the war. Indian and American scholars have accepted the view that the role of the INA in Indian independence was vital, particularly the political impact of the subsequent Delhi trials.[27] Louis Allen, however, believed their role was less crucial, pointing out that the mood of the British people at the time – as evinced by their overwhelming rejection of Winston Churchill at the polls in July 1945 in favour of a reforming Labour government – had no interest in or intention of using force to repress Indian nationalism. The mood of post-war Britain has to be taken into account; the British, though triumphant, were dog tired of war, and this 'was the most important single factor in the British withdrawal, more so than anything that happened in India itself'.[28] This attitude came to a head in January 1946, when the ground crews of a number of RAF stations near Calcutta went on strike over delays in repatriation. The men offered no violence: indeed, they were formally respectful to their officers. They simply refused to obey orders until they received reassurances that their demands would be met. The implications of the incident were obvious: the British were no longer interested in governing an empire.[29] And as Partap Narain points out, when the Royal Indian Navy mutinied on 18 February and the Parachute Regiment in Malaya demanded immediate demob, it was plain the British were quite ready to leave. 'No further proof is necessary to repudiate INA's role in attaining our freedom.'[30]

The Python repatriation scheme rapidly denuded Burma and India of British troops. Suddenly orders were arriving for Release Groups to proceed for embarkation, first to India then to Britain. 'Whilst we were happy for them to be on their way home,' recalled one regimental history, 'it was a sad day in many ways for it did seem that the break-up of our efficient and highly trained "Family" was now starting ... To part with them after so many years together, perhaps never to meet again, was quite a wrench.'[31] With everyone going home it was not easy to say goodbye, not only between British comrades. 'Often in those days', said John Hill,

> we would be marching along, and on passing an Indian unit, someone would rush out and shake hands with a man in the ranks; or when halted some of the Gurkhas would come over, and grinning hugely, would utter a word, perhaps Kinu, Kabwet or Mandalay – and then we knew they had been with us there.[32]

Scott Gilmore found himself in charge of a trainload of soon to be released Tommies,

> singing, singing songs they had chorused nostalgically many times before to keep their spirits up. This time their spirits needed no lifting ... 'Waltzing Matilda', 'I Belong to Glasgow', 'Take Me Back to Dear Old Blighty', 'She was Poor But She Was Honest', and, especially appropriate, 'They Say There's a Troopship Just Leaving Bombay (Bless 'Em All)' ... For now they

really were headed homeward to Blighty, to sweethearts, mums and home fires.[33]

At the Homeward Bound Trooping Depot in Deolali, near Bombay, men were issued with a pamphlet called *Westward Bound: Advice and Help for your Journey Home.* Page 1 listed 'Duties to be carried out and jobs for which volunteers are required': listed first were the three least popular jobs in a soldier's life: guards, camp maintenance and working parties. Little wonder that waiting any longer for transport home than seemed absolutely necessary would send men 'doolaly'. Blighty was still far away. The camp's three cinemas changed their programme every three days and in one film a GI hero, on leave after winning the war in Burma, wooed the heroine with 'Gee Kid, we must get together. It's three months since I even saw a white woman!' The performance was brought to a premature end as the audience, many of whom had not seen a white woman for three years, tore the place to pieces.[34] For Denis Gudgeon it was only when reaching Merryfield Airfield at Taunton with some lengths of silk for his parents, and being made to pay duty by HM Customs and Excise, that 'I knew I was home!'[35]

However, for many British officers of Indian regiments it was different. With independence approaching, they were obviously surplus to requirements, but it took longer while the complicated arrangements were made. In July 1946 John Shipster finally took leave of 7th/2nd Punjab Regiment at Singapore after five and a half years overseas. He felt enormous sadness,

> for I had deep feelings of affection for all our Indian soldiers – Muslim, Sikh and Dogra. They had served the Raj with unstinting loyalty and were prepared, when called upon, to die for their Regiment (I say 'Regiment' quite deliberately, for that is where their focus of loyalty lay). Surat Singh, my young Sikh orderly, accompanied me and my baggage to the docks. He bade me farewell, saluted and said the Sikh battle cry '*Sat Sri Akal*' (God is strong), which I had heard so often. I didn't dare look back.[36]

On 3 January 1948 2nd Royal Berkshires left Rangoon on HMS *Scythia*, the last British battalion to leave the country. No one came to wave them off.[37]

Burma had changed. Set to write the history of NCAC, Edward L. Fischer noted that America's arrival in northern Burma was noticeable 'and a little disheartening. Tribesmen whose customs, dress, and ways of life were the same as those followed by their ancestors the night that Christ was born, soon began wearing olive drab caps, khaki shirts, and GI shoes, and eating from cans.'[38] Late in 1945 Muriel Degaa Upfill had to return to the

USA from India. Her adopted daughter Minty (Araminta was the nearest English equivalent to her Burmese name, which meant 'Bright Star') went back to Burma with Mi Mi Khaing as her guardian. Muriel promised to return when there was peace: but there was to be no peace. Maurice Maybury returned to help restore the administration of his beloved Burma, a task achieved with remarkable speed.[39] But its purpose now was to facilitate the transition to independence, a process fraught with difficulty. The AFO split on 19 August 1945, when the Communists left and Aung San headed the Anti-Fascist Peoples Freedom League (AFPFL).

The formulation of post-war British policy in Burma was tardy and uncertain because the colonial authorities struggled to understand the profound changes that had taken place. In Rangoon the price of eggs was forty-eight times what it had been three years earlier.[40] London's attention was focused largely on military matters and it assumed that the disastrous reduction in Burma's productive capacity – several million acres of rice land returned to semi-jungle and the cattle population reduced by a third – must be made good before any political measures could effectively be implemented. London completely failed to appreciate the new sense of national solidarity born of wartime suffering. While thoughtful Burmese understood that the shortage of technical, administrative and business experience was an obstacle, the elimination of British and Indian business interests left opportunities they were keen to exploit, and few wanted to postpone independence.[41] Churchill had been so anti-independence that he blocked repeated efforts by the exiled Burmese government to gain a statement on it until May 1945. The military authorities were equally harsh: in their view any Burmese collaborating with the Japanese was a traitor. The government-in-exile at Simla, including British civil servants, was sympathetic to the nationalist point of view and smarted under the aspersions cast on it by military and government in India on the usefulness of its 'holiday' activities during the Japanese occupation.[42] But two liberalizing factors were to hand: Mountbatten was inclined to promote the co-operation of moderate nationalist elements, and in July 1945 Clement Atlee's newly elected Labour government was far more sympathetic to Indian and Burmese aspirations than Churchill's administration had been. Atlee's election was an enormous surprise to Americans but not to the British, who were determined not to go back to where they were before the war. Most British soldiers were children of the depression and many came from slums. They were often stunted (the tallest in David Murray's platoon of 1st Camerons was 5 feet 9 inches); they expected nothing and were surprised by any kindness or interest shown in them. Their country had given them nothing more than the ability to read and write, and they wanted something better in their post-war world.[43]

Mountbatten knew that Burma might have to serve as a base for future operations and that he must work with the Burmese.[44] He protected Aung San from elements within the Burma government, something that was not lost on the Burmese, and his PR department gave Aung San wide publicity as an 'example of patriotic resistance within the British Empire'.[45] On leaving Burma in 1946, Dorman-Smith noted: 'We must, I think, accept as a fact that Aung San is the most important figure in Burma today. Everyone appears to trust and admire him ... his troops adore him and will do anything he says ... He has no ambition.'[46] On the latter point, however, Dorman-Smith was wrong: Aung San had one driving ambition, which was independence for his people.[47] It was Burma's misfortune to have been used as a base for the Japanese 'March on Delhi' and to have suffered from concentrated Allied air attacks against railways and other transportation facilities from 1943 onwards. All the cities along the main north–south axis suffered partial demolition, and the countryside was strewn with ordnance left by both sides. Burma paid a heavy price in destruction and dislocation for being a battlefield and the Burmese who sought to lead their country to the sunny uplands of independence found they had to take over a ruined country.[48] Akyab and Mandalay were mere shells; in Rangoon the railway station had been obliterated and many of the better buildings ruined or badly damaged. Those left were now in military hands, which were far from gentle. The British and Indians were greater vandals than the Japanese had been; parquet flooring and staircases were commonly used for firewood. The manager of a bank returned to find Indian troops using the hall as a cookhouse, with open fires on the marble paving. Owners of property had great difficulty in claiming compensation even where it was technically possible.[49]

Elections for constituent assemblies were duly held on 7 April 1947 and the AFPFL won an overwhelming majority to govern once independence was granted on 4 January 1948. On 19 July 1947 Pat Molloy was working in the Secretariat building when he was startled by machine-gun fire, followed by the sound of screeching tyres. He ran to investigate and, seeing an open doorway, found two soldiers prostrate. 'This was the doorway to the Council Chamber. I looked through and saw an unbelievable scene of carnage. Dead bodies were sprawled across the Council table in chairs or fallen under the table!'[50] Aung San and seven associates had been assassinated. Checks on stores were practically non-existent and Captain David Vivian, 'a small rat-like fellow', the sort 'who always remain in the Army

when better men are anxious to return to their peace time posts', was care-
less whom he sold weapons to, and this included U Saw.[51] But U Saw's
house was being watched and the police arrived soon after he had filled the
automatic that killed his rival with liquor and drunk from the barrel. The
trial was drawn-out but U Saw remained cheerful. When he stepped onto
the gallows he bid his gaolers 'Good morning', laughing as he mounted
the steps to the noose. Vivian was arrested and convicted for his part and
gaoled in Insein but then released in 1949, when Karen rebels occupied the
town. He stayed with them producing arms until killed by a Burma Army
patrol on 12 August 1950.[52]

Able and honest politicians were rare in Burma, and the country never
recovered from the shock. British commercial enterprises went to the
Burmese with terms favouring the latter. Emile Foucar was dismayed to be
presented with a form early in 1948, having practised law in Rangoon for
quarter of a century. 'Was it for this,' he asked, 'registration as foreigners, that
a few brief years ago many thousands of our race had died in the dark jungles and on the dusty stubble of those sunbaked paddy lands?'[53] Communist
insurrections and army mutinies in 1948 were followed by rebellions that
quickly spread among the Karens, Mons and other ethnic groups. As fighting raged on the doorstep of Rangoon, the parliamentary government of U
Nu only just survived. Following a few years of weak and ineffective 'democratic' government, a military coup under General Ne Win seized power in
1962 and Burma disappeared behind a bamboo curtain erected by the Burma
Socialist Programme Party. Far from quelling opposition, Ne Win's tactics
created a new cycle of insurgencies. At one stage the deposed prime minister U Nu also took up arms with the Karens and Mons in the Thai border-
lands, while China lent military backing to the Communist Party of Burma
via the mountainous north-east. The military has ruled with appalling
incompetence and venality ever since, 'a dotty combination of wholesale
nationalism, chauvinism, Buddhism and rejection of the modern world'.[54]
For seven years Muriel Degaa Upfill received regular letters from Minty,
who became a nurse and married. One carried a poignant message:
'Mummy, I'd love to see you, but I don't want you to come back. They treat
foreigners badly, and when you leave I'll never see you again.' Then all letters ceased. Finally, in 1964 she learned that Minty had died and Mi Mi
Khaing and her husband, Sao San Mong, were under house arrest.[55]

In July 1988 the 77-year-old Ne Win suddenly resigned, triggering pro-
democracy protests across the country that were crushed that September
when the military seized power, rebranding themselves the State Law and
Order Restoration Council. The old royal term Myanma, or the colloquial

'Bama' (corrupted to Burma), was decreed to represent only where Burmans lived until 1989, when the military government changed their mind and the country's name to Myanmar. They continued to persecute activists while promising elections, which were held in May 1990. The National League for Democracy, led by Aung San Suu Kyi – Aung San's daughter, who was two years old when he was murdered – won 392 out of 485 seats. But the junta refused to relinquish power and placed her under house arrest. She was awarded the Nobel Peace Prize in 1991. In 1995 Suu Kyi was released, but in 1999 she refused to accept the conditions imposed for her to visit her sick British husband, who subsequently died of cancer. The military continued to attack and arrest activists, and Suu Kyi was once more put under house arrest.[56] And still the hill peoples – Karens, Kachins, Shans, Mons and Muslim Arakanese – resist, the bitter testament to the success of SOE and OSS. And across the border to the west the Nagas have fought ever since independence from Britain for independence from India, a forgotten legacy of the forgotten war.[57]

Compton Mackenzie, on a visit to research his history of the campaign in 1948, found little at Sinzweya to remind him of recent events, 'except a few slit trenches gradually filling up. Cattle are grazing tranquilly. We sat beneath a tree and surveyed a scene of Arcadian peace.'[58] For most British and Americans, Burma rapidly faded from view, leaving only memories:

> a flooded foxhole, a battle-dress blouse drenched with sweat and rain, a leaky basha, an indescribable bush-hat, mepacrine tablets, rations dropping from a Dakota, a sudden burst of Bren fire shattering the silence of the jungle, the peculiar tinny crack of a Jap rifle, a tuktoo calling in a poongyikaung, stewed goat and tinned potatoes.[59]

For them at least the war was over, and Kimura's sword hung over Slim's mantelpiece, 'where I had always intended that one day it should be'.[60] John Shipster hoped that 'I was unscathed by my experiences, but even now I still sometimes wake up shouting after dreaming of Japanese encounters. There can be few things more frightening than close-quarter fighting in the dark against an enemy as ruthless as the Japanese.'[61] But society forgets all too quickly. The Union flag was raised over Rangoon by an Indian soldier, Mohammed Munsif Khan. After partition he worked in the Pakistan embassy in Beijing, then went to join his son in Britain. Owing to an administrative error he was stopped at Heathrow airport and the Home Office refused his application to stay. Disgusted by the deportation order, he returned his medals, including the Burma Star.[62] But Winifred Beaumont 'had the memory of many warm, if short, friendships with men and women of other races', and she had a souvenir, a piece of tin with 'the words "Lest We Forget" pricked out in holes made by a nail and the heel of a boot. A soldier's tribute to a dead comrade. Like a bad conscience, it lies at the bottom of my trunk, reminding me of a promise made and never kept.'[63]

# Notes

| AMSM | Army Medical Services Museum, Aldershot |
|------|------|
| AWM | Australian War Memorial, Canberra |
| BA | Broadlands Archive, Hartley Library, University of Southampton |
| CAC | Churchill Archives Centre, Churchill College, Cambridge |
| GM | The Gurkha Museum, Winchester |
| IWM | Imperial War Museum, London |
| LHCMA | Liddell Hart Centre for Military Archives, King's College, London |
| NA | National Archives, Washington DC |
| NAM | National Army Museum, London |
| NRHC | Northamptonshire Regiment History Committee, Museum and Art Gallery, Northampton |
| OIOC | Oriental and India Office Collection, British Library, London |
| PRO | Public Record Office, Kew |
| RAFM | Royal Air Force Museum, Colindale, London |
| RAHT | Royal Artillery Historical Trust, Firepower Museum, Woolwich |
| RCSM | Royal Corps of Signals Museum, Blandford Forum |
| RDSGM | Royal Scots Dragoon Guards Museum, Edinburgh |
| RHQDD | Regimental Headquarters, The Devonshire and Dorset Regiment, Exeter |
| RWKM | Queen's Own Royal West Kent Regiment Museum, Maidstone |
| SGM | Soldiers of Gloucestershire Museum, Gloucester |
| SRM | Staffordshire Regiment Museum, Lichfield |
| SOAS | School of Oriental and African Studies, London |
| TM | The Tank Museum, Bovington |
| WRM | Worcestershire Regiment Museum, Worcester |

## INTRODUCTION

1. S. Brookes, *Through the Jungle of Death*, p. ix.
2. F. N. Trager (ed.), *Burma*, p. 1.
3. R. Humphreys, *To Stop a Rising Sun*, p. 141.
4. R. Callahan, *Burma 1942–45*, pp. 161–4.
5. L. Allen, *Burma*, pp. 630–6, xix.
6. R. Storry, *A History of Modern Japan*, chaps. 7–10.

7. R. Baker, *Burma Post*, pp. 139—40.
8. Callahan, p. 32.
9. B. Tuchman, *Sand against the Wind*, p. 436.
10. E. L. Rasor, *The China—Burma—India Campaign 1931—1945*, p. 38.
11. Callahan, pp. 25—6. For a full account of America's pre-war views on a campaign in mainland China, see Edward J. Miller, *War Plan Orange*.
12. Tuchman, p. 213.
13. C. E. Lucas-Phillips, *The Raiders of Arakan*, Foreword.
14. N. N. Prefer, *Vinegar Joe's War*, p. 2.
15. J. Masters, *The Road past Mandalay*, p. 161.
16. Mountbatten of Burma, *Report to the Combined Chiefs of Staff*, p. 277.
17. C. Ogburn, *The Marauders*, p. 232.
18. IWM 17955/5, Major John Winstanley.
19. W. Pennington, *Pick up your Parrots and Monkeys*, p. 346.
20. J. Hill, *China Dragons*, p. 170.
21. G. MacDonald Fraser, *Quartered Safe Out Here*, p. 125.
22. D. Wilson, *The Sum of Things*, p. 127.
23. J. Nunneley, *Tales from the King's African Rifles*, pp. vii, 204. On the other hand, when asked if they would like to join the Burma Campaign Fellowship Group, all the former members of 9th Border Regiment declined, despite the fact that many held strong Christian beliefs. For a full discussion of attitudes to wartime enemies see Ian Buruma's *The Wages of Guilt: Memories of War in Germany and Japan*.
24. See, for example, E. Fursden, 'A Pilgrimage to Kohima and Imphal: 97 and More Remember', in *Army Quarterly and Defence Journal*, 124 (July 1994), pp. 295—9.
25. W. Beaumont, *A Detail on the Burma Front*, p. 107.
26. The Kohima Epitaph was composed by Major John Etty-Leal, GSO II at Headquarters 2nd Division, as an adaptation from one written during the First World War by J. Maxwell Edmonds, himself inspired by a Classical epigram commemorating the Spartans who held the pass at Thermopylae in 480 BC (G. S. MacKenzie, 'So Who *Really* Wrote the Kohima Epitaph?', in *Soldier*, 5 February 1996, and letter from N. L. Rylatt to *Soldier*, 18 March 1996). The memorial itself was created by men of 2nd Division, the principal feature being a great monolith brought down by Naga tribesmen. It was designed by Lieutenant J. W. Ferrie RE, a Glasgow architect, and most of the engraving was done by Craftsman M. Cresswell REME with tools provided by Sapper C. D. Shirley RE. It was unveiled at a ceremony in November 1944. The original copper plates with the roll of honour were replaced by stone when local bandits stole the originals to make bullets (G. Forty, *XIV Army at War*, p. 46n.). Today Garrison Hill, not far from the cemetery, is the site of a striking Catholic cathedral, built as a memorial.

# 1 BURMA AND THE BRITISH

1. J. Lunt, 'A Hell of a Licking', p. 23; Imperial Sunset, p. 347.
2. M. M. Khaing, Burmese Family, p. 111.
3. Founded in 1865, it became perhaps the greatest single commercial inland water transportation operation in the world. For a history of this extraordinary colonial enterprise see A. McCrae and A. Prentice, Irrawaddy Flotilla. See also A. McCrae et al., Tales of Burma, for a series of first-hand accounts of pre- and early-war Burma.
4. Lunt, 'A Hell of a Licking', pp. 31–3.
5. Begun in October 1937 and completed in early 1939, it was 'a magnificent piece of engineering, built by Chinese labour, not with bulldozers and mechanical equipment, but with picks and shovels, wielded by thousands of people. Hewn mostly out of the solid rock of the mountain sides, the debris was removed, on their heads, by women with small wicker baskets … Thousands must have died' (M. C. Cotton, Hurricanes over Burma, p. 288). Indeed, as many as four out of every five coolies – men, women and children – died from bombs, exposure and sickness. The story of this astonishing achievement is told in Tan Pei-ying's The Building of the Burma Road, and Squadron Leader Gerald Samson's The Burma Road.
6. L. Allen, Burma, pp. 7–9.
7. S. W. Short, On Burma's Eastern Frontier, p. 15.
8. See N. R. Chakravarti, The Indian Minority in Burma: The Rise and Decline of an Immigrant Community.
9. For a scholarly history of Burma, see J. F. Cady, A History of Modern Burma, which provides a detailed overview of Burmese history up to the immediate post-war period, and D. G. E. Hall, Burma. Accounts of the British occupation of Burma can be found by Godfrey Harvey, British Rule in Burma 1824–1942, and Terence Blackburn, The British Humiliation of Burma. For a thorough examination of the political and social consequences of the conquest, see Thant Myint-U, The Making of Modern Burma. For detailed military accounts, see George Bruce, Burma Wars, 1824–86; Major Snodgrass's eyewitness account of The Burmese War (1824–1826); William Laurie, The Second Burmese War: A Narrative of Operations at Rangoon (first published in 1863 and since reissued); and Anthony Stewart's account of the Third Burma War, The Pagoda War.
10. M. Glover, That Astonishing Infantry, pp. 92–3.
11. Cady, p. 125.
12. Cady, pp. 138–41. Dacoit, defined legally, referred to armed robbery involving five or more people, but was employed generally to refer to any such civil or guerrilla activity. D. E. Omissi, The Sepoy and the Raj, p. 220.
13. For an account of the rice-milling business in the 1930s, see C. Lorimer, 'Rice Paddy – and Some By-Products', in McCrae et al., Tales of Burma.
14. Cady, pp. 156–63.
15. M. Collis, The Journey Outward, pp. 121–2. Collis's four autobiographical

books provide an excellent description of Burma in the first half of the twentieth century. Other autobiographical accounts of pre- and early-war Burma include A. J. S. White's *The Burma of 'AJ'*, Maurice Maybury's *Heaven-Born in Burma*,vol. 1, *The Daily Round*, and the memoirs of another civil servant, L. Glass's *The Changing of Kings*. S. M. Morris (ed.), *Long Ago, Far Away: The Burma Diaries of Doris Sarah Eastman*, is the diary of a teacher during the First World War and 1920s; P. Elliott's *The White Umbrella* describes life through the eyes of a Shan princess sold into marriage; M. Hearsey, *Land of Chindits and Rubies*, was written by an Anglo-Burmese married to an Irish Burma policeman. Another Burma policeman, Bill Tydd, published his memoirs of service between 1929 and 1942, *Peacock Dreams*. Harold Braund's *Distinctly I Remember* and Emile Foucar's *I Lived in Burma* are the memoirs of a magistrate and solicitor respectively. Neville Windsor, born in Pegu, describes the effects of war in a typical Eurasian family in *Burma: Land of my Dreams*. J. H. Williams in *Elephant Bill* describes the pre-war working life in the teak forests with its elephants. See also Charles Braimer Jones, *Not Forgetting the Elephants*, and Gordon Hunt's *The Forgotten Land*. There are descriptions of various businesses in Alistair McCrae et al., *Tales of Burma*, and Nicholas Greenwood (ed.), *Shades of Gold and Green: Anecdotes of Colonial Burmah 1886–1948*. Muriel Sue Degaa Upfill's *An American in Burma 1930–1942* gives the most lively description of Rangoon and Pegu, while Harry S. Hengshoon, the son of a Chinese businessman, describes his childhood in Bassein and Rangoon in *Green Hell*. Katherine Read with John Ballou describes life in a missionary hospital in *Bamboo Hospital*. Among fictional accounts of pre-war Burma the most famous is George Orwell's *Burmese Days*. Other fictional accounts include Maurice Collis's *She Was a Queen* (1951) and *Siamese White* (1965) and F. Tennyson Jesse's *The Lacquer Lady* (1929).

16. Cady, pp. 170–5.

17. For a full account of the development of Burmese nationalism and the British response to separation, see Albert D. Moscotti, *British Policy and the Nationalist Movement in Burma, 1917–37*.

18. M. Collis, *Trials in Burma*, p. 209.

19. Cady, pp. 307–9; Foucar, pp. 14, 24, 209–10; and J. Becka, *The National Liberation Movement in Burma during the Japanese Occupation Period (1941–1945)*, pp. 34–43.

20. See Robert H. Taylor, *Marxism and Resistance in Burma, 1942–1945*, pp. 1–92, for a discussion of the significance of Communist ideas in Burmese nationalism, before and during the war.

21. Khaing, pp. 94–8. See also K. Sein and J. A. Withey, *The Great Po Sein*, for a description of Burmese puppet theatre before and during the war.

22. Cady, pp. 382–3. Aung San's daughter the Nobel Peace Prize winner Aung San Suu Kyi wrote a short personal pen portrait of the father she hardly knew – *Aung San of Burma* – in 1982. Aung San's own writings, heavily edited, were published by Dr Maung Maung in 1962 under the same title. For a recent, detailed and thorough appraisal of Aung San's contribution to the Burmese

independence movement, see Angeline Naw, *Aung San and the Struggle For Burmese Independence*.

23. Dr Maung Maung, *To a Soldier Son*, p. 12.
24. C. McPhedran, *White Butterflies*, pp. 80–1.
25. A. Draper, *Dawns like Thunder*, p. 21.
26. Churchill was obviously racist, but US President Franklin D. Roosevelt – the champion of colonial people – later wrote to Churchill to say he had never liked the Burmese, 'and you people must have had a terrible time with them for the last fifty years … I wish you could put the whole bunch of them into a frying pan with a wall around I and let them stew in their own juice.' C. T. Thorne, *Allies of a Kind*, pp. 5–6.
27. For the most complete recent biography of Chiang, see Jonathan Fenby's *Generalissimo*.
28. Cady, p. 412.
29. There are a number of biographies of Chandra Bose. *The Lost Hero*, by Mihir Bose, is lively, while Gerard Corr's *The War of the Springing Tigers* tries to link him with a mutiny in 1915. Perhaps the best is Hugh Toye's *The Springing Tiger*. More recent is Leonard A. Gordon's definitive dual biography of Subhas and his brother Sarat, *Brothers against the Raj*. See also S. C. Maikap, *Netaji Subhas Chandra Bose and Indian War of Independence*.
30. E. L. Fischer, *The Chancy War*, pp. 60–1.
31. Ba Maw, *Breakthrough in Burma*, pp. 61–2.
32. H. G. Wells, *Travels of a Republican Radical in Search of Hot Water*, pp. 84–8.
33. A. J. Barker, *The March on Delhi*, p. 21.
34. Ba Maw, pp. 114–5. Ba Maw had already been sounded out through his dentist, another Suzuki, who put him in touch with various naval officers.
35. Cady, pp. 420–1. On Burmese loyalty, the British preferred to claim disturbances were inspired by economic rather than political tension, since this did not reflect so badly on imperial self-image (F. Furedi, 'The Demobilized African Soldier', in D. Killingray and D. Omissi, *Guardians of Empire*, p. 184). Ministry of Information officials were instructed to 'stress that Burman dissatisfaction with British rule, in so far as it is implied in the collaboration of certain elements with the Japanese, is due principally to economic causes' (OIOC M-3–863, 'Extract from MOI Guidance no. 65, dated 8 April 1942').
36. M. Collis, *Last and First in Burma (1941–1948)*, p. 22.
37. I. Morrison, *Grandfather Longlegs*, pp. 62–9; Naw, pp. 62–3. Controversy over Aung San's secret departure from Burma remains, with Ba Maw dissenting from the generally accepted view.
38. Naw, pp. 62–3; L. Allen, *Burma*, pp. 17–20. See also Document no. 1, 'Plan for the Burma Operation Drawn by Colonel Suzuki Keiji, Chief of the Minami Organ, December 1941', in Trager (ed.), pp. 27–31. For the complete story of this mission see Izumiya Tatsuro, *The Minami Organ*, and Yoon W-Z., 'Japan's Scheme for the Liberation of Burma: The Role of the Minami Kikan and the Thirty Comrades', and OIOC MS Eur C614, 'A

History of the Minami Organ, compiled 1944, by Col. Sugii Mitsuru of the Burma National Army Advisory Dept, translated by H. Takahashi 1954, Giving an Outline Account of the Burma Independence Army 1935–42 (Ch. XXII missing)', and Ike Nobutaka, *Japan's Decision for War, Records of the 1941 Policy Conferences* (especially p. 122, the demand for closing the Burma Road by the Army Staff).

39. Cady, p. 438. For a list of the 'thirty comrades', see Trager (ed,), pp. 239–41.

40. Ba Maw, p. 139: L. Allen, *Burma*, pp. 557–9.

41. Cady, p. 437; Burma Intelligence Bureau, *Burma during the Japanese Occupation*, vol. 1, pp. 1–3.

42. P. Lowe, *Great Britain and the Origins of the Pacific War*, pp. 8–10, 134–5.

43. He had retired in 1937 and been recalled to service on the outbreak of war in Europe; at sixty-two he was too old for the task and often fell asleep during meetings. S. W. Kirby, *The War against Japan*, vol. 1, p. 56.

44. PRO CAB 65/23, 'War Cabinet Conclusions, confidential annex, 21 July 1941 (41) 72–(41) 107 1941 July 21–Oct. 30'; W. S. Churchill, *The Second World War*, vol. 3, pp. 161–72.

45. J. Kennedy, *The Business of War*, p. 108; PRO WO 106/2620, 'Malaya Campaign: Comments by Major-General Playfair: War Office Correspondence 1943 Nov–1944 Apr'.

46. PRO CAB 80/18, 'Memoranda nos. 701–750 1940 Sept. 2–Sept.15'; CAB 80/24, 'Report of the Singapore Defence Conference 1940'; CAB 79/8, 'Far East Tactical Appreciation and Report of Singapore Defence Conference'.

47. F. F. Liu, *A Military History of Modern China*, pp. 175–6.

48. PRO CAB 44/324, 'Draft Narrative of the First Burma Campaign December 1941–May 1942'.

49. McLeod was serving out the last four years of his service. Nearly sixty and with 'a white moustache, bronzed face and very tired eyes', he knew delay was the best that might be achieved. Lunt, '*A Hell of a Licking*', pp. 43, 62.

50. Sir A. Cochrane, 'Burma in Wartime', *Asiatic Review*, XXXVII (1941), pp. 681–94.

51. IWM 97/36/1, Lieutenant-Colonel I. C. G. Scott.

52. The best biography of Wavell remains John Connell's two-parter, *Wavell: Scholar and Soldier* (London, Collins, 1964) and *Wavell: Supreme Commander*. See also Ronald Lewin, *The Chief*, and Harold E. Raugh, *Wavell in the Middle East 1939–1941*.

53. Universally known as 'the Auk', Auchinleck was one of the most underrated British soldiers of the war, largely due to his being overshadowed in the Middle East by the egocentric Bernard Law Montgomery. For biographies, see John Connell, *Auchinleck: A Biography of Field Marshal Sir Claude Auchinleck*; Richard Parkinson, *The Auk: Auchinleck Victor at Alamein*; and Philip Warner, *Auchinleck: The Lonely Soldier*.

54. B. H. Liddell Hart (ed.), *The Rommel Papers*, p. 146. According to Rommel, Wavell was the 'only British general who showed a touch of genius'.

55. Connell, *Wavell: Supreme Commander*, p. 29.

56. B. Prasad (ed.), *The Retreat from Burma 1941–42*, p. 31.

57. T. Carew, *The Longest Retreat*, p. 11; Cady, pp. 412–9.

58. A. Wavell, *Despatch by the Supreme Commander*, p. 11; PRO WO 106/2666, 'Comment on Wavell's Dispatches by War Office'.

59. Kirby, vol. 2, pp. 10–11.

60. R. Spurr, *Let the Tiger Turn Tail: Spurr's War*, p. 41.

61. H. Probert, *The Forgotten Air Force*, pp. 82–3, 85.

62. D. G. E. Hall, p. 167.

63. No comprehensive history of the Burma Rifles as a regiment has been written, although shortly after the war *Standing Orders of the Second Battalion the Burma Rifles: With a Short Record of the Battalion* was published. See Lunt, *Imperial Sunset*, pp. 347–70, and 'The Burma Rifles', in *Journal of the Society of Army Historical Research*, LXXVI/307, 1998, pp. 202–7, written by a former officer of Burma Rifles, in which he discusses service with them and their wartime performance. Ann Purton's *The Safest Place* is the story of an army bride of the Burma Rifles. Her husband, Humphrey, served in the 4th Battalion, then the 5th.

64. Like the Burma Rifles, most such units have no histories except seemingly one, which served with distinction throughout the war: OIOC MS Eur Photo Eur 157, Histories of the Chin Hills Battalion 1894–1933 and 1942.

65. For a good overview of Burma's forces 1937–42, see http:homepages. force9.net/rothwell/burmaweb/index.htm.

66. Lunt, *Imperial Sunset*, is an overview of such service worldwide.

67. Kirby, vol. 2, pp. 8–9.

68. L. B. Oatts, *The Jungle in Arms*, p. 40.

69. Lunt, 'A Hell of Licking', pp. 45, 56.

70. Kirby, vol. 2, pp. 11–13.

71. PRO CAB 106/25, 'A Record of The 1st Bn. Gloucestershire Regt. (The 28th) in Burma, 1938–1942'.

72. For a superb soldier's description of life in India pre-war, see J. W. Pennington's *Pick up your Parrots and Monkeys*, chaps. 5–7.

73. PRO CAB 106/25.

74. J. Gaylor, *Sons of John Company*, pp. 53–4.

75. The best single-volume histories of the Indian Army are Philip Mason's *A Matter of Honour* and S. L. Menezes's *Fidelity and Honour: The Indian Army from the Seventeenth to the Twenty-First Century*. For detailed emphases on social aspects, subsistence and military justice, see David Omissi, *The Sepoy and the Raj: The Indian Army 1860–1940*, and H. S. Bhatia (ed.), *Military History of British India 1607–1947*; for the developments of the early twentieth century, see K. M. L. Saxena, *The Military System of India (1900–1939)*. For a comprehensive survey presenting both British and Indian perspectives, see T. A. Heathcote, *The Military in British India*. For a good concise overview of the Indian Army during the two World Wars, see Ian Sumner's *The Indian Army 1914–1947*.

76. Heathcote, p. 94.

77. S. H. A. Rizvi, *Veteran Campaigners: A History of the Punjab Regiment 1759–1981*, p. 98.

78. J. Shipster, *Mist on the Rice-Fields*, p. 19. For a full description of all the classes of Indian soldier and their homelands, see J. C. G. Lever, *The Sowar and the Jawan*.

79. S. Gilmore and P. Davis, *A Connecticut Yankee in the 8th Gurkha Rifles*, pp. 92–3.

80. F. W. Perry, *The Commonwealth Armies: Manpower and Organization in Two World Wars*, pp. 97–8.

81. C. Chevenix Trench, *The Indian Army and the King's Enemies 1900–1947*, pp. 134–5.

82. D. P. Marston's *Phoenix from the Ashes* is a study of development of the Indian Army through the cauldron of the Burma campaign, starting with the establishment of the IMA and indianization, and showing how by 1945 it was significantly different from 1939 – flexible, innovative, more culturally representative and highly professional.

83. Perry, p. 115. Compton Mackenzie quotes figures for 1 July 1939 of 183,000 Indian troops commanded by 2,978 British and 528 Indian officers and by 1 July 1945 over 2,250,000 men, 37,187 British and 13,355 Indian officers (*Eastern Epic*, p. 1). It was unquestionably the largest all-volunteer army in history.

84. See Marston, chap. 2, 'The Gathering Storm: Expansion of the Indian Army, 1939–41', and B. Prasad (ed.), *Expansion of the Armed Forces and Defence Organization*.

85. D. Atkins, *The Reluctant Major*, p. 97.

86. H. B. Rattenbury, *China–Burma Vagabond*, p. 252.

## 2 JAPAN AND CHINA

1. For a discussion of how Western intervention following Commodore William Perry's expedition of 1853 produced a military revolution in Japan, see Meirion and Susie Harries, *Soldiers of the Sun*.

2. H. K. Beale, *Theodore Roosevelt and the Rise of America to World Power*, p. 174.

3. P. Elphick, *Far Eastern File*, p. 20.

4. There are numerous studies of Japanese policy and the road to war. Michael A. Barnhart, in *Japan Prepares for Total War*, discusses her search for economic security and the gradual moulding of that quest into an attempt to acquire a resource-rich zone on mainland Asia; this desire developed into one for empire and then for war.

5. Lowe, pp. 4–6.

6. E. Niderost, 'Dress Rehearsal for a World War', in *WWII History*, vol. 2/6, November 2003, pp. 36–45.

7. D. Wilson, *When Tigers Fight*, pp. 6–7. For those wishing to investigate the Sino-Japanese War in detail, see James Hsiung and Steve Levine's *China's*

*Bitter Victory* or Hsu Long-hsuen's mammoth *History of the Sino-Japanese War (1937–1945)*; condensed from 100 volumes into 642 pages, it gives the history from the Nationalist side, starting with the Mukden Incident in 1931, covering 23 campaigns, 1,117 battles and 9 million casualties, and concluding that the war was started by the Communists and the Soviet Union.

8. Lowe, pp. 10–11. For a biography see L. Mosley, *Hirohito: Emperor of Japan*. For more recent revisionist treatments see Edward Behr's *Hirohito*, Peter Wetzler's *Hirohito and War* and Herbert P. Bix's *Hirohito and the Making of Modern Japan*.

9. L. Allen, *Burma*, pp. 284–5.

10. W. H. Chamberlin, *Japan over Asia*, pp. 16, 275.

11. Lin Y., *Vigil of a Nation*, p. 637.

12. A. Hino, *Hana to Heitai*, p. 59.

13. The most comprehensive study is Iris Chang, *The Rape of Nanking*. See also Honda Katsuichi, *The Nanjing Massacre*, a detailed investigation into the actions of the Japanese Army in raping and killing in various military operations, especially at Nanking. The author demonstrates the efforts of right-wing Japanese, including many government officials – both behind the crimes and subsequently – to cover them up.

14. D. Wilson, *When Tigers Fight*, pp. 38–9.

15. M. Boatner, *Biographical Dictionary of World War II*, p. 567.

16. H. Foster Snow, *Inside Red China*, pp. 316–7.

17. P. Lowe, p. 103.

18. In the six months to May 1940 this amounted to some £2 million worth, 38 per cent of which was of American origin and 37 per cent from the USSR. Only 3.4 per cent was of British Empire origin. See PRO FO 371/24666, 'Supplies of War Materials to China'. For contemporary accounts of the road and its operations see R. Slater, *Guns through Arcady*; C. Yee, *The Men of the Burma Road*; N. Smith, *The Burma Road*; N. Bradley, *The Old Burma Road*; and H. D. Friber, *West China and the Burma Road*.

19. P. Lowe, pp. 139–40, 150–2.

20. F. Dorn, *Walkout; With Stilwell in Burma*, p. 20.

21. D. Wilson, *When Tigers Fight*, pp. 9–10.

22. W. Elsbree, *Japan's Role in Southeast Asian Nationalist Movements, 1940–1945*, pp. 8–11.

23. O. C. Spencer, *Flying the Hump*, pp. 26–7, 34.

24. I. Lyall Grant and K. Tamayama, *Burma 1942: The Japanese Invasion*, pp. 27–8.

25. Journalist Vanya Oakes covers Chennault and the Tigers in *White Man's Folly*, (pp. 220–30). For the most complete, detailed and fascinating recent description of Chennault and his unit, see Daniel Ford *Flying Tigers*. Accounts by unit members include Robert L. Scott, *God is My Co-Pilot*, and C. R. Bond and T. H. Anderson, *A Flying Tiger's Diary*. See also Bruce Gamble, *Black Sheep One: The Life of Gregory 'Pappy' Boyington*. For an early account of the unit see R. Whelan, *The Flying Tigers*.

26. L. Stowe, *They Shall Not Sleep*, p. 143.

27. O. J. Greenlaw, *The Lady and the Tigers*, pp. 148–9. For a biography of Madame Chiang, see Emily Hahn, *The Soong Sisters*. For a full family biography see S. Seagrave, *The Soong Dynasty*.

28. See Wayne G. Johnson and Don van Cleve (eds.), *Chennault's Flying Tigers*, and, for an account by an AVG armament technician with 3rd Squadron including much technical detail on the P-40 aircraft and its armament, Charles Baisden, *Flying Tiger to Air Commando*. The same subject is also covered in detail in Carl Molesworth, *P-40 Warhawk Aces of the CBI*, and Frederick A. Johnson, *P-40 Warhawk*. See also Terrill J. Clements, *American Volunteer Group Colours and Markings*.

29. L. Stowe, pp. 62–85.

30. Lowe, pp. 230–1.

31. PRO FO 371/35957, 'Events Leading up to War with Japan 1943'.

32. Tojo finally became Minister of War in July 1941 and Prime Minister that October. The militarists had finally triumphed and war soon followed, with Tojo exercising unquestioned control over Japan's civil and military establishments until his resignation on 18 July 1945. Boatner, p. 568.

33. N. Ike, *Japan's Decision for War*, pp. 263–4. For a thorough appraisal of Anglo-Japanese relations in the early war years see K. Sato, *Japan and Britain at the Crossroads, 1939–1941*.

34. F. C. Jones, *Japan's New Order in East Asia: Its Rise and Fall 1937–1945*, pp. 79, 87, 140–1, 148–9, 218, 234, 238, 242–6, 351.

35. Elsbree, pp. 15–17. For a discussion of how Thailand accommodated the Japanese and secretly negotiated with Americans and British, see E. B. Reynolds, *Thailand and Japan's Southern Advance, 1940–1945*.

36. F. C. Jones, pp. 330, 402.

37. L. Allen, *Burma*, pp. 11–12.

38. M. Collis, *Last and First in Burma (1941–1948)*, pp. 32–4, 37–9, 47–8, 68–9, 209.

39. It has been suggested he did this because, much impressed by the arrival at Singapore of *Repulse* and *Prince of Wales*, he wanted to see whether the British would intercept and destroy the fleet before formally agreeing to the Japanese request for non-resistance and transit facilities. A. Gilchrist, *Malaya 1941*, p. 49.

40. J. B. Haseman, *The Thai Resistance Movement during the Second World War*, pp. 35–6.

41. PRO CAB 106/25, 'A Record of The 1st Bn. Gloucestershire Regt. (The 28th) in Burma. 1938–1942'.

42. K. Tamayama and J. Nunneley, *Tales by Japanese Soldiers*, p. 26.

43. See Oliver Lindsay, *The Lasting Honour*; Tim Carew, *The Fall of Hong Kong*; Ted Ferguson, *Desperate Siege*; and, for the best and most recent account, Philip Snow, *The Fall of Hong Kong*.

44. D. Wilson, *When Tigers Fight*, pp. 188, 192.

45. Terauchi commanded Southern Army throughout the war and was therefore responsible for Burma and Thailand and the railway built between them with slave and PoW labour. Boatner, p. 558.

46. See Document no. 2, 'Matters Concerning the Enforcement of Strategy in Burma. Drawn up and Issued by the Southern Forces, February 6, 1942', in Trager (ed.), pp. 31–3.

47. LHCMA Brooke-Popham Papers, Confidential Memorandum, Dec 1941, V/5/50.

48. R. E. Sherwood, *Roosevelt and Hopkins*, p. 449.

49. H. Lory, *Japan's Military Masters*, p. 201. See also M. and S. Harries, *Soldiers of the Sun*. For comprehensive guides to the Japanese Army's training, equipment and organization during the Second World War see George Forty's superb *Japanese Army Handbook 1939–1945*. See also A. J. Barker, *Japanese Army Handbook 1939–1945*, and H. Saburo, *Kogun: The Japanese Army in the Pacific War*.

50. S. Ienaga, *Japan's Last War*, p. 49.

51. Barker, *The March on Delhi*, p. 74.

52. E. J. Drea, 'In the Army Barracks of Imperial Japan', *Armed Forces and Society*, vol. 15/3, Spring 1989, p. 337.

53. Ienaga, pp. 157–9.

54. G. Armstrong, *The Sparks Fly Upward*, p. 137.

55. PRO WO 208/2505, 'ATIS Enemy Publication 237 03.12.44 "Personal Punishment and military discipline"'; WO 208/2603, 'ATIS Enemy Publication 336 "Extra-legal punishment"'.

56. A. D. Coox, 'High Command and Field Army: The Kwantung Army and the Nomohan Incident 1939', *Military Affairs*, Oct 1969, pp. 302–12.

57. M. Tsuji, *Singapore: The Japanese Story*, p. 22.

58. See J. Fitzpatrick, *The Bicycle in Wartime*, chap. 6.

59. Harries and Harries, pp. 272–3.

60. B. Bond (ed.), *Chief of Staff: The Diaries of Lieutenant-General Sir Henry Pownall*, vol. 2, p. 67.

61. C. F. Romanus and R. Sunderland, *Stilwell's Mission to China*, chap. 2; Tuchman, pp. 240–5.

62. T. V. Soong was the only son of Charlie Soong, two years older than Madame Chiang. He studied economics at Harvard, then worked for an international banking firm before returning to China, where he took over the Central Bank of Canton in 1935. When the Sino-Japanese War expanded in 1937, he served as finance minister, then foreign minister, but he did not get on well with Chiang and fell from grace in 1943.

63. C-t. Liang, *General Stilwell in China 1942–1944*, pp. 24–5.

64. J. A. Goette, *Japan Fights for Asia*, p. 79.

65. Prefer, p. 14.

66. L. I. Bland and S. R. Stevens (eds.), *The Papers of George Catlett Marshall*, vol. 3, p. 140.

67. Liang, p. 3.

68. R. J. Aldrich, *Intelligence and the War against Japan: Britain, America and the Politics of Secret Service*, pp. 201–2.
69. IWM P149, Brig. L. F. Field.

## 3 INVASION

1. Lyall Grant and Tamayama, pp. 49–50.
2. Lunt, 'A Hell of a Licking', pp. 88–90.
3. C. Shores and B. Cull with Y. Izawa, *A Bloody Shambles*, vol. 1, p. 241; and Lyall Grant and Tamayama, p. 51. For a detailed and thorough appraisal of air operations during the 1942 campaign, see Shores and Cull with Izawa, vol. 1, chap. 7, and vol. 2, chaps 7 and 9.
4. W. S. Churchill, vol. 3, p. 564.
5. NAM 7808–96, 'History of 202 (L of C) Area 1942–1946'; J. Connell, *Wavell: Supreme Commander*, pp. 53, 60.
6. Lyall Grant and Tamayama, p. 40.
7. Connell, *Wavell: Supreme Commander*, p. 62.
8. Lewin, p. 159.
9. A view shared by both Hutton and Smyth. See Prasad (ed.), *Retreat from Burma, 1941–42*, p. 254.
10. Connell, *Wavell: Supreme Commander*, p. 66.
11. J. Helsdon Thomas, *Wings over Burma*, p. 19.
12. P. F. Geren, *Burma Diary*, pp. 3–7.
13. C. Delachet Guillon, *Daw Sein. Les dix mille vies d'une femme birmane*, pp. 152–5.
14. PRO CAB 106/25, 'A Record of The 1st Bn. Gloucestershire Regt. (The 28th) in Burma, 1938–1942.'
15. RAHT MD/1454, 'Notes concerning 3 Indian Light Anti-Aircraft Battery, in the Withdrawal from Burma January to March 1942', by Lt.-Col. C. H. T. MacFetridge.
16. A. Stewart, *The Underrated Enemy*, pp. 140–1; Shores and Cull, with Izawa, p. 249.
17. M. C. Cotton, *Hurricanes over Burma*, pp. 125–6, 129. For the memoirs of two other 17 Squadron members, see Barry Sutton, *Jungle Pilot*, and Hedley Everard, *A Mouse in My Pocket*. For a history of 136 Squadron, see Vivian K. Jacobs, *The Woodpecker Story*.
18. Connell, *Wavell: Supreme Commander*, p. 22.
19. Lunt, 'A Hell of a Licking', pp. 82–3.
20. W. S. Churchill, vol. 4, p. 53. The British sent a unit to China, 204 Military (Commando) Mission, including many Australians, ostensibly to train the Chinese in guerrilla warfare. It fought no battles and won no awards but was wasted by disease before finally being withdrawn. For a full account see Ian Adamson, *The Forgotten Men*, and William Noonan, *Lost Legion*. For a personal view see J. Friend, *The Long Trek*.

21. W. S. Churchill, vol. 4, p. 388.

22. Connell, *Wavell: Supreme Commander*, p. 71. Dill was to continue to play an important role as head of the British military mission to Washington, where he built a crucially important relationship with Marshall. See Alex Danchev, *Very Special Relationship: Field Marshal Dill and the Anglo-American Alliance, 1941–44.*

23. A. Bryant, *The Turn of the Tide*, p. 295.

24. A. Stewart, p. 145.

25. Khaing, p. 8.

26. This is one of twelve 'phoenix' units selected for study in Daniel P. Marston's *Phoenix from the Ashes.*

27. Carew, *The Longest Retreat*, p. 60.

28. NAM 7711–232, 'With the 4th Sikhs in Burma 1942–43: A Personal Account, by Lt-Col. I. A. J. Edwards-Stuart'.

29. Lunt, '*A Hell of a Licking*', pp. 88–90. An interesting contemporary portrait of Smyth is provided by Eve Curie, who met him during the campaign (*Journey among Warriors*, pp. 320–4).

30. P. Carmichael, *Mountain Battery*, pp. 3–4; A. B. Howard, 'Screw Guns in Action 1940–1945: 12 (Poonch) Indian Mountain Battery', *The Journal of the Royal Artillery*, LXXIII/2, June 1946, pp. 107–14; RAHT MD/1422, 'Extracts from the Battery Histories of: 2 (Derajat) Mtn Bty RA; 9 (Muree) Ind Mtn Bty I Arty; 12 (Poonch) Mtn Bty RA; 16 (Zhob) Mtn Bty RA; 19 (Maymyo) Mtn Bty RA; 21 Mtn Bty'; MD/3042, 'Personal Account of 5th Mountain Battery in the Retreat from Burma', by Brig. W. H. H. Wilberforce.

31. J. Smyth, *Milestones*, p. 169.

32. Lunt, '*A Hell of a Licking*', p. 86.

33. OIOC MS Eur D1034, letter to Maurice Collis, 11 Nov 1955.

34. LHCMA Hutton Papers, 'Rangoon 1941–42, A Personal Record'. (Also held at IWM 97/3/1, Lt.-Gen. Sir Thomas Hutton.)

35. Lunt, '*A Hell of a Licking*', pp. 95–100; OIOC MS Eur Photo Eur 289, memoir by Bernard Fletcher Kane of his life and career in Burma Posts and Telegraphs Dept 1937–50; IWM 85/16/1, Col. B. F. Kane (extracts of same).

36. V. A. Subramanyam, *The Signals*, pp. 43–4.

37. L. Allen, *Burma*, pp. 23–4.

38. Tamayama and Nunneley, p. 30.

39. Lyall Grant and Tamayama, pp. 53–4.

40. Ba Maw, p. 141. See Dorothy Hess Guyot, 'The Burma Independence Army: A Political Movement m Military Garb', in J. Silverstein (ed.), *Southeast Asia in World War II.*

41. RCSM 916.6, 'Military Histories Far East, Communications in Burma'.

42. Prasad (ed.), *The Retreat from Burma 1941–42*, p. 51n.

43. Lyall Grant and Tamayama, p. 65. For the effect on the civilian population see Maybury, vol. 2, pp. 75–84.

44. PRO WO 172/926, 'War Diary 1/9 Jat Regt. 1942 Jan–May'.

45. Lyall Grant and Tamayama, p. 70. As Martin Caidin points out, air combat records for the early days of the war are notoriously unreliable, with many discrepancies between claims and losses. He also discusses AVG tactics. See M. Caidin, *Zero Fighter*, pp. 100, 102-4.

46. PRO CAB 122/649, 'Employment of AVG in Burma and China'.

47. Cotton, p. 122.

48. Lunt, '*A Hell of a Licking*', p. 108.

49. The extraordinary story of Major Hugh Seagrim is told in Ian Morrison's *Grandfather Longlegs*.

50. Lunt, '*A Hell of a Licking*', pp. 111-12.

51. NAM 7711-232.

52. Lunt, '*A Hell of a Licking*', p. 114.

53. C. H. T. MacFetridge, 'The Light Anti-Aircraft Battery in the Withdrawal from Burma, January–May 1942', *The Journal of the Royal Artillery*, CIX/1, March 1982, p. 44; M. Farndale, *History of the Royal Regiment of Artillery*, p. 83.

54. Carmichael, p. 42. See also C. H. T. MacFetridge and J. P. Warren, *Tales of the Mountain Gunners*.

55. Tuchman, pp. 248-9; Spencer, p. 40.

56. Kirby, vol. 4, p. 88.

57. Connell, *Wavell: Supreme Commander*, pp. 133, 160; B. Bond (ed.), *Chief of Staff*, vol. 2, pp. 87, 89; Lunt, '*A Hell of a Licking*', pp. 120-1.

58. LHCMA, Hutton Papers, Smyth to Hutton, 8 Feb 1942.

59. Lunt, '*A Hell of a Licking*', pp. 123, 154.

60. Sakurai was respected by his officers for his decisiveness, integrity and scrupulous personal behaviour. One staff officer of 55th Division said his character 'would remind you of the grace and grandeur of Mount Fuji', adding 'he was well conversant with the power of the British-Indian forces and the geography of the Burma battlefields' (L. Allen, *Sittang*, pp. 3–5). For an interesting pen portrait by his ADC, Lieutenant Sugimoto Eiichi, see Tamayama and Nunneley, pp. 112-6.

61. W. Hingston, *Never Give Up*, p. 155.

62. This is one of the twelve 'phoenix' units in Daniel P. Marston's *Phoenix from the Ashes*.

63. PRO CAB 106/172, 'Martaban–Sittang Bridge. Letters from Lt.-Col. H. A. Stevenson (commanding 3rd/7th Gurkha Rifles)'.

64. The Armoured Car Section, Rangoon Battalion, BAF, was equipped with four Rolls-Royce India Pattern armoured cars, each equipped with a single Vickers .303-inch machine-gun. Two cars were damaged beyond repair trying to reach Martaban on 9 February. The third was lost on the retreat from Bilin to Mokpalin on 21 February; the last car was lost on 22 February by the Sittang Bridge. PRO WO 172/310, 'War Diary 2 Rangoon Bn. 1939 Sep–1942 Feb'.

65. G. Evans and A. Brett-James, *Imphal*, pp. 42-3.

66. Draper, p. 72.

67. Tamayama and Nunneley, pp. 33–4.

68. Another 229 were captured, while 5 officers, 3 VCOs and 65 men managed to escape. Japanese losses were given as 17 dead and 33 wounded. W. S. Thatcher, *The Tenth Baluch Regiment in the Second World War*, pp. 324–6; Carew, *The Longest Retreat*, pp. 87–94; IWM 20457, Brig. J. Randle; Marston, pp. 64–6.

69. IWM 77/153/1, Captain H. B. Toothill; C. R. L. Coubrough, *Memories of a Perpetual Second Lieutenant*, pp. 19–33.

70. Dogras came from the Himalayan foothills around Kangra and Jammu, mostly yeoman farmers scraping a living from terraced hills. Their isolation kept them Hindu while their neighbours embraced Islam and they were intensely proud of their Rajput origin, referring to themselves as such in their own country. *India's Fighting Men*, p. 5.

71. Lyall Grant and Tamayama, pp. 87–97.

72. Tuchman, p. 237.

73. A. C. Wedemeyer, *Wedemeyer Reports!*, pp. 151–2.

74. Hingston, pp. 159–76; G. Fitzpatrick, *No Mandalay, No Maymyo*, pp. 69–71, 285–6.

75. *Memoir of 214 Infantry Regiment*, quoted in Lyall Grant and Tamayama, p. 101.

76. OIOC MS Eur Photo Eur 011 Telegrams, dated 8 Dec 1941–3 May 1942, chiefly relating to the Japanese invasion of Burma.

77. J. Connell, *Wavell: Supreme Commander*, p. 181.

## 4 DISASTER ON THE SITTANG

1. Lunt, '*A Hell of a Licking*', p. 127.

2. PRO WO 172/369, 'Burma Headquarters G.S. 1942 Jan.–Feb., Apr.–May'.

3. C. N. Barclay, *The History of the Duke of Wellington's Regiment 1919–1952*, pp. 113–5. See also IWM 99/48/1, Brigadier A. D. Firth.

4. Lunt, '*A Hell of a Licking*', pp. 138–40; Probert, p. 87; C. N. Barclay, *The Regimental History of The 3rd Queen Alexandra's Own Gurkha Rifles*, vol. 2, *1927–1947*, pp. 26–7.

5. GM W2, 'Diary of Lt. D. H. West, 1/7 GR'.

6. Ironically, Smyth was one officer who did not recognize these tactics for what they were. He later recorded that he thought his headquarters was the target of such a diversion on 21 February. J. Smyth, *Before the Dawn*, pp. 180–1.

7. Colonel Mackenzie described his experiences in *Operation Rangoon Jail*.

8. GM W2, 'Diary of Lt. D. H. West, 1/7 GR'.

9. Lyall Grant and Tamayama, pp. 125–6.

10. R. M. Maxwell, *Desperate Encounters*, pp. 238–41.

11. Barclay, *The Regimental History of The 3rd Queen Alexandra's Own Gurkha Rifles*, vol. 2, *1927–1947*, p. 30; PRO WO 172/966, 'War Diary 1/7 and 3/7 Gurkha Rifles 1942 Feb.–May.'

12. Smyth, *Milestones*, p. 190. The detailed story of the Sittang bridge disaster is

most thoroughly examined by Louis Allen in *Burma*, pp. 36–44, 644–51. See also Farndale, pp. 88–90; R. P. Pakenham-Walsh, *History of The Corps of Royal Engineers*, vol. 9, p. 162.

13. Chevenix Trench, p. 206; Barclay, *The Regimental History of The 3rd Queen Alexandra's Own Gurkha Rifles*, vol. 2, *1927–1947*, pp. 31–3.

14. Carew, *The Longest Retreat*, p. 131.

15. Lunt, '*A Hell of a Licking*', p. 144.

16. J. M. Brereton and A. C. S. Savory, *The History of the Duke of Wellington's Regiment (West Riding) 1702–1992*, p. 306. See also IWM 99/48/1, Brigadier A. D. Firth.

17. GM G533/7 GR Historical Records, Personal Accounts of Actions 1942 ('Personal Account of Events in the Sittang Battle, Lt.-Col. S. F. Harvey-Williams').

18. J. P. Cross and B. Gurung (eds.), *Gurkhas at War*, p. 70.

19. Carew, *The Longest Retreat*, pp. 134–45; Barclay, *The History of The Duke of Wellington's Regiment 1919–1952*, p. 118; Hingston, *Never Give Up*, p. 193.

20. Lunt, '*A Hell of a Licking*', p. 145.

21. PRO CAB 106/172, 'Account of Defence of Martaban and the Sittang Bridge Burma 1942 Feb., by Lieutenant-Colonel H. A. Stevenson, Commanding Officer 3rd Battalion 7th Gurkha Rifles, including sketch map and extract from diary'.

22. Hingston, p. 195; Carew, *The Longest Retreat*, p. 145; G. D. Sheffield, *The Redcaps*, pp. 133–4.

23. LHCMA, Hutton Papers, 'Rangoon 1941–42, A Personal Record'.

24. Smyth, *Before the Dawn*, p. 157.

25. LHCMA, Hutton Papers, 'Rangoon 1941–42, A Personal Record'.

26. Smyth, *Milestones*, p. 141.

27. IWM 99/73/1 Hutton Papers, Smyth to Hutton, 4 Feb 1942.

28. Lunt, '*A Hell of a Licking*', pp. 151–2.

29. IWM Misc 66, item 1022, letter to Ronald Lewin, 20 July 1981.

30. Next to this paragraph, Auchinleck pencilled 'Right!' PRO WO 106/2659, 'Diary Lt.-Col. W. E. V. Abraham'.

31. LHCMA, Hutton Papers, 'Rangoon 1941–42, A Personal Record'.

32. Some sixty-five stayed to work first at Maymyo and then Shwebo, often under bombing and helping out in their spare time at the hospital, dressing wounds and carrying out the dead. They were finally sent to Myitkyina by train then flown to Assam. C. Mackenzie, *Eastern Epic*, pp. 518–19.

33. NAM 5912–161–3, 'Evacuation from Rangoon of the W.A.S.(B)'. The Under-Secretary of the Home Department was Fielding Hall, son of the writer Harold, and steeped in the Buddhist tradition. Working under tremendous strain, he was at a loss to know what to do with his charges and, with many warders and attendants having already fled, reluctantly decided to release them. This proved erroneous as the Japanese had not yet arrived. Later, appalled by what he had done, he took his own life leaving a note trailing in despair. 'I know I made a bad mistake. I thought I was doing the right

thing. I am ...' (L. Glass, *The Changing of Kings: Memories of Burma 1934–1949*, p. 139).

34. Khaing, p. 131.

35. See M. S. Degaa Upfill, *An American in Burma 1930 to 1942*.

36. NAM 7711–232, 'With the 4th Sikhs in Burma 1942–43: A Personal Account by Lt.-Col. I. A. J. Edwards-Stuart'. See also OIOC MS Eur D750, 'Account of the evacuation of Rangoon by the Chartered Bank of India and other banks at the end of February 1942 dated 14 July 1942'.

37. See A. A. Mains, *The Retreat from Burma*, chaps. 3 and 4; and G. Rodger, *Red Moon Rising*.

38. P. Collister, *Then a Soldier*, p. 91. See also IWM 83/46/1, Major P. Collister, and NAM 9002–9, Major Peter Collister.

39. PRO CAB 106/25, 'A Record of The 1st Bn. Gloucestershire Regt. (The 28th) in Burma, 1938–1942'.

40. Shores and Cull, with Izawa, *Bloody Shambles*, vol. 2, pp. 268–9; IWM 01/22/1, W. Jepson.

41. Lunt, '*A Hell of a Licking*', p. 162.

42. Draper, p. 10; W. G. Burchett, *Bombs over Burma*, p. 75.

43. Carew, *The Longest Retreat*, pp. 151–3; M. Collis, *Last and First in Burma*, p. 105.

44. Lyall Grant and Tamayama, p. 107.

45. IWM 02/54/5 & 3A, Major-General Sir John Winterton, 'Papers relating to Allied operations in Burma include reports on Army/Air Force co-operation, operations by Chinese forces, oilfields denial and the Allied withdrawal together with copies of various despatches'.

46. W. S. Churchill, vol. 4, pp. 166–7, 169. There are a number of biographies of Alexander, the best being Nigel Nicolson's *Alex: The Life of Field Marshal Earl Alexander of Tunis*.

47. Field Marshal Viscount Alexander, *The Alexander Memoirs*, pp. 92–5.

48. LHCMA, Hutton Papers, Wavell to Hutton, 2 July 1942.

49. Connell, *Wavell: Supreme Commander*, pp. 190–200.

50. LHCMA, Hutton Papers, 'Rangoon 1941–42, A Personal Record'.

51. Lyall Grant and Tamayama, pp. 154–5.

52. IWM 87/14/1, Lt.-Col. A. G. Dunn; Lunt, '*A Hell of a Licking*', pp. 164–5.

53. Short, p. 54.

54. They separated again after five days. Barclay, *The History of The Duke of Wellington's Regiment 1919–1952*, p. 121.

55. G. M. O. Davy, *The Seventh and Three Enemies*, p. 219. For the best technical guide to the Stuart, or 'Honey', as it was known to the British, see Stephen Zaloga's *M3 & M5 Stuart Light Tank 1940–1945*.

56. TM RH.872 RTR:38, 'Mandalay and Beyond, a Personal Story of the 2nd RTR in Burma 1942', by Major Arthur J. Fearnley.

57. R. Clarke, *With Alex at War: From the Irrawaddy to the Po 1941–1945*, p. 15.

58. PRO CAB 106/17, 'Burma Campaign 1942 Report on Ops. of 1/11 Sikhs'; P. G. Bamford, *1st King George V's Own Battalion, The Sikh Regiment*, pp.

78-9: This is one of the twelve 'phoenix' units in Daniel P. Marston's *Phoenix from the Ashes*.

59. S. Dun, *Memoirs of the Four-Foot Colonel*, p. 25.

60. B. R. Mullaly, *Bugle and Kukri. The Story of the 10th Princess Mary's Own Gurkha Rifles*, p. 201.

61. G. M. Fortreath, *Pipes, Kukris and Nips*, p. 60.

62. D. Twiston Davies (ed.), *The Daily Telegraph Book of Military Obituaries*, pp. 380-8; TM RH.872 RTR:38.

63. Although the Japanese tanks were also armed with 37mm guns, these were a short-barrelled weapon and utterly ineffective. Lyall Grant and Tamayama, p. 159.

64. Davy, pp. 234-6; Carew, *The Longest Retreat*, pp. 172-3; D. Twiston Davies (ed.), pp. 145-50.

65. Carew, *The Longest Retreat*, pp. 168-9.

66. GM, Major D. S. Day, '1/4 GR Officer's Association Newsletter No. 40'.

67. A. Wagg, *A Million Died*, p. 53. The question of compensation was fought over for years afterwards until the House of Lords found in the company's favour in 1964 (Carew, *The Longest Retreat*, pp. 155-7).

68. Barclay, *The History of The Duke of Wellington's Regiment 1919-1952*, pp. 122-3.

69. When darkness fell after four and a half hours the 28th's B Company was reduced to just six NCOs and fourteen men. PRO CAB 106/25, 'A Record of The 1st Bn. Gloucestershire Regt. (The 28th) in Burma, 1938-1942'; E. W. C. Sandes, *From Pyramid to Pagoda*, pp. 23-5.

70. T. Dillon, *Rangoon to Kohima*, p. 32.

71. SGM 33/G13A, 'COs Accounts Operations of 1st, 2nd, 5th Bns, 1940-42'.

72. LHCMA, Hutton Papers, 'Rangoon 1941-42, A Personal Record'.

73. NAM 7709-6, '2nd Bn. 13th F. F. Rifles War History (Unofficial) January 1942-November 1946'; W. E. H. Conden, *The Frontier Force Rifles*, pp. 181-2. This is one of the twelve 'phoenix' units in Daniel P. Marston's *Phoenix from the Ashes*.

74. Lyall Grant and Tamayama, pp. 178-82; L. Allen, *Burma*, pp. 55-7; Farndale, p. 93.

75. PRO CAB 106/17; Bamford, pp. 81-4.

76. Davy, pp. 240-1.

77. IWM AL 5185, '214th Infantry Regiment at Taukkyan, 7 March 1942, Interrogation of Commanders and Staff officers. Tokyo, April 1951'.

78. Lunt, '*A Hell of a Licking*', pp. 167-8.

79. Imperial General Headquarters, order nos. 590, 603; Official History, *Imperial General Headquarters, Army*, vol. 3, p. 436, quoted in Lyall Grant and Tamayama, p. 188.

## 5 ENTER SLIM

1. Mains, *The Retreat from Burma*, p. 62.
2. Collister, pp. 92-3, 96.
3. SGM 33/G13A, 'The 28th in Burma 1941-1943'.
4. Dillon, p. 27. This account of the 28th was written by the Adjutant and is a plain, matter-of-fact account.
5. G. Tyson, *Forgotten Frontier*, p. 35. These figures are only estimates and different ones occur in the same source.
6. M. C. Nickerson, *Burma Interlude*, p. 105.
7. Rodger, p. 63.
8. Carmichael, p. 28.
9. Lunt, '*A Hell of a Licking*', p. 173.
10. L. Stowe, p. 116.
11. Brookes, p. 2; Maybury, vol. 2, p. 121.
12. E. C. V. Foucar, *I Lived in Burma*, p. 131. By now Foucar had been commissioned and was serving as Services Public Relations Officer at Army Headquarters. As such he regularly came into contact with correspondents such as George Rodger, Jack Belden and O. D. Gallagher. He was a success, according to the far from uncritical Australian Wilfred Burchett (*Bombs over Burma*, p. 71).
13. M. Calvert, *Fighting Mad*, p. 54.
14. PRO ADM 1/11798, 'Force "Viper" – Account of Operations in Burma Campaign Period 8 February-31 May 1942'. See also A. Cecil Hampshire, 'The Saga of "Force Viper"', in *On Hazardous Service*, based on an earlier article in the *RUSI Journal*.
15. Calvert, *Fighting Mad*, pp. 55-66.
16. Liang C-t, pp. 33-5.
17. M. Collis, *Last and First in Burma*, p. 122.
18. F. Eldridge, *Wrath in Burma*, pp. 47, 92; Ho Y-c, *The Big Circle*, p. 5n.
19. H. W. Baldwin, *Great Mistakes of the War*, p. 60.
20. J. Stilwell, *The Stilwell Papers*, pp. 60, 78, 85.
21. Short, p. 63.
22. O. D. Gallagher, *Retreat in the East*, p. 182.
23. L. Stowe, p. 124.
24. Tuchman, pp. 264-5.
25. R. Lyman, 'The Appointment of Slim to Burma Corps – March 1942', in *Slim, Master of War*, pp. 265-8.
26. Slim's own memoirs of his early career, *Unofficial History*, are perceptive and amusing. The best biography of Slim remains Ronald Lewin's *Slim: The Standardbearer*, while first Geoffrey Evans (*Slim as Military Commander*) and recently Robert Lyman (*Slim, Master of War*) have examined his military career in Burma in detail.
27. W. J. Slim, *Defeat into Victory*, p. 23.
28. Shores and Cull, with Izawa, vol. 2, pp. 286, 346-7.

29. NAM 7302–44–2, 'Personal Diary of events in Burma prior to and during the campaign with an account of the retreat through the Hukong Valley (May–June 1942), by Major E. H. Cooke, I. A., 2nd Comd, 9th Bn, The Burma Rifles'. James Lunt described Cooke as 'one of the best of the original Burma Rifles', having spent a week jungle training with him before the war. 'He made me a stew of delicious mushrooms, taught me the name of every bird and butterfly we saw, and also taught me how to swim mules across torrential rivers … Poor "Cookie"; only in Burma would he have found his *métier*, and only perhaps in the Burma Rifles, where eccentricity was part of everyday life' (Lunt, *A Hell of a Licking*', p. 57).

30. Carmichael, pp. 75, 77.

31. Muriel Sue Degaa Upfill visited Toungoo before the war: 'Traces of its glory still remain in ancient ruins and beautiful pagodas, in the wide moat and pleasant gardens. Of its origin, nothing is known save from legend and the surviving chronicles of the Burmese kings.' Degaa Upfill, p. 58.

32. Carew, *The Longest Retreat*, pp. 204–5.

33. Field Marshal Earl Alexander, 'Report', in A. P. Wavell, *Operations in Burma from 15 December 1941 to 20 May 1942*; Field Marshal Viscount Alexander, *The Alexander Memoirs*, p. 94.

34. Lyall Grant and Tamayama, pp. 190–2.

35. Rodger, p. 88.

36. For a biography of Seagrave, see Sue Mayes Newhall, *The Devil in God's Old Man*.

37. Geren, pp. 25–6.

38. GM, 'History of 17 Indian Division, July 1941 to December 1945'.

39. Cotton, p. 283.

40. Shores and Cull, with Izawa, vol. 2, p. 351.

41. M. Charlton, *Mandalay and Beyond*, p. 30.

42. K. Hemingway, *Wings over Burma*, p. 162; Baisden, pp. 50–1; IWM 12822/4, Flight Lieutenant Arthur Hughes.

43. Prasad (ed.), *The Retreat from Burma 1941–42*, pp. 377–8; Probert, pp. 92–3; IWM 17567/3, Pilot Officer James Thirlwell.

44. Lunt, *A Hell of a Licking*', p. 187. 'Bobs' was the affectionate nickname given to Field Marshal Earl Roberts of Kandahar, Commander-in-Chief India 1885–93.

45. Lunt, 'Toungoo 21 March 1942', in *Charge to Glory*, pp. 9–10.

46. Lyall Grant and Tamayama, pp. 204–5.

47. It cost them 2 officers and 15 men killed and 9 men wounded; PRO CAB 106/25, 'A Record of The 1st Bn. Gloucestershire Regt. (The 28th) in Burma, 1938–1942'.

48. A detailed account of 1st Glosters' action is given in Dillon, pp. 67–71.

49. L. Allen, *Burma*, pp. 62–3.

50. Sandes, pp. 27–8; Tamayama and Nunneley, pp. 64–5.

51. TM MH.5 RH.837, Hus Major M. J. E. Patteson, 'Survival at Shwedaung'; IWM 65/56/1, Major R. A. Hemelryk.

52. Lyall Grant and Tamayama, pp. 208-14.

53. Davy, p. 267; IWM 86/72/1, Captain E. N. Sheppard; IWM 75/75/1 a. Morrison; IWM 85/35/1, L. E. Tutt.

54. Collister, pp. 101-2; Dillon, pp. 72-8.

55. Tamayama and Nunneley, pp. 63-4.

56. PRO WO 172/694, 'War Diary 7th Queen's Own Hussars 1942 Jan-May'; IWM 67/279/1, Major P. H. Cleere.

57. LHCMA, Hutton Papers, 'Rangoon 1941-42, A Personal Record'.

58. J. Leasor, *The Marine from Mandalay*, pp. 45-7; A. C. Hampshire, *On Hazardous Service*, pp. 113-5.

59. Lyall Grant and Tamayama, pp. 220-6.

60. Brookes, pp. 12-13.

61. Cotton, p. 294.

62. PRO CAB 122/298, 'India and Burma 1940-1943'; *China Airlift - The Hump*, vol. 4, pp. 371-2.

63. Shores and Cull, with Izawa, vol. 2, p. 361.

64. Lunt, '*A Hell of a Licking*', pp. 198-9.

65. PRO CAB 106/17, 'Burma Campaign 1942 Report on Ops. of 1/11 Sikhs'.

66. Stilwell, p. 76.

67. Liang C-t, p. 37; Tuchman, pp. 279-80.

68. This is based on a report by Major Chappell of the Burma Military Police to Cowan on 2 April that a large column of Japanese troops was crossing the river at Prome. It was widely discounted at the time and in the official histories but has subsequently been confirmed as Sakurai's intention. Lyall Grant and Tamayama, pp. 226, 228-30.

69. PRO WO 172/966, 'War Diary 1/7th and 3/7th Gurkha Rifles 1942 Feb-May'.

70. Lyall Grant and Tamayama, pp. 233-9; Tamayama and Nunneley, pp. 71-4.

71. Lunt, '*A Hell of a Licking*', pp. 202-3; J. M. Brereton, *The 7th Queen's Own Hussars*, p. 187.

72. U Nu, *Burma under the Japanese*, pp. 1-2.

73. Cady, p. 440.

74. Davy, p. 294; G. Fitzpatrick, pp. 110-11.

## 6 STRUGGLE ON THE PLAIN

1. C. Mackenzie, *Eastern Epic*, p. 504; I. M. Jack, *A Soldier's Tale*, pp. 16-18.

2. For a full account of the action off Ceylon in April 1942 see Michael Tomlinson's *The Most Dangerous Moment*.

3. Elsbree, pp. 32-4; G. R. Collis, *The Eagle Soars*, p. 25.

4. For a biography see Donald McIntyre, *Fighting Admiral*.

5. In fact, Somerville was warned of the Japanese threat to Ceylon on 28 March by sigint and withdrew the fleet to 'Port T', its secret hideaway at Addu Atoll in the Maldives, sending the merchant shipping in Colombo to Cochin in

south-west India, When nothing happened on 2 and 3 April, Somerville decided the code-breakers were wrong and sent *Cornwall* and *Dorsetshire* back to Colombo and *Hermes* and *Vampire* back to Trincomalee. M. Smith, *The Emperor's Codes*, pp. 162–3.

6. This Catalina of 413 Squadron had only arrived from Pembroke Dock two days earlier. Squadron Leader L. J. Birchall RCAF and his crew spent the rest of the war as prisoners, Birchall gaining an OBE for his courageous work on behalf of his fellow PoWs (M. Tomlinson, pp. 84–8, 94–100, 189–90).

7. Shores and Cull, with Izawa, vol. 2, p. 397.

8. N. L. R. Franks, *Hurricanes over the Arakan*, pp. 61–4; G. R. Collis, pp. 14–19.

9. A light cruiser and two destroyers picked up the survivors the following day, rescuing 1,122 officers and men. See Ken Dimbleby's *Turns of Fate: The Drama of HMS 'Cornwall' 1939–1942*.

10. Franks, *Hurricanes over the Arakan*, pp. 65–70.

11. Shores and Cull, with Izawa, vol. 2, pp. 412–26; Caidin, p. 120; H. Besley, *Pilot–Prisoner–Survivor: Six Years in Uniform*, pp. 50–1.

12. See 'Burma and Andaman Invasion Operations Mar 42–Apr 42, Japanese Monograph no. 79', in D. S. Detwiler and C. B. Burdick (eds.), *War in Asia and the Pacific 1937–1949*, vol. 5, pp. 5–10 (also at IWM AL 5193).

13. On 4 March 1944 Australian Prime Minister John Curtin sought assurance regarding Japanese naval moves and received them. 'Our battleship squadron in Ceylon is well posted. Our shore-based aircraft are strong.' R. A. Pearson, *Australians at War in the Air 1939–1945*, p. 63.

14. Tuchman, p. 285.

15. Burma Intelligence Bureau, vol. 1, pp. 4, 23; vol. 2, pp. 154–5.

16. Cady, p. 441n; Tun Pe, *Sun over Burma*, pp. 23–7.

17. Burma Intelligence Bureau, vol. 1, pp. 1, 3–4, 59.

18. U Nu, pp. 20–1.

19. Rodger, pp. 93–6.

20. Carmichael, pp. 96–7.

21. See OIOC MS Eur Photo Eur 419, account by John Revill Case, Manager, British Burmah Petroleum Company Ltd, of the demolition of the Company's installations in face of the Japanese invasion, and of the British evacuation from Burma.

22. A description of the particular supply problems the armoured units faced is given in TM 04.201.1, 'Seconds Out!' vol. 2, a history of 2nd Royal Tank Regiment, compiled by Sgt K. Chadwick, pp. 237–44.

23. Dillon, pp. 92–3.

24. Lunt, '*A Hell of a Licking*', pp. 209–10.

25. Prasad (ed.), *The Retreat from Burma 1941–42*, p. 269; T. O. Thompson, 'Burma Retreat, 1942 – Part II', *Journal of the Royal Army Medical Corps*, XC/2, 1948; Carmichael, p. 123.

26. Colonel F. J. Biddulph, Director of Transportation, had only arrived in Rangoon from India on 27 January and recommended the Irrawaddy Flotilla Company be militarized three days later – too late to be practicable.

Equally, it was only now that the Burma Railways Battalion, BAF, was embodied, by which time many junior staff had already deserted. PRO CAB 44/324, 'Draft Narrative of the First Burma Campaign December 1941–May 1942'.

27. Windsor, pp. 27–8.

28. Dr Maung Maung, *To a Soldier Son*, pp. 18–19. For some reason not apparent, Maung Maung gives the date as 23 April.

29. Rodger, p. 98.

30. Tuchman, p. 282.

31. G. Fitzpatrick, pp. 124, 131–3.

32. J. Belden, *Still Time to Die*, p. 12.

33. Berrigan's full report can be read in Wagg, chap. 11.

34. Lunt, '*A Hell of a Licking*', pp. 212–3; R. B. Deedes, *Historical Records of The Royal Garwhal Rifles*, vol. 2, *1923–1947*, pp. 54–6.

35. Lyall Grant and Tamayama, p. 251; Tamayama and Nunneley, pp. 105–8.

36. Slim, *Defeat into Victory*, p. 65. For a brief biography of Sun's war service see N. Fong, *Burma War and General Sun Li-jen*.

37. TM RH.872 RTR:38, 'Mandalay and Beyond, a Personal Story of the 2nd RTR in Burma 1942', by Major Arthur J. Fearnley.

38. F. Fox, *The Royal Inniskilling Fusiliers in the Second World War*, pp. 40–1.

39. Hingston, p. 217, M. Ahmad, *Heritage*, pp. 244–7.

40. J. Finnerty, *All Quiet on the Irrawaddy*, p. 104.

41. Carew, *The Longest Retreat*, p. 236.

42. Major Brian Montgomery was on Slim's staff and overhead the conversation. Lewin, *Slim*, p. 94.

43. Slim, *Defeat into Victory*, p. 68.

44. Dillon, p. 100.

45. Carmichael, pp. 167–8; Farndale, pp. 98–100; Sandes, pp. 29–31.

46. G. Fitzpatrick, pp. 186–7.

47. Slim, *Defeat into Victory*, p. 72.

48. Liang C-t, p. 40.

49. C. L. Chennault, *Way of a Fighter*, pp. 148–9.

50. Tuchman, p. 283.

51. IWM AL 827/3, 'Short History of 18 Japanese Division'; AL 5231, 'Japanese 1st Tank Regiment Burma 1942. Organization and Movements'; AL 5242, '1st Tank Regiment in Burma; March–August 1942. Organization, Strength and Operations'.

52. P. Elliott, *The White Umbrella*, pp. 126–7.

53. H. Rodriguez, *Helen of Burma*, pp. 12, 68.

54. Stilwell, p. 90.

55. R. Clarke, p. 29.

56. C. B. Jones, p. 71.

57. Maybury, vol. 2, pp. 130–4, 155–6.

58. Slim, *Courage and Other Broadcasts*, pp. 39–40.

59. J. Kennedy, *The Business of War*, p. 209.

60. IWM 81/21/1, Col. B. J. Amies; NAM 8002–3, '33 Indian Years 1915–1947'. See also OIOC MS Eur E418 Amies Collection.

61. He subsequently had no regrets. This incident was investigated by *The Observer* in 1984 and subsequently the Serious Crime Squad of Scotland Yard following a question in the House of Commons by Tam Dalyell MP. No action was taken. G. Fitzpatrick, pp. 200–06.

62. OIOC MS Eur R195, tape recording of interview by Ralph Esmond Selby Tanner (1990).

63. PRO ADM 1/11798, 'Force "Viper" – Account of Operations in Burma Campaign Period 8 February–31 May 1942'.

64. NAM 7711–232, 'With the 4th Sikhs in Burma 1942–43: A Personal Account', Lt.-Col. I. A. J. Edwards-Stuart.

65. Lewin, *Slim*, p. 98 n.1.

66. Lyall Grant and Tamayama, p. 268.

67. C. Mackenzie, *Eastern Epic*, p. 480.

68. Burchett, *Bombs over Burma*, pp. 85–8; Burchett, *Trek Back from Burma*, pp. 102–5. See also Curie, pp. 336–9.

69. Short, pp. 112–3.

70. Brookes, pp. 23, 28, 30–1. In *A Corner of Heaven* Chin Lee, the former secretary to Sawbwa Fang Yu-chi, describes his life in Mangshih and the arrival of the refugee family Brookes.

71. Slim, *Defeat into Victory*, p. 86; Mains, *The Retreat from Burma*, pp. 84–5.

72. Calvert, *Fighting Mad*, pp. 81–3.

73. Lyall Grant and Tamayama, pp. 272–8. In fact, only one span was brought down and another later collapsed. Attempts to deceive the Japanese in Burma frequently failed owing to their woefully inefficient intelligence service, which commanders frequently ignored. See A. D. Coox, 'Flawed Perception and its Effect upon Operational Thinking: The Case of the Japanese Army, 1937–41', in M. I. Handel (ed.), *Intelligence and Military Operations*.

74. Slim, *Defeat into Victory*, p. 86.

75. Lunt, '*A Hell of a Licking*', p. 235.

76. Slim, *Defeat into Victory*, pp. 91–2; M. I. Qureshi, *The First Punjabis*, p. 382.

77. Lunt, '*A Hell of a Licking*', pp. 241–3.

78. NAM 7709–64, '2nd Bn. 13th F. F. Rifles War History (Unofficial) January 1942–November 1946'; Deedes, pp. 54–6.

79. Lunt, '*A Hell of a Licking*', p. 245.

80. Slim, *Defeat into Victory*, p. 96.

81. Lyman, p. 53.

82. NAM 7302–44–2, 'Personal Diary of Events in Burma prior to and during the Campaign with an Account of the Retreat through the Hukong Valley (May-June 1942) by Major E. H. Cooke, I.A., 2nd Comd, 9th Bn, The Burma Rifles'.

83. McPhedran, p. 301.

84. Calvert, *Fighting Mad*, p. 77.

85. The Thais had great difficulty supplying their Northern Army and suffered

greatly from sickness, especially malaria. In 1945 they disbanded it *in situ* and it straggled homewards pursued by 93rd Division, itself now reduced to a force of bandits under a warlord. Lyall Grant and Tamayama, p. 281.

## 7 RETREAT

1. Kirby, vol. 1, pp. 208—9.
2. Carmichael, pp. 212—3.
3. TM 04.201.1, '"Seconds Out!" vol. 2, A History of 2nd Royal Tank Regiment', compiled by Sgt K. Chadwick, p. 234.
4. McCrae and Prentice, pp. 143—6. See also IWM 80/8/1, F. A. Malcolm and OIOC MS Eur E375, 'Irrawaddy Flotilla Company Collection', including business papers, correspondence, articles, photographs, drawings and paintings, of and relating to the Irrawaddy Flotilla Company with descriptions by Company employees of the retreat from Burma.
5. Slim, *Defeat into Victory*, p. 105.
6. Calvert, *Fighting Mad*, pp. 92—4, 100—2.
7. C. H. T. MacFetridge, 'The Light Anti-Aircraft Battery in the Withdrawal from Burma', *The Journal of the Royal Artillery*, CIX/1, March 1982, pp. 46—9; 'Battle of Shwegyin', in *Tales from the Burma Campaign*, pp. 24—6; IWM 89/1/1, Lt.-Col. C. H. T. MacFetridge.
8. PRO WO 172/960, 'War Diary 2nd/5th Gurkha Rifles 1942 Jan—May, Sept—Dec'; Barclay, *The Regimental History of The 3rd Queen Alexandra's Own Gurkha Rifles*, vol. 2, *1927—1947*, pp. 43—5.
9. Chevenix Trench, pp. 214—5.
10. McCrae and Prentice, p. 147.
11. PRO CAB 44/324, 'Draft Narrative of the First Burma Campaign December 1941—May 1942'.
12. Collister, pp. 112—4.
13. PRO AIR 23/1924, 'Despatch on Air Operations in Burma and the Bay of Bengal Covering the Period January 1st to May 22nd 1942 by Air Vice-Marshal D. F. Stevenson CBE, DSO, MC'. No. 31 Squadron was formed in 1915 and in October 1942 sired 194 Squadron at Lahore, whereafter a healthy rivalry developed to between the two, to the subsequent benefit of air supply (Franks, *First in the Indian Skies*, p. 88).
14. A. R. Tainsh, ... *And Some Fell by the Wayside*, pp. 1—2.
15. McPhedran, pp. 33—4.
16. NAM 7302—44—2, 'Personal Diary of Events in Burma prior to and during the Campaign with an Account of the Retreat through the Hukong Valley (May—June 1942), by Major E. H. Cooke, I.A., 2nd Comd, 9th Bn, The Burma Rifles'. See also IWM 88/4/1, Lt.-Col. A. D. Stoker.
17. R. H. Gribble, *Out of the Burma Night*, p. 9.
18. Tyson, p. 30.
19. This project monopolized practically all the local transport and the planters

had to provide all doctors and medical facilities from Tea Garden resources (NAM 7808–96, 'History of 202 (L of C) Area 1942–1946'; J. H. Williams, *Elephant Bill*, p. 152).

20. SOAS E Coll C/31 H. Tinker, 'The Forgotten Long March: The Indian Exodus from Burma, 1942'.

21. Carew, *The Longest Retreat*, p. 255.

22. PRO CAB 44/324; GM, 'History of 17 Indian Division, July 1941 to December 1945'.

23. GM, 'History of 17 Indian Division, July 1941 to December 1945'.

24. Davy, pp. 300–01.

25. These were ten 25-pounders, eleven 3.7-inch mountain guns and four 2-pounders. W. E. Duncan, H. F. Ellis, R. L. Banks and N. Scarfe (eds.), *The Royal Artillery Commemoration Book*, p. 86.

26. Lyman, pp. 56–8.

27. Slim, *Defeat into Victory*, pp. 109–10.

28. Carew, *The Longest Retreat*, pp. 263–4.

29. See H. Mackay, 'One Long Picnic', in A. McCrae et al., *Tales of Burma*.

30. G. Fitzpatrick, pp. 261, 265.

31. PRO CAB 106/25, 'A Record of The 1st Bn. Gloucestershire Regt. (The 28th) in Burma, 1938–1942'.

32. SGM 32/G13, 'The 28th in Burma 1941–1943'.

33. Carew, *The Longest Retreat*, pp. 266–7.

34. Calvert, *Fighting Mad*, p. 107.

35. Carmichael, p. 234.

36. Slim, *Defeat into Victory*, pp. 111–2.

37. A. J. F. Doulton, *The Fighting Cock*, pp. 20–1; Maybury, vol. 2, p. 168.

38. Lunt, '*A Hell of a Licking*', p. 263.

39. Humphreys, pp. 102–3.

40. Mains, *The Retreat from Burma*, pp. 110–11.

41. Stilwell, pp. 95–106; Fischer, *The Chancy War*, pp. 108–13.

42. Burchett, *Trek Back from Burma*, p. 272.

43. Chennault, p. 161.

44. Romanus and Sunderland, *Stilwell's Mission to China*, p. 139.

45. Liang C-t, p. 41.

46. Ho Y-c, pp. 23–34.

47. Tuchman, p. 299.

48. The celebrated anthropologist Edmund Leach first met Noel Stevenson in 1938 while Stevenson was engaged in writing a diploma thesis based on his work with the BFS. Stevenson became Leach's main contact and adviser when the latter arrived in Burma in August 1939. See S. L. Tambiah, *Edmund Leach: An Anthropological Life*, pp. 40–6.

49. J. Barnard, *The Hump*, pp. 149, 161.

50. F. Clifford, *Desperate Journey*, p. 59.

51. Leasor, p. 112.

52. NAM 7302–44. See also C. J. Goodman, 'Personal Experiences of the

Retreat to India in 1942, by Motor Transport from Heho to Myitkyina (April 20 to May 6) and then on Foot via the Hukawng Valley and Pangsao Pass to Ledo in Assam (May 7 to June 16) of C. J. Goodman, Capt., R.E.', in L. Allen, *Burma*, pp. 85–9.

53. Gribble, p. 73; V. J. Moharir, *History of The Army Service Corps (1939–1945)*, pp. 330–3.
54. Brookes, p. 96.
55. Clifford, pp. 91–4.
56. Tainsh, p. 121.
57. S. F. Russell, *Muddy Exodus*, p. 35.
58. Tyson, p. 52.
59. Gribble, pp. 85–6.
60. NAM 7302–44.
61. McPhedran, pp. 40, 44, 45.
62. NAM 7302–44.
63. McPhedran, pp. 96–7.
64. Gribble, p. 127.
65. NAM 7302–44.
66. Clifford, p. 166.
67. McPhedran, p. 102.
68. Leasor, p. 141.
69. Tyson, p. 40.
70. SOAS E Coll 3 C/31. See also chap. 3, 'With the Yunnan–Burma Railway workforce on the Hukawng Valley refugee trail, 19 April to 23 May 1942', in H. S. Hengshoon, *Green Hell*, pp. 23–34.
71. Brookes, pp. xvi–xviii, 175–6.
72. Tyson, chaps. 11–13.
73. The 1931 census showed 1,017,825 Indians in Burma, of whom 617,521 were born there. Before the fall of Rangoon, 70,000 were evacuated by sea; in April and May 4,801 were evacuated by air; at least 400,000 made the trek overland. Between 100,000 and 200,000 passed over the Taungup Pass and entered India via Chittagong, Many died on the way; the remainder travelled through central Burma. Estimates range as high as 100,000 (some higher but these are obviously just guesses). The official death toll is only 4,268 but is more probably around 50,000. Of those that left, no more than half tried subsequently to return. SOAS E Coll 3 C/31 H. Tinker. See also N. R. Chakravarti, *The Indian Minority in Burma: The Rise and Decline of an Immigrant Community*.

## 8 PLANS AND TRANSFORMATIONS

1. A. P. Wavell, *The Good Soldier*, p. 10.
2. J. H. Williams, p. 163.
3. Cady, p. 440.

4. M. Baird-Murray, *A World Overturned*, pp. 64, 71–2.

5. Becka, pp. 81–6.

6. Morrison, pp. 70–2, 183–201.

7. Becka, pp. 91–101. See Doc. No. 25, 'Summary of the Establishment of the Burma Defense Army. Drafted by the Commander of the Hayashi Army Group. August 9, 1942', in Trager (ed.), pp. 105–8.

8. Lyall Grant and Tamayama, p. 251.

9. IWM AL 425 SEATIC, Historical Bulletin no. 246, 'Burma–Siam Railway': Doc. no. 65. 'Summary for the Construction of the Burma–Thailand Railway. Instruction from the Imperial General Headquarters to the Southern Forces. June 20, 1942', in Trager (ed.), pp. 231–2; C. A. Kinvig, *River Kwai Railway*, pp. 23–4, 38–9, 41. There is a vast literature of this appalling episode. Major-General Clifford Kinvig's fiftieth anniversary account is the best historical overview, balancing the various personal accounts (at least those published up to 1992) with a thorough and extremely detailed study of the wider subject: the ideal starting-point for further study. See also: G. F. Kershaw, *Tracks of Death*; Tom Ingelse, *The Story of a Railway*; and Kevin Patience, 'Guide to the Death Railway', and Winston G. Ramsey, 'The Death Railway', in *After the Battle*, 26 (1979), pp. 13–20, 1–12, 21. General Australian accounts include: *Nippon Very Sorry – Many Men Must Die*; Hank Nelson, *Prisoners of War*; K. Bradley, *Hellfire Pass Memorial*; Gavan McCormack and Hank Nelson (eds.), *The Burma–Thailand Railway*; together with James McClelland, *Names and Particulars of all Australians Who Died While Prisoners of War on the Burma Death Railway*. There is a brief account of two of the affected regiments in their respective histories: see W. N. Nicholson, *The Suffolk Regiment 1928 to 1946*, pp. 213–26, and W. E. Underhill, *The Royal Leicestershire Regiment, 17th Foot, A History of the Years 1928 to 1956*, pp. 118–29. See also Don Wall and Clem Seale, *Singapore and Beyond*, as it affected an Australian unit.

10. IWM 93/7/2, Captain C. E. Escritt.

11. E. E. Dunlop, *The War Diaries of Weary Dunlop*, p. 176.

12. F. A. E. Crew, *The Army Medical Services, Campaigns*, vol. 5, *Burma*, p. 22.

13. Kinvig, *River Kwai Railway*, pp. 78–9; L. G. Holmes, *Four Thousand Bowls of Rice: A Prisoner of War Comes Home*, p. 34.

14. Lyall Grant and Tamayama, p. 332.

15. Iida noticed that the Japanese companies that followed the army into Burma were mere concession grabbers, thinking only of the long-term exploitation of the future and not of transferring economic power to the Burmese. 'Japanese of this kind kept pouring into Burma', he wrote, 'and swaggered and strutted about – what kind of impression must that have made on the Burmese?' L. Allen, *Burma*, p. 562.

16. Elsbree, pp. 18–24, 26–34; Becka, pp. 105, 107–9; F. C. Jones, *Japan's New Order in East Asia*, pp. 333–7.

17. U Khin, *U Hla Pe's Narrative of the Japanese Occupation of Burma*, p. 15.

18. Elsbree, pp. 38–41. See document no. 9, 'Instructions to the Members of

the Military Administration Department Delivered by Iida Shojiro, the Commander of Hayashi Army Group, to the Members of the Military Administration Department. March 23, 1942', in Trager (ed.), p. 59.

19. Cady, pp. 445-8, Doc. No. 30. 'Military Order No. 21. Issued by Iida Shojiro, the Commander of Burma Area Forces. August 1, 1942, Rangoon', in Trager (ed.), p. 122.

20. M. Collis, *Last and First in Burma (1941-1948)*, pp. 55-7, 71-2, 143-4. Figures vary regarding this human upheaval, but Becka (p. 79) suggests around half the Eurasian and Indian population – 10,000 Anglo-Burmese and Anglo-Indians and 350,000 Indians, plus some 12,000 Europeans – had left the country. See also Paul H. Krasotka's comprehensive study 'The Impact of the Second World War on Commercial Rice Production in South-East Asia' and Kurosawa Aiko's 'Transportation and Rice Distribution in South-East Asia during the Second World War', in P. H. Krasotka (ed.), *Food Supplies and the Japanese Occupation of South-East Asia*.

21. Tun Pe, p. 40.

22. Becka, pp. 110-12.

23. P. Elliott, pp. 132-3.

24. H. R. Corpe, *Prisoner beyond the Chindwin*, pp. 51-2.

25. R. Lamont-Brown, *Kempeitai*, p. 35. See also G. Hicks, *The Comfort Women*.

26. U Nu, pp. 51-3, 56-7. For a biography of this most important figure in wartime and post-war Burma, see Richard A. Butwell's *U Nu of Burma* and his autobiography *Saturday's Son*, pp. 102-13.

27. Cady, pp. 450-1; U Nu, pp. 86-7.

28. Tuchman, p. 307; A. Chandra, *Indian Army Triumphant in Burma*, p. xiv.

29. *Merrill's Marauders*, p. 5.

30. Romanus and Sunderland, *Stilwell's Mission to China*, p. 251.

31. Chennault, p. 214.

32. See Hugh Cave, *Wings across the World*.

33. Mains, *The Retreat from Burma*, p. 80; Burchett, *Bombs over Burma*, p. 29.

34. PRO CAB 120/493, 'Burma Operations 13 May 1942-3 August 1943'.

35. Connell, *Wavell: Supreme Commander*, pp. 236-7; Prasad (ed.), *The Reconquest of Burma*, vol. 1, pp. 17-23.

36. Mains, *Field Security*, pp. 69-84.

37. NAM 7808-96, 'History of 202 (L of C) Area 1942-1946'.

38. R. F. H. Nalder, *The Royal Corps of Signals*, pp. 331, 334.

39. Liang C-t, p. 44.

40. B. Tuchman, pp. 317-8; Romanus and Sunderland, *Stilwell's Mission to China*, pp. 104-8.

41. Romanus and Sunderland, *Stilwell's Mission to China*, pp. 227-8.

42. PRO CAB 121/681, 'Reconquest of Burma July 1942-June 1943'.

43. Later a total of 64 and then 83 squadrons was agreed. By the end of 1942 1,443 aircraft were available, but many of these were non-operational. H. St G. Saunders, *The Royal Force 1939-1945*, vol. 3, p. 299.

44. PRO CAB 121/681.

45. G. Moorehouse, *India Britannica*, p. 242.

46. Connell, *Wavell; Supreme Commander*, p. 23.

47. A. Stewart, p. 199.

48. H. Evans, *Thimmaya of India*, pp. 180–1.

49. C. Somerville, *Our War*, pp. 11–12, 118.

50. H. Evans, p. 181.

51. P. Hart, *At the Sharp End*, pp. 119–20.

52. H. Trevelyan, *The India We Left*, p. 114.

53. Collister, p. 175.

54. C. Branson, *British Soldier in India*, p. 118.

55. C. Mackenzie, *Eastern Epic*, pp. 526–8; Pakenham-Walsh, vol. 9, pp. 179–81.

56. Liang C–t, p. 80.

57. J. M. Vesely, *Unlike Any Land You Know*, p. 42. For an overview of bomber units and operations in CBI see Eric Munday, *USAAF Bomber Units Pacific 1941–45*. See also Thurzal Q. Terry, *Strangers in their Land* (9th Bomb Squadron); Charles S. Nicholls, *The Record, History of the Eleventh Bombardment Squadron (M), Three Hundred Forty First Bombardment Group (M), Fourteenth Air Force, United States Air Forces*; David K. Hayward (ed.), *Eagles, Bulldogs & Tigers* (22nd Bomb Squadron); MacKay H. Nelson, *Diary of Bomb Squadron* (391st Bomb Squadron); and Thomas H. Clare and Irma M. Clare, *Lookin' Eastward* (Chaplain for the 341st Bomb Group (M)).

58. Kinvig, *River Kwai Railway*, pp. 107–8, 115–7.

59. M. Howard, *Grand Strategy*, vol. 4, pp. 39–91.

60. J. W. Dunn, 'The Ledo Road', in B. W. Fowle (ed.), *Builders and Fighters: U.S. Army Engineers in World War II*, p. 329.

61. This was undertaken by Colonel John C. Arrowsmith, Chief Engineer to Lieutenant-General Raymond A. Wheeler, Commanding General, Services of Supply, China-Burma-India, with 45th Engineer General Service Regiment and 823rd Engineer Aviation Battalion assisted by native labour superintended by HQ Eastern Army. However, neither Wheeler nor Arrowsmith was satisfied with British assistance or the supply of labour. Equipment maintenance was also a major problem, with new machinery only arriving in dribbles. L. Anders, *The Ledo Road*, pp. 20–1, 37–41, 53.

62. PRO CAB 79/24, 'Minutes of Meetings nos. 301–361 1942 Oct. 26–Dec. 31, Chiefs of Staff Committee, 19.12.42'; CAB 121/681.

63. Eldridge, p. 149.

64. American writers such as Tuchman and Anders tend to agree, assuming that administrative problems were little more than difficulty in shuffling papers. Given America's 'can-do' spirit and brilliance at improvisation, this is perhaps understandable. Wavell was a past master at making ends meet with hardly any resources at all, but India was bottom of the pile and north-east India lacked any sort of transportation system to bring forward what little was allocated. PRO CAB 121/681, 'Reconquest of Burma July 1942–June 1943'.

65. Romanus and Sunderland, *Stilwell's Mission to China*, p. 244, n.67.

66. Romanus and Sunderland, *Stilwell's Mission to China*, p. 259; Liang, C-t, p. 104.

67. Romanus and Sunderland, *Stilwell's Mission to China*, p. 270.

68. A. Bryant, *The Turn of the Tide*, p. 494.

69. Tuchman, pp. 359–61; W. F. Craven and J. L. Cate (eds.), *The Army Forces in World War II*, vol. 4, *The Pacific: Guadalcanal to Saipan August 1942 to July 1944*, chap. 13. For a biography of Arnold, see Thomas M. Coffey, *HAP: The Story of the U.S. Air Force and the Man Who Built It*, and his own account of his war service, *Global Mission*.

70. Liang, C-t, pp. 107–8, 129–32.

71. The British provided rations and fuel while, apart from Bren guns and carriers, all arms and equipment supplied to the Chinese would be American. The Americans set up their own medical staff which proved a huge success, led by Gordon Seagrave among others. By judicious staff appointments under Brigadier-General Frederick McCabe, they made rapid progress. Tuchman, p. 327.

72. Liu, pp. 183–5; Ho Y-c, pp. 45–6.

73. Eldridge, p. 146.

74. Fischer, *The Chancy War*, pp. 29–30.

75. G. Seagrave, *Burma Surgeon Returns*, pp. 15–27.

76. Anders, p. 57.

77. Nalder, *The Royal Corps of Signals*, pp. 393–4.

78. IWM 133299/8, Lieutenant D. F. Neil.

79. C. MacFetridge, 'The Indian Army in Burma: A Personal Reminiscence', in Smurthwaite (ed.), p. 63.

80. NAM 7302–44–1, 'The Story of the Burma Rifles, Major C. M. Enriquez'.

81. Perry, pp. 108–10; Marston, pp. 79–86.

82. A number of radio announcers were known by this name, most commonly Iva Ikuro Toguri, who was born in 1916 in California, and an American citizen of Japanese descent. She was trapped while visiting an aunt in Tokyo at the start of the war and married a Portuguese named d'Aquino. She later claimed to have been coerced into making the 15-minute daily broadcasts as 'Anna', for which she received $40 a month. Boatner, p. 569.

83. Atkins, *The Reluctant Major*.

84. Nalder, *The History of British Army Signals in the Second World War*, p. 99.

85. Gaylor, pp. 249–51; S. Jagota, *History of the Corps of Electrical and Mechamcal Engineers*, pp. 26–31, chaps. 4–5.

86. Gaylor, pp. 249–53; Prasad (ed.), *Expansion of the Armed Forces and Defence Organization*, pp. 106–8.

87. C. Evans, *A Doctor in XIVth Army*, p. 98.

## 9 DONBAIK

1. Branson, p. 118.
2. Prasad (ed.), *The Reconquest of Burma*, vol. 1, pp. 55–6. The story of Z Force is told in G. Evans, *The Johnnies*, whose name derived from their being known as BOJs (British Officer Johnnies). For a personal account see also J. Mackay, 'Denied Ordinary Rites', in McCrae et al., *Tales of Burma*. For V Force operations later in the war, see J. Bowen, *Undercover in the Jungle*.
3. See OIOC MS Eur E390, 'North Arakan 1942', by Peter Murray, dated 1980, detailing the collapse of British administration in the area, with a brief historical introduction and a short account of subsequent events.
4. A. Irwin, *Burmese Outpost*, p. 40. See also IWM 88/19/1, J. S. Fletcher.
5. See the official history by Charles Cruickshank, *SOE in the Far East*. For descriptions of agents raising Shans and Kachins also Ian Fellowes-Gordon, *The Battle for Naw Seng's Kingdom*.
6. See B. Phillips, *KC8 Burma*, based largely on Bob Phillips's diary. They were supported by a company of 7th/14th Punjabis. See *Fourteenth Punjab Regiment*, pp. 51–2.
7. M. Miles, *A Different Kind of War*, pp. 76–8; R. Dunlop, *Behind Japanese Lines*, pp. 69, 88.
8. For biographies of Donovan, see Anthony Cave-Brown, *The Last Hero*, and Corey Ford, *Donovan and the OSS*.
9. R. Dunlop, pp. 29–41, 121–35, 151–64, 206–8. For a full account of the work of the fifty-one Columban Fathers working as missionaries in Upper Burma in 1936–1979, including their experiences during the Second World War, see Fischer's *Mission in Burma: The Columban Fathers' Forty-three Years in Kachin Country*.
10. C. B. Jones, p. 87.
11. Connell, *Wavell: Supreme Commander*, pp. 241–2. See also IWM P139, Lieutenant-General N. M. S. Irwin.
12. Prasad (ed.), *The Arakan Operations 1942–45*, pp. 8–10; M. Hickey, *The Unforgettable Army*, pp. 73–4.
13. L. Allen, *Burma*, pp. 94–5.
14. IWM 82/27/1, Sir Henry Jones.
15. IWM AL 827/1, 'History of 55 Japanese Division. Outline of Operations'.
16. L. Allen, *Burma*, pp. 96–8.
17. Prasad (ed.), *The Arakan Operations 1942–45*, pp. 24–9. A detailed account of the adventures of Major Denis Holmes, a V Force officer whose unit operated in the Arakan, is given in Lucas-Phillips, *The Raiders of Arakan*.
18. Slim, *Defeat into Victory*, p. 152.
19. Fox, p. 48; Ahmad, pp. 257–60; Tamayama and Nunneley, pp. 124–8. See also OIOC MS C519, 'Holiday on Full Pay', by Lt.-Col. Lionel Heathcote Landon, and MS Eur R194, taped interview, given 1990, by Lt.-Col. Lionel Heathcote Landon; IWM 80/2/1, Lt.-Col. L. H. Landon by the commander of 8th (Lahore) Mountain Battery at Donbaik.

20. Prasad (ed.), *The Arakan Operations 1942–45*, pp. 36–9; Farndale, p. 128.

21. C. T. Atkinson, *A History of The 1st (P.W.O.) Battalion The Dogra Regiment 1887–1947*, pp. 151–3; R. D. Palsokar, *A Historical Record of the Dogra Regiment*, p. 207. Second/1st Punjabis is one of the twelve 'phoenix' units in Daniel P. Marston's *Phoenix from the Ashes*, pp. 86–91.

22. B. Perrett, *Tank Tracks to Rangoon*, p. 80.

23. Rizvi, p. 13; Ahmad, pp. 261–5.

24. Ever since then, in memory of their exploits, 8th/6th Rajputana Rifles have celebrated 3 February as their battalion day. D. S. Chand, *The Rajputana Rifles*, p. 24.

25. GM G23/G46, 'The Japanese Morale. Compiled from Translation Extracts and Captured Jap Documents'.

26. Fox, p. 49; Qureshi, pp. 315–8; Ahmad, pp. 265–7.

27. Nalder, *The History of British Army Signals in the Second World War*, pp. 91–2, 95–6.

28. RCSM 916.6, 'Military Histories Far East, Communications in Burma'.

29. For a full discussion of Japanese Army water transport see M. Parillo, *The Japanese Merchant Marine in World War II*, pp. 177–94.

30. They would ultimately amount to the Burma Flotilla (later numbered 59th); 16th and 17th Motor Torpedo Boat Flotillas RN; 55th and 56th Fairmile Flotillas RIN using locally constructed craft; 49th Fairmile Flotilla SANF; 36th and 37th Fairmile Flotillas with mixed SA and RN crews; 13th and 14th Fairmile Flotillas RN, plus assorted other craft, with mostly RIN crews and RAN and RNZN officers. O. A. Goulden, *From Trombay to Changi's A Helluva Way: The Story of Arakan Coastal Forces*, pp. 34–6. See also OIOC MS Eur C388, 'Coral Strand', by Lt. Ivor John N. Jukes RINVR, describing his experiences with Arakan Coastal Forces, *c.* 1943–4.

31. Lyman, pp. 89–90.

32. Prasad (ed.), *The Arakan Operations 1942–45*, pp. 36–9, 57–61.

33. E. Johnson, *A Brief History of the Machine-Gun Battalion The Jat Regiment 1941–1946*, p. 101.

34. Prasad (ed.), *The Arakan Operations 1942–45*, pp. 65, 69–71.

35. Franks, *Hurricanes over the Arakan*, p. 154.

36. A. S. Turner, *An Engineer in the War*, pp. 66–7.

37. C. A. C. Sinker and D. P. St C. Rossier, *The History of the First Battalion The Lincolnshire Regiment in India, Arakan, Burma and Sumatra*, pp. 11–13.

38. The unit had been started by renowned war correspondent George Steer, whose despatches to *The Times* alerted the world to the horrors of aerial bombardment following the atrocity at Guernica during the Spanish Civil War. See Nicholas Rankin's excellent biography *Telegram from Guernica*, pp. 217, 220–4.

39. Glover, p. 200.

40. IWM 98/23/1, S. J. Raggatt.

41. GM G23/G46, 'The Japanese Morale. Compiled from Translation Extracts and Captured Jap Documents'.

42. See R. A. G. Nicholson, 'Sugar 5. Arakan 1943', *Journal of the Royal Artillery*, LXXVI/1, 1949; Farndale, p. 130; Glover, pp. 200-4.

43. SOAS E Coll 3 E/28, '1939–1945 The Unsung Heroes: A Personal Account by 5186455 Fusilier W. C. Smith, 1st Battalion Royal Welch Fusiliers'; IWM 16603, Sergeant C. D. Jones.

44. According to another eyewitness, Graves was killed before the sergeant was wounded. SOAS E Coll M/89, G. H. Davies, 'My Memories of the Burma War 1943', but Sergeant Reuben Jones 89 himself recalled that both he and the Bren gunner were wounded and 'Graves went on alone' before being hit (Nunneley, *Tales from the Burma Campaign*, p. 57).

45. IWM 10165, Company Sergeant Major M. McClane.

46. Rankin, pp. 234-7.

47. IWM 98/8/1, Captain D. C. Rissik.

48. Glover, p. 204; A Muir, *The First of Foot*, pp. 144-5; S. W. McBain, *A Regiment at War*, p. 29.

49. L. Allen, *Burma*, pp. 103-6; Slim, *Defeat into Victory*, pp. 153-4.

50. J. Thompson, *The Imperial War Museum Book of the War in Burma 1942–45*, pp. 54-9.

51. This fed doubts at the time of Japanese claims that British shelling had killed the brigadier, but it has since been confirmed by the medical officer who attended him. Tamayama and Nunneley, pp. 136-42; L. Allen, *Burma*, pp. 110-11; G. H. Davies, 'Memories', *Y Ddraig Goch: The Journal of The Royal Welch Fusiliers*, XXII/4, St David's Day, 1982.

52. See R. A. G. Nicholson, 'Indin April 6th, 1943. A Gunner Battle', *Journal of the Royal Artillery*, LXXVI/1, 1949; Farndale, p. 133.

53. Nalder, *The Royal Corps of Signals in the Second World War*, p. 395.

54. Prasad (ed.), *The Arakan Operations 1942–45*, p. 81.

55. Sinker and Rossier, p. 19.

56. PRO WO 203/1167, 'Report by Comd 71 Ind Inf Bde. Notes on Lessons from the Operations in Arakan 1943'.

57. C. T. Atkinson, pp. 157-8.

58. Prasad (ed.), *The Arakan Operations 1942–45*, pp. 84-5.

59. PRO CAB 121/681, 'Reconquest of Burma July 1942–June 1943'.

60. Prasad (ed.), *The Arakan Operations 1942–45*, p. 88.

61. Lewin, *Slim*, pp. 123-4.

62. Giffard had been senior general on the Army list when appointed. He lacked the dazzling personality to spark the soldiers' enthusiasm, but they liked him and called him 'Pop'. Lewin, *Slim*, p. 124; Slim, *Defeat into Victory*, pp. 164-5.

63. These figures vary considerably from Japanese figures, which record Allied dead as 4,789 and 483 PoWs. Their own losses amounted to 611 dead, 1,165 wounded: some 30 per cent of those taking part. L. Allen, *Burma*, p. 113.

64. Crew, pp. 122-3.

65. Kirby, vol. 3, pp. 32-3.

66. Charles Evans served with two different IMFUs. See his *A Doctor in XIVth Army*.

67. Armstong, pp. 138, 140.

68. J. S. G. Blair, *In Arduis Fidelis*, p. 328.

69. The drug even had an operational dimension, leading to what became called 'Tactics of Malaria Warfare', enabling the British to fight where malaria was prevalent while the Japanese could not. While aerial photography showed mosquito breeding areas, from March 1945 onwards Japanese prisoners were asked about malaria and the state of quinine supplies and had blood samples taken. During the ensuing monsoon the Japanese could be manoeuvred into malarial areas and his resupply route for quinine blocked, with a breakdown expected 4–6 weeks later. J. S. G. Blair, p. 329.

70. PRO WO 203/1167.

71. Crew, p. 678; B. Shephard, *A War of Nerves*, pp. 221–2.

72. PRO WO 203/1171, 'Appreciation of the Situation in Burma by Lieut.-Gen. Kawabe (Shozo) GOC-in-C 15th Army in Burma Made at Rangoon, 7 June 1943'.

73. J. S. G. Blair, p. 330.

74. G. W. Robertson, '*The Rose & the Arrow*', p. 173.

75. Humphreys, p. 12.

76. Atkins, *The Forgotten Major*, p. 57n.

77. G. C. Griffiths, 'The Railway Corridor and Before: With the 2nd Battalion in Burma', *Y Ddraig Goch: The Journal of The Royal Welch Fusiliers*, XXII/4, St David's Day, 1982, p. 52.

78. Shipster, p. 64.

79. J. Hudson, *Sunset in the East*, p. 22.

80. Franks, *Hurricanes over the Arakan*, p. 210.

81. Cotton, p. 175.

82. Hart, pp. 111–12.

83. SRM Acc. no. 5491, '1st Bn. India and Burma 1939–1945'; H. Cook, *The North Staffordshire Regiment*, p. 118.

83. Kirby, vol. 3, pp. 44–53.

## 10 WINGATE

1. *SEAC*, 4 June 1944.

2. Prasad (ed.), *The Reconquest of Burma*, vol. 1, p. 13.

3. Calvert, *Fighting Mad*, p. 66. Wingate has had numerous biographers. Although occasionally prone to hyperbole, the most recent and thorough is John Bierman and Colin Smith's *Fire in the Night*. The best of the early biographies is Christopher Sykes's, *Orde Wingate: A Biography* (1959), which shows his drive, initiative and unpredictability: a bizarre war hero. In contrast, he came under vitriolic attack from the official historian, S. Woodburn Kirby (*The War against Japan*, vol. 3, pp. 220–3.) Various writers have since set out to redress the balance. Derek Tulloch's *Wingate in Peace and War* (1972), written by Wingate's best friend, was the first attempt to refute the

unbalanced view and neglect of the official history. Tulloch accused Mountbatten and Slim of being critical of Wingate and extended praise for him and his accomplishments, noting that the Japanese admitted how disruptive Chindit operations had been to their own. Bernard Fergusson reviewed Tulloch's book ('The Wingate "Myth": Review Article', *The Journal of the Royal United Services Institute*, 117, September 1972, pp. 75–6) and other related publications with observations about 'those who would denigrate Wingate', Fergusson having himself been accused by Michael Calvert of 'denying him thrice' following publication of *The Trumpet in the Hall 1930–1958*, in 1970 (see pp. 172–91).

Some years later Sir Robert 'Bobby' Thompson wrote in his memoirs: 'The whole assessment was no more than a hatchet job by little men who could not have competed with Wingate either in military argument or in battle' *(Make for the Hills*, p. 73.) With Peter Mead he wrote 'Wingate – The Pursuit of Truth', *Army Quarterly and Defence Journal*, 108/3, pp. 333–40, and Mead wrote 'Orde Wingate and the Official Historians', in the *Journal of Contemporary History*, 14 January, 1979, pp. 55–82. Mead was a staff officer with Wingate, and these were further efforts to rehabilitate him from the attacks of the official historians, although some of Mead's formulations were absurdities. (See also Peter Mead, *Wingate and the Historians*.) Shelford Bidwell, historian of the second expedition, then took up the argument in 'Wingate and the Official Historians: An Alternate View'(*Journal of Contemporary History*, 15 April 1980, pp. 245–56), later expanded in Peter Mead and Shelford Bidwell, 'Orde Wingate: Two Views', *Journal of Contemporary History*, 15 July, 1980, pp. 401–4.

In 1982 former Chindits produced a series of personal tributes in 'Major General O. C. Wingate D.S.O. An Appreciation of the Planner and Leader of the Chindit Campaigns in 1943 and 1944 behind the Japanese Lines in Burma during World War II. Compiled by Members of the Chindits Old Comrades Association United Kingdom 1982. For private circulation only' (NAM Class 92Win, acc. no. 33303). Some dozen years later David Rooney followed this with 'A Grave Injustice: Wingate and the Establishment', *History Today*, 44, March 1994, pp. 11–13. He claimed manipulated documents and missing evidence, especially by Kirby, which he followed up with his book *Wingate and the Chindits*. Other studies include Luigi Rossetto, *Major General Orde Charles Wingate and the Development of Long Range Penetration*, which notes that Wingate's widow refused to allow access to his papers owing to abuse by previous researchers and, curiously, that the NAM and IWM contained nothing on the Chindits (he can't have looked far); and Trevor Royle, *Orde Wingate* (1995). Royle's book was sanctioned by the Wingate family and is both an analysis of his shifting reputation and a comparison with Montgomery.

4. Fergusson, *Beyond the Chindwin*, pp. 20–1.
5. GM, '2nd King Edward VII's Own Goorkhas, 3rd Battalion Records 1940–43', Brigadier Bernard Fergusson letter to Brigadier Philip Panton, 10

September 1946. Some thought him mad, a proposition discussed by Richard Rhodes-James, *Chindit*, pp. 87–91.

6. O. C. Wingate, 'Report on Operations of 77th Indian Infantry Brigade in Burma February to June 1943 by Brigadier O. C. Wingate' (hereafter, Wingate, 'Report'). Copies can be found at PRO CAB 106/51; CAB 106/46; AIR 23/1943; IWM 97/120/6–12 Major-General O. C. Wingate Papers; GM, '2nd King Edward VII's Own Goorkhas, 3rd Battalion Records, 1940–43'; and OIOC.

7. PRO AIR 41/36, 'Air Historical Branch Narrative, The Campaign in the Far East', p. 140.

8. Bierman and Smith, p. 234.

9. See J. J. Burke-Gafney, *The Story of The King's Regiment 1914–1948*, part 3, chap. 2.

10. IWM 15486/4, Private C. A. W. Aves. See also IWM 85/34/1, Private R. V. Hyner; IWM 80/49/1 Private L. F. Grist, and OIOC MS Eur C861.

11. Fergusson, *Beyond the Chindwin*, p. 47.

12. GM, '2nd King Edward VII's Own Goorkhas, 3rd Battalion Records, 1940–43', Brigadier Bernard Fergusson letter to Brigadier Philip Panton, 10 September 1946; Lt. R. P. Wormell letter to Lt.-Col. A. L. Fell, Comdt, 2nd Gurkha Rifles, no date.

13. G. R. Stevens, *History of the 2nd King Edward VII's Own Goorkha Rifles (The Sirmoor Rifles)*, vol. 3, *1921–1948*, pp. 200–1.

14. GM, '2nd King Edward VII's Own Goorkhas, 3rd Battalion Records, 1940–43'; 'One More River', by D. F. Neill, quoted in H. James, *Across the Threshold of Battle*, p. 39.

15. Masters, *The Road past Mandalay*, p. 157. A view shared by Terence O'Brien, *Out of the Blue*, p. 22.

16. NAM 7302–44–1, 'The Story of the Burma Rifles, by Major C. M. Enriquez'.

17. P. Stibbé, *Return via Rangoon*, p. 25.

18. IWM 15486/4, Private C. A. W. Aves.

19. Wingate, 'Report'.

20. J. S. G. Blair, p. 358, n. 12.

21. Bierman and Smith, p. 257.

22. P. Chinnery, *March or Die*, p. 29.

23. IWM 133299/8, Lieutenant D. F. Neill.

24. D. F. Neill, 'One More River', quoted in H. James, pp. 42–3.

25. In an unusual move, Wavell requested this promotion, which Churchill had been pleased to see he got in the New Year's list. Lewin, *The Chief*, pp. 207–8.

26. Calvert, *Fighting Mad*, p. 134.

27. Irwin had as GOC Eastern Army also been involved in the development of Wingate's force. It was he who drew up the original operational instruction that was then issued under its name. But he was less enthusiastic that it be employed except as part of a larger operation and took no part in the final decision to begin. L. Allen, *Burma*, pp. 124–6.

28. *Daily Express*, 21 May 1943.

29. Bierman and Smith, p. 271.

30. Doulton, pp. 50–2.

31. C. J. Rolo, *Wingate's Raiders*, p. 61; Fergusson, *Beyond the Chindwin*, pp. 58–9.

32. Stibbé, p. 51.

33. D. Halley, *With Wingate in Burma*, p. 54.

34. IWM AL 827/6, 'History of Burma Area Army (outline).'

35. D. S. Detwiler and C. B. Burdick (eds.), *War in Asia and the Pacific 1937–1949*, vol. 6/6, 'Burma Operations Record 15th Army Operations in Imphal Area and Withdrawal to Northern Burma', Japanese Monograph no. 134, p. 16; IWM AL 827/13 'History of Japanese 15th Army'.

36. SOAS E Coll G/37, 'Effect on the Japanese Army of Wingate's Invasion of North Burma in the Spring of 1943, by Lt.-Gen. Mutuguchi and Lt.-Col. Fujiwara'; 'Report on the Interrogation concerning the 1st Wingate Expedition, February 1943, of Lt.-Gen. Mutaguchi, Lt.-Gen. Tanaka, and various regimental commanders and staff officers'. (Also IWM 82/15/1, Major-General G. W. Symes.)

37. GM, '2nd King Edward VII's Own Goorkhas, 3rd Battalion Records, 1940–43', no. 4 Column War Diary; IWM 96/12/1, Colonel B. B. G. Bromhead.

38. GM, '2nd King Edward VII's Own Goorkhas, 3rd Battalion Records, 1940–43', no. 2 Column War Diary; D. F. Neill, 'One More River'.

39. Wingate, 'Report'.

40. Fergusson, *Beyond the Chindwin*, pp. 95–100.

41. H. James, p. 90.

42. Fergusson, *Beyond the Chindwin*, pp. 107–14.

43. SOAS E Coll G/37: L. Allen, *Burma*, pp. 133–6.

44. Wingate, 'Report'.

45. Calvert, *Prisoners of Hope*, p. 126.

46. H. James, p. 128.

47. SOAS E Coll G/37.

48. Fergusson employed the officer in his headquarters and he was later reinstated. There were also at least two instances of flogging for falling asleep on sentry duty during the expedition: the only form of field punishment available (Bierman and Smith, pp. 288–9). Men were also flogged for stealing rations, although the only incident investigated involved 2nd York and Lancaster Regiment during the second expedition. See PRO WO 172/4394, War Diary: 14 Air Landing Brigade: H.Q. 1944 Nov., Dec.'; P. Sharpe, pp. 209–10; J. Shaw, *Special Force: A Chindit's Story*, p. 209; T. O'Brien, *Out of the Blue*, pp. 134–5.

49. R. Painter, *A Signal Honour*, p. 46.

50. Fergusson, *Beyond the Chindwin*, p. 143.

51. J. Thompson, *The Imperial War Museum Book of War behind Enemy Lines*, pp. 142, 157.

52. IWM 133299/8, Lieutenant D. F. Neill.

53. Calvert, *Fighting Mad*, p. 129.
54. IWM 15486/4, Private C. A. W. Aves.
55. Cross and Gurung (eds.), p. 73.
56. Painter, p. 55.
57. Wingate, 'Report'.
58. NAM 7302–44–4, 'Tribute to Burma Rifles, Part Played in Wingate Expedition'.
59. P. Narain, *Subedar to Field Marshal*, p. 171. This story is probably apocryphal.
60. Rolo, p. 139.
61. Bierman and Smith, pp. 302n., 305.
62. H. James, p. 187.
63. Halley, p. 183.
64. After the war she continued to serve with the renamed Queen Alexandra's Royal Army Nursing Corps, and in the early 1950s was matron of the British Military Hospital at Taiping in North Malaya, renowned for her cheerful efficiency and still plying patients with champagne when she thought it would help. There came a time when all could see she was losing weight and a consultant confirmed what she already knew: she was dying of cancer and had only weeks to live. Before flying home to spend her final days with relatives, she was the calm, elegant and radiant centre of a farewell party at the Divisional Headquarters mess, where she sipped her favourite champagne and smoked a cigarette through a long holder. With her strong faith and with no sign of despair or foreboding, she left the party in high spirits, never to return. Hickey, pp. 93, 261.
65. GM, '2nd King Edward VII's Own Goorkhas, 3rd Battalion Records, 1940–43', Lt. R. P. Wormell, letter to Lt.-Col. A. L. Fell, Comdt, 2nd Gurkha Rifles, no date; IWM 92/39/1, Lt. R. A. Wilding.
66. Stibbé, pp. 126–7.
67. Prasad (ed.), *The Reconquest of Burma*, vol. 1, p. 136.
68. Fergusson, *Beyond the Chindwin*, p. 241.
69. Stevens, *History of the 2nd King Edward VII's Own Goorkha Rifles (The Sirmoor Rifles)*, vol. 3, *1921–1948*, p. 231.
70. Bierman and Smith, p. 308.
71. PRO CAB 106/170, 'Extracts from the Wingate Papers'.
72. IWM 66/197/1, Major K. D. Gilkes Papers, General Sir Claude Auchinleck, covering letter to 'Report on Operations of 77th Indian Infantry Brigade in Burma February to June 1943', in J. Thompson, *The Imperial War Museum Book of War behind Enemy Lines*, pp. 170–1.
73. J. Thompson, *The Imperial War Museum Book of War behind Enemy Lines*, p. 168.
74. Wingate, 'Report'.
75. GM, '2nd King Edward VII's Own Goorkhas, 3rd Battalion Records, 1940–43', War Diary no. 4 column.
76. PRO AIR 41/36, 'Air Historical Branch Narrative, the Campaign in the Far East, vol. 3', pp. 93–6.

77. IWM 12352, Major W. Scott.
78. W. W. Russell, *Forgotten Skies*, pp. 47–8; Franks, *First in the Indian Skies*, pp. 116–7.

## 11 SUPREMO

1. The area was also home to the Chin Hills Battalion BFF. See OIOC Ms Eur E250, 'History of the Chin Hills Battalion Military Police'.
2. Turner, pp. 73–4.
3. Sandes, p. 45; S. Verma and V. K. Anand, *The Corps of Indian Engineers 1939–1947*, pp. 102–6; Evans and Brett-James, p. 45.
4. Chandra, pp. 75–6.
5. Atkins, *The Forgotten Major*, pp. 3–8, 42; Pakenham-Walsh, vol. 9, pp. 192–4.
6. PRO WO 203/1167, Report by Comd 71 Ind Inf Bde. Notes on Lessons from the Operations in Arakan 1943'.
7. Slim, *Defeat into Victory*, p. 538. See Detwiler and Burdick (eds.), vol. 3, *Command, Administration and Special Operations, 5, Principles of Night Combat [Night Combat Study Part I]*.
8. PRO WO 203/2607, 'Lessons From Operations'. This appears to be a reference to one of Wavell's sayings. Wavell, p. 47.
9. P. Davis, *A Child in Arms*, pp. 30–2.
10. Cameron had served with the KOYLI at Gallipoli during the First World War and afterwards joined the Gurkhas, commanding 2nd/5th during the retreat. He was known as 'Snow White' since the experience of having to abandon some of his beloved riflemen at the Sittang disaster turned his hair pure white. Evans and Brett-James, p. 117.
11. During the attempts to retake No. 3 Stockade, Havildar Gaje Ghale of 2nd /5th Royal Gurkhas won the VC. GM G9 '2/5RGR (FF) Phase of 2/5th History 8/42 – 5/44'. Prasad (ed.), *The Reconquest of Burma*, vol. 1, pp. 67–72; J. N. Mackay, *A History of The 4th Prince of Wales's Own Gurkha Rifles*, vol. 3, *1938–1948*, p. 132; *History of the 5th Royal Gurkha Rifles (Frontier Force)*, pp. 209–24.
12. T. Farrant, 'Fifty Years Ago', in *The Lion and The Dragon*, regimental magazine of The King's Own Royal Border Regiment, 10/1, 1993, p. 48.
13. The full load tables for a battalion's mules are to be found in 9th Border's war diary. Mules 1–4 carried signals stores; 5–20 the battalion's 3-inch mortars; 21–2 pioneer stores; 23–38 companies' reserve ammunition; 39–50 platoon 2-inch mortar mules; 51–62 were light machine-gun mules. Jeeps carried less immediate necessities such as dubbin, hurricane lamps and stationery. PRO WO 172/2501, 'War Diary 9 Border 1943 Jan.– Dec.'.
14. *History of the 5th Royal Gurkha Rifles (Frontier Force)*, p. 295.
15. Maxwell, pp. 251–5.
16. IWM 77/51/2 & 2A, Captain D. H. Cozens; OIOC MS Eur B386, 'Bamboos and Partisans', by Major Hamilton Simonds-Gooding. One levy

was issued a 12-bore shotgun, which he exchanged for a flintlock musket manufactured in 1685. Villagers made ammunition for these museum pieces using 'any old iron' and explosives reputedly from charcoal mixed with wine and dried in the sun. Later the army had to purchase black powder and lead bars and drop these in the Chin Hills, as Lee-Enfield rifles could not be spared (Evans and Brett-James, p. 44).

17. Gilmore and Davis, p. 107.

18. See Ursula Graham Bower's memoir *Naga Path*. For personal accounts of serving with the Chin Levies, see Harold Braund, *Distinctly I Remember*, and Desmond Kelly, *Kelly's Burma Campaign: Letters from the Chin Hills*.

19. Morrison, pp. 84–90, 202–12. Pagani's story is told in Robert Hamond's *The Flame of Freedom*.

20. Morrison, pp. 95–105, 113. For a personal account by an American flyer, see John Boyd with Gareth Garth, *Tenko! Rangoon Jail*. See also Rowan T. Thomas, *Born in Battle*, pp. 56–150.

21. F. C. Jones, pp. 353–4.

22. The IIL was formed by Major Fujiwara Iwaichi's F. Kikan, the Japanese intelligence agency responsible for supporting Asian liberation movements, and Giani Pritam Singh, a Sikh missionary who formed a branch in Bangkok shortly before hostilities in December 1941 (IWM AL 827/9 SEATIC Bulletin no. 240, 'Translation of Essays by Lt.-Col. Fujiwara Iwaichi on Burma Campaign, March 1943 onwards'). The INA was first formed in February 1942 by F. Kikan and the IIL.

23. W. S. Desai, *India and Burma*, pp. 79–80.

24. Elsbree, pp. 158–9.

25. Becka, pp. 123–5; Doc. no. 38, 'Treaty of Alliance between Japan and Burma. Signed on August 1, 1943, Rangoon' (p. 152); Doc. no. 39, 'Japan–Burma Secret Military Agreement. Signed on August 1, 1943, Rangoon (p. 153); Doc. no. 40, 'Detail Describing the Japan–Burma Secret Military Agreement. Signed on August 1, 1943, Rangoon (pp. 154–5); Doc. no. 43, 'Declaration of Independence of Burma. Proclaimed by the President, Burma Constituent Assembly. August 1, 1943, Rangoon' (pp. 164–8); Doc. no. 44. 'Declaration of War. Proclaimed by the Head of the State of Burma (Ba Maw). August 1, 1943, Rangoon' (pp. 168–70), in Trager (ed.).

26. Trager (ed.), p. 164.

27. P. Elliott, p. 135.

28. L. Allen, 'The Japanese Occupation of South East Asia (I)', *Durham University Journal*, XXXIII/1, December 1970, p. 14.

29. Cady, p. 461.

30. Opposition to independence was centred on Colonel Iishi Akio, Senior Staff Officer of the General Affairs Section at Southern Army, who cited the example of Wang Ching-wei, head of the Chinese collaborationist government in Nanking. L. Allen, *Burma*, pp. 560–1.

31. Tun Pe, pp. 54–8, 75.

32. Cady, pp. 467–9.

33. Burma Intelligence Bureau, vol. 1, p. 19. Ne Win was formerly known as Thakin Shu Maung. Cady, pp. 455–6. See also On Kin's *Burma under the Japanese*, and U Tun Pe's *Sun over Burma*.

34. W. S. Churchill, vol. 4, p. 793; vol. 6, p. 143.

35. Sherwood, p. 716.

36. 'Except for the fact that he was a stout hearted fighter, suitable to lead a brigade of Chinese scallywags, I could see no qualities in him. He was a Chinese linguist, but had little military knowledge and no strategic ability of any kind. His worst failing, however, was his deep rooted hatred of anybody or anything British! It was practically impossible to establish friendly relations with him or the troops under his command. He did a vast amount of harm by vitiating the relations between Americans and British in both India and Burma. Chennault … a fine fighting man, but of limited ability, who added little to the useful discussions of the day.' A. Danchev and D. Todman (eds.), *War Diaries, 1939–1945*, pp. 403–4.

37. Chennault, p. 220.

38. Bryant, *The Turn of the Tide*, p. 624.

39. Tuchman, pp. 369–73.

40. It was a convoluted process that brought Wavell to the viceroyalty, either by chance or perhaps default. Lewin, *The Chief*, pp. 215–20.

41. OIOC MS Eur C588 minute, 20 June 1943, by Leo Amery, Secretary of State for India and Burma, to the Prime Minister on the need for reducing the strength of the Indian Army and increasing pay; also a cipher telegram to the Viceroy, commenting on Auchinleck's views on the limits of troop reduction: PRO CAB 66/36 WP(43) 197; CAB 65/34 (43) 47–(43) 90 1943 Apr. 1–June 29.

42. Kirby, vol. 2, p. 383.

43. Connell, *Auchinleck*, pp. 755–8.

44. Marston, pp. 95–103.

45. *The Jungle Book*, Military Training Pamphlet No. 9, India, 4th edn, September 1943. For a description of the curriculum in a training battalion, see Conden, *The Frontier Force Regiment*, pp. 448–50, 587–9.

46. *Warfare in the Far East*, Military Training Pamphlet No. 52, War Office, 1944.

47. Collister, p. 166.

48. Perry, pp. 111–12. For development of India as a base for offensive operations including port expansion, see Prasad (ed.), *Expansion of the Armed Forces and Defence Organization*, and Kirby, vol. 2, pp. 299–300, 489–91; vol. 3, pp. 17–19, 27, 313; vol. 4, pp. 16–17; vol. 5, 77–9.

49. W. S. Churchill, vol. 5, p. 507.

50. Bryant, *Triumph in the West*, p. 691.

51. W. S. Churchill, vol. 5, p. 62; M. Gilbert, *Road to Victory*, p. 465.

52. Later officially called 5307th Composite unit (Provisional), it was made famous as 'Merrill's Marauders' after the name of its first commander (see Chapter 13). At 772 pages long, the most astonishingly detailed history of Galahad is *Spearhead: A Complete History of Merrill's Marauders Rangers*, by

James E. T. Hopkins with John M. Jones. Another excellent, concise but well-illustrated account is Alan Baker's *Merrill's Marauders*.

53. Tuchman, pp. 382–4.
54. Barker, *The March on Delhi*, p. 44. For biographies of Mountbatten there are Richard Hough's informal study *Mountbatten: A Hero of our Time* and Ian McGeoch's *A Princely Sailor*, which gives a military study. However, Philip Ziegler's official biography, *Mountbatten*, is 'so thorough, so circumspect, so fair, so impeccably researched that there will be no need for any other' (A. Cooke, *The New Yorker*, 9 September 1985, p. 108).
55. Ziegler, *Mountbatten*, pp. 219–22; McGeoch, p. 97; M. Howard, *Grand Strategy*, vol. 4, p. 578.
56. O. Harvey, *War Diaries*, p. 286.
57. Ziegler, *Mountbatten*, pp. 230–6.
58. G. Evans, *Slim as Military Commander*, p. 105; Callahan, p. 68.
59. R. Lyman, 'The Appointment of Slim to Eastern Army – October 1943', in *Slim, Master of War*, appx 2, pp. 269–72.
60. Lewin, *Slim*, p. 129.
61. E. P. MacIntosh, *Sisterhood of Spies*, p. 191.
62. S. Bidwell, *The Chindit War*, p. 32.
63. Stilwell. p. 230.
64. Fischer, *The Chancy War*, pp. 189–90; Ziegler, pp. 243–5.
65. W. S. Churchill, vol. 5, p. 78.
66. Ziegler, *Mountbatten*, pp. 262–7.
67. Bryant, *Triumph in the West*, p. 46.
68. Tuchman, pp. 401–6.
69. Romanus and Sunderland, *Stilwell's Command Problems*, p. 65.
70. Bryant, *Triumph in the West*, p. 108.
71. Tuchman, pp. 407–9.
72. Romanus and Sunderland, *Stilwell's Command Problems*, p. 80.
73. The first edition was published on 10 January 1944. It was the first such paper of its kind and many reputable journalists worked on it, representing all three services. Although restricted by paper shortages to four pages, it was an instant success and continued to be so over two and a half years and 852 editions, the last one published in Singapore on 15 May 1946.
74. R. Arnold, *A Very Quiet War*, p. 153. Arnold was Deputy Director of Public Relations at SEAC; Ziegler, *Mountbatten*, pp. 253–5.
75. D. Wilson, *The Sum of Things*, p. 102; Hough, pp. 178–9; J. Leyin, *Tell Them of Us: The Forgotten Army – Burma*, pp. 126–7.
76. G. W. Robertson, p. 172.
77. Lyman, pp. 76–80.
78. Lewin, *Slim*, p. 136; D. Rooney, *Burma Victory*, pp. 24, 174.
79. Somerville was a sea dog of the old school and made no secret of the fact that it was he who ran the Navy in the Far East, and he was quite prepared to put reservations on orders issued to him by a junior. Ziegler, *Mountbatten*, pp. 238–40.

80. P. Ziegler (ed.), *Personal Diary of Admiral the Lord Louis Mountbatten*, p. 19.
81. NAM 7808-96, 'History of 202 (L of C) Area 1942-1946'.
82. GREF was authorized on 20 March 1943 to take over the main road and air-field projects. By the end of the year it had expanded to 26,000 men and later reached 100,000 with half in 80 engineer units and another half ITA and other civilian labourers together with 7 GPT companies formed into 7th MT Regiment under command of CRIASC, 202 Area. Verma and Anand, pp. 120-5.
83. NAM 7808-96; E. T. C. Gordine, *A Patriot's Boast*, pp. 94-5.
84. Leasor, pp. 155-8.
85. P. Moon (ed.), *Wavell: The Viceroy's Journal*, p. 53; Lewin, *Slim*, pp. 226-7. Ironically, while the famine irretrievably damaged the British reputation as efficient administrators, Bengal had an Indian Congress provincial government at the time.
86. Bryant, *Triumph in the West*, p. 158.
87. C. Evans, p. 41.
88. Leyin, p. 72.

## 12 THE MARCH ON DELHI

1. PRO WO 172/4884, appx 'D' to 'War Diary, Jan 1944. 4th Bn Royal West Kent Regiment War Diary, Jan–Dec 1944'.
2. IWM 93/14/12; P425 Brig. Sir Philip Toosey, 'Report on Prisoner of War Camps in Malaya and Thailand.' See Chapter 10, 'Speedo-Worko', in Kinvig, *River Kwai Railway*.
3. Kinvig, *River Kwai Railway*, pp. 104-5.
4. PRO WO 203/1171, 'Appreciation of the Situation in Burma by Lieut.-Gen. Kawabe (Shozo) GOC-in-C 15th Army in Burma Made at Rangoon, 7 June 1943'.
5. PRO WO 208/3924, 'Memo by Lt.-Col. J. Figgess, UK Liaison Mission, Tokyo: "Enquiry for Historical Section of Cabinet Office" 26 May 1948'. His true level of enthusiasm is not clear. According to Joyce Lebra, when Bose called on the imprisoned Mohan Singh, he replied, 'My name carries enough weight. When I appear in Bengal everyone will revolt. Wavell's whole army will join me' (*Jungle Alliance*, p. 124). But Singh avers that he listened with some scepticism (*A Soldier's Contribution to Independence*, p. 266).
6. PRO WO 208/149, 'Report on Operations in Burma 1943-5'.
7. L. Allen, *Burma*, p. 154.
8. Detwiler and Burdick (eds.), vol. 6/6, 'Burma Operations Record 15th Army Operations in Imphal Area and Withdrawal to Northern Burma', Japanese monograph no. 134, pp. 18, 27.
9. Craven and Cate (eds.), vol. 4, pp. 468-84; Kinvig, *River Kwai Railway*, pp. 155-7.
10. Detwiler and Burdick (eds.), vol 6/6, 'Burma Operations Record 15th Army

Operations in Imphal Area and Withdrawal to Northern Burma', Japanese Monograph no. 134, pp. 30–1, 42–7.

11. For a biographical account of Mutaguchi and his turbulent relationship with Sato, see 'Mutaguchi and the March on Delhi', in Swinson, *Four Samurai*, pp. 115–50.

12. IWM AL 5074, 'Japanese Monograph 133. Burma Operations Record: Outline of Burma Area Line of Communication'.

13. Kinvig, *River Kwai Railway*, p. 164; Ba Maw, p. 295.

14. IWM AL 5074.

15. Vesely, pp. 99–122.

16. IWM AL 5035, 'SEATIC Bulletin 242, Japanese Generals Answers to Questionnaire, 1946'.

17. On 1 December 1943 B-24s of 7th Bombardment Group (H) raided Rangoon harbour and railway yards in the area. During the briefing 'a hush fell over the room, for the crews respected the danger they would be facing'. They were engaged by Japanese fighters for 70 minutes, a theatre record, and six American bombers were lost. E. R. Evans, *Combat Cameraman China–Burma–India*, pp. 38–43.

18. B. Peacock, *Prisoner on the Kwai*, pp. 133–4; IWM AL 827/3, 'History of 54 Japanese Division'.

19. R. Rivett, *Behind Bamboo*, p. 197.

20. For Yamauchi, see Barker, *The March on Delhi*, pp. 275–6; L. Allen, *Burma*, pp. 247, 296–8; IWM 827/11, 'History of 15 Japanese Division from March 1944'.

21. Later Japanese historians would attribute their overall defeat in Burma to the disastrous assumption, taken long before their divisions crossed the Chindwin, after Naka assured them tanks would not be encountered. At the last table exercise before the offensive started at Maymyo between 22 and 26 December the operation was treated as though they would not be, although neither Sato nor Yanagida was present. Only at the last moment as the division crossed the Chindwin did Naka admit he was wrong, but it was too late to make changes, and as Takagi Toshiro states, Naka's mistake would lead directly to the deaths of thousands of Japanese soldiers whose rotting corpses would litter the hillsides and jungle west of the Chindwin in the summer of 1944. With battalions diverted to assist containing the Chindits, 15th Division was seriously understrength and, having replaced the guns normally used with mountain guns of 1908 vintage (with only 200 rounds per gun), seriously short of firepower. Detwiler and Burdick (eds.), vol. 6/6, 'Burma Operations Record 15th Army Operations in Imphal Area and Withdrawal to Northern Burma', Japanese Monograph no. 134, p. 136; L. Allen, *Burma*, pp. 247–8, 260.

22. IWM Al 827/6, 'History of Burma Area Army (outline)'.

23. IWM AL 456; AL 5036 SEATIC Hist. Bull. No. 243, 'History of Japanese 28th Army'; Detwiler and Burdick (eds.), vol. 7/1, 'Burma Operations Record: 28th Army Operations in Akyab Area (November 1943–September 1945', Japanese Monograph no. 132, p. 6.

24. Kirby, vol. 3, pp. 78–9: IWM AL 827/4, 'History of 2 Japanese Division'; Al 827/3, 'History of 54 Japanese Division'; Al 827/1, 'History of 55 Japanese Division. Outline of Operations'; AL 827/2, 'History of 56 Japanese Division'.

25. L. Allen, *Burma*, p. 285.

26. IWM AL 5009/7, 'Reports of SEATIC Interrogators: Lt.-Gen. Sato Kotoku, Cmdr 31 Division'.

27. L. Allen, *Burma*, p. 286.

28. Barker, *Japanese Army Handbook 1939–1945*, p. 116.

29. Tamayama and Nunneley, p. 157.

30. SOAS E Coll 3 B/37 Captain J. C. Smyth, 'Notes on the Burmese Campaign compiled from Japanese Sources. Unpublished 1946'.

31. Evans and Brett-James, p. 86.

32. Barker, *Japanese Army Handbook 1939–1945*, pp. 116–7.

33. Tamayama and Nunneley, p. 175.

34. Prasad (ed.), *The Reconquest of Burma*, vol. 1, p. 82.

35. PRO WO 172/4427, 'War Diary 63rd Indian Infantry Brigade 1944 Jan.–Dec.'; Rizvi, p. 79; Barclay, *The Regimental History of The 3rd Queen Alexandra's Own Gurkha Rifles*, vol. 2, *1927–1947*, pp. 61–4; Mackay, *A History of The 4th Prince of Wales's Own Gurkha Rifles*, vol. 3, *1938–1948*, p. 152; Mullaly, *Bugle and Kukri*, pp. 213–4; Duncan, Ellis, Banks and Scarfe (eds.), pp. 12–13; Doulton, pp. 69–73.

36. Chandra, p. 81.

37. LHCMA Gracey Papers 1/8, 17 Nov 1943.

38. D. K. Palit, *Sentinels of the North-East*, pp. 131–44.

39. Slim, *Defeat into Victory*, pp. 179–89.

40. Rooney, *Burma Victory*, pp. 29–31.

41. See George Markham's *Japanese Infantry Weapons of World War Two*. For a comparative study of infantry and support weapons used by the two sides, see M. Baldwin, 'Infantry Weapons in the Far East', in D. Smurthwaite (ed.), *The Forgotten War*.

42. GM G23, 'Chin Hills Operation Notes and Imphal Ops'.

43. PRO WO 172/4318, 'War Diary 20th Indian Division 1944 Jan.–Jun. Instruction No. 2'; Chandra, p. 82.

44. PRO WO 172/4427, 'War Diary 63rd Indian Infantry Brigade 1944 Jan.–Dec.'

45. A tall, suave and highly ambitious officer, in his 1958 autobiography Wedemeyer describes being 'eased out to Asia' as Mountbatten's Deputy Chief of Staff for planning (*Wedemeyer Reports!*, p. 249), and Mountbatten referred to him as 'a tricky customer but very loyal to me' (Hough, p. 171).

46. See John G. Martin's complete history of combat cargo, *It Began at Imphal*. This includes considerable technical detail on the aircraft flown as well as full operational histories of the units. See also the same author's *Through Hell's Gate to Shanghai: History of the 10th Combat Cargo Squadron, 3rd Combat Cargo Group, CBI Theater, 1944–1946*.

47. Lyman, pp. 171–6.

48. G. J. Thomas, *Eyes for the Phoenix*, pp. 78–84; A. Clayton, *Forearmed*, pp. 179–81.

49. Franks, *The Air Battle of Imphal*, pp. 20–1, 43–4. This is the best reference for details of the air fighting, laced with numerous quotes from participants. For a semi-fictionalized account, see O. Moxon, *The Last Monsoon*.

50. Vincent was a popular and familiar figure to the army as well as the air force. G. Evans and A. Brett-James, p. 193.

51. Tulihal was 4,000 yards long, owing to a misunderstanding between the British, who talked of airfield length in yards, and the Americans, who talked of feet; but this proved of great benefit to Operation Thursday when heavily loaded Dakotas took off and landed at both ends. Evans and Brett-James, pp. 195–6.

52. See John Stanaway's *P-38 Lightning Aces of the Pacific and CBI*, and *Mustang and Thunderbolt Aces of the Pacific and CBI*.

53. Evans and Brett-James, p. 112.

54. PRO WO 172/4652, 'War Diary 129 Fd Regt RA Jan.–Dec. 1944'.

55. Since divisions were normally commanded by a lieutenant-general, it was common practice in Japanese doctrine to give command of any large detachments to the commander of the infantry group, a major-general. In this case it was based on III/213th Regiment with two additional companies from 215th Regiment, 33rd Engineer Regiment (a battalion strength unit) and initially two battalion detached from 15th Division (II/51st and III/60th). L. Allen, *Burma*, p. 206.

56. LHCMA Gracey Papers 1/11, 'Account of Operations against Kyaukchaw Position, 17–25 Jan 44'; NRHC 569, 'The Northamptonshire Regt. Burma December 1943–April 1945, Compiled by Lt.-Col. D. E. Taunton, D.S.O.'.

57. PRO WO 203/682, '1944 Mar. Kyaukchaw to Dathkyauk Awk Operation on 10 Feb. 1944: An Account'; WO 203/684, 'Kyaukchaw Battle'; W. J. Jervois, *The History of the Northamptonshire Regiment*, pp. 247–53; H. J. Huxford, *History of the 8th Gurkha Rifles*, p. 204.

58. Conden, *The Frontier Force Rifles*, pp. 395–8. This is one of the twelve 'phoenix' units in Daniel P. Marston's *Phoenix from the Ashes*, pp. 142–5.

59. Evans and Brett-James, pp. 132–3.

60. Farndale, pp. 175–6; P. J. Shears, *The Story of The Border Regiment 1939–1945*, pp. 39–40.

61. Evans and Brett-James, pp. 175–7; L. Allen, *Burma*, pp. 209–11.

62. A. C. Bickersteth, *ODTAA*, p. 65; Mullaly, *Bugle and Kukri*, pp. 334–43.

63. J. H. Williams, p. 186.

64. This, as David Rooney notes, raises a significant question; if Slim's strategy was to withdraw to the Imphal plain and fight there, why did Fourteenth Army continue to pour supplies forward? Rooney, *Burma Victory*, pp. 42–5.

65. Roberts went on to become Quartermaster General before retirement. Evans and Brett-James, p. 31.

66. Doulton, pp. 78, 83.

67. 'During the morning of the 13th', Kirby, vol. 3, p. 111; 'Soon after half past eight in the evening', Evans and Brett-James, p. 114; 'At 2040 hours on 13 March', Prasad (ed.), *The Reconquest of Burma*, vol. 1, p. 190.

68. C. Peterson, *Unparalleled Danger, Unsurpassed Courage*, p. 152.

69. Rooney, *Burma Victory*, p. 35.

70. Evans and Brett-James, pp. 122–6.

71. Lyall Grant, *Burma: The Turning Point*, p. 62. This provides an excellent, very thoroughly researched and detailed account of the crucial battles fought by 17th Indian Division to extract itself from peril.

72. Atkins, *The Forgotten Major*, p. 81.

73. NAM, 'History of 9th Battalion The Border Regiment'; Shears, pp. 139–40.

74. Moharir, p. 381; Pakenham-Walsh, vol. 9, pp. 213–4; IWM P461, Captain C. Satchell (45th Mule Company RIASC); GM, 'History of 17 Indian Division, July 1941 to December 1945'; Sandes, pp. 58–60; Farndale, pp. 178–9.

75. Such was the effect of 17th Indian Division's skilful withdrawal that Yanagida – never enthusiastic about the Imphal operation – was prompted to send a signal to Mutaguchi that there could be no question of taking Imphal in three weeks as ordered and that, with the onset of the monsoon, they were inviting tragedy. Mutaguchi's response was furious. Yanagida had spent almost his entire career on the staff and was deeply affected by his division's casualties, later shutting himself up in his tent. He had also clashed with his Chief of Staff, Colonel Tanaka Tetsujiro, a tough character inclined towards Mutaguchi's outlook. Following the battle of Tongzang, Yanagida asked his intelligence officer's opinion of future operations, after which Tanaka very loudly told him not to listen to his divisional commander's complaints. L. Allen, *Burma*, pp. 199–205.

76. Kirby, vol. 3, p. 450; Lyall Grant, *Burma: The Turning Point*, pp. 67–70.

77. Romanus and Sunderland, *Stilwell's Command Problems*, p. 175.

78. Ziegler, *Mountbatten*, pp. 271–2; B. Bond (ed.), p. 151.

79. The RAF were to send twenty-five, but the unit involved, 216 Squadron, could not manage this. PRO AIR 41/64, 'Air Historical Branch Narrative, The Campaign in the Far East', pp. 103–6.

80. By the time he relinquished command in July 1944, Briggs had probably been in close contact with the enemy for longer than any other British commander. Among his post-war appointments he was Commander-in-Chief, Burma. Evans and Brett-James, pp. 153, 155–8. He was, according to Christison, 'stolid, methodical, slow to think, express himself and act, but extremely sound and conventional'. IWM 82/15/1, General Sir Philip Christison Bt.

81. *Wings of the Phoenix*, p. 176. 194 Squadron was formed from 31 Squadron in October 1943 and a healthy rivalry soon existed between them. For histories see: D. A. Briscoe, *The Friendly Firm Remembers*; D. Williams, *194 Squadron Royal Air Force*; and RAFM B3687, 'History of No. 194 Squadron 1943–1945'.

82. Franks, *The Air Battle of Imphal*, p. 37.

83. Sandes, pp. 220–1.

84. Brett-James, *Ball of Fire*, pp. 300–1.

85. Colvin, *Not Ordinary Men*, pp. 24–5.

86. Swinson, *Kohima*, p. 35.

87. Colvin, p. 34.

88. Graham Bower, *Naga Path*, p. 153.

89. The brigade was formed from volunteers at Delhi in October 1941, comprising 151st (British), 152nd (Indian) and 153rd (Gurkha) Battalions. In 1942 151st Battalion went to the Middle East following a number of scrapes with Americans. (It was renumbered 156th and eventually fought at Arnhem, where it was reduced to eleven men.) It was replaced by another Gurkha battalion – 154th – in October 1942, based on the remnants of 3rd/7th Gurkhas, but this was not at Sangshak. See K. C. Praval, Chapter 4, 'India Raises her First Para Brigade', in *India's Paratroops (A History of the Parachute Regiment of India)*, pp. 18–26; F. G. Nield, *With Pegasus in India: The Story of 153 Gurkha Parachute Battalion*; 'Indian Airborne Reminiscences', *The Journal of the Royal Army Medical Corps*, XCI/6, December 1948.

90. L. Allen, *Burma*, pp. 220–1n.

91. Farndale, p. 180.

92. IWM AL 5236, 'Battle at Sangshak, 22–28 March 1944. Report by Japanese Research Division Received under 38 of 18 October 1955'.

93. This was a raw unit of the Nepalese Army restricted to service within India. It was not heavily engaged during the battle and there are disagreements as to its performance. PRO WO 203/36, 'Nepalese Troops Employment in 14 Army'.

94. Tamayama and Nunneley, p. 161.

95. There is no record of this message in IV Corps War Diary, and three days later Slim held a conference with Scoones and Stopford of XXXIII Corps, at which he decided to defend Kohima. Had he known then that an entire division was heading towards it, he would surely not have allowed the sacrifice of the small garrisons at Jessami and Kharasom, nor sent units piecemeal into Kohima. Rooney, *Burma Victory*, pp. 55–6.

96. They included many outstanding young men, including undergraduate contemporaries of Richard Hillary, author of *The Last Enemy*, and part of a set known as 'the long-haired boys' at Oxford in the 1930s. Few survived the war. The full story of this important battle took forty years to emerge in Harry Seaman's excellent and moving book, *The Battle at Sangshak*. See also OIOC MS Eur C770, 'Account by Maj. Victor H. Brookes of the battle of Sangshak, Mar 1944'.

97. Seaman, p. 82.

98. Scoones was less than generous to Hope-Thomson in his despatches and Louis Allen in *Burma* was extremely critical of him, based on a single eye-witness account given years later, going on to say that Lieutenant-Colonel Jackie Trim of 4th/5th Mahrattas took over and Hope-Thompson [*sic*]

'grasped his tube of toothpaste, convinced it was his pistol' (J. Lunt, 'The Sangshak Cover-Up', *Army Quarterly and Defence Journal*, 119/3, July 1989). The story of 4th/5th Mahrattas' break-out and of Lieutenant-Colonel Trim is also to be found in M. G. Abhankyar, *Valour Enshrined*, pp. 425-41. Their successor, The Maratha Light Infantry, was granted the unique honour 'Sangshak' in the 1960s and 4th Battalion celebrates 'Sangshak Day' as its battalion day (J. Gaylor, *Sons of John Company*, pp. 203-4).

99. Detwiler and Burdick (eds.), vol. 6/6, 'Burma Operations Record 15th Army Operations in Imphal Area and Withdrawal to Northern Burma', Japanese Monograph no. 134, p. 119.
100. L. Allen, *Burma*, pp. 248-51.

## 13 STILWELL IN THE NORTH

1. H. Leonard, *Burma Mission: Company 'D' 13th Mtn Med Bn*, p. 11.
2. T. White and A. Jacoby, *Thunder out of China*, p. 154.
3. L. T. Camp, *Lingering Fever*, p. 41.
4. Tuchman, pp. 377-8.
5. Fischer, *The Chancy War*, pp. 176-8.
6. Spencer, pp. 63, 100-06. This provides the best single-volume overview of Hump operations written by a participant. For personal accounts see: J. Gen Genovese, *We Flew Without Guns*; Edwin Lee White, *Ten Thousand Tons by Christmas*; and Eleanor Lapsley, *A Memory of David Lapsley*. For a colour photo album, see Jeff L. Ethell and Don Downie, *Flying the Hump*.
7. Craven and Cate (eds.) vol. 4, pp. 412-3.
8. E. Sevareid, *Not So Wild a Dream*, p. 260.
9. Spencer, pp. 46-7. Although most flights were by Americans, RAAF squadrons carried 7,500 tons in November 1943, more than ATC that month. For an overview of Australian participation in Burma air operations, see G. Odgers, *Australia in the War of 1939-1945*, series 3, *Air*, vol. 2, *Air War against Japan 1943-1945*, chap. 16.
10. PRO AIR 41/36, 'Air Historical Branch Narrative, The Campaign in the Far East, vol. 3', pp. 56-7; Anders, pp. 28-9.
11. Peers and Brelis, pp. 107-9, 123; Eldridge, pp. 174-6.
12. M. R. D. Foot and J. M. Langley, *MI9*, pp. 274-5.
13. PRO WO 203/1171, 'Appreciation of the Situation in Burma by Lieut.-Gen. Kawabe (Shozo) GOC-in-C 15th Army in Burma. Made at Rangoon, 7 June 1943'.
14. Stilwell, p. 308.
15. Liu, p. 189.
16. Romanus and Sunderland, *Stilwell's Command Problems*, p. 11.
17. Anders, p. 77.
18. J. Bykofsky and H. Larson, *United States Army in World War II, The Technical Services, The Transportation Corps: Operations Overseas*, p. 568.

19. NAM 7808–96, 'History of 202 (L of C) Area 1942–1946'; Bykofsky and Larson, pp. 568–71.

20. For Pick's background see Boatner, p. 429.

21. U. Lee, *United States Army in World War II, Special Studies, The Employment of Negro Troops*, pp. 618–9.

22. Fischer, *The Chancy War*, pp. 30–1; W. B. Sinclair, *Confusion beyond Imagination*, vol. 1, p. 228.

23. Anders, pp. 88–104.

24. NA Capt James R. Nagel, RG 407, CABN 464–0.20, 'Jungle Mission', quoted in E. R. Craine, *Burma Roadsters*, pp. 85–7.

25. They were relieved in due course by 684th AAA Separate MG Battery, another to precede Galahad. *Ex-CBI Roundup*, December 1985, p. 25.

26. PRO WO 203/2672, 'The North Burma Campaign Ledo to Myitkyina: A Background History'.

27. Ho Y-c, pp. 64–6.

28. Tuchman, pp. 393–4.

29. PRO WO 203/2672.

30. Anders, p. 101.

31. Anders, pp. 102–3.

32. In April 1944 the total Allied ground strength in theatre was 1,189,000, of which 15 per cent was American. Of this, however, less than one per cent were combatants. Of operational air forces, some 40 per cent of 73,000 men were American (although only 28 per cent if non-operational strengths are counted). Barker, *The March on Delhi*, p. 269.

33. Tuchman, p. 415.

34. G. S. Seagrave, *Burma Surgeon Returns*, p. 94.

35. Romanus and Sunderland, *Stilwell's Command Problems*, pp. 122–8.

36. 'He was the kind of man', said Stilwell, 'who would ensure there was no fighting.' Tuchman, p. 424.

37. PRO PREM 3/53/4, Hollis to Ismay, concrete no. 696, 2 September 1943.

38. Slim, *Defeat into Victory*, pp. 178–9.

39. Romanus and Sunderland, *Stilwell's Command Problems*, p. 29.

40. PRO WO 203/2672.

41. For Tanaka, see Tuchman, p. 416, and Boatner, p. 555.

42. Tuchman, p. 423.

43. T. Sun, *The Art of War*, p. 109.

44. Tuchman, p. 419.

45. OIOC MS Eur C850, 'With Detachment 101 U.S. Army, the Burmese Underground Movement', by Kyaw Win Maung (alias Wali Mohamed).

46. Kachin Rangers were masters of ambush, and claimed to inflict casualties at a rate of 25 to 1. See Peers and Brelis, pp. 120–32; R. Dunlop, pp. 21–3. For further personal narratives of Detachment 101 operatives, see J. S. Fletcher, *Secret War in Burma*, and Sharon E. Karr, *Traveler of the Crossroads*.

47. R. Hilsman, *American Guerrilla*, pp. 137–8, 297–8. Hilsman's unit comprised a Chinese and a Karen company with a Shan scout platoon (300 men in total).

The Chinese company was commanded by Bill Brough from Newcastle upon Tyne, who began the war as a conscientious objector and enrolled in a Quaker medical unit in China before joining Seagrave's unit. His Karen company was commanded by two Burma Rifles officers. Their tasks were to gather intelligence and to harass, ambush and disrupt Japanese supplies. See his memoir, *To Reason Why*.

48. W. Langer, *In and out of the Ivory Tower*, p. 187.
49. R. B. Laidlaw, 'The OSS and the Burma Road 1942–45', in R. Jeffreys-Jones and A. Lownie (eds.), *North American Spies*, p. 119.
50. H. Feis, *The China Tangle*, p. 127.
51. Tuchman, p. 428.
52. W. S. Churchill, vol. 5, pp. 560–1, 573.
53. Tuchman, pp. 429–31. Tuchman is, however, wrong to say this Japanese move was provoked by Stilwell ferreting around in north Burma.
54. Tuchman, p. 432.
55. For Merrill, see Boatner, pp. 361–2.
56. Ogburn, p. 61.
57. R. Dunlop, p. 275; J. B. George, *Shots Fired in Anger*, p. 460.
58. F. Owen, *Campaign in Burma*, p. 84. For the memoir of a newsman at war serving as combat cameraman with Tenth Air Force, see E. R. Evans, *Combat Cameraman China–Burma–India*.
59. P. Smart, letter to *Burman News*, 1994, quoted in Prefer, p. 29.
60. Fischer, *The Chancy War*, p. 142; Ogburn, p. 72.
61. Sherman L. Glass was a veterinary officer who worked as a liaison officer with the British and Chinese. His *Who Stoled My Mule?* is an excellent account of the problems of setting up Galahad with its animal transport and its subsequent support. H. L. Hames has written a tribute to these animals, *The Mules' Last Bray*, both in CBI and in the US Forest Service, which made extensive use of them before everything was mechanized after the war.
62. Prefer, p. 44.
63. Tuchman, p. 434.
64. IWM AL 1063, 'Operation of 18 Japanese Division in Kamaing and Walawbum, Burma, by Lt.-Gen. Tanaka Shinichi, Commander 18 Division, May 1949'. For detailed descriptions of the march to and battle at Walawbum, using many first-hand accounts, see Hopkins with Jones, chaps. 8 and 9, and also A. D. Baker, pp. 44–72.
65. D. Richardson, 'The Dead End Kids', *The Best of Yank, The Army Weekly*, p. 92. For a description of Japanese tactics and American reaction to them, including an excellent line-drawn illustration, see George, pp. 481–5.
66. Prefer, pp. 82–3.
67. J. Girsham with L. Thomas, *Burma Jack*, pp. 145–6.
68. Ziegler, *Mountbatten*, p. 247.
69. Hopkins with Jones, pp. 113–5, 135–7; L. E. Weston, *The Fightin' Preacher*, pp. 124–5.
70. R. Arnold, p. 153.

71. Ho Y-c, p. 92.

72. Tuchman, p. 434.

73. Eldridge, p. 202; Ziegler, *Mountbatten*, p. 271.

74. Eldridge, p. 216.

75. *Time*, 21 October 1946.

76. Tuchman, p. 437.

77. Tuchman, pp. 421–2; Camp, p. 121.

78. Romanus and Sunderland, *Stilwell's Command Problems*, p. 308.

79. A. D. Baker, pp. 74–89.

80. Prefer, pp. 100–1.

81. Tuchman, pp. 440–1.

82. Ogburn, p. 183. See Hopkins with Jones, chap. 10.

83. C. N. Hunter, *Galahad*, p. 88. See Hopkins with Jones, chap. 11.

84. George, p. 499.

85. IWM AL 1063, 'Operation of 18 Japanese Division in Kamaing and Walawbum, Burma, by Lt.-Gen. Tanaka Sinichi, Commander 18 Division, May 1949'. See also AL 1064, 'Interrogation Report of Gen. Tanaka Sinichi, Commander 18 Division, Burma, January 1948'; AL 5009/3, 'Report of SEATIC Interrogator Lt.-Gen. Tanaka Sinichi, Cmdr 18 Division'.

86. Prefer, pp. 103–8.

87. George, pp. 524–6.

88. See Hopkins with Jones, chap. 13; A. D. Baker, pp. 90–109.

89. J. E. T. Hopkins, H. G. Stelling and T. S. Voohees, 'The Marauders and the Microbes', in J. A. Stone (ed.), *Crisis Fleeting*, p. 322.

90. Prefer, pp. 114–7.

91. PRO WO 203/2672.

92. Romanus and Sunderland, *Stilwell's Command Problems*, p. 310.

93. D. Abbott, 'Nphum Ga Retold', *Burman News*, November 1993.

94. Prefer, pp. 122–4.

95. Hopkins with Jones, p. 448.

96. Tuchman, pp. 443–4.

97. Romanus and Sunderland, *Stilwell's Command Problems*, p. 200.

98. Weston, pp. 153–5.

99. Ogburn, pp. 5, 216; Hopkins with Jones, p. 90.

100. Hopkins with Jones, chap. 16.

101. Ogburn, p. 227.

## 14 THE ADMIN BOX

1. A. Lewis, *Letters to My Wife*. This was Alun Lewis's last letter home before his tragic death on 5 March 1944, aged twenty-six. Lewis's first collection of poems, *Raider's Dawn*, was published in 1942, and a posthumous collection, *Ha! Ha! Among the Trumpets*, introduced by his friend (through correspondence) Robert Graves, in 1945. In his preface to Lewis's collection *In*

*the Green Tree* (1948) he is described by A. L. Rowse as 'one of the two best poets' of the Second World War. Although his death was officially declared an accident, J. Pikonlis's biography of the young poet discusses the possibility of suicide (*Alun Lewis: A Life*, pp. 265-6): But William Proll, who went to Lewis's immediate aid, remained convinced it was an accident ('Forgotten Army is Recalled by Bill', *South Wales Argus*, 7 July 1995). However, as Professor Gwyn Jones noted, it is of little real importance: the important thing was the loss of another young life and to Anglo-Welsh literature.

2. Franks, *Spitfires over the Arakan*, pp. 50-9.

3. Probert, pp. 158-60. Among the obsolescent types they replaced were Mohawks, which 5 and 155 Squadrons had been operating for eighteen months. For the story of these units see G. Beauchamp, *Mohawks over Burma*, and the memoir of 5 Squadron pilot Oliver Moxon, *Bitter Monsoon*.

4. Franks, *Fighter Pilot's Summer*, pp. 196, 198.

5. McGeoch, pp. 112-3; Ziegler, *Mountbatten*, pp. 248-9.

6. Craven and Cate (eds.), vol. 4, p. 502.

7. Nalder, *The History of British Army Signals in the Second World War*, p. 101; Nalder, *The Royal Corps of Signals*, p. 457.

8. For Christison, see his unpublished memoir, 'Life and Times of General Sir Philip Christison Bt' (IWM 82/15/1).

9. This followed a suggestion by Giffard during a visit to the War Office in December 1942 after the Torch landings had secured French North Africa and removed the threat to West Africa. A. Haywood and F. A. S. Clarke, *History of the Royal West African Frontier Force*, p. 373.

10. Humphreys, p. 8.

11. R. Street, *Another Brummie in Burma*, p. 21.

12. C. Boyd and A. Yoshida, *The Japanese Submarine Force in World War II*, p. 159; Tomlinson, p. 188.

13. Nunneley, *Tales from the King's African Rifles*, pp. 118-21; Humphreys, pp. 49-50.

14. C. Somerville, *Our War*, pp. 204-5.

15. Woolner was an excellent commander with a flair for accuracy and personally fearless, having won three MCs in the First World War. Unfortunately Christison developed a very poor impression of the fine qualities of African troops, and their contribution has only recently been properly recorded by John Hamilton, a former RWAFF officer, who takes great exception in *War Bush* to much of Christison's memoir; see IWM 82/15/1. However, Michael Hickey chooses Christison's less favourable opinion of Woolner (*The Unforgettable Army*, pp. 110-11).

16. Each brigade had an auxiliary group, a self-administered infantry unit approximately 1,600 strong (reduced after experience from an original war establishment of some 2,200), including 23 British officers and 28 British NCOs. SOAS E Coll K/103, 'History of 3rd Auxiliary Group, Gold Coast Regiment, Royal West African Frontier Force, 81st (W.A.) Division, May

1941–December 1945. By Major E. S. Stafford.' (Also IWM 97/36/1 Major E. S. Stafford.)

17. They had been there throughout the monsoon and were exhausted by patrolling, disease and skirmishing. W. L. Hailes and J. Ross, *The Jat Regiment*, pp. 269–75; SOAS E Coll 3 D/8; J. A. L. Hamilton, *War Bush*, pp. 52–9.

18. It was based on Headquarters 111th Regiment with two companies (about 400 men) from 55th Reconnaissance Regiment (who called themselves 'The Last Cavalry', but were, in fact, mounted infantry), III/111th Regiment, II/143rd Regiment, and a composite unit made of reinforcements for 144th Regiment. Kirby, vol. 3, p. 152 n.3.

19. Brett-James, *Report My Signals*, p. 87.

20. Shipster, pp. 29–30.

21. Franks, *Spitfires over the Arakan*, pp. 114, 137, 145.

22. M. R. Roberts, *Golden Arrow*, pp. 45–6; *Fourteenth Punjab Regiment*, pp. 24–5.

23. Brett-James, *Ball of Fire*, pp. 260–2; G. W. Robertson, p. 175. This is an excellent regimental history of 136th (1st West Lancashire) Field Regiment, RA (TA).

24. Street, *A Brummie in Burma*, pp. 22, 24; IWM 81/2/1, Ray Street.

25. H. Gunning, *Borderers in Battle*, pp. 211–8; E. V. R. Bellers, *The History of The 1st King George V's Own Gurkha Rifles (The Malaun Regiment)*, vol. 2, pp. 172–6; Perrett, *Tank Tracks to Rangoon*, p. 82n.

26. G. Betham and H. V. R. Geary, *The Golden Galley*, pp. 267–9.

27. PRO WO 203/1793, 'Report by HQ 5th Ind Div on the First Battle of Razabil Fortress'; Ahmad, pp. 286–9.

28. Hickey, p. 145.

29. Lyman, pp. 151–2.

30. IWM 82/15/1, General Sir Philip Christison Bt.

31. A. Farrar-Hockley, *The Army in the Air*, pp. 147–50; H. J. Parham and E. M. G. Bellfield, *Unarmed into Battle*, pp. 110–13.

32. Sadly this brave and enterprising officer was killed towards the end of the 1944 Arakan campaign. Roberts, pp. 45–6; H. Maule, *Spearhead General*, p. 244. 55th Forward Observation Squadron was one of six in 303rd Indian Brigade, the operational formation that implemented deception schemes under D Force, commanded from January 1944 by Lieutenant-Colonel P. E. X. Turnbull, using simulators and sound equipment. They also performed a variety of other tasks. Finally formed officially in September 1944, it expanded to eight companies, three British, two Punjabi Mussulmen and one each of Jats, Sikhs and Pathans, assigned roughly one per corps by January 1945. There were also two light scout car companies operating sonic equipment, although these did not stand up well to jungle conditions. See PRO WO 203/33, 'Deception Organisation: Correspondence and Reports'; and P. Turnbull, 'D Force Burma 1943–45: Distracting the Japanese in Burma', in *War Monthly*, 47, December 1977.

33. IWM AL 827/1, 'History of 55 Japanese Division. Outline of Operations'; L. Allen, *Burma*, pp. 170–4.

34. Sakurai, no relation to 28th Army's command.er, was renowned for his eccentric social behaviour, but also had a reputation for ruthlessness. Hickey, pp. 102–3.

35. Messervy repeatedly explained of his name: 'The accent is not on the "Mess" but the "Serve".' He is unusual for such a relatively junior commander in having had a biography written of him, Henry Maule's uncritical *Spearhead General*.

36. G. D. Sheffield, p. 136.

37. IWM 82/15/1, General Sir Philip Christison Bt.

38. IWM AL 5295, 'Report (English Translation) on 55th Division Operations, Arakan, February 1944, by Lt.- Gen. Hanaya, Divisional Commander'.

39. RCSM 916.6, 'Military Histories Far East, Report on Operations, Burma 33 Corps'.

40. Divisional Signals lost 8 officers, 7 British and 90 Indian soldiers killed or missing, never to be seen again. And while the British say all code books and other important documents were destroyed, the Japanese found numerous documents including some in Japanese and a copy of Sakurai's operational order for Ha-Go. Nalder, *The Royal Corps of Signals*, p. 452n.; L. Allen, *Burma*, pp. 175–7, 182.

41. IWM 80/11/1, Major N. H. Weddle.

42. For the story of the gunner battle see Farndale, pp. 154–62.

43. G. W. Robertson, p. 178.

44. Armstrong, pp. 145–6.

45. G. Evans, *The Desert and the Jungle*, pp. 126–7. This is a personal account of its author's war experiences.

46. In an address to the Royal Empire Society on 6 February 1946, Slim was quite emphatic in stating that when 7th Indian Division was surprised 'we had the answer and our plans already ready to meet the danger'. This view was not shared by an RIASC air supply officer, who was offended by Slim's failure to credit the air supply organization for its improvisation during the battle. He wrote a detailed article, 'A Footnote to Air Supply in Fourteenth Army' by 'Air Coy' in the *RIASC Journal*, November 1946, pp. 9–11. This prompted Major-General Snelling to write a letter to the editor to say: 'Improvisation it was, but I would suggest at a higher level than the Co[mpan]y' (*RIASC Journal*, February 1947, p. 93). 'Air Coy' would not be denied, however. He replied via the editor that 'the great bulk of the hard work fell to the RIASC side of air supply, and it was curious how little knowledge of (and recognition of) these units existed often in high circles' (*RIASC Journal*, May 1947, p. 104). The article and letters make interesting reading.

47. Probert, pp. 168–72; D. J. Innes, *Beaufighters over Burma*, p. 93.

48. Franks, *Spitfires over the Arakan*, pp. 157–8, 165, 172; Franks, *First in the Indian Skies*, pp. 104–6; Saunders, *Royal Air Force 1939–1945*, pp. 318–22. For a personal account of service with 62 Squadron, see Doug Sutcliffe's *Airborne over Burma*, also IWM 12288/4, Flying Officer Cecil Brathwaite.

49. T. Grounds, *Some Letters from Burma*, pp. 73–4. This book is based on Grounds's letters home but also on many other 25th Dragoon sources to form a very effective, if personalized, regimental history. See also IWM 91/16/1, T. Grounds; 87/38/2, Capt. L. M. Taylor; 93/29/1, J. McKnight.

50. IWM 87/35/1, W. Adrain. 4th/8th Gurkhas is one of the twelve 'phoenix' units in Daniel P. Marston's *Phoenix from the Ashes*.

51. Perrett, *Last Stand! Famous Battles against the Odds*, p. 163.

52. G. Evans, *The Desert and the Jungle*, pp. 134–9.

53. Sandes, pp. 171–2; IWM 10469, Lieutenant-Colonel G. H. Cree.

54. Roberts, pp. 48–9; Betham and Geary, pp. 256–7; Farndale, pp. 151–2.

55. P. Turnbull, *Battle of the Box*, p. 90.

56. Leyin, pp. 167–9; Palsokar, *The Grenadiers*, pp. 209–10.

57. Sandes, pp. 172–3; Maule, pp. 284–5; Brett-James, *Ball of Fire*, p. 286.

58. Slim, *Defeat into Victory*, p. 241.

59. Gilmore and Davis, pp. 139–40; Huxford, pp. 198–200; Marston, pp. 128–31.

60. Irwin, p. 119.

61. Gunning, pp. 219–27.

62. IWM 82/15/1, General Sir Philip Christison Bt; Sinker and Rossier, p. 34.

63. Sandes, pp. 176–7; G. Evans, *The Desert and the Jungle*, p. 150; Leyin, pp. 192–3.

64. Qureshi, p. 324.

65. Leyin, p. 185; G. W. Robertson, pp. 208–9.

66. L. Allen, *Burma*, p. 186.

67. Tamayama and Nunneley, p. 148.

68. Slim, *Defeat into Victory*, pp. 246–7.

69. The Japanese also made a grave error in believing the main British force was holed up at Sinzweya, failing to notice 9th, 33rd and 114th Indian Brigades to the north. Fortunately the British were equally inept since these took little part in the battle, and allowed Sakurai Column subsequently to withdraw. Detwiler and Burdick (eds.), vol.7/1, 'Burma Operations Record: 28th Army Operations in Akyab Area (November 1943–September 1945', Japanese Monograph no. 132, pp. 25–6.

70. Armstrong, p. 165.

71. IWM 93/29/1, J. McKnight.

72. Leyin, pp. 183–4. The composer Bernard Stevens admired Branson as an artist and a man of action. Although also in the Army, he managed to compose a 'Symphony of Liberation' which he dedicated to Branson, and which was played at the Royal Albert Hall by the London Philharmonic Orchestra under Malcolm Sargent. Branson had 'feelings for his fellow men that expressed themselves in an idealism' that led to his joining the International Brigade that fought on the Republican side against Franco during the Spanish Civil War, where he was taken prisoner and spent eight months in a concentration camp. 'The sincerity of his ideals was beyond question.' His

death was a great loss to the whole regiment, and he left behind a baby daughter he had never seen (Grounds, p. 151).

73. This unit came from 11th (East African) Division and was used because his own 81st Reconnaissance Regiment was carrier-borne and unsuited to the terrain, operating on the main Arakan front instead. See Chapter 2, 'Advance to Kyauktaw', and Chapter 14, 'The "Good Old Days" of 81 (WA) Divisional Recce Regiment', in J. A. L. Hamilton, *War Bush*.

74. E. W. Maslen-Jones, *Fire by Order*, p. 13.

75. IWM 87/37/1, Captain D. M. Cookson.

76. Colvin, p. 146.

77. IWM 97/36/1, Lieutenant J. A. L. Hamilton.

78. Somerville, p. 222.

79. SOAS E Coll 3 D/3, C. G. Bowen, '"West African Way" The Story of the Burma Campaigns 1943–1945 5th Bn. Gold Coast Regt. 81 West African Division'.

80. IWM 87/37/1, Captain D. M. Cookson. The dominant language in the Nigeria and Gold Coast Regiments before the war had been Hausa, but in Sierra Leone and Gambia no one language predominated and so the 'pidgin' dialect that had developed over the centuries was a useful *lingua franca*. It also assisted those officers in the division who were Polish, and could thus converse with both soldiers and fellow officers quite easily (J. A. L. Hamilton, pp. 32–3).

81. IWM AL 5009/9, 'Report of SEATIC Interrogators: Lt.-Gen. Sakurai Tokutaro, Cmdr 55 Division'.

82. Hamilton, pp. 90–5.

83. SOAS E Coll 3 D/3.

84. Christison seems to have paid little attention to the West Africans, nor to have made much effort to do so. He failed to visit the division during the withdrawal, although Snelling, the highest-ranking staff officer at Fourteenth Army, managed to do so. As the administrative chief, his support for the division was crucial. And in K. C. Christofas, '81 (West African) Division – Report on Experience on Air Supply, January to June 1944', there is a fine exposition on the first organization set up to run air supply for a normal formation on a long-term basis. Hamilton, pp. 108–13, 117–42; IWM 92/15/1, Major P. B. Poore; 91/8/1, Major J. A. Chapman; J. F. Macdonald, *The War History of Southern Rhodesia*, pp. 496–7.

85. PRO WO 203/1793; WO 203/1175, '1944 Mar. Razabil area of Arakan: Report on Assaults by Infantry Supported by Tanks, Artillery and Air on Japanese Positions'. Bamford, p. 107; Roberts, pp. 107–8; Marston, pp. 132–4.

86. R. B. Lockhart, *The Marines Were There*, pp. 188–90.

87. NAM 7709–6, '2nd Bn. 13th F. F. Rifles War History (Unofficial) January 1942–November 1946'; IWM 97/36/1, Major D. E. Gardiner; 97/36/1, Captain I. A. Wallace; N. C. E. Kendrick, *The Story of The Wiltshire Regiment (Duke of Edinburgh's)*, pp. 164–5; Betham and Geary, p. 172.

88. The next day the tunnel was occupied with a large 'XXIV' sign above what was now called '24th Tunnel'. Two years later earth from Tredegar Hill was brought back in a casket and retained in the chambers of Tredegar District Council. G. A. Brett, *History of the South Wales Borderers and The Monmouthshire Regiment*, pp. 22–4; M. Gillings, *The Shiny Ninth*, p. 38.

89. Krishen Tewari of 25th Indian Division Signals watched the Gurkhas' assault: 'Beautiful sight – it is etched in my memory.' Somerville, p. 225; Ahmad, pp. 305–8; Deedes, p. 119; Nunneley (ed.), *Tales from the Burma Campaign*, pp. 105–6.

90. IWM 97/36/1, Major D. E. Gardiner; Marston, pp. 134–7.

91. IWM 87/37/1, Captain D. M. Cookson.

92. At the end of his detailed account of these actions – based largely on primary sources – John Hamilton contrasts it with the story in the official history and as related by Christison in his memoirs, concluding that nobody reading either would realize that Hubforce was under XV Corps command, and would gain the impression that Indian Army troops were good while African and Indian State Forces (as represented by the Tripura Rifles) were bad. He suggests this may have been due to the excision of an appendix describing Hubforce operations by Christison from Woolner's report written in July, and Kirby's failure to consult any primary sources below corps level. Hamilton, pp. 165–85.

## 15 THURSDAY

1. R. D. van Wagner, *Any Time, Any Place, Any Where*, p. 20. This is the most useful reference on this original unit and Operation Thursday. It also gives full technical details of the various aircraft being operated and excellent photographic coverage, mainly courtesy of the 1st Air Commando Association. For individual squadron histories see James V. Meisel, *72nd Airdrome Squadron*, and Roy F. Kappel, *Whispering Wings over Burma* (5th Liaison Squadron). See also Craven and Cate (eds.), vol. 4, pp. 503–8.

2. See Maurice Horn, *'Introducing Terry and the Pirates'*.

3. L. J. Thomas, *Back to Mandalay*, pp. 10, 14–19, 76–7. Lowell Thomas's book tells the story of 1st Air Commando, mainly through Cochran's own words.

4. P. D. Chinnery, *Any Time, Any Place*, pp. 17, 27. This book is not restricted to Chindit operations.

5. Van Wagner, p. 52.

6. GM Diary/Draft History no. S5, 'Report on Operations Carried out by Special Force – Oct '43 to Sept. '44'.

7. Tulloch, p. 136.

8. PRO WO 172/4261, 'War Diary: Special Force and 3 Indian Division: G. Special Force 1944 Jan., Mar.–Dec.'.

9. IWM 82/15/1, Major-General G. W. Symes.

10. J. Thompson, *The Imperial War Museum Book of War behind Enemy Lines*, pp. 183–4.

11. Bierman and Smith, p. 339. Among Cochran's glider pilots was Jackie Coogan, former child actor, whom was introduced to Desmond Whyte. 'Schoolboy memories raced back to Charlie Chaplin plus small boy in cloth cap. A tall muscular man grasped my hand, almost lifting me off the ground, with the remark, "Don't say it. They all tell me I just can't be the Kid"' (WL RAMC 1830, D. Whyte, 'A Trying Chindit', in *British Medical Journal*, 285, 18-25 December 1982). Coogan was seen changing the landing light directions during the second night to help incoming aircraft avoid smashed-up gliders, 'risking his neck to save lives. I've never seen that in any of the reports I've read, but Bob Bendick and Charlies Russhon saw him in the darkness' (E. R. Evans, *Combat Cameraman China–Burma–India*, p. 81).

12. Wingate was constantly evolving fresh ideas and this came quite late in the day, after the quotation from Zechariah 9: 12, which prefixed his Training Note no. 8, 'Strongholds'. The version Calvert quotes in *Prisoners of Hope* (p. 274) does not agree with the Authorized and Revised Versions of the Bible, which have 'Turn *you* to the strong hold, ye prisoners of hope.' Hamilton, pp. 263-4.

13. PRO WO 203/1833, '77th Indian Infantry Brigade: Operations in Burma'.

14. 'Everything is propaganda', he said Fergusson, *The Wild Green Earth*, p. 73.

15. Tulloch, pp. 147-8.

16. IWM 84/21/1, Lt.-Col. D. M. C. Rose.

17. IWM 66/187/1, Major R. P. J. Dobney.

18. J. Thompson, *The Imperial War Museum Book of War behind Enemy Lines*, p. 179; Fergusson, *The Trumpet in the Hall*, pp. 175-6.

19. O'Brien, *Out of the Blue*, p. 24; 'Wingate – a Flawed Hero', *Sunday Telegraph*, 11 March 1984.

20. IWM 80/49/1, Lieutenant J. R. Sealy.

21. Calvert, *Fighting Mad*, p. 137.

22. PRO CAB 106/170, 'Extracts from the Wingate Papers'.

23. Lyman, pp. 187-8.

24. Ziegler, *Mountbatten*, p. 276.

25. J. Thompson, *The Imperial War Museum Book of War behind Enemy Lines*, pp. 184-7.

26. L. J. Thomas, pp. 124-5; Van Wagner, p. 52; R. E. Prather, *Easy into Burma*, p. 27.

27. Chinnery, *Air Commando*, p. 7.

28. P. Sharpe, *To Be A Chindit*, chap. 9. See also: IWM 80/49/1, N. P. Aylen; W. E. Underhill, *The Royal Leicestershire Regiment, 17th Foot, A History of the Years 1928 to 1956*, pp. 185-91.

29. IWM 18269/9, Captain J. W. Dell.

30. W. J. Cooper, *Desert Sand to Jungle Trail*, p. 135. For an account of 2nd Queen's, including accounts by members of 21 and 22 Columns, see *Operations of the 1st and 2nd Battalions The Queen's Royal Regiment in Burma during World War Two*, pp. 16-28. For further accounts by members of 2nd Queen's see also IWM 92/28/1, H. Atkins, and 93/4/1, G. Hill.

31. Bidwell, p. 136. Bidwell's is the most thorough and considered overall military account of the 1944 operation.
32. Conden, *The Frontier Force Regiment*, p. 477.
33. L. J. Thomas, p. 156.
34. IWM 82/15/1, Major-General G. W. Symes, Diary.
35. Slim, *Defeat into Victory*, p. 216.
36. O'Brien, *Out of the Blue*, pp. 56–9.
37. L. J. Thomas, pp. 161–6; E. R. Evans, p. 77–81.
38. Bierman and Smith, pp. 348–50; Tulloch, pp. 200–01. In his own memoirs Slim says that he took Wingate aside and calmed him, but Bierman and Smith note that no other witness to the scene agrees with his description of it, written as it was ten years later (*Defeat into Victory*, p. 235). Wingate's anxiety was perfectly natural as he was convinced the Chinese had betrayed his secret, their security being notoriously lax (B. Prasad (ed.), *Reconquest of Burma*, vol. 1, p. 337; Lewin, *Slim*, p. 163; Bierman and Smith, pp. 381–4; D. Tulloch, p. 148). However, Wingate was certainly ignorant of the possibilities of air photos or he would have requested Fourteenth Army Photographic Intelligence Unit to maintain a regular inspection. Besides, Piccadilly was the site of Michael Vlasto's casualty evacuation flight in 1943, and photos of it had already been published in *Life*.
39. SOAS E Coll 3 G/26, Revd Donald Mackay, 'A Padre with the Chindits'. See also IWM 84/36/1, Major F. Turner.
40. Calvert, *Fighting Mad*, p. 143.
41. R. Campbell Begg and P. H. Liddle (eds.), *For Five Shillings a Day*, p. 351.
42. B. Towill, *Chindit Chronicle*, p. 20.
43. Calvert, *Fighting Mad*, p. 145; Calvert, *Prisoners of Hope*, p. 29. The latter was first published by Jonathan Cape in 1952 and is a detailed description of 77th Brigade on the second Chindit expedition. *Fighting Mad*, first published in 1965 and since revised, contains many of the same anecdotes. See also J. Hallam, *The History of The Lancashire Fusiliers 1939–45*, pp. 109–21; IWM 80/49/1, Lt.-Col. H. N. F. Patterson; and IWM 80/49/1, Capt. J. R. Sealy.
44. Calvert, *Prisoners of Hope*, p. 32; Prather, pp. 36–42.
45. Calvert, *Fighting Mad*, pp. 146–7.
46. G. Donaldson, *Did I Take the Right Turning?*, p. 76.
47. Bidwell, *The Chindit War*, p. 110.
48. L. Allen, *Burma*, p. 316.
49. H. R. K. Gibbs, *Historical Record of the 6th Gurkha Rifles*, vol. 2, p. 124.
50. L. J. Thomas, pp. 195–6; Van Wagner, pp. 59–60; Franks, *The Air Battle of Imphal*, pp. 28–35.
51. 'The officers', noted Richard Rhodes-James, 'with the contempt of sentimentality that they always affected, were apt to laugh at these stirring little pieces, and they were apt to convey some of this cynicism to the men. This was dangerous as the men for the most part worshipped Wingate and it was a direct blow to their idol. I think that secretly we were ashamed of our scorn.' Rhodes-James, *Chindit*, p. 79.

52. L. Allen, *Burma*, pp. 326–8.
53. Detwiler and Burdick (eds.), vol.6/6, 'Burma Operations Record 15th Army Operations in Imphal Area and Withdrawal to Northern Burma', Japanese Monograph no. 134, pp. 149–50.
54. Lunt, *Imperial Sunset*, p. 318.
55. Calvert, *Fighting Mad*, p. 153; Calvert, *Prisoners of Hope*, p. 51; Twiston Davies (ed.), pp. 387–91.
56. IWM 80/49/1, Lieutenant N. Durant. This account, written as a long letter to his family not long afterwards, was published in a 1995 booklet, *Experiences of the Second World War in Burma*, together with the experiences of Dr William Bullock, who served with the West Africans in Arakan.
57. Cairns was a Somerset Light Infantry subaltern attached to the South Staffords. He was recommended for a VC but the citation was lost in the air crash that killed Wingate. After the war his father wrote to the CO of 1st South Staffords asking that his son's case be reconsidered, following a BBC broadcast on 10 December 1948. With eyewitness accounts from Calvert and his column commander a submission was made through the War Office to the King. The posthumous award was made on 20 May 1949. W. L. Vale, *History of the South Staffordshire Regiment*, p. 409.
58. S. R. Nicholls, 'Account of the Role of the Field Gunners in the 1944 Chindit Campaign', *The Journal of The Royal Artillery*, CXVI/1, March 1989, pp. 72–83; RAHT MD/1463, 'Guns over Burma – The Story of Special Forces Battery RA', by Capt. J. F. Brown (Also at IWM 95/34/1, Captain J. F. Brown); Farndale, pp. 184–5.
59. RCSM 916.6, 'Military Histories Far East, Burma'.
60. L. Allen, *Burma*, pp. 332–7.
61. IWM 97/20/6–12, Wingate Papers, Mountbatten to Wingate, 17 March 1944.
62. Bidwell, *The Chindit War*, pp. 142–6.
63. Later there was a breakdown in 45th Reconnaissance Regiment. Sharpe, pp. 217–8, 220–35; Underhill, pp. 192–200; O. F. Sheffield, *The York and Lancaster Regiment 1919–1953*, pp. 103–6.
64. Calvert, *Prisoners of Hope*, p. 62.
65. Rhodes-James p. 206.
66. IWM 87/37/1, Captain R. Tatchell. For discussions of the circumstances surrounding Wingate's death see: R. S. Sansome, *Bamboo Workshop*, pp. 117–29; L. Allen, *Burma*, pp. 344–52. For a complete account see Dennis Hawley's *The Death of Wingate and Subsequent Events*.
67. Bidwell, *The Chindit War*, pp. 160–1, 169; Tulloch, p. 236; Slim, *Defeat into Victory*, p. 269.
68. Calvert, *Fighting Mad*, p. 163.
69. IWM 11619/3, Private F. W. Merchant.
70. IWM AL 457 SEATIC Hist. Bull. no.244, 'History of 33rd Army'; Detwiler and Burdick (eds.), vol.6/6, 'Burma Operations Record 15th Army Operations in Imphal Area and Withdrawal to Northern Burma', Japanese Monograph no. 134, pp. 146–7.

71. GM, Diary/Draft History no. S5; Report on Operations Carried Out by Special Force – Oct '43 to Sept. '44; Vale, p. 410.

72. J. Shaw, *The March Out*, p. 28. James Jesse Shaw was a pre-war regular who served with Royal Fusiliers and Welsh Guards before joining the Royal West African Frontier Force. His entertaining memoirs, *Special Force: A Chindit's Story*, covers this service as well as his Chindit adventures. For an overview of 3rd (West African) Brigade's operations, see Hamilton, pp. 266–309. See also Charles Carfrae's *Chindit Column*, Three further memoirs by members of 7th Nigeria are held at the IWM: 89/9/1, Lt.-Col. C. P. Vaughan; 99/21/1, Maj. I. F. R. Ramsey; 99/21/1, Capt. D. E. Arnold. See also 99/12/1, A. M. Gainer, who served with 6th Nigeria in the same brigade.

73. Campbell Begg and Liddle (eds.), p. 364.

74. J. Shaw, *The March Out*, p. 74.

75. Masters, *The Road past Mandalay*, p. 193.

76. Campbell Begg and Liddle (eds.), p. 354.

77. Lieutenant-Colonel J. R. 'Jumbo' Morris of 'Morrisforce' had been appointed to this position but was 140 miles away, and he only took over after the Chindits had been withdrawn, although he rather pompously assumed the rank immediately. O'Brien, *Out of the Blue*, p. 153.

78. Masters, *The Road past Mandalay*, pp. 213–4. See also IWM 91/9/1, Major D. S. McCutcheon (a brief history of 3rd/4th Gurkhas during Thursday), and 91/1/1 & 1A, Lt.-Col. I. L. Simpsons (Diary of the CO of 3rd/4th Gurkhas and Commander of 40 Column).

79. IWM 80/49/1, Lieutenant N. Durant.

80. WL RAMC 1830.

81. Chinnery, *Any Time, Any Place*, pp. 29–30. See also IWM 67/411/1, A. G. G. Oliver.

82. Much to the annoyance of Colin Mackenzie, the chief of Force 136, who thought it absurd not to make use of his men already in the area. He was especially annoyed because Slim was starting to criticize Force 136 for carrying out private guerrilla operations in the area rather than assisting Fourteenth Army with intelligence, and he gave it short shrift. O'Brien, *The Moonlight War*, pp. 55–6. See also: PRO WO 203/4332, 'Force 136: Operational Reports 1944 Nov.–1945 Nov.'; WO 203/5748, 'Clandestine Operations: Miscellaneous Papers 1944 July–1946 Feb.'; SOAS E Coll 3 G/49 D. C. Herring, 'DAH Force: Report on Operations in the Kachin Hills March–July 1944' (also at IWM 80/49/1 Lt.-Col. D. C. Herring).

83. GM G26, 'Report on L.R.P. G. Operations of 94 Coln 4/9th GR during 1944, by Lt.-Col. P. C. Cane, MC'. (Also at IWM 84/21/1, Lt.-Col. P. C. Cane; see also 80/49/1, Lieutenant Colonel A. F. Harper.)

84. O'Brien, *Out of the Blue*, pp. 168–70; J. Thompson, *The Imperial War Museum Book of War behind Enemy Lines*, pp. 224–6.

85. Masters, *The Road past Mandalay*, p. 219.

86. J. Shaw, *The March Out*, p. 41.

87. W. F. Jeffrey, *Sunbeams like Swords*, p. 70.

88. Carfrae, p. 119.

89. PRO WO 201/5221, SACSEA Reports and Correspondence Apr–Sept 1944'.

90. GM Diary/Draft History no. S5, 'Report on Operations Carried Out by Special Force – Oct '43 to Sept. '44'.

91. J. Thompson, *The Imperial War Museum Book of War behind Enemy Lines*, pp. 227; IWM 12352/4, Lt.-Col. W. P. Scott; Farndale, pp. 185–6.

92. Masters, *The Road past Mandalay*, pp. 233–4.

93. IWM AL 827/5, 'Short History of 53 Japanese Division'.

94. Masters, *The Road past Mandalay*, p. 241.

95. IWM 80/49/1, Revd. W. H. Miller.

96. J. Shaw, *The March Out*, p. 53.

97. S. Leathart, *With the Gurkhas*, p. 101.

98. L. J. Thomas, p. 243.

99. IWM 80/49/1, Lt.-Col. P. H. Morris.

## 16 KOHIMA: THE SIEGE

1. Quoted in Franks, *First in the Indian Skies*, p. 131.

2. J. Costello, *The Pacific War*, p. 466.

3. IWM AL 5009/7, 'Report of SEATIC Interrogators: Lt.-Gen. Sato Kotoku, Cmdr 31 Division'.

4. Kirby, vol. 3, p. 299.

5. H. H. Richards, 'Kohima – How I Got There', *Firm and Forester*, 8/3, April 1985, pp. 204–7.

6. The numbers of non-combatants and size of the garrison vary between sources: Arthur Campbell talks of 1,500 (*The Siege*, p. 53), Anthony Brett-James of 2,900 (*Ball of Fire*, p. 306), while Bisheswar Prasad refers to 3,500 men (*Reconquest of Burma*, vol.1, p. 276). The total was probably around 2,500, including around 1,000 non-combatants. Barker, *The March on Delhi*, p. 173.

7. The Shere Regiment did not perform well once it lost its British officers to other tasks. PRO WO 203/36, 'Nepalese Troops, Employment in 14 Army'.

8. For which special praise is due to the Indian Pioneers, who laboured constantly before the battle and carried the wounded during it. Barker, *The March on Delhi*, p. 173.

9. C. Mackenzie, *All over the Place*, p. 69.

10. PRO WO 172/4507, 'War Diary 202 L of C Area 1944 Jan.–Dec.'.

11. PRO CAB 44/190, 'Section 7, Chapter "J", Campaigns in the Far East, The War Against Japan, Central (Chindwin) Front November 1943 to December 1944, Book III (The Third of Three). The Battle of Kohima. Final Phase of the Battle of Imphal, Exploitation and Pursuit to the Chindwin. Brigadier M. R. Roberts'.

12. PRO WO 172/4884, 'War Diary 4th Royal West Kent Regiment 1944 Jan.–Dec.'.

NOTES TO PAGES 258-62

13. Lyman, p. 207.

14. Barker, *The March on Delhi*, p. 171n.; J. Hedley, *Jungle Fighter*, p. 32.

15. Swinson, *Kohima*, p. 42.

16. As they did so, Lieutenant-Colonel F. N. 'Tim' Betts of V Force was making his laborious way back towards British lines. J. Thompson, *The Imperial War Museum Book of the War in Burma 1942–1945*, pp. 138–40; Palit, *Sentinels of the North-East*, pp. 144–8.

17. P. Steyn *The History of The Assam Regiment*, pp. 66, 70–4.

18. Colvin, pp. 42–52.

19. Swinson, *Kohima*, pp. 51–2. Unlike with British units serving in Indian formations, there was a mutual loathing between the Indian Army and 2nd Division. The latter was a pre-war regular formation, and although most of its personnel were wartime conscripts, it retained its character, as did its constituent units. The Japanese soon identified them as 'from Yorkshire' because the divisional badge was the Crossed Keys of York, although it contained no units from that county but battalions from other fine regiments. The men detested India and Indians, who were all 'wogs'; they referred to Indian Army officers as 'wog' officers, even if they were white. In this respect the division felt that it was looked down on by the Indian Army and had 'picked up the tab' for the snobbery and condescension with which British Army officers customarily treated their Indian Army counterparts before the war: 'One didn't speak to these people in peacetime' was a common attitude fostered in return by Indian Army officers (David Murray, interview with author, 26 June 2003).

20. Swinson, *Kohima*, p. 56.

21. This joke 'did not go down well with the General concerned'. SOAS E Coll 3 M/75, H. C. Smith '"Hostilities Only": Tales of an Amateur Soldier in World War II'.

22. A Campbell, *The Siege*, pp. vii, 210.

23. E. B. Stanley Clarke and A. T. Tillot, *From Kent to Kohima*, p. 77.

24. Colvin, p. 63. Colvin talks of the garrison being attacked by 13,000 Japanese. But this appears based on a Japanese regiment comprising 5,000 men, which is an overstatement even before accounting for losses. In reality 31st Division never concentrated more than around 9,000 to attack Kohima, although this still represents a considerable superiority.

25. Campbell, pp. 49–50; C. E. Lucas-Phillips, *Springboard to Victory*, pp. 132–3.

26. Qureshi, pp. 295–6.

27. Kirby, vol. 3, p. 301.

28. Swinson, *Kohima*, p. 62.

29. PRO WO 172/4884.

30. Swinson, *Kohima*, p. 60; Lucas-Phillips, *Springboard to Victory*, pp. 118–9.

31. Colvin, p. 74.

32. PRO WO 172/4884.

33. For Miyazaki see Barker, *The March on Delhi*, p. 273.

34. L. Allen, *Burma*, pp. 227–8.

35. Barker, *The March on Delhi*, p. 174.

36. IWM AL 5009/7.
37. Campbell, pp. 66–7.
38. PRO WO 172/4884; Ahmad, pp. 324–7.
39. Swinson, *Kohima*, p. 69; L. Allen, *Burma*, p. 270.
40. Campbell, pp. 72–3.
41. Lucas-Phillips, *Springboard to Victory*, pp. 149–51; Colvin, pp. 86–8.
42. Richard de Courtenay Yeo was, according to his comrade, John Mellors, 'an endearing innocent', but his actions in this battle were crucial. J. Mellors, *Shots in the Dark*, p. 125; Farndale, p. 198.
43. PRO WO 203/4637, 'Imphal and Kohima, Personal Narratives and Reports'.
44. Lucas-Phillips, *Springboard to Victory*, pp. 167–8; Colvin, pp. 71, 95; Campbell, p. 107.
45. RWKM Corporal H. F. Norman, Diary (also at IWM 81/16/1, H. F. Norman).
46. IWM 81/2/1, R. Street.
47. Lucas-Phillips, *Springboard to Victory*, pp. 155–6; Colvin, pp. 80, 88–9.
48. Humphreys, p. 29.
49. Campbell, p. 92.
50. Lucas-Phillips, *Springboard to Victory*, pp. 144–6; MacFetridge and Warren (eds.), pp. 152–74.
51. Tamayama and Nunneley, *Tales by Japanese Soldiers*, p. 172.
52. L. Allen, *Burma*, p. 237.
53. Barker, *The March on Delhi*, p. 177.
54. Swinson, *Kohima*, p. 81.
55. For Grover see Colvin, pp. 129–30.
56. Kirby, vol. 3, p. 303.
57. PRO CAB 44/190.
58. Hart, pp. 146–7.
59. The Japanese had moved troops to cover the rear of the position but they had not had time to dig in properly and these broke and ran – a very rare occurrence (D. Murray, interview with author, 26 June 2003).
60. Swinson, *Kohima*, p. 89.
61. Barker, *The March on Delhi*, p. 175.
62. Franks, *The Air Battle of Imphal*, p. 124; Franks, *First in the Indian Skies*, p.108; Saunders, *Royal Air Force 1939–1945*, pp. 326–7.
63. Probert, p. 187.
64. IWM 17955/5, John Winstanley.
65. RWKM, Corporal H. F. Norman, Diary.
66. Prasad (ed.), *Reconquest of Burma*, vol. 1, p. 279.
67. PRO WO 203/2683, '33rd Indian Corps Account of Operations vol. 1. 1 April 1944–22 June 1944'.
68. Swinson, *Kohima*, p. 92.
69. L. Allen, *Burma*, pp. 238, 260–4.
70. Swinson, *Kohima*, p. 142.

71. Carbonell died in early May of gas gangrene following a severe wound. Colvin, pp. 138, 203.
72. L. Allen, *Burma*, p. 287; Slim, *Defeat into Victory*, p. 311.
73. Colvin, p. 102.
74. WRM V. F. S. Hawkins, 'Operations of the 5 Infantry Brigade, 2 Division in Assam, 30 March–12 May 1944, with Special Reference to the Battle of Kohima, October 1946' (also at IWM P104, Brigadier V. F. S. Hawkins).
75. Tamayama and Nunneley, p. 169.
76. PRO WO 172/4451, '161st Indian Brigade War Diary Jan–Dec 1944'; Narain, pp. 168–9.
77. Brett-James, *Ball of Fire*, p. 321.
78. Campbell, p. 203.
79. Qureshi, p. 298.
80. PRO WO 203/2683; D. Rissik, *The D.L.I. at War*, p. 186.
81. Swinson, *Kohima*, p. 103.
82. Campbell, p. 208.
83. Stanley Clarke and Tillot, p. 250.
84. Swinson, *Kohima*, p. 104.
85. Colvin, pp. 126–7.

## 17 IMPHAL

1. Belden, *Still Time to Die*, p. 8.
2. R. Wilson, *The Imphal Shrimps, from 'High Appreciations: Recollections of a Captain'* (not paginated).
3. Hickey, p. 150.
4. Lewin, *Slim*, p. 173. The most comprehensive account of this confusion is Geoffrey Evans and Anthony Brett-James, *Imphal: A Flower on Lofty Heights*.
5. L. Allen, *Burma*, p. 194.
6. J. Thompson, *The Lifeblood of War*, p. 90.
7. Evans and Brett-James, pp. 182–4; Rooney, *Burma Victory*, p. 11.
8. D. R. Mankekar, *Leaves from a War Reporter's Diary*, p. 61.
9. PRO WO 203/1718, 'Lushai Brigade: An Official History by Historian Brigadier P. C. Marindin'. See also NAM '1939–1945' (54), 'McCall's Total Defence Scheme in Lushai Hills', an article in *The Assam Review and Tea News*, 34/4, December 1945, among others on the ITA and the physical properties of tea soil.
10. Probert, pp. 188–94; Saunders, pp. 318–22.
11. These were: (Hurricanes) 113 Squadron; (Spitfires) 81, 136, 607 (County of Durham) (See RAFM B3015, 'A Winged Lion, Salient: The Story of no. 607 (County of Durham) Squadron, Royal Auxiliary Air Force'), and at Silchar, 615 Squadrons; (Vengeances) 82, 84, 110 and 7 IAF Squadrons. Japanese fighter *sentais* (Oscars): 50th, 64th, 87th and 204th Squadrons; Bombers (Dinahs): 8th, 12th and 62nd, (Kates) 34th Squadron. Franks, *The Air Battle*

*of Imphal*, pp. 47, 53, 60. Although plagued by a negative press, army reports on Vengeance support were unequivocal in their praise of its accuracy and effectiveness. For a detailed description of the Vultee Vengeance and its operations at Imphal by 7 and 8 Squadrons IAF and 82 and 84 Squadrons RAF, see P. C. Smith, *Vengeance! The Vultee Vengeance Dive Bomber*, and *Jungle Dive-Bombers At War*, chap. 5.

12. Perrett, *Tank Tracks to Rangoon*, pp. 82n., 135–6. For a qualitative description of the various types of armour used in the campaign, see G. Forty, 'Tank Tracks in the Jungle', in Smurthwaite (ed.).

13. Evans and Brett-James, pp. 209–10.

14. Pakenham-Walsh, p. 218; RSDGM CB 15 C114, 'The Reminiscences of Four Members of "C" Squadron 3rd Carabiniers (Prince of Wales Dragoon Guards)'. C. D. Johnson has pieced together the detail of what happened in Lion Box between 4 and 7 April down to section level, in *The Forgotten Army's Box of Lions*. There were elements of Artisan Works and Quarrying companies, GPT companies, some 70 men from 27th/5th Mahratta Light Infantry (a garrison unit) and some 1,500 men in a reinforcement camp. His account conveys the piecemeal nature of the fighting, which it describes from both sides, and lists the names, ranks and ages of all those on the Allied side who were killed.

15. G. D. Sheffield, p. 138.

16. K. C. Mehra, *A History of The Army Ordnance Corps 1775–1974*, pp. 224–5; Moharir, pp. 388–90.

17. Evans and Brett-James, p. 41.

18. W. L. Hailes and J. Ross, *The Jat Regiment*, pp. 290–2; Brett-James, *Ball of Fire*, p. 333; NAM 6411/47–1, 'Scrapbook, kept by Col. Becher, W.W.II. Concerning 3/9 Jat Regiment: April 1944'.

19. Corporal Arthur Freer was a wireless operator in B Squadron Leader's tank. His book *Nunshigum* describes the battle in some detail in a novelistic style (also IWM 19822/12, Corporal Arthur Freer). C. T. Atkinson, pp. 170–3; Oatts, *I Serve*, pp. 266–7; Evans and Brett-James, pp. 215–25; L. Allen, *Burma*, pp. 253–60; Perrett, *Tank Tracks to Rangoon*, p. 117. Craddock received a DCM and Ranbir Singh an IOM (C. Peterson, *Unparalleled Danger Unsurpassed Courage*, p. 110); a DSO, three MCs and two MMs were also awarded for this action. Ever since then 13 April has been celebrated by B Squadron and its successor in the Royal Scots Dragoon Guards (Carabiniers and Greys), when it parades without officers under the SSM.

20. L. Allen, *Burma*, p. 258.

21. IWM AL 5236, 'Report on Operations I/60th Infantry Regiment at Imphal March–July 1944'.

22. Evans and Brett-James, pp. 226–8; Farndale, pp. 201–2.

23. Chandra, pp. 90–2.

24. Some references say five were lost; possibly Troop Carrier Command lost two. Two were shot down by Captain Takiguchi Hiroshi of 204th *Sentai*. Franks, *The Air Battle of Imphal*, pp. 89–90, 98.

25. Franks, *The Air Battle of Imphal*, pp. 146, 184; J. G. Littlejohn, *Royal Air Force Days*, pp. 80, 95; IWM 11366/4, Flight Lieutenant Owen Parry.

26. P. C. Smith, *Jungle Dive-Bombers at War*, pp. 76–7.

27. Cross, *Jungle Warfare*, p. 61.

28. Since his first operation at Donbaik, George Steer had raised and trained another four such units, each with an establishment of sixty. The modern successor unit, 15th (UK) Information Support Group, is proud to claim descent from Steer's unit among others. Rankin, pp. 238–40, 245–6.

29. M. G. Abhankyar, *Valour Enshrined*, pp. 452–3.

30. Doulton, p. 128. The IFBU joined in the defence of Scraggy and proved more effective than originally anticipated in terms of propaganda. They broadcast programmes prepared by Korean-trained propagandists and sentimental Japanese music of a sort now banned in Japan. Steer reported that of fifty to sixty broadcast days, only four times were they fired upon. Four times Japanese raised white flags: one was fired on and the other three not reported until the following day. On two occasions when positions were attacked following broadcasts, prisoners were taken who did not resist, saying they would have surrendered earlier had they been able to, and on all other occasions the positions were found empty. See PRO WO 203/3312, 'Propaganda: Indian Field Broadcasting Units'.

31. K. W. Cooper, *The Little Men*, pp. 14–15.

32. TM RH(54).8 IAC 7 Cav; MH.5, 'On Such Small Things'; NAM Ind. Cav. 7 Cav. '7th Light Cavalry in the Manipur Campaign March–August 1944', pp. 4–8. This is one of the twelve 'phoenix' units in Daniel P. Marston's *Phoenix from the Ashes*, pp. 147–9.

33. This attack cost the Devons 19 dead and 68 wounded, but 68 Japanese bodies were counted and many more had been dragged away. Jeremy Taylor, *The Devons*, pp. 177–80; W. J. P. Aggett, *The Bloody Eleventh*, pp. 342–5; J. Thompson, *The Imperial War Museum Book of the War in Burma 1942–1945*, pp. 197–202 (see also IWM 20476/3, Private William Palmer; 19901/3, Corporal Stanley May; 19603/2, Private William Savage; and 19771/3, Private Rendell 'Ray' Dunn); Bickersteth, p. 79; Mullally, *Bugle and Kukri*, pp. 351–5; Conden, *The Frontier Force Rifles*, pp. 401–4.

34. L. Allen, *Burma*, pp. 222–7.

35. J. Hudson, p. 87.

36. Painter, p. 89; RAHT MD/1844, 'Field Artillery in Jungle Warfare', by Capt. I. M. Ferguson MC RA.

37. Jeremy Taylor, pp. 181–3.

38. Painter, p. 101.

39. Noronha received an MC, and four MMs were also awarded. E. G. Pythian-Adams, *The Madras Regiment 1758–1958*, p. 239. 4th/3rd Madras is one of the twelve 'phoenix' units in Daniel P. Marston's *Phoenix from the Ashes*, pp. 145–7.

40. Bellers, pp. 191–9.

41. Conden, *The Frontier Force Rifles*, p. 399.

42. P. Moon (ed.), *Wavell: The Viceroy's Journal*, p. 49; Philip Mason, *A Matter of Honour*, p. 502. In another version Jim Allan relates the same story, but this

time it occurs in the Admin Box and the wag is a 2nd West Yorks sergeant (*In the Trade of War*, p. 85). Since, as with so many such stories, these accounts are at least second- or even third-hand, one must assume they are apocryphal.

43. Between 1 and 10 May the Devons lost 200 killed wounded and missing. Jeremy Taylor, pp. 185–7.

44. Swinson, *Kohima*, p. 143.

45. BA S145,6 May 1945.

46. Lewin, *Slim*, p. 188.

47. Kirby, vol. 3, p. 310.

48. Lyman, *Slim*, pp. 20–1.

49. Bellers, pp. 201–7; Shears, p. 43; D. Sutherland, *Tried and Valiant*, pp. 198–200; Conden, *The Frontier Force Rifles*, pp. 404–6.

50. W. Bugler, *The Story of 114*, pp. 112–4; RAHT MD /1945, 'My War in the Far East 1943–46', by S/Sgt R. A. Wickstead.

51. Mullaly, *Bugle and Kukri*, pp. 316–9.

52. The AFS was created in 1915 as a volunteer ambulance and transport corps with the French armies. Under its Director-General, Stephen Galatti, it performed the same service in 1940 until the fall of France, when its ambulance sections were sent to the British and Free French. In Africa, Europe and India–Burma the AFS deployed 437 ambulances and 891 men. It suffered 27 fatalities and 78 wounded. In India their commander was Lieutenant-Colonel Chauncey B. Ives. (For the full story of this extraordinary organization see G. Rock, *History of the American Field Service, 1920–1955*.)

53. Doulton, pp. 151–5; J. Sym, *Seaforth Highlanders*, pp. 278–83; J. Stockman, *Seaforth Highlanders*, pp. 208–9; Farndale, pp. 215–6.

54. Somerville, pp. 254–6; IWM 18370/7, Major Dinesh Chandra Misra; A. M. Sethin and V. Katju, *Traditions of a Regiment*, pp. 284–6; D. S. Chand, *The Rajputana Rifles*, p. 25; R. de R. Channer, 'FOO, Imphal June 1944', *Gunner*, August 1994, pp. 16–17.

55. J. P. Lawford and W. E. Catto, *Solah Punjab*, pp. 226–30; J. Croft, 'A Company Commander at Imphal', *Journal of the Society for Army Historical Research*, LXXII, spring 1994, no. 289, pp. 26–8.

56. J. Hudson, p. 90.

57. The Burma Star was awarded for service in the Burma Campaign between 11 December 1941 and 2 September 1945 inclusive. Qualification required, for the navy, six months' operational service in the Bay of Bengal including the Straits of Malacca; for the army, shore-based naval personnel and air force ground personnel, the requirement was service in any part of Burma, Bengal or Assam, and in China and Malaya from 10 February 1942 to 2 September 1945, or one operational sortie for aircrew. For an overview of British decorations awarded during the campaign see L. Smurthwaite, 'In Recognition of Gallant and Distinguished Service: Gallantry and Campaign Awards to British and Commonwealth Forces in The Far East 1941–1945', in Smurthwaite (ed.).

58. PRO WO 203 4637, '1944 Apr.–Aug. Imphal and Kohima Campaigns: Personal Narratives'.

59. This represented a typical sapper task during the campaign. It existed as a 109-mile mule track open to jeeps only with constant maintenance, crossing four mountain ranges up to 6,000 feet high and five rivers, four of them over suspension bridges averaging 300 feet long and 150 feet high. In July and September 1942 Lieutenant-Colonel G. P. Chapman with about 150 officers and men of 82nd Anti-Tank Regiment with Naga labour had improved this bridle path into something like a road which could just take a jeep. See Chapman's account, *The Lampi*.

60. Slim inaccurately gives the impression that all twenty of the volunteers perished, but in fact they sustained few losses and received a hero's welcome when they returned to their unit. Evans and Brett-James say three Japanese were involved (on the night April 15/16); one jumping to his death and two killed in the explosion. Slim, *Defeat into Victory*, pp. 328–9; Rooney, *Burma Victory*, p. 156; Evans and Brett-James, pp. 244–5.

61. Huxford, p. 210; Marston, pp. 150–2; Jervois, pp. 265–9; NRHC 'To Burma: "I Was Not To Reason Why"', by Denis A. Short. This excellent extensive memoir provides an extensive, detailed account of the drudgery, strains and horrors of life on Point 5846. J. Thompson, *The Imperial War Museum Book of the War in Burma 1942–1945*, pp. 205–7.

62. TM RH.88 150 RAC: 3024, 'Account of Action on Imphal Plain', by Sgt C. C. Cusworth; O. F. Sheffield, p. 257.

63. IWM 17583, Lieutenant D. S. Day.

64. Huxford, p. 210.

65. Perrett, *Tank Tracks to Rangoon*, p. 129.

66. TM RH.88 150 RAC: 3024, 'Account of Action on Imphal Plain', by Sgt C. C. Cusworth.

67. Evans and Brett-James, pp. 246–50, 262–5.

68. See R. A. Cooper, *'B' Company 9th Battalion The Border Regiment*, another fine example of writing from what was surely the most literary regiment of the campaign.

69. Sandes, p. 64; Mullaly, *Bugle and Kukri*, pp. 224–30.

70. Initially this comprised eight 25-pounders from 9th Field Regiment, four 3.7-inch Howitzers from 23rd Indian Mountain Regiment, six 6-pounders from 203rd Anti-Tank Battery and three Bofors from 165th Light Anti-Aircraft Battery, under the command of Lieutenant-Colonel Roger Lumpton. Evans and Brett-James, p. 245.

71. Jervois, pp. 270–1; Evans and Brett-James, pp. 251–61.

72. Evans and Brett-James, pp. 266–8.

73. J. B. Chaplin, *Action in Burma, 1942–1945*, pp. 81–2; J. M. Hepper, 'A Light Mountain Regiment in the Imphal Campaign, 29th Indian Light Mountain Regiment', *The Journal of the Royal Artillery*, LXXIV/1, March 1947, pp. 74–80.

74. Rooney, *Burma Victory*, pp. 159–61.

75. Evans and Brett-James, p. 305.

76. RSDGM CB08 C63, 'An Account of the Operations of The 32nd Indian Infantry Brigade, Part III, Bishenpur and The Silchar Track, April to July 1944'; Barclay, *The Regimental History of the 3rd Queen Alexandra's Own Gurkha Rifles*, pp. 71-3.

77. IWM 19822/12, Corporal Arthur Freer; Rooney, *Burma Victory*, pp. 162-3.

78. Evans and Brett-James, p. 274.

79. Bellers, pp. 207-13.

80. For the story of the wartime Japanese language school based at the School of Oriental and African Studies, which trained interpreters and intelligence officers in crash courses, including Louis Allen who was on Translators V (the fifth batch), see S. Oba, *The 'Japanese' War*.

81. Rooney, *Burma Victory*, p. 164; L. Allen, *Burma*, pp. 278-81.

82. Sandes, *From Pyramid to Pagoda*, pp. 66-7.

83. Barclay, *The Regimental History of The 3rd Queen Alexandra's Own Gurkha Rifles*, pp. 173-8; Doulton, pp. 155-6.

84. Carew, *Longest Retreat*, p. 252.

85. G. Rock, *History of the American Field Service, 1920-1955*, p. 515.

86. Praval, *Valour Triumphs*, pp. 122-3.

87. IWM 15335/3, Lieutenant Michael Martin; *History of the 5th Royal Gurkha Rifles (Frontier Force)*, pp. 261-4.

88. Slim, *Defeat into Victory*, p. 337.

89. Major R. A. Adams was awarded an MC in this action, after which Slim wrote to Savory to say he thought 1st/11th Sikhs and 1st/4th Gurkhas were the best battalions in the army. Bamford, pp. 111-5; F. T. Birdwood, *The Sikh Regiment in the Second World War*, pp. 320-4; Betham and Geary, pp. 206-7; C. T. Atkinson, pp. 161-3; C. L. Proudfoot, *We Lead*, pp. 77-8; W. N. Nicholson, *The Suffolk Regiment 1928 to 1946*, pp. 175-7.

90. Pakenham-Walsh, pp. 218-9; Doulton, p. 142.

91. He returned to Tokyo in June 1944 and was put on the reserve list but recalled to active service in April 1945 and appointed garrison commander of Kwantung Province in China. Detained by the Russians after the capitulation, he died in Siberia some time after the war's end. Barker, *The March on Delhi*, p. 276.

92. Shibata took over 15th Division on 10 June 1944 after promotion to lieutenant-general. Barker, *The March on Delhi*, pp. 273-4. See IWM AL 5009/4, 'Reports of SEATIC Interrogators: Lt.-Gen. Shibata Uichi, Cmdr 15 Division'.

93. For Terauchi see Boatner, p. 558.

94. L. Allen, *Burma*, pp. 260-6.

95. RSDGM CB 04 C33 no. 2 of 2, 'Account of the Attack on the Mobdung Front Features, 5/15 June '44. By Captain I. E. Morgan – 3rd Carabiniers'; CB 15 C114; W. N. Nicholson, pp. 179-84.

96. The cost had been high; in a week's fighting the Jats lost 33 dead and 111 wounded. Hailes and Ross, pp. 297-300.

97. Evans and Brett-James, pp. 312–4.
98. Sansome, p. 111; Franks, *The Air Battle of Imphal*, pp. 191–3; L. Allen, *Burma*, p. 306.
99. L. Allen, *Burma*, pp. 309–14.

## 18 KOHIMA: THE BATTLE

1. P. R. Boyle and J. Musgrave-Wood, *Jungle, Jungle Little Chindit*, p. 65.
2. Lieutenant-Colonel W. A. Bickford, 'Kohima: The Second Phase', *Army Quarterly*, LI, October 1945, p. 45. (See also IWM DS/MISC/95, Colonel W. A. Bickford).
3. Mankekar, p. 85.
4. Throughout they were supported by 117,194 and 216 Squadrons RAF, which flew 782 sorties to drop supplies, of which 560 were successful, losing three aircraft. Briscoe, pp. 59, 62. For the most complete account of a column in this brigade see W. A. Wilcox, *Chindit Column 76*. Losses were so severe that it had to amalgamate with its sister 33 Column from 2nd Duke of Wellington's Regiment. A previously unpublished manuscript called 'Epic in Nagaland', by Major Paul Haskins, is partly reproduced in D. Williams, *194 Squadron Royal Air Force*, pp. 43–6. See also IWM 10041/3, Flight Sergeant Douglas Williams; 12559/3, Warrant Officer Deryck Groocock; 12376/3, Pilot Officer Joe Simpson. Major Haskins, who served with 44 Column, based on 1st Essex, had hoped to publish it but this was sadly never achieved. The manuscript notes and correspondance relating to it are held at the Essex Regiment Museum in Chelmsford. Also in 23rd LRP Brigade was 60th Field Regiment RA serving as infantry. See J. Bartlett and J. Benson, *All the King's Enemies*; IWM 94/26/1, F. H. A. Howe; W. E. Duncan et al., *The Royal Artillery Commemoration Book*, pp. 127–31; Terence Weiler, 'Tales from the Naga Hills', in Nunneley (ed.), *Tales from the Burma Campaign*, pp. 28–30. See also C. N. Barclay, *The History of The Duke of Wellington's Regiment 1919–1952*, pp. 136–49; T. A. Martin, *The Essex Regiment 1929–1950*, pp. 102–22; P. J. Shears, *The Story of The Border Regiment 1939–1945*, pp. 75–7; and D. Sutherland, *Tried and Valiant*, pp. 201–5.
5. Mankekar, p. 147.
6. Wilcox, p. 102.
7. L. Allen, *Burma*, pp. 268–9; Rissik, p. 189. See also IWM 91/8/1, Major D. C. Rissik; DS/MISC/65, Major P. L. Rome; 92/28/1, D. P. Wilson.
8. Swinson, *Kohima*, pp. 108–9.
9. Rissik, pp. 190–1.
10. Swinson, *Kohima*, pp. 116–7.
11. This 'commando' was formed from within 2nd Division to handle boats in the planned landings in south Arakan; when these operations were cancelled, it was decided to keep the unit on for commando tasks and pathfinding in the jungle. It was never incorporated in War Establishments and was peculiar,

while it existed, to 2nd Division, and commanded by Major A. K. MacGeorge of The Royal Scots. PRO CAB 44/190, 'Section 7, Chapter "J", Campaigns in the Far East, The War against Japan, Central (Chindwin) Front November 1943 to December 1944, Book III (The Third of Three). The Battle of Kohima. Final Phase of the Battle of Imphal, Exploitation and Pursuit to the Chindwin. Brigadier M. R. Roberts'; A. Muir, *The First of Foot*, pp. 162-3.

12. Hart, pp. 153-6.

13. Crew, p. 299; Colvin, p. 175.

14. Swinson, *Kohima*, pp. 123-5. See also the memoir by the Medical Officer of 7th Worcesters, Leslie Willson, *A Son of the Raj*.

15. Swinson, *Kohima*, p. 129.

16. Colvin, p. 135.

17. In contrast, the Japanese thought they had been hit with 11,500 British artillery rounds during a single two-day engagement. L. Allen, *Burma*, p. 286.

18. D. Murray, interview with the author, 26 June 2003.

19. 45th Cavalry, a war-raised regiment, was originally tasked with patrolling the Corps Line of Communication, carrying supplies and protecting the Zubza box. Colvin, p. 151n.

20. Swinson, *Kohima*, p. 134.

21. O. G. W. White, *Straight on for Tokyo*, pp. 101, 108.

22. C. Whiting, *The Poor Bloody Infantry*, p. 211.

23. The accuracy of bunker-busting medium guns was remarkable. They would fire at about 1,500 yards range with a high charge (to give high muzzle velocity for accurate direct shooting). With their third round they would be accurately ranged on the bunker and the fifth round with a slight-delayed action fuse would explode inside. After destruction, the industrious Japanese would rebuild them overnight, only to be destroyed again a few days later. They also built dummy and alternative positions. (Stanley Clarke and Tillot, pp. 61-2.)

24. J. McCann, *Echoes of Kohima*, p. 330; Colvin, pp. 164-5.

25. Hart, pp. 162-3.

26. Glover, pp. 210-11.

27. Swinson, *Kohima*, pp. 126-9, 139-40.

28. That night alone 5th Brigade demanded (and received the next morning): 1,600 blankets, 100 coils barbed wire, 1,000 gauzes, 10 rolls flannelette, 30 battledress suits, 50 cardigans, 120 bales fodder, 100 gallons petrol, 50 gallons high octane, 150 razors, 160 Indian Type compo rations, 1,000 water sterilizing kits, 4 drums mosquito cream, 4 drums dubbin, 60 three-inch mortar rounds (HE), 60 three-inch mortar rounds (Smoke), 20 mule loads of tinned jam, and fruit, 15 mule loads of vegetables, 16 gallons of rum, 100 pairs of boots and 18 mailbags. No wonder Slim replied when asked why he didn't 'fling a couple of divisions' across the Chindwin that 'only amateurs fling divisions ... Not professional soldiers.' Swinson, *Kohima*, pp. 140-1.

29. O. G. W. White, p. 103.

30. Muir, pp. 170-1. See also 'Kohima, 1944', in McBain, pp. 45-70.

31. Swinson, *Kohima*, pp. 147–8, 152.
32. IWM 91/21/1, Captain J. H. Howard.
33. S. White, '*Strike Home*', p. 72.
34. Hart, pp. 182–6.
35. IWM 16970/46, Sergeant Bert Fitt.
36. WRM, V. F. S. Hawkins, 'Operations of the 5 Infantry Brigade, 2 Division in Assam, 30 March–12 Amy 1944, with Special Reference to the Battle of Kohima, October 1946'; Hallam, p. 126.
37. Colvin, pp. 166–70.
38. O. G. W. White, p. 106.
39. Rissik, p. 193; S. D. Shannon, '*Forgotten No More*': 2nd Battalion DLI at Kohima 1944, p. 26.
40. Glover, p. 213.
41. Swinson, *Kohima*, p. 166.
42. Hart, p. 189.
43. Glover, p. 213.
44. Swinson, *Kohima*, pp. 169–72.
45. NAM Acc. no. 33653, Captain F. T. Burnett, 'Keeping up with the Hunt'; NAM 731–68, four copies of *Fauji Ahkbar*.
46. Palit, *Major General A. A. Rudra*, p. 279.
47. Qureshi, p. 326.
48. IWM 16970/46, Sergeant Bert Fitt.
49. Hart, pp. 191–6.
50. The bath unit was an *ad hoc* arrangement run by Headquarters 2nd Division's Administrative Branch. The Divisional engineers devised a water-heating system and water supply with REME modified vehicles. The bather sat in a 44-gallon drum halved lengthways filled with hot water, and after soaping himself stood up to be hosed down by an operator. The unit's manpower was drawn from the infantry battalions from those incapacitated or considered too old for service in the forward area (some of them over thirty!) D. Murray, interview with the author, 26 June 2003.
51. Swinson, *Kohima*, pp. 175–7.
52. F. Clarke, *The Road to Spiderpore*, p. 156.
53. Colvin, p. 184.
54. Roberts, pp. 128–30; *Operations of the 1st and 2nd Battalions the Queen's Royal Regiment in Burma during World War Two*, pp. 11–13.
55. Swinson, *Kohima*, pp. 180–4.
56. W. Miles, *The Life of a Regiment*, p. 375.
57. M. A. Lowry, *An Infantry Company in Arakan and Kohima*, p. 116; Twiston Davies (ed.), pp. 83–6.
58. Rizvi, p. 66.
59. PRO WHO 203/1777, Report on Ops Kohima 1 Queen's at Kohima May 444/15 Punjab at Kohima May 44 Op Squash–May 44 (Maungdaw Hills) 14 Baluch – ditto – BARFORCE History of Dec 43–Apr 44 2 Div at Kohima Apr–May 44'.

60. As was commonly the case with machine-gun battalions, it fought as numerous small detachments grouped with line battalions according to task. A detailed account of the unit's actions during the battle was written shortly afterwards by Rex King-Clark, the second-in-command (who was effectively Commanding Officer as the CO was away). It was published over 50 years later as *The Battle for Kohima 1944*.

61. D. Wilson, *The Sum of Things*, p. 117.

62. P. K. Kemp, *History of The Royal Norfolk Regiment 1919–1951*, pp. 82–3.

63. Swinson, *Kohima*, p. 195.

64. The Dorset's CO recalled to a Fourteenth Army observer: 'We took over on April the 26th and fifteen casualties while we were taking over, which showed us we were up against something pretty tough. I made a recce with the company commanders after dusk and at three next morning I sent two companies round the left of the garden … They stayed there for five days, for the last three of those days being fired at over open sights by a Jap 75 [mm] on Treasury Hill. We used to run rations to them in an armoured car right past the Jap bunkers separating them from the rest of us, and we brought out the wounded the same way. The Japs in the bunker couldn't fire on the armoured car, but they rolled grenades down which didn't hurt it … There were of course many quiet days, days when we tried little stunts and got the odd couple of Japs. Once for some reason one of them waved a yellow and white flag tied to a bamboo. We shot his hand off. It'll show you how close they were when I tell you that one day a Jap deepening his dugout started shovelling soil into one of ours. We threw a grenade at him.' PRO WHO 203/4637.

65. O. G.W. White, p. 111.

66. Perrett, *Tank Tracks to Rangoon*, p. 143; IWM 17265/5, Sergeant Henry William Cook; IWM 15334/4, Lieutenant Lintorn Trevor Highlett.

67. PRO WO 203/4367, '1944 Apr.–Aug. Imphal and Kohima Campaigns: Personal Narratives'.

68. Bellers, pp. 221–2.

69. Swinson, *Kohima*, pp. 202, 204–5, 206–7.

70. Glover, pp. 214–5.

71. IWM 20456/30, Major David Wilson.

72. Scott had missed a kick aimed at a Japanese grenade that landed near by. At Kohima, 2nd Royal Norfolks lost 11 officers and 79 men killed, with 13 officers and 150 men wounded. P. K. Kemp, *History of The Royal Norfolk Regiment 1919–1951*, p. 85. See also IWM 17353/17, Lieutenant Maurice Franses; 17534/23, Company Sergeant-Major Walter Gilding; 15609/4, Private William John Cron.

73. Colvin, pp. 197–9, 205–6; Palit, *Major-General A. A. Rudra*, p. 265.

74. Shipster, p. 55.

75. Lowry, p. 120.

76. Swinson, *Kohima*, p. 222.

77. Bellers, pp. 222–8.

78. L. Allen, *Burma*, pp. 284–9.
79. Swinson, *Kohima*, p. 211.
80. L. Allen, *Burma*, p. 289.
81. Swinson, *Kohima*, pp. 232–4, 236.
82. L. Allen, *Burma*, pp. 289–96.
83. D. Rissik, p. 197; Perrett, *Tank Tracks to Rangoon*, p. 143; Evans and Brett-James, p. 327.

# 19 MONSOON

1. Humphreys, p. 176.
2. Jagota, pp. 74–5.
3. Humphreys, p. 12.
4. AMSM File 37, 'The Evacuation of a Casualty from a Remote Part of Burma'. The story of the Gurkha is probably apocryphal. Slim told it to a Burma Star Association Reunion at the Albert Hall, but it apparently referred to the battle of Imphal and the Gurkha was going to use his kukri (M. Hickey, *The Unforgettable Army*, p. 186).
5. Shipster, p. 43.
6. Street, *Another Brummie in Burma*, p. 84.
7. Bamford, p. 116; Evans and Brett-James, pp. 285–6.
8. Atkins *The Forgotten Major*, p. 108; G. W. Robertson, p. 166.
9. T. F. Hankin, *From Bootle to Burma*, p. 113; A. W. Munn, *A Fragment of Life (The Burma Episode)*, p. 182; Leyin p. 99; Franks, *First in the Indian Skies*, p. 109.
10. Humphreys, pp. 74–6.
11. R. Arnold, pp. 122–3; Tuchman, p. 452.
12. J. Hudson, p. 55.
13. Hart, pp. 197–8.
14. Hart, p. 158.
15. *Tik Hai*, 9th Border Regiment Association Newsletter (no numbering).
16. Hickey, pp. 92.
17. J. Hainsworth, 'Forgotten Heroines: The Women's Services in the Far East', in Smurthwaite (ed.), p. 83.
18. Humphreys, p. 78.
19. M. Robertson, *Sister Sahibs*, p. 38. See also: Diane Sloggett, *Angels of Burma*; Angela Bolton, *The Maturing Sun*; and Jean Bowden, *Grey Touched with Scarlet*, pp. 171–84.
20. Hickey, p. 94.
21. Humphreys, p. 96.
22. SOAS E Coll 3 M/83, Capt. L. S. Beswick, 'Two Roads in Burma'.
23. Fischer, *The Chancy War*, pp. 38–9.
24. Collister, p. 90.
25. Hill, pp. 166–7.

26. SOAS E Coll 3 B/37, Capt. J. C. Smyth, 'Notes on the Burma Campaign Compiled from Japanese Sources'; GM G46, 'Payagi Interrogation Report no. 8. Miscellaneous Questions from Twelfth Army Directive'.

27. Leyin, p. 180.

28. Joe Milner deals with this theme in his 'factionalized' account of Chindit operations, *To Blazes with Glory: A Chindit's War*.

29. Maslen-Jones, p. 110.

30. G. Hanley, *Monsoon Victory*, p. 117.

31. G. C. Griffiths, 'The Railway Corridor and Before: With the 2nd Battalion in Burma', *Y Ddraig Goch: The Journal of The Royal Welch Fusiliers*, XXII/4, St David's Day, 1982.

32. Cross, *Jungle Warfare*, p. 42.

33. A. W. Munn, p. 57.

34. Hill, p. 100.

35. NAM 5912-161-4, *A 'Wasbie' in Burma*, N. S. B. Clayton. See also OIOC WAS(B) 1943–46; MS Eur D859 Ussher Collection; Letters and Photographs of Miss Marjorie E Ussher; IWM 94/51/1, Mrs J. Morton; 82/26/1, Miss E. P. Cheverton. For the story of the WAS(B), an excellent booklet by Sally and Lucy Jaffé called *Chinthe Women* is available for £5 from Rock Hill Cottage, Chipping Norton, Oxon, OX7 5BA. See also Kathleen Vellacott Jones, *The Wasbies*, which contains a complete list of all members, 1942–1946, and her personal memoir (as Kathleen Vellacott), *Ticket to Burma*.

36. J. Hudson, p. 64.

37. Out of the line in August, 1st Royal Welch Fusiliers held an inter-company choir competition; they beat 506th Field Company 6–0 at rugby and 2–0 at soccer. They also beat the Divisional Royal Artillery 14–0 at rugby but lost to 16th Field Regiment 1–3 at soccer. They were entertained by 'The Green Flies' concert party and inspected by Wavell, who said he was very pleased to see representatives of his old brigade and to see them looking so well. C and D Companies held a *Brains Trust* and the Colville Mobile Canteen presented *Desert Song*, starring Dennis Morgan and Irene Manning. C and D Company then held another *Brains Trust*, reportedly even more successful than the first! But a security intelligence report noted the men's disappointment at the comparatively few shows by the Divisional Mobile Cinema and Concert Party – they had hoped for one per week; enthusiasm was great for those arranged at company level. PRO WO 172/4925, 'War Diary 1st Royal Welch Fusiliers Jan.–Dec.1944'.

38. SOAS E Coll 3 E/38, Michael A. Demetriadi, 'Correspondence and Notes 1958–1960, relating to 1st Battalion The Royal Welch Fusiliers at Kohima and Elsewhere'. G. W. Robertson, pp. 231–2; Leyin, pp. 221–3; A. E. Clarke, *Return to Singapore*, pp. 17–18; E. R. Evans, pp. 112–8.

39. Street, *A Brummie in Burma*, p. 66.

40. A. Sutherland Brown, *Silently into the Midst of Things*, p. 73.

41. Shipster, p. 61.

42. Spencer, p. 122.

43. Hill, pp. 94-5.

44. G. Coulthard, *From Private to Trooper Back to Private*, p. 153. This is an extremely funny account of the pointlessness of so much of army life and, although the dialogue cannot have been remembered after fifty years, it rings true. It is also likely that he saw the film after his unit returned from Burma. *Objective, Burma*, also called *Operation Burma* (Warner Bros, 1945), starred Errol Flynn, William Prince, James Brown and George Tobias, and was directed by Raoul Walsh and produced by Jerry Wald. It portrays long-range penetration operations in Burma, culminating in a walk-out. *Distant Drums* (1951) is set in the nineteenth century, replacing the Japanese with Native Americans.

45. A. Massie, 'Burma and the British Soldier', in Smurthwaite (ed.), p. 56.

46. Gilmore and Davis, p. 227.

47. Gilmore and Davis, pp. 228-9.

48. Forty, *XIV Army at War*, p. 57.

49. Briscoe, pp. 78-9. See also: Saunders, pp. 318-22; R. A. Pearson, pp. 73-5.

50. D. Smurthwaite, 'Behind the Front: Logistics and the Maintenance of Fourteenth Army', in Smurthwaite (ed.), pp. 132-3.

51. Rooney, *Burma Victory*, p. 65.

52. Doulton, p. 138.

53. Littlejohn, p. 95.

54. M. Anglo, *Service Newspapers of the Second World War*, p. 72.

55. Spencer, p. 123. For other personal accounts of Combat Cargo operations see: Gerald A. White, *The Great Snafu Fleet*; and William E. Smith (ed.), *Second Troop Carrier Squadron, China–Burma–India, World War II, January 1943–December 1945*.

56. Crew, p. 324.

57. Evans and Brett-James, p. 204; Franks, *The Air Battle of Imphal*, p. 202.

58. Franks, *The Air Battle of Imphal*, p. 175.

59. PRO AIR 41/41/64, 'Air Historical Branch Narrative, The Campaign in the Far East', appx 20.

60. An air task force, although the latter, due to combine 1st Air Commando and 3rd Combat Cargo, never came into being. Craven and Cate (eds.), vol. 5, pp. 204-7.

61. Sansome, pp. 112-3.

62. SOAS E Coll 3 M/83, Capt. L. S. Beswick, 'Two Roads in Burma'.

63. Chapman, p. 6.

64. Hanley, p. 46.

65. G. W. Robertson, pp. 236-7.

66. For an overview of operational intelligence in Burma, see Clayton, pp. 183-9, 190.

67. During the retreat in 1942 air recce had been provided on an *ad hoc* basis with individual aircraft fitted with cameras from various squadrons, including the AVG, but mainly by 28 Squadron RAF and 1 Squadron IAF at Toungoo and

forming no. 3 PRU based in India after the retreat, which was renumbered 681 Squadron on 25.01.43, operating Hurricanes and then Spitfires. In late 1943 a new squadron was formed with Mosquitos, 684 to be fully operational by April 1944 under 171 Wing and joined by US 9th PR Squadron based at Barrackpore operating independently under Tenth Air Force. The Americans then formed 8th Photo Reconnaissance Group when 20th Tactical Reconnaissance Squadron arrived in March. See G. J. Thomas, *Eyes for the Phoenix*, passim.

68. Sigint in the Far East seems to have provided considerable information regarding strengths and supplies, but less on Japanese commanders' intentions. British sigint operations were centred on the Wireless Experiment Centre in Delhi, effectively an outstation of Bletchley Park, which operated 88 substations across India intercepting Japanese signals. At Barrackpore, Intelligence School 'C' provided immediate sigint for Fourteenth Army and the Tactical Air Intelligence Section at Comilla provided detailed air intelligence for 3rd Tactical Air Force, with a squadron of USAAF P-38 Lightnings ready to operate snap missions which enjoyed spectacular success, shooting down 135 aircraft and destroying others on the ground. A Special Liaison Unit was set up in early 1944 to pass high-level Ultra sigint to Slim. Ultra information received from the Japanese was much the same as that received from the German Army in Europe: operational and movement orders, strength returns and locations of Japanese formations which not only formed useful targets for the air but gave Slim a complete order of battle of the Japanese forces. To provide sigint support there was a Special Wireless Group (around 12 officers and 300 men) at Fourteenth Army and Special Wireless Companies (about a third the size) with each corps and at various other locations. (M. Smith, pp. 199–202, 230, 280, 282, 294, 301–2.)

69. In August V Force Headquarters was disbanded to provide staff for the Lushai Brigade and then steadily run down until June 1945, when it was finally disbanded. PRO WO 203/464, 'V Force: A Force of Officers to Raise and Lead Bands of Guerrillas from the Tribes of Assam-Burma border: Organisation'.

70. NAM Ind Inf 3 Regt., 'The Story of the 4th Bn., The Madras Regiment in the Burma Campaign, 1943–'45'.

71. Peers and Brelis, p. 39; R. Harris-Smith, *OSS*, pp. 288, 296–7; Thorne, pp. 338, 454; Aldrich, p. 201.

72. For a full account of the operations of 357 and 358 Squadrons in support of clandestine missions by SOE, ISLD, Z Force, D Division, E Group and OSS, see D. G. Morris, *Beyond the Irrawaddy and the Salween*. See also OIOC MS Eur R135, taped interview by Carlyle Edmund Seppings, Burma Army 1941–45, Burma Police 1945–50, chiefly on his wartime experiences with the ISLD as an undercover agent in Burma, and in the Burma Police after the war, including his surveillance of the nationalist politician U Saw.

73. GS I(d) was formally taken over by SEAC in March 1944 and renamed D Division along the lines of 'A' Force in the Middle East. In fact the unit's official designation was Force 456 but it was known as D Division for the rest of

the war. It had a staff (on paper) of 32 officers, 30 other ranks and 9 secretarial staff. PRO CAB 154/99, 'Strategic Deception in the War against Japan'; A. Stripp, *Codebreaker in the Far East*, pp. 179–91; R. Arnold, pp. 93–7.

74. O'Brien, *The Moonlight War*, pp. 19–21.

75. PRO WO 203/33, 'Deception Organisation: Correspondence and Reports'; Howard, pp. 205–18; O'Brien, *The Moonlight War*, pp. 153, 287–8, 305–6. Stripp, pp. 179–91.

76. Becka, pp. 167–9, 178, 180. See also Chapter 19 in F. S. V. Donnison, *British Military Administration in the Far East*.

77. M. Collis, *Last and First in Burma (1941–1948)*, pp. 209–10.

78. C. Cruickshank, *SOE in the Far East*, pp. 176–7.

79. Kirby, vol. 4, p. 33.

80. Bowen, p. 104.

81. T. A. Martin, *The Essex Regiment 1929–1950*, p. 118.

82. RHQDD, 'The 1st Bn in Burma 1943–1945', by Major P. V. Nepean MC; Jeremy Taylor, *The Devons*, pp. 253–8.

83. SOAS E Coll 3 M/75, H. C. Smith, '"Hostilities Only": Tales of an Amateur Soldier in World War II'.

84. Shipster, p. 59.

85. Detwiler and Burdick (eds.), vol. 6/6, 'Burma Operations Record 15th Army Operations in Imphal Area and Withdrawal to Northern Burma', Japanese Monograph no.134, p. 164.

86. J. Clabby, *The History of The Royal Army Veterinary Corps 1919–1961*, pp. 147–9; Captain Yamashita Seiryo, 'Horse and Oxen', in Tamayama and Nunneley, pp. 187–92.

87. Clabby, p. 158. The reminiscences of two RAVC officers can be found in J. D. Parkinson and R. B. Hornby, *Along O' My Old Brown Mule*.

88. Maule, pp. 324–5.

89. Roberts, p. 146.

90. Swinson, *Kohima*, p. 251.

91. F. C. Jones, H. Borton and B. R. Pearn, *The Far East 1942–1946*, p. 123; R. J. C. Butow, *Japan's Decision to Surrender*, p. 31n.6. For Koiso see Boatner, p. 287.

92. Swinson, *Kohima*, p. 245.

93. For Kawabe, Kimura, Tanaka and Mutaguchi see Boatner, pp. 267, 275, 387, 555; and Swinson, *Four Samurai*, p. 252.

94. Such a clearance was unprecedented at such a high level in the Japanese Army. L. Allen, *Burma*, p. 386.

95. Lyman, p. 225.

96. Swinson, *Kohima*, pp. 242–3.

97. L. Allen, *Burma*, p. 275.

98. Whiting, p. 212.

## 20 MYITKYINA AND MOGAUNG

1. *CBI Round-up*, quoted in Tuchman, p. 508.
2. E. J. King and W. M. Whitehill, *Fleet Admiral King*, p. 541.
3. Tuchman, pp. 446–7.
4. IWM AL 827/5, 'Short History of 53 Japanese Division'.
5. See Hopkins with Jones, chaps. 15 and 16.
6. Prefer, pp. 133–9.
7. Fellowes-Gordon, *The Battle for Now Seng's Kingdom*, p. 120.
8. Stilwell, p. 296.
9. W. S. Churchill, vol. 5, p. 569.
10. Romanus and Sunderland, *Stilwell's Command Problems*, p. 233.
11. Craven and Cate (eds.), vol. 5, p. 207; Romanus and Sunderland, *Stilwell's Command Problems*, pp. 228–30.
12. IWM 97/20/6–12, Major-General O. C. Wingate Papers: Major J. F. F. Barnes.
13. Romanus and Sunderland, *Stilwell's Command Problems*, p. 230.
14. Chan W-L, *Burma*, p. 59. See Hopkins with Jones, chaps. 20–22.
15. Masters, *The Road past Mandalay*, p. 249.
16. GM Diary/Draft History no. S5: 'Report on Operations Carried Out by Special Force – Oct '43 to Sept. '44'.
17. Masters, *The Road past Mandalay*, p. 255.
18. Masters, *The Road past Mandalay*, pp. 257–9.
19. O' Brien, *Out of the Blue*, p. 236.
20. J. Thompson, *The Imperial War Museum Book of War behind the Enemy Lines*, p. 238.
21. IWM 84/21/1, Major P. C. Cane – Morrisforce War Diary; IWM 97/1/1, Maj. B. G. Kinloch.
22. J. Shaw, *The March Out*, p. 128.
23. D. Bednall, *Sun on my Wings*, pp. 113–4.
24. Designed by Major Kenneth Robertson RE, they were built from local resources with essential parts flown in, using six (later nine) sapper platoons and operated in three squadrons forming the 'Indawgyi Grand Fleet' – *Ark Royal, Vindictive, Valiant, Vanguard*; *Revenge, Renown and Resolution*; *Barham, Benbow and Blenheim* – and used for casualty evacuation. K. E. Robertson, 'Indawgyi', *The Royal Engineers Journal*, LXII, September 1948; Pakenham-Walsh, pp. 231–3.
25. Masters, *The Road past Mandalay*, pp. 265–7.
26. He was able to get all his priceless letters out of Burma by protecting them in cellophane and an anti-gas wallet. J. Shaw, *The March Out*, pp. 103–4, 177.
27. Towill, p. 72.
28. Masters, *The Road past Mandalay*, p. 269.
29. IWM 80/49/1, Revd W. H. Miller.
30. J. Shaw, *The March Out*, p. 105; Barclay, *The History of The Cameronians (Scottish Rifles)*, p. 153.

31. G. S. Seagrave, *Burma Surgeon Returns*, p. 137.

32. O'Brien, *Out of the Blue*, p. 31.

33. Ogburn, p. 279. This unattributed remark appears in numerous memoirs of the campaign. 'For an American to qualify for evacuation through sickness he had to display a temperature in excess of 102 degrees (Fahrenheit) for three consecutive days. So desperate was the need for anyone who could pull a trigger. Galahad survivors were vomiting most of their K-rations and some fell asleep during battle' (J. P. Davies, *Dragon by the Tail*, p. 293).

34. O. Gruhzit-Hoyt, *They Also Served*, p. 232.

35. This now comprised 42nd, 88th, 89th and 150th Chinese Regiments, Galahad, 209th and 236th Engineer Combat Battalions, Morrisforce and W and X Troops, 69th Light Anti-Aircraft Regiment RA. On 29 June Hunter took over and 149th Chinese Regiment began to arrive as well as a K9 or War Dog Company, of which the Japanese became very afraid, although a tiger made short work of two of them. PRO WO 203/2672, 'North Burma Campaign: A Background History'.

36. Prefer, p. 166; Hopkins with Jones, pp. 635-45, 651-6.

37. SOAS E Coll 3 F/4, R. F. Bates, 'Memories of Military Service (A Teenager in Burma)'.

38. Romanus and Sunderland, *Stilwell's Command Problems*, p. 242.

39. Ogburn, p. 279; SOAS E Coll 3 F/4.

40. Chan W-L, p. 68.

41. J. Shaw, *The March Out*, p. 150.

42. Calvert, *Fighting Mad*, p. 176.

43. Bidwell, *The Chindit War*, p. 268.

44. IWM 80/49/1, Lieutenant N. Durant.

45. Among the casualties was Major Archie Wavell, son of the Viceroy, who was hit in the wrist and almost had his hand ripped off. Calmly he walked back and took his turn awaiting evacuation until Lentaigne ordered Calvert to fly him out immediately, threatening him with dismissal if he failed. Calvert supposed this was for two reasons: the Viceroy may not have been aware that the second Chindit operation pursued a different policy towards its wounded than the first in that they were to be evacuated rather than abandoned; and it looked to Calvert from the map that the offensive might appear stalled and they could not risk the Viceroy's son falling into the hands of the Japanese and INA. Calvert, *Prisoners of Hope*, p. 211.

46. Allmand, attached from the Indian Armoured Corps, was suffering from trench foot and should have already been evacuated. Gibbs, pp. 144, 149-51; NAM Acc. no. 8101-78, 'Documents Relating to Capt. Michael Allmand, Indian Armoured Corps attached 3/6 Gurkha Rifles, who won the Victoria Cross in Burma in June 1944'.

47. Cross and Gurung (eds.), p. 111.

48. As Shelford Bidwell says, 'in the history of infantry fighting the feat of 77th Brigade is unsurpassed'. Bidwell, *The Chindit War*, pp. 273-4.

49. IWM 9942/21, Brig. M. Calvert.

50. Calvert, *Fighting Mad*, pp. 181–2; Calvert, *Prisoners of Hope*, p. 252.
51. Hamilton, pp. 301–5.
52. Towill, p. 129.
53. Chan W-L, p. 86.
54. Prefer, p. 170.
55. Masters, *The Road past Mandalay*, pp. 281–2.
56. For a short biography see Lyle Wilkes, *Festing – Field Marshal*.
57. *History of The East Lancashire Regiment in the War 1939–1945*, p. 256.
58. SOAS E Coll 3 K/32, G. Foster, '36th Division, The Campaign in North Burma – 1944–45'; Pakenham-Walsh, pp. 233–7.
59. M. Gilbert, *Road to Victory: Winston S. Churchill 1941–1945*, pp. 883–5.
60. McGeoch, p. 107.
61. Ziegler, *Mountbatten*, pp. 279–80.
62. PRO WO 203/2672.
63. R. Arnold, p. 130.
64. Tuchman, pp. 474–5.
65. BA C324 SACSEA Personalities Report, para. 98.
66. Most were later captured by Kachin rangers but four died on the retreat, two being shot when mistaken for Japanese soldiers. The Japanese employed some 3,200 women in Burma through private contractors including 2,800 Koreans, almost all coerced into prostitution. Significant numbers of Burmese women, including many volunteers who believed Japanese promises of Burmese independence, were also employed. Hicks, pp. 138–40.
67. L. Allen, *Burma*, pp. 381–5.
68. Fischer, *The Chancy War*, pp. 164–5.
69. Ogburn, p. 277.
70. Two of the regiment's medical officers, Major James E. T. Hopkins and Captain Henry G. Stelling, wrote a scathing report on the conditions affecting the formation that combined with a report by Colonel Tracey S. Voorhees of the Judge Advocate General Corps, comprised 'The Marauders and the Microbes: A Record of Righteous Indignation' and was commonly known as the 'Hopkins Report'. Failure to evacuate sick men were described as 'more dynamite than the Patton Incident', and confidence in theatre commanders described as 'zero'. The report can be seen in J. H. Stone (ed.) (WL RAMC 1332(P)).
71. Bidwell, *The Chindit War*, p. 279. For an account of this unit, see Chapter 11, 'Ghosts in the Jungle', in M. Richardson, *Fighting Tigers*. See also IWM 89/1/1, Lieutenant-Colonel F. R. Wilford.
72. IWM 80/49/1, Brig. P. H Graves-Morris; 98/3/1, Maj. R. P. J. Dobney.
73. J. Shaw, *The March Out*, pp. 190–1.
74. Gillings, pp. 59–64; Brett, pp. 38–40.
75. J. Shaw, *The March Out*, pp. 195–6.
76. Gillings, pp. 65–9; IWM P146, W. N. Elliott.
77. Calvert, *Fighting Mad*, p. 183.
78. Rhodes-James, p. 179.

79. Blair, pp. 332–3.

80. Hickey, pp. 138–9.

81. They were known as the 'Honeymooners' because they came from The Bedfordshire and Hertfordshire Regiment, or 'Beds and Hearts'. IWM 80/49/1, Maj. R. J. Bower; Crew, p. 188; Blair, p. 333.

82. This was since, writing years later, Mutaguchi said the Chindits 'put a great obstacle in the way of our Imphal plan and were an important reason for its failure'. Tulloch, pp. 264–5; SOAS E Coll G/37, G. W. Symes, 'Some Views of the Wingate Expeditions of 1943 and 1944 from the Japanese Standpoint'.

83. Sir Robert 'Bobby' Thompson, RAF liaison officer on both Chindit expeditions (the first 76 pages of his memoir, *Make for the Hills*, are devoted to them) and prominent in the later successful defeat of the Communist insurgency in Malaya, suggests in his foreword to Peter Mead's *Wingate and the Historians* that a crude analogy might be if the Germans landed two airborne divisions in southern England two days after D-Day. This is spurious however. The Allies in both cases enjoyed total air supremacy, and such a nuisance would have been crushed within days. Moreover, Burma Area Army's Chief of Staff later insisted: 'All Japanese troops were disposed for the Imphal operation, all arrangements made, all supplies, etc. dumped. The Chindits affected none of this, and none of those troops were diverted.' (IWM AL 827/8, 'Intelligence Report on Wingate Expeditions 1943 and 1944. Interrogation of General Kimura, Lt.-Gen. Naka and Major Kaetsu by Burma Command intelligence officer, 28 March 1946'.) But Burma Area Army's supply officer and 15th Division's Chief of Staff did acknowledge that 2nd Transport Headquarters plans were completely frustrated by them, and as a result neither 15th nor 31st Division received any further supplies for emergencies once their 25-day allocation ran out. IWM AL 5224, '2nd Wingate Operations, Questionnaire and Answers. Prepared by Military Historical Division, Tokyo.'; AL 5080, 'History of 2nd Field Transport HQ Burma August 1943 to End of War'.

84. Monograph 134 in Japanese Defence Archives, quoted in Tulloch, p. 264.

85. Ziegler, *Mountbatten*, p. 247.

86. Ogburn, p. 289; Masters, *The Road past Mandalay*, pp. 286–9.

87. IWM 80/49/1, Lieutenant-Colonel A. F. Harper. (See also Harper's memoir, *Horse and Foot*.)

88. O'Brien, *Out of the Blue*, p. 49.

89. In assisting Stilwell as agreed at Quebec, Wingate's master plan to capture Indaw did not coincide with his superiors; nor was it realistic. He was explicitly told no more troops would be available to garrison it, and his insistence on the attempt might be read as an attempt to present Slim with a *fait accompli*, perhaps one that would appeal to Churchill and lead to his replacing Slim. Calvert believed a bastion at Indaw acting as a base for six Chindit brigades would have achieved more than on the Imphal front; but Imphal was vital ground, Indaw was not. J. Thompson, *The Imperial War Museum Book of War*

*behind Enemy Lines*, p. 256; *The Imperial War Museum Book of the War in Burma 1942-1945*, pp. 268-70.

90. IWM 96/42/1, General Sir Geoffry Scoones; J. Thompson, *The Lifeblood of War*, pp. 95-6.

91. Ziegler, *Mountbatten*, p. 276.

92. Romanus and Sunderland, *Stilwell's Command Problems*, pp. 329-60.

93. Liu, p. 216.

94. Tuchman, pp. 452-3; Liang C-t, p. 176.

95. IWM AL 827/25, Japanese Account of Burma Operations, December 1941 to August 1945 (Report by Japanese Officers Submitted to HQ 12 Army)'.

96. When Marshall visited London in June, Brooke told him Stilwell must go because of poor relations with the three service chiefs, his handling of the Chindits, and his limey-hating attitude. Marshall's anger flared: 'Brooke, you have three C-in-Cs in India,' he exclaimed, 'none of them want to fight. We have one man who will fight and you want him taken out. What the hell kind of business is this?' Although enraged by Marshall's attitude, Brooke's acknowledgement that all three service chiefs were being recalled at Mountbatten's insistence deprived Marshall of an issue. Tuchman, p. 467.

97. RSDGM CB13 C95, 'Burma Notes Eastern Command.'

98. Hsu Long-hsuen and Chang M-k, pp. 409-10.

99. In the battles for Lungling and Tengchung the Chinese lost 37,133 dead to the Japanese 13,620. Romanus and Sunderland, *Time Runs Out in CBI*, pp. 354-60, 394-8.

100. D. Webster, *The Burma Road*, pp. 275-6.

101. Tuchman, pp. 489-92.

102. IWMAL 827/25, 'Japanese Account of Burma Operations, December 1941 to August 1945 (Report by Japanese Officers Submitted to HQ 12 Army)'.

103. Liang C-t argues that the war situation in China was not as bad as Marshall maintained and that China would have been better served by strengthening Chennault's Fourteenth Air Force. Liang C-t, pp. 239-41.

104. Tuchman, p. 494.

105. Instrumental in the recall was Roosevelt's new envoy to Chungking, Patrick Jay Hurley, who was in Chungking as Roosevelt's personal envoy and, recognizing the message as an ultimatum, asked to present it to Chiang in order to soften the blow. Stilwell could not pass up the opportunity it presented. Ronald Lewin described CBI as the 'greatest theatre of illusions', and says the greatest fool was 'the bone-headed Patrick Hurley' ('World War II: A Tangled Web', *Journal of the Royal United Services Institute*, 127, December 1982, p. 19). For Hurley see Boatner, p. 244. For a full biography see R. D. Buhite, *Patrick Hurley and American Foreign Policy*.

106. For Sultan and Wheeler see Boatner, pp. 549-50, 608-9.

107. Tuchman, pp. 500-2.

108. Professor Liang Chin-tung points out that there was major misunderstanding between Chiang and Stilwell as to his precise role: Stilwell and the American government regarded his primary position as representative of

American Forces in China and his role as Chief of Staff of the China Theatre as secondary; the Chinese regarded these positions as reversed. Furthermore, they thought Stilwell's actions should be subordinate to the Supreme Commander China Theatre, as designated by Britain and America – Chiang. As such, Chiang was responsible for all military matters including US Forces in theatre, which caused grave difficulties from the outset, and became increasingly complicated and retrograde up to Stilwell's recall. The second reason for the recall was differences in strategy between Chiang and Stilwell. Chiang had to consider the situation affecting China while Stilwell, as commander of Chinese forces in Burma, was limited to essentially local interests, and obsessed with vindicating the humiliation of 1942. When the Ichi-Go offensive was launched, Chiang regarded it as a life and death matter and recalled forces from northern Burma to central China. Stilwell bitterly opposed this as it reduced his own strength. Liang C-t, pp. 24, 50, 64, 77.

109. B. Tuchman, p. 512.

## 21 PURSUIT

1. Nunneley, *Tales from the King's Afrian Rifles*, p. 163.
2. Kirby, vol. 4, pp. 14–16.
3. Slim, *Defeat into Victory*, pp. 373–5.
4. R. Ryder, *Oliver Leese*, pp. 200–01.
5. Ziegler, *Mountbatten*, pp. 286–7. For Browning see Boatner, p. 66.
6. Ryder, p. 203.
7. Slim, *Defeat into Victory*, p. 385.
8. Ryder, p. 209.
9. Slim, *Defeat into Victory*, p. 388.
10. For a biography of Leese see Ryder, although this somewhat glosses over his problems in Asia, especially the 'sacking' of Slim.
11. RAFM Peirse Papers, Folder 23, E17a, 13 May 1944; Warner, pp. 263–4; Ziegler, *Mountbatten*, p. 237.
12. Probert, pp. 223–5.
13. PRO AIR 41/64, 'Air Historical Branch Narrative, The Campaign in the Far East,' appx 33, 34; Craven and Cate (eds.), vol. 5, p. 232.
14. See Richard Townshend Bickers, *Ginger Lacey: Fighter Pilot*.
15. Probert, pp. 232–5. See also Harry Horner, *No Tigers in our Jungle*.
16. Hames, p. 31.
17. Prefer, pp. 187–92.
18. SOAS E Coll 3 F/4, R. F. Bates, 'Memories of Military Service (A Teenager in Burma)'.
19. CAC Slim Papers, File 3/2.
20. Mountbatten of Burma, *Report to the Combined Chiefs of Staff*.
21. The Air Historical Branch holds an unpublished biography of Bandon called *The Abandoned Earl*, by Michael Seth-Smith.

22. Prasad (ed.), *The Arakan Operations 1942–45*, pp. 213–4.

23. Hanley, p. 108.

24. IWM AL 827/25, 'Japanese Account of Burma Operations, December 1941 to August 1945 (report by Japanese officers submitted to HQ 12 Army)'.

25. L. Allen, *Burma*, pp. 392–4.

26. Kinvig, *River Kwai Railway*, pp. 175–6.

27. Parillo, pp. 137–43.

28. D. McIsaac (ed.), *The United States Strategic Bombing Survey*, vol. 9, p. 104.

29. L. Allen, *Burma*, p. 391.

30. Craven and Cate (eds.), vol. 5, pp. 236–40; Saunders, pp. 342–7.

31. 'In the monsoon you had fantastic thunderstorms, towering cu-nims; air currents, low cloud bases, and violent rain', noted Flight Sergeant Deryck Groocock of 194 Squadron. 'We flew so many times to these places [jungle strips]. We knew just about every inch of our area of Burma, so we knew which valleys we could fly up without coming to a dead end. Often there were clouds on the mountaintops, and you had to fly up a valley underneath.' IWM 12559/3, Warrant Officer D. W. Groocock.

32. For Blackburn, see Probert, pp. 202–3, 207–9.

33. For the history of 27 Squadron see David Innes's *Beaufighters over Burma* (written by an Australian former member). See also Chaz Bowyer, *The Flying Elephants*. For 177 Squadron's history, see Atholl Sutherland Brown, *Silently into the Midst of Things* (written by a Canadian former member). For a full account of the RCAF, see J. R. W. Gwynne-Timothy, *Burma Liberators – the RCAF in SEAC*, and T. W. Melnyk, *Canadian Flying Operations in South-East Asia 1941–1945*. For the history of 435 and 436 Squadrons RCAF, which operated Dakotas, see *Canucks Unlimited* and W. C. Law (ed.), *Chinthe: Canadians over Burma*.

34. Kinvig, *River Kwai Railway*, p. 179.

35. Probert, p. 205.

36. R. Jordan, *To Burma Skies and Beyond*, pp. 73–4, 80, 102.

37. C. H. Fritsche, 'B-24 Liberator', in R. Higham and C. Williams (eds.), *Flying Combat Aircraft of the USAAF and USAF*, p. 55.

38. Bob Bergin describes one such mission against the bridges crossing the Kwai Yai at Kanchanaburi, Thailand, on 3 April 1945 in 'Mission to the River Kwai', *Air Classics*, 35, June 1999, pp. 10–12.

39. Kinvig, *River Kwai Railway*, pp. 182–3.

40. Sutherland Brown, pp. 145–6.

41. SOAS E Coll 3 B/37, Captain J. C. Smyth, 'Notes on the Burmese Campaign compiled from Japanese sources. Unpublished 1946'; 'Burma Operations Record: 28th Army Operations in Akyab Area (November 1943–September 1945), Japanese Monograph no. 132', in Detwiler and Burdick (eds.), vol. 7/1, pp. 45–6.

42. G. J. Thomas, p. 101.

43. Hanley, p. 27. The division comprised ten battalions of King's African Rifles: three each from Uganda and Nyasaland (now Malawi) and two each from

Kenya and Tanganyika (now Tanzania), with a battalion from Northern Rhodesia (now Zambia), and included a Belgian casualty clearing station from Congo.

44. Turner, p. 92; Hanley, pp. 20–2, 52.

45. Nunneley (ed.), *Tales from the Burma Campaign*, p. 61.

46. C. Roetter, *Psychological Warfare*, pp. 136–7.

47. L. Allen, *Burma*, p. 396; Evans and Brett-James, *Imphal*, pp. 76–83, 89.

48. PRO WO 203/467, 'Burma Intelligence Corps: Organization'.

49. Hanley, pp. 35–6.

50. J. Hudson, p. 100.

51. Nunneley, *Tales from the King's African Rifles*, p. 140.

52. Cross and Gurung (eds.), p. 120.

53. SOAS E Coll 3 W/12, Manabu Wada, 'Drifting down the Chindwin: A Story of Survival' (published in abridged form in Tamayama and Nunneley, pp. 172–86).

54. Swinson, *Kohima*, p. 244.

55. At Imphal this had enjoyed relatively good communications and reinforcements, amounting to five battalions including II/51st Regiment, 1/60th Regiment, 61st Regiment (less one battalion) and I/213th Regiment. See Kirby, vol. 4, p. 41n.

56. Malcolm Page, *KAR: A History of The King's African Rifles*, p. 144; Hanley, p. 60.

57. H. Moyse-Bartlett, *King's African Rifles*, pp. 617–8.

58. Somerville, p. 257. For a brief discussion of East African soldiers, with particular regard to gunners, see H. E. Fernyhough, 'East African Artillery', *The Journal of the Royal Artillery*, LXXV/1, March 1948, pp. 24–30.

59. Moyse-Bartlett, pp. 630–4; Hanley, pp. 145–9.

60. IWM 79/29/1, Lieutenant-Colonel K. H. Collen.

61. Nunneley, *Tales from the King's African Rifles*, p. 189.

62. Lyman, p. 238; PRO WO 203/1718, 'Lushai Brigade: An Official History by Historian Brigadier P. C. Marindin'.

63. SOAS E Coll 3 W/6, Nishiji Yasumasa, 'Those Forsaken by God: The Retreat from Imphal'. Accompanying this story are some incredibly powerful charcoal sketches, which are reproduced in Tamayama and Nunneley, pp. 196–212.

64. RSDGM CB 15 C114, 'The Reminiscences of Four Members of "C" Squadron 3rd Carabiniers (Prince of Wales's Dragoon Guards)'.

65. C. T. Atkinson, p. 177.

66. Brett-James, *Ball of Fire*, pp. 365–6.

67. SOAS E Coll 3 M/87, Capt. L. S. Beswick, 'Two Roads in Burma'.

68. Brett-James, *Report My Signals*, p. 197.

69. SOAS E Coll 3 M/29, P. H. Gadsdon, 'An Amateur at War'.

70. RSDGM CB 15 C116.3, Kennedy Peak, Burma 1944'.

71. Qureshi, p. 334; Marston, pp. 152–4.

72. C. Evans, p. 76; Pakenham-Walsh, pp. 238–42.

73. Callahan, p. 141.

NOTES TO PAGES 353−8

74. SOAS E Coll 3 B 37, Captain J. C. Smyth, 'Notes on the Burmese Campaign Compiled from Japanese Sources. Unpublished 1946'.

75. For air operations in north Burma, see Craven and Cate (eds.), vol. 5, pp. 240−6.

76. J. G. Truitt, 'The Irrawaddy Bridge, Ledo Road', *The Military Engineer*, 35, October 1945; Anders, pp. 144−8, 154, 182.

77. Sinclair, pp. 249−50.

78. Prefer, pp. 195−6, 200−6.

79. Romanus and Sunderland, *Time Runs Out in CBI*, p. 126.

80. Spencer, p. 156.

81. Jeremy Taylor, pp. 249−50. See also IWM 85/34/1, N. G. Plumb.

82. Hanley, pp. 214−5.

83. Bamford, p. 128. See also IWM 95/35/1, Lieutenant-Colonel W. L. Farrow.

84. Kirby, vol. 4, pp. 143−5; Gillings, pp. 74−9; J. C. Kemp, *The History of The Royal Scots Fusiliers 1919−1959*, pp. 120−2; *History of The East Lancashire Regiment in the War 1939−1945*, pp. 260−2.

85. At least they had a tremendous Christmas, with plentiful fresh pork, goose, chicken and fish, which they caught with grenades. SOAS E Coll 3 E/53, 'Ledo to Mandalay: A Diary of the North Burma Campaign 1944−45: "A" Company 9th Battalion, The Royal Sussex Regiment'; Gillings, pp. 86−92.

86. J. Henslow, *A Sapper in the Forgotten Army*, p. 105.

87. Jagota, p. 84.

88. The name was chosen by Barlow and refers to the former Royal House of Scotland, the Stuarts. It was presented to the Indian Military Academy at Dehra Dun in 1949 as a trophy. Proudfoot, *We Lead*, pp. 69, 83−4; Palsokar, *The Grenadiers*, pp. 212−13.

89. Jagota, p. 88.

90. Hill, p. 36.

91. NAM 625.7 (591), 'The Design and Construction of the Tamu−Kalewa road, Burma' by R. S. Colquhoun; J. H. Williams, p. 130.

92. Lord Birdwood, *The Worcestershire Regiment 1922−1950*, p. 119.

93. Jervois, pp. 285; NRHC, Denis A. Short, 'To Burma: "I Was Not To Reason Why"', pp. 184−5.

94. Slim, *Defeat into Victory*, p. 379.

95. Lewin, *Slim*, p. 212.

96. Henslow, p. 165; Roberts, p. 182.

97. 'Report on Chindwin River Gunboats' by Lt.-Cdr. G. S. Penman BRNVR, in AWM 940.5450941 G786 no. 42, 'Burma 1941−1945 Naval operations, Admiralty Battle Summary no. 42, Tactical and Staff Duties Division, 1948, pp. 143−8'; Forty, *XIV Army at War*, p. 100.

98. In June 1944, with SEAC planning various amphibious operations, a small-operations group was formed to control the beach reconnaissance and other advance operations. The Special Boat Section and SRU were both active on the Irrawaddy. See G. B. Courtney, *SBS in World War II: The Story of the Original Special Boat Section of the Army Commandos*, and B. S. Wright, *The*

*Frogmen of Burma: The Story of the Sea Reconnaissance Unit.* See also IWM 93/1/1, Lieutenant Commander A. I. Hughes.

99. It was named 'Grub' bridge after the small son of Colonel F. Seymour-Williams. Pakenham-Walsh, pp. 243–7.

100. Slim was gazetted KCB and the others KBE on 28 September 1944 for their service in the battles of Ngakyedauk Pass, Imphal and Kohima. Kirby, vol. 4, p. 161.

101. Slim, *Defeat into Victory*, p. 369.


## 22 ARAKAN

1. Martin Page (ed.), *'Kiss Me Goodnight, Sergeant Major'*, p. 123

2. 'Burma Operations Record: 28th Army Operations in Akyab Area (November 1943–September 1945), Japanese Monograph no. 132', in Detwiler and Burdick (eds.), vol. 7/1, pp. 47–8.

3. Prasad (ed.), *The Arakan Operations 1942–45*, pp. 169–73; IWM 14148/10, Captain D. F. Neill.

4. GM Maj.-Gen. F. J. Loftus Tottenham CBE DSO, 'Walkabouts and Laughabouts in the Raj'. For Loftus Tottenham, see Twiston Davies (ed.), pp. 22–4.

5. SOAS E Coll 3 D/9, P. J. Jeffreys, 'Burma 1944–1945: Memories of the 2nd Kaladan Campaign 5th (West African) Brigade & 81st (West African) Div.'.

6. See M. S. Clarke, *Kaladan Mortars*. (See also IWM 94/41/1, Major M. S. Clarke.)

7. SOAS E Coll 3 D/9, P. J. Jeffreys.

8. Hamilton, pp. 201–21.

9. C. R. A. Swynnerton, *A Short History of The 1st (West African) Infantry Brigade in the Arakan 1944–45*, p. 86; Haywood and Clarke, pp. 470–1.

10. P. van Straubanzee, *Desert, Jungle and Dale*, pp. 71, 80; Hamilton, p. 224.

11. Havildar Singh was an Ahir, a 'non-martial' class not previously enlisted in the Indian Army. Equally, the VC is rarely awarded to gunners. Palit, pp. 306–7; Farndale, p. 240.

12. Thatcher, p. 500.

13. Prasad (ed.), *The Arakan Operations 1942–45*, pp. 196–202.

14. This was a Madrassi unit whose members spoke several languages, mostly Tamil and Telegu. Few, if any, knew Urdu, which had caused complications when it was first raised. SOAS E Coll 3 D/7, '7th Indian Field Regiment Royal Indian Artillery: A Narrative 1943–1947'; R. J. Lewendon, 'Personal Reminiscences of the Arakan', *The Journal of The Royal Artillery*, CXVI/1 March 1989, pp. 40–4.

15. Perrett, *Tank Tracks to Rangoon*, p. 80.

16. McCrae et al., *Tales of Burma*, pp. 161–2.

17. AWM 940.5450941 G786 no. 42, 'Burma 1941–1945 Naval Operations, Admiralty Battle Summary no. 42, Tactical and Staff Duties Division, 1948';

Goulden, *From Trombay to Changi's a Helluva Way: The Story of Arakan Coastal Forces*, pp. 116–8.

18. McCrae et al., *Tales of Burma*, pp. 164–7.

19. D. J. E. Collins, *Official History of the Indian Armed Forces in the Second World War 1939–45: The Royal Indian Navy*, p. 295.

20. SOAS E Coll 3 D/4, 'Arakan Assignment. The Story of 82nd West African Division'.

21. Becka, pp. 190–1, 193, 207–8.

22. Prasad (ed.), *The Arakan Operations 1942–45*, p. 214; E. R. Evans, pp. 133–4.

23. IWM 82/15/1, General Sir Philip Christison Bt.

24. Parham and Bellfield, pp. 132–3; Duncan, Ellis, Banks and Scarfe (eds.), p. 93.

25. T. Mackenzie, *44 (R.M.) Commando, Achnacarry to the Arakan*, pp. 91–2.

26. G. H. Gill, *Royal Australian Navy*, p. 564.

27. R. McKie, *Echoes from Forgotten Wars*, p. 163; Mankekar, pp. 107–10.

28. O. F. Sheffield, pp. 236–8.

29. Deedes, p. 153.

30. Lawford and Catto, p. 262.

31. SOAS E Coll 3 D/4.

32. IWM 4383/4, Major-General H. C. Stockwell.

33. Gill, pp. 567–70. The story of the COPPs, which made surveys on beaches for subsequent landings, is told by B. Strutton and M. Pearson in *The Secret Invaders*. For details of SRU operations see A. C. Hampshire, *Undercover Sailors*, pp. 113–8.

34. The guns were manned by 37/47 Battery of 27th Field Regiment and became known as HMS *Enterprise* and HMS *Fighter* (after E and F Troops), and the craft were crewed by IWT personnel. They supported the landings at Kangaw and Ruywa as part of the deception plan. (Duncan, Ellis, Banks and Scarfe (eds.), pp. 112–3.)

35. Prasad (ed.), *The Arakan Operations 1942–45*, pp. 236–42; J. G. Pocock, *The Spirit of a Regiment*, pp. 76–9; Thatcher, pp. 478–9; O. F. Sheffield, pp. 238–40; Deedes, p. 156; Mankekar, pp. 112–7; IWM 14148/10, Captain D. F. Neill.

36. H. Evans, pp. 205–6.

37. Prasad (ed.). *The Arakan Operations 1942–45*, pp. 248–52; K. C. Praval, *Valour Triumphs*, pp. 130–3; Betham and Geary, pp. 179–83; Thatcher, pp. 510–14; Mankekar, pp. 121–5.

38. Prasad (ed.), *The Arakan Operations 1942–45*, p. 253; Spurr, pp. 116–20.

39. PRO WO 203/360, '25 Indian Division, 2 Punjab Regiment: Account of Operations for Period 1945 Jan.–Feb.'.

40. H. Evans, p. 223; Praval, *Valour Triumphs*, pp. 134–5.

41. C. Peterson, *Unparalleled Danger Unsurpassed Courage*, pp. 119, 121; Praval, *Valour Triumphs*, pp. 134–5. On 27 October 1945 19th Hyderabad Regiment was renamed 19th Kumaon Regiment, and shortly afterwards regimental numbers (apart from the Punjab regiments) were dropped. The battalion's successor, 8th Bn The Kumaon Regiment, still celebrates 7 February as 'Kangaw Day'.

42. SOAS E Coll 3 D/4; Swynnerton, pp. 28–9.

43. Knowland was formerly of The Royal Norfolk Regiment and had only just joined 1st Commando. IWM 20614/3, Private V. G. H. Ralph; T. Mackenzie, pp. 106–7; Lockhart, pp. 192–4.

44. Nunneley, *Tales from the Burma Campaign*, p. 114.

45. Lawford and Catto, pp. 265–6; Prasad (ed.), *The Arakan Operations 1942–45*, pp. 255–7.

46. Prasad (ed.), *The Arakan Operations 1942–45*, p. 261.

47. Franks, *First in the Indian Skies*, pp. 131–3.

48. IWM 82/15/1, General Sir Philip Christison Bt.

49. T. Blore, *Commissioned Barges*, pp. 208–9; Deedes, p. 142.

50. Sinker and Rossier, p. 51.

51. Lockhart, p. 191.

52. Prasad (ed.), *The Arakan Operations 1942–45*, pp. 268–73.

53. *RAC Journal*, 1, 1946–7, p. 390; R. D. Palsokar, *The Grenadiers*, pp. 204–5.

54. Deedes, p. 143.

55. Sinker and Rossier, pp. 53–5.

56. Prasad (ed.), *The Arakan Operations 1942–45*, pp. 274–81; Farndale, p. 256.

57. N. McWhirter and R. McWhirter (eds.), *The Guinness Book of Records*, p. 222; Swynnerton, pp. 37–8; Duncan, Ellis, Banks and Scarfe (eds.), pp. 110–12.

58. The Commandos had suffered an unusually high proportion of casualties with head injuries, a fact pointed out to Christison on a visit by Edwina, Lady Mountbatten. This he ascribed to their insistence on wearing their green berets rather than helmets and was only overcome by a direct order from Mountbatten. IWM 82/15/1, General Sir Philip Christison Bt.

59. Prasad (ed.), *The Arakan Operations 1942–45*, pp. 282–5.

60. Duncan, Ellis, Banks and Scarfe (eds.), p. 114.

61. Prasad (ed.), *The Arakan Operations 1942–45*, pp. 294–5.

62. J. G. Pocock, pp. 82–5; Abhankyar, pp. 477–8; Thatcher, pp. 481–3; Deedes, p. 157.

63. G. R. Stevens, *History of the 2nd King Edward's Own Goorkhas*, p. 256.

64. Lawford and Catto, pp. 267–73; Prasad (ed.), *The Arakan Operations 1942–45*, pp. 298–300.

65. On their way back from the battle for Hill 170 and Tamandu 7th/16th Punjab Regiment found a small abandoned boy, about five years old, whom Subedar Ghazan Khan took care of, and in due course took him to his village after the war. In 1983 the boy finally met his brother for the first time after thirty-eight years separation. Rizvi, p. 89.

66. Ahmad, p. 386; Marston, pp. 179–81.

67. G. Powell and J. Powell, *The History of the Green Howards*, p. 200.

68. J. Allan, *In the Trade of War*, pp 123–4.

69. Allan, pp. 131–2. For a description of battle exhaustion, see: D. Sheil-Small, *Green Shadows*, pp. 175–6; R. A. Cooper, p. 141.

70. Prasad (ed.), *The Arakan Operations 1942–45*, pp. 304–7.

71. L. Allen, *Sittang*, pp. 63–5.

## 23 ACROSS THE IRRAWADDY

1. Morrison, pp. 133–9.
2. For other accounts of life in Rangoon gaol see: C. R. L. Coubrough, *Memories of a Perpetual Second Lieutenant*, pp. 93–4; Besley, pp. 75–88; IWM 97/6/1, Flight Lieutenant C. A. Kidd.
3. L. Hudson, *The Rats of Rangoon*, pp. 58–61.
4. Morrison, pp. 154–5.
5. Lamont-Brown, *Kempeitai*, p. 101.
6. Cady, pp. 465, 473–4, 478–82.
7. PRO WO 203/58, 'Arming of Anti-Fascist Organisation: Operational Reports 1945 Jan.–Apr.'; WO 203/4332, 'Force 136: Operational Reports 1944 Nov.–1945 Nov.'; Aldrich, pp. 334–6.
8. F. C. Jones, *Japan's New Order in East Asia*, pp. 356–7.
9. Elsbree, pp. 72–5; U Nu, pp. 93–7, 107–8.
10. CAC Slim Papers, File 3/2.
11. When one of the official historians, Brigadier M. R. Roberts, asked him how he gained this notion, Slim said it arose naturally out of staff discussions at Fourteenth Army. (G. Evans, *Slim as Military Commander*, p. 187.) He did not know who first mentioned Meiktila, but this characteristically modest assessment possibly hides its origin. Wingate had suggested to Mountbatten and Slim in March 1944 that one possible use of the reserve Chindit brigades would be Meiktila via Pakkoku. PRO WO 203/187, 'LRP Correspondence'; 'Forecast of Possible Developments of Thursday by Commander Special Force', 13 March 1944.
12. Bithess was hessian rolls 50 yards long and a yard wide, treated with bitumen and laid to overlap by 8 inches, then packed tight and cambered by laying the two outsized trips first and then building up from the edge to the centre. It was very expensive since each yard of road required a gallon of petrol and a gallon of diesel but it worked. By December four roads were available to the Chindwin and 'Bill' Williams's elephants had helped build them all. J. H. Williams, pp. 236–7, 279; Pakenham-Walsh, pp, 243–5. For an overview of administrative developments in India and Assam, and in preparation for Capital, see Kirby, vol. 4, chaps. 2, 9.
13. G. Evans, *Slim as Military Commander*, p. 190.
14. He sent Leese an appreciation on 17 December and gave verbal orders to his Corps Commanders on the 18th, confirmed in writing the following day, two days before sending Leese the detailed appreciation and plan. Lewin, *Slim*, pp. 209–13; Kirby, vol. 4, p. 168; Callahan, pp. 156–8. Richard Ryder in his biography of Leese tries to give him the credit but is unconvincing (*Oliver Leese*, pp. 217–34).
15. PRO WO 203/298, 'Fourteenth Army Operation Capital Planning Papers'.
16. McGeoch, pp. 131–3; Romanus and Sunderland, *Stilwell's Command Problems*, p. 99.
17. Kirby, vol. 4, appx 20, pp. 501–5.

18. D. Hart-Davis, *Peter Fleming*, p. 285.
19. In five months' fighting 11th (East African) Division had lost 26 British all ranks and 233 Africans dead, 95 and 976 wounded, and 7 and 35 missing. Malcolm Page, p. 158; Farndale, pp. 226–7.
20. This scheme was almost certainly conceived and planned by Slim and Fourteenth Army staff rather than by Fleming. RCSM 916.6, 'Military Histories Far East, Signals Effort 14th Army WW2, Folio 1 of 4, Report on Signal Deception Measures Adopted during Operations of the Fourteenth Army Dec 44–Mar 45'; Subramanyam, pp. 5–7; PRO AIR 41/64, 'Air Historical Branch Narrative, The Campaign in the Far East', pp. 366–7; O'Brien, *The Moonlight War*, pp. 169–73.
21. G. Hartcup, *Camouflage*, pp. 115–6.
22. Jervois, pp. 290–305; NRHC, Denis A. Short, 'To Burma: "I Was Not To Reason Why"', pp. 198–218.
23. L. Allen, *Burma*, pp. 409–11.
24. IWM 20520/4, Captain Frederick Rowley; Pakenham-Walsh, pp. 262–3; Kirby, vol. 4, pp. 178, 184–6.
25. D. S. Chand, *The Rajputana Rifles*, p. 26; C. E. N. Lomax, *The History of The Welch Regiment 1919–1951*, pp. 150–2.
26. Mountbatten of Burma, *Report to the Combined Chiefs of Staff*, para. 423; L. Allen, *Burma*, pp. 403–4.
27. Each division included a battalion of Vickers medium machine-guns but although very powerful weapons they were vulnerable at close quarters. In all 2nd Royal Berkshire lost 9 officers and 90 men killed and wounded at Kabwet but at least 250 Japanese were killed. Hill, pp. 74–92 (also IWM 91/13/1, Major L. J. L. Hill); G. Blight and M. Dempsey, *The Royal Berkshire Regiment (Princess Charlotte of Wales's) 1920–1947*, pp. 361–70 (much of the detail here is provided by John Hill); F. T. Birdwood, *The Sikh Regiment in the Second World War*, pp. 393–5; L. Allen, *Burma*, pp. 404–5.
28. Feis, p. 275.
29. The first convoy of 113 vehicles along the road included fifty-five war correspondents in thirty-three jeeps. It was an eventful journey as there were still plenty of Japanese around. Fischer, *The Chancy War*, pp. 49–60.
30. Spencer, p. 174. It had officially been operational for 1,074 days and had lost an aircraft and its crew for each of them. *China Airlift – The Hump*, vol. 4, pp. 354–5.
31. U. Lee, p. 617.
32. Mary Penick Motley (ed.), *The Invisible Soldier*, p. 133.
33. J. Randolph, *Marsmen in Burma*, p. 136.
34. Prefer, pp. 223–39.
35. P. J. Faggion, letter, *Burman News*, November 1994.
36. Randolph, p. 197.
37. Prefer, p. 252. The 475th were deactivated in China on 1 July 1945. They were reactivated and deactivated during the 1950s, and in 1969 Galahad's

colours were presented to 75th Ranger Regiment, which traced its origins to 5307th Composite Unit (Provisional) and continues the unit's traditions (Hopkins with Jones, pp. 733–4).

38. C. R. B. Knight, *Historical Records of The Buffs*, pp. 338–40.

39. Chevenix Trench, p. 279.

40. Armstrong, p. 215.

41. Brett, p. 60.

42. Chevenix Trench p. 279; P. Narain, p. 174.

43. The British official history puts the entry as 8 January, while the Indian history gives the 7th as when the lead patrol of 5th/10th Baluch arrived. Either way, there was some confusion as to which formation was responsible for the task. Kirby, vol. 4, p. 177; Prasad (ed.), *The Reconquest of Burma*, vol. 2, p. 490; L. Allen, *Burma*, pp. 401–3; O. G. W. White, p. 201; Rissik, p. 204; Oatts, *I Serve*, pp. 272–6.

44. Kirby, vol. 4, pp. 174–5.

45. G. D. Sheffield, pp. 140–1.

46. Armstrong, p. 191.

47. G. W. Robertson, pp. 249–51.

48. *4/8th Gurkha Rifles News Chronicle*, no. 2, 1945, local distribution, p. 3, quoted in Gilmore and Davis, *A Connecticut Yankee in the 4/8th Gurkha Rifles*, p. 182.

49. N. G. Hiscox, *Under Two Flags*, p. 90.

50. Hanley, p. 132.

51. J. Dewar McLintock, *The Manipur Road*, p. 93.

52. Gilmore and Davis, pp. 182–4; Probert, pp. 245–51. See also: Patrick Davis, pp. 118–22; Sheil-Small, pp. 57–60.

53. Shipster, p. 63. The exchange rate was fixed at 16 rupees to the pound.

54. Kirby, vol. 4, pp. 180–2.

55. IWM AL 827/13, 'History of Japanese 15 Army'.

56. G. J. Thomas, p. 130.

57. 'Burma Operations Record: 28th Army Operations in Akyab Area (November 1943–September 1945), Japanese Monograph no. 132', in Detwiler and Burdick (eds.), vol. 7/1, p. 95.

58. Maule, pp. 340–1.

59. Wright, pp. 179–86; Hampshire, *Undercover Sailors*, pp. 97–111; R. MacLaren, *Canadians behind Enemy Lines, 1939–1945*, pp. 302–7.

60. They accounted for an estimated 1,200 Japanese, while their own casualties amounted to 18 British officers and soldiers and 151 Africans killed, with 23 British and 420 Africans wounded – the heaviest of any East African brigade. Malcolm Page, pp. 160–3.

61. Proudfoot, *We Lead*, pp. 85–6.

62. Jervois, pp. 309–15; NRHC, Denis A. Short, pp. 219–31; IWM 20474/5, Lieutenant Peter Noakes; 84/18/1, R. R. Haslam; P474, E. Williams.

63. They were 4 VCOs and 42 IORs killed, 1 BO, 3 VCOs and 115 IORs wounded, 1 non-combatant and 3 IORs missing. Conden, *The Frontier Force*

*Rifles*, pp. 412–16; Marston, pp. 186–9.

64. Conden, *The Frontier Force Rifles*, pp. 408–11; NAM 8102–63, 'Documents Relating to 14/13 FFR and their Unique Headdress'. Proudfoot, *We Lead*, pp. 86–8.

65. K. W. Cooper, p. 48.

66. 'Gathering our last reserves of strength, we stumbled across the corpse-strewn fields and through the Burmese graveyard into Satpangon. Among the rubble, beneath the ruined pagodas and burnt-out bashas the dead of the Battalion lay sprawled around the bunkers they had silenced; the living lay among them speechless, worn out, beyond anything, and watched with sunken eyes as we joined them.' K. W. Cooper, pp. 71–9: In this action 2nd Border lost 1 officer and 21 dead, 39 wounded. Shears, p. 49; Sutherland, pp. 198–200.

67. Nunneley (ed.), *Tales from the Burma Campaign*, pp. 87–8. See also A. Murray, 'The Crossing of the Irrawaddy by 4 Corps February 1945', *The Royal Engineers Journal*, LXI, 1947.

68. G. Evans, *The Desert and the Jungle*, p. 146; Maule, p. 342.

69. Mullaly, *The South Lancashire Regiment The Prince of Wales's Volunteers*, p. 453.

70. Henslow, p. 147.

71. Mullaly, *The South Lancashire Regiment The Prince of Wales's Volunteers*, p. 457.

72. Sheil-Small, p. 69.

73. It seems the latter had mistaken an assault river crossing in small 12-man boats for an amphibious landing in large craft, and their commanding officer had only been concerned with what would happen when they disembarked. According to the official history 2nd South Lancs were selected because of their experience in amphibious operations gained in Madagascar in 1942. Henslow, pp. 148–57; Kirby, vol. 4, p. 257n.; W. Miles, p. 387.

74. Bamford, pp. 129–35; Marston, pp. 189–91; G. W. Robertson, pp. 257–8, 266; J. Thompson, *The Imperial War Museum Book of the War in Burma 1942–1945*, pp. 298–303.

75. Armstrong, p. 225. Sir James Scott wrote, 'Pagan is in many respects the most remarkable religious city in the world. Jerusalem, Rome, Kiev and Benares cannot boast the multitude of temples and the lavishness of design and ornament that makes marvellous the deserted capital on the Irrawaddy, the whole place is thickly studded with pagodas of all sizes and shapes, and the very ground is so heavily covered with crumbling remnants and vanished shrines, that according to the popular saying, you cannot move foot or hand without touching a sacred thing' (*Burma from the Earliest Times to the Present Day*). Alas, the city was virtually obliterated in an earthquake in 1975.

76. Prasad (ed.), *The Reconquest of Burma*, vol. 2, pp. 286–8.

77. Verma and Anand, pp. 190–1.

78. Lord Birdwood, p. 185.

79. 'Why Our Soldiers Faced Bullets in Vain: Dunkirk Boats Too Rotten to Cross Irrawaddy', *Daily Herald*, 5 March 1945; Pakenham-Walsh, pp. 262–3.

80. D. Murray, interview with the author 26 March 2003. Glover, pp. 244–5; Pennington, pp. 304–9.
81. O. G. W. White, p. 236; Saunders, p. 354.
82. Ronald Lewin contrasts it with Montgomery's crossing of the Rhine. *Slim*, p. 221.

## 24 MANDALAY AND MEIKTILA

1. Martin Page (ed.), *'Kiss Me Goodnight, Sergeant Major'*, p. 168.
2. O. F. Sheffield, p. 264; J. G. Pocock, p. 70n.
3. Masters, *The Road past Mandalay*, pp. 297–301.
4. C. E. N. Lomax, p. 155.
5. Painter, p. 144.
6. Masters, *The Road past Mandalay*, p. 308.
7. IWM AL 827/20, 'Interrogation of General Kimura Hyotaro in Changi Jail, 1st April 1946. Reference Operations in Burma'.
8. Blight and Dempsey, pp. 381–92; O. F. Sheffield, pp. 260–2; L. Allen, *Burma*, pp. 406–7.
9. Hill, pp. 115, 120.
10. It would have been sooner, but Rees refused to bomb the sacred places having served there before the war and knowing their importance, although the Indian official history notes a 'lot of machine-gun fire was poured from the air'. Prasad (ed.), *Reconquest of Burma*, vol. 2 p. 354.
11. Sutherland Brown, pp. 185–6.
12. 'Morale in the battalion was supposed not to be good and the sick rate was high. I had been told that I was not only to look after the wounded but to cut down on the numbers sent back each day because of complaints due mainly to fear and strain.' The battalion had seen long service in India before the war and although many of its number had been lost in action or to sickness or had otherwise left, many more remained who had seen action during the previous year's battles while many others were completely new to the weariness and ferocity of close quarter battle. C. Evans, pp. 122, 130.
13. Kirby, vol. 4, pp. 292–4.
14. 'There has been a tendency to rush operations; natural among troops who had been fighting the Japanese for two years with inadequate support weapons and whose experience taught them that if once allowed to consolidate, the Japanese were extremely difficult to dislodge. Considerably more thought should be devoted to DECEPTION on all levels, and every available method, both natural and artificial, should be utilized.' RSDGM CB 04 C34, Lt.-Col. John Ashton, 'Account of 3 DG Advance from Imphal to Rangoon 1944–45. Summary of the Main Lessons from the Operation of Tanks during the Present Campaign'.
15. B. A. T. Hammond, 'The Train', *The Gunner*, 292, March 1995, pp. 34–6.
16. G. W. Robertson, p. 290; Prather, pp. 89–90.

17. J. S. G. Blair, pp. 335-6.

18. Fort Dufferin, the former palace of the kings of Ava, was named after the Viceroy of India, the Marquess of Dufferin, who had added 'and Ava' to his title when Burma was conquered in the Pagoda War 1885-6. Captain Basil Hamilton-Temple-Blackwood, the 4th marquess, was working with an IFBU when he was killed in March 1945 by a mortar bomb between Mandalay and Ava, in an incident recorded by the SEAC Film Unit. Rankin, p. 239; Lunt, *Jai Sixth!*, p. 52n.

19. A full description of Fort Dufferin and the building of Mandalay can be found in F. Tennyson Jesse's novel *The Lacquer Lady* and E. C. V. Foucar's *They Reigned in Mandalay*.

20. 'The operation I intend is one of surprise', declared Rees, 'a silent start and rapid seizing of the bridgehead, NOT the forcing of an entry at all costs by bludgeon methods. If the surprise operation at reasonably light cost is not possible owing to enemy vigilance and preparations, then it will not be pressed home at all costs.' Prasad (ed.), *The Reconquest of Burma*, vol. 2, p. 359.

21. IWM 20520/4, Captain Frederick Rowley.

22. G. D. Sheffield, p. 142.

23. RAFM AC/76/32. This is the draft of Vincent's memoirs and the line was excised from the published version. S. F. Vincent, *Flying Fever*, p. 174.

24. He was accompanied by Lieutenant-Colonel O. G. W. White of 2nd Dorsets, who noted his regiment already held the honour 'Ava' from the First Burma War. O. G. W. White, pp. 266-7.

25. Maybury, vol. 3, p. 43.

26. C. Evans, p. 142; Jeremy Taylor, *The Devons*, pp. 273-4.

27. Masters, *The Road past Mandalay*, p. 310.

28. J. Dewar McLintock, *The Manipur Road*, p. 101.

29. This is one of the twelve 'phoenix' units in Daniel P. Marston's, *Phoenix from the Ashes*.

30. Long before the Meiktila plan came to maturity Alasdair Tuck, the Brigade Major, was showing Slim around the brigade when Slim asked him what was the most important thing about the use of armour. Tuck gave the standard training pamphlet reply about mobility, firepower and saving of infantry lives when Slim stopped him and said: 'Those are expected of it, but the *most* important thing is *reliability*.' L. Allen, *Burma*, p. 426.

31. Palsokar, *The Grenadiers*, pp. 225-7.

32. Ahmad, pp. 358-62.

33. M. Smeeton, *A Change of Jungles*, pp. 89-91.

34. Maule, pp. 351-2.

35. Masters, *The Road past Mandalay*, p. 303.

36. Barclay, *The Regimental History of The 3rd Queen Alexandra's Own Gurkha Rifles*, pp. 80-4.

37. SOAS E Coll 3 B/37, Captain J. C. Smyth, 'Notes on the Burmese Campaign Compiled from Japanese sources. Unpublished 1946'.

38. IWM 5009/1, Gen. Kimura Hyotaro Cmdr Burma Area Army; 5009/2

Lt.-Gen. Tanaka Shinichi, C. of S. Burma Area Army; L. Allen, *Burma*, pp. 429–35; H. Mitchell, *Against the Odds*, pp. 51–6; IWM AL 457 SEATIC Bulletin no. 244, 'History of Japanese 28th Army' 1946 Oct. 1.

39. Romanus and Sunderland, *Time Runs Out in CBI*, pp. 225–6.

40. Ziegler, *Mountbatten*, pp. 289–90; Mountbatten of Burma, *Report to the Combined Chiefs of Staff*, pp. 134–5; Lewin, *Slim: The Standardbearer*, p. 224.

41. He flew in a USAAF B-25 when the RAF refused, saying it was too risky; they would fly anyone but him. On 1 May a Dakota taking him to look at Rangoon was hit by light anti-aircraft fire and forced to turn back. Slim, *Defeat into Victory*, pp. 442–3, 446, 493.

42. Slim, *Defeat into Victory*, pp. 449–50.

43. Cross and Gurung, p. 99.

44. NAM Ind. Cav. 9H Acc. no. 28070, 'Royal Deccan Horse, Account of Operations in Burma January to May 1945'.

45. Thatcher, pp. 349–50.

46. He was on attachment from 2nd Green Howards. Sandes, pp. 77–9; W. A. T. Synge, *The Story of the Green Howards*, p. 374.

47. L. Allen, *Burma*, p. 442.

48. GM G46 Payagi Interrogation Report no. 7, 'A Japanese Account of Battle of Meiktila – March 1945'.

49. MacDonald Fraser, pp. 88–9.

50. Chand was awarded an immediate MC during this battle. Chevenix Trench, pp. 283–4; Palsokar, *The Grenadiers*, pp. 223–5.

51. GM G46 Payagi Interrogation Report no. 7; Palsokar, pp. 86–92; J. D. Hookway (ed.), *M & R*, pp. 47–50.

52. Franks, *First in Indian Skies*, p. 134.

53. Brett-James, *Ball of Fire*, p. 402.

54. IWM 80/38/1, Captain Jack Scollen; Parham and Bellfield, *Unarmed into Battle*, pp. 137–8; Farndale, pp. 279–81.

55. Alasdair Tuck said: 'Punch Cowan was a splendid Infantry General but he did not really understand the tanks problems and he or his staff kept on asking for *one* tank to accompany an infantry patrol. It took some time for it to sink in that a troop of three was the minimum tank team, if we were not to get too many knocked out.' L. Allen, *Burma*, p. 449.

56. 'The flags were prized trophies. They were of white silk, with a large red sun centred, and beautiful red characters around. We asked for their return once the characters on them had been interpreted.' Patrick Davis, pp. 154–5.

57. Prasad (ed.), *The Reconquest of Burma*, p. 329.

58. GM G46 Payagi Interrogation Report no. 7.

59. M. Baird-Murray, *A World Overturned*, p. 113.

60. Becka, pp. 139, 211–23.

61. Dr Maung Maung, *To a Soldier Son*, p. 57.

62. PRO WO 203/513, '1945 Mar.–Apr. Burma Rising'.

63. L. Allen, *Sittang*, p. 24.

64. Mountbatten of Burma, *Report to the Combined Chiefs of Staff*, pp. 139–45.

65. Pennington, p. 317.
66. Hill, pp. 109–10.
67. Mountbatten of Burma, *Report to the Combined Chiefs of Staff*, p. 140; Proudfoot, p. 90; Mullaly, *Bugle and Kurki*, pp. 375–7.
68. Nunneley (ed.), *Tales from the Burma Campaign*, p. 136.
69. Rizvi, p. 67; Roberts, p. 199; Mullaly, *The South Lancashire Regiment The Prince of Wales's Volunteers*, pp. 466–70; Bellers, *The History of The 1st King George V's Own Gurkha Rifles (The Malaun Regiment)*, pp. 263–5.
70. Kirby, vol. 4, pp. 363–6.
71. O. G. W. White, pp. 275–6.
72. Palsokar, *The Grenadiers*, p. 223; W. Miles, p. 391.
73. Ahmad, pp. 364–5.
74. L. Allen, *Burma*, pp. 462–3.
75. Smeeton, pp. 108–9.
76. IWM 20457/34, Brigadier John Randle.
77. Barclay, *The Regimental History of The 3rd Queen Alexandra's Own Gurkha Rifles*, pp. 86–7; Peterson, p. 139.
78. L. Allen, *Burma*, pp. 464–7.
79. Slim, *Defeat into Victory*, p. 496.

## 25 RANGOON

1. Y. Aida, *Prisoner of the British*, p. 7.
2. Mountbatten of Burma, *Report to the Combined Chiefs of Staff*, p. 145; Slim, *Defeat into Victory*, p. 481.
3. Prasad (ed.), *The Reconquest of Burma*, vol. 2, p. 417.
4. Lewin, *Slim*, p. 231.
5. PRO AIR 41/64, 'Air Historical Branch Narrative, The Campaign in the Far East', appx 36; WO 203/866, '1944 Mar. Air Supply for maintenance of 14 Army'.
6. Lyman, *Slim, Master of War*, p. 245.
7. L. Allen, *Burma*, pp. 459–61.
8. Mountbatten of Burma, *Report to the Combined Chiefs of Staff*, p. 153.
9. Brett-James, *Ball of Fire*, pp. 414–6; L. Allen, *Burma*, pp. 468–72; W. Miles, pp. 400–1; Hailes and Ross, pp. 318–9; C. T. Atkinson, pp. 181–2; O. F. Sheffield, pp. 215–7; Perrett, *Tank Tracks to Rangoon*, p. 226.
10. Oatts, *I Serve*, p. 283.
11. 16th Light Cavalry made a 3,500 mile dash from Quetta to reach Dimapur by 15 February 1945, going on to operate its armoured cars with 255th Indian Tank Brigade. Proudfoot, *History of the 16th Light Cavalry [Armoured Corps]*, p. 160.
12. PRO WO 203/1815, 'Armoured Corps: Report on Operations by 8 Cavalry Regiment'; H. G. Rawlinson, *History of 8th King George V's Own Light Cavalry*, pp. 129–30.

13. Chandra, p. 217.

14. Masters, *The Road past Mandalay*, p. 313; see Chapter 7, 'Campaign's End: A Transformed Army', in D. P. Marston, *Phoenix from the Ashes*.

15. S. C. Gupta, *History of the Indian Air Force 1933–1945*, p. 177.

16. PRO WO 203/53, 'Clandestine Organizations: Administration, Control, and Co-ordination 1945 Jan.–Mar.'.

17. Mountbatten of Burma, *Report to the Combined Chiefs of Staff*, p. 173.

18. Morrison, pp. 158–65.

19. Cross and Gurung, pp. 124–5.

20. IWM 11037/4, Maj. R. A. Rubinstein. See also 82/52/1, Lt.-Col. J. E. S. Smallwood; P463, Maj. J. P. Lucas.

21. L. Allen, *Burma*, p. 473.

22. Cruickshank. pp. 189–90; IWM 86/29/1, D. Gibbs.

23. SOAS E Coll 3 M/87, Capt. L. S. Beswick, 'Two Roads in Burma'.

24. Conditions in the internment camps were terrible, with many women subjected to brutal beatings, or made to 'entertain' Japanese officers. Celia was a girl of three when interned by the Japanese. Her little brother died of dysentery while her mother was made to work washing uniforms and bandages for the Japanese with other women in the camp. 'My mother and the other women were marched several miles every day, with an escort, to a river (these memories still haunt my mother and reduce her to tears at the age of 85), where they stood waist-deep in the rushing water to wash filthy bandages, medical dressings and Japanese uniforms caked in blood. She remembers women being washed away during the monsoon floods, and the Japanese guards doing nothing to help them. She remembers bored guards watching the women, then selecting one and shouting, "You!", and raping her. She remembers once passing a group of men p[risoners], my father among them, mending the road, and the screaming guards flailing around with their bayonets to prevent them speaking to each other.' But when her father joined them, covered in bayonet wounds, they were befriended by a guard who smuggled food to them and shortly before leaving for the front at Maymyo gave Celia a scarf that had been sent to him, covered in red stitches. He said each was a blessing and it would protect her: www.war-experience.org/collections/civilians/alliedbrit/celia/index.html.

25. Corpe, pp. 152–3.

26. O. F. Sheffield, pp. 262–3; Bellers, pp. 267–8.

27. Praval, *Valour Triumphs*, pp. 137–8; Farndale, pp. 226–7, 232–4; Knight, pp. 342–9; Bellers, pp. 243–4; Gillings, pp. 105–9.

28. SOAS E Coll 3 M/75, H. C. Smith, '"Hostilities Only": Tales of an Amateur Soldier in World War II'.

29. Prasad (ed.), *The Reconquest of Burma*, vol. 2, p. 402; Slim, *Defeat into Victory*, p. 501.

30. NAM Ind. Cav. 9H Acc. no. 28070, 'Royal Deccan Horse, Account of Operations in Burma January to May 1945'.

31. TM – RH.(54).5255 ITB; MH.5(591), 'Operational Research Group

Report on Crew Casualties and Tank Battle Damage Sustained by 255 Indian Tank Brigade (Feb–May) 1945'; Proudfoot, *History of the 16th Light Cavalry [Armoured Corps]*, pp. 169–70.

32. PRO WO 203/1795, '254 and 255 Indian Tank Brigades: Report on Operations from 1945 Jan.–Mar.'.

33. Jagota, pp. 109–19; PRO WO 203/354, 'The Fighting RIEME: Operation Reports by Various Officers – Series of Short Reports of Minor Contacts with Jitter Parties and Stragglers'.

34. Sansome, p. 8.

35. Gilmore and Davis, p. 202.

36. C. Evans, p. 149.

37. Conden, *The Frontier Force Regiment*, p. 425.

38. Since crossing the Irrawaddy 17th Indian Division had suffered 719 killed, 2,767 wounded and 71 missing. It had killed over 10,000 of the enemy and captured 211 guns, but taken only 167 prisoners. J. Thompson, *The Imperial War Museum Book of the War in Burma 1942–1945*, p. 383.

39. L. Allen, *Sittang*, pp. 30–4.

40. K. P. Mackenzie p. 182; C. R. L. Coubrough, *Memories of a Perpetual Second Lieutenant*, pp. 122–36; Besley, pp. 89–103.

41. GM, 2nd King Edward VII's Own Goorkhas, 3rd Battalion Records, 1940–43, 'From Tonmakeng to Tenko', by D. F. G. Gudgeon, quoted in H. James, *Across the Threshold of Battle*, p. 198; Stibbé, pp. 203–22.

42. L. Hudson, p. 186; L. Allen, *Burma*, pp. 481–7.

43. T. B. H. Otway, *The Second World War 1939–1945*, pp. 381–3.

44. Kirby, vol. 4, pp. 395–6.

45. The anonymous divisional historian, aware of the feelings roused by the snatching of laurels at the moment of triumph from Fourteenth Army, felt it was a fitting reward 'for the two years of gruelling obscurity in the Arakan' an obscurity perpetuated by Louis Allen, who completely ignores XV Corps after the Admin Box battle and in 1945. It had been 'doing an indispensable job in disrupting the Japanese supply lines and building up the air and sea communications necessary to nourish the main body of South-East Asia forces fighting their way down the interior of Burma'. *Tiger Head*, p. 36; IWM 97/7/1, Captain W. S. Knight.

46. Goulden, *The 13th and 14th Fairmile Flotillas in Burma*, p. 129.

47. S. C. Pickford, *Destination Rangoon*, p. 279.

48. Spurr, pp. 128–9. See also OIOC MS Eur C388, 'To Rangoon and Beyond', by Lt. Ivor John N. Jukes RINVR, on HMIS *Kistna*'s part in the retaking of Burma.

49. PRO WO 208/1057, 'Japanese Order of Battle April 1943 to August 1945'; Sinker and Rossier, p. 59. G. D. Sheffield, p. 143.

50. G. Evans, *Slim as Military Commander*, p. 212.

51. IWM AL 827/20, 'Interrogation of General Kimura Hyotaro in Changi Jail, 1st April 1946. Reference Operations in Burma'.

52. McKie, p. 117.

53. Browning felt Leese fancied himself a second Montgomery but lacked the talent. The egotistical Montgomery had written to Leese soon after his appointment that 'Dickie Mountbatten came to see me the other day. He is a most delightful person but I feel his knowledge of how to make war is not very great!! You ought to go out there as his Army C-in-C, and keep him on the rails!' N. Hamilton, *Monty: Master of the Battlefield*, p. 804. Leese thus expected to be in charge but instead found Slim to be so and serving a sharper man in Mountbatten than himself. Ziegler, *Mountbatten*, p. 293.

54. IWM 82/15/1, General Sir Philip Christison Bt.

55. A. Danchev and D. Todman (eds.), *War Diaries, 1939–1945*, p. 692; Layman, pp. 255–7.

56. Allan, p. 65.

57. Hill, p. 145.

58. Brett-James, *Report My Signals*, p. 180.

59. MacDonald Fraser, pp. 35–7.

60. Lewin, *Slim*, p. 241.

61. Smurthwaite (ed.), p. 49.

62. Ziegler, *Mountbatten*, p. 294.

63. Undoubtedly it was a fierce and desperate fight, and what may have happened is that, in order to commemorate it, the Commanding Officer and Company Commander agreed that one of the surviving wounded should receive an award and Lachhiman was selected. Denis Sheil-Small knew him well, having trained and served with him (*Green Shadows*, pp. 166–7).

64. Slim, *Defeat into Victory*, p. 519.

65. NAM WWII Far East 1945 12 Army Acc. no. 2828, 'History of the Twelfth Army from its Formation on 28th May, 1945 to the End of Operations September, 1945'. This provides a summary of operations by brigade and appendices on artillery, engineers, signals, air support, RAF and clandestine operations and the military administration of Burma. It also has a transcript of the surrender formalities 11–13 September 1945. By now, Japanese manpower amounted to just 62,000, with 2,700 sick in hospital.

66. RSDGM CB 04 C34, Lt.-Col. John Ashton, 'Account of 3 DG Advance from Imphal to Rangoon 1944–45'.

67. PRO WO 203/4404, 'Patriotic Burmese Forces and Anti-Fascist Organisation Burma'; S. Tucker, *Burma*, pp. 59–60.

68. Immediately following the war 20th Indian Division was sent to Saigon to secure the surrender of Japanese forces in French Indo-China and came into conflict with patriotic forces. See P. M. Dunn, *The First Vietnam War*.

69. See Haseman.

70. Aida, pp. 141–2.

71. L. Allen, *Sittang*, pp. 47–9.

72. 'Burma Operations Record: 28th Army Operations in Akyab Area (November 1943–September 1945), Japanese Monograph no. 132', in Detwiler and Burdick (eds.), vol. 7/1, p. 200. See also Nagai Hideko, 'Nurses Escaped from Hell', and Ikeda Fusako, 'Japanese Nurse in a British

Hospital', in Tamayama and Nunneley, pp. 227–36, 236–42.

73. Eventually thirty-eight varieties of edible grass were identified, but salt short-age was the main problem. In the tropics sweating causes the body to lose large amounts which if not replaced lead to exhaustion, heat cramps and dehydration. The Indian Army had calculated that an average man with unlimited water (which was no problem for 28th Army) would need 2 grammes of salt per hour when working and half a gramme at rest. Sufficient supplies might have been stored in the Yomas before Kimura fled the city but this was not done and Sakurai's men had to find substitutes; one was a sour sauce from mangoes eaten with rice. Grass, bamboo shoots, lizards and sour mango sauce might have kept the body going, but little more. Bamboo also enabled the Japanese to build at least temporary accommodation. L. Allen, *Sittang*, pp. 78–84; L. Allen, *Burma*, pp. 488–91.

74. PRO AIR 23/2885, E8; Saunders, pp. 361–3.

75. Mackay, *A History of The 4th Prince of Wales's Own Gurkha Rifles*, p. 359.

76. Baird-Murray, pp. 119–21.

77. IWM 95/33/1, Lieutenant W. S. Farrow.

78. J. Thompson, *The Imperial War Museum Book of the War in Burma 1942–1945*, pp. 393–9.

79. L. Allen, *Sittang*, pp. 49–56.

80. J. Randle, 'An Ad Hoc Elephant Battery in WW2', *Durbar: Journal of the Indian Military Historical Society*, 19/1, pp. 25–6.

81. Although Louis Allen's *The Last Battle* is the most complete history of the breakout, he also treats it and the aftermath thoroughly from the Japanese point of view in *Burma*, pp. 492–534.

82. NAM 6308–12, 'RA 17 Ind Div Account of Ops 5 May 1945 to the Japanese Surrender'; G. W. Robertson, pp 294–306; RAHT MD/2494, 'An Artillery OP in Burma May–August 1945', by Lt. R. A. Arthur MBE.

83. Prasad (ed.), *The Reconquest of Burma*, vol. 2, pp. 454–5; L, Allen, *Sittang*, appx A., pp. 239–46.

84. Praval, *Valour Triumphs*, p. 143.

85. Masters, *The Road past Mandalay*, pp. 314–5.

86. IWM 11760/5, Maj. A. Trofimov.

87. J. Randle, 'The Girls', *Durbar: Journal of the Indian Military Historical Society*, 19/4, pp. 136–7.

88. Palsokar, *A Historical Record of the Dogra Regiment*, pp. 229–30; F. T. Birdwood, pp. 393–5; Bamford, pp. 147–51; Huxford, p. 210; Bellers, pp. 279–81.

89. Bidwell, *Gunners at War*, pp. 228–9.

90. L. Allen, *Sittang*, pp. x–xi.

91. E. Gordon, *Miracle on the River Kwai*, p. 162.

## 26 RETURN

1. MacDonald Fraser, pp. 217–21.
2. Patrick Davis, p. 250.
3. SOAS E Coll 3 M/17, J. F. Clifford, 'The Hills of Bishenpur and Advance into Central Burma'.
4. SOAS E Coll 3 P/3, 'The Strategy of the South-East Asia Campaign, a Lecture Given by Admiral the Viscount Mountbatten of Burma to the Royal United Services Institute on Wednesday, 9th October, 1946'.
5. Harries and Harries, pp. 384–8. Terauchi had suffered a stroke on 10 April 1945, prompted by bad news on all fronts, but partially recovered and remained in post until Emperor Hirohito ordered him home in early August. On 10 August, just before he was due to leave, he learned from US commercial radio of surrender negotiations and, after the emperor made his surrender broadcast on the 15th, was instrumental in persuading his subordinates to comply. Not being fully in command of his faculties and unable to travel (which Mountbatten's doctor confirmed in Saigon), Mountbatten – who could not be seen to deal with less than the senior enemy commander – sent Browning to sign the surrender documents in Rangoon on 28 August and in Singapore on 12 September. Terauchi sent for his ceremonial swords, one dating to 1292, which he surrendered to Mountbatten on 30 November 1945 in Saigon, and proved a solicitous prisoner – obviously with not long to live – who would normally have committed suicide. He died at Johore Bahru in Malaya on 12 June 1946. L. Allen, *Burma*, pp. 543–52.
6. NAM WWII Far East 1945 12 Army Acc. no. 2828, 'History of the Twelfth Army from its Formation on 28th May 1945 to the End of Operations September 1945'.
7. Kirby, vol. 5, p. 252.
8. OIOC MS Eur R144, taped interview (1983) by Lieutenant-Colonel B. M. Montgomery.
9. L. Allen, *Sittang*, p. 232.
10. L. Allen, *Sittang*, p. 113; *Burma*, pp. 536–43.
11. Dr Maung Maung, *To a Soldier Son*, pp. 78–9.
12. SOAS E Coll 3 E/17, B. Kendall, 'I Was There! With the British 2nd Division'.
13. D. Ripley, 'Incident in Sima', *Yale Review*, winter 1947, 34/2, p. 273.
14. Kinvig, *River Kwai Railway*, pp. 195–6.
15. Kinvig, *River Kwai Railway*, pp. xiii–xiv. Since the war very many personal memoirs of surviving the railway have been published. Many are laced with deep bitterness and hatred at the appalling treatment received, which in some cases totally blighted the post-war lives of the sufferers; some were written on psychiatric advice as catharsis for the deep psychological scars inflicted; others display forgiveness for their tormentors. These accounts are usually deeply personal and centred on the camps in which the author lived, their knowledge of the wider story of the railway being limited to rumour.

The Imperial War Museum and Australian War Memorial hold numerous accounts of life on the railway, some of which have since been published. Britons personal accounts include A. G. Allbury, *Bamboo and Bushido*, Len Baynes, *Kept: The Other Side of Tenko*, James Bradley, *Towards the Setting Sun*, Reginald Burton, *Railway of Hell, Capture and Forced Labour*, John T. Barnard, *The Endless Years*, J. Coast, *Railroad of Death*, Mary Davey, *Back to Burma*, John Durnford-Slater, *Branch Line to Burma*, Ernest Gordon, *Miracle on the Kwai*, Robert Hardie, *The Burma–Siam Railway*, Harry Howarth, *Where Fate Leads*, Arthur Lane, *When You Go Home* (which lists 22,602 British service men and women who died as prisoners of war), Eric Lomax, *The Railway Man*, Andy Milliken, *From the Kwai to the Kingdom*, Stanley Pavillard, *Bamboo Doctor*, Basil Peacock, *Prisoner on the Kwai*, Gerald Reminick, *Death's Railway*, Ian Skidmore, *Marines Don't Hold Their Horses*, W. F. Sollman, *Memories of the Thai–Burma Railway* and Thomas Pounder, *Death Camps of the River Kwai*. Australian personal accounts include Sir Edward 'Weary' Dunlop's *War Diaries* and (with James Boyle) *Railroad to Burma*. Other Australian accounts include Stan Arneil, *One Man's War*, Les Atkinson, *My Side of the Kwai*, Russell Braddon, *The Naked Island*, Hugh V. Clarke, *A Life for Every Sleeper*, E. R. Hall, *The Burma–Thailand Railway of Death*, Leslie Hall, *The Blue Haze*, Linda Goetz Holmes, *Four Thousand Bowls of Rice*, Mary Jahne, *From Red Gums to Bamboo*, Douglas McLaggan, *The Will to Survive*, Roy Mills, *Doctor's Diary and Memoir*, J. Mitchell, *The Moon Seemed Upside Down*, Ray Parkin, *Into the Smother* (book 2 of his *Wartime Trilogy*), Ian Denys Peek, *One Fourteenth of an Elephant*, Philippa Poole, *Of Love and War*, Rohan Rivett, *Behind Bamboo*, 'Eugene' in Patricia Shaw, *Brother Digger*, John Stewart, *To the River Kwai*, John Towers, *The Tale of a Tojo Tourist*, John 'Bill' Toon, *Hellfire*, and Roy H. Whitecross, *Slaves of the Sons of Heaven*. Artwork books include Jack Chalker (illustrator) and Sir Edward Dunlop (introduction), *Burma Railway Artist*, and Ronald Searle, *To the Kwai and Back*, and Fred Ransome Smith, *Lest We Forget*. Dutch accounts include Frank van Henneker, *Gentle Heroes*, Joop Hulsbus, *En de Zon Werd Rood*, Wim Kan, *Burmadagboek 1942–1945*, and Hendrick L. Leffelaar and E. van Witsen, *Werkers aan de Burma-Spoorweg*, Loet Velmans, *Long Way Back to the River Kwai*, and Chaim Nussbaum, *Chaplain on the River Kwai*, by a Dutch rabbi who served as a chaplain in the prisoner camps along the Kwai river from 1942 to 1945. For the contrasting story of a Japanese prisoner in British hands see Aida Yuji, *Prisoner of the British*, and for the extraordinary story of the escape from internment in India by two Germans in 1944 (although they did not get back to Germany until after the war), see Rolf Magener *Prisoner's Bluff*. (For American accounts see following note.)

16. H. R. Charles, *Last Man Out*, p. 87. This is a moving story, and a cathartic one for its author. Another survivor's tale from USS *Houston* is William Jacob Weissinger, *Attention, Fool!* Joan and Clay Blair Jr's *Return from the River Kwai* tells the story of 2,000 prisoners and their journey on a 'Hell Ship'. For an

overview of American experiences on the railway see Robert S. La Forte and Ronald E. Marcello (eds.), *Building the Death Railway*, and Cornelis B. Evers, *Death Railway*, Personal accounts include a number by members of 2nd Battalion, 131st Field Artillery Regiment, Texas National Guard, including Hollis G. Allen, *The Lost Battalion*, Benjamin Dunn, *The Bamboo Express*, Clyde Fillmore, *Prisoner of War*, Cornel Lumiere, *Red Runs the River Kwai*, Dick Scroggs, *The Soapman and the Railroad of Death*, Reuben Stone, *The Light behind the Clouds*, Horace G. Teel, *Our Days Were Years*, and Kyle Thompson, *A Thousand Cups of Rice*.

17. Charles, p. 171.
18. H. T. Cook and T. F. Cook, *Japan at War*, p. 103.
19. E. Gordon, p. 69.
20. Kinvig, *River Kwai Railway*, pp. 202–7.
21. Cook and Cook, pp. 420–7. (Clifford Kinvig incorrectly says Abe was hanged; *River Kwai Railway*, p. 208.)
22. NAM 9107-160, Captain D. W. T. Ballance.
23. Chevenix Trench, pp. 290–1.
24. Tamayama and Nunneley, p. 245.
25. Morrison, p. 171.
26. Prasad, *Expansion of the Armed Forces and Defence Organization*, p. 438; Philip Mason, pp. 513–4; Slim, *Defeat into Victory*, p. 323.
27. When they surrendered, INA prisoners were sent back to India, interrogated and 'sorted' into 'black' (confirmed traitors), 'grey' (dubious) and 'white': the blacks were earmarked for trial, greys discharged and whites offered reinstatement (Palit, *Major-General A. A. Rudra*, pp. 276–7).
28. L. Allen, Postface to I. Fujiwara (trans. Y. Akashi), *F. Kikan*, pp. 312–3.
29. A. Stewart, *The Underrated Enemy*, pp. 204–5.
30. Politically the mantle of Netaji Subhas Chandra Bose is important in Bengal for vote gathering. He was 'a great man', but lauding the exploits of the INA against the Indian Army is highly dangerous. Much misinformation has been published in India since about the INA's success. Narain, pp. 217, 220–1.
31. G. W. Robertson, p. 308.
32. Blight and Dempsey, pp. 416.
33. Gilmore and Davis, p. 242.
34. J. A. Baty, *Surgeon in the Jungle War*, p. 194.
35. GM 2nd King Edward VII's Own Goorkhas, 3rd Battalion Records, 1940–43, 'From Tonmakeng to Tenko'', by D. F. G. Gudgeon, quoted in H. James, *Across the Threshold of Battle*, p. 198.
36. Shipster, p. 87.
37. Blight and Dempsey, *The Royal Berkshire Regiment (Princess Charlotte of Wales's) 1920–1947*, p. 416.
38. Fischer, *The Chancy War*, p. 89.
39. Maybury, vol. 3, p. 30.
40. Parillo, p. 218.
41. Cady, p. 485.

42. M. Collis, *Last and First in Burma (1941–1948)*, pp. 187–91.

43. D. Murray, interview with the author, 26 June 2003.

44. Mountbatten's difficult position is examined in Peter Dennis, *Troubled Days of Peace*.

45. PRO WO 203/4404; Naw, pp. 128–30; Aldrich, p. 336.

46. M. Collis, *Last and First in Burma (1941–1948)*, p. 251.

47. Trager (ed.), p. 24.

48. Cady, p. 478.

49. Foucar, *I Lived in Burma*, p. 189.

50. S. Molloy, *Burma Bride*, pp. 199–200.

51. Foucar, *I Lived in Burma*, p. 199; OIOC MS Eur R135, taped interview by Carlyle Edmund Sweepings, Burma Army 1941–45, Burma Police 1945–50 (chiefly on his wartime experiences with the Inter-Services Liaison Department as an undercover agent in Burma, and his work in the Burma Police after the war, including his surveillance of U Saw).

52. Foucar, *I Lived in Burma*, pp. 201–3; see also U Maung, *Burmese Nationalist Movements 1940–1948*, chaps. 7–10, and J. H. McEnery, *Epilogue in Burma*, pp. 108–14.

53. Foucar, *I Lived in Burma*, p. 9.

54. 'J. Casey, Nobel Prisoner of Rangoon', *Daily Telegraph*, 15 January 1991.

55. Degaa Upfill, pp. 212–4.

56. Ne Win ('Brilliant as the Sun') dominated the political landscape of Burma in a 26-year era of isolation from the outside world. But by the time he stepped down in 1988, the country had collapsed to become one of the world's ten poorest nations. But, in private, Aung San had begun to express concerns about his wartime comrade, which his daughter Aung San Suu Kyi referred to many years later. 'My father didn't build up the Burmese army in order to suppress the people', she said. *The Guardian*, 6 December 2002.

57. http://news.bbc.co.uk/1/hi/world/from_our_own_correspondent/32885.stm; http://news:bbc.co.uk/1/hi/world/south_asia/3372513.stm.

58. C. Mackenzie, *All over the Place*, p. 143.

59. NAM Ind Inf. 3 Regt., 'The Story of the 4th Bn., The Madras Regiment in the Burma Campaign, 1943–45'.

60. Slim, *Defeat into Victory*, p. 534.

61. Shipster, p. 38.

62. *Sunday Times*, 27 June 1982.

63. Beaumont, p. 160.

# Bibliography

## HISTORICAL SOURCES

*A Happy Family: The Story of The Twentieth Indian Division*, New Delhi, Roxy Press, 1946

*A Short War History of 'A' Squadron, 146 Regiment Royal Armoured Corps (The Duke of Wellington's) 1940–1946 United Kingdom–India–Burma–Sumatra*, Medan, Typ. Varekamp, 1946

Abhyankar, M. G., *Myth Exploded: Being the Analysed and Collated Review of the Operations in Burma from October 1943 to September 1945*, Dehra Dun, Natraj Publishers, 1955

——, *Valour Enshrined: A History of the Maratha Light Infantry, 1768–1947*, New Delhi, Orient Longmans, 1971

Adams, G. P., *The Thailand to Burma Railway*, Poole, Ashley, 1978

Adamson, L., *The Forgotten Men*, London, G. Bellard and Sons, 1965

Aggett, W. J. P., *The Bloody Eleventh – History of the Devonshire Regiment*, vol. 3, *1914–1969*, Exeter, Devonshire and Dorset Regiment, 1995

Ahmad, M., *Heritage: The History of The Rajput Regiment 1778–1947*, Fategarh, The Commandant, The Rajput Regimental Centre, 1989

Aida, Y. (trans. H. Ishiguro and L. Allen), *Prisoner of the British: A Japanese Soldier's Experiences in Burma*, London, The Cresset Press, 1966

Aldrich, R. J., *Intelligence and the War against Japan: Britain, America and the Politics of Secret Service*, Cambridge, Cambridge University Press, 2000

Alexander, Field Marshal Viscount, *The Alexander Memoirs*, ed. J. North, London, Cassell, 1962

Allan, J. R., *In the Trade of War*, Tunbridge Wells, Parapress, 1994

Allbury, A. G., *Bamboo and Bushido: An Authentic Narrative*, London, Robert Hale, 1956

Allen, H. G., *The Lost Battalion*, Jacksboro, TX, Herald, 1963

Allen, L., *Burma: The Longest War 1941–45*, London, Phoenix Press, 2000

——, *Sittang: The Last Battle; The End of the Japanese in Burma, July–August 1945*, London, Macdonald, 1976

Alsop, J. W., and Platt, A., *'I've Seen the Best of It': Memoirs*, New York, Norton, 1992

Anand, V., *Indian Heroes and Heroines of World War II – A Brief History*, London, Institute for Media Communications, 1995

Anders, L., *The Ledo Road: General Joseph W. Stilwell's Highway to China*, Norman, OK, University of Oklahoma Press, 1965

Anglo, M., *Service Newspapers of the Second World War*, London, Jupiter, 1972

Armstrong, G., *The Sparks Fly Upward: An Experience*, East Wittering, Gooday Publishers, 1991

Arneil, S. F., *One Man's War*, Sydney, S. F. Arneil, 1980

Arnold, H. H., *Global Mission*, New York, Harper, 1949

Arnold, R., *A Very Quiet War*, London, Rupert Hart-Davis, 1962

Atkins, D., *The Forgotten Major: In the Siege of Imphal*, Pulborough, Toat Press 1989

——, *The Reluctant Major*, Pulborough, Toat Press, 1986

Atkinson, C. T., *A History of The 1st (P. W. O.) Battalion The Dogra Regiment 1887–1947, 37th Dogras, 1887–1922 1st (P. W. O.) Bn., 17th Dogra Regt., 1922–1945*, Southampton, The Camelot Press, 1950

Atkinson, L., *My Side of the Kwai: Reminiscences of an Australian Prisoner of War of the Japanese*, Kenthurst, NSW, Kangaroo Press, 2001

Auchinleck, C., *Operations in the Indo–Burma Theatre Based on India from 21st June 1943 to 15th November 1943*, London, HMSO, 1948

Aung San Suu Kyi, *Aung San of Burma: A Biographical Portrait by his Daughter*, Edinburgh, Kiscadale, 1991

Ba Maw, *Breakthrough in Burma: Memoirs of a Revolution 1939–46*, New Haven, CT, Yale University Press, 1968

Ba U, *My Burma: The Autobiography of a President*, New York, Taplinger, 1959

Baggaley, J., *Chindit Story*, London, Panther, 1955

Bailey, N. J., *Thailand and the Fall of Singapore*, London, Westview, 1986

Baird-Murray, M., *A World Overturned: A Burmese Childhood 1933–1947*, London, Constable, 1997

Baisden, C., *Flying Tiger to Air Commando*, Atglen, PA, Schiffer Military History, 1999

Baker, A. D., *Merrill's Marauders*, London, Pan/Ballantine, 1972

Baker, R., *Burma Post*, Worthing, Churchgate, 1989

Baldwin, H. W., *Great Mistakes of the War*, New York, Harper, 1950

Bamford, P. G., *1st King George V's Own Battalion, The Sikh Regiment: The 14th King George's Own Ferozepore Sikhs 1846–1946*, Aldershot, Gale & Polden, 1948

Barclay, C. N., *The History of The Cameronians (Scottish Rifles)*, vol. 3, *1933–1946*, London, Sifton Praed, 1948

——, *The History of The Duke of Wellington's Regiment, 1919–1952*, London, William Clowes and Son, 1953

——, *The Regimental History of the 3rd Queen Alexandra's Own Gurkha Rifles*, vol. 2, *1927–1947*, London, William Clowes and Son, 1953

Barker, A. J., *Japanese Army Handbook 1939–1945*, Shepperton, Ian Allen, 1979

——, *The March on Delhi*, London, Faber and Faber, 1963

Barnard, J., *The Hump: The Greatest Untold Story of the War*, London, Corgi, 1961

Barnard, J. T., *The Endless Years ... Written during his Captivity*, London, Chantry Publications, 1950

Barnhart, M. A., *Japan Prepares for Total War: The Search for Economic Security, 1919–1941*, Ithaca, NY, Cornell University Press, 1987

Barrett, C., *Wings of an Angel*, London, Minerva Press, 2001

Bartlett, J., and Benson, J., *All the King's Enemies: The Remarkable Deeds of the 'Lincolnshire Gunners'*, Boston, Richard Kay, 2000

Baty, J., *Surgeon in the Jungle War*, London, William Kimber, 1979

Baynes, L. L., *Kept: The Other Side of Tenko*, London, Star, 1985

Beale, H. K., *Theodore Roosevelt and the Rise of America to World Power*, Baltimore, MD, Johns Hopkins University Press, 1956

Beamish, J., *Burma Drop*, London, Elek, 1958

Beard, G., *The Long, Long Road: Mt. Isa to the Burma Railway and Back* [no publishing details, 2000]

Beasley, W. G., *Japanese Imperialism 1894–1945*, Oxford, Oxford University Press, 1987

—— *The Modern History of Japan*, London, Weidenfeld & Nicolson, 1963

Beaton, C., *Far East*, London, B. T. Batsford, 1945

Beauchamp, G., *Mohawks over Burma*, Leicester, Midland Counties, 1985

Beaumont, W., *A Detail on the Burma Front*, London, BBC, 1977

Becka, J., *The Nationalist Liberation Movement in Burma during the Japanese Occupation Period (1941–1945)*, Prague, Oriental Institute in Academia, 1983

Bednall, D., *Sun on my Wings*, Pembroke Dock, Paterchurch, 1989

Behr, E., *Hirohito: Behind the Myth*, London, Penguin, 1990

Belden, J., *Retreat with Stilwell*, London, Cassell, 1943

——, *Still Time To Die*, London, Victor Gollancz, 1945

Bell, A. C., *History of The Manchester Regiment, First and Second Battalions, 1922–1948*, Altrincham, John Sherratt and Son, 1954

Bellers, E. V. R., *The History of The 1st King George V's Own Gurkha Rifles (The Malaun Regiment)*, vol. 2, *1920–1947*, Aldershot, Gale & Polden, 1956

Benedict, R., *The Chrysanthemum and the Sword: Patterns of Japanese Culture*, London, Routledge and Kegan, 1967

Besley, H., *Pilot–Prisoner–Survivor: Six Years in Uniform*, Toowoomba, QLD, Darling Downs Institute Press, 1986

Betham, G., and Geary, H. V. R., *The Golden Galley: The Story of The Second Punjab Regiment 1761–1947*, Oxford, 2nd Punjab Regiment Officers' Association, 1956

Bevan, A. J., *The Story of Zarak Khan*, London, Jarrold & Sons, 1949

Bhatia, H. S. (ed.), *Military History of British India 1607–1947*, New Delhi, Deep and Deep, 1977

Bhonsle, R. K., *The Japanese Offensive 1941–43: An Analytical Study*, New Delhi, Himalayan Books, 1990

Bickersteth, A. C., *ODTAA: Being Extracts from the Diary of an Officer who Served with the 4/10th Gurkha Rifles in Manipur and Burma*, Aberdeen, privately printed at Aberdeen University Press, 1953

Bidwell, S., *The Chindit War: The Campaign in Burma 1944*, London, Hodder and Stoughton, 1979

——, *Gunners at War*, London, Arrow, 1972

Bierman, J., and Smith, C., *Fire in the Night: Wingate of Burma, Ethiopia, and Zion*, London, Pan, 2001

Bingham, J., *U Thant: The Search for Peace*, London, Victor Gollancz, 1966

Birdwood, F. T., *The Sikh Regiment in the Second World War*, Norwich, Jarrold & Sons, no date

Birdwood, Lord, *The Worcestershire Regiment 1922–1950*, Aldershot, Gale & Polden, 1952

Bix, H. P., *Hirohito and the Making of Modern Japan*, London, HarperCollins, 2001

Blackburn, T., *The British Humiliation of Burma*, Bangkok, Orchid Press, 2000

Blair J., and Blair, C., Jr., *Return from the River Kwai*, New York, Simon, 1979

Blair, J. S. G., *In Arduis Fidelis: Centenary History of The Royal Army Medical Corps*, Edinburgh, Scottish Academic Press, 1998

Bland, L. I., and Stevens, S. R. (eds.), *The Papers of George Catlett Marshall*, Baltimore, MD, Johns Hopkins University Press, 1991

Blight, G., and Dempsey, M., *The History of The Royal Berkshire Regiment (Princess Charlotte of Wales's) 1920–1947*, London, Staples Press, 1953

Blore, T., *Commissioned Barges: The Story of the Landing Craft*, London, Hutchinson, no date

Boatner, M., *The Biographical Dictionary of World War II*, Novato, CA, Presidio, 1996

Bolton, A., *The Maturing Sun: An Army Nurse in India, 1942–1945*, London, Imperial War Museum, 1986

Bond, B. (ed.), *Chief of Staff: The Diaries of Lieutenant-General Sir Henry Pownall*, vol. 2, *1940–1944*, London, Leo Cooper, 1974

Bond, C. R., and Anderson, T. H., *A Flying Tiger's Diary*, College Station, TX, Texas A & M University Press, 1984

Booth, J. R., and Hobbs, J. B., *Ninth Battalion, Fourteenth Punjab Regiment, Raised 1st April, 1941, Disbanded 8th July, 1947: India, Ceylon, Burma, French Indo-China, Sarawak, India*, Cardiff, Western Mail and Echo Ltd, 1948

Bose, M., *The Lost Hero: A Biography of Subhas Bose*, London, Quartet, 1982

Bowden, J., *Grey Touched with Scarlet: The War Experiences of the Army Nursing Sisters*, London, Robert Hale, 1959

Bowen, J., *Undercover in the Jungle*, London, William Kimber, 1978

Bowyer, C., *The Flying Elephants: A History of No. 27 Squadron, Royal Flying Corps – Royal Air Force, 1916–69*, London, Macdonald, 1972

Boyd, C., and Yoshida, A., *The Japanese Submarine Force in World War II*, Shrewsbury, Airlife, 1995

Boyd J., with Garth, G., *Tenko! Rangoon Jail: The Amazing Story of Sgt. John Boyd's Survival as POW in a Notorious Japanese Prison Camp*, Paducah, KY, Turner, 1996

Boyington, C., *Baa Baa Black Sheep*, New York, Arno Press, 1972

Boyle, J., and Dunlop, E. E., *Railroad to Burma*, St Leonard's, NSW, Allen & Unwin, 1993

Boyle, P., and Musgrave-Wood, J., *Jungle, Jungle, Little Chindit*, London Hollis and Carter, 1946

Braddon, R., *The Naked Island*, London, Werner Laurie, 1952

Bradley, J. R., *Cyril Wild: The Tall Man Who Never Slept*, Fontwell, Woodfield, 1991

——, *Towards the Setting Sun: An Escape from the Thailand–Burma Railway*, Chichester, Philimore, 1982

Bradley, K., *Hellfire Pass Memorial: Thai–Burma Railway*, Bangkok, Australian–Thai Chamber of Commerce, 1990

Bradley, N., *The Old Burma Road: A Journey on Foot and Muleback*, London, Heinemann, 1945

Branson, C., *British Soldier in India: The Letters of Clive Branson*, London, Communist Party of Great Britain, 1944

Braund, H. E. W., *Distinctly I Remember: a Personal Story of Burma*, Mt Eliza, VIC, Wren, 1972

Brayley, M., *The British Army 1939–45 (3)*, Men-at-Arms 374, Oxford, Osprey, 2002

Brereton, J. M., *The 7th Queen's Own Hussars*, London, Leo Cooper, 1975

——, and Savory, A. C. S., *The History of the Duke of Wellington's Regiment (West Riding) 1702–1992*, Halifax, The Duke of Wellington's Regiment (West Riding), 1993

Brereton, L. H., *The Brereton Diaries: The War in the Air in the Pacific, Middle East and Europe, 3 October 1941–8 May 1945*, New York, Morrow, 1946

Brett, G. A., *History of The South Wales Borderers and The Monmouthshire Regiment*, part 5, *The 6th Battalion The South Wales Borderers 1940–1945*, Pontypool, Hughes and Son, 1956

Brett-James, A., *Ball of Fire: The Fifth Indian Division in the Second World War*, Aldershot, Gale & Polden, 1951

——, *Report My Signals*, London, Hennel Locke, 1948

Briscoe, D. A., *The Friendly Firm Remembers: Stories by the Members of 194 Squadron RAF in South East Asia*, Victoria, BC, Fotoprint, 2000

Bristow, R. C. B., *Memories of the British Raj: A Soldier in India*, London, Christopher Johnson, 1974

Brooke-Popham, R., *Operations in the Far East from 12th October 1940–27th December 1941*, London, HMSO, 1948

Brookes, S., *Through the Jungle of Death: A Boy's Escape from Wartime Burma*, London, John Murray, 2000

Brough, B., *To Reason Why ...*, Newcastle upon Tyne, Hickory Tree Press, 2001

Browne, C., *Tojo: The Last Banzai*, New York, Holt, Rinehart and Winston, 1967

Bruce, G., *Burma Wars, 1824–86*, London, Rupert Hart-Davis, 1973

Bryant, A., *The Turn of Tide 1939–1943: A Study Based on the Diaries and Autobiographical Notes of Field Marshal The Viscount Alanbrooke K. G., O. M.*, London, Collins, 1956

——, *Triumph in the West 1943–1946: Based on the Diaries and Autobiographical Notes of Field Marshal The Viscount Alanbrooke K. G., O. M.*, London, Collins, 1959

Bugler, W., *The Story of 114: An Informal History of the 114th (Sussex) Field Regiment (one-time Jungle Field Regiment) R. A., (T.A.)*, F. Taylor, no date

Buhite, R. D., *Patrick Hurley and American Foreign Policy*, Ithaca, NY, Cornell University Press, 1973

Bullock, W., and Durant, N., *Experiences of the Second World War in Burma*, Winchester, George Mann, 1995

Burchett, W. G., *At the Barricades: The Memories of a Rebel Journalist*, London, Macmillan, 1981

——, *Bombs over Burma*, Melbourne, F. W. Cheshire, 1944

——, *Trek Back from Burma*, Allahabad, Kitabistan, no date

——, *Wingate's Phantom Army*, Bombay, Thacker, 1944

——, *Wingate Adventure*, Melbourne, F. W. Cheshire, 1944

Burke-Gaffney, J. J., *The Story of The King's Regiment 1914–1948*, Liverpool, Sharpe and Kellet for The King's Regiment, 1954

*Burma Campaign Memorial Library: A Collection of Books and Papers about the War in Burma 1942–1945*, London, School of Oriental and African Studies, 2001

*Burma during the Japanese Occupation*, Simla, Government of India Press, vol. 1, 1943; vol. 2, 1944

*Burma Handbook*, Simla, Government of India Press, 1943

Burma Intelligence Bureau, *Burma during the Japanese Occupation*, 2 vols, Simla, Government of Burma, 1943–4

Burton, R., *Railway of Hell: A Japanese POW's Account of War, Capture and Forced Labour*, Barnsley, Leo Cooper, 2002

Buruma, I., *The Wages of Guilt: Memories of War in Germany and Japan*, London, Vintage, 1995

Butow, R. J. C., *Japan's Decision to Surrender*, Stanford, CA, Stanford University Press, 1954

——, *Tojo and the Coming of War*, Stanford, CA, Stanford University Press, 1961

Butwell, R. A., *U Nu of Burma*, Stanford, CA, Stanford University Press, 1963

Bykofsky, J., and Larson, H., *United States Army in World War II, The Technical Services, The Transportation Corps: Operations Overseas*, Washington, DC, Office of The Chief of Military History, United States Army, 1957

Byrd, M., *Chennault: Giving Wings to the Tiger*, Tuscaloosa, AL, University of Alabama Press, 1987

Cady, J. F., *A History of Modern Burma*, Ithaca, NY, Cornell University Press, 1958

Caidin, M., *Zero Fighter*, London, Macdonald, 1970

Callahan, R., *Burma 1942–45: The Politics and Strategy of the Second World War*, London, Davis-Poynter, 1978

Calvert, M., *Fighting Mad*, Shrewsbury, Airlife, 1996

——, *Prisoners of Hope*, London, Leo Cooper, 1971

——, *Slim*, London, Pan/Ballantine, 1973

——, *The Chindits: Long Range Penetration*, London, Pan/Ballantine, 1973

Camp, L. T., *Lingering Fever: A World War II Nurse's Memoir*, Jefferson, NC, McFarland & Co., 1997

Campbell, A., *The Siege: A Story from Kohima*, London, George Allen and Unwin Ltd, 1956

Campbell Begg, R., and Liddle, P. H. (eds.), *For Five Shillings a Day: Personal Histories of World War II*, London, HarperCollins, 2000

Cane, P., *Chinese Chindits*, Aldershot, Gale & Polden, 1948

*Canucks Unlimited: The Record in Story and Picture of the History, Life and Experiences of the Men of the 436 R.C.A.F. Squadron: India-Burma 1944–45*, Toronto, Rous and Mann (printers), no date

Carew, T., *All This and a Medal Too*, London, Constable, 1954

——, *The Longest Retreat: The Burma Campaign*, London, Hamish Hamilton, 1969

——, *The Fall of Hong Kong*, London, Anthony Blond, 1960

Carfrae, C., *Chindit Column*, London, William Kimber, 1985

Carmichael, P., *Mountain Battery*, Bournemouth, Devin, 1983

Cattanach, J., *The Jeep Track: The Story of the 81st West African Division Fighting on the Arakan Front in Burma*, London, Regency Press, 1990

Cave, H., *Wings across the World: The Story of the Air Transport Command*, New York, Dodd, Mead, 1945

Cave-Brown, A., *The Last Hero – Wild Bill Donovan: The Biography and Political Experience of Major General William J. Donovan, Founder of the OSS and 'Father' of the CIA, from His Personal and Secret Papers and Diaries of Ruth Donovan*, New York, Times, 1982

Chaikin, R. B., *'To My Memory Sing' – A Memoir Based on Letters and Poems from Sol Chick Chaikin, an American Soldier in China–Burma–India during World War II*, Monroe NY, Library Research Associates, 1997

Chakravarti, N. R., *The Indian Minority in Burma: The Rise and Decline of an Immigrant Community*, Oxford, Oxford University Press, 1971

Chalker, J., and Dunlop, E. E., *Burma Railway Artist: The War Drawings of Jack Chalker*, Barnsley, Leo Cooper, 1994

Chamberlin, W. H., *Japan over Asia*, London, Duckworth, 1938

Chan W.-L., *Burma: The Untold Story*, Novato, CA, Presidio, 1986

Chand, D. S., *The Rajputana Rifles*, New Delhi, Reliance Publishing House, 1995

Chandra, A., *Indian Army Triumphant in Burma: The Burmese Campaign 1941–45*, Delhi, Atma Ram & Sons, 1984

Chang, I., *The Rape of Nanking: The Forgotten Holocaust of World War II*, London, Penguin, 1998

Chaphekar, S. G., *A Brief History of the Burma Campaign, 1943–45*, Poona, Mahrashtra Militaristic Board, 1955

Chaplin, J. B., *Action in Burma, 1942–1945*, London, P. F. Smith, 1984

Chapman, G. P., *The Lampi: A Story about Some Gunners*, Calcutta, Thacker Spink & Co., 1944

Charge, D. H., *The Beginning of the End: A Story about the Chindits in Burma*, Swindon, Forces Publishing Service, 1995

Charles, H. R., *Last Man Out: Surviving the Burma Railroad*, Ramsbury, The Crowood Press, 1989

Charlton, M., *Mandalay and Beyond: Tales from a Medical Airman's Diary*, Braunton, Merlin, 1996

Chaudhuri, P., *9th Gurkha Rifles – A Regimental History (1817 to 1947)*, New Delhi, Vision Books, 1984

Chennault, C. L. (ed. R. Hotz), *Way of a Fighter: The Memoirs of Claire L. Chennault*, New York, G. P. Putnam's Sons, 1949

Chevenix Trench, C., *The Indian Army and the King's Enemies 1900–1947*, London, Thames and Hudson, 1988

Chhina R., *The Indian Distinguished Service Medal*, New Delhi, Invicta India, 2001

*China Airlift – The Hump: China's Aerial Lifeline, the Beginning of the China–Burma–India Hump Pilots Association*, Popular Bluff, MO, Hump Pilots Association, 3 vols, 1980, 1983, 1992

*China Airlift – The Hump*, vol. 4, China–Burma–India Hump Pilots Association, Paducah, KN, Turner, 1997

Chinnery, P. D., *Any Time, Any Place: Fifty Years of the USAF Air Commando and Special Operations Forces 1944–1994*, Shrewsbury, Airlife, 1994

——, *March or Die*, Shrewsbury, Airlife, 1997

——, *Air Commando: Inside the Air Force Special Operations Command*, New York, St Martin's Press, 1997

Christian, J. L., *Burma*, London, William Collins, 1952

——, *Burma and the Japanese Invader*, Bombay, Thacker, 1945

Churchill, T. B. L., *Commando Crusade*, London, William Kimber, 1987

Churchill, W. S., *The Second World War*, vol. 3, *The Grand Alliance*, London, Cassell, 1950

——, *The Second World War*, vol. 4, *The Hinge of Fate*, London, Cassell, 1951

Clabby, J., *The History of The Royal Army Veterinary Corps 1919–1961*, London, J. A. Allen, 1963

Clare, T. H., and Clare, I. M., *Lookin' Eastward: A G.I. Salaam to India*, New York, Macmillan, 1945

Clarke, A. E., *Return to Singapore*, Swindon, Forces Publishing Service, 1995

Clarke, F., *The Road to Spiderpore*, Taunton, Rocket Publishing, 1995

Clarke, H. V., *A Life for Every Sleeper: A Pictorial Record of the Burma–Thailand Railway*, St Leonard's, NSW, Allen & Unwin, 1986

Clarke, M. S., *Kaladan Mortars: A Walk on a Knife-Edge*, Fontwell, Woodfield, 1994

Clarke, R., *With Alex at War: From the Irrawaddy to the Po 1941–1945*, Barnsley, Leo Cooper, 2000

Clayton, A., *Forearmed: A History of the Intelligence Corps*, London, Brassey's (UK), 1993

Cleaver F., *The Long Way Home – An Account of Florence Cleaver's Journey out of Burma in 1942*, ed. J. Roberts, Matlock, Aubrex, 1993

Clements, T. J., *American Volunteer Group Colours and Markings*, Aircraft of the Aces 41, Oxford, Osprey, 2001

Clifford, F., *Desperate Journey*, London, Hodder and Stoughton, 1979

Clune, F., *Song of India*, Sydney, Invincible Press, 1946

Coast, J., *Railroad of Death*, London, The Commodore Press, 1946

Cochrane, S., *Chindit: Special Force, Burma 1944*, Philadelphia, PA, Xlibris, 2000

Coffey, T. M., *HAP: The Story of the U.S. Air Force and the Man Who Built It: General Henry H. 'Hap' Arnold*, New York, Viking, 1982

Cohen, S. P., *The Indian Army: Its Contribution to the Development of a Nation*, Delhi, Oxford University Press, 1990

Coll, B. D., Keith, J. E., and Rosenthal, H. H., *United States Army in World War II, The Technical Services, The Corps of Engineers: Troops and Equipment*, Washington, DC, Office of The Chief of Military History, United States Army, 1958

Collier, B., *The War in the Far East 1941–45 – A Military History*, London, Heinemann, 1969

Collins, D. J. E., *Official History of the Indian Armed Forces in The Second World War 1939–45: The Royal Indian Navy*, New Delhi, Combined Inter-Services Historical Section (India and Pakistan), 1964

Collins, L., and Lapierre, D., *Freedom at Midnight*, London, Collins, 1975

Collis, G. R., *The Eagle Soars*, Bishop Auckland, The Pentland Press, 1998

Collis, M., *Last and First in Burma (1941–1948)*, London, Faber and Faber, 1956

——, *Lords of the Sunset*, London, Faber and Faber, 1938

——, *Into Hidden Burma: An Autobiography*, London, Faber and Faber, 1953

——, *The Journey Outward: An Autobiography*, London, Faber and Faber, 1952

——, *Trials in Burma*, Harmondsworth, Penguin, 1945

Collister, P., *Then a Soldier*, Worthing, Churchman Publishing, 1985

Colvin, J., *Not Ordinary Men: The Story of the Battle of Kohima*, London, Leo Cooper, 1995

Conden, W. E. H., *The Frontier Force Regiment*, Aldershot, Gale & Polden, 1962

——, *The Frontier Force Rifles*, Aldershot, Gale & Polden, 1953

Connell, J., *Auchinleck: A Biography of Field Marshal Sir Claude Auchinleck*, London, Cassell, 1959

——, *Wavell: Supreme Commander 1941–1943*, London, Collins, 1969

Cook, H., *The North Staffordshire Regiment (Prince of Wales's) (The 64th/98th Regiment of Foot)*, London, Leo Cooper, 1970

Cook, H. T., and Cook, T. F., *Japan at War: An Oral History*, London, Phoenix Press, 2000

Cooper, K. W., *The Little Men: A Platoon's Epic Fight in the Burma Campaign*, London, Robert Hale, 1973

Cooper, R. A., *'B' Company 9th Battalion The Border Regiment 48 Brigade 17th Indian (Light) Division IV Corps 14th Army South East Asia Command: One Man's War in Burma 1942–1944 Recalled in Hospital in 1945*, London, Dennis Dobson, 1978

Cooper, W. J., *Desert Sand to Jungle Trail: One Man's War 1940–1946*, Minster Lovell, Bookmarque, 1997

Corpe, H. R., *Prisoner beyond the Chindwin*, London, Arthur Barker, 1955

Corbett, J., *Jungle Lore*, Oxford, Oxford University Press, 1953

——, *My India*, London, Reprint Society, 1963

Corr, G. H., *The War of the Springing Tigers*, London, Osprey, 1975

Costello, J., *The Pacific War 1941–1945*, London, Collins, 1981

Cotton, M. C., *Hurricanes over Burma*, including *The Memoirs of Wing Commander 'Bunny' Stones, DFC*, London, Grub Street, 1995

Coubrough, C. R. L., *Memories of a Perpetual Second Lieutenant*, York, Wilton 65, 1999

Coulthard, G., *From Private to Trooper Back to Private*, Bishop Auckland, The Pentland Press, 1994

Courtney, G. B., *SBS in World War II: The Story of the Original Special Boat Section of the Army Commandos*, London, Robert Hale, 1983

Craine, E. R., *Burma Roadsters: The 464th CA AA Bn in China–Burma–India*, Tucson, AZ, Western Research Company, 1992

Craven, W. F., and Cate, J. L. (eds.), *The Army Air Forces In World War II*, vol. 4, *The Pacific: Guadalcanal to Saipan August 1942 to July 1944*, Chicago, IL, University of Chicago Press, 1950

——, *The Army Air Forces In World War II*, vol. 5, *The Pacific: Matterhorn to Nagasaki June 1944 to August 1945*, Chicago, IL, University of Chicago Press, 1953

Crew, F. A. E., *The Army Medical Services: Campaigns*, vol. 5, *Burma*, London, HMSO, 1966

Crosby, M. G. M., *Irregular Soldier*, Guernsey, XB Publications, 1993

Cross, J. P., *Jungle Warfare: Experiences and Encounters*, London, Arms and Armour, 1989

——, and Gurung B. (eds.), *Gurkhas at War: The Gurkha Experience in their Own Words, World War II to the Present Day*, London, Greenhill, 2002

Crosthwaite, C., *The Pacification of Burma*, London, Frank Cass, 1960

Crozier, B., *The Rebels: A Study of Post War Insurrections*, London, Chatto and Windus, 1960

Cruickshank, C., *SOE in the Far East*, Oxford, Oxford University Press, 1983

Curie, E., *Journey among Warriors*, London, Heinemann, 1943

*Dagger Division: Story of the 19th Indian Division*, Bombay, G. S. Borker, 1946

Danchev, A., *Very Special Relationship: Field Marshal Dill and the Anglo-American Alliance*, London, Brassey's, 1986

——, and Todman, D. (eds.), *War Diaries 1939–1945: Field Marshal Lord Alanbrooke*, London, Weidenfeld & Nicolson, 2001

Das, C. N., *The Rajputana Rifles: Brief History*, New Delhi, Reliance Publishing, 1995

Daugherty, L. J., *Fighting Techniques of a Japanese Infantryman 1941–1945: Training, Techniques and Weapons*, Staplehurst, Spellmount, 2002

Davey, M., *Back to Burma: For the Love of John*, London, Rathgar Press, 1995

Davies, J. P., *Dragon by the Tail: American, British, Japanese, and Russian Encounters with China and One Another*, New York, W. W. Norton, 1972

Davies, P. N., *The Man Behind the Bridge: Colonel Toosey and the River Kwai*, London, Athlone, 1991

Davis, Patrick, *A Child in Arms*, London, Buchan and Enright, 1985

Davis, Paxton, *A Boy's War*, Winston-Salem, NC, John F. Blair, 1990

Davy, G. M. O., *The Seventh and Three Enemies: The Story of World War II and the 7th Queen's Own Hussars*, Cambridge, W. Heffer and Sons, 1952

Daws, G., *Prisoners of the Japanese: POWs of World War in the Pacific: The Powerful Untold Story*, London, Robson, 1994

Day-Lewis, T. (ed.), *Last Letters Home*, London, Macmillan, 1995

Deedes, R. B., *Historical Records of The Royal Garwhal Rifles*, vol. 2, *1923–1947*, Dehra Dun, The Army Press, 1962

Degaa Upfill, M. S., *An American in Burma 1930–1942: The Memoirs of Muriel Sue Degaa Upfill*, Tempe, AZ, Arizona University Press, 1999

Delachet Guillon, C., *Daw Sein. Les dix mille vies d'une femme birmane*, Paris, Seuil, 1978

Dennis, P., *Troubled Days of Peace: Mountbatten and South-East Asia Command, 1945–46*, Manchester, Manchester University Press, 1987

Denny, J. H., *Chindit Indiscretion*, London, Christopher Johnson, 1956

Desai, W. S., *India and Burma: A Study*, Bombay, Orient Longmans, 1954

Detwiler, D. S., and Burdick, C. B. (eds.), *War in Asia and the Pacific 1937–1949*, 15 vols., New York, Garland, 1980

Dewar McClintock, J., *Manipur Road: The Story of the Mandalay Campaign*, London, Brown, Watson Ltd, no date

Dhillon, G. S., *From My Bones: Memoirs of Col. Gurbaksh Singh Dhillon of the Indian National Army (Including the Red Fort Trial)*, New Delhi, Aryan Books International, 1998

Dillon, T., *Rangoon to Kohima*, Gloucester, Regimental Headquarters The Gloucestershire Regiment, 1979

Dimbleby, K., *Turns of Fate: The Drama of HMS 'Cornwall' 1939–1942*, London, William Kimber, 1984

Dod, K. C., *United States Army in World War II, The Technical Services, The Corps of Engineers: The War against Japan*, Washington, DC, Office of The Chief of Military History, United States Army, 1966

Donaldson, G., *Did I Take the Right Turning?*, Bishop Auckland, The Pentland press, 1999

Donnison, F. S. V., *British Military Administration in the Far East 1943–1946*, London, HMSO, 1956

——, *Burma*, London, Ernest Benn, 1970

Dorn, F., *Walkout: With Stilwell in Burma*, New York, Thomas Y. Crowell, 1971

Doulton, A. J. F., *The Fighting Cock: Being the History of The 23rd Indian Division 1942–1947*, Aldershot, Gale & Polden, 1956

Draper, A., *Dawns like Thunder: The Retreat from Burma 1942*, London, Leo Cooper, 1987

Dreyer, E. L., *China at War, 1901–1949*, London, Longman, 1995

Dulat, J. S., *Partners in Victory: Mountbatten, Slim and the Campaign in Burma 1942–45*, New Delhi, ABC Publishing, 1983

Dull, P. S., *Battle History of the Imperial Japanese Navy, 1941–45*, Wellingborough, Patrick Stephens, 1978

Dun, S., *Memoirs of the Four-Foot Colonel*, Ithaca, NY, Cornell University, 1980

Duncan, W. E., Ellis, H. F., Banks, R. L., and Scarfe, N. (eds.), *The Royal Artillery Commemoration Book 1939–1945*, London, G. M. Bell and Sons, 1950

Dunlop, E. E., *The War Diaries of Weary Dunlop: Java and the Burma–Thailand Railway 1942–1945*, London, Penguin, 1991

Dunlop, R., *Behind Japanese Lines, With the OSS in Burma*, Chicago, IL, Rand-McNally, 1979

——, *Donovan: America's Master Spy*, Chicago, IL, Rand-McNally, 1982

Dunn, B., *The Bamboo Express*, Chicago, Adams, 1979

Dunn, P. M., *The First Vietnam War*, London, Hurst, 1985

Durnford, S. J. H., *Branch Line to Burma*, London, Macdonald, 1958

Ebury, S., *Weary: The Life of Sir Edward Dunlop*, London, Viking, 1994

Ehrman, J., *Grand Strategy*, vol. 5, *August 1943–September 1944*, London, HMSO, 1956

——, *Grand Strategy*, vol. 6, *September 1944–August 1945*, HMSO, London, 1956

Eldridge, F., *Wrath in Burma: The Uncensored Story of General Stilwell and International Maneuvers in the Far East*, New York, Doubleday, 1946

Elliott, J. G., *A Roll of Honour: The Story of The Indian Army 1939–1945*, London, Cassell, 1965

Elliott, P., *The White Umbrella*, Bangkok, Post, 1999

Ellis, J., *The Sharp End of War: The Fighting Man in World War II*, Newton Abbot, David & Charles, 1980

Elphick, P., *Far Eastern File: The Intelligence War in the Far East 1930–1945*, London, Hodder & Stoughton, 1997

Elsbree, W., *Japan's Role in Southeast Asian Nationalist Movements, 1940–1945*, Cambridge, MA, Harvard University Press, 1953

Ethell, J. L., and Downie, D., *Flying the Hump: In Original World War II Color*, Osceola, WI, Motorbooks, 1995

Evans, C., *A Doctor in XIVth Army: Burma 1944–1945*, Barnsley, Leo Cooper, 1998

Evans E. R., *Combat Cameraman China–Burma–India*, Pittsburgh, PA, Dorrance Publishing, 1996

Evans, G., *Slim as Military Commander*, London, Batsford, 1969

——, *The Desert and The Jungle*, London, William Kimber, 1959

——, *The Johnnies*, London, Cassell, 1964

——, and Brett-James, A., *Imphal: A Flower on Lofty Heights*, London, Macmillan, 1962

Evans, H., *Thimayya of India: A Soldier's Life*, New York, Harcourt, Brace and Co., 1960

Everard, H., *A Mouse in My Pocket: Memoirs of a Fighter Pilot*, Picton, Ontario, privately printed, no date

Evers, C. B., *Death Railway: The Stirring Account of the Building of the Infamous Burma–Siam Railway and the Lives of the Men Who Died Constructing It*, Bangkok, Craftsman, 1993

Fadoyebo, I., *A Stroke of Unbelievable Luck*, ed., D. Killingray, Madison, WI, University of Wisconsin, 1999

Farndale, M., *History of The Royal Regiment of Artillery: The Far East Theatre 1939–1945*, London, Brassey's, 2002

Farrar-Hockley, A., *The Army in the Air. The History of the Army Air Corps*, Stroud, Alan Sutton, 1994

Fay, P. W., *The Forgotten Army: India's Armed Struggle for Independence 1942–1945*, Ann Arbor, MI, University of Michigan Press, 1995

Feis, H., *The China Tangle: The American Effort in China from Pearl Harbor to the Marshall Mission*, Oxford, Oxford University Press, 1953

Fellowes-Gordon, I., *Amiable Assassins: The Story of the Kachin Guerrillas of North Burma*, London, Robert Hale, 1957

——, *The Battle for Naw Seng's Kingdom: General Stilwell's North Burma Campaign and its Aftermath*, London, Leo Cooper, 1971

Fenby, J., *Generalissimo: Chiang Kai-shek and the China He Lost*, London, Free Press, 2003

Ferguson, T., *Desperate Siege: The Battle of Hong Kong*, Toronto, Doubleday, 1980

Fergusson, B., *Beyond the Chindwin: Being an Account of the Adventures of Number Five Column of the Wingate Expedition into Burma, 1943*, Barnsley, Leo Cooper, 1995

——, *Return to Burma*, London, Collins, 1962

——, *The Black Watch and the King's Enemies*, London, Collins, 1950

——, *The Wild Green Earth*, London, Collins, 1946

——, *The Trumpet in the Hall 1930–1958*, London, Collins, 1970

——, *Wavell: Portrait of a Soldier*, London, Collins, 1961

Fielding Hall, H., *Burmese Palace Tales*, Bangkok, White Lotus Press, 1997

——, *The Soul of a People*, Bangkok, Orchid Press, 1995

Fillmore, C., *Prisoner of War: History of the Lost Battalion*, Wichita Falls, TX, Nortex, 1973

Finnerty, J., *All Quiet on the Irrawaddy*, Bognor Regis, New Horizon, 1979

——, *All Hell on the Irrawaddy*, Bognor Regis, Anchor, 1985

Fischer, E. L., *Mission in Burma – The Columban Fathers' Forty-three Years in Kachin Country*, New York, Seabury, 1980

——, *The Chancy War: Winning in China, Burma, and India, in World War Two*, New York, Orion, 1991

Fitzpatrick, G., *No Mandalay No Maymyo (79 Survive): Unique Episodes in British History*, Lewes, Book Guild, 2001

Fitzpatrick, J., *The Bicycle in Wartime: An Illustrated History*, London, Brassey's (UK), 1998

Fletcher, J. S., *Secret War in Burma*, Austell, GA, J. S. Fletcher, 1997

Fong, N. (trans. R. Quan), *Burma War and General Sun Li-Jen*, Hong Kong, Tai Yuan Publishing, 1964

Foot, M. R. D., and Langley, J. M., *M19: The British Secret Service that Fostered Escape and Evasion 1939–1945 and its American Counterpart*, London, The Bodley Head, 1979

Ford, C., *Donovan and the OSS*, London, Robert Hale, 1970

Ford, D., *Flying Tigers: Claire Chennault and the American Volunteer Group*, Washington, DC, Smithsonian Institution, 1991

Fortreath, G. M., *Pipes, Kukris and Nips*, Edinburgh, The Pentland Press, 1991

Forty, G., *Japanese Army Handbook 1939–1945*, Stroud, Sutton Publishing, 1999

——, *XIV Army at War*, Shepperton, Ian Allen, 1982

Foster, R. C. G., *History of the Queen's Royal Regiment*, vol. 8, *1924–1948*, Aldershot, Gale & Polden, 1953

Foster Snow, H. (Nym Wales), *Inside Red China*, New York, Doubleday, 1939

Foucar, E. C. V., *I Lived in Burma*, London, Dennis Dobson, 1956

——, *They Reigned in Mandalay*, London, Dennis Dobson, 1946

*Fourteenth Punjab Regiment: A Short History 1939–1945*, London and Bradford, Lund Humphries, no date.

Fowle, B. W., *Builders and Fighters: U.S. Army Engineers in World War II*, Fort Belvoir, VA, Office of History, United States Army Corps of Engineers, 1992

Fox, F., *The Royal Inniskilling Fusiliers in the Second World War. A Record of the War as Seen by The Royal Inniskilling Fusiliers, Three Battalions of Which Served*, Aldershot, Gale & Polden, 1951

Franks, N. R. L., *First in the Indian Skies*, London, Life Publications, 1981

——, *Hurricanes over the Arakan*, Wellingborough, Patrick Stephens, 1989

——, *Spitfires over the Arakan*, London, William Kimber, 1988

——, *The Air Battle of Imphal*, London, William Kimber, 1985

——, and Richey, P., *Fighter Pilot's Summer*, London, Grub Street, 1993

Freer, A. F., *Nunshigum: On the Road to Mandalay*, Bishop Auckland, The Pentland Press, 1995

Friber, H. D., *West China and the Burma Road*, Minneapolis, MN, Augsburg, 1941

Friend, J., *The Long Trek*, London, Frederick Mueller, 1957

Fujiwara, I. (trans. Akashi Yoji), *F. Kikan: Japanese Army Intelligence Operations in South-east Asia during World War II*, Hong Kong, Heinemann Asia, 1983

Gallagher, O. D., *Retreat in the East*, London, George G. Harrap & Co., 1942

Gamble, B., *Black Sheep One: The Life of Gregory 'Pappy' Boyington*, Novato, CA, Presidio, 2000

Gander, T. J., *Medium Tank M3 to M3A5: General Lee/Grant*, Tanks in Detail 4, Hersham, Ian Allan, 2003

Garforth-Bles, G. D., and Clarke, S. D., *Now or Never – the Story of the 4th Bn. The Madras Regiment in the Burma Campaign 1943–'45*, Calcutta, Thacker's Press, 1945

Gavin, D., *Quiet Jungle – Angry Sea: My Escapes from the Japanese*, Luton, Lennard, 1989

Gaylor, J., *Sons of John Company: The Indian and Pakistan Armies 1903–1991*, Tunbridge Wells, Spellmount, 1992

Geddes, M., *Remembering Weary*, Ringwood, VIC, Viking, 1996

Genovese, J. G., *We Flew without Guns*, Philadelphia, PA, Winston, 1945

George, J. B., *Shots Fired in Anger: A Rifleman's View of the War in the Pacific, 1942–1945, including the Campaign on Guadalcanal and Fighting with Merrill's Marauders in the Jungles of Burma*, Washington, DC, National Rifle Association of America, 1981

Geren, P. F., *Burma Diary*, Deland, FL, Everett Edward Inc., 1968

Gibbs, H. R. K., *Historical Record of the 6th Gurkha Rifles*, vol. 2, Aldershot, Gale & Polden, 1955

Gibson, P. S., *Durban's Lady in White: An Autobiography*, Northaw, Aedificamus Press, 1991

Giffard, G., *Operations in Burma and North-East India from 16th November, 1943 to 22nd June, 1944*, London, HMSO, 1951

——, *Operations in Assam and Burma, 23rd June 1944 to 12th November 1944*, London, HMSO, 1951

Gilbert, M., *Winston S. Churchill*, vol. 7, *Road to Victory, 1941–1945*, London, Heinemann, 1986

Gilchrist, A., *Malaya 1941: The Fall of a Fighting Empire*, London, Robert Hale, 1992

Gill, G. H., *Australia In the War of 1939–1945*, series 2, *Navy*; vol. 2, *Royal Australian Navy 1942–1945*, Canberra, Australian War Memorial, 1968

Gillings, M., *The Shiny Ninth: 9th Battalion The Royal Sussex Regiment 1940–1946*, Wittering, The Pinwe Club, 1986

Gillison, D., *Australia In The War of 1939–1945*, series 3, *Air*, vol. 1, *Royal Australian Air Force 1939–1942*, Canberra, Australian War Memorial, 1962

Gilmore, S., and Davis, P., *A Connecticut Yankee in the 8th Gurkha Rifles: A Burma Memoir*, London, Brassey's, 1995

Girsham, J., with Thomas, L. J., *Burma Jack*, New York, W. W. Norton, 1971

Glass, L., *The Changing of Kings: Memories of Burma 1934–1949*, London, Peter Owen, 1985

Glass, S., *Who Stoled My Mule?*, Athens, OH, The Lawhead Press, 1984

Glover, M., *That Astonishing Infantry: Three Hundred Years of the History of the Royal Welch Fusiliers (23rd Regiment of Foot) 1689–1989*, London, Leo Cooper, 1989

Goette, J. A., *Japan Fights for Asia*, London, MacDonald, 1945

*Golden Arrow: The Story of the 7th Indian Division*, Bombay, G. S. Borker, 1946

Goldingham, J. C., *Letters from John: India Command and S.E.A.C. 1942–1945*, Oxford, Joseph Vincent, 1946

Goodacre, R., *With the Fighting Cock and the Black Cat in India and Burma: A History of 82nd Anti-Tank Regiment (and 82nd Anti-Aircraft/Anti-Tank Regiment) Royal Artillery, 1941–1945*, Banstead, Ray Goodacre, 2002

Gordine, E. T. C., *A Patriot's Boast*, Ilfracombe, Arthur H. Stockwell, 1975

Gordon, E., *Miracle on the River Kwai*, London, Collins, 1963

Gordon, L. A., *Brothers against the Raj: A Biography of Sarat and Subhas Chandra Base*, New York, Columbia University Press, 1990

Gosh, K. K., *The Indian National Army: Second Front of the Indian Independence Movement*, Meerut, Meenakshi, 1969

Gould, T., *Imperial Warriors: Britain and the Gurkhas*, London, Granta, 1999

Goulden, O. A., *From Trombay to Changi's A Helluva Way: The Story of the Arakan Coastal Forces*, London, The Chameleon Press, 1987

——, *The 13th and 14th Fairmile Flotillas in Burma: With the 34th They Sailed from Pembroke Dock, Most Got to Rangoon and Some Got to Bangkok*, London, The Chameleon Press, 1989

Graham Bower, U., *Naga Path*, London, John Murray, 1952

Grant, P., *A Highlander Goes to War: A Memoir 1939–1945*, Edinburgh, The Pentland Press, 1995

Greenlaw, O. J., *The Lady and the Tigers*, New York, E. P. Dutton, 1943

Greenwood, N. (ed.), *Shades of Gold and Green: Anecdotes of Colonial Burmah 1886–1948*, New Delhi, Asian Educational Services, 1998

Gribble, R. H., *Out of the Burma Night. Being the story of a fantastic journey through the wilderness of the Hukawng valley and the forest clad mountain of the Naga tribes people at the time of the Japanese invasion of Burma*, Calcutta, Thacker Spink, 1944

Griffiths, A. L., *Black Cats and Bush Hats: Burma 1943–45, Recalled with Some Laughter and Some Tears by Cpl A. L. Griffiths, 9th Border Rgt., 17th Indian Div., 14th Army*, Harrow, Frank Richards (printers), 1991

Grimsey, R., *Tobruk to Belsen via Burma, A Soldier's Story*, Stowmarket, Capella, 1987

Grounds, T., *Some Letters from Burma: The Story of the 25th Dragoons at War*, Tunbridge Wells, Parapress, 1994

Gruhzit-Hoyt, O., *They Also Served: American Women in World War II*, New York, Birch Lane Press, 1995

Gunning, H., *Borderers in Battle. The War Story of The King's Own Scottish Borderers*, Berwick upon Tweed, Martin's Printing Works, 1948

Gupta, P. S., and Deshpande, A. (eds.), *The British Raj and its Armed Forces, 1857–1939*, New Delhi, Oxford University Press, 2002

Gupta, S. C., *Official History of The Indian Armed Forces in The Second World War 1939–45, History of the Indian Air Force 1933–1945*, New Delhi, Combined Inter-Services Historical Section (India and Pakistan), 1961

Guthrie, D., *Jungle Diary*, London, Macmillan, 1946

Gwyer, J. M. A., and Butler, J. R. M., *Grand Strategy*, vol. 3, *June 1941–August 1942*, London, HMSO, 1964

Gwynne-Timothy, J. R. W., *Burma Liberators – the RCAF in SEAC*, 2 vols, Toronto, Next Level Press, 1991

Haggie, P., *Britannia at Bay: The Defence of the British Empire against Japan 1931–1941*, Oxford, Oxford University Press, 1981

Hahn, E., *The Soong Sisters*, London, Robert Hale, 1942

Hailes, W. L., and Ross, J., *The Jat Regiment: A History of The Regiment 1803–1947*, Bareilly, The Commandant, Jat Regimental Centre, 1965

Hall, D. G. E., *Burma*, London, Hutchinson's University Library, 1956

Hall, E. R., *The Burma–Thailand Railway of Death*, Armadale, NSW, Graphic Books, 1981

Hall, L. G., *The Blue Haze: Incorporating the History of 'A' Force Groups 3 & 5, Burma–Thai Railway 1942–1943*, Kenthurst, NSW, Kangaroo Press, 1996

Hallam, J., *The History of the Lancashire Fusiliers 1939–45*, Stroud, Alan Sutton, 1993

Halley, D., *With Wingate in Burma: Being the Story of the Adventures of Sergeant Tony Aubrey of the King's (Liverpool) Regiment during the 1943 Wingate Expedition to Burma*, London, Hodge, 1945

Hames, H. L., *The Mules' Last Bray: World War II and U.S. Forest Service Reminiscences*, Missoula, MO, Pictorial Histories Publishing Company, 1996

Hamilton, J. A. L., *War Bush: 81 (West African) Division in Burma 1943–1945; North Arakan, Kaladan, Mowdok, Tinma, Myohaung, Chindits 1944, Burma 1943–45*, Norwich, Michael Russell, 2001

Hamilton, N., *Monty: Master of the Battlefield, 1942–44*, London, Hamish Hamilton, 1983

Hamond, R., *The Flame of Freedom: Corporal R. A. S. Pagani's Escape from the Railway of Death*, London, Leo Cooper, 1988

Hampshire, A. C., *Undercover Sailors: Secret Operations of World War II*, London, William Kimber, 1985

——, *On Hazardous Service*, London, William Kimber, 1974

Handel, M. I. (ed.), *Intelligence and Military Operations*, London, Frank Cass, 1990

Hankin, T. F., *From Bootle to Burma*, London, Pen Press, 1996

Hanley, G., *Monsoon Victory*, London, Transworld, 1958

Hardie, R., *The Burma–Siam Railway: The Secret Diary of Dr Robert Hardie, 1942–45*, London, IWM, 1983

Harper, A. F., *Horse and Foot: The Story of a Cavalry Subaltern. India, 1914–1955. A Young Man's Memories*, York, Quack's Books, 1995

Harries, M., and Harries, S., *Soldiers of the Sun: The Rise and Fall of the Imperial Japanese Army 1868–1945*, London, Heinemann, 1991

Harris-Smith, R., *OSS: The Secret History of America's First Central Intelligence Agency*, Berkeley, CA, University of California Press, 1972

Hart, P., *At the Sharp End: From Le Paradis to Kohima, 2nd Battalion The Royal Norfolk Regiment*, Barnsley, Pen and Sword, 1998

Hartcup, G., *Camouflage: A History of Concealment and Deception in War*, Newton Abbot, David & Charles, 1979

Hart-Davis, D., *Peter Fleming: A Biography*, London, Jonathan Cape, 1974

Harvey, G., *British Rule in Burma 1824–1942*, London, Faber and Faber, 1942

Harvey, O., *War Diaries, 1941–45*, ed. J. Harvey, London, Collins, 1978

Haseman, J. B., *The Thai Resistance Movement during the Second World War*, DeKalb, IL, Northern Illinois Center for Southeast Asian Studies, 1978

Hastings, D. J., *Bombay Buccaneers: Memories and Reminiscences of the Royal Indian Navy*, London, British Association for Cemeteries in South East Asia, 1986

——, *The Royal Indian Navy 1612–1950*, Jefferson, NC, McFarland and Co., 1988

Havers, N., *March On! An Infantry Battalion in England, India and Burma 1941–1945*, Worcester, Square One, 1992

Hawley, D., *The Death of Wingate and Subsequent Events*, Braunton, Merlin, 1994

Hay, J., *On Big Flowery Hill: A Soldier's Journal of a Secret Mission into Occupied China, 1942*, Reading, Two Rivers Press, 2000

Hayter, A., *The Second Step*, London, Hodder and Stoughton, 1962

Hayward, D. K. (ed.), *Eagles, Bulldogs and Tigers: History of the 22nd Bomb Squadron in China–Burma–India*, Huntington Beach, CA, 22nd Bomb Squadron Association, 1997

Haywood, A., and Clarke, F. A. S., *The History of the Royal West African Frontier Force*, Aldershot, Gale & Polden, 1964

Hearsey, M., *Land of Chindits and Rubies*, London, M. A. Leverston-Allen, 1982

Heath, I., *The North-East Frontier 1837–1901*, Men-at-Arms 324, Oxford, Osprey, 1999

Heathcote, T. A., *The Indian Army: The Garrison of British Imperial India 1822–1922*, Newton Abbot, David and Charles, 1974

——, *The Military in British India: The Development of British Land Forces in South Asia, 1600–1947*, Manchester History of the British Army Series, Manchester University Press, 1995

Hedley, J., *Jungle Fighter: Infantry Officer, Chindit and S. O. E. Agent in Burma, 1941–1945*, Brighton, Tom Donovan, 1996

Helsdon Thomas, J., *Wings over Burma*, Bognor Regis, New Horizon, 1984

Hemingway, K., *Wings over Burma*, London, Quality Press, 1944

Henderson, W., *From China Burma India to the Kwai*, Waco, TX, Texian Press, 1991

Hengshoon, H., *Green Hell: Unconventional Warfare in the CBI*, Huntington Beach, CA, B & L Lithograph, 2000

Hennecker, F. V., *Gentle Heroes*, Bundaberg, QLD, Margaret and Hans van Hennecker, 1990

Henry, M., *The US Army in World War II (I) The Pacific*, Men-at-Arms 342, Oxford, Osprey, 2000

Henslow, J., *A Sapper in the Forgotten Army*, Petersfield, J. Henslow, 1986

Hess, G. R., *America Encounters India, 1941–1947*, Baltimore, MD, Johns Hopkins University Press, 1971

Hickey, M., *The Unforgettable Army: Slim's XIVth Army in Burma*, Staplehurst, Spellmount, 1992

Hicks, G., *The Comfort Women: Japan's Brutal Regime of Enforced Prostitution in the Second World War*, New York, W. W. Norton, 1994

Higham, R., and Williams, C. (eds.), *Flying Combat Aircraft of the USAAF and USAF*, vol. 2, Ames, IO, Iowa State University Press, 1978

Hill, J., *China Dragons: A Rifle Company at War, Burma 1944–1945*, London, Blandford, 1991

Hilsman, R., *American Guerrilla: My War behind Enemy Lines*, Washington, DC. Brassey's (US), 1990

Hingston, W., *Never Give Up, being Volume V, The History of the King's Own Yorkshire Light Infantry 1919–1942*, London and Bradford, Lund Humphries, 1950

Hino, A., *Hana to Heitai*, Tokyo, Shinchosha, 1953

Hiscox, N. G., *Under Two Flags*, Edinburgh, The Pentland Press, 1997

*History of The East Lancashire Regiment in the War 1939–1945*, Manchester, H. Rawson and Co., 1953

*History of the 5th Royal Gurkha Rifles (Frontier Force)*, vol. 2, *1929–1947*, Aldershot, Gale & Polden, 1956

Hobbs, J. E. O., *Burma Remembered*, Worthing, J. E. O. Hobbs, 1985

Hodson, J. L., *War in the Sun*, London, Victor Gollancz, 1942

Hogan, D. W., *India-Burma (The U.S. Army Campaigns of World War II)*, Washington, DC, Government Printing Office, 1992

——, *U.S. Army Special Operations in World War II*, Collingdale, PA, Diane Publishing Company, 1992

Holden-Reid, B., and White, J. (eds,), *American Studies: Essays in Honour of Marcus Cunliffe*, Basingstoke, Macmillan, 1991

Holmes, L. G., *Four Thousand Bowls of Rice: A Prisoner of War Comes Home*, St Leonard's, NSW, Allen & Unwin, 1993

Hookway, J. D. (ed.), *M & R: A Regimental History of the Sikh Light Infantry, 1941–1947*, Bath, J. D. Hookway, 1999

Hopkins, J. E. T., with Jones, J. M., *Spearhead: A Complete History of Merrill's Marauders Rangers*, Baltimore, MD, Galahad Press, 1999

Horn, M., *'Introducing Terry and the Pirates': Terry and the Pirates China Journey*, New York, Gelman-Nostalgia, 1977

Horner, H., *No Tigers in our Jungle: Life in the Royal Air Force Regiment in South-East Asia Command 1943–1945*, London, Excalibur Press, 1982

Hough, R., *Mountbatten: Hero of our Time*, London, Weidenfeld & Nicolson, 1980

Houghton Brodrick, A., *Beyond the Burma Road*, London, Hutchinson, 1944

Howard M., *Grand Strategy*, vol. 4, *August 1942–September 1943*, London, HMSO, 1972

——, *British Intelligence in the Second World War*, vol. 5, *Strategic Deception*, London, HMSO, 1990

Howarth, H., *Where Fate Leads*, Ross Anderson Publications, 1983

Hoyt, E. P., *Merrill's Marauders*, Los Angeles, CA, Pinnacle, 1980

Ho Y-c, *The Big Circle*, New York, Exposition Press, 1948

Hsiung, J. C., and Levine, S. I., *China's Bitter Victory: The War with Japan, 1937–1945*, Armonk, NY, M. E. Sharpe, 1993

Hsu Long-hsuen and Chang M-k (trans. Wen H-l), *History of the Sino-Japanese War (1937–1945)*, Taipei, Chung Win, 1971

Htin, A., *The Stricken Peacock: Anglo-Burmese Relations 1752–1948*, The Hague, Martin Nijhoff, 1952

Hudson, J., *Sunset in the East: Fighting against the Japanese through the Siege of Imphal and alongside them in Java 1943–1946*, Barnsley, Leo Cooper, 2002

Hudson, L., *The Rats of Rangoon*, London, Leo Cooper, 1987

Hulsbus, J., *En de Zon Werd Rood: De Ondergang van Nederlands Indië en de Hel van Birma Spoorweg, 1941–1945*, Baam, Hollondia, 1986

Humphreys, R., *To Stop a Rising Sun: Reminiscences of Wartime in India and Burma*, Stroud, Alan Sutton, 1996

Hunt, G., *The Forgotten Land*, London, Geoffrey Bles, 1967

Hunt, R., *Shadowless Lamp: Memoirs of an RAMC Surgeon*, London, William Kimber, 1971

Hunter, C. N., *Galahad*, San Antonio, TX, Naylor, 1963

Hutton, J. H., *The Angami Nagas*, London, Macmillan, 1924

Huxford, H. J., *History of the 8th Gurkha Rifles*, Aldershot, Gale & Polden, 1952

Ienaga, S., *Japan's Last War*, Oxford, Blackwell's, 1979

Ike, N., *Japan's Decision for War: Records of the 1941 Policy Conferences*, Stanford, CA, Stanford University Press, 1967

*India's Fighting Men*, New Delhi, Interservices Public Relations Directorate, 1945

Ingelse, T., *The Story of a Railway: Thailand–Burma Railway 1942–45*, The Hague, Museum voor het Onderwijs, 1983

Innes, D., *Beaufighters over Burma: No. 27 Squadron, RAF, 1942–45*, Poole, Blandford Press, 1985

Irwin, A., *Burmese Outpost*, London, Collins, 1945

Izumiya, T. (trans. U Tun Aung Chain), *The Minami Organ*, Rangoon, Universities Press, 1981

Jack, I. M., *A Soldier's Tale*, Wedmore, Stanley Castle, 1995

Jacob, A., *A Traveller's War: A Journey to the Wars in Africa, India and Russia*, London, Collins, 1944

Jacobs, V. K., *The Woodpecker Story: As Told by Members of No. 136 (Fighter) Squadron RAF 'The Woodpeckers'*, Edinburgh, The Pentland Press, 1994

Jaffé, S., and Jaffé, L., *Chinthe Women: Women's Auxiliary Service Burma 1942–1946*, Chipping Norton, Chinthe Women, 2001

Jagota, S., *History of the Corps of Electrical and Mechanical Engineers*, New Delhi, The Corps of Electrical and Mechanical Engineers, 1981

Jahne, M., *From Red Gums to Bamboo*, Greensborough, VIC, Wordweavers, 2001

James, H., *Across the Threshold of Battle: Behind Japanese Lines with Wingate's Chindits, Burma 1943*, Lewes, Book Guild, 1993

James, W., *They Sent Me an Invitation So I Went to WWII*, Houston, TX, Emerald Ink Publishing, 1998

Jeffrey, W. F., *Sunbeams like Swords*, London, Hodder and Stoughton, 1951

Jeffreys, A., *British Infantryman in the Far East 1941–1945*, Warrior 66, Oxford, Osprey, 2003

Jeffreys-Jones, R., and Lownie, A. (eds.), *North American Spies: New Revisionist Essays*, Lawrence, KS, University of Kansas Press, 1991

Jervois, W. J., *The History of the Northamptonshire Regiment: 1934–1948*, Northampton, Northamptonshire Regimental History Committee, 1953

Johnson, C. D., *The Forgotten Army's Box of Lions*, Norwich, C. D. Johnson, 2001

Johnson, E., *A Brief History of the Machine-Gun Battalion, The Jat Regiment 1941–46*, Bangalore, Higginbothams, 1947

Johnson, F. A., *P-40 Warhawk*, Osceola, WI, Motorbooks, 1999

Johnson, W. G., and van Cleve, D. (eds.), *Chennault's Flying Tigers A Pictorial History of the American Volunteer Group (The Original Flying Tigers) China Air Task Force 14th Air Force 1941–1945*, vol. 1, Silver Bay, MN, 14th Air Force Association, 1982

Jones, C. B., *Not Forgetting the Elephants*, Lewes, Book Guild, 1983

Jones, F. C., *Japan's New Order in East Asia: Its Rise and Fall 1937–1945*, New York, AMS Press, 1978

Jones, F. C., Borton, H., and Pearn, B. R., *The Far East, 1942–1946*, Oxford, Oxford University Press, 1955

Jones, L. R., *A Pilot's Story of Flying in War and Peace*, Glebe, NSW, Fast Books, 1996

Jordan, R., *To Burma Skies and Beyond: An Airman's Story*, London, Janus Publishing Company, 1995

Jowett, P., *The Japanese Army 1931–45 (2)*, Men-at-Arms 369, Oxford, Osprey, 2002

——, *Chinese Civil War Armies 1911–49*, Men-at-Arms 306, London, Osprey, 1997

Judson, E., *Adoniram Judson, D. D., His Life and Labours*, London, Hodder and Stoughton, 1883

Kadel, R. J. (ed.), *'Where I Came in … ' in China, Burma, India*, Paducah, KY, Turner, 1986

Kan, W., *Burmadagboek 1942–1945*, Amsterdam, Arbeiderspers, 1986

Kappel, R. F., *Whispering Wings over Burma; The Jungle Angles*, Elk Creek, NE, R. F. Kappel, 1998

Karaka, D. F., *With The Fourteenth Army*, London, Dorothy Crisp, 1945

Karr, S. E., *Traveler of the Crossroads: The Life of Adventurer Nicol Smith*, Jacksonville, OR, Log Cabin, 1996

Kase, T., *Eclipse of the Rising Sun*, ed. D. Nelson, London, Jonathan Cape, 1951

Kaul, B. M., *The Untold Story*, Bombay, Allied Publishers, 1967

Keegan J. (ed.), *Churchill's Generals*, London, Weidenfeld and Nicolson, 1991

Kelly, D., *Kelly's Burma Campaign: Letters from the Chin Hills*, London, Tiddim Press, 2003

Kemp, J. C., *The History of The Royal Scots Fusiliers 1919–1959*, Glasgow, Robert MacLehose & Co., The University Press, Glasgow, for The Royal Scots Fusiliers, 1963

Kemp, P. K., *History of The Royal Norfolk Regiment 1919–1951*, vol. 3, Norwich, Regimental Association of The Royal Norfolk Regiment, 1953

——, and Graves, J., *The Red Dragon: The Story of The Royal Welch Fusiliers 1919–1945*, Aldershot, Gale & Polden, 1960

Kennedy, J., *The Business of War*, London, Hutchinson, 1957

Kendrick, N. C. E., *The Story of The Wiltshire Regiment (Duke of Edinburgh's) The 62nd and 99th Foot (1756–1959) The Militia and The Territorials, The Service Battalions and All Those Others Who Have Served or Been Affiliated with The Moonrakers*, Aldershot, Gale & Polden, 1963

Kershaw, G. F., *Tracks of Death: The Burma–Siam Railway*, Lewes, Book Guild, 1992

Khaing, M. M., *Burmese Family*, London, Longmans, 1946

Khan, S. N., *My Memories of I.N.A. and its Netaji*, Delhi, Rajkamal, 1946

Khera, P. N., *The Official History of the Indian Armed Forces in the Second World War: Technical Services – Ordnance and I.E.M.E.*, Delhi, Combined Inter-Services Historical Section, India and Pakistan, 1962

Khin, U., *U Hla Pe's Narrative of the Japanese Occupation of Burma*, Ithaca, NY, Cornell University Press, 1961

Kiani, M. Z., *India's Freedom Struggle and the Great INA*, New Delhi, Reliance, 1994

Killingray, D., and Omissi, D., *Guardians of Empire: The Armed Forces of the Colonial Powers c. 1700–1964*, Manchester, Manchester University Press, 1999

King, E. J., and Whitehill, W. M., *Fleet Admiral King: A Naval Record*, New York, W. W. Norton, 1952

King-Clark, R., *The Battle for Kohima 1944: The Narrative of The 2nd Battalion, The Manchester Regiment, the Machine Gun Battalion of the British 2nd Division*, Cheshire, Fleur-de-Lys Publishing, 1995

Kinvig, C. A., *River Kwai Railway: The Story of the Burma–Siam Railroad*, London, Brassey's (UK), 1992

——, *Death Railway*, London, Pan/Ballantine, 1973

Kirby, S. W., *The War against Japan*, vol. 1, *The Loss of Singapore*, London, HMSO, 1957

——, *The War against Japan*, vol. 2, *India's Most Dangerous Hour*, London, HMSO, 1958

——, *The War against Japan*, vol. 3, *The Decisive Battles*, London, HMSO, 1961

——, *The War against Japan*, vol. 4, *The Reconquest of Burma*, London, HMSO, 1965

——, *The War against Japan*, vol. 5, *The Surrender of Japan*, London, HMSO, 1969

Knight, C. R. B., *Historical Records of The Buffs Royal East Kent Regiment (3rd Foot) Formerly Designated The Holland Regiment and Prince George of Denmark's Regiment 1919–1948*, London, The Medici Society, 1951

Koenig, W. J., *Over the Hump: Airlift to China*, London, Pan/Ballantine, 1972

Krasotka, P. H. (ed.), *Food Supplies and the Japanese Occupation in South-East Asia*, Basingstoke, Macmillan, 1998

La Forte, R. S., and Marcello, R. E. (eds), *Building the Death Railway: The Ordeal of American POWs in Burma, 1942–1945*, Wilmington, DE, Scholarly Resources Inc., 1992

Lackersteen, D., *Diamonds in the Dust: Tales of the Evacuation of Burma*, Allahabad, Kitabistan, 1944

Lal, P. C., *My Years with the IAF*, New Delhi, Lancer International, 1986

Lamont-Brown, R., *Kempeitai: Japan's Dreaded Military Police*, Stroud, Sutton, 1998

Lane, A., *When You Go Home*, Stockport, Arthur Lane, 1993

Langer, W., *In and Out of the Ivory Tower*, New York, Watson, 1977

Lapsley, E., *A Memory of David Lapsley: October 13, 1919–January 2, 1944*, New Haven, CT, E. Lapsley, 1951

Larkin, E., *Secret Histories: A Journey through Burma Today in the Company of George Orwell*, London, John Murray, 2004

Laurie, W. F. B., *The Second Burmese War: A Narrative of Operations at Rangoon*, Bangkok, Orchid Press, 2002

Law, W. C. (ed.), *Chinthe: Canadians over Burma*, Victoria, BC, Diggen-Hibben (printers), no date

Lawford, J. P., and Catto, W. E., *Solah Punjab*, Aldershot, Gale & Polden, 1967

Lawson, A. A., *Life in the Burmese Jungle*, Lewes, Book Guild, 1983

Le Butt, P., *We Too Can Die: Tales of the Chindits*, London, Robert Anscombe, 1947

Leasor, J., *The Marine from Mandalay*, London, House of Stratus, 2001

Leathart, S., *With the Gurkhas: India, Burma, Singapore, Malaya, Indonesia, 1940–1959*, Edinburgh, The Pentland Press, 1996

Lebra, J., *Jungle Alliance: Japan and the Indian National Army*, Singapore, Donald Moore for Asia Pacific Press, 1971

Lee, C-y., *A Corner of Heaven: My Burmese Reminiscences*, London, W. H. Allen, 1960

Lee, U., *United States Army in World War II, Special Studies, The Employment of Negro Troops*, Washington, DC, Office of The Chief of Military History, United States Army, 1966

Leese, O., *Operations in Burma from 12th November 1944 to 15th August 1945*, London, HMSO, 1951

Leffelaar, H. L., and van Witsen, E., *Werkers aan de Burma-Spoorweg: Ledere Twee Dwarsliggers een Mensenleven, 414 Kilometer en 200000 Doden*, Wever, Franeker, 1982

Leicester, L. A., *Flights into the Night: Reminiscences of a World War Two RAF Wellington Pilot*, Manchester, Crécy, 2000

Leonard, H., *Burma Mission: Company 'D' 13th Mtn Med Bn.*, Allentown, PA, Herman Leonard, 1946

Lever, J. C., *The Sowar and the Jawan: The Soldiers of the Former Indian Army and their Homelands*, Ilfracombe, Arthur H. Stockwell, 1981

Levett, R., *The Girls*, Hawthorn, VIC, N. S. Hudson, 1997

Lewin, R., *Slim: The Standardbearer*, London, Leo Cooper, 1976

———, *The Chief: Field Marshal Lord Wavell Commander-in-Chief and Viceroy 1939–1947*, London, Hutchinson, 1980

Lewis, A., *Letters to My Wife*, Bridgend, Seren Books, 1989

*Lewisham Gunners: A Centenary History of 291st (4th London) Field Regiment R. A. (T. A.) formerly 2nd Kent R. G. A. (Volunteers)*, Chatham, W. and J. Mackay & Co., 1962

Leyin, J., *Tell Them of Us: The Forgotten Army – Burma*, Stanford-le-Hope, Lejins, 2000

Liang C-t., *General Stilwell in China 1942–44: The Full Story*, New York, St John's University Press, 1972

Liddell Hart, B. H. (ed.), *The Rommel Papers*, London, Collins, 1953

Lin, Y., *Vigil of a Nation*, London, Heinemann, 1946

Lindsay, O., *The Lasting Honour: The Fall of Hong Kong 1941*, London, Hamish Hamilton, 1978

Lindsell, R. A., *A Short History of Queen Victoria's Own Madras Sappers and Miners during World War II 1939–1945*, Bangalore, Hosali Press, 1947

Lindo, J., *From Dingle to Delhi*, Liverpool, Handel Publishing, no date

Litner, B., *Burma in Revolt: Opium and Insurgency since 1948*, Boulder, CO, Westview Press, 1994

Littlejohn, J. G., *Royal Air Force Days: Never a Dull Moment*, London, Avon, 1998

Liu, F. F., *A Military History of Modern China 1924–1949*, Princeton, NJ, Princeton University Press, 1956

Lockhart, R. B., *The Marines Were There: The Story of the Royal Marines in the Second World War*, London, Putnam, 1950

Lohbeck, D., *Patrick J. Hurley*, Chicago, IL, Henry Regnery, 1956

Lomax, C. E. N., *The History of The Welch Regiment 1919–1951*, Cardiff, Western Mail and Echo, 1952

Lomax, E., *The Railway Man*, London, Vintage, 1996

Lory, H., *Japan's Military Masters*, New York, Viking Press, 1943

Lowe, P., *Great Britain and the Origins of the Pacific War: A Study of British Policy in East Asia 1937–1941*, Oxford, Clarendon Press, 1977

Lowry, M. A., *An Infantry Company in Arakan and Kohima*, Aldershot, Gale & Polden, 1950

Lucas-Phillips, C. E., *Springboard to Victory*, London, William Heinemann 1966

——, *The Raiders of Arakan*, London, William Heinemann, 1971

Lumiere, C., *Red Runs the River Kwai*, West Palm Beach, FL, Flamingo, 1976

Lunt, J., *'Hell of a Licking': The Retreat from Burma 1941–2*, London, Collins, 1986

——, *Charge to Glory*, New York, Harcourt Brace, 1960

——, *Imperial Sunset: Frontier Soldiering in the 20th Century*, London, Macdonald, 1981

——, *Jai Sixth! The Story of the 6th Queen Elizabeth's Own Gurkha Rifles 1817–1994*, London, Leo Cooper, 1994

Lyall Grant, I., *Burma: The Turning Point*, Chichester, The Zampi Press, 1993

——, and Tamayama, K., *Burma 1942: The Japanese Invasion – Both Sides Tell the Story of a Savage Jungle War*, Chichester, The Zampi Press, 1999

Lydall, E., *Enough of Action*, Lewes, Book Guild, 1996

Lyman, R., *Slim, Master of War: Burma and the Birth of Modern Warfare*, London, Constable & Robinson, 2004

McBain, S. W., *A Regiment at War: The Royal Scots (The Royal Regiment) 1939–1945 (including the Canadian Scottish Regiment)*, Edinburgh, The Pentland Press, 1988

McCann, J., *Echoes of Kohima*, Oldham, John McCann, 1989

McClelland, J., *Names and Particulars of all Australians Who Died While Prisoners of War on the Burma Death Railway and Who are Buried in the Thanbyuzant War Cemetery, Burma*, Silverdale, NSW, J. McClelland Research, 1990

——, *Names and Particulars of all Australians Who Died While Prisoners of War on the Burma Death Railway and Who are Buried in the Kanchanaburi War Cemetery, Thailand*, Silverdale, NSW, J. McClelland Research, 1990

McCleod, D., *History of the 130th Field Regiment, Royal Artillery and its Burma Campaign*, Billingham, D. McCleod, 1996

McCormack, G., and Nelson, H. (eds), *The Burma–Thailand Railway: Memory and History*, St Leonard's NSW, Allen & Unwin, 1993

McCrae, A., et al., *Tales of Burma*, Paisley, James Paton, 1981

——, and Prentice, A., *Irrawaddy Flotilla*, Paisley, James Paton, 1978

Macdonald, J. F., *The War History of Southern Rhodesia*, vol. 2, Salisbury, Government of Southern Rhodesia, 1950

Macdonald, R., *Dawn like Thunder*, London, Hodder and Stoughton, 1944

MacDonald Fraser, G., *Quartered Safe Out Here: A Recollection of the War in Burma*, London, HarperCollins, 1995

McEnery, J. H., *Epilogue in Burma, 1945–48: The Military Dimension of British Withdrawal*, Tunbridge Wells, Spellmount, 1990

MacFetridge, C. H. T., and Warren, J. P., (eds.), *Tales of the Mountain Gunners*, London and Edinburgh, William Blackwood and Sons, 1973

McGee, G. A., *The History of the 2nd Battalion, Merrill's Marauders: Northern Burma Campaign of 1944*, Braunfels, TX, G. A. McGee, 1987

McGeoch, I., *The Princely Sailor: Mountbatten of Burma*, London, Brassey's, 1996

MacHorton, I., and Maule, H., *Safer than a Known Way: One Man's Epic Struggle against Japanese and Jungle*, London, Odhams, 1958

McIntosh, E. P., *Sisterhood of Spies: The Women of the OSS*, Annapolis, MD, Naval Institute Press, 1998

McIntyre, D., *Fighting Admiral: The Life and Battles of Admiral of the Fleet Sir James Somerville*, London, Evans Brothers, 1961

McIssac, D. (ed.), *The United States Strategic Bombing Survey*, vols 7–10, New York, Garland, 1976

Mackay, J. N., *A History of the 4th Prince of Wales's Own Gurkha Rifles*, vol. 3, *1938–1948*, London and Edinburgh, William Blackwood and Sons, 1952

——, *History of the 7th Duke of Edinburgh's Own Gurkha Rifles*, London and Edinburgh, William Blackwood and Sons, 1962

McKay, R. R., *The Last of the Dozen*, Edinburgh, The Pentland Press, 1996

McKelvie, R., *The War in Burma*, London, Methuen, 1948

Mackenzie, C., *Eastern Epic*, vol. 1, *September 1939–March 1943, Defence*, London, Chatto and Windus, 1951

——, *All over the Place: Fifty Thousand Miles by Sea, Air, Road and Rail*, London, Chatto and Windus, 1949

Mackenzie, K. P., *Operation Rangoon Jail*, London, Cristopher Johnson, 1954

Mackenzie, T., *44 (R.M.) Commando, Achnacarry to the Arakan: A Diary of the Commando at War, August 1943 to March 1947*, Brighton, Tom Donovan, 1996

McKie, R., *Echoes from Forgotten Wars*, Sydney, William Collins, 1980

McLaggan, D., *The Will to Survive: A Private's View as a P.O.W.*, Kenthurst, NSW, Kangaroo Press, 1995

MacLaren, R., *Canadians behind Enemy Lines, 1939–1945*, Vancouver, BC, University of British Columbia Press, 1981

McPhedran, C., *White Butterflies*, Canberra, Pandanus Books, 2002

McWhirter, N., and McWhirter, R. (eds.), *The Guinness Book of Records*, Enfield, Guinness Superlatives, 1972

Magener, R. (trans. B. Creighton), *Prisoner's Bluff*, London, Rupert Hart-Davis, 1954

Maikap, S. C., *Netaji Subhas Chandra Bose and Indian War of Independence*, Calcutta, Punascha, 1998

Mains, A. A., *Field Security: Very Ordinary Intelligence*, Chippenham, Picton, 1992

——, *Sandhurst to the Khyber 1932–1940: Pre-war Service with Gurkhas*, Durham, Memoir Club, 1999

——, *The Retreat from Burma: An Intelligence Officer's Personal Story*, London, W. Foulsham, 1973

Majumdar, B. N., *Administration in The Burma Campaign (1941–1945)*, Delhi, Clifton & Co., 1952

Mankekar, D. R., *Leaves from a War Reporter's Diary*, New Delhi, Vikas Publishing, 1977

Markham, G., *Japanese Infantry Weapons of World War Two*, London, Arms and Armour Press, 1976

Marston, D. P., *Phoenix from the Ashes: The Indian Army in the Burma Campaign*, Westport, CT, Praeger, 2003

Martin, J. G., *It Began at Imphal: The Combat Cargo Story*, Manhattan, KS, Sunflower University Press, 1988

——, *Through Hell's Gate to Shanghai: History of the 10th Combat Cargo Squadron, 3rd Combat Cargo Group, CBI Theater, 1944–1946*, Athens, OH, Lawhead, 1983

Martin, T. A., *The Essex Regiment 1929–1950*, Brentwood, Essex Regiment Association, 1952

Maslen-Jones, E. W., *Fire by Order: Recollections of Service with 656 Air Observation Post Squadron in Burma*, Barnsley, Leo Cooper, 1997

Mason, Paul D., *Nicolson VC*, Ashford, Geerings, 1991

Mason, Philip, *A Matter of Honour: An Account of The Indian Army, its Officers and Men*, London, Jonathan Cape, 1974

Masters, J., *Bugles and a Tiger: A Personal Adventure*, London, Michael Joseph, 1956

——, *The Road past Mandalay*, London, Michael Joseph, 1961

Matthews, G., *The Re-conquest of Burma 1943–1945*, Aldershot, Gale & Polden, 1966

Maule, H., *Spearhead General: The Epic Story of General Sir Frank Messervy, and his Men in Eritrea, North Africa and Burma*, London, Odhams, 1961

Maung Maung, Dr, *Aung San of Burma*, The Hague, Marthinus Nijhoff, 1962

——, *A Trial in Burma: The Assassination of Aung San*, The Hague, Martinus Nijhoff, 1962

——, *To a Soldier Son*, Rangoon, Sarpay Beikman, 1974

Maung Maung, U., *Burmese Nationalist Movements 1940–1948*, Edinburgh, Kiscadale, 1989

Maurice, D., *From Cradle to War: 'My First Three Decades, 1915–1945'*, Edinburgh, The Pentland Press, 1998

Maxwell, R. M., *Desperate Encounters: Stories of The 5th Royal Gurkha Rifles of the Punjab Frontier Force*, Edinburgh, The Pentland Press, 1986

Maybury, M., *Heaven-Born in Burma*, vol. 1, *The Daily Round*, Castle Cary, Folio Hadspen, 1984

——, *Heaven-Born in Burma*, vol. 2, *Flight of the Heaven-Born*, Castle Cary, Folio Hadspen, 1985

——, *Heaven-Born in Burma*, vol. 3, *Swan-Song of the Heaven-Born*, Castle Cary, Folio Hadspen, 1986

Mayes Newhall, S., *The Devil in God's Old Man*, New York, W. W. Norton, 1969

Mead, P., *Wingate and the Historians*, Braunton, Merlin, 1987

Mehra, K. C., *A History of The Army Ordnance Corps 1775–1974 (A Saga of Two Centuries)*, Allahabad, Wheeler, 1990

Meisel, J. V., *72nd Airdrome Squadron: Firsr Air Commando Group*, Tucson, AZ, J. V. Meisel, 1994

Mellors, J., *Shots in the Dark*, London, Magazine Editions, 1974

Melnyk, T. W., *Canadian Flying Operations in South-East Asia 1941–1945*, Ottawa, Ministry of Supply and Services Canada, 1976

Menezes, S. L., *Fidelity and Honour: The Indian Army from the Seventeenth to the Twenty-First Century*, New Delhi, Viking, 1993

Mennim, A. M., *An Indian Odyssey*, York, Croft Press, 1997

*Merrill's Marauders*, Washington, DC, US War Department, History Section, 1945

Michie, A., *Retreat to Victory*, London, George Allen and Unwin, 1942

Miles, M., *A Different Kind of War*, New York, Doubleday, 1967

Miles, W., *The Life of a Regiment*, vol. 5, *The Gordon Highlanders 1919–1945*, Aberdeen, Aberdeen University Press, 1961

Miller, E. J., *War Plan Orange: The U.S. Strategy to Defeat Japan, 1897–1945*, Annapolis, VA, Naval Institute Press, 1991

Milliken, A., *From the Kwai to the Kingdom*, Basingstoke, Marshalls, 1985

Mills, R. M., *Doctor's Diary and Memoir; Pond's Party, F Force, Thai–Burma Railway*, New Lambton, NSW, R. M. Mills, 1994

Mitchell, H., *Against the Odds*, Lewes, Book Guild, 1990

Mitchell, J. (ed.), *The Moon Seems Upside Down: Letters of Love and War; Letters of Arthur Alan Mitchell 1939–1945*, St Leonard's, NSW, Allen & Unwin, 1995

Moharir, V. J., *History of the Army Service Corps (1939–1946)*, New Delhi, Sterling, 1979

Molesworth, C., *P-40 Warhawk Aces of the CBI*, Oxford, Osprey, 2000

Molesworth, G., *The History of The Somerset Light Infantry (Prince Albert's) 1919–1945*, Taunton, Regimental History Committee, 1951

Molloy, S., *Burma Bride*, Knebworth, Able, no date.

Moon, P. (ed.), *Wavell: The Viceroy's Journal*, London, Oxford University Press, 1973

Moon, T. N., and Eifler, C. F., *The Deadliest Colonel*, New York, Vantage, 1975

Moorehouse, G., *India Britannica*, London, Harvill Press, 1983

Morris, D. G., *Beyond the Irrawaddy and the Salween: RAF Special Duty Missions in the South East Asia Theatre of War 1944–45*, Gardenvale, VIC, Mostly Unsung Military History Research and Publications, 1996

Morris, S. M. (ed.), *Long Ago, Far Away: The Burma Diaries of Doris Sarah Eastman*, London, Minerva, 1994

Morrison, I., *Grandfather Longlegs: The Life and Gallant Death of Major H. P. Seagrim G.C., D.S.O., M.B.E.*, London, Faber and Faber, 1947

Moscotti, A. D., *British Policy and the Nationalist Movement in Burma, 1917–37*, Honolulu, University of Hawaii Press, 1974

Moser, D., *China–Burma–India*, Alexandria, VA, Time-Life, 1978

Mosley, L., *Gideon Goes to War: The Story of Major-General Orde Charles Wingate*, London, A. Barker, 1955

——, *Hirohito: Emperor of Japan*, London, Weidenfeld and Nicolson, 1966

Motley, M. P. (ed.), *The Invisible Soldier: The Experience of the Black Soldier, World War II*, Detroit, MI, Wayne State University Press, 1975

Mountbatten of Burma, Earl, *Report to the Combined Chiefs of Staff – South-East Asia 1943–1945*, London, HMSO, 1951

Moxon, O., *Bitter Monsoon: The Memoirs of a Fighter Pilot*, London, Robert Hale, 1955

Moyse-Bartlett, H., *King's African Rifles. A Study of the Military History of East and Central Africa, 1890–1945*, Aldershot, Gale & Polden, 1956

Muir, A., *The First of Foot: The History of The Royal Scots (The Royal Regiment)*, Edinburgh, The Royal Scots History Committee, 1961

Mullaly, B. R., *Bugle and Kukri. The Story of the 10th Princess Mary's Own Gurkha Rifles*, London and Edinburgh, William Blackwood and Sons, 1957

——, *The South Lancashire Regiment The Prince of Wales's Volunteers*, Bristol, The White Swan Press, no date

Munday, E., *USAAF Bomber Units Pacific 1941–45*, Airwar 22, London, Osprey, 1979

Munkman, J., *The River Posts*, Lewes, The Book Guild, 1992

Munn, A. W., *A Fragment of Life (The Burma Episode)*, London, Avon, 1996

Munn, M., *Stars at War*, London, Robson, 1996

Murphy, R. L., *Last Viceroys: The Life and Times of Rear-Admiral the Earl of Mountbatten of Burma ...*, London, Jarrolds, 1949

Murrell, E., *For Your Tomorrow*, Dorchester, Plush Publishing, 1999

Nalder, R. F. H., *The History of British Army Signals in the Second World War*, London, Royal Signals Institution, 1953

——, *The Royal Corps of Signals: A History of its Antecedents and Development (circa 1800–1955)*, London, Royal Signals Institution, 1958

Narain, P., *Subedar to Field Marshal*, New Delhi, Monas Publications, 1999

Naw, A., *Aung San and the Struggle for Burmese Independence*, Chiang Mai, Silkworm, 2001

Nelson, H., *Prisoners of War: Australians under Nippon*, Crow's Nest, NSW, ABC Enterprises, 1990

Nelson, M. H., *Diary of a Bomb Squadron*, Cedar Rapids, UT, Rollographics, 1997

Nicholls, C. S., *The Record, History of the Eleventh Bombardment Squadron (M), Three Hundred Forty-First Bombardment Group (M), Fourteenth Air Force, United States Air Forces*, Nashville, TN, Harris, 1945

Nicholson, W. N., *The Suffolk Regiment 1929 to 1946*, Ipswich, East Anglian Magazine, no date.

Nickerson, M. C., *Burma Interlude*, Honolulu, HA, Topgallant, 1989

Nicolson, N., *Alex: The Life of Field Marshal Earl Alexander of Tunis*, London, Weidenfeld and Nicolson, 1973

Nield, E., *With Pegasus in India: The Story of 153 Gurkha Parachute Battalion*, Nashville, TN, The Battery Press, no date

*Nippon Very Sorry – Many Men Must Die: Submission to the United Nations Commission on Human Rights (ECOSOC Resolution 1503); Authorised by the Queensland Ex-POW Reparation Committee*, Brisbane, Boolarong Publications, 1990

Nu, U (trans. J. S. Furnivall), *Burma under the Japanese: Pictures and Portraits*, London, Macmillan, 1954

——, *Saturday's Son*, New Haven, CT, Yale Univesity Press, 1975

Nunneley, J. (ed.), *Tales from the Burma Campaign 1942–1945*, Petersham, Burma Campaign Fellowship Group, 1998

——, *Tales From the King's African Rifles: A Last Flourish of Empire*, London, Cassell, 2000

Nussbaum, C., *Chaplain on the River Kwai: The Story of a Prisoner of War*, New York, Shapolsky, 1988

O'Brien, T., *Out of the Blue: A Pilot with the Chindits*, London, Collins, 1984

——, *The Moonlight War: The Story of Clandestine Operations in South-East Asia, 1944–1945*, London, Collins, 1987

O'Diear, J., *Touching the Clouds: The General Claire Chennault Story*, Alexander, NC, Alexander Books, 1996

Oakes, V., *White Man's Folly*, Boston, MA, Houghton Mifflin, 1943

Oatts, L. B., *The Jungle in Arms*, London, William Kimber, 1962

——, *I Serve – Regimental History of the 3rd Carabiniers (Prince of Wales's Dragoon Guards)*, Norwich, Jarrold and Son, 1966

Oba, S., *The 'Japanese' War: London University's WWII Secret Teaching Programme and the Experts Sent to Help Beat Japan*, Folkestone, Japan Library, 1995

Odgers, G., *Australia in the War of 1939–1945*, series 3, *Air*, vol. 2, *Air War against Japan 1943–1945*, Canberra, Australian War Memorial, 1957

Ogburn, C., *The Marauders*, London, Hodder and Stoughton, 1960

Oliver, F. R., *Our Colonels are Methodist*, Braunton, Merlin, 1987

Omissi, D., *The Sepoy and the Raj: The Indian Army 1860–1940*, Basingstoke, Macmillan, 1994

On Kin, *Burma under the Japanese*, Lucknow, Lucknow Publishing House, 1947

*Operations of the 1st and 2nd Battalions The Queen's Royal Regiment in Burma during World War Two*, Guildford, The Queen's Royal Surrey Regiment Musem, 1991

Otway, T. B. H., *The Second World War 1939–1945; Airborne Forces*, London, The War Office, 1951

Oung, K., *Who Killed Aung San?*, Bangkok, White Lotus, 1996

Owen, F., *The Campaign in Burma*, London, HMSO, 1946

——, *Burma: A Miracle in Military Achievement*, Calcutta, SEAC, 1945

Page, Malcolm, *KAR: A History of The King's African Rifles and East African Forces*, Barnsley, Leo Cooper, 1998

Page, Martin (ed.), *'Kiss Me Goonight, Sergeant Major': The Songs and Ballads of World War II*, London, Hart-Davis, MacGibbon, 1973

Painter, R., *A Signal Honour: With the Chindits and the XIVth Army in Burma*, Barnsley, Leo Cooper, 1999

Pakenham-Walsh, R. P., *History of The Corps of Royal Engineers*, vol. 9, *1938–1948, Campaigns in Sicily and Italy: The War against Japan: North-West Europe 1944–45: Minor and Non Operational Areas: Post-War 1945–48*, Chatham, The Institution of the Royal Engineers, 1958

Palit, D. K., *History of The Regiment of Artillery, Indian Army*, London, Leo Cooper, 1972

——, *Major General A. A. Rudra: His Service in Three Armies and Two World Wars*, New Delhi, Reliance, 1997

——, *Sentinels of the North-East: The Assam Rifles*, New Delhi, Palit and Palit, 1984

Palsokar, R. D., *A Historical Record of the Dogra Regiment: A Saga of Gallantry and Valour, 1858–1981*, Faizabad, The Commandant, Dogra Regimental Centre, 1982

——, *History of the 5th Gorkha Rifles (Frontier force)*, vol. 3, *1858 to 1991*, Shillong, The Commandant, 58 Gorkha Training Centre, 1991

——, *History of The Sikh Light Infantry*, vol. 2, Fategarh, The Commandant, The Sikh Light Infantry Regimental Centre, 1997

——, *'The Bihar Warriors': A History of the Bihar Regiment 1758–1986*, Ranchi, The Commandant, The Bihar Regimental Centre, 1986

——, *The Grenadiers: A Tradition of Valour*, Jabalour, The Commandant, The Grenadiers Regimental Centre, 1981

Parham, H. J. and Belfield, E. H. G., *Unarmed into Battle: The Story of the Air Observation Post*, Winchester, Warren and Son, 1956

Parillo, M., *The Japanese Merchant Marine in World War II*, Annapolis, MD, Naval Institute Press, 1993

Park, K., *Air Operations in South-East Asia from 1st June 1944 to the Reoccupation of Rangoon, 2nd May 1945*, London, HMSO, 1951

Parkin, R., *Ray Parkin's Wartime Trilogy (Out of the Smoke, Into the Smother and The Sword and the Blossom)*, Melbourne, Melbourne University Press, 2000

Parkinson, J. D., and Hornby, R. B., *Along O' My Old Brown Mule*, Lancaster, Holden, 1996

Parkinson, R., *The Auk: Auchinleck Victor at Alamein*, London, Granada, 1977

Pavillard, S. S., *Bamboo Doctor*, London, Macmillan 1960

Payne, R., *China Awake*, London, Heinemann, 1947

Pe, M. T., *What Happened in Burma: The Frank Revelations of a Young Burmese Revolutionary Leader who has Recently Escaped from Burma to India*, Kitibistan, Allhabad Law Journal Press, 1943

Peacock, B., *Prisoner on the Kwai*, London, William Blackwood and Sons, 1966

Peacock, G., *The Life of A Jungle Walla: Reminiscences in the Life of Lieut.-Col. E. H. Peacock, D.S.O., M.C.*, Ilfracombe, Arthur H. Stockwell, no date

Pearcy, A., *Dakota at War*, Shepperton, Ian Allen, 1982

Pearson, G., *Brief History of the K.G.V.'s Own Bengal Sappers and Miners Group R.I.E. (August 1939–July 1946)*, Roorkee, 1947

Pearson, R. A., *Australians at War in the Air 1939–1945*, vol. 2, *Coastal Command, The Fleet Air Arm, Middle East & Mediterranean, South-East Asia, South-West Pacific, Ground Staff, The Tactical Air Force*, Kenthurst, NSW, Kangaroo Press, 1995

Peek, I. D., *One Fourteenth of an Elephant; A Memoir of Life and Death on the Burma–Thailand Railway*, Sydney, Pan Macmillan Australia, 2003

Peers, W. R. and Brelis, D., *Behind The Burma Road*, London, Robert Hale, 1963

Peirse, R., *Air Operations in South-East Asia from 16th November, 1943 to 31st May, 1944*, London, HMSO, 1951

Pennington, J. W., *Pick up your Parrots and Monkeys and Fall in Facing the Boat*, London, Cassell, 2003

Perrett, B., *Tank Tracks to Rangoon: The Story of British Armour in Burma*, London, Robert Hale, 1978

——, *Last Stand! Famous Battles against the Odds*, London, Arms and Armour, 1991

——, *Seize and Hold: Master Strokes on the Battlefield*, London, Arms and Armour, 1994

Perry, F. W., *The Commonwealth Armies: Manpower and Organization in Two World Wars*, Manchester, Manchester University Press, 1988

Peterson, C., *Unparalleled Danger, Unsurpassed Courage: Recipients of the Indian Order of Merit in the Second World War*, Reston, VA, C. Peterson, 1997

Phillips, B., *KC8 Burma*, Manhattan, KS, Sunflower University Press, 2000

Philpott, B., *RAF Combat Units SEAC 1941–45*, Airway 23, London, Osprey, 1979

Pickford, S. C., *Destination Rangoon*, Denbigh, Gee & Son, 1989

Pikonlis, J., *Alun Lewis – A Life*, Bridgend, Poetry Wales Press, 1984

Pocock, J. G., *The Spirit of a Regiment, being The History of 19th King George V's Own Lancers 1921–1947*, Aldershot, Gale & Polden, 1962

Pocock, T., *Fighting General: The Public and Private Campaigns of General Sir Walter Walker*, London, Collins, 1973

Poole, P., *Of Love and War: The Letters and Diaries of Captain Adrian Curlews and his Family 1939–1945*, Sydney, Collins, 1988

Popham, H., *F.A.N.Y. The Story of the Women's Transport Service 1907–1984*, London, Leo Cooper with Secker and Warburg, 1984

Pounder, T., *Death Camps of the River Kwai*, St Ives, United Writers Publications, 1977

Powell, G., and Powell, J., *The History of the Green Howards: Three Hundred Years of Service*, Barnsley, Leo Cooper, 2002

Prasad, B. (ed.), *The Official History of the Indian Armed Forces in the Second World War: Campaigns in the Eastern Theatre: The Arakan Operations 1942–45*, Delhi, Combined Inter-Services Historical Section (India and Pakistan), 1954

——, *The Official History of the Indian Armed Forces in the Second World War: Campaigns in Eastern Theatre: The Reconquest of Burma*, vol. 1, Delhi, Combined Inter-Services Historical Section (India and Pakistan), 1958

——, *The Official History of the Indian Armed Forces in the Second World War: Campaigns in Eastern Theatre: The Reconquest of Burma*, vol. 2, Delhi, Combined Inter-Services Historical Section (India and Pakistan), 1959

——, *The Official History of the Indian Armed Forces in the Second World War: Campaigns in Eastern Theatre: The Retreat From Burma 1941–42*, Delhi, Combined Inter-Services Historical Section (India and Pakistan), 1952

——, *The Official History of the Indian Armed Forces in the Second World War: Defence of India: Policy and Plans*, Delhi, Combined Inter-Services Historical Section (India and Pakistan), 1963

——, *The Official History Of The Indian Armed Forces in the Second World War: Expansion of the Armed Forces and Defence Organization*, Delhi Combined Inter-Services Historical Section (India and Pakistan), 1956

Prather, R. E., *Easy into Burma*, Dayton, OH, Russel E. Prather, 1977

Praval, K. C., *India's Paratroopers (A History of the Parachute Regiment of India)*, London, Leo Cooper, 1975

——, *Valour Triumphs – A History of the Kumaon Regiment*, Faridabad, Thompson Press (India), 1976

Prefer, N. N., *Vinegar Joe's War: Stilwell's Campaigns for Burma*, Novato, CA, Presidio, 2000

Prendergast, J. H., *Prender's Progress: A Soldier in India, 1931–1947*, London, Cassell, 1979

Probert, H., *The Forgotten Air Force: The Royal Air Force in the War against Japan 1942–1945*, London, Brassey's (UK), 1995

Proudfoot, C L., *We Lead: 7th Light Cavalry, 1784–1990*, New Delhi, Lancer International, 1991

——, *History of 16th Light Cavalry [Armoured Corps]*, Calcutta, Hooghly Print Co., 1976

Purton, A., *The Safest Place*, Wells-next-the-Sea, L. H. Purton, 1982

Pythian-Adams, E. G., *The Madras Regiment 1758–1958*, Wellington (India), Defence Services Staff College, 1958

Qureshi, M. I., *The First Punjabis: History of the First Punjab Regiment 1759–1956*, Aldershot, Gale & Polden, 1958

Randolph, J., *Marsmen in Burma*, Houston, TX, John Randolph, 1946

Rankin, N., *Telegram from Guernica: The Extraordinary Life of George Steer, War Correspondent*, London, Faber and Faber, 2003

Rao, U. S., *Reminiscences of an INA Soldier*, Magalore, Sharada, 1986

Rasor, E. L., *The China–Burma–India Campaign, 1931–1945: Historiography and Annotated Bibliography*, Westport CT, Greenwood, 1998

Rattenbury, H. B., *The China–Burma Vagabond*, London, Frederick Mueller, 1946

Rawlinson, H. G., *History of 8th King George V's Own Light Cavalry*, Aldershot, Gale & Polden, 1948

Rayment, J., *Temporary Gentleman: 'Sapper' Field Company 81st Division, Royal West African Frontier Force, Burma Campaign, 1943–1945*, Winchester, George Mann, 2003

Read, K. L., with Ballou, R. L., *Bamboo Hospital*, Philadelphia and New York, J. B. Lippincott, 1961

Reminick, G., *Death's Railway: A Merchant Mariner POW on the River Kwai*, Benicia, CA, Glencannon Press, 2002

Reynolds, E. B., *Thailand and Japan's Southern Advance, 1940–1945*, Basingstoke, Macmillan Press, 1994

Rhodes-James, R., *Chindit*, London, John Murray, 1980

Richardson, M., *Fighting Tigers: Epic Actions of the Royal Leicestershire Regiment*, Barnsley, Leo Cooper, 2002

Rillstone, T., *... And Behold We Live: Days of Danger in Wartime Burma*, Essendon, VIC, St Columban's Mission Society, no date.

Rissik, D., *The D.L.I. at War; The History of The Durham Light Infantry 1939–1945*, Brancepeth Castle, The Depot The Durham Light Infantry, 1952

Rivett, R., *Behind Bamboo*, London, Angus and Robertson, 1966

Rizvi, S. H. A., *Veteran Campaigners: A History of the Punjab Regiment, 1759–1981*, Lahore, Wajidalis, 1984

Roberts, M. R., *Golden Arrow: The Story of the 7th Indian Division in the Second World War 1939–1945*, Aldershot, Gale & Polden, 1952

Robertson, G. W., *'The Rose & The Arrow', A Life Story of 136th (1st West Lancashire) Field Regiment Royal Artillery 1939–1946*, Dorchester, Friary Press, 1986

Robertson, J., *Maymyo – More Far: A Walk out of Burma – 1942*, Banbury, Norman Hudson, 1999

Robertson, M., *Sister Sahibs*, Lewes, Book Guild, 1987

Robins, F. C., *Overseas Diary: India and Burma, World War II*, ed. R. M. Robins, Gainesville, MO, Rumaro Press, 1990

Rock, G., *History of the American Field Service, 1920–1955*, New York, American Field Service, 1956

Rodger, G., *Red Moon Rising*, London, The Cresset Press, 1943

Rodriguez, H., *Helen of Burma*, London, Collins, 1983

Roetter, C., *Psychological Warfare*, London, Batsford, 1974

Rolo, C. J., *Wingate's Raiders: An Account of the Incredible Adventure that Raised the Curtain on the Battle for Burma*, London, George G. Harper, 1944

Romanus, C. F. and Sunderland, R., *United States Army in World War II, China–Burma–India Theater, Stilwell's Mission to China*, Washington, DC, Office of The Chief of Military History, United States Army, 1953

——, *United States Army in World War II, China–Burma–India Theater, Stilwell's Command Problems*, Washington, DC, Office of The Chief of Military History, United States Army, 1956

——, *United States Army in World War II, China–Burma–India Theater, Time Runs Out in CBI*, Washington, DC, Office of the Chief of Military History, United States Army, 1959

Rooney, D., *Burma Victory: Imphal and Kohima March 1944 to May 1945*, London, Cassell, 1992

——, *Mad Mike: A Life of Michael Calvert*, London, Leo Cooper, 1996

——, *Wingate and the Chindits: Redressing the Balance*, London, Arms and Armour, 1994

Rose, D., *Off the Record: The Life and Letters of a Black Watch Officer*, Staplehurst, Spellmount, 1996

Rossetto, L., *Major General Orde Charles Wingate and the Development of Long Range Penetration*, Manhattan, KS, MA/AH Publications, 1982

Royle, T., *Orde Wingate: Irregular Soldier*, London, Weidenfeld and Nicolson, 1995

Russell of Liverpool, Lord, *The Knights of Bushido: A Short History of Japanese War Crimes*, London, Greenhill, 2002

Russell, S. F., *Muddy Exodus: An Account of the Evacuation from Upper Burma in May 1942 and the Flight of Refugees through the Hukawng Valley to Safety in India*, Rugby, P. R. Russell, no date.

Russell, W. W., *Forgotten Skies: The Story of the Air Forces in India and Burma*, London, Hutchinson, 1945

——, *The Friendly Firm, A History of 194 Squadron, Royal Air Force*, 194 Squadron RAF Association, 1972

Ryder, R., *Oliver Leese*, London, Hamish Hamilton, 1987

Saburo, H. (with Alvin D. Coox), *Kogun: The Japanese Army in the Pacific War*, Quantico, VA, The Marine Corps Association, 1959

Samson, G., *The Burma Road*, London, London China Society, 1946

Samson, J., *Chennault*, New York, Doubleday, 1987

Sandes, E. W. C., *From Pyramid to Pagoda: The Story of The West Yorkshire Regiment (The Prince of Wales's Own) in the War 1939–1945 and Afterwards*, London, F. J. Parsons, 1952

Sansome, R. S., *The Bamboo Workshop: The History of The RAF Repair and Salvage Units India/Burma 1941–1946*, Braunton, Merlin Books, 1996

Sareen, T. R., *Japan and the Indian National Army*, New Delhi, Mounto, 1996

Sato, K., *Japan and Britain at the Crossroads, 1939–1941: A Study in the Dilemmas of Japanese Diplomacy*, Tokyo, Senshu University Press, 1986

Saunders, H. St G., *The Royal Air Force*, vol. 3, *The Fight is Won*, London, HMSO, 1975

Savage, J. R., *A Guest of the Emperor*, Moorooka, QLD, Boolarong Press, 1995

Saxena, K. M. L., *The Military System of India (1900–1939)*, New Delhi, Reliance, 1999

Schlaefli, R., *Emergency Sahib*, London, R. J. Leach, 1992

Scott, J. G., *Burma from the Earliest Times to the Present Day*, London, T. Fisher Unwin, 1924

Scott, R. L., *God is My Co-Pilot*, Garden City, NY, Blue Ribbon, 1944

——, *Flying Tiger: Chennault of China*, New York, Doubleday, 1953

Scott Daniell, D., *Cap of Honour, The Story of the Gloucestershire Regiment*, Bristol, White Lion, 1975

Scroggs, D., *The Soapman and the Railroad of Death*, New York, Dorrance, 1976

Seagrave, G. S., *Burma Surgeon*, New York, W. W. Norton, 1943

——, *Burma Surgeon Returns*, New York, W. W. Norton, 1946

Seagrave, S., *The Soong Dynasty*, London, Sidgwick and Jackson, 1985

Seaman, H., *The Battle at Sangshak: Burma, March 1944*, London, Leo Cooper, 1989

Searle, R., *To the Kwai and Back*, London, Collins, 1986

Seiker, F., *Lest We Forget: Life as a Japanese P. O. W.; Sketches and Comments*, Worcester, Bevere Vivis Gallery Books, 1995

Sein, K. and Withey, J. A., *The Great Po Sein*, Bloomington, IN, Indiana University Press, 1965

Sethin, A. M., and Katju, V., *Traditions of a Regiment: The Story of the Rajputana Rifles*, New Delhi, Lancers Publishing, 1983

Sevareid, E., *Not So Wild a Dream*, New York, Athenum Publishing, 1978

Shannon, S. D., *'Forgotten No More': 2nd Battalion DLI at Kohima 1944*, ed. I. Watson, Durham, County Durham Books, 1994

Sharpe, P., *To Be a Chindit*, Lewes, Book Guild, 1995

Shaw, J., *The March Out: The End of the Chindit Adventure*, London, Rupert Hart-Davis, 1953

——, *Special Force: A Chindit's Story*, Gloucester, Alan Sutton, 1996

Shaw, P., *Brother Digger: The Sullivans, 2nd AIF*, Melbourne, VIC, Greenhouse, 1984

Shears, P. J., *The Story of The Border Regiment: 1939–1945*, London, Nisbet & Co., 1948

Sheffield, G. D., *The Redcaps: A History of the Royal Military Police and its Antecedents from the Middle Ages to the Gulf War*, London, Brassey's (UK), 1994

Sheffield, O. F., *The York and Lancaster Regiment 1919–1953*, vol. 3, Aldershot, Gale & Polden, 1956

Sheil-Small, D., *Green Shadows: A Gurkha Story*, London, William Kimber, 1982

Shephard, B., *A War of Nerves: Soldiers and Psychiatrists 1914–1994*, London, Pimlico, 2002

Sherwood, R. E., *Roosevelt and Hopkins*, New York, Harper, 1948

Shipster, J., *Mist on the Rice-Fields: A Soldier's Story of the Burma Campaign 1943–45 and Korean War 1950–51*, Barnsley, Leo Cooper, 2000

Shores, C. and Cull, B., with Izawa, Y., *Bloody Shambles*, vol. 1, *The Drift to War to the Fall of Singapore*, London, Grub Street, 1992

——, *Bloody Shambles*, vol. 2, *The Defence of Sumatra to the Fall of Burma*, London, Grub Street, 1992

Short, S. W., *On Burma's Eastern Frontier*, London and Edinburgh, Marshall, Morgan and Scott, 1945

Shrivastava, V. K., *The Rajputana Rifles*, New Delhi, Lancer, 2000

Sigal, L. V., *Fighting to a Finish: The Politics of War Termination in the United States and Japan, 1945*, Ithaca, NY, Cornell University Press, 1988

Silverstein, J. F. (ed.), *Southeast Asia in World War II: Four Essays*, New Haven, CT, Yale University Press, 1966

Sinclair, W. B., *Confusion beyond Imagination, China-Burma-India in World War II*, Book 1, *Jungle, Paddy and Mountain Heroes, Awarded and Unrewarded Mud, Gravel, Ruts and Rocks*, Coeur d'Aiene, ID, Joe F. Whitley, 1986

Singh, B., *Independence and Democracy in Burma, 1945–1952: The Turbulent Years*, Michigan Papers on South and Southeast Asia, No. 40, Ann Arbor, MI, Michigan University Press, 1992

Singh, G., *Japanese Offensive*, Jalandar, ABS Publications, 1990

Singh, M., *Soldiers' Contribution to Indian Independence: The Epic of the Indian National Army*, New Delhi, Army Educational Stores, 1974

Singh Mangat, G., *Indian National Army, Role in India's Struggle for Freedom*, New Delhi, Classical, 1991

Sinker, C.A.C., and Rossier, D. P. St C., *The History of the First Battalion The Lincolnshire Regiment in India, Arakan, Burma and Sumatra, September 1939 to October 1946*, Lincoln, Keyworth & Sons, 1949

Sivaram, M., *The Road to Delhi*, Rutland, VT, Charles E. Tuttle, 1966

Skidmore, I., *Marines Don't Hold Their Horses*, Shepperton, Ian Allen, 1981

Skinner, H. A., *'Guest' of the Imperial Japanese Army (1942–45)*, Littlehampton, Harold A. Skinner, 1993

Slater, R., *Guns through Arcady: Burma and the Burma Road*, Sydney, Angus and Robertson, 1941

Slim, W., *Courage and Other Broadcasts*, London, Cassell, 1957

——, *Defeat into Victory*, London, Cassell, 1956

——, *Unofficial History*, London, Cassell, 1959

Sloggett, D., *Angels of Burma*, Edinburgh, The Pentland Press, 2000

Smeeton, M., *A Change of Jungles*, London, Rupert Hart-Davis, 1962

Smith, B. F., *Shadow Warriors: OSS and the Origins of CIA*, London, André Deutch, 1983

Smith, E. D., *Battle for Burma*, London, Batsford, 1979

Smith, F. R., *Lest We Forget: Working on the Thai–Burma Railway of Death: Drawings*, Kangaroo Flat, VIC, Mulqueen Printers, 1992

Smith, M., *The Emperor's Codes: Bletchley Park and the Breaking of Japan's Secret Ciphers*, London, Bantam, 2001

Smith, N., *The Burma Road*, New York, Garden City Publications, 1940

Smith, P. C., *Jungle Dive-Bombers at War*, London, John Murray, 1987

——, *Vengeance! The Vultee Vengeance Dive Bomber*, Shrewsbury, Airlife, 1986

Smith, R. H., *OSS: The Secret History of America's First Central Intelligence Agency*, Berkeley, CA, University of California Press, 1972

Smith W. E. (ed.), *Second Troop Carrier Squadron. China-Burma-India, World War II, January 1943–December 1945: A Compilation of Official Logs or Diaries and a Collection of Photographs*, Cullman, AL, Gregath, 1987

Smurthwaite, D. (ed.), *The Forgotten War: The British Army in the Far East 1941–1945*, London, National Army Museum, 1992

Smyth, J., *Before the Dawn, A Story of Two Historic Retreats (Dunkirk 1940, Burma 1942)*, London Cassell, 1957

——, *Milestones*, London, Sidgwick and Jackson, 1979

——, *The Only Enemy: An Autobiography*, London, Hutchinson, 1959

Snodgrass, Major, *The Burmese War (1824–1826)*, Bangkok, Avon Publishing, 1997

Snow, P., *The Fall of Hong Kong: Britain, China and the Japanese Occupation*, New Haven, CT, Yale University Press, 2003

Sollman, W. F., *Memories of the Thai–Burma Railway*, Bangkok, Yodying Sophon, 1974

Somerville, C., *Our War: The British Commonwealth and the Second World War*, London, Weidenfeld & Nicolson, 1998

Spector, R. H., *Eagle against the Sun: The American War with Japan*, Harmondsworth, Penguin, 1987

Spencer, O. C., *Flying the Hump: Memories of an Air War*, College Station, TX, Texas A & M University Press, 1992

Spurr, R., *Let the Tiger Turn Tail: Spurr's War*, Edinburgh, Mainstream, 1992

Stanaway, J., *P-38 Lightning Aces of the Pacific and CBI*, Aircraft of the Aces 14, Oxford, Osprey, 1997

——, *Mustang and Thunderbolt Aces of the Pacific and CBI*, Aircraft of the Aces 26, Oxford, Osprey, 1999

*Standing Orders of the Second Battalion the Burma Rifles: With a Short Record of the Battalion*, Aldershot, Gale & Polden, 1948

Stanley Clarke, E. B., and Tillot, A. T., *From Kent to Kohima: Being the History of The 4th Battalion The Queen's Own Royal West Kent Regiment (T. A.) 1939–1947*, Aldershot, Gale & Polden, 1951

Stevens, G. R., *The 9th Gurkha Rifles*, vol. 2, *1937–1947*, The Regimental Association (U.K.) 9th Gurkha Rifles, 1953

——, *History of the 2nd King Edward VII's Own Goorkhas, The Sirmoor Rifles*, vol. 3, *1921–1948*, Aldershot, Gale & Polden, 1952

——, *The 9th Gurkha Rifles, 1937–47*, London, Butler and Tanner, 1953

Stevenson, D. F., *Air Operations in Burma and the Bay of Bengal, January 1st to May 22nd, 1942*, HMSO, 1948

Stewart, A., *The Underrated Enemy: Britain's War with Japan, December 1941–May 1942*, London, William Kimber, 1987

Stewart, A. T. Q., *The Pagoda War: Lord Dufferin and the Fall of the Kingdom of Ava, 1885–6*, London, Faber and Faber, 1972

Stewart, J., *To The River Kwai: Two Journeys, 1943, 1979*, London, Bloomsbury, 1988

Steyn, P., *The History of The Assam Regiment*, vol. 1, *1941–1947*, Calcutta, Orient Longmans, 1959

Stibbé, P., *Return via Rangoon: A Young Chindit Survives the Jungle and Japanese Captivity*, London, Leo Cooper, 1995

Stilwell, J., *The Stilwell Papers*, ed. T. H. White, London, Macdonald, 1949

Stimson, H. L., and Bundy, M., *On Active Service in Peace and War*, New York, Harper, 1948

Stockman, J., *Seaforth Highlanders: A Fighting Soldier Remembers (1939–1945)*, Somerton, Crécy, 1987

Stone, J. H. (ed.), *Crisis Fleeting: Original Reports on Military Medicine in India and Burma in the Second World War*, Washington, DC, Office of the Surgeon General, 1969.

Stone, R., *The Light Behind the Clouds*, Waco, TX, Texian Press, 1992

Stones, D., *Operation Bograt: From France to Burma*, Tunbridge Wells, Spellmount, 1990

Storry, R., *A History of Modern Japan*, Harmondsworth, Penguin, 1960

Stowe, J. A., *Siam Becomes Thailand: A Story of Intrigue*, London, Hurst, 1991

Stowe, L., *They Shall Not Sleep*, New York, Alfred A. Knopf, 1945

Street, R., *A Brummie in Burma: Once upon a Wartime*, Grantham, Barny Books, 1995

——, *Another Brummie in Burma*, Grantham, Barny Books, no date

Stripp, A., *Codebreaker in the Far East*, London, Frank Cass, 1989

Strutton, B., and Pearson, M., *The Secret Invaders*, London, Hodder and Stoughton, 1958

Subramanyam, V. A., *The Signals: A History of the Corps of Signals*, Delhi, Macmillan India, 1986

Sumner, I., *The Indian Army 1914–1947*, Elite 75, Oxford, Osprey, 2001

Sun, T. (trans. S. B. Griffith), *The Art of War*, Oxford, Oxford University Press, 1963

Sutcliffe, D. H., *Airborne over Burma*, Upton upon Severn, D. H. Sutcliffe and The Self Publishing Association, 1988

Sutherland, D., *Tried and Valiant: The History of The Border Regiment (The 34th and 55th Regiments of Foot) 1702–1959*, London, Leo Cooper, 1972

Sutherland Brown, A., *Silently into the Midst of Things: 177 Squadron Royal Air Force in Burma 1943–1945; History and Personal Narratives*, Lewes, Book Guild, 1997

Sutton, B., *Jungle Pilot*, London, Macmillan, 1946

Sweet-Escott, B., *Baker Street Irregular*, London, Methuen, 1965

Swinson, A., *Four Samurai: A Quartet of Japanese Army Commanders in the Second World War*, London, Hutchinson, 1968

——, *Kohima*, London, Cassell, 1966

Swynnerton, C. R. A., *A Short History of The 1st (West African) Infantry Brigade in the Arakan 1944–45*, Lagos, Ife-Olu Printing Works, 1949

Sykes, C., *Orde Wingate: A Biography*, London, Collins, 1959

Sym, J., *Seaforth Highlanders*, Aldershot, Gale & Polden, 1962

Synge, W. A. T., *The Story of The Green Howards 1939–1945*, Richmond, The Green Howards, 1952

Tainsh, A. R., *... And Some Fell by the Wayside: An Account of the North Burma Evacuation*, Bombay, Orient Longmans, 1948

Tamayama, K., and Nunneley, J., *Tales by Japanese Soldiers of the Burma Campaign 1942–1945*, London, Cassell, 2000

Tambiah, S. J., *Edmund Leach: An Anthropological Life*, Cambridge, Cambridge University Press, 2002

Tan, P-y., *The Building of the Burma Road*, London, McGraw-Hill, 1945

Taylor, C. G., *The Forgotten Ones of 'South East Asia Command' and Force 136*, Ilfracombe, Arthur H. Stockwell, 1989

Taylor, E., *Front-line Nurse, British Nurses in World War II*, London, Robert Hale, 1997

Taylor, Jeremy, *The Devons; A History of the Devonshire Regiment, 1685–1945*, Bristol, White Swan Press, 1951

Taylor, Joe G., *Air Supply in the Burma Campaigns*, USAF Historical Studies no. 75, USAF Historical Division, Research Studies Institute, Air University, 1957

Taylor, R. H., *Marxism and Resistance in Burma, 1942–1945: Thein Pe Myint's Wartime Traveler*, Athens, OH, Ohio University Press, 1984

Teel, H. G., *Our Days Were Years: History of the Texas Lost Battalion*, Quanah, TX, Nortex, 1978

Tennyson Jesse, F., *The Story of Burma*, London, Macmillan, 1946

Terrell, R., *Civilians in Uniform: A Memoir 1937–1945*, London, The Radcliffe Press, 1998

Terry, T. Q., *Strangers in their Land: CBI Bombardier, 1939–1945*, Manhattan, KS, Sunflower University Press, 1992

Tewari, K. K., *A Soldier's Voyage of Self-Discovery*, Pondicherry, All India Press, no date

Thatcher, W. S., *The Tenth Baluch Regiment in the Second World War*, Abbottabad, Baluch Regimental Centre, 1980

*The Best of Yank, The Army Weekly*, New York, World, 1945

*The 'Black Cat' Division: An Account of the Achievements of the Famous 17th Indian Division in Burma during the Second World War*, New Delhi, Roxy Press, 1946

*The 'Fighting Fifth': History of the 5th Indian Division*, Delhi, R. W. Pearce, 1946

*The RAF and the Far East War 1941–1945*, Bracknell Paper no. 6, *A Symposium on the Far East War, 24 March 1995, Sponsored Jointly by the Royal Air Force Historical Society and the Royal Air Force Staff College Bracknell*, Bracknell, Royal Air Force Historical Society, 1995

*The Story of The 25th Indian Division: The Arakan Campaign*, Bombay, G. S. Borker, 1946

*The Twenty-Third Indian Division: An Illustrated Story Telling of the Division's Exploits and Achievements from 1942 until 1945*, New Delhi, 1945

Thomas, G. J., *Eyes for the Phoenix: Allied Aerial Photo-Reconnaissance Operations South-East Asia 1941–1945*, Aldershot, Hikoki, 1999

Thomas, L. J., *Back to Mandalay*, Worcester, Frederick Mueller, 1952

Thomas, R. T., *Born in Battle: Round the World Adventures of the 513th Bombardment Squadron*, Philadelphia, PA, Winston, 1945

Thompson, H. L., *New Zealanders with the Royal Air Force*, vol. 3, *Mediterranean and Middle East, South-east Asia*, Wellington, War History Branch, Department of Internal Affairs, 1959

Thompson, J., *The Imperial War Museum Book of War behind Enemy Lines*, London, Sidgwick and Jackson, 1998

——, *Imperial War Museum Book of the War in Burma 1942–45: A Vital Contribution to Victory in the Far East*, London, Sidgwick and Jackson, 2002

——, *The Lifeblood of War: Logistics in Armed Conflict*, London, Brassey's (UK), 1991

Thompson, K., *A Thousand Cups of Rice: Surviving the Death Railway*, Austin, TX, Eakin Publications, 1994

Thompson, P., *How the Japanese Army Fights*, London, Penguin, 1942

Thompson, R., *Make for the Hills: Memories of Far Eastern Wars*, London, Leo Cooper, 1989

Thorne, C. G., *Allies of a Kind: The United States, Britain, and the War against Japan, 1941–1945*, Hamish Hamilton, 1978

*Tiger Head: The Story of The 26th Indian Division*, Bombay, G. S. Borker, 1946

Tinker, H., *Burma: The Struggle for Independence, 1944–48*, London, HMSO, 1984

——, *The Union of Burma: A Study of the First Years of Independence*, 4th edn, Oxford, Oxford University Press, 1967

Tobey, P. L., *The Sitapur Incident: The Americans and Chinese Meet the Japanese in Burma: 1944*, Lincoln, RI, Andrew Mowbray Inc., 1987

Tomlinson, M., *The Most Dangerous Moment*, London, Mayflower/Granada Publishing, 1979

Toon, J. W. H., *Hellfire: The Story of One Man's Survival on the Burma–Thailand Death Railway*, Melbourne, World Holidays, 1995

Towers, J., *The Tale of a Tojo Tourist*, Toowoon Bay, NSW, J. Towers, 1997

Towill, B., *A Chindit's Chronicle*, Lincoln, NE, Another's Choice, 2000

Townshend Bickers, R., *Ginger Lacey: Fighter Pilot*, London, Robert Hale, 1997

Toye, H., *The Springing Tiger. A Study of a Revolutionary*, London, Cassell, 1959

Trager, F. N. (ed.) (trans. Yoon W-Z., assisted by T. T. Winant), *Burma: Japanese Military Administration, Selected Documents, 1941–1945*, Philadelphia, PA, University of Philadelphia Press, 1971

Trevelyan, H., *The India We Left*, London, Macmillan, 1972

Tsuji, M., *Singapore: The Japanese Story*, London, Constable, 1962

Tuchman, B., *Sand against the Wind: Stilwell and the American Experience in China 1911–45*, London, Macdonald Futura, 1981

Tucker, S., *Burma: The Curse of Independence*, London, Pinto, 2001

Tulloch, D., *Wingate in Peace and War: An Account of the Chindit Commander*, London, Macdonald, 1972

Tun Pe, U., *Sun over Burma*, Rangoon, Rasika Ranjani Press, 1949

Turnbull, P., *Battle of the Box*, Shepperton, Ian Allen, 1979

Turner, A. S., *An Engineer in the War: Bomb Disposal, Jungle, Sikhs*, Taunton, Onyx Publishing, 1998

Twiston Davies, D. (ed.), *The Daily Telegraph Book of Military Obituaries*, London, Grub Street, 2003

Tyson, G., *Forgotten Frontier*, Calcutta, W. H. Targett, 1945

Underhill, W. E., *The Royal Leicestershire Regiment, 17th Foot: A History of the Years 1928 to 1956*, Plymouth, Underhill (Plymouth) Ltd, 1957

Vale, W. L., *History of the South Staffordshire Regiment*, Aldershot, Gale & Polden, 1969

Van Straubanzee, P., *Desert, Jungle and Dale*, Edinburgh, The Pentland Press, 1991

Van Wagner, R. D., *Any Place, Any Time, Any Where: The 1st Air Commandos in WWII*, Atglen, PA, Schiffer, 1998

Vellacott, K., *Ticket to Burma*, Sydney, The Shakespeare Head, no date

Vellacott Jones, K., *The Wasbies: The Story of the Women's Auxiliary Service (Burma)*, London, War Facts, 1946

Velmans, L., *Long Way back to the River Kwai: Memories of World War II*, New York, Arcade, 2003

Verma, S., and Anand, V. K., *The Corps of Indian Engineers 1939–1947*, Delhi, Historical Section, Ministry of Defence, 1974

Vesely, J. M., *Unlike Any Land You Know: The 490th Bomb Squadron in China–Burma–India*, Lincoln, NE, Writers' Club Press, 2000

Vincent S. F., *Flying Fever*, Norwich, Jarrolds, 1972

Virk, D. S., *Indian Army Post Offices in the Second World War*, New Delhi, Army Postal Service Association, 1982

Vorley, J. S., and Vorley, H. M., *The Road from Mandalay*, Windsor, Wilton 65, 2002

Wagg, A., *A Million Died! A Story of War in the Far East*, London, Nicholson and Watson, 1943

Ward, S. P. G., *Faithful: The Story of The Durham Light Infantry*, London, Thomas Nelson and Son, 1962

Ward Fay, P., *The Forgotten Army: Armed Struggle for Independence 1942–1945*, Calcutta, Rupa, 1994

Warner, P., *Auchinleck: The Lonely Soldier*, London, Buchan and Enright, 1981

Waterford, V., *Prisoners of the Japanese in World War II; Statistical History, Personal Narratives and Memorials Concerning POWs in Camps and Hellships, Civilian Internees, Asian Slave Laborers and Others Captured in the Pacific Theater*, Jefferson, NC, McFarland & Co., 1994

Wavell, A. P., *Despatch by the Supreme Commander of the ABDA Area to the Combined Chiefs of Staff on the Operations in the South-West Pacific 15th January 1942 to 25th February 1942*, London, HMSO, 1948

——, *Operations in Burma from 15 December 1941 to 20 May 1942 and including the Reports of Lieutenant-General T. J. Hutton and General the Honourable Sir Harold R. L. G. Alexander*, London, HMSO, 1948

——, *Operations in Eastern Theatre, Based on India, from March 1942 to 31 December 1942*, London, HMSO, 1946

——, *Operations in India Command, 1 January 1943 to 20 June 1943*, London, HMSO, 1948

——, *The Good Soldier*, London, Macmillan, 1948

Webster, D., *The Burma Road: The Epic Story of the China–Burma–India Theater in World War II*, New York, Farrar, Strauss and Giroux, 2003

Wedemeyer, A. C., *Wedemeyer Reports!*, New York, Holt, 1958

Weissinger, W. J., *Attention, Fool!*, Austin, TX, Eakin Publications, 1998

Wells, H. G., *Travels of a Republican Radical in Search of Hot Water*, Harmondsworth, Penguin, 1939

Weston, L. E., *The Fightin' Preacher*, Cheyenne, WY, Vision Press, 1992

Wetzler, P., *Hirohito and War: Imperial Tradition and Military Decision Making in Prewar Japan*, Honolulu, HA, University of Hawaii Press, 1998

Whelan, R., *The Flying Tigers: The Story of The American Volunteer Group*, Sydney, Angus and Robertson, 1944

White, A. J. S., *The Burma of 'AJ': Memories of AJS White C.M.G. O.B.E. Indian Civil Service 1922–1937 Secretary-General of the British Council 1940–1947*, London, BACSA, 1991

White, E. L., *Ten Thousand Tons by Christmas*, St, Petersburg, FL, Valkyrie, 1977

White, G. A., *The Great Snafu Fleet: 1st Combat Cargo/344 Airdrome/326th Troop Carrier Squadron in WW II's CBI Theater*, Philadelphia, PA, Xlibris, 2000

White, O. G. W., *Straight on for Tokyo: The War History of The 2nd Battalion The Dorsetshire Regiment (54th Foot)*, Aldershot, Gale & Polden, 1948

White, S., *'Strike Home': The Royal Bucks. Yeomanry 1794–1967*, Leicester, S. White, 1992

White, T., and Jacoby, A., *Thunder out of China*, New York, William Sloan, 1946

Whitecross, R. H., *Slaves of the Sons of Heaven: The Personal Story of an Australian Prisoner of the Japanese during the Years 1942–1945*, London, Corgi, 1980

Whitehead, J., *Escape to Fight On: With No. 204 Military Mission in China*, London, Robert Hale, 1990

——, *Far Frontiers: People and Events in N.E. India, 1857–1947*, London, BACSA, 1989

Whiting, C., *The Poor Bloody infantry*, London, Guild, 1987

Wilcox, W. A., *Chindit Column 76*, London, Longmans, Green, 1945

Wilkes, L., *Festing – Field Marshal*, Lewes, Book Guild, 1991

Williams, D., *194 Squadron Royal Air Force: 'The Friendly Firm'*, Braunton, Merlin, 1987

Williams, G., *The Frank Owen Story*, London, Square One, 1993

Williams, J. H., *Elephant Bill*, London, Rupert Hart-Davis, 1950

Willis, G. R. T., *No Hero, Just a Survivor; A Personal Story with Beaufighters and Mosquitos of 47 Squadron RAF over the Mediterranean and Burma 1943–1945*, Huddersfield, Robert Willis Associates, 1999

Willson, L., *A Son of the Raj*, Bishop Auckland, The Pentland Press, 1996

Wilmot, A. J., *27th R. A. – Only Jungle and the Japanese*, Peterborough, A. J. Wilmot, 1990

Wilson, D., *The Sum of Things*, Staplehurst, Spellmount, 2001

Wilson, D., *When Tigers Fight: The Story of the Sino-Japanese War 1937–45*, London, Hutchinson, 1982

Wilson, R., *The Imphal Shrimps, from 'High Appreciation: Recollections of a Captain'*, Chester, R. Wilson, 1962

——, *Tailpiece at Tamu, from 'High Appreciation: Recollections of a Captain'*, Chester, R. Wilson, 1960

Windsor, N. R., *Burma: Land of My Dreams*, Sidcup, Jasmine Publications, 1996

*Wings of the Phoenix: The Official Story of the Air War in Burma*, London, HMSO, 1949

Woodruff, P., *The Men Who Ruled India*, vol. 2, *The Guardians*, London, Jonathan Cape, 1954

Wright, B. S., *The Frogmen of Burma: The Story of the Sea Reconnaissance Unit*, London, William Kimber, 1970

Yee, C., *The Men of the Burma Road*, London, Methuen, 1942

Zaloga, S., *M3 & M5 Stuart Light Tank 1940–1945*, New Vanguard 33, Oxford, Osprey, 1999

Ziegler, P., *Mountbatten: The Official Biography*, London, Collins, 1985

——, (ed.), *Personal Diary of Admiral The Lord Louis Mountbatten, Supreme Allied Commander, South-East Asia, 1943–1946*, London, Collins, 1988

Zhang, C., and Liu, J., *An Illustrated History of China's War of Resistance against Japan*, Beijing, Foreign Languages Press, 1995

Zimmerman, P. B., *From Plow to Pen*, Los Angeles, CA, Paul B. Zimmerman, no date

## OTHER

Aldiss, B. W., *The Soldier Erect, or Further Adventures of the Hand-Reared Boy*, London, Corgi, 1974

Andrews, E. M., *The Patrol*, London, Cassell, 1956

Andrews, J. C., *Such Are the Valiant*, London, John Spencer, no date

Andrews, L. W., *Death March*, London, Corgi, 1960

——, *Of Lesser Renown*, London, Cassell, 1958

——, *Tattered Battalion*, London, Cassell, 1957

——, *The Scarlet Shield*, London, Corgi, 1957

Baillie, P., *Chindwin Monsoon*, London, Brown, Watson Ltd, 1958

Bates, H. E., *The Purple Plain*, London, Michael Joseph, 1947

——, *The Jacaranda Tree*, London, Michael Joseph, 1948

Baxter, W., *Look Down in Mercy*, London, Heinemann, 1951

——, *The Image and the Search*, London, Heinemann, 1953

Beck, H., *The Hero Machine*, New York, NAL, 1967

Bell, G., *Sideshow: The Unforgettable Story of the Forgotten Army*, London, Frederick Mueller, 1953

Bickers, R. T., *Jungle Pilot*, London, Brown, Watson Ltd, no date

Black, D., *Fantastic Journey*, London, Cassell, 1944

Blake, I., *Marine H SBS: The Burma Offensive*, Sutton, Severn House Publishers, 1997

Blankenship, W. D., *Tiger Ten*, New York, Putnam, 1976

Bonham, F., *Burma Rifles: A Story of Merrill's Marauders*, New York, Thomas Y. Crowell, 1960

Boulle, P. H. (trans. X. Fielding), *The Bridge on the River Kwai*, New York, Vanguard, 1954

Bowen, R. S., *Red Randall in Burma*, New York, Grosset and Dunlap, 1945

Boyington, G., *Tonya*, Indianapolis IN, Bobbs-Merrill, 1960

Braddon, R., *End of a Hate*, London, Cassell, 1958

Bragg, M., *The Soldier's Return*, London, Hodder and Stoughton, 1999

Brelis, D., *The Mission*, New York, Pocket Books, 1959

Brendon, G., *The Charm of Mambas*, London, William Heinemann, 1958

Buck, P. S., *The Promise*, London, Methuen, 1944

Butterworth, S., *Three Rivers to Glory*, London, Hutchinson, 1956

Carew, T., *Man for Man*, London, Constable, 1955

Catherall, A., *The River of Burning Sand*, London, Collins, 1947

Chamales, T. T., *Never so Few*, New York, Scribner, 1957

Chang, C. T., *Burma Road*, Singapore, Malaysia Publications, 1964

Clifford, F., *A Battle is Fought to be Won*, London, Hamish Hamilton, 1960

——, *Honour the Shrine*, Coronet Books, 1972

Collis, M., *Siamese White*, London, Faber and Faber, 1965

——, *She Was a Queen*, London, Faber and Faber, 1951

Cooper, B., *Van Langeren Girl*, New York, Vanguard Press, 1960

Crook, W., *Four Days*, New York, Antheneum, 1979

Crumpler, G. H., *Under the Burmese Pagoda*, Pt Lookout, MO, School of the Ozarks, 1975

Cruttwell, F., *A Kind of Fighting*, London, Dent, 1959

Davis, F. M., *Bamboo Camp #10*, Derby, CT, Monarch Books, 1962

Davis, P., *Two Soldiers*, Simon & Schuster, 1956

Donald, A. A., *Burma Victory and Other Poems*, Ilfracombe, Arthur H. Stockwell, 1947

Donaldson, D. H., *The Lone Chindit*, London, Robert Hale, 1967

Elder, R., *After My Own Fashion*, London, Longmans, Green & Co., 1949

Eyre, D. C., *Foxes Have Holes*, London, Robert Hale, 1949

Fenn, C., *The Golden Rule of General Wong*, London, Arthur Barker, 1960

Ford, D., *Remains*, Lincoln, NE, iUniverse, 2000

Forster, R., *The Flute of Aoska*, London, Eyre & Spottiswoode, 1955

Forsyth, R. A., *Squadron Will Move*, London, Macmillan, 1947

Friend, J., *The Long Trek*, London, Frederick Muller, 1957

George, S. C., *Burma Story*, London, Frederick Warne, 1948

Gordon, J. W., *Wings from Burma to the Himalayas*, Memphis, TN, Global Press, 1987

Griffin, S., *Burma Road Calling!*, London, Harrap, 1943

Griffin, W. E. B., *The Last Heroes*, New York, Jove Publications, 1998

Hanley, G., *See You in Yasukini*, London, William Collins, 1969

Horsely, D., *Living Dead*, London, Brown, Watson Ltd, 1959

Howard, A. T., *Rangoon Episode*, London, John Spencer, no date

Hunt, G., *One More River*, London, William Collins, 1965

Jackson, R., *The Rising Sun*, Sutton, Severn House Publishers, 1999

Johnston, G. H., *Death Takes Small Bites*, London, Victor Gollancz, 1948

——, *The Far Face of the Moon*, New York, Morrow, 1964

Johnston, J., *Patrol of the Dead*, London, Arthur Barker, 1955

King, D., *The Brave and the Damned*, New York, Paperback, 1966

Kynoch, J., *Banzai Kohima*, Stubbington, Hants, Charnwood Publications, 1997

Leasor, J., *Nothing to Report*, London, Viking, 1955

Lee C-R., *A Gesture Life*, London, Granta, 1999

Leslie, C., *The Golden Stairs*, New York, Doubleday, 1968

Macbeth, G., *The Katana: A Novel*, New York, Simon and Schuster, 1981

Maddock, R. B., *One More River*, London, Nelson, 1963

Mannin, E., *The Living Lotus*, New York, Putnam, 1956

Marks, J. M., *Ayo Gurkha!*, Oxford, Oxford University Press, 1971

Mason, R., *The Wind Cannot Read*, London, Hodder and Stoughton, 1946

Maung, T., *The Chindits and the Stars*, London, Regency, 1971

McCann, J., *Kohima, An Historic Village: And Other Short Stories*, Chadderton, J. McCann, 1988

Miller, L. O., *Assignment: Burma*, Dorset, NY, Dorchester Publishing, 1980

Milner, J., *To Blazes with Glory: A Chindit's War*, Gaskell, 1995

Moxon, O., *After the Monsoon*, London, Robert Hale, 1958

——, *The Last Monsoon*, London, Elmfield Press, 1957

Nathanson, E. M., *A Dirty Distant War*, New York, Viking Penguin, 1987

O'Diear, J., *Season of the Tigers*, Alexander, NC, Alexander Books, 1995

Orwell, G., *Burmese Days*, London, Penguin, 1989

Phillips, J. A., *Pagoda*, London, The Bodley Head, 1953

Pugh, M., *The Chancer*, London, Hutchinson, 1959

Reeman, D., *Dust on the Sea*, London, Heinemann, 1999

Rennie, D. J., *Penetration Force*, London, John Spencer, 1959

Roland, P. K., *Banzai*, London, John Spencer, 1959

Ross, K., *Ricky & Co, Air Commandos*, Cambridge, Cambridge University Press, 1946

Ruthin, M., *Jungle Nurse*, London, Dennis Dobson, 1960

Scanlan, J., *Davis*, Garden City NY, Doubleday, 1969

Scott, G. L., *Burma Mission*, London, John Spencer, no date

Scott, J. M., *Where the River Bends*, London, Heinemann, 1962

Scott, P., *Johnny Sahib*, London, Granada Publishing, 1979

——, *The Mark of the Warrior*, London, Granada Publishing, 1979

Shute, N., *The Chequer Board*, London, William Heinemann, 1947

Sibly, J., *You'll Walk to Mandalay*, London, Jonathan Cape, 1960

Slimming, J., *The Pass*, New York, Harper, 1962

Stanford, J. K., *Last Chukker*, London, Faber and Faber, 1941

——, *Reverie of Qu-Hai and Other Stories*, London, William Blackwood & Son, 1951

Stuart, V., *Life Is Destiny*, London, Robert Hale, 1958

Suyin, H., *A Many-Splendoured Thing*, London, Jonathan Cape, 1952

Takeyama, M. (trans. H. Hibbett), *Harp of Burma*, Rutland, VT, Charles E. Tuttle, 1968

Tan, A., *The Kitchen God's Wife*, New York, Putnam, 1991

Tarmey, M., *When You Go Home: The Bloody Battle of Kohima Ridge*, London, Corgi, 1975

Taylor, T., *Born of War*, New York, McGraw-Hill, 1988

Tennyson Jesse, F., *The Lacquer Lady*, London, Heinemann, 1929

Tumbull, P., *One Bullet for the General*, London, Collins, 1969

——, *The Last of Men*, London, Hutchinson, 1960

——, *Like an Abominable Branch*, London, Hurst and Blackett, 1947

Vroman, B. F., *Linger Not at Chebar*, Angel Press of Wisconsin, 1992

Wakeford, L. H. and Wakeford, J., *Brown Men's Jungle*, London, E. J. Arnold, 1951

Wallace, J. H., *A Walk in the Forest*, London, Brown, Watson Ltd,

Wehl, D., *The Moon Upside Down*, London, Barrie, 1948

Williams, H. E. (ed.), *The Stars: Anthology of Poems*, Boston, Richard Kay, 1990

# Index

The ranks quoted are generally the highest cited in the text.

Abbott, Pte W., 56
Abe Hiroshi, 2nd Lt, 426–7
Adams, Maj M.B. ('Bill'), 388
Adams, Maj R.A., 310
Admin Box, battle for, 228–34, 236
Akyab Island, 2, 12, 77, 80, 88, 90, 131, 140, 144, 180, 344, 364, 365, 368
Alexander, Lt-Col L.A., 159, 163, 164
Alexander, Lt-Gen Hon. Sir Harold, 57, 65, 67, 69, 70, 72, 75, 77–9, 83–6, 93, 98–101, 103–6, 110, 112, 179–80
Alison, Col John, 239, 241
All Burma School Movement, 14
All Burma Youth League, 375
Allan, Lt Jim, 372–3, 416
Allen, Capt L., 202
Allen, Louis, 427–9
Allied Air Command, South-East Asia, 222
All-India Radio, 191
Allmand, Capt Michael, 332
Alston-Roberts-West, Brig Michael, 301
American Field Service (AFS), 312
American Office of Strategic Services (OSS), 64, 139, 375, 418; Detachment 101, 210, 322.
American Volunteer Group (AVG) see United States Forces
American–British–Dutch–Australian Command (ABDA), 46, 66
Amery, Leo, 57, 177, 178
Amies, Col Basil, 100
Andrews, Cpl, 388
Anstice, Brig J.H., 81, 82, 93

Anti-Fascist Organisation (AFO; Burmese political coalition), 321, 375, 403, 430
Anti-Fascist People's Freedom League (AFPFL), 430, 431
Arakan, 12, 13, 45, 73, 133, 140, 150, 170, 177, 213, 222, 226, 344, 359–73
Arakan Defence Army (later Patriotic Army of Burma – Arakan Division), 364
Aram, Pte, 199
Arcadia Conference (Washington, 1941–2), 38, 40, 46
Arkell, Capt J.W., 171–2
Armstrong, Lt-Col Geoffrey, 229, 384
Arnold, Lt-Gen Henry H. ('Hap'), 132, 194, 222, 239, 241, 379
Arnold, Capt Ralph, 334
Ashton, Lt-Col John, 418
Assam, 13, 70, 73, 100, 101, 112, 126, 133
Atkins, Capt David, 135
*Atlantis* (German raider), 32
Atlee, Clement, 430
Aubrey, Sgt Tony, 161, 166
Auchinleck, FM Sir Claude John Eyre, 2, 19, 168, 177, 261
Aung San, 15, 17–18, 34–5, 122, 176, 375, 403, 417, 418, 430, 431
Aung San Suu Kyi, 433
*Automedon* (liner), 32
Auxiliary Forces Institute (AFI), 315
Aves, Pte Charles, 156, 157, 165

Ba Maw, Dr, 15, 16, 17, 34, 123–4, 174–6, 188, 375, 413, 414

Ba Sein (Thakin politician), 17, 34–5, 175
Bagot, Lt-Gen Charles, 70, 82
Bahadur, Rfn Amrit, 52
Baho government (puppet regime), 122
Baird-Murray, Maureen, 121–2, 420
Balance, Capt Derek, 427
Baldwin, AM John, 247, 280
Ballinger, Lt-Col G.A., 60
Bandon, AVM, Earl of, 344
Banzai Hideki, Maj, 421
Barker, A.J., 234
Barlow, Brig A.E., 83
Barlow, Lt-Col Jack, 356, 404
Barnard, Jack, 114
Barnes, Maj J.F.F., 326
Barrett, Gnr Allan, 316
Barrowclough, Gnr Harry, 316
Bates, Pte Richard F., 330
Baz, Sub Moghal, 422
Beable, Sgt Ed, 64–5
Bears, Arthur, 234
Beattie, Alexander, 110, 118–19
Beaumont, Nurse Winifred, 7, 433–4
Belden, Jack, 272
Bell, Capt Tony, 394
Bell, Flt Sgt J.V., 268
Bell, Lt C.W., 353
Bentley-Smith, Lt, 152
Berrigan, Darrel, 96
Beswick, Capt Leslie, 312, 410
Bickersteth, Lt Anthony, 196
Bickford, Lt-Col Wilbur, 290
Bilin (river), 55, 56, 58, 62
Blackburn, Wg Cdr James, 347
Blaker, Maj Jim, 332–3
Blue, Pte Clyde, 381
Boatner, Brig-Gen Haydon L., 207–9,
    328, 330
Bose, Rash Behari, 175
Bose, Subhas Chandra, 16, 17, 174, 175,
    187, 188, 414, 427
Bourke, Brig John, 48, 52, 59, 62
Bowen, Maj Charles, 235
Bowen, Capt John, 321
Bower, Ursula Graham, 173, 200
Boyd, William L., 31–2
Braidwood Dolloff, Phyllis, 330
Branson, Sgt Clive, 129, 137, 234–5

Braund, Mr Justice Harold, 110, 119
Brereton, Maj-Gen Lewis, 90
Brett, Lt-Gen George H., 43, 44
Brett-James, Capt Anthony, 224, 352, 417
Briggs, Maj-Gen Harold, 199
Brimah, Pte Aziz, 223
British and Commonwealth Forces:
  Allied Land Forces South-East Asia
    (ALFSEA), 182, 342, 417
  Armies: 11th Army Group, 182, 194,
    321; Twelfth Army, 416, 417,
    419–20, 422, 424; Fourteenth Army,
    3, 182, 193–5, 234, 273, 297, 310,
    324, 342, 344, 357, 370, 371, 373,
    378, 379, 380, 386, 390, 398, 403,
    407, 410–12, 414, 416; Eastern
    Army (earlier Eastern Command),
    133, 140
  Corps: Burcorps (Burma Corps), 76,
    77, 81, 84–6, 93, 95, 102, 104, 111;
    IV, 112, 126, 127, 133, 135, 159, 164,
    170, 193, 195, 197, 200, 202, 303,
    378, 379, 383, 386, 394, 404, 405,
    411, 421; XV, 133, 140, 149, 222,
    223, 226, 228, 237, 240, 344, 365,
    370, 379; XXX, 341; XXXIII, 273,
    344, 353, 378, 379, 386, 404, 410,
    411, 417
  Divisions: 1st Burma (later 39th
    Indian), 22, 43, 67, 70, 76, 77, 78,
    79, 86, 93, 95–6, 100, 102–3, 134;
    2nd, 6, 140, 149–50, 260, 266, 271,
    297, 305, 323, 357, 383, 386, 389–90,
    393, 395; 3rd Indian (Special Force),
    239, 241, 325–7, 337; 5th Indian,
    195, 199, 202, 222, 224–6, 228, 229,
    236, 267, 275–7, 287, 318, 344, 351,
    379, 401, 409–11, 425; 7th
    Australian, 56, 65; 7th Indian, 152,
    222, 224–6, 228, 229, 233, 277, 297,
    299, 384, 386, 388, 396, 404, 405,
    420; 8th Australian, 56; 11th (East
    African), 324, 344, 348–9, 379; 14th
    Indian, 131–3, 140–1, 143, 144,
    147–8, 150; 15th Indian, 189, 226;
    17th Indian, 43, 47, 53, 58, 62, 66,
    67, 69, 74, 76, 77, 81, 84, 86, 93,
    95–6, 100, 102, 105, 110–11, 133,

134, 170–2, 193–7, 198, 202, 275,
282–6, 289, 379, 385–7, 396, 404,
405, 411, 413, 421, 422, 424; 18th,
42, 63; 19th Indian, 355–7, 378, 380,
383, 386, 390–2, 395, 396, 398, 418;
20th Indian, 170, 193–6, 275, 277,
278, 281, 282, 286, 357, 379, 383,
386–8, 390, 393, 403, 411; 23rd
Indian, 110, 113, 133, 134, 159, 197,
200, 201, 275–8, 281, 324, 349; 25th
Indian, 134, 237, 344, 361, 364, 366,
368, 370, 372; 26th Indian, 133, 134,
143, 147, 148, 152, 228, 229, 232,
233, 237, 242, 355, 361, 364, 366,
368, 370, 372, 415; 36th Indian, 134,
229, 237, 326, 327, 333, 335, 354,
380, 382–3, 398; 70th, 133, 148, 240,
241; 81st (West African), 222 & n,
223, 237; 82nd (West African), 222
& n, 359, 361, 363, 365–7, 370–3;
Assam Line of Communications
Area (later 202nd Line of . . .), 126

Brigades: 1st Burma, 22, 77, 95, 96,
103; 1st Indian, 281; 2nd Burma, 22,
46–7, 48, 51, 52, 53, 55, 59, 67, 77,
102; 2nd (West African), 371; 3rd
Commando, 364, 366, 370; 3rd
(West African), 223, 242, 250, 251,
254, 258, 327, 329, 332, 335; 4th
Indian, 147, 148, 233, 237, 291, 292,
294–7, 302, 304, 369, 370, 372, 409;
5th Indian, 266, 292, 293, 295, 296,
301, 390, 395, 405; 5th (West
African), 360; 6th Indian, 141, 147,
148; 6th (West African), 131, 140,
144, 145, 266, 270, 291, 296, 302,
360; 7th Armoured, 59, 67, 77, 81n,
83, 93, 96, 102, 103, 105, 106; 9th
Indian, 288–90, 228, 229, 230, 236,
275, 276, 380, 401, 402; 10th Indian,
77; 13th Indian, 22, 77, 103; 14th
(LRP), 250, 251, 253, 327, 329, 332,
335; 15th, 251; 16th Indian, 22, 48,
50, 54–6, 58, 59, 60, 61, 81–2, 83,
84; 16th (LRP), 253; 22nd (East
African), 372; 23rd (LRP), 148, 240,
290, 297; 28th (East African), 384,
387; 29th, 127–8, 333; 29th Indian,

355; 36th Indian, 148, 369; 37th
Indian, 197, 277, 281; 44th Indian,
47; 45th Indian, 47; 46th Indian, 47,
55, 59, 60, 67; 47th Indian, 141–2,
143, 147, 148; 48th Indian, 55, 56,
58, 59, 69, 83, 84, 86, 95, 102, 105,
107, 172, 193, 284, 396, 399, 400,
402, 406; 49th Indian, 201, 278, 289;
50th Indian Tank, 133, 370; 50th
Indian Parachute, 200–1, 242, 286,
414; 51st Indian, 361 & n, 364, 365,
366; 55th Indian, 141–2, 143, 144,
148; 62nd Indian, 380, 392; 63rd
Indian, 67, 68, 70, 81–2, 83, 84, 101,
103, 110, 170, 191–3, 284–5, 396,
399, 400, 405, 406; 64th Indian, 380,
391; 71st Indian, 143, 147, 148,
369–70; 72nd, 237, 333, 336, 355;
74th Indian, 366, 371, 372; 77th
Indian, 156, 159, 242, 253, 254, 327,
331–2, 333; 80th Indian, 286; 88th
Indian, 141; 89th Indian, 170,
225–7, 230, 232, 233, 277, 287; 98th
Indian, 380, 392; 99th Indian, 398,
400, 405, 406; 100th Indian, 196,
286, 387; 111th (LRP), 159, 248,
251–3, 327, 329, 332, 333; 114th
Indian, 28, 233, 304, 384; 116th
Indian, 178; 123rd Indian, 141–3,
202, 225, 231, 233, 237, 275, 288–9,
409, 410; 150th Indian, 178; 161st
Indian, 22, 225, 236, 258, 260, 266,
269, 270, 277, 291, 296; 254th
Indian Tank, 275, 380, 356; 255th
Indian Tank, 396, 411; 268th
Lorried Indian, 297, 304, 355, 378,
390, 393, 411; Lushai, 297; Barcol,
356; Claudcol, 405–6; Dah Force
(LRP), 253; Morrisforce (LRP),
327–8; Strike Force (battle group),
81 & n, 82–3

Royal Armoured Corps:
3rd Carabiniers (Prince of Wales's
Dragoon Guards), 196, 275, 276,
285, 287, 289, 351, 353, 394, 395,
409
7th Queen's Own Hussars, 68–9, 70,
71, 82–3, 87, 106 & n

British and Commonwealth Forces (*cont.*)
  Royal Armoured Corps (*cont.*)
    25th Dragoons, 225, 229–34, 237
    2nd Battalion, The Royal Tank
      Regiment, 67, 68, 81n, 82, 86,
      95, 356
    116th Regiment RAC (Gordon
      Highlanders), 396
    146th Regiment RAC (Duke of
      Wellington's), 142, 369, 372
    149th Regiment RAC (York and
      Lancaster), 237, 267, 292
    150th Regiment RAC (King's Own
      Yorkshire Light Infantry), 267,
      282, 391, 393, 411
    45th Reconnaissance Regiment,
      Reconnaissance Corps, 250
  Indian Armoured Corps:
    Probyn's Horse (5th King Edward
      VII's Own Lancers), 396–7, 398,
      405
    7th Light Cavalry, 278, 288, 289,
      356, 391, 404
    8th King George V's Own Light
      Cavalry, 409
    Royal Deccan Horse (9th Horse),
      396, 398, 399
    Prince Albert Victor's Own (11th
      Frontier Force), 409
    16th Light Cavalry, 297, 398, 405
    19th King George V's Own Lancers,
      366, 371
    Central India Horse, 81
    45th Cavalry, 293
  Royal Artillery: 414th Battery (Essex
    Yeomanry), Royal Horse Artillery
    (TA), 82–3; 18th (Self-Propelled)
    Field Regiment, 404; 99th Field
    Regiment (Royal Buckinghamshire
    Yeomanry) (TA), 295, 394; 114th
    (Sussex) Field Regiment (TA),
    280–1, 412–13; 136th Field
    Regiment (1st West Lancashire)
    (TA), 234, 384; 129th (Lowland)
    Field Regiment (TA), 198; 158th
    Field Regiment, 113, 201; 160th
    Field Regiment, 370; 6th Medium
    Regiment, 230; 100th Anti-

Tank/Anti-Aircraft Regiment
    (Gordon Highlanders), 299; 36th
    Light Anti-Aircraft Regiment, 228;
    69th Light Anti-Aircraft Regiment,
    326; 8th (Belfast) Heavy Anti-
    Aircraft Regiment (SR), 230; 656th
    Air Observation Post Squadron, 226
  Indian Artillery: 2nd (Derajat)
    Mountain Battery, 261; 12th
    (Poonch) Mountain Battery, 47, 51,
    52; 15th (Jhelum) Mountain Battery,
    65, 201; 20th Mountain Battery, 261;
    28th Mountain Battery, 65; 24th
    Mountain Regiment, 261, 266; 30th
    Mountain Regiment, 360, 361; 1st
    Field Regiment, 67, 82 86; 7th Field
    Regiment, 361; 3rd Light Anti-
    Aircraft Battery, 45, 47, 51, 107; 8th
    Heavy Anti-Aircraft Battery, 45
  East African Artillery: 301st Field
    Regiment, 222; 302nd Field
    Regiment, 351–2
  Engineers: 24th Field Company, Royal
    Bombay Sappers and Miners, 47, 60;
    30th Field Company, Queen
    Victoria's Own Madras Sappers and
    Miners, 383, 427; 56th Field
    Company Queen Victoria's Own
    Madras Sappers and Miners, 56; 60th
    Field Company Queen Victoria's
    Own Madras Sappers and Miners,
    47, 51; 323rd Field Park Company,
    288; 8th (Sikh) Battalion, 144;
    Malerkotla Field Company (Indian
    States Forces), 58, 60, 96; Military
    Engineering Services (MES), 184;
    General Reserve Engineering Force
    (GREF), 184; Pioneer Corps
    (India), 135, 351, 368
  British Infantry:
    The Royal Scots (The Royal
      Regiment): 1st Battalion, 146,
      295, 298–9, 300, 302
    The Queen's Royal Regiment (West
      Surrey): 1st Battalion, 299, 300;
      2nd Battalion, 243
    The Buffs (Royal East Kent
      Regiment): 2nd Battalion, 383

The King's Own Royal Regiment (Lancaster): 2nd Battalion, 254–5

The Royal Warwickshire Regiment, 76

The King's Regiment (Liverpool): 1st Battalion, 254, 255; 13th Battalion, 156, 158

The Royal Norfolk Regiment: 2nd Battalion, 129, 151, 267, 295, 296, 299, 302

The Lincolnshire Regiment: 1st Battalion, 145, 148, 152, 232, 332, 369, 370, 415

The Devonshire Regiment: 1st Battalion, 278, 279, 322, 355, 368, 393

The Suffolk Regiment: 2nd Battalion, 288, 289, 410

The West Yorkshire Regiment (The Prince of Wales' Own): 1st Battalion, 68, 70, 82, 87, 170, 284, 287, 399, 414; 2nd Battalion, 182, 199, 230, 232–3, 258, 275, 289

The Leicestershire Regiment: 2nd Battalion, 250; 7th Battalion, 335

The Green Howards (Princess Alexandra's Own Regiment of Yorkshire): 2nd Battalion, 372

The Lancashire Fusiliers: 1st Battalion, 247, 332; 1/8th Battalion, 294, 296, 304

The Royal Scots Fusiliers: 1st Battalion, 355

The Royal Welch Fusiliers: 1st Battalion, 13, 145–7, 269, 294, 296–7, 302, 390; 2nd Battalion, 313

The South Wales Borderers: 6th Battalion, 237, 260, 335, 383

The King's Own Scottish Borderers (Edinburgh Regiment): 2nd Battalion, 225, 232, 255

The Cameronians (Scottish Rifles): 1st Battalion, 69, 81n, 86, 246, 255, 327, 328 & n, 392

The Royal Inniskilling Fusiliers: 1st Battalion, 77, 96, 97, 141, 142

The Gloucestershire Regiment: 1st Battalion, 20, 35, 45, 64, 70, 72, 80, 81 & n, 82, 83, 102, 111, 172

The Worcestershire Regiment: 7th Battalion, 266, 296, 301, 305, 390

The East Lancashire Regiment: 2nd Battalion, 336

The Duke of Wellington's Regiment (West Riding): 2nd Battalion, 58, 59, 62, 63, 67, 70, 81 & n, 83

The Border Regiment: 2nd Battalion, 280, 388; 9th Battalion, 172, 198, 284, 311, 398

The Royal Sussex Regiment, 157; 9th Battalion, 335–6, 355, 383

The South Staffordshire Regiment: 1st Battalion, 248–9, 331, 332

The Dorset Regiment: 2nd Battalion, 293, 294, 296, 300, 304, 390, 405

The South Lancashire Regiment (Prince of Wales' Volunteers): 2nd Battalion, 388–9

The Welch Regiment: 2nd Battalion, 392

The Essex Regiment: 1st Battalion, 322

The Northamptonshire Regiment: 1st Battalion, 196, 282–3, 284, 357

The Royal Berkshire Regiment (Princess Charlotte of Wales's): 1st Battalion, 145, 271, 290, 291, 296, 302; 2nd Battalion, 380, 393, 429

The Queen's Own Royal West Kent Regiment: 4th Battalion, 258, 260 & n, 261–5, 269, 271, 322

The King's Own Yorkshire Light Infantry: 2nd Battalion, 20, 51, 53, 55, 61, 62, 67, 95, 96, 100, 111

The Oxfordshire and Buckinghamshire Light Infantry: 6th Battalion, 363, 371

The Manchester Regiment: 2nd Battalion, 300

The North Staffordshire Regiment (The Prince of Wales's): 1st Battalion, 152

British and Commonwealth Forces (*cont.*)
British Infantry (*cont.*)
The York and Lancaster Regiment:
2nd Battalion, 335; 7th Battalion,
410; 9th Battalion, 365, 371
The Durham Light Infantry: 2nd
Battalion, 146, 271, 291, 294, 296,
302
The Seaforth Highlanders (Ross-
shire Buffs, Duke of Albany's): 1st
Battalion, 110, 166, 197, 281
The Queen's Own Cameron
Highlanders: 1st Battalion, 267,
293, 296, 301, 390
1st Commando, 368
142nd Independent Commando
Company, 161
143rd Special Service Company, 292
Indian Infantry:
1st Punjab Regiment: 1st Battalion,
1, 266, 297, 300, 351; 2nd
Battalion, 142, 144, 202, 233, 353;
5th Battalion, 369
2nd Punjab Regiment: 2nd
Battalion, 367; 3rd Battalion, 236,
288, 289, 401; 7th Battalion, 24,
232, 302, 322, 429
3rd Madras Regiment: 4th Battalion,
279
4th Bombay Grenadiers: 2nd
Battalion (King Edward's Own),
368, 369; 3rd Battalion, 230, 391;
4th Battalion, 396–7, 400–1,
405
5th Mahratta Light Infantry: 4th
Battalion, 201, 277; 6th Battalion,
159; 17th Battalion, 359, 371
6th Rajputana Rifles: 5th Battalion
(Napier's), 278, 281; 8th Battalion,
144
7th Rajput Regiment: 1st (Queen
Victoria's Own) Light Infantry
Battalion, 141; 2nd Battalion
(Prince Albert Victor's), 80, 96,
237, 369, 372; 4th Battalion, 224,
263, 270, 293, 296; 6th Battalion,
400, 405, 424
8th Punjab Regiment, 23n; 2nd

Battalion, 148, 383; 5th (Burma)
Battalion, 141
9th Jat Regiment, 198; 1st Royal
Battalion (Light Infantry), 50, 62,
107; 3rd Battalion, 236, 276, 289;
5th Battalion, 223
10th Baluch Regiment: 5th
Battalion (King George's Own)
(Jacob's Rifles), 380, 383, 395; 7th
Battalion, 54–5, 282, 399, 406,
420; 14th Battalion, 359, 371;
16th Battalion, 341, 366–7
11th Sikh Regiment: 1st Battalion
(King George V's Own)
(Ferozepore Sikhs), 67, 71, 224,
237, 287–8, 355, 380, 387, 389,
401, 420; Machine-Gun Battalion,
393, 450
12th Frontier Force Regiment: 4th
Battalion (Sikhs), 47, 51, 56, 58,
60, 62, 63, 67, 82, 100, 413; 9th
Battalion, 278–9
13th Frontier Force Rifles: 2nd
Battalion, 70, 82, 103, 237, 372,
373; 8th Battalion, 369, 397; 14th
Battalion, 196, 387
14th Punjab Regiment: 3rd
Battalion, 289; 4th Battalion, 224,
352; 9th Battalion, 196, 283
15th Punjab Regiment: 1st
Battalion, 3, 140, 148; 4th
Battalion, 299, 300, 302, 303,
388, 389, 404, 420; 6th Battalion,
424
16th Punjab Regiment: 1st
Battalion, 193, 282; 7th Battalion,
236, 365, 368, 372
17th Dogra Regiment: 1st Battalion
(Prince of Wales's Own), 142,
276, 288, 289, 351; 5th Battalion,
55, 61, 62, 84
18th Garwhal Rifles: 1st Battalion,
369–70; 4th Battalion, 365
19th Hyderabad Regiment: 1st
Battalion (Russell's), 383, 421; 2nd
Battalion (Berar), 287; 4th
Battalion, 128; 8th Battalion,
366–7

Assam Regiment: 1st Battalion, 109, 200, 258, 259, 269, 271

Assam Rifles: 3rd (Chin Hills) Battalion, 258, 269

152nd Parachute Battalion, 202

153rd Parachute Battalion, 201, 202

Patiala Infantry (Indian State Forces): 1st Battalion, 166, 282

Gurkha Infantry:

1st King George V's Own Gurkha Rifles (The Malaun Regiment), 410; 3rd Battalion, 279; 4th Battalion, 225, 280, 295, 297, 298, 300, 301, 303

2nd King Edward VII's Own Goorkha Rifles (The Sirmoor Regiment), 410; 3rd Battalion, 156-7 & n, 162, 165, 167, 359, 366, 371-2

3rd Queen Alexandra's Own Gurkha Rifles: 1st Battalion, 60, 61, 67, 86, 107, 193, 406; 3rd Battalion, 287

4th Prince of Wales's Own Gurkha Rifles, 111; 1st Battalion, 59, 60, 61, 62, 69, 86, 172, 193, 283; 3rd Battalion, 172-3; 4th Battalion, 392-3

5th Royal Gurkha Rifles (Frontier Force), 67; 2nd Battalion, 67, 86, 87, 107, 171, 172, 197, 284-5, 287; 3rd Battalion, 172, 198

6th Gurkha Rifles: 1st Battalion, 76, 77, 395, 402; 3rd Battalion, 248, 249, 331-2

7th Gurkha Rifles, 107; 1st Battalion, 50, 67, 69, 86, 107, 264, 284, 399, 415; 3rd Battalion, 54, 61, 62, 67

8th Gurkha Rifles, 158; 1st Battalion, 237, 415; 3rd Battalion, 196, 282, 283; 4th Battalion, 230, 232, 417, 420

9th Gurkha Rifles, 410; 3rd Battalion, 242, 254, 255, 332, 337; 4th Battalion, 253

10th Gurkha Rifles, 20n, 156; 1st Battalion, 68, 193, 195, 284; 3rd Battalion, 281; 4th Battalion, 196, 278

African Infantry:

11th East African Scouts, 231, 236

King's African Rifles: 4th (Uganda) Battalion, 351; 11th (Kenya) Battalion, 350; 22nd (Nyasaland) Battalion, 351; 26th (Tanganyika Territory) Battalion, 351; 71st (Somaliland) Battalion, 350

Nigeria Regiment: 4th Battalion, 360; 5th Battalion, 372; 7th Battalion, 254; 12th Battalion, 253

Gold Coast Regiment: 5th Battalion, 223, 235, 361; 7th Battalion, 235, 236

Sierra Leone Regiment: 1st Battalion, 360

Gambia Regiment: 1st Battalion, 236, 237-8

Royal Army Service Corps (RASC), 394

Royal Army Medical Corps (RAMC), 394

Queen Alexandra's Imperial Military Nursing Service (QAIMNS), 312

Royal Indian Army Service Corps (RIASC), 134-5; 309th General Purpose Transport Company, 135, 171

Indian Army Ordnance Corps (IAOC), 135

Indian Electrical and Mechanical Engineers (IEME), 135, 356, 357, 412

Indian Army Medical Corps (IAMC), 135; 41st Indian General Hospital, 7, 310; 53rd Indian General Hospital, 256; 66th Indian General Hospital, 310; No.1 Malaria Field Laboratory, 149; Malaria Forward Treatment Units, 149-50; 7th Indian Malaria Forward Treatment Unit (IMFTU), 353

British and Commonwealth Forces (*cont.*)
Indian Medical Service, 135
Indian Medical Department, 135
Indian Hospital Corps, 135
Pioneer Corps (India), 135, 351, 368
Corps of Military Police (India), 135
Women's Auxiliary Service (Burma), 63, 314
Women's Auxiliary Corps (India), 135–6
Burma Intelligence Corps, 349
55th Observation Sqn (deception unit), 226
Indian Field Broadcasting Unit (IFBU), 145, 146, 278
Burma Army:
Burma Rifles: 1st Battalion, 51, 96, 115, 166; 2nd Battalion, 42, 47, 49; 3rd Battalion, 47, 49, 51, 59, 60, 63, 67; 4th Battalion, 61, 67; 5th Battalion, 80, 95, 96; 6th Battalion, 47, 49; 7th (Burma Police) Battalion, 47, 51, 96; 8th (Frontier Force) Battalion, 47, 48, 51, 52, 61, 67; 9th (Reserve) Battalion, 78, 108; 12th (Lower Burma) Battalion, 96
Burma Regiment: 1st Battalion, 258, 302, 389; 4th Battalion, 205
Burma Auxiliary Force (BAF), 20–1
Burma Defence Force, 20–1
Burma Frontier Force (BFF), 19, 20–1, 81, 85, 116, 134; FF2, 42, 59; Kohine Battalion, 49
Burma Intelligence Corps, 349
Burma Military Police, 20, 68, 134
Nepalese Army: Kalibahadur Regiment, 201; Shere Regiment, 258
Other Units: West India Regiment, 76; Birmingham University Officers' Training Corps, 76
Royal Air Force:
Indian Air Force (IAF; *later* RIAF), 409; Combined Army Air Transport Organization (CAATO), 222, 344

Groups: 221 Gp, 195, 222, 240, 343; 224 Gp, 222, 224, 343, 344; 231 Gp, 347; 267 Gp, 46
Wings: 177 Wing, 222, 247; 293 Wing, 318; 901 Wing, 393
Squadrons: 1 Sqn (Indian Air Force), 46, 77, 195; 5 Sqn, 195; 11 Sqn, 90; 17 Sqn, 46, 77, 80, 84, 343; 27 Sqn, 347; 28 Sqn, 46, 77, 195, 319; 31 Sqn, 108, 168–9, 229, 240, 268, 401; 45 Sqn, 46, 77; 47 Sqn, 347; 60 Sqn, 20; 62 Sqn, 229; 67 Sqn, 20, 45, 77; 81 Sqn, 229, 240, 248; 94 Sqn, 277; 110 Sqn, 415; 113 Sqn, 46, 77; 135 Sqn, 46, 77; 136 Sqn, 144; 139 Sqn, 77, 88; 152 Sqn, 289; 155 Sqn, 348; 159 Sqn, 347; 177 Sqn, 347, 348, 393; 194 Sqn, 199, 229, 240; 205 Sqn, 277; 211 Sqn, 348; 357 Sqn, 320; 490 Sqn, 189; No. 3 Photographic Reconnaissance Unit, 319; 656 Air Observation Post Sqn, 364; 517 Air Ministry Experimental Station (radar unit), 20
Royal Navy, 89, 90, 143, 144, 415; Eastern Fleet, 88; Headquarters Coastal Force, 143; *Athelstane* (Fleet Auxiliary), 90; *Cornwall*, HMS, 89; *Dorsetshire*, HMS, 89; *Formidable*, HMS, 89; *Hermes*, HMS, 89, 90; *Hollyhock*, HMS, 90; *Indomitable*, HMS, 37, 89; *Indus*, HMIS, 90; *Ladybird*, HMS, 29; *Narbada*, HMIS, 363; *Pamela* (gunboat), 357; *Pathfinder*, HMS, 370; *Phoebe*, HMS, 344; *Prince of Wales*, HMS, 37; *Queen Elizabeth*, HMS, 364, 369, 415; *Ramsay*, HMAS, 365; *Repulse*, HMS, 37; *Richelieu* (Free French warship), 415; *Rita* (RM boat), 74; *Scythia*, HMS, 429; *Una* (gunboat), 357; *Vampire*, HMAS, 90; *Vita*, HMAS (hospital ship), 90; *Warspite*, HMS, 89; Combined Operations Pilotage Party (COPP), 366; Sea Reconnaissance Unit (SRU), 358; 42nd (Royal Marines) Commando,

364–5; 44th (Royal Marines) Commando, 237; Burma Royal Naval Volunteer Reserve, 20

*British Sergeant* (tanker), 90

Bromhead, Maj George, 162

Brooke, Gen Sir Alan, 46, 176–8, 180, 280, 334, 341, 342, 416–17

Brookes, Stephen, 1, 84, 101–2, 116, 118, 119

Brook-Popham, ACM Sir Robert, 18, 22, 37

Brooks, Tom, 2, 116

Brown, Flt Lt Athol Sutherland, 348

Brown, Col Rothwell H., 206

Brown, Lt-Col W.F. ('Bruno'), 200

Browning, Lt-Gen Frederick ('Boy'), 342, 416

Brownless, Capt P.P.S., 321–2

Burchett, Wilfred, 65, 101, 113

Burma Campaign Fellowship Group, 6

Burma Frontier Service, 51

Burma Independence Army (BIA; *later* Burma National Army (BNA); *later* Burma Defence Army (BDA); *then* Burmese Patriotic Forces), 49, 74, 81, 82, 90–1, 122, 124, 174, 176, 207, 321, 375, 403, 418, 421, 424

Burma Road, 93, 130, 338, 354, 380; strategic value, 3, 12, 16, 30, 31, 33, 63, 71, 79, 84, 140; Gokteik viaduct, 34, 104, 163, 164

Burma Royal Naval Volunteer Reserve, 20, 144

Burma Socialist Programme Party, 432

Burma Star Association, 2, 6

Burma–Thailand Railway, 122–3, 124, 130, 173, 186, 188, 347, 425–6

Burmah Oil Company, 13, 69, 96

Burmans (ethnic Burmese), 12 & n, 13, 20, 87, 100, 115

Burnett, Capt F.T., 297

Bush Warfare School, 74, 114

Busk, Mike, 253

Cady, John, 7

Cairns, Lt George, 249

Calcutta, 12, 65, 70, 77, 113

Calistan, Maj Albert, 269

Callahan, Professor Raymond, 2, 3

Calvert, Brig Mike, 74, 104, 106–7, 112, 114, 155, 161–5, 168, 246, 247, 248–9, 287, 331, 332, 336, 337

Cameron, Brig R., 171, 172

Camp Robert W. Landis, 344

Cane, Maj Peter, 253, 328

Carbonell, Lt J.A.C., 269

Carew, Capt Tim, 287

Carfrae, Maj Charles, 254

Carmichael, Lt Pat, 73, 78, 91, 97, 105, 112

Carr, 2nd Lt Peter, 111–12

casualties: treatment of, 309–12, 336–7

Cavendish, Brig Ronnie, 145, 146, 147

*CBI Roundup* (newspaper), 354

Ceylon, 88, 89

Chan Won-Loy, Capt, 326–7

Chand, Capt Sobha, 400–1

Chandra, Anil, 409

Chapman, Lt-Col G.P., 319

Charles, Marine Robert H., 425

Chatfield, Admiral of the Fleet, Lord, 28

Chennault, Brig-Gen Claire L., 32, 50, 77, 98, 113–14, 125–6, 132, 176, 211, 334

Cherry Society (Japanese military faction), 187

Chiang Kai-shek, Generalissimo, 4, 16, 19, 30–2, 37, 40–1, 43, 56, 74–5, 85–6, 98, 114, 127, 130–2, 176, 180–1, 211, 334, 338–80; *see also* Stilwell

Chiang, Madam (Soong Mei-Ling) 16, 31, 32, 41, 43, 95

Chiangi Gaol, 122

*Chicago Daily News*, 33

Chin Hills, 12, 170, 171, 194, 273

Chin Levies (intelligence group), 173, 191

China Air Task Force, 126

China National Air Corporation (CNAC), 31

Chindits *see* Wingate

Chindwin (river), 11, 12, 93, 102, 105, 109, 156, 246, 351, 378

Chinese Forces:
  Armies: 1st Army, 354; 5th Army, 67,
    77, 78, 79, 85, 99, 101, 114; 6th
    Army, 75, 77, 85, 93, 98, 114; 66th
    Army, 5; Y Force (later Chinese
    Expeditionary Force (CEF)), 74–5,
    127, 180, 181, 209, 211, 215, 217,
    218, 243, 334, 338, 339, 354, 380; X
    Force (also Ramargh Force), 127,
    181, 354
  Divisions: 14th, 217; 18th, 210; 22nd,
    86, 114, 209, 215, 325, 354, 355;
    30th, 209, 354; 36th, 339, 357; 38th,
    96 & n, 100, 103, 114, 181, 208,
    209, 213, 217; 49th, 98; 50th, 217,
    354, 355; 55th, 98; 93rd, 43, 98, 104;
    96th, 98, 114–15; 116th, 339; 130th,
    339; 198th, 339; 200th, 79, 99, 114
  Regiments: 1st Provisional Tank
    Group, 213; 12th Engineer, 207;
    65th, 209; 88th, 213; 113th, 215,
    216; 114th, 331, 382; 150th, 326
  Others: US/CC 1st Provisional Tank
    Group, 209, 215
Chinese Army in India (CAI; also
  Ramgarh force), 206, 207
Chins (Burmese minority ethnic group),
  20, 52
Chittagong, 12, 13, 80, 144, 186, 363
Choke, Ken, 409
Christison, Capt J.A.A., 70, 195
Christison, Lt-Gen Philip, 222, 225, 226,
  228, 229, 232, 233, 236, 342, 344, 358,
  359, 364, 366, 368–9, 370, 371, 416
Chungking, 41, 43, 74, 85, 114
Churchill, Winston S., 3, 18, 38, 40,
  42–3, 46, 56–7, 65, 95, 126, 132,
  148–9, 168, 176–8, 240, 280, 321, 341
Clarke, Capt Rupert, 67
Clayton, Nancy ('Bubbles'), 314
Clifford, J. Francis, 423
Cloak (deception plan) see Irrawaddy
Coath, Capt Tom, 265
Cochran, Col Phil, 239, 240, 241–2, 243,
  246, 248, 255
Cochrane, V-Adm the Hon. Sir
  Archibald, 19
Collen, Lt-Col K.H., 351

Collingwood, Brig George, 388
Collis, Maurice, 13–14, 17
Collister, Lt Peter, 72, 83, 129, 178, 312
Colombo, 74, 88, 89
Colvin, John, 200
Congress Party, 128, 200
Connolly, Tpr M.L., 353
Control Faction (Japanese military
  faction), 29
Conway, FO Gordon, 144, 224
Cook, CSM, 267
Cooke, Maj Edward, 78, 108–9, 115–18
Cookson, Capt David, 235, 237–8
Cooper, Bill, 243
Cooper, Lt K.W., 388
Cooper, Maj R.A., 286
Co-Prosperity Sphere, Greater East Asia
  (Japanese), 31, 123, 124
Corlett, Lt John, 259
Corpe, Hilda, 410
Cotton, Sqn Ldr Monty ('Bush'), 46, 151
Coughlin, Col John G., 375
Coulthard, Pte G., 316
Cowan, Maj-Gen David Tennant
  ('Punch'), 54, 62, 66, 80, 81, 84,
  195–198, 284–6, 399–400, 402, 405,
  413
Craddock, SSM, 276
Craigie, Sir Robert, 33
Crowther, Sgt Bill, 61
Crowther, Maj-Gen W.A., 421
Crumpacker, Edgar D., 318
Cuming, Brig A.E., 191–2
Cumming, Lt J.A., 111–12
Cunningham, Adm Sir Andrew, 179
Curtin, John (PM of Australia), 56–7
Cusworth, Sgt C.C., 282–3

D Division (intelligence group), 379
Daily Express, 159, 168
Daily Herald, 390
Daily Mail, 168
Dass, 2nd Lt Mehar, 52
Davies, 2nd Lt Dickie, 129
Davies, Brig H.L. ('Taffy'), 60
Davies, Nurse Martha, 310
Davis, Maj Patrick, 402, 423
Dawson, Brig J.A., 344

Day, Lt Donald, 283
Degaa Upfill, Minty, 429–31, 432
Degg, Maj Ron, 248
Dell, Capt James, 243
Dempsey, Gen Sir Miles, 417
Dent-Smith, L Cpl C., 170
Detachment 101 see American Office of
    Strategic Services
Dill, Gen Sir John, 19, 20, 46
Dillon, Capt Terence, 70
Dimapur (Manipur Road), 73, 109, 110,
    112, 113, 118–19, 131, 135, 256, 258,
    260, 266, 290
Din, Nk Fazal, 399
Din, Sub Mata, 367
Dobama Asionye ('We Burmese' Society),
    14
Dolan, Tom, 286
Donald, Lt-Col A.A. ('Archie'), 72, 137
Donaldson, Gp Capt George, 247
Donbaik see Arakan
Donovan, Col William ('Wild Bill'), 64,
    139
Dorman-Smith, Lady, 65, 103
Dorman-Smith, Rt Hon. Sir Reginald,
    19–20, 43, 47–8, 55, 56, 63, 65, 67, 75,
    85, 99, 101, 321, 431
Dorn, Brig-Gen Frank ('Pinky'), 30–1,
    214, 218
Douglas, ACM Sir Sholto, 179
Doyle, Marine William, 115, 118
Drive Away the Fascist Japanese Marauders
    (AFO manifesto), 375
Drum, Lt-Gen Hugh A., 41
Dunlop, Lt-Col Edward ('Weary'), 123
Dunlop, Maj George, 162
Durant, Lt Norman, 249, 252, 331
Dyer, Lt-Col Jerry, 54

East Asia Youth League, 125, 176, 375
East India Company, 13, 23, 24
Edward, Lt-Col W.D. ('Donny'), 47
Edwards, CSM John, 313
Edwards-Stuart, Lt-Col I.A.J., 51
Eifler, Carl F., 139
Ekin, Brig Roger, 47, 52, 53, 56, 61, 111
Emmett, Maj George, 162
Erikson, Lt H., 206

Eureka Conference (Tehran, 1943), 181
Evans, Capt Charles, 185, 353, 393–4,
    396, 412
Evans, Brig-Gen Frederick W., 222, 230,
    232, 388
Evans, Brig Geoffrey, 228, 230
Evans, Lt Glyn, RN, 415
Evans, Tpr John, 230
Everard, PO Hedley ('Snooks'), 80

Faggion, Pfc Peter J., 382
Faithfull, Maj C.K.T., 83
Farrow, Lt, 420
Fearnley, Lt Arthur, 68, 96
Ferguson Hoey, Maj Charles, 232
Fergusson, Maj Bernard, 156, 161, 162,
    163, 164, 167, 241–2, 243, 250
Ferrying Command (later Air Transport
    Command (ATC)), 52, 125–6, 127
Festing, Maj-Gen Francis Wogan, 333
Fiddament, Pte Dick, 151–2
Field, Brig L.F., 41
Finnerty, Sgt John ('Tim'), 96–7
Fischer, Edward L., 43, 312
Fitt, Sgt Bert ('Winkie'), 297–8
Fitzpatrick, Lt Gerald, 95, 97, 100, 111
Followers (Non-Combatant Enrolled),
    72n, 300
Force 'Viper', 74
Forster, Mr Leslie, 69
Fort Dufferin (Mandalay), 101, 392,
    394–5
Fort Hertz (Putao), 114, 118, 159, 166,
    205, 206
Fortreath, Maj G.M., 68
Foucar, Emile, 432
4th/8th Gurkha Rifles News Chronicle,
    384
Fowler, Maj Tony ('Raj'), 299
Fox, Cpl, 62
Fraser, Adm Sir Bruce, 343
Freedom Bloc see Thakin Party
Friend, Flt Sgt Albert, 251–2
Frink, Lt-Col H.R.C. ('Frinkie'), 229,
    230
Fujida, L Cpl, 142, 145–6
Fulton, Maj R., 350
Fumimaro, Prince Konoye, 33

Gadsdon, Maj Peter, 352
Galahad *see* United States Forces:
    Ground: 5307th Composite Unit
    (Provisional)
Gallagher, O.D., 75
Gardiner, Capt David, 237
Gardiner, Ritchie, 119, 320
Garrod, AM Sir Guy, 343
*Gazette of India* (newspaper), 17
Genfi, Pte Kofi, 235
George, Lt John B., 216
Geren, Paul, 79–80
'Gert' and 'Daisy' (entertainers), 311, 328
Ghandi, Mohandas K. (Mahatma), 56,
    128, 186
Ghonse, Signalman Syed, 48
Gibson, Perla Siedle, 222
Giffard, Gen Sir George, 149, 182, 195,
    209, 242, 280, 341–3
Giles, Maj Ken, 165
Gilliam, Neil, 281, 287
Gilmore, Maj Scott, 232, 316, 385, 428–9
Girsham, Jack, 213
Goddard, Maj-Gen Eric, 43, 66–7, 101
Goddard, Gp Capt Henry, 289
Gordon, Ernest, 240
Goschen, Brig Willie, 295, 299, 300
Gracey, Maj-Gen Douglas, 193, 196–7,
    278–9, 387, 393, 394, 403–4
Grant, Maj-Gen Ian Lyall, 198
Graves, Lt David, 146
Graves-Morris, Lt-Col, 255
Gribble, R.H., 116, 118
Grover, Maj-Gen John, 266, 267, 269,
    291, 292, 294, 297, 299, 301–2, 305,
    323
Gudgeon, Maj Denis, 414, 429
*Gunseikanbu* (Japanese military
    government), 123
Gurung, Rfn Bahn Bhagra, 371–2
Gurung, Rfn Lachhiman, 417
Gurung, Rfn Lalbahadur, 61
Gurung, Nk Sunbahadur, 197
Gyaw, Lt Ba, 173

Hafiz, Jem Abdul, 276
*Hai Lee* (Norwegian freighter), 17
Haines, CSM W., 270

Hamilton, Lt John, 235
Hanaya Tadashi, Lt-Gen, 226, 228, 233,
    236, 237
Hankin, Thomas, 310
Hanley, Gerald, 319, 349, 385
Harada Munaji, Col, 82
Harkabir, C.H.M., 406
Harman, Lt Carter, 253
Harman, L Cpl John, 264
Harper, Capt Alec, 337
Harvey, Oliver, 179
Harvey-Williams, Maj S.F., 61
Hasted, Brig Bill, 357
Hasten, Maj Donald, 270
*Hastings* (steamer), 74
Hawkins, Brig Victor, 266, 269, 271, 292,
    294, 300
Hayashi Yoshihide, Maj-Gen, 250, 252
Hazell, Sgt Fred, 129, 150, 267, 292
Hedley, Capt John, 421
*Heinrich Jenson* (steamer), 70
Hekking, Dr Henri, 425
Helliwell, Arthur, 390
Hely, Brig A.F. ('Tim'), 228, 231
Hemingway, FO Kenneth, 80
Henslow, Lt John, 355–6, 388–9
Herring, Lt-Col D.C., 253
Hiatt, Lt-Col Wright, 208
Hickey, Michael, 336
Hill, Maj John, 5–6, 315, 356, 380, 417,
    428
Hilsman, Roger, 210
Hiraku Masao, 266
Hirohito, Emperor, 29, 423
Hiscox, Gnr Norman, 384–5
Hla Pe, U., 123
Ho Chi Minh, 418
Ho Ying-chin, Gen, 98
Hobson, Lt-Col Pat, 228
Hodson, Sgt Wallace, 280
Hogan, Sqn Ldr Guy, 195
Holt, LA Bert, 89
Honda Masaki, Lt-Gen, 251, 338, 339,
    401, 405–6, 409, 424
Hong Kong, 28, 176
Honjo Seikei, Capt, 49
Hope-Thomson, Brig M.R.T. ('Tim'),
    200–1, 202

Horner, Lt Sam, 294
Horsford, Lt-Col Derek, 303
Horwood, Lt John, 196
Howard, Capt John, 295, 298
Hubforce (taskforce), 237
Hudson, Lt John, 151, 279, 311, 314, 349
Hugh-Jones, Brig Noël, 59, 60, 62
Hukawng valley, 93, 101, 109, 116–17, 130, 181, 211
Hume, Maj John, 52
'Hump, the' (China–Burma air route), 31–2, 85, 115, 125, 132, 176, 199, 204–6, 211, 288, 354, 381
Humphreys, A.J., 222
Hunter, Col Charles, 211, 215–18, 326
Hutcheon, Chief Engineer William, 106
Hutton, Lt-Gen Thomas, 43, 46, 47–8, 50–6, 59, 60, 62, 63, 65–7, 77, 83

Igarishi Kisaku, Master Sgt, 318
Iida Shojiro, Lt-Gen, 37, 53, 66, 71, 79, 101, 123, 186
Imahara Kanichi, 2nd Lt, 399
Imanishi, Sgt-Maj, 292
Imperial Way (Japanese military faction), 187
Imphal, 7, 43, 101, 110, 111, 113, 256; siege of, 186–203, 272–89
India Tea Association (ITA), 109, 111, 184, 317
Indian Independence League (IIL), 174, 175
Indian National Army (INA), 4, 128–9, 174 & n, 175, 187, 200, 225, 236, 386, 389, 405, 411, 414, 427–8; Ghandi Brigade, 279
intelligence activities, 88, 137–40, 319–20
Irrawaddy (river), 11, 77, 78, 81, 93, 102–3, 164, 346, 354, 373, 374–90, 400
Irrawaddy Flotilla Company, 11, 67, 106, 108, 173, 363
Irwin, Capt Anthony, 137, 139
Irwin, Lt-Gen Noel, 112, 133, 140, 141, 145, 147, 179
Iwakuro Hideo, Maj-Gen, 190, 346, 422

Jacob, Alaric, 159, 168
Jagmal, Nk, 367

James, 2nd Lieut, Harold, 158, 162, 164, 166
James, Capt J.C.S., 356
Japan–Burma Association, 17
Japanese Forces:
  Imperial Japanese Navy: *Akagi*, HIJMS, 90; *I-27* (submarine), 223
  Armies:15th, 37, 48, 53, 71, 161, 163, 187, 280, 324, 338, 339, 346, 378, 386, 397, 398, 402, 405, 409, 418; 25th, 37, 42; 28th, 190, 223, 236, 338, 339, 359, 386, 404, 418, 419, 421, 423; 33rd, 190, 251, 337, 338, 354, 359, 378, 402, 406, 409, 418, 419, 424; Army Group Phoenix, 418
  Divisions: 2nd, 188, 190, 236, 338, 339, 397, 411; 5th Air, 221, 224, 273, 386; 15th, 189, 199, 202, 247, 256, 275, 277, 286, 289, 305, 322, 344, 350, 380, 386, 392, 410, 418; 18th, 71, 78, 98, 102, 161, 163, 186, 189, 190, 209, 216, 251, 337, 354, 394, 400–2, 405, 406, 420; 31st, 161, 188–19, 199, 201, 256, 262, 275, 286, 289, 323, 344, 350, 405; 33rd ('White Tigers'), 37, 53 & n, 55, 66, 78, 80, 81, 98, 103, 141, 186, 189, 196, 256, 282–5, 322, 344, 355, 397, 405; 36th, 411; 38th, 208; 49th, 346, 398, 400, 401, 405; 53rd, 251, 254, 287, 325, 338, 380, 386, 397, 400, 405, 420; 54th, 188–190, 287, 323, 369, 370–1, 419; 55th, 37, 42, 48, 53, 55, 66, 69, 78, 79, 98, 101, 141, 143, 147, 190, 404, 418; 56th, 37, 71, 79, 103, 161, 163, 164, 190, 217, 251, 338, 339, 382, 418
  Brigades: 7th Brigade (Air), 221; 24th Independent Mixed, 188, 250, 251, 411, 418; 105th Independent Mixed, 190, 411
  Regiments: 1st Tank, 98; 4th Infantry, 382; 5th Artillery, 404; 5th Railway, 426, 427; 13th Artillery, 31; 14th Tank, 98, 400; 16th Infantry, 397; 21st Artillery, 189; 36th Anti-Aircraft, 398; 51st Infantry, 275–7; 52nd Airfield, 398; 55th Reconnaissance,

Japanese Forces (*cont.*)
  Regiments (*cont.*)
    236, 354, 360, 401, 402; 55th
    Artillery, 49; 56th Infantry, 213, 354;
    58th Infantry, 201, 202, 261, 262,
    291, 302, 304; 60th Infantry, 202,
    247, 275, 277, 392; 67th Infantry,
    392; 84th Airfield, 398; 112th
    Infantry, 55, 66, 69, 79, 141, 142,
    208, 233, 404; 119th Infantry, 400;
    121st Infantry, 369; 124th Infantry,
    295, 305; 138th Infantry, 259, 262,
    264, 266, 291, 411; 143rd Infantry,
    42, 55, 56, 66, 68, 79; 151st Infantry,
    287; 154th Infantry, 287, 367–8;
    213th Infantry, 141, 196, 279, 285,
    379; 214th Infantry, 55, 56, 69, 70,
    81, 84, 86, 191, 282, 284–7; 215th
    Infantry, 54, 55, 59, 82, 84, 86, 95,
    198, 282, 285, 286
  Battalions: I/35th, 216; I/51st, 380;
    II/51st, 249; I/55th, 163, 164;
    II/55th, 164; III/55th, 163; I/56th,
    400; II/56th, 164; III/56th, 164;
    III/58th, 201, 266; III/111th, 236;
    III/112th, 49; I/114th, 216;
    III/114th, 249; II/128th, 331;
    III/128th, 331; II/143rd, 144, 232;
    III/143rd, 232; II/146th, 254;
    I/151st, 331; III/151st, 277; I/168th,
    398; II/168th, 398; III/213th, 144;
    III/214th, 70; I/215th, 86; II/215th,
    54, 81, 86; III/215th, 83; II/416th,
    164
  Other Units: 1st Railway Materials
    Workshop, 122; 2nd Field Transport,
    398, 400; 11th Disease Prevention
    and Water Supply Unit, 96; 13th
    Naval Base Unit, 190; 50th Air
    Regiment (*Sentai*), 318; 107th Lines
    of Communications Hospital, 398
Japanese Surrendered Personnel (JSP), 427
Jarrett, Capt Jimmy, 364
Jeffreys, Peter, 360
Jeffries, Maj John, 159, 161
Jenkinson, Maj C.R., 151
Johnson, Gnr W., 151, 309
Johnson, Lt, 233

Johnston, Maj Duncan, RM, 74, 100
Jones, C Sgt, 335
Jones, Fus, 59, 146
Jones, Sgt Reuben, 89, 146
Jones, Charles Braimer, 99
Jones, Brig J.K. ('Jonah'), 50, 54, 61
Jones, Paul, 210
Jones, Tom, 91
Jordan, Sqn Ldr Reg ('Lucky'), 347
Joubert de la Ferté, AM Sir Philip, 379
Judge, Lt Karamjit Singh, 404
Judson College (Rangoon), 79, 417
Jung Bahadur (PM of Nepal), 24
jungle warfare training, 47, 70, 171, 172,
  176–8, 321

Kachins (Burmese ethnic group), 12, 20,
  51, 52, 119, 134, 210, 215, 219, 320,
  433
Kalewa, 73, 93, 101, 102, 106, 107, 110
Kameyama Shosaku, Lt, 190, 201, 263
*Kamikaze*, 413 & n, 415
Kanir, Home, 350
Karen National Association, 13
Karens (Burmese ethnic group), 12, 13,
  20, 51, 68, 115, 320, 374–5, 409–10,
  421, 432, 433
Kasuya, Maj-Gen, 398, 399–400
Katamura Shihachi, Lt-Gen, 323, 398
Kawabe Masakazu (or Shozo), Lt-Gen,
  150, 161, 186–7, 206, 256, 288, 289,
  323, 339
Kawamata Koji, L Cpl, 35
KC 8 (intelligence group), 139
Kelly, Sgt E.P. ('Ted'), 284
Kelly, Capt Sean, 291
*Kempeitai* (Japanese military police), 124,
  173, 174, 374–5, 410, 418
Kerr, Lt John, 162
Khaing Mi Mi, 64, 430, 432
Khan, Mohammed Munsif, 433
Khan, Capt Rahim, 70
Khan, Nk Sher, 352
Khati, Dalbahadur, 410
*Khedive Ismail*, SS, 223
Kimura Heitaro (or Hoyotaro), Lt-Gen,
  323, 339, 346, 348, 358, 378, 387, 392,
  404, 409, 413, 416, 433

King, Adm Ernest J., 132, 176, 181, 325
Kinloch, Capt Bruce, 60
Kinnison, Lt-Col Henry L., 326
Knight, Lt Jack L., 382
Knowland, Lt George, 368
Knowles, Capt Stewart, 363
Koba Dai, Col, 163, 236
Koba Force (Japanese formation), 223
Koba Hiroshi, Col, 223
Koga Takeshi, Lt-Gen, 143, 147
Kohima, 6, 7: siege, 256–71; battle,
    290–305; see also Imphal
Koiso Kuniaki, Gen, 323
Kokubu Shozo, 34
Kondo Nobutake, V-Adm, 88
Kunming (China), 3, 12, 32, 115, 127
Kunomura Momoyo, Maj-Gen, 187, 190,
    305

Lacey, Sqn Ldr James ('Ginger'), 343
Lama, Rfn Ganju, 289
Langer, William, 210
Lashio, 3, 12, 53, 79, 80, 84, 98, 101, 115
Laverty, Lt-Col John ('Texas Dan'), 260,
    261, 262, 263, 264
Lawson, Capt John, 158, 394
Layton, Adm Sir Geoffrey, 88–9
Leathart, Capt Scott, 255
Ledo Road, 130, 133, 179, 206–8, 211,
    343, 353, 380
Leese, Lt-Gen Sir Oliver, 341–2, 344,
    371, 375, 378–9, 395, 403, 407, 409,
    416–17
Leigh-Mallory, ACM Sir Trafford, 343
Lentaigne, Brig W.D.A. ('Joe'), 248, 251,
    253, 327, 332
Leonard, Lt-Col R.G., 68
Lethbridge, Brig J.S. ('Tubby'), 417
Lewin, Ronald, 179
Lewis, Lt Alun, 221
Ley, Maj Hugh, 230
Leyin, Tpr John, 185, 235
Li Shi Fu, 339
Liao Yao-hsiang, 132, 218, 219, 325
Life (magazine), 169
Linlithgow, Victor, Marquis of, 17, 57
Lloyd, Maj-Gen Wilfred, 140, 141, 144,
    147, 149

Lo Chin-ying, Gen, 75, 86, 113
Loftus Tottenham, Maj-Gen F.J., 303
Lomax, Maj-Gen Clive, 147, 232
long range penetration (LRP), 156, 195,
    196, 241, 242–55, 321–2; see also
    United States Forces: Ground: 5307th
    Composite Unit; Merrill; Wingate
Longmore, Lt Peter, 198
Love, Maj S.W.A. ('Bwana'), 42
Lowry, Maj Martin, 303
Lubeck, Capt, 226
Lung Yun, Gen, 31–3
Lunnon-Wood, Flt Sgt, 348
Lunt, Lt James, 11, 21, 46–8, 51, 52, 58,
    64, 73, 80–1, 100
Lutz, Maj, 414
Lynn, Vera, 310

MacAllindon, Fr Denis, 139
McCann, Pte John, 294
McClane, CSM Martin, 146
McCrae, Alister, 363–4
McCrindle, Capt Eric, 115, 174, 374
MacDonald Fraser, L Cpl George, 6, 400,
    417
McDowell, Sgt John R., 354
MacFetridge, Maj Charles, 134
McGeary, Matron Agnes, 166–7
McGee, Lt George A., 320
Mackay, Capt Revd Donald, 246
Mackay, Capt Hamish, 111
MacKenzie, Colin, 375
Mackenzie, Compton, 433
Mackenzie, Col Kenneth, 53, 60, 414
McKie, Roy, 365, 416
McKnight, Tpr J., 234
Mackrell, Gyles, 119–20
McLeod, Maj-Gen D.K., 19, 43, 63
McLintock, J. Dewar, 385, 396
McNaught, Lt-Col Jock, 293, 300
McPhedran, Colin, 15, 103, 108, 117,
    118
McPhedran, Ethel, 118
McPhedran, Robert, 103–4, 117, 118
Maddox, Cpl, 74
Magee, Pat, 415
Magruder, Brig-Gen John, 40–1, 114,
    125

Magwe, 64, 66, 77, 80, 84, 86, 95–6, 108
Mains, Maj Tony, 64, 72
Malaria Forward Treatment Units
    (MFTU), 149–50
Malaya, 3, 18, 31, 33–4, 37, 43, 47, 71,
    417
Malloy, Pat, 431
Maloney, RSM Jim, 231
Manabu Wada, Senior Pte, 191
Mandalay, 12, 16, 45, 71, 74–5, 78, 80,
    94–5, 99, 100, 102, 391–5
Manekshaw, Capt S.H.J.F. ('Sam'), 60
Marayama Shizuo, 324
'March on Delhi' (Japanese), 186–203,
    431
Marment, Maj Arthur, 300, 303
Mars Task Force see US Forces: Ground
Marshall, Gen George C., 41, 132, 176,
    178, 181, 209, 215, 218, 339–40, 398–9
Martin, Rear-Admiral Bernard, 344
Maruyama Fusayasu, Col, 216, 217
Maslen-Jones, Capt Ted, 313
Masters, Lt-Col John, 157, 252, 253–4,
    327, 328, 333, 337, 392, 396, 409, 421
Mather, Capt John, 295
Matsui Hideji, Maj-Gen, 411
Matsumoto, Sgt Roy, 218
Matsumura Hiroshi, Col, 247–8
Matsuo Hideji, Maj-Gen, 414
Matsuyama, Lt-Gen, 164
Maude, Gen Sir F.S., 76, 77
Maung Maung, Dr, 94, 424–5
Maung Tun, 167
Maungdaw, 140–1, 148–9, 152, 237, 361
May, Pte Bert, 311
Maybury, Maurice, 395, 430
Maymyo, 73, 74, 77, 84, 85, 101, 102,
    104, 115
Meiktila, 78, 90, 93, 101, 378, 379, 386,
    396–406, 416
Merchant, Pte William, 251
Mercury (aircraft), 334
Merrill, Brig-Gen Frank D., 211–12, 215,
    217, 219–20, 326, 330; see also Galahad;
    Stilwell
Messervy, Lt-Gen Frank, 225, 226, 229,
    232, 383, 386, 387, 388, 411
Metcalfe, Capt Revd Neville, 69

Miller, Padre, 329
Miller, Capt Revd W.H., 255, 329
Milne, Brig Ian, 149
Minami Kikan (Minami Organisation),
    17–18, 49
Misra, Maj Dinesh ('Danny'), 281
Mitchell, Lt-Col T.W.M., 388–9
Miyawaki Kosuke, Col, 141
Miyazaki Shigesaburo, Maj-Gen, 201,
    202, 262, 291, 305, 323
Mizukami Genzu, Maj-Gen, 334–5
Molvom, 288, 289
monsoon, 309, 359, 415
Montgomery, Lt-Col Brian, 100, 424
Morton, John, 106
Moulmein, 12, 20, 37, 45, 46–8, 50–3, 55
Mountbatten, Vice-Admiral Lord Louis,
    2, 4, 179, 181 & n, 182, 209, 211, 214,
    242, 279–80, 334, 416–18, 430–1
Munn, Lt A.W., 313
Murada, Col, 284
Murie, Chief Engineer Jack, 107
Murray, Lt David, 430
Musoma, Mutili, 350
Mutaguchi Renya, Lt-Gen, 161, 163,
    186, 187, 188, 189, 199, 269, 284, 288,
    289, 301, 323, 324
Myitkyina, 11, 93, 131–2, 161, 180, 208,
    211, 217, 325–334

Nagas (ethnic group), 12, 119, 173, 259,
    292, 323, 433
Nagazawa Kanichi, Maj-Gen, 404
Nagel, Capt James R., 207
Nagumo Chuichi, Vice-Admiral, 88–9,
    90
Nair, Capt M. ('Bosco'), 297
Naka Eitaro, Lt-Gen, 190, 354, 401
Nakai Buhachiro, Cpl, 49
Narain, Partap, 428
National League for Democracy (Burma),
    433
Nawin Chaung, 84
Ne Win, 176, 432
Neale, Sqn Ldr Robert H., 77
Nehru, Jawarla, 16, 17, 187
Neill, Lt Dominic ('Nick'), 133–4, 157,
    158, 162

Nepean, Maj Patrick, 322
Nettlefield, Maj John, 261, 271
*New Burma* (newspaper), 34
Ni, Daw (cousin of Dr Ba Maw), 15
Nicholson, Maj-Gen C.G.G., 323
Nicholson, Maj James, 349
Nickerson, Marjorie, 73
Nimmo, Capt Bill, 409
Nimmo, Maj Jimmy, 115, 174, 374, 409
Nishiji Yasumasa, 351
Norman, Cpl Harold, 264–5, 268
Noronha, Capt R.S., 279
North, Clive, 119
North China Railway Company, 37
Northern Combat Area Command
    (NCAC), 380, 429
Nphum Ga, battle of, 217, 218
Nu, U. (Thakin politician), 91, 410, 432
Nunneley, Lt John, 6, 349–51

O'Brien, Flt Lt Terence, 327, 320
O'Callaghan, Lt-Col Denis, 134
Octagon Conference (Quebec, 1944),
    240, 242, 341
Office of Strategic Services (OSS), 64,
    139, 375, 418; Detachment 101, 210
Officer, Col W.J., 150
Ogburn Jr., 2nd Lt Charlton, 5, 212, 219,
    330, 335, 337
Ogburn, Lt Eric, 296
O'Hara, Maj Chris, 234
Old, Brig-Gen William D., 52, 222, 229,
    243
Omoto Kimio, Col, 276–7
*Ontario* MV, 357
Operation Anakim, 127, 132, 177
Operation Anvil, 181
Operation Axiom, 210, 211
Operation Buccaneer, 180, 181
Operation Cannibal, 127
Operation Capital, 334, 341, 343, 357
Operation Champion, 180
Operation Character (Force 136), 409–1
Operation Cudgel, 224, 234, 236
Operation Culverin, 180
Operation Dracula, 180, 334, 341, 407–8,
    414
Operation Duffy, 395

Operation Error, 102
Operation Extended Capital, 378–9, 407,
    414
Operation Ha-Go (Japanese), 190, 226,
    233
Operation Ichi-Go (Japanese), 334, 338,
    346
Operation Jericho, 224
Operation Lightning, 364
Operation Longcloth *see* Wingate
Operation Mai (Japanese), 419
Operation Mailfist, 407
Operation Nation (Force 136), 409
Operation Navvy (Tiddim road), 170,
    171, 351, 353
Operation Nipoff (Japanese repatriation),
    427
Operation Passport, 366
Operation Ravenous, 127
Operation Roger, 407
Operation Romulus, 344, 364
Operation Saucy (North Burma
    Campaign), 176
Operation Stamina, 318
Operation Stencil (deception) *see*
    Irrawaddy (river)
Operation Talon, 344
Operation Thursday *see* Wingate
Operation U-Go (Japanese; *earlier*
    Operation 21), 186, 187, 190, 288
Operation Yacht, 42
Operation Zipper, 407, 416
Oriental Mission (special operations), 51
Owen, Lt-Col Basil, 62
Owen, Frank, 81
Ozawa Jisabura, V-Adm, 89, 90

Padam Sing Rai, L Nk, 69
Pagani, Cpl R.A.S., 173
Painter, Capt Robin, 165–6, 279, 392
Park, ACM Keith, 343, 419
Patterson, Maj R.A.K., 365
Patteson, Lt M.J.E. ('Kildare'), 82
Paw Tun, Sir, 35
Pawsey, Charles, 259, 265
Pearce, Maj-Gen C.F.B., 321, 355
Pearl Harbor, 33, 37, 88
Peers, William R., 210

Pegu (Burma), 13, 53, 59, 62, 66, 67, 68, 69, 78
Peirse, ACM Sir Richard, 70, 127, 222, 280, 334, 343
Pennington, Capt William, 5, 403
People's Revolutionary Party (Burmese Nationalist/pro-Japanese group), 18, 49; see also Aung San
Percival, Lt-Gen A.E., 37
Pert, Brig Claud, 405–6
Phibun, Soggram, 35, 188
Phylatoff, Pte V., 64
Pick, Col Lewis A. ('Old Mud and Ruts'), 207, 208
Pickford, Lt Sydney, 415
Po Hla, Saw, 173
Pong, Pte Kweku, 360–1
Pound, Adm Sir Dudley, 37
Power, V-Adm Sir Arthur, 343
Pownall, Lt-Gen Sir Henry, 37, 40, 182, 341, 342
Presterly, Pfc George C., 330
Pringle, Maj R.C., 249
prisoners of war, 5–6, 83, 87, 97, 122, 128, 130, 168, 186, 230, 425–6
Project 9 (later 1st Air Commando Group), 239–40, 255
Project CA281 (also Project 9), 239
Prome, 66, 74, 80, 81, 83, 84, 85
Pu, U., 17
Pugh, Lt-Col Lewis, 323
Pun, Nk Lachhiman, 406
Pun, Rfn Tulbahadur, 332
Punch (magazine), 54
Pyinmana, 79–80, 85, 86, 98
Pyle, Ernie, 319

Qadir, Maj Ghulam, 351
Quadrant Conference (Quebec, 1943), 178
Queen Mary (liner), 178

Rafiq, Jemadar Mohammed, 270
Rahman, Capt Attiqur, 63
Rai, Nk Agansing, 287
Rajwade, M.R., 383
Ram, Sepoy Bhanderi, 361
Ram, Sowar Jot, 278

Ram, Sub Tiru, 276
Ramsay, Lt-Cdr J.M., RAN, 365
Randle, Capt Jack, 296–8
Randle, Maj John, 406, 420–2
Randolph, Capt Revd Roy, 265
Rangoon, 3, 11, 12, 14, 16, 32, 37, 43, 45, 49, 50, 55, 59, 69, 90; Japanese capture, 63–4, 67–72, 88; Allied capture, 407–22, 425
Rangoon Defence Force (Japanese), 414
Ranking, Maj-Gen R.P.L., 258, 259
Ransome, Sgt George, 72
rations, 150–1, 213, 241–2, 313–14, 317–18, 336
Rattenbury, Harold, 25–6
Rau, Capt R.M., 383, 427
Rawlley, Maj Naveen, 270
Raymond, Lt Claude, 372
Recovery of POW's and Internees (RAPWI), 425
Red Cross Voluntary Aid Detachment (VAD), 312
Rees, Maj-Gen T.W. ('Pete'), 357, 378, 380, 387, 391, 392, 394, 395
Rees, Capt W.D., 147, 396
Reizan Kannon Temple (Kyoto), 1
repatriation (British), 428–31
Rhodes-James, Capt Richard, 250
Richards, Col Hugh, 258, 259, 261, 262, 265, 268, 270, 271
Rissik, Capt David, 146–7
Roberts, Maj-Gen Ouvry, 197, 200
Robertson, George, 15
Robertson, Nurse Marian, 312
Robinson, Maj Jack, 62
Robinson, Sgt William, 311
Rodger, George, 73, 79, 91, 94
Rodriguez, Nurse Helen, GM, 98–9
Roebuck, L Cpl, 62
Rome, Lt Pat, 291
Rooke, Lt Christopher, 247, 252
Roosevelt, President Franklin D., 3–4, 18–19, 30–1, 38, 40, 46, 52, 56, 85, 90, 132, 176, 184, 334, 339–40
Roosevelt, President Theodore, 28
Rowley, Capt Frederick, 380, 395
Rubinstein, Dick, 410

Russell, Lt-Col John E., 206–7
Russell, Stanley Farrant, 116

*Sagaing* (freighter), 90
Sakano Toshiyuki, L Cpl, 234
Sakuma Takanobu, Col, 70, 284–7
Sakurai Shozo (*also* Seizo), Lt-Gen, 53,
    59, 86, 102–3, 105, 190, 223, 232, 233,
    373, 404, 411, 419, 424
Sakurai Tokutaro, Maj-Gen, 226, 233,
    237
Salomons, Brig J.A., 402
Salween (river), 11, 12, 37, 48, 51, 53, 54
Sandeman, Capt Sandy, 81
Sao Hearn Hkam, Princess, 98, 175
Sao San Mong, 432
Sato Katoku, Lt-Gen, 188, 190, 201, 202,
    256, 258–9, 269, 291, 301, 303–5,
    323–4
Sato Misao, Maj, 83
Satterthwaite, Pte Albert, 311
Saunders, Wg Cdr A.E., 415
Saunders, Lt-Col Peter, 302
Savage, Lt-Col William J., 208
Savory, Maj-Gen Reginald, 2, 177
Saw Pe Tha, 122
Saw, U., 17, 34–5, 432
Scollen, Capt Jack, 401
Scoones, Lt-Gen Geoffry, 164, 193,
    194–8, 202, 275, 276, 280–1, 287, 319,
    342–3, 355, 358
Scott, Lt C.G., 19
Scott, Maj-Gen J. Bruce, 22, 77, 78, 95,
    97, 103, 105
Scott, Maj Michael, 169
Scott, Lt-Col Robert, 295, 300
Scott, Capt Walter, 69
*SEAC* (newspaper), 181, 298
Seagram, Maj Hugh, 51, 173, 374–5
Seagrave, Dr Gordon, 79–80, 113, 133,
    207, 209
Sealy, Lt J.R., 242
Sein, Daw, 45
Sen, Lt-Col L.P. ('Bogy'), 361n
Sevareid, Eric, 205
Sextant Conference (Cairo, 1943), 180,
    241
Shah, L Nk, 365

Shan States, 34, 43, 51, 53, 67, 77, 79, 85,
    98, 103, 124, 174, 403
Shans (Burmese hill people), 12, 433
Shapland, Brig J.D., 302
Sharp, Arthur, 375
Sharp, Richard, 301
Shaw, Sgt James, 251, 255, 328–9, 335
Sheil-Small, Maj Denis, 389
Shepley, James, 212
Sheridan, Ann, 344
Shibata Uichi, Lt-Gen, 288
Shimeyoki Masatsu, Capt, 421
Shipster, Maj John, 224, 302–3, 310, 315,
    322, 429, 433
Short, Stanley, 101
Shuttleworth, Maj, 247
Singapore, 3, 18, 21–2, 32, 40, 43, 53, 55,
    56, 90
Singh, Maj Amrit, 413
Singh, Lt Bahadur, 405
Singh, Hav Bharat, 421
Singh, Nk Gian, 404
Singh, Capt Mohan, 174–5
Singh, Nk Nand, 237
Singh, Hav Parkash, 141
Singh, Jem Prakash, 387
Singh, Sub Ram Sarup, 353
Singh, Sub Ranbir, 276
Singh, Hav Umrao, 361
Sittang (river and valley), 11, 48, 58–63,
    66, 83, 86, 421
Slim, Lt-Gen William ('Uncle Bill'), 2–3,
    76–7, 95–7, 99–100, 111, 147, 149,
    179, 182, 246, 280, 337, 378, 416–17
Smart, Phil, 212
Smeeton, Lt-Col Miles, 398, 405–6
Smith, Maj Harry, 322, 411
Smith, Lt L.C., 360
Smith, Fus W.C., 146
Smyth, Maj-Gen J.G. ('Jackie'), 47, 48,
    50, 52–6, 59, 60, 62, 63, 65, 77
Snelling, Maj-Gen A.H.J. ('Grocer Alf'),
    225, 226
Snow, Lt-Col J.F., 355
Soe U. (Thakin politician), 320
Somerville, Admiral Sir James, 89, 182,
    343
Songkrai (POW camp), 426–7

Soong, Mei-Ling *see* Chiang, Madam
Soong Tzu-vun (T.V. Soong), 41
South-East Asia Command (SEAC), 179, 180, 221, 321, 325, 338, 370
Special Force *see* British and Commonwealth Forces: Divisions: 3rd Indian Division
Special Operations Executive (SOE), 139 & n; Force 136, 139, 319–21, 364, 375, 403, 421
Spencer, Otha C., 205, 315
Spencer, Sgt Richard, 265
Spink, Maj E.E., 355
Spurr, Sub-Lt Russell, RINVR, 20, 415
Stanbridge, Flt Lt Brian, 401
State Law and Order Restoration Council (Burma), 432–3
Steer, Maj George, 146
Stevenson, AVM Donald, 45–6, 47, 70
Stevenson, Lt-Col H.A., 54, 62
Stevenson, Lt-Col Noel, 51, 114
Stibbé, Lt Philip, 157, 161, 167
Stilwell, Maj-Gen Joseph W. ('Vinegar Joe'), 41, 52, 74–5, 85–6, 95, 98–101, 103, 113–14, 127, 133, 176–9, 181, 206–19, 249, 326–7, 329–34, 337–40, 344, 380–1
Stock, Roger, 291
Stockwell, Maj-Gen Hugh, 365–6
Stone, Sqn Ldr 'Bunny', 80, 84
Stopford, Lt-Gen Montagu, 258–60, 266, 269, 292, 297, 299, 304, 323, 386, 394, 410, 417, 424
Stowe, Leland, 32–3, 75
Stratemeyer, Maj-Gen George E., 222
Street, Pte Raymond, 224–5, 265, 315
Stuart, James ('Fighting Father'), 114 & n, 139
Sultan, Lt-Gen Daniel, 340, 354
*Sun* (Burmese pro-Japanese newspaper), 34
Sun Li-jen, Lt-Gen, 96–7, 103, 114, 130, 206, 207–9, 218, 330
Sunwar, Jaharman, 399
Suzuki Keiji, Col (*aka* Minami Masuyo), 17–18, 49, 122
Suzuki Tadashi, Capt, 54

Swaine, Bob, 383
Swinson, Capt Arthur, 260, 267, 292, 298, 304
Symbol Conference (Casablanca, 1943), 132
Symes, Maj-Gen G.W., 240

Ta Naga, 161
Tai An-lan, Maj-Gen, 79
Takahashi Hachiro, Capt, 403
Takaze Numata, Lt-Gen, 189
Takeda, Maj-Gen, 254
Takeuchi Yutaka, Lt-Gen, 48, 49–50
Tamarkan (POW camp), 186
Tamu, 73, 107, 109, 110, 121
Tamura Masataro, 413, 414
Tanahashi Seizo, Col, 143, 233–4
Tanaka Nobuo, Maj-Gen, 285, 287, 398, 401, 402
Tanaka Sinichi, Lt-Gen, 209, 213, 217, 323–4, 325
Tanner, 2nd Lt Ralph, 100
Tapa, Rfn Chhabe, 332
Tatchell, Capt Rodney, 250
Tavoy, 20, 37, 47, 49
Taylor, Capt Bill, 243
Tenasserim, 11, 12, 37, 43, 49, 71
tennis court, battle of *see* Kohima
Terauchi Hisaichi, FM, Count, 37, 77, 186, 288, 323, 339, 423–4
Tewari, Lt Krishen, 128
Thailand, 12, 33–4, 35, 42, 46; advance on Shan States, 104
Thakin Party (Burmese nationalist party), 15, 17, 20, 34–5, 87, 90–1
Than Tun, 375, 403
Thapa, Sub Netrabahadur, 287
Thapa, Rfn Thilbahadur, 165
Thapa, Hav Tilbir, 164
Thein Maung, 34
Thimayya, Lt-Col K.S. ('Timmy'), 28–9, 361n, 366
'Thirty Comrades' (*also* 'Thirty Heroes'), 18, 49
Thomas, L Acn J. Helsdon, 45
Thompson, Arthur Bell (*aka* Francis Clifford), 115, 116, 118, 174, 409–10
Thompson, Maj-Gen Sir Julian, 164, 337

Thompson, Maj-Gen Treffry, 53
Thorat, Lt-Col S.P.P., 361n, 367
Thornton, Len, 223, 310
Thornton, Lt P., 142
Tighe, Lt-Col S.C.H., 401
Tilly, Lt James, 213
*Time Life* (magazine), 212
Tojo Hideki, Gen, 30, 33, 123, 174 175 323
Toosey, Lt-Col Peter, 186
Toothill, Capt Bruce, 55
Total War Research Institute, 123
Toungoo, 32, 46, 67, 72, 74, 75, 77, 78, 79, 81, 83, 85
Towill, Capt Bill, 342
Townsend, Flt Lt Edmund, 205
Trevelyan, Humphrey (*later* Lord), 129
Trident Conference (Washington, 1943), 43, 176
Trincomalee, 88, 90
Tripartite Axis Pact (Japan/Germany/Italy, 1940), 31, 33
Trofimov, Aubrey, 421
Tsuji Masanobu, Col, 398, 406
Tu Lu-ming, Gen, 75, 78–9, 86
Tuchman, Barbara, 3, 211
Tulloch, Brig Derek, 240, 241, 250–1, 337
Tun Oke (Thakin politician), 122
Turner, Maj A.S., 144
Turner, Sgt Victor, 287
Twidle, Maj Bob, 393

Uga Takeshi, Col, 401
United Pongyi Association, 125
United States Forces:
  US Navy: *Houston*, USS, 425
  Ground: 5th Infantry Regiment, 330; 14th Infantry Regiment, 330; 33rd Infantry Regiment, 212, 330; 124th Cavalry Regiment, 343, 381; 330th Engineer General Services Regiment, 133; 475th Infantry Regiment, 343, 344, 354; 900th Airborne Engineer Company, 243, 247; 5303rd (Provisional) Combat Troops, 207; 5307th Composite Unit (Provisional) 'Galahad'/

Merrill's Marauders, 178, 207, 211–20, 325, 326, 329–30, 335, 343–4; 1st Battalion, 18, 326; 2nd Battalion, 215–18; 3rd Battalion, 213, 215–19; 5332nd Brigade (Provisional) Mars Task Force, 343–4, 354, 381, 382; 98th Field Artillery Battalion, 217; 209th Combat Engineer Battalion, 207; 464th Anti-Aircraft Battalion, 207; 612th Field Artillery Battalion (pack), 343; 613th Field Artillery Battalion (pack), 343; 879th Engineer Aviation Battlion, 326; Northern Combat Area Command (NCAC), 207, 209, 343, 357; Photographic Reconnaissance Unit, 318
  Air: Allied Air Command, South-East Asia, 222; Assam–Burma–China Ferrying Command (*later* Ferrying Command; *then* Air Transport Command (ATC)), 13, 52, 125–6, 127, 224; Tenth Air Force, 52, 85, 90, 125, 129–30, 222, 255, 318, 326, 339, 354; Fourteenth Air Force, 132, 338, 339; Strategic Air Force (SAF), 318; 7th Heavy Bombardment Group, 130, 347, 348; 12th Bombardment Group, 347; 23rd Fighter Group (*earlier* AVG), 125; 341st Medium Bombardment Group, 130; 443rd Group, 222; American Volunteer Group (AVG; 'Flying Tigers'), 32, 46, 50, 59, 77, 84–5, 125; No. 1 Air Commando ('Cochran's Flying Circus'), 241 & n; 293rd Wing, 318; 11th Sqn, 130; 22nd Sqn, 130; 436th Sqn, 130; 490th Sqn, 130; 490th Bombardment Sqn, 206; 491st Sqn, 130; 492nd Sqn, 130; 493rd Sqn, 130, 348
Upfill, Murial Degaa, 64, 432

V Force (intelligence group), 137–8, 141, 148, 173, 193, 197, 210, 236, 320
van Straubanzee, Lt-Col Philip, 360

Vandivert, Bill, 169
Vincent, AVM Stanley, 195, 343, 395
Vivian, Capt David, 431–2
Vlasto, FO, 169

Wait, Lt Reginald ('Rex'), 267, 404
Wakeley, Maj-Gen Victor, 59
Wales, Nym, 30
Walker, V-Adm H.T.C., 415
Walsh, Maj-Gen George, 416
Walwyn, Lt-Col C.E.B., 360
war criminal trials, 426
Warren, Brig Frederick ('Daddy'), 26,
    259, 261, 262, 269, 352
Watanabe Masao, Lt-Gen, 79
Wavell, FM Sir Archibald, 19, 42–3, 46,
    53, 57, 66, 84, 100, 121, 126, 130, 140,
    155, 159, 168, 184
Webber, Capt F.D., 107
Wedemeyer, Maj-Gen Albert, 194, 211,
    214, 326, 340, 357, 398
Wei Li-huang, Gen, 338
Weingartner, Lt Victor J., 213
Welch, Father, 116
Wessels, Brig-Gen Theodore F., 330,
    331
West, Lt D.H., 59, 60
Weston, Lt Logan, 219
Weston, Lt William, 399
Wheeler, Lt-Col L.G., 166
Wheeler, Lt-Gen Raymond A., 340
White, Flt Sgt Dick, 315
White, Maj Geoffrey, 294, 300
Whittaker, Pfc Anthony, 382
Whyte, Capt Desmond, 69, 252
Wickham, Brig John, 68
Wilcox, W.A., 291
Wild, Cyril, 426
Willey, Brig-Gen John P., 344, 382
Williams, Col, 146
Williams, Lt-Col Humphrey, 145
Williams, J.H. ('Elephant Bill'), 121, 196,
    357

Williams, Bandsman Les, 61
Williams, Lt Wynn, 191
Willshaw, Sgt Arthur, 158
Wilson, Capt David, 6, 181, 300
Wilson, Capt Richard ('Tug'), 272
Winant, Ambassador John, 179
Winch, Cpl H. ('Harry'), 368
Wingate, Maj-Gen Orde, 74, 155–70,
    178–9, 182, 187, 213, 223, 239–55,
    287, 331, 335, 336–7
Winstanley, Maj John, 5, 268
Winter, Maj-Gen John, 65
Wood, Maj-Gen E.C., 109–10, 116
Woods, Hugh, 31
Woolner, Maj-Gen C.G., 223, 235, 236
Wormell, Lt R.P., 167

X Force see Chinese Forces

Y Force see Chinese Forces
Yamamoto Isoruku, Admiral, 33, 229,
    350
Yamamoto Tsunoro, Maj-Gen, 196, 280
Yamashita Tomyuki, Gen, 37
Yamauchi Masafumi, Lt-Gen, 189, 202,
    277, 286–7, 288
Yanagida Motozo, Lt-Gen, 186, 197, 284,
    285, 288
Yasukuni Temple (Tokyo), 38
Yenangyaung, 78, 93, 95–7, 100, 103
Yeo, Maj Richard, 262, 264
Yomas Intelligence Service, 80
Yomiuri (Japanese newspaper), 17
Yoshifuku, Capt, 291
Yoshino Suichiro, Lt, 427
Yosuke, Matsouka, 33
Young, Capt Jock, 259–60
Young, Lt-Col John, 261, 262, 263
Yubang Ga, 209
Yuji, Pte Aida, 418
Yukihiko Imai, 200

Z Force (intelligence group), 137, 319